Ubuntu

24.04
LTS
Desktop

Applications
and
Administration

To Augie, Wally, and Howie

Ubuntu 24.04 LTS Desktop: Applications and Administration
Richard Petersen

Surfing Turtle Press

Alameda, CA

www.surfingturtlepress.com

Please send inquiries to: editor@surfingturtlepress.com

ISBN-13   978-1-949857-43-6

Copyright 2024 by Richard Petersen. All rights reserved.

Printed in the United States of America.

Except as permitted under the Copyright Act of 1976, no part of this publication may be reproduced or distributed in any form or by any means, or stored in a database or retrieval system, without the prior written permission of the publisher, with the exception that the program listings may be entered, stored, and executed in a computer system, but they may not be reproduced for publication.

Information has been obtained by Surfing Turtle Press from sources believed to be reliable. However, because of the possibility of human or mechanical error by our sources, Surfing Turtle Press, the author Richard Petersen, or others, Surfing Turtle Press does not guarantee the accuracy, adequacy, or completeness of any information and is not responsible for any errors or omissions or the results obtained from use of such information.

Limit of Liability and Disclaimer of Warranty: The publisher and the author make no representation or warranties with respect to the accuracy or completeness of the contents of this work and specifically disclaim all warranties, including without limitation warranties of fitness for a particular purpose. The information and code in this book is provided on "as is" basis. No warranty may be created or extended by sales or promotional materials. The advice and strategies contained herein may not be suitable for every situation. This work is sold with the understanding that the publisher is not engaged in rendering legal, accounting, or other professional services. Surfing Turtle Press and anyone else who has been involved in the creation or production of the included code cannot and do not warrant the performance or results that may be obtained by using the code.

Trademark Acknowledgements

UNIX is a trademark of The Open Group

Microsoft and MS-DOS are registered trademarks of Microsoft Corporation

IBM and PC are registered trademarks of the International Business Machines Corporation

Fedora is a trademark of Red Hat, Inc.

Ubuntu is a trademark of Canonical, Inc.

ubuntu®, ◉, and **kubuntu®** are trademarks of Ubuntu, Canonical, Inc.

The Ubuntu Font Family provides libre/open fonts (TTF) for Ubuntu, **http://font.ubuntu.com/**

See **https://ubuntu.com** for more information

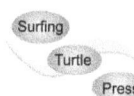 is a trademark of Surfing Turtle Press

Preface

This book covers the Ubuntu 24.04 LTS (Noble Numbat) release, focusing on applications and administrative tools. The emphasis here is on what users will face when using Ubuntu, covering topics like installation, applications, software management, the Ubuntu desktops (GNOME, MATE, and KDE), shell commands, network connections, and system administration tasks. Ubuntu 24.04 LTS introduces several new features, as well as numerous smaller modifications. It is a long-term support release. The Ubuntu desktop, which uses GNOME, is examined in detail, along with Snap and APT package management.

The Ubuntu desktop uses a Dock and an Activities overview to manage access to applications and devices. In addition, Ubuntu 24.04 LTS desktop is based on GNOME 46, with several desktop configuration tools and the Settings dialog. In addition, features such as workspaces, extensions, and the GNOME Files file manager, are covered. The Kubuntu desktop, which uses KDE, provides a different interface using plasma containers to support panels, menus, activities, configuration tools, and widgets. Ubuntu MATE is based on the traditional GNOME 2 desktop, buy with alternative menus, panel layouts, and a dock.

Part 1 focuses on getting started, covering Ubuntu information and resources, using Ubuntu Live USB/DVD drives, installing and setting up Ubuntu, upgrading Ubuntu, basic use of the desktop interface, and connecting to wired and wireless networks. Repositories and their use are covered in detail, along with the Snap system for managing Snap packages. Ubuntu Snap package management with the App Center and the **snap** command, as well as APT package management with Gnome Software, the Synaptic Package Manager, and the **apt** and **apt-get** commands.

Part 2 focuses in on office, multimedia, mail, Internet, and social media applications such as the Evolution and Thunderbird email applications, the Videos media player, the Rhythmbox music player, and the LibreOffice office suite. The section includes coverage of the sound settings, Firefox Web browser, and FTP applications.

Part 3 covers the Ubuntu, Kubuntu, and Ubuntu MATE in detail. It also covers other Ubuntu flavors including Xubuntu, Lubuntu, Ubuntu Cinnamon, and Ubuntu Unity desktops. The Ubuntu desktop features a Dock, Activities overview, Applications overview, and a new System menu with Quick Setting buttons. The Kubuntu desktop is examined which is based on the KDE desktop with features such as widgets, activities, panels, menus, desktop effects, and the Discover software manager. Ubuntu MATE provides traditional GNOME 2 panels, but with alternative menus and panel layouts. It also provides a dock. All the desktops are different, but all access and install software from the Ubuntu APT software repositories and the Ubuntu Snap Store. All are also official Ubuntu Flavors, different desktops but the same compatible software, most of which can run on any of the flavors. The BASH shell interface is also explored, with its command editing, folder navigation, and file operations.

Part 4 deals with administration topics, first discussing system tools like the GNOME system monitor, the Disk Usage Analyzer, Seahorse, and Disk Utility. Then a detailed chapter on Ubuntu system administration tools is presented, covering tasks such as managing users and file systems, Bluetooth setup, network folder sharing, backups, and printing. The network connections chapter covers a variety of network tasks, including manual configuration of wired and wireless connections, and firewalls (the Gufw and FirewallD applications).

Overview

Preface	5
Overview	7
Contents	9

Part 1: Getting Started

1. Ubuntu 24.04 LTS Introduction	29
2. Installing Ubuntu	45
3. Usage Basics: Login, Desktop, Network, and Help	77
4. Installing and Updating Software: Snap and APT	157

Part 2: Applications

5. Office Suites, Editors, and E-mail	213
6. Graphics and Multimedia	247
7. Internet Applications	275

Part 3: Desktops

8. Ubuntu Desktop — 295

9. Kubuntu (KDE Plasma) — 341

10. Ubuntu MATE — 407

11. Ubuntu Flavors — 473

12. Shells — 493

Part 4: Administration

13. System Tools — 527

14. System Administration — 557

15. Network Connections — 613

Table Listing — 661

Figure Listing — 665

Index — 685

Contents

Preface 5

Overview 7

Contents 9

Part 1: Getting Started

1. Ubuntu 24.04 LTS Introduction 29

    Ubuntu 24.04 LTS 31
    Ubuntu 24.04 LTS Key Changes 32
    Ubuntu Releases 34
    Ubuntu Desktop and Server 34
    Ubuntu Flavors 36
    Ubuntu Live USB/DVD 37
        Ubuntu Live USB drive 38
    Ubuntu Software 39
    Ubuntu Help and Documentation 40
        help.ubuntu.com 41
        discourse.ubuntu.com 41
        Ubuntu news and blog sites 42
        Linux documentation 42
    Open Source Software 42
    Linux 43

2. Installing Ubuntu 45

Install Discs 46
Using BitTorrent: Transmission 47
Metalinks 47
Zsync 47
Installing Multiple-Boot Systems 47
Hardware Requirements 48
Installation Overview 48
Installation with the Ubuntu Desktop USB/DVD 49
Welcome and Language 50
Accessibility 52
Keyboard Layout 53
Internet connection 54
Try or install Ubuntu (direct install only) 54
Type of Installation, Interactive or Automated Install 55
Applications: Default and Extended selections 55
Optimize your computer: proprietary software 56
Disk setup 57
No detected operating systems 57
Advanced Features: LVM, Encryption, and ZFS 58
Encrypt the disk 60
Detected Ubuntu operating system 61
Detected other operating systems with free space 62
Detected another operating system using entire disk (resize) 62
Manual installation 63
Creating new partitions on a blank hard drive manually 63
Ready to install 67
Select your timezone 68
Create your account 68
Install Progress 69
Upgrading 71
Upgrade over a network from Ubuntu 20.04 and 23.10 71
Upgrading to a new release with apt-get 73
Recovery, rescue, and boot loader re-install 73
Recovery Mode (Advanced Options menu) 73
Re-Installing the Boot Loader 74

3. Usage Basics: Login, Desktop, Network, and Help 77

Accessing Your Ubuntu System 78
- GRUB Boot Loader 78
- The GNOME Display Manager: GDM 80
- The System menu 82
- Lock Screen 84
- Logging Out and Switching Users 85
- Poweroff 86
- Accessing Linux from the Command Line Interface 86

The Ubuntu Desktop 87
- Ubuntu (GNOME) 88
- Files File Manager 91
- Ubuntu Customization with GNOME Tweaks: Themes, Icons, Fonts, and Startup Applications 92

Network Connections 95
- NetworkManager Wired Connections 96
- NetworkManager Wireless Connections 96
- Configuring Network Connections with GNOME Settings 98

Settings 101
- Accessibility (Universal Access) 105
- Appearance 106
- Apps 107
  - Default Apps 108
  - Removable Media 109
  - App Permissions, Associations (file and link types), and Storage 110
- Color Profiles (GNOME Color Manager) 113
- Displays (Resolution, Rotation, Scaling, and Night Light) 114
- Keyboard 116
- Mouse and Touchpad 117
- Multitasking 120
- Notifications 121
- Search 123
- Online Accounts 123
- Power 124
  - powertop and tuned 127
- Privacy & Security 127
- Sharing 130

System 131
    Regions & Language 131
    Date & Time 133
    Users 136
    Remote Desktop 136
    Secure Shell 138
    About (System Information) 139
  Ubuntu Desktop: Icons, Dock, and Tiling 140
File Manager Search 142
Accessing File Systems and Devices 142
  Accessing Archives from GNOME: File Roller 143
  Mounting ISO Disk Image files: Disk Image Mounter 144
  File Manager CD/DVD Creator interface 144
  ISO Image File Writing with Disk Utility and Brasero 144
Startup Applications Preferences 145
Display Configuration and Additional Drivers 146
Help Resources 147
  Ubuntu Desktop Guide 147
  Context-Sensitive Help 150
  Application Documentation 150
  The Man Pages 150
  The Info Pages 150
Terminal Window 150
  GNOME Console: GNOME 4.2 154
Command Line Interface 154

4. Installing and Updating Software: Snap and APT 157

Installing Software Packages: APT and Snap 158
Software Package Types 159
Ubuntu Package Management Software 160
Snaps Packages 162
Managing Snap: App Center and the snap command 162
  Snap Channels: tracks and risk levels 167
  Snap Confinement 168
  Snap Revisions: revert 172
  Snap Package Configuration 173
  Snap and systemd 174

  Snap and Services 174
  App Center for Snap 175
 APT: Deb Package Management.. 181
  Ubuntu APT Repositories 181
   APT Repository Components 182
   APT Repositories 182
   APT Ubuntu Repository Configuration file: ubuntu.sources and sources.list.d 183
   APT Software Repositories managed with Software & Updates.................... 185
  App Center for APT (Debian) packages... 187
  GNOME Software 189
  Synaptic Package Manager: APT only.. 191
   Properties.. 193
   Installing packages 193
   Removing packages 194
   Search filters 194
  GNOME Software for separate DEB packages.. 195
  Source code files... 195
  DEB Software Packages 195
  Managing software with apt and apt-get... 196
  Updating packages (Upgrading) with apt... 197
  Command Line Search and Information: dpkg-query and apt-cache tools 198
  Managing non-repository packages with dpkg... 199
  Using packages with other software formats 200
 Updating Ubuntu 200
  Updating Snaps 200
  Updating Ubuntu APT software with Software Updater.....................................202
  Configuring Updates with Software & Updates...204
 Firmware Updater 206
 Flatpak..207
 Installing and Running Windows Software on Linux: Wine.......................................208

Part 2: Applications

5. Office Suites, Editors, and E-mail 213
 LibreOffice 214
 Calligra..216
 GNOME Office Applications..217

Running Microsoft Office on Linux: Wine and CrossOver 218
Document Viewers, and DVI) 219
E-book Readers: FBReader, Foliate, and Calibre 220
Notes 222
GNOME Clocks and Weather 223
GNOME Characters and Fonts 224
GNOME Calendar 225
Editors 226
    GNOME Text Editors: Text Editor and Gedit 226
        GNOME Text Editor 226
        GNOME Gedit 227
    The nano text editor 228
    KDE Editor: Kate 229
    The Emacs Editor 229
    The Vi Editor: Vim and Gvim 229
Database Management Systems 233
    SQL Databases (RDBMS) 233
    LibreOffice Base 233
    MySQL 234
        MariaDB 234
    PostgreSQL 234
E-Mail Clients 234
    Thunderbird 235
    Evolution 237
    The KDE Mail Client: KMail 239
    Command Line Mail Clients 240
        Mutt 240
        Mail 240
    Notifications of Received Mail 241
    Accessing Mail on Remote Mail Servers 241
    Mailing Lists 242
    MIME: /etc/mime.types 242
Usenet News 243
    Newsreaders 244
        Binary Newsreaders and Grabbers 245
        slrn 245
    News Transport Agents 246

6. Graphics and Multimedia 247

Graphics Applications 248
Photo Management: Shotwell, Photos, and Camera (Snapshot) 249
GNOME Graphics Applications 252
KDE Graphics Applications 254
X Window System Graphic Programs 255
Multimedia 255
Multimedia support 255
GStreamer 257
GStreamer Plug-ins: the Good, the Bad, and the Ugly 257
GStreamer MP3 Compatibility: iPod 258
Music Applications 258
CD/DVD Burners 261
Video Applications 261
Video and DVD Players 261
Videos Plugins 265
DVD Video support 266
PiTiVi and Shotcut Video editors 266
TV Players 268
DVB and HDTV support 268
Kaffeine DVB and ATSC tuning 268
Xvid (DivX) and Matroska (mkv) on Linux 269
Ubuntu Studio 269
Sound 269
Volume Control 270
Settings Sound 270
PulseAudio server and applications 272

7. Internet Applications 275

URL Addresses 276
Web Browsers 277
The Firefox Web Browser 277
GNOME Web (Epiphany) 280
Chromium 281
Links and Lynx: Line-Mode Browsers 282
Java for Linux 282
BitTorrent Clients (transmission) 283

- FTP Clients 284
  - Network File Transfer: FTP 285
  - Web Browser–Based FTP 285
  - GNOME Desktop FTP 286
  - FileZilla 287
  - gFTP 288
  - wget 288
  - curl 288
  - ftp 289
  - lftp 290
- Social Networking 290
  - Instant Messenger 290
    - Pidgin 291
  - VoIP Applications 291
    - Skype 291
  - GNOME Maps 292

Part 3: Desktops

8. Ubuntu Desktop 295

- GNOME 296
- The Ubuntu GNOME Desktop 296
  - Top Bar 297
  - System Menu 298
  - Desktop menu and Desktop folder 299
  - Activities Overview 300
  - Ubuntu Dock and GNOME Dash 302
  - Window Thumbnails 304
  - Applications Overview 306
    - Overview Application Folders 307
  - Activities Search 309
  - Managing Windows 310
  - Workspaces 315
  - Notifications and Message dialog 318
  - Desktop Customization with GNOME Tweaks: Themes, Icons, Fonts, and Startup Applications 319
  - Desktop Customization: manually placing application launchers on the Desktop 320

GNOME Help Browser	321
The Files File Manager	322
Home Folder Subfolders	322
File Manager Windows	322
File Manager adaptive feature for narrow widths	325
File Manager Sidebar and Tools menu	327
Tabs	329
Displaying and Managing Files and Folders	329
Navigating in the File Manager	330
Managing Files and Folders	331
Renaming Files	332
Compress and Archive Files	333
Copying Files	334
Grouping Files	334
Opening Applications and Files MIME Types	335
File and Folder Properties	335
File Manager Preferences	337
File Manager Search	338

9. Kubuntu (KDE Plasma) 341

KDE Plasma 5 and Kubuntu 24.04 LTS	343
Installing Kubuntu	343
SDDM	344
The Plasma Desktop	345
The KDE Help Center	347
Desktop Menu and Display Configuration	347
Edit Mode	348
Desktop Backgrounds (Wallpaper)	349
Themes	350
Leave KDE	351
The Main Menu - Application Menus	353
Application Launcher	354
Application Menu	357
Application Dashboard	359
KRunner	360
Removable Devices: Device Notifier	361
KDE Network Connections: NetworkManager	362

- Desktop Widgets (Plasmoids) 364
  - Managing desktop widgets 364
  - Folder and Icon Widgets 366
- Activities 366
  - Activity Switcher Widgets for the Desktop and Panel 370
- KDE Windows 373
- Task Managers 374
  - Icon-only Task Manager 376
  - Task Manager 378
  - Window List 379
- Applications 379
- Virtual Desktops: Pager and Overview 380
  - Pagers 380
  - Overview Effect 382
- KDE Panel 384
  - KDE Panel Widgets 385
  - KDE System Tray 387
- KDE Panel Configuration 388
- Desktop Effects 389
- KDE File Manager: Dolphin 393
  - Navigating Folders 399
  - Copy, Move, Delete, Rename, and Link Operations 399
  - Search Bar and Filter Bar 400
    - Search Bar 400
    - Filter Bar 401
  - FTP 401
- KDE Configuration: KDE System Settings 402
- Plasma Software Management: Discover 405

10. Ubuntu MATE 407

- Ubuntu MATE Help and Documentation 408
- MATE Applications 409
- The MATE Desktop 410
  - Indicator Applet Configuration 412
  - MATE Components 414
  - Drag-and-Drop Files to the Desktop 416
  - MATE Tweak 417

- Applications on the Desktop ... 417
- The Desktop Menu ... 418
- Windows ... 419
- Window List ... 420
- Workspace Switcher ... 421
- MATE Panel Layouts ... 423
  - Familiar Layout ... 424
  - Traditional Layout ... 424
  - Redmond Layout ... 425
  - Cupertino Layout ... 425
  - Mutiny Layout ... 426
  - Pantheon Layout ... 426
  - Contemporary Layout ... 427
- MATE Panel Menus ... 427
  - Brisk Menu ... 428
  - Brisk Menu with dash layout ... 429
  - Classic and Compact Menus ... 430
  - Plank Applet (dock) ... 431
- MATE Panel ... 434
  - Panel Properties ... 435
    - Displaying Panels ... 435
    - Moving and Hiding Expanded Panels ... 436
    - Unexpanded Panels: Movable and Fixed ... 436
    - Panel Background ... 437
  - Panel Objects ... 437
    - Moving, Removing, and Locking Objects ... 437
    - Adding Objects ... 438
    - Application Launchers ... 438
    - Adding Drawers ... 438
    - Adding Menus ... 439
    - Adding Folders and Files ... 439
    - Adding Applets ... 439
- Caja File Manager ... 439
  - Home Folder Sub-folders and Bookmarks ... 440
  - File Manager Windows ... 440
  - File Manager Side Pane ... 443
  - Tabs ... 445
  - Displaying Files and Folders ... 445

- File manager tools and menus ... 446
- Navigating in the file manager ... 447
- Caja File Manager Search ... 450
- Managing Files and Folders ... 450
  - Using a file's pop-up menu ... 450
  - Renaming Files ... 451
  - Grouping Files ... 451
  - Opening Applications and Files MIME Types ... 452
- File and Folder Properties ... 452
- Caja Preferences ... 454

Control Center ... 455
MATE Preferences ... 455
- About Me: photo, name, and password ... 457
- Appearance ... 458
  - Desktop Background ... 458
  - Desktop Themes ... 459
- Assistive Technologies ... 460
- Bluetooth Manager and Adapters ... 461
- Displays ... 462
- File Management: Default Applications for Media ... 463
- Fonts ... 464
  - Configuring Fonts ... 465
  - Adding Fonts ... 465
- Mouse and Keyboard Preferences ... 465
- MATE Power Management ... 466
- Popup Notifications ... 467
- Preferred Applications for Web, Mail, Accessibility, and terminal windows ... 468
- Screen Saver and Lock ... 469
- Sound ... 470
- Time and Date Manager ... 471

11. Ubuntu Flavors ... 473

Xubuntu (Xfce) ... 474
Lubuntu (LXQT) ... 477
Ubuntu Studio ... 480
Ubuntu Budgie ... 481
Ubuntu Cinnamon ... 484

Ubuntu Unity..488

12. Shells 493

The Command Line...494
    Command Line Editing 495
    Command and Filename Completion 497
History 498
    History Events 498
Filename Expansion: *, ?, [ ] 500
    Matching Multiple Characters 502
    Matching Single Characters 502
    Matching a Range of Characters..503
    Matching Shell Symbols 503
    Generating Patterns 504
Standard Input/Output and Redirection 504
    Redirecting the Standard Output: > and >>..505
    The Standard Input..506
    Redirecting the Standard Error: >&, 2>, |& 507
    Pipes: | 508
Linux Files 509
The File Structure 511
    Home Directories...511
    Pathnames..512
    System Directories 513
Listing, Displaying, and Printing Files: ls, cat, more, less, and lpr............................513
    Displaying Files: cat, less, and more..513
    Printing Files: lpr, lpq, and lprm 514
Managing Directories: mkdir, rmdir, ls, cd, pwd...515
    Creating and Deleting Directories...515
    Displaying Directory Contents 515
    Moving Through Directories 516
    Referencing the Parent Directory 516
File and Directory Operations: find, cp, mv, rm, ln 517
    Searching Directories: find 517
        Searching the Working Directory 519
        Locating Directories..519
    Copying Files..520

Contents

Moving Files 521
Copying and Moving Directories 522
Erasing Files and Directories: the rm Command 522
Links: the ln Command 522
    Symbolic Links 523
    Hard Links 523

Part 4: Administration

13. System Tools 527

GNOME System Monitor 528
Managing Processes 529
Glances 531
Scheduling Tasks 532
    KDE Task Scheduler 532
Logs 533
Disk Usage Analyzer 533
Virus Protection 535
Hardware Sensors 536
Disk Utility and Udisks 536
Plymouth 539
Managing keys with Seahorse 539
    Passwords and Keys 540
    Keyrings 540
    Creating a new GPG key 541
    Keyservers 544
    Importing Public Keys 544
    Sharing Keys 547
Logical Volume Manager 548
    LVM Structure 548
    LVM Tools: using the LVM commands 549
        Managing LVM Physical Volumes with the LVM commands 549
        Managing LVM Groups 550
        Activating Volume Groups 551
        Managing LVM Logical Volumes 551
    Steps to create a new LVM group and volume 552
    Steps to add a new drive to an LVM group and volume 553

- LVM Device Names: /dev/mapper ... 553
  - Using LVM to replace drives ... 553
    - LVM Snapshots ... 554
- OpenZFS ... 555

14. System Administration ... 557

- Ubuntu Administrative Tools ... 558
- /etc/hostname and hostnamectl ... 559
- Controlled Administrative Access ... 559
  - sudo ... 560
    - sudo command ... 560
    - sudo configuration ... 560
  - Root User Access: root and su ... 562
  - PolicyKit ... 563
- Users (Settings | System | Users) ... 564
- Users and Groups ... 568
  - New Users (Users and Groups) ... 570
  - Groups (Users and Groups) ... 572
  - Passwords ... 572
- Managing Services ... 573
- File System Access ... 573
  - Access to Internal Linux File Systems ... 573
  - Access to Windows NTFS File Systems on Local Drives ... 574
  - Zero Configuration Networking: Avahi and Link Local Addressing ... 574
  - Access to Linux Local Network Shared File Systems with mDNS ... 574
  - Access to Windows Local Network Shared File Systems ... 577
  - Shared Folders for your network (nautilus-share, Samba, and smbpasswd) ... 578
  - Accessing Samba Shares from Windows ... 582
  - File and Folder Permissions ... 583
  - Automatic file system mounts with /etc/fstab ... 585
- Bluetooth ... 586
- DKMS ... 591
- Editing Configuration Files ... 592
- GRUB 2 ... 592
- Backup Management: Deja Dup, rsync, BackupPC, and Amanda ... 597
  - Deja Dup (Backups) ... 597
  - Individual Backups: archive and rsync ... 601

BackupPC 602
Amanda 603
Printing 603
Printers: Settings 604
Remote Printers 606
Print Settings (system-config-printer) 607

15. Network Connections 613

Network Connections: Dynamic and Static 614
NetworkManager 615
User and System-Wide Network Configuration: NetworkManager 616
NetworkManager Manual Configuration using GNOME Settings 617
Settings Wi-Fi tab 617
Settings Network tab (wired) 620
NetworkManager Manual Configuration Using Network Connections: nm-connection-editor 625
NetworkManager wireless router, using your wireless connection as a Hotspot and for a Hidden Network. 628
Managing Network Connections with nmcli 629
Dial-up PPP Modem Access: wvdial 633
Netplan 634
Netplan configuration file 635
Configure a network with systemd-networkd 637
The systemd-networkd Netplan configuration file 638
Netplan wireless configuration for systemd-networkd 640
Switching between systemd-networkd and network-manager 641
Firewalls 642
Important Firewall Ports 643
Setting up a firewall with ufw 643
Gufw 644
ufw commands 647
ufw rule files 649
FirewallD and firewall-config 649
GNOME Nettool 654
Predictable and unpredictable network device names 655
Network device path names 656
Renaming network device names with udev rules 658
Renaming network device names for systemd-networkd with systemd.link 659

Table Listing **661**

Figure Listing **665**

Index **685**

Part 1: Getting Started

Introduction
Installation
Usage Basics
Managing Software

ubuntu

1. Ubuntu 24.04 LTS Introduction

Ubuntu Releases
Ubuntu 24.04 LTS
Ubuntu Release
Ubuntu Flavors
Ubuntu Live DVD and USB
App Center
Ubuntu Help and Documentation
Open Source Software
History of Linux and UNIX

Ubuntu Linux is currently one of the most popular end-user Linux distributions (**https://ubuntu.com**). Ubuntu Linux is managed by the Ubuntu foundation, which is sponsored by Canonical, Ltd (**https://canonical.com**), a commercial organization that supports and promotes open source projects. Ubuntu is based on Debian Linux, one of the oldest Linux distributions, which is dedicated to incorporating cutting-edge developments and features (**https://www.debian.org**). Mark Shuttleworth, a South African and Debian Linux developer, initiated the Ubuntu project. Debian Linux is primarily a Linux development project, trying out new features. Ubuntu provides a Debian-based Linux distribution that is stable, reliable, and easy to use.

Ubuntu is designed as a Linux operating system that can be used easily by everyone. The name Ubuntu means "humanity to others." As the Ubuntu project describes it: "Ubuntu is an African word meaning 'Humanity to others", or "I am what I am because of who we all are." The Ubuntu distribution brings the spirit of Ubuntu to the software world."

The official Ubuntu philosophy lists the following principles.

1. Every computer user should have the freedom to download, run, copy, distribute study, share, change, and improve their software for any purpose, without paying licensing fees.
2. Every computer user should be able to use their software in the language of their choice.
3. Every computer user should be given every opportunity to use software, even if they work under a disability.

The emphasis on language reflects Ubuntu's international scope. It is meant to be a global distribution that does not focus on any single market. Language support has been integrated into Linux in general by its internationalization projects, denoted by the term i18n.

Making software available to all users involves both full accessibility supports for users with disabilities as well as seamless integration of software access using online repositories, making massive amounts of software available to all users at the touch of a button. Ubuntu also makes full use of Linux's automatic device detection ability, greatly simplifying installation as well as access to removable devices and attached storage.

Ubuntu aims to provide a fully supported and reliable, open source and free, easy to use and modify, Linux operating system. Ubuntu makes the following promises about its distribution.

Ubuntu will always be free of charge, including enterprise releases and security updates.

Ubuntu comes with full commercial support from Canonical and hundreds of companies around the world.

Ubuntu includes the very best translations and accessibility infrastructure that the free software community has to offer.

Ubuntu USB/DVDs contain only free software applications; we encourage you to use free and open source software, improve it and pass it on (Ubuntu repositories contain some proprietary software like vendor graphics drivers that is also free).

Ubuntu 24.04 LTS

Ubuntu 24.04 LTS introduces several new features, as well as numerous smaller modifications. It is a long-term support release based on the Linux 6.8 kernel. The Ubuntu repositories support several major desktops, including the Ubuntu Desktop (GNOME), Kubuntu (KDE), and Ubuntu MATE. You can think of Ubuntu as a multi-desktop system, where the same repositories support different desktops. The Ubuntu Desktop features the GNOME user interface with a dock, applications overview, activities overview, and System menu. Referred to as the Ubuntu desktop, GNOME is the default desktop (see Figure 1-1). It is based on GNOME 46.

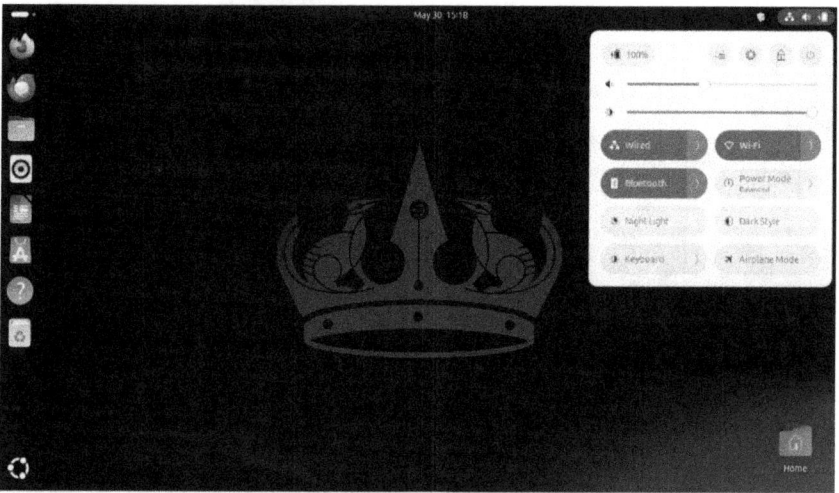

Figure 1-1: Ubuntu 24.04 LTS Ubuntu Desktop

For documentation check:

https://help.ubuntu.com/

Check the Ubuntu Release Notes for an explanation of changes.

https://wiki.ubuntu.com/NobleNumbat/ReleaseNotes

For basic tutorials of Ubuntu tasks such as installation and setting up Samba, see the Ubuntu tutorials site.

https://ubuntu.com/tutorials/

Ubuntu 24.04 LTS provides a default selection of applications to install. Only the Web browser and a few utilities are installed, instead of a full set of applications (see Figure 1-2). There are no office, multimedia, graphic, or sound applications installed. You can choose the "Default selection" option during the Installation processes on the Applications screen. There are two options: "Default selection" and "Extended selection". The "Default selection" option is already selected. For to an extended set of applications, such as office and multimedia applications, choose the "Extended selection" option.

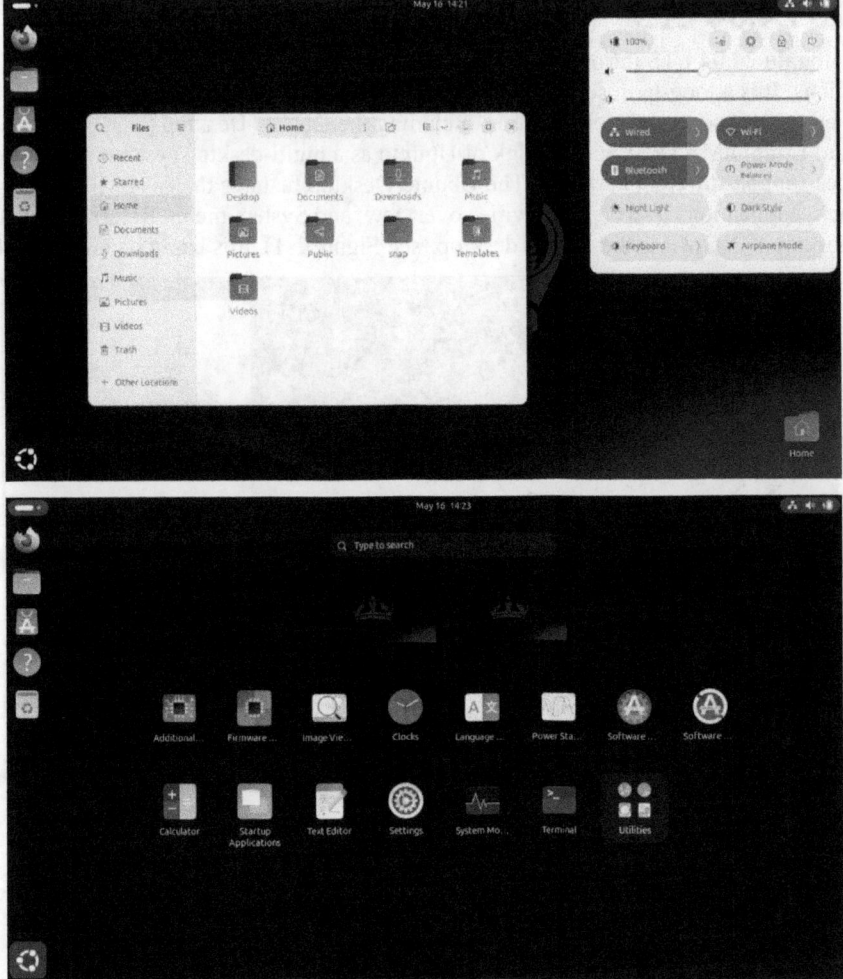

Figure 1-2: Ubuntu 24.04 LTS Ubuntu Desktop, Default selection

Ubuntu 24.04 LTS Key Changes

Several key changes have been made for the 24.04 LTS release.

Ubuntu uses GNOME 46, which implements major changes to the desktop and file manager.

For Ubuntu 24.04, the Ubuntu Desktop Installer (ubuntu-desktop-installer) has been reworked and is now renamed the Ubuntu Bootstrap Installer (ubuntu-desktop-bootstrap).

During installation, the minimal install of applications is now the default. During the installation processes on the Applications screen, there are two options: "Default selection" and "Extended selection". The "Default selection" option (minimal) is already selected. For to an extended set of applications, such as office and multimedia applications, choose the "Extended selection" option.

Installation supports the ZFS file system. ZFS support remains experimental.

Installation supports full disk encryption using a TPM (Trusted Platform Module) controller on your motherboard to physically encrypt your hard drive. Full disk encryption is still experimental.

A separate Firmware Updater application now manages firmware updates separately.

The default audio server is now PipeWire instead of PulseAudio

The Nautilus folder sharing extension is no longer installed by default. You can install it from a terminal window with **sudo apt install nautilus-share** command. This will also install the Samba server if it is not already installed. Once installed, only then does a Sharing Options entry appear in a folder's context menu (right-click).

GNOME 46 features a completely reworked System menu using Quick Settings buttons for basic network and desktop settings, such as turning wired, Wi-Fi, and Bluetooth connections on and off. Menu buttons on the right side of some of the Quick Settings buttons, display menus within the System menu such as selecting a Wi-Fi connection, a Bluetooth device, or a power mode. There are also buttons at the top for accessing the Power Off menu, lock screen, and Settings.

Apps Center is the software manager used for the Ubuntu Desktop. It is designed to primarily manage Snap packages, though it will also install APT packages. For APT packages, you can still use the **apt** commands to manage packages, as well as GNOME Software or the older Synaptic Package Manager.

The file manager (Nautilus) supports a grid view with a button to switch between grid and list views.

The file manager menus have been reworked and repositioned. The View menu only provides sorting options. The tools menu has been moved to the top of the sidebar and holds entries for changing the icon size, new tabs, new windows, showing hidden files, and opening the file manager Preferences. The folder menu button is a vertical ellipses located on the right side of the location bar. It has entries for new folder, open with, reload, edit location, add bookmark, open in terminal, and Properties.

The file manager has a Search Everywhere function, activated by a looking glass button on the top left of the header bar. This search will search all your folders. The traditional folder search searches your current folder and subfolders.

The file manager properties and preferences dialogs have been re-designed.

The activities button is now a set of elongated dots, one for each workspace that you have. The highlighted one indicates your current workspace.

Text Editor can directly edit files with administrative access. To open files that require administrative access you are prompted for your password.

Numerous applications are installed as Snap applications, though many GNOME applications still use APT. There are Snap versions of LibreOffice, vlc, Celluloid, and

Thunderbird. Some GNOME applications such as Video player and Rhythmbox are still APT (Deb packages).

Snap is the primary package manager for Ubuntu. It uses the snapd daemon to install, update, and run Snap installed applications. With Ubuntu 24.04, the snap-store application is managed by the App Center software manager. The App Center installs Snap packages by default, though it can also manage Debian (APT) packages. To install the APT version, select the Debian version from the App Center Search's "Filter by' menu. The App Center cannot manage Flathub packages. If you want to install from the Flathub repository, you should install the original GNOME Software software manager, available on the APT repository as **gnome-software** and on the App Center as Software.

Ubuntu Releases

Ubuntu provides both long-term and short-term support releases. Long-term support releases (LTS), such as Ubuntu 24.04, are released every two years. Short-term releases, such as Ubuntu 23.04, are provided every six months between the LTS versions. They are designed to make available the latest applications and support for the newest hardware. Each has its own nickname, like Noble Numbat for the 24.04 LTS release. The long-term support releases are supported for three years for desktops and five years for servers, whereas short-term support releases are supported for 18 months. In addition, Canonical provides limited commercial support for companies that purchase it.

Installing Ubuntu is easy to do. A core set of applications are installed, and you can add to them as you wish. Following installation, additional software can be downloaded from online repositories. There are only a few install screens, which move quickly through default partitioning, user setup, and time settings. Hardware components such as graphics cards and network connections are configured and detected automatically. With the App Center (installed by default), you can find and install additional software with the click of a button.

The Ubuntu distribution of Linux is available online at numerous sites. Ubuntu maintains its own site for the desktop edition at **https://ubuntu.com/desktop** You can download the current release of Ubuntu Linux from **https://ubuntu.com/download/desktop**.

Ubuntu Desktop and Server

The Ubuntu Desktop edition provides desktop functionality for end users. The Ubuntu Desktop release provides a Live USB/DVD using the GNOME desktop. Most users would install this version. You can download the Ubuntu Desktop from the Download page, which you can access from the Ubuntu site (**https://ubuntu.com**) by clicking on the Download menu and choosing Desktop. The page address is:

```
https://ubuntu.com/download/desktop
```

For upgrade instructions, click on the "Software Updater" link in the "From an older version" section.

```
https://ubuntu.com/tutorial/tutorial-upgrading-ubuntu-desktop
```

To open the Alternative Download page, click on the "Alternative downloads and torrents" link below the Download button.

```
https://ubuntu.com/download/alternative-downloads
```

The Alternative Downloads page provides information on BitTorrent files for downloading the Ubuntu 24.04 LTS DVD release.

Table 1-1 lists the websites where you can download ISO images for the desktop and server. ISO images can be downloaded directly or by using a BitTorrent application like Transmission. Metalink downloads are also supported which make effective use of mirrors. If you have already downloaded a pre-release ISO image, like a beta version, you can use zsync to download just the final changes, greatly reducing download times.

Those who want to run Ubuntu as a server, to provide an Internet service such as a website, would use the Ubuntu Server edition. The Server edition provides only a simple command line interface; it does not install the desktop. It is designed primarily to run servers. Keep in mind that you could install the desktop first, and later download server software from the Ubuntu repositories, running them from a system that also has a desktop, though there are overhead costs for a server running a desktop. You do not have to install the Server edition to install and run servers. You can download the Server edition from the Ubuntu Server download page, which you can access from the Ubuntu site (**https://ubuntu.com**). The page address is:

```
https://ubuntu.com/download/server
```

URL	Internet Site
https://ubuntu.com/download/	Primary download site for Desktop and Server DVDs
http://releases.ubuntu.com/noble/	Download site for Desktop DVD and Server CDs, including alternate install methods like torrent, zsync, and metalink.
http://cdimages.ubuntu.com/releases/noble/release/	Download site for Ubuntu DVDs for Apple powerpc, arm, and IBM z systems.
http://cdimages.ubuntu.com/	Download site for all Ubuntu flavors, including Kubuntu, Ubuntu MATE, Ubuntu Cinnamon, Xubuntu, and Ubuntu Studio. Check also their respective websites.

Table 1-1: Ubuntu DVD ISO Image locations

The releases site provides a DVD download page with download files for BitTorrent, zsync, and metalink, as well as a direct download link.

```
http://releases.ubuntu.com/noble/
```

Apple powerpc, ARM, and IBM z compatible Ubuntu Desktop DVDs can also be downloaded from cdimages site:

```
http://cdimages.ubuntu.com/releases/noble/release/
```

Ubuntu Flavors

Ubuntu supports several desktops, known as flavors, each designed for a distinct group of users or functions. Flavors install different collections of software such as the Xfce (Xubuntu) or MATE desktops, the KDE desktop (Kubuntu), servers, educational software, and multimedia applications.

Ubuntu Flavor	Description
Kubuntu	Live USB/DVD and Install using the KDE desktop, instead of GNOME, **https://www.kubuntu.org**. Add to Ubuntu desktop with the **kubuntu-desktop** metapackage.
Ubuntu MATE	Uses the MATE desktop, **https://ubuntu-mate.org.** Add to Ubuntu desktop with the **ubuntu-mate-desktop** metapackage.
Xubuntu	Uses the Xfce desktop instead of GNOME, **http://xubuntu.org**. Useful for laptops.
Lubuntu	Lightweight version of Ubuntu based on the LXDE desktop, **https://lubuntu.me/**
Ubuntu Studio	Ubuntu desktop with multimedia and graphics production applications, **https://ubuntustudio.org**. Add to Ubuntu desktop with the **ubuntustudio-desktop** metapackage
Ubuntu Kylin	Ubuntu Desktop for Chinese users
Ubuntu Budgie	The Budgie desktop based on the Ubuntu desktop, **https://ubuntubudgie.org**
Ubuntu Cinnamon	Cinnamon desktop developed for Linux Mint, **https://ubuntucinnamon.org/**
Edubuntu	Ubuntu for education, **https://www.edubuntu.org/**
Ubuntu Unity	Uses the older Ubuntu Unity desktop, **https://ubuntuunity.org**

Table 1-2: Ubuntu Flavors

Ubuntu Flavors have the same Ubuntu packages but use either a different desktop or a specialized collection of software for certain groups of users. Kubuntu uses the KDE desktop instead of GNOME. Xubuntu is a stripped down and highly efficient desktop using the Xfce desktop, ideal for low power use on laptops and smaller computer. Edubuntu provides educational software that can be used with a specialized Edubuntu server, providing educational software on a school network. Ubuntu Studio provides a collection of multimedia and image production software. Lubuntu is based on the LXDE desktop, providing a very lightweight version of Ubuntu. Ubuntu MATE uses the MATE desktop. Ubuntu Kylin is the Ubuntu Desktop for Chinese users. Ubuntu Unity is based on the older Unity desktop previously developed by Ubuntu. Ubuntu Cinnamon uses the Cinnamon desktop developed for Linux Mint. Table 1-2 lists websites where you can download ISO images for the various flavors.

You can download flavors from their respective websites, or from **http://releases.ubuntu.com**. The Ubuntu site spells flavors as flavours. The links for their sites are available at:

```
https://ubuntu.com/download/flavours
```

The versions featuring different desktops are listed here.

https://www.kubuntu.org   KDE desktop version

https://ubuntu-mate.org   MATE desktop version

https://xubuntu.org   Xfce desktop version

https://lubuntu.me/   LXDE desktop version

https://ubuntubudgie.org/   Budgie desktop version

https://ubuntuunity.org/   Ubuntu Unity desktop version

https://ubuntucinnamon.org/   Cinnamon desktop version

https://www.edubuntu.org/   Ubuntu desktop configured for educational support

https://ubuntustudio.org/   Ubuntu Studio with applications for graphics and multimedia

You can find out more about flavors (flavours) at: **https://ubuntu.com/download/flavours**, which you can access from the Ubuntu site (**https://ubuntu.com**). Click the Download menu, choosing Ubuntu Flavours. Links to their websites are provided on the Ubuntu Flavours page, where you can then download their live/install DVDs. All these flavors can be downloaded from their respective websites, as well as from:

```
http://releases.ubuntu.com/
```

The **http://releases.ubuntu.com** and **http://cdimages.ubuntu.com** sites hold both BitTorrent and full image files for the flavors they provide. The **http://releases.ubuntu.com** site also provides downloads from multiple mirrors and zsync files for synchronizing downloads. Keep in mind that most of these flavors are released as Live USB/DVD discs, 64 bit versions.

Ubuntu Live USB/DVD

The Ubuntu Desktop USB/DVD can operate as a Live session (the Server edition does not), so you can run Ubuntu from any DVD or USB drive. New users can also use the Live-USB/DVD to try out Ubuntu to see if they like it. The Ubuntu Desktop USB/DVD will run as a Live session automatically using Ubuntu as the desktop. To create a Live USB, you install the Ubuntu Desktop ISO image to a USB drive using a USB creator application such as Startup Disk Creator on Ubuntu or the Fedora Media Writer on Windows or MAC systems.

The Desktop Live USB/DVD provided by Ubuntu includes a basic collection of software packages. You will have a fully operational Ubuntu desktop (see Figure 1-3). You have the full set of administrative tools, with which you can add users, change configuration settings, and even add software, while the Live session is running. When you shut down, the configuration information is lost, including any software you have added. Files and data can be written to removable devices like USB drives, DVD write discs, and network drives, letting you save your data during a Live session.

When you start up the Ubuntu Desktop USB/DVD, the startup screen is displayed, with the "Try Ubuntu" option selected. This option starts up a Live session, and will start automatically after a few seconds. The Live USB/DVD desktop is then displayed (see Figure 1-2) and you are logged in as the **ubuntu** user. The Dock on the left side displays icons for installing Ubuntu, the Web browser (Firefox), Thunderbird mailer, Rhythmbox music player, LibreOffice writer, the App

Center, and Ubuntu desktop help. The desktop shows icons for the home folder (ubuntu), the trash, and an Install Ubuntu icon. On the top bar to the right is the System menu with entries for network connections, which you can configure for wireless access, as well as a power button for shutting down your system.

You can save files to your home folder, but they are temporary and disappear at the end of the session. Copy them to a DVD, USB drive, another removable device, or to a network file system (if you have network access) to save them.

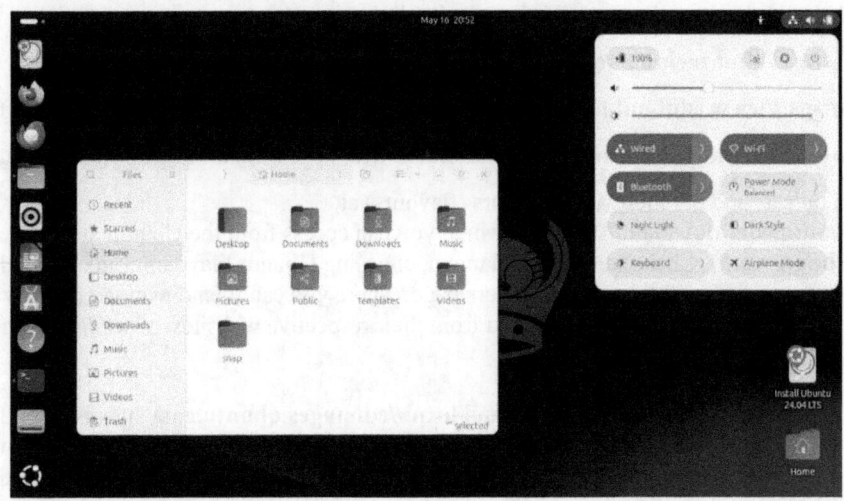

Figure 1-3: Ubuntu Live USB/DVD

All the Live USB/DVDs also function as install discs for Ubuntu, providing a collection of software, and installing an Ubuntu operating system that can be expanded and updated from Ubuntu online repositories. An Install icon lets you install Ubuntu on your computer, performing a standard installation to your hard drive. From the Live session desktop, double-click the Install Ubuntu icon on the desktop or dock to start the installation.

Ubuntu Live USB drive

On Ubuntu, you can use the USB Startup Disk Creator utility to install any Ubuntu disc image on a USB drive. The USB Live/install drive is generated using the DVD image that you first have to download. Check the Ubuntu tutorial on create a Live USB drive.

https://ubuntu.com/tutorial/tutorial-create-a-usb-stick-on-ubuntu

Note: Alternatively, you could download and use the Fedora Media Writer to create the USB drive. The Fedora Media Writer can be installed on Windows and Mac operating systems. If you do not already have an Ubuntu system, you could use the Fedora Media Writer to create your Ubuntu USB drives on Windows or Mac. If you access the Fedora download site from a Windows system, the download button downloads the Fedora Media Writer for Windows, **https://getfedora.org/en/workstation/download/**.

Click "Startup Disk Creator" icon on the Applications overview to open the Make Startup Disk window with an entry at the top to select an ISO image and an entry below to select the USB drive to use. Click the Other button to locate a specific disk image to use. Then click the "Make Startup Disk" button to install the ISO on the USB drive.

The "Make Startup Disk" operation will not erase any data already on your USB drive. You can still access it, even Windows data. The Ubuntu Live OS will coexist with your current data, occupying available free space.

To boot from the Live USB, be sure your computer (BIOS) is configured to boot from the USB drive. The Live USB drive will then start up just like the Live DVD, displaying the install screen with options to try Ubuntu or install it.

When you create the Live USB drive, you have the option to specify writable memory. This will allow you to save files to your USB drive as part of the Ubuntu Live operating system. You can save files to your Document or Pictures directory and then access them later. You can also create new users, and give those users administrative permission, just as you would on a normally installed OS. With the Settings User Accounts tool, you could even have the new user be the automatic login, instead of the **ubuntu** user. In effect, the Ubuntu Live USB drive becomes a portable Ubuntu OS. Even with these changes, the Ubuntu Live USB remains the equivalent of a Live DVD, just one that you can write to. There is no GRUB boot loader. You still use the install start up screen. In addition, you cannot update the kernel.

If you want a truly portable Ubuntu OS, just perform a standard installation to a USB drive, instead of to a hard drive. You will have to create a new clean partition on the USB drive to install to. You would either reduce the size of the current partition, preserving data, or simply delete it, opening up the entire drive for use by the new Ubuntu OS.

Ubuntu Software

All Linux software for Ubuntu is currently available from online repositories. You can download applications for desktops, Internet servers, office suites, and programming packages, among others. Software packages are distributed primarily through the official Ubuntu repository. Downloads and updates are handled automatically by your desktop software manager and updater. Many popular applications are included in separate sections of the repository. During installation, your system is configured to access Ubuntu repositories. You can update to the latest software from the Ubuntu repository using the software updater.

A complete listing of software packages for the Ubuntu distribution, along with a search capability is located at:

https://packages.ubuntu.com

In addition, you could download from third-party sources software that is in the form of compressed archives or in DEB packages. DEB packages are archived using the Debian Package Manager and have the extension **.deb**. Compressed archives have an extension such as **.tar.gz**. You also can download the source version and compile it directly on your system. This has become a simple process, almost as simple as installing the compiled DEB versions.

There are two software management systems supported and used by Ubuntu 24.04, the older APT (Advanced Package Tool) software management system that uses DEB packages, and the newer Snap system that uses Snap packages. Snap is the new package format that will eventually replace the deb package management system on Ubuntu. The packages are called **snaps**. With Snap, the software files for an application are not installed in global folders. They are installed in one separate location, and any dependent software and libraries are included as part of the Snap package.

Due to licensing restrictions, multimedia support for popular operations like MP3, DVD, and DivX are included with Ubuntu in a separate section of the repository called multiverse. Ubuntu includes on its restricted repository NVIDIA and AMD vendor graphics drivers. Ubuntu also provides as part of its standard installation, the generic X.org drivers that will enable your graphics cards to work.

All software packages in the Ubuntu repositories are accessible directly with the App Center and the Synaptic Package Manager, which provide easy software installation, removal, and searching. The App Center will support both APT and Snap packages, but gives priority to Snap packages.

Ubuntu Help and Documentation

A great deal of help and documentation is available online for Ubuntu, ranging from detailed install procedures to beginner questions (see Table 1-3). The documentation for Ubuntu 24.04 LTS is located at **https://help.ubuntu.com/**. The Firefox Web browser start page displays links for two major help sites: Ubuntu documentation at **https://help.ubuntu.com** and Ubuntu Community at **https://help.ubuntu.com/community**. Check the Ubuntu tutorials site (**https://ubuntu.com/tutorials/**) for basic tutorials on different Ubuntu tasks Tutorials for Ubuntu topics and tasks, such as running the Live USB/DVD, setting up Samba, Install the Ubuntu desktop, and configuring the Apache Web server.

Site	Description
https://help.ubuntu.com/	Help pages and install documentation
https://packages.ubuntu.com	Ubuntu software package list and search
https://discourse.ubuntu.com.org	Ubuntu Discourse site
https://askubuntu.com	Ask Ubuntu Q&A site for users and developers (community based)
https://ubuntu.com/tutorials/	Tutorials for Ubuntu topics and tasks
http://fridge.ubuntu.com	News and developments
http://planet.ubuntu.com	Member and developer blogs
https://ubuntu.com/blog	Latest Ubuntu news
http://www.tldp.org	Linux Documentation Project website
https://help.ubuntu.com/community	Community Documentation
https://lists.ubuntu.com	Ubuntu mailing lists

Table 1-3: Ubuntu help and documentation

In addition, there are blog and news sites as well as the standard Linux documentation. Ubuntu Community features Ubuntu documentation, support, blogs, and news. A Contribute section links to sites where you can contribute for development, artwork, documentation, and support. The Ask Ubuntu site is a question and answer site based on community support, which provides answers to many common questions (**https://askubuntu.com**). For mailing lists, check **https://lists.ubuntu.com**. There are lists for categories like Ubuntu announcements, community support for specific flavors, and development for areas like the desktop, servers, or mobile implementation.

help.ubuntu.com

Ubuntu-specific documentation is available at **https://help.ubuntu.com**. Here, on listed links, you can find specific documentation for different releases. Always check the release help page first for documentation, though it may be sparse and cover mainly changed areas. For 24.04 LTS the Documentation section provides the Ubuntu Desktop Guide (Desktop) and the Ubuntu Server Guide. The Ubuntu Desktop Guide covers the GNOME interfaces and is the same guide installed with your desktop, accessible as Help (Applications overview).

```
https://help.ubuntu.com/stable/ubuntu-help/index.html
```

One of the more helpful pages is the Community Help page, **https://help.ubuntu.com/community**. Here you will find detailed documentation on the installation of all Ubuntu releases, using the desktop, installing software, and configuring devices. Always check the page for your Ubuntu release first. The page includes these main sections:

Installation: Link to Install page with sections on desktop, server, and alternate installations.

Hardware: Sections on managing hardware. Links to pages on drives and partitions, input devices, wireless configuration, printers, sound, and video.

Further Topics: Links to pages on system administration, security, and troubleshooting, servers, networking, and software development.

Ubuntu Flavors: Links to documentation on different Ubuntu versions such as Lubuntu and Kubuntu.

discourse.ubuntu.com

The Ubuntu Discourse site provides online support and discussion for users. Categories covers areas such as support, announcements, projects, and documentation. The Project Discussion category covers specific support areas like desktop, server, cloud, and the snap store. The "Support and Help" category provides an area where users can obtain answers to questions. You can use the search feature to find discussions on your topic of interest. You can also sort by latest and recent posts.

```
https://discourse.ubuntu.com
```

Ubuntu news and blog sites

Several news and blog sites are accessible from the News page at **https://wiki.ubuntu.com/Home**.

http://fridge.ubuntu.com The Fridge site lists the latest news and developments for Ubuntu. It features the Weekly newsletter, latest announcements, and upcoming events.

http://planet.ubuntu.com Ubuntu blog for members and developers

https://ubuntu.com/blog Ubuntu news

Linux documentation

The Linux Documentation Project (LDP) has developed a complete set of Linux manuals. The documentation is available at the LDP home site at **http://www.tldp.org**. The Linux documentation for your installed software will be available in your **/usr/share/doc** directory.

Open Source Software

Linux is developed as a cooperative Open Source effort over the Internet, so no company or institution controls Linux. Software developed for Linux reflects this background. Development often takes place when Linux users decide to work together on a project. Most Linux software is developed as Open Source software. The source code for an application is freely distributed along with the application. Programmers can make their own contributions to a software package's development, modifying and correcting the source code. As an open source operating system, the Linux source code is included in all its distributions and is freely available. Many major software development efforts are also open source projects, as are the KDE and GNOME desktops along with most of their applications. You can find more information about the Open Source movement at **https://opensource.org**.

Open source software is protected by public licenses that prevent commercial companies from taking control of open source software by adding modifications of their own, copyrighting those changes, and selling the software as their own product. The most popular public license is the GNU General Public License (GPL) provided by the Free Software Foundation. Linux is distributed under this license. The GNU General Public License retains the copyright, freely licensing the software with the requirement that the software and any modifications made to it are always freely available. Other public licenses have been created to support the demands of different kinds of open source projects. The GNU Lesser General Public License (LGPL) lets commercial applications use GNU licensed software libraries. The Qt Public License (QPL) lets open source developers use the Qt libraries essential to the KDE desktop. You can find a complete listing at **https://opensource.org**.

Linux is currently copyrighted under a GNU public license provided by the Free Software Foundation (see **http://www.gnu.org/**). GNU software is distributed free, provided it is freely distributed to others. GNU software has proved both reliable and effective. Many of the popular Linux utilities, such as C compilers, shells, and editors, are GNU software applications. In addition, many open source software projects are licensed under the GNU General Public License (GPL). Most of these applications are available on the Ubuntu software repositories. Chapter 4 describes in detail the process of accessing these repositories to download and install software applications from them on your system.

Under the terms of the GNU General Public License, the original author retains the copyright, although anyone can modify the software and redistribute it, provided the source code is included, made public, and provided free. In addition, no restriction exists on selling the software or giving it away free. One distributor could charge for the software, while another could provide it free of charge. Major software companies are also providing Linux versions of their most popular applications.

Linux

Linux is a fast, stable, and open source operating system for PCs and workstations that features professional-level Internet services, extensive development tools, fully functional graphical user interfaces (GUIs), and a massive number of applications ranging from office suites to multimedia applications. Linux was developed in the early 1990s by Linus Torvalds, along with other programmers around the world. As an operating system, Linux performs many of the same functions as UNIX, Macintosh, and Windows. However, Linux is distinguished by its power and flexibility, along with being freely available. Most PC operating systems, such as Windows, began their development within the confines of small, restricted personal computers, which have become more versatile and powerful machines. Such operating systems are constantly being upgraded to keep up with the ever-changing capabilities of PC hardware. Linux, on the other hand, was developed in a different context. Linux is a PC version of the UNIX operating system that has been used for decades on mainframes and is currently the system of choice for network servers and workstations.

Technically, Linux consists of the operating system program referred to as the kernel, which is the part originally developed by Linus Torvalds. However, it has always been distributed with a large number of software applications, ranging from network servers and security programs to office applications and development tools. Linux has evolved as part of the open source software movement, in which independent programmers joined to provide free quality software to any user. Linux has become the premier platform for open source software, much of it developed by the Free Software Foundation's GNU project. Most of these applications are also available on the Ubuntu repository, providing packages that are Debian compliant.

Linux operating system capabilities include powerful networking features, including support for Internet, intranets, and Windows networking. As a norm, Linux distributions include fast, efficient, and stable Internet servers, such as the Web, FTP, and DNS servers, along with proxy, news, and mail servers. Linux has everything you need to set up, support, and maintain a fully functional network.

Linux is distributed freely under a GNU General Public License (GPL) as specified by the Free Software Foundation, making it available to anyone who wants to use it. GNU (which stands for "GNU's Not Unix") is a project initiated and managed by the Free Software Foundation to provide free software to users, programmers, and developers. Linux is copyrighted, not public domain. The GNU General Public License is designed to ensure that Linux remains free and, at the same time, standardized. Linux is technically the operating system kernel, the core operations, and only one official Linux kernel exists. Its power and stability have made Linux an operating system of choice as a network server.

Originally designed specifically for Intel-based personal computers, Linux started out as a personal project of computer science student Linus Torvalds at the University of Helsinki. At that time, students were making use of a program called Minix, which highlighted different UNIX features. Minix was created by Professor Andrew Tanenbaum and widely distributed over the Internet to students around the world. Torvalds's intention was to create an effective PC version of UNIX for Minix users. It was named Linux, and in 1991, Torvalds released version 0.11. Linux was widely distributed over the Internet, and in the following years, other programmers refined and added to it, incorporating most of the applications and features found in standard UNIX systems. All the major window managers have been ported to Linux. Linux has all the networking tools, such as FTP file transfer support, Web browsers, and the whole range of network services such as email, the domain name service, and dynamic host configuration, along with FTP, Web, and print servers. It also has a full set of program development utilities, such as C++ compilers and debuggers. Given all its features, the Linux operating system remains small, stable, and fast.

Linux development is overseen by The Linux Foundation (**https://www.linuxfoundation.org**), which is a merger of The Free Standards Group and Open Source Development Labs (OSDL). This is the group with which Linux Torvalds works to develop new Linux versions. Linux kernels are released at **https://www.kernel.org/**.

ubuntu

2. Installing Ubuntu

Install Discs
Installation Overview
Installation with the Ubuntu Desktop DVD
Recovery
Re-Installing the Boot Loader

Installing Ubuntu Linux is a very simple procedure, using just a few screens with default entries for easy installation. A pre-selected collection of software is installed. Most of your devices, like your display and network connection, are detected automatically. The most difficult part would be a manual partitioning of the hard drive, but you can use automatic partitioning for fresh installs, as is usually the case.

For Ubuntu 24.04, the Ubuntu Desktop Installer (ubuntu-desktop-installer) has been reworked and is now renamed the Ubuntu Bootstrap Installer (ubuntu-desktop-bootstrap).

See the Ubuntu documentation for a detailed reference on the Ubuntu installer, as well as details for PC, PowerPC, and ARM. As of this printing, the installation guide for Ubuntu 24.04 is not yet published, but, when ready, should be available at:

https://help.ubuntu.com

Install Discs

In most cases, installation is performed using an Ubuntu Desktop USB/DVD that will install the Ubuntu desktop, along with a pre-selected set of software packages. The Ubuntu Desktop USB/DVD is also designed to run from a USB drive or DVD disc, while providing the option to install Ubuntu on your hard drive. You can download the ISO disc image from the Ubuntu download site. The Ubuntu Desktop USB/DVD has only a 64-bit version.

https://ubuntu.com/download/desktop

You can also download the Ubuntu ISO images for both the desktop from:

https://releases.ubuntu.com/noble

Ubuntu releases	Description
Ubuntu Desktop Live/Install USB/DVD	Primary Ubuntu release, Ubuntu desktop, can be burned to either DVD disc or USB drive.
Ubuntu Server DVD	Server-only installation, no desktop, command line interface
Ubuntu Cloud	Cloud based install for OpenStack

Table 2-1: Ubuntu releases

Ubuntu tailors its installs by providing different install ISO images for different releases and versions (see Table 2-1). These include the Desktop ISO image, the Server ISO image designed for servers, and the Mac ISO image for Apple desktops.

Desktop DVD Run as a Live DVD or install Ubuntu Linux with the Ubuntu desktop and a standard set of applications.

Desktop USB Run as Live USB or install Ubuntu Linux with the Ubuntu desktop and a standard set of applications, uses the Ubuntu Desktop DVD ISO image installed on a USB drive.

Server install USB/DVD Install Ubuntu with a standard set of servers; this uses the command line interface (no desktop). Can use either a DVD or USB disk.

Using BitTorrent: Transmission

Most current Linux and Windows systems support BitTorrent for downloading. BitTorrent provides an efficient, safe, and fast method for downloading large files. Various BitTorrent clients are available, including one from the original BitTorrent developer. Transmission is the preferred Ubuntu BitTorrent application. BitTorrent relies on making multiple connections that can use up bandwidth quickly. The BitTorrent files for all versions (Desktop and Server) can be found at the primary download sites, along with direct downloads:

http://releases.ubuntu.com/24.04

Metalinks

Metalinks are XML files that work like mirror lists, allowing download clients to easily choose a fast mirror and perform a more controlled download. You would need to use a download client that supports metalinks, like KGet, **gget**, or **aria2**. For more information about using metalink with Ubuntu, see:

https://wiki.ubuntu.com/MetalinkIsoDownloads

For general information see.

https://en.wikipedia.org/wiki/Metalink

A metalink file will have the extension **.metalink**. Metalink files for the Ubuntu releases are available at:

http://releases.ubuntu.com/24.04/

Zsync

Ubuntu also provides zsync downloads for its Ubuntu ISO images. The **zsync** program operates like **rsync**, but with very little overhead. It is designed for distributing a single file to many locations. In effect, you are synchronizing your copy to the original. The zsync program is designed to download just those parts of the original file that the downloaded copy needs. It uses a **.zsync** file that has the name of the ISO image you want to download. You can download **.zsync** files for Ubuntu ISO images from the **http://releases.ubuntu.com/noble/** download page.

The **zsync** program is useful for users who have already download a pre-release version of an Ubuntu ISO image, such as the beta version. You would rename the beta image file to that of the new release, and then perform a zsync operation on it using the appropriate **.zsync** file provided by the Ubuntu download page. Only those parts of the final version that differ from the beta version would be downloaded, greatly reducing the actual amount of data downloaded.

You can install **zsync** using the **apt install** command. For more information, see the zsync Man page and the Zsync site: **http://zsync.moria.org.uk/**. For information on how to use zsync with Ubuntu, see:

https://ubuntu-tutorials.com/2009/10/29/use-zsync-to-update-existing-iso-images/

Installing Multiple-Boot Systems

The GRUB boot loader already supports multiple booting. Should you have both Ubuntu and Windows systems installed on your hard disks, GRUB will let you choose to boot either the

Ubuntu system or a Windows system. During installation, GRUB will automatically detect any other operating systems installed on your computer and configure your boot loader menu to let you access them. You do not have to perform any configuration yourself.

If you want a Windows system installed on your computer, you should install it first. Windows would overwrite the boot loader installed by a previous Ubuntu system, cutting off access to the Linux system. If you installed Windows after having installed Ubuntu, you will need to re-install the Ubuntu GRUB boot loader. See the section at the end of this Chapter on re-installing the boot loader. There are several ways you can do it, most very simple.

If you have already installed Windows on your hard drive and configured it to take up the entire hard drive, you can select the "Install alongside" option during installation to free up space and set up Ubuntu partitions.

Tip: You can also use the Ubuntu Live USB/DVD to start up Ubuntu and perform any necessary hard disk partitioning using GParted.

Hardware Requirements

Most hardware today meets the requirements for running Ubuntu. Ubuntu can be installed on a wide variety of systems, ranging from the very weak to the very powerful. The install procedure will detect most of your hardware automatically. You will only need to specify your keyboard, though a default is automatically detected for you. You can check the Ubuntu System Requirements page at **http://help.ubuntu.com** for details:

`https://help.ubuntu.com/community/Installation/SystemRequirements`

Installation Overview

Installing Ubuntu involves several processes, including creating Linux partitions, loading the Ubuntu software, selecting a time zone, and creating a user account. The installation program used for Ubuntu is a screen-based program that takes you through all these processes, step-by-step, as one continuous procedure. You can use either your mouse or the keyboard to make selections. When you finish with a screen, click the Next button at the bottom to move to the next screen. If you need to move back to the previous screen, click Back. You can also press TAB, the arrow keys, SPACEBAR, and ENTER keys to make selections.

Installation is a straightforward process. A graphical installation is easy to use, providing full mouse support.

Most systems today already meet hardware requirements and have automatic connections to the Internet.

They also support booting a DVD-ROM disc or USB drive, though this support may have to be explicitly configured in the system BIOS.

If you are installing on a blank hard drive or on a drive with free space, or if you are performing a simple update that uses the same partitions, installing Ubuntu is a simple process. Ubuntu also features an automatic partitioning function that will perform the partitioning for you.

Chapter 2: Installation **49**

A preconfigured [...] u will not even have to select packages.

For a quick insta[...] nstallation process by placing your DVD disc in the DVD dr[...] starting up your system. To boot from the USB disk, you m[...] ot disk (F12 at start up on many computers). Graphical ins[...] ing the instructions in each window as you progress. Installatio[...]

1. **Welcome** A def[...] English, so you can usually just click Next.
2. **Accessibility** Ch[...] need.
3. **Keyboard Layout** [...] an usually just click Next.
4. **Internet connectio**[...] ch as wired, wireless, or hidden wireless.
5. **Type of installation** [...] ated. Interactive is the default and the one most users w[...] Next.
6. **Applications** On t[...] se a Default selection that installs just the opera[...] d the web browser, or an Extended selection tha[...] plications.
7. **Optimize your comp**[...] ch as proprietary drivers such as Nvidia, and third party [...]
8. **Disk setup** For auto[...] options, depending on what other operating systems [...] rd drive. For drives that have other operating systems [...] hem or, if Ubuntu 20.04 or 21.10 is installed, choos[...] ntire disk. In all cases, you can also choose to partiti[...] Something else" option). As soon as you click the "In[...] tallation begins.
9. **Disk setup: Manual par**[...] hing only, in which you set up partitions yourself. Ot[...]
10. **Select your timezone** U[...] or select your city from the drop-down menu.
11. **Create your account** Se[...] ur computer, as well as a password for that user. You [...] ally.

After the installation comple[...] stem. You will then be asked to remove your USB/DVD dis[...]

Installation with the U[...]VD

The Ubuntu Desktop DVD/U[...] rom the DVD/USB (Live DVD/USB) and installing Ubunt[...] d then initiate an installation, or install directly. Attach y[...] Ubuntu DVD disc in the DVD drive before you start your comp[...] onfigured to boot from

Part 1: Getting Started

the USB drive or from the DVD drive. If you are using a DVD, most computers are already set up to boot first from the DVD drive. To boot from the USB drive, you may have to either temporarily select the boot disk (F12 at start up on many computers), or configure your BIOS to boot from the USB drive. After you start your computer, the installation program starts up.

On most screens, a Next button is displayed on the lower-right corner of an installation screen. Once finished with a screen, click Next to move on. In some cases, you will be able to click a Back button to return to a previous screen. As each screen appears in the installation, default entries will be selected, usually by the auto-probing capability of the installation program. If these entries are correct, you can click Next to accept them and go on to the next screen.

You have two ways to begin the install. You can start the installation directly or you can first start up the Ubuntu Live session. The advantage of the Live session is that you will be able to configure your network access and any other devices you have. Most users will not need to perform any configuration. In this case, you could perform a direct install, instead of starting the live session. With a direct install, the System menu, located at the top-right of the screen, is available, but it only allows you to choose the Wi-Fi connections. You cannot perform any network configuration.

The Live session is a fully functional Ubuntu system. Configuration options are listed in the System menu (top right side) (see Figure 2-1). If your computer has a wired connection, it will already be configured for you and the Wired entry will show that you are connected. For a Wi-Fi connection you will have to choose a connection to use. Click the Wi-Fi entry to expand to a menu showing all available Wi-Fi networks near you. Choose the one you want to use. Should you have to perform more detailed network configurations, choose the "Wired Settings" or "Wi-Fi Settings" entries the respective menus. To perform other configurations, open the Settings dialog, by clicking the Setting button (gear image) at the top right of the System menu.

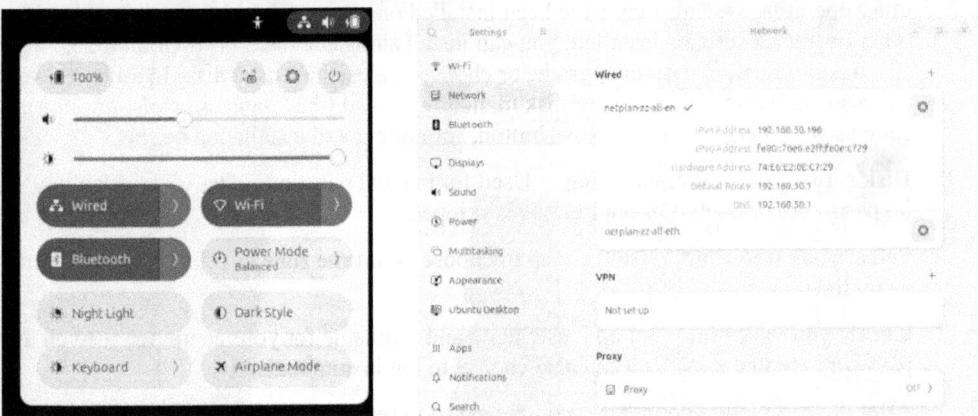

Figure 2-1: Ubuntu Live session System menu and Wired Network configuration

Welcome and Language

When the Ubuntu Desktop USB/DVD first boots, a text screen first appears with the following options.

```
Try or Install Ubuntu
Ubuntu (safe graphics)
Boot from next volume
UEFI Firmware Settings
```

An asterisk appears before the selected entry. Use the up and down arrows to move between entries, and press ENTER to choose one. The UEFI Firmware Settings entry starts up your computer's BIOS settings.

The " Ubuntu" and "Ubuntu (safe graphics)" entry starts an automatic disk checking process, which you can cancel by pressing CTRL-c. As the system starts up, the Ubuntu logo is displayed along with your computer's logo.

Ubuntu as a Live session will start, displaying the Welcome screen of the install process (see Figure 2-2). An Ubuntu Bootstrap button is displayed at the bottom of the Welcome screen. You can click it to hide the desktop showing only the install screen and the top bar. You can continue with the installation directly if you want. To re-display the desktop, you can click on the activities button on the top left side of the top bar.

Figure 2-2: Install screen for Ubuntu Desktop USB/DVD

Should you want to use the live session instead, you can close the install Welcome window and use Ubuntu as a live session from your USB/DVD disk. To later install Ubuntu, click the "Install Ubuntu" icon on the desktop or on the dock (the Ubuntu icon at the top) (see Figure 2-3). The Install window opens to the Welcome screen for choosing your language.

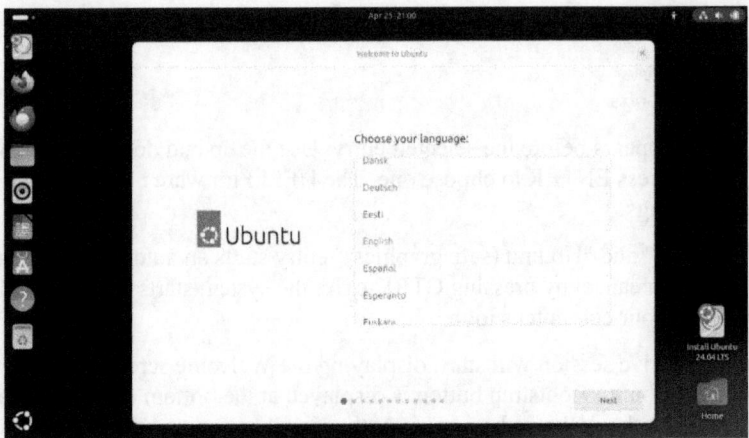

Figure 2-3: Live USB/DVD (Desktop) with Install icon

On the Welcome screen, select the language you want from the list on the left. A default language will already be selected, usually English (see Figure 2-4). Click the Next button to start up the installation.

Figure 2-4: Install Welcome and Language screen

Accessibility

On the Accessibility screen you can chooses several accessibility enhancements should you need them during installation. Links to configuration dialogs are shown for Seeing, Hearing, Typing (see Figure 2-5), Pointing and clicking, and Zoom. If you do not need any of these, just click Next.

Chapter 2: Installation **53**

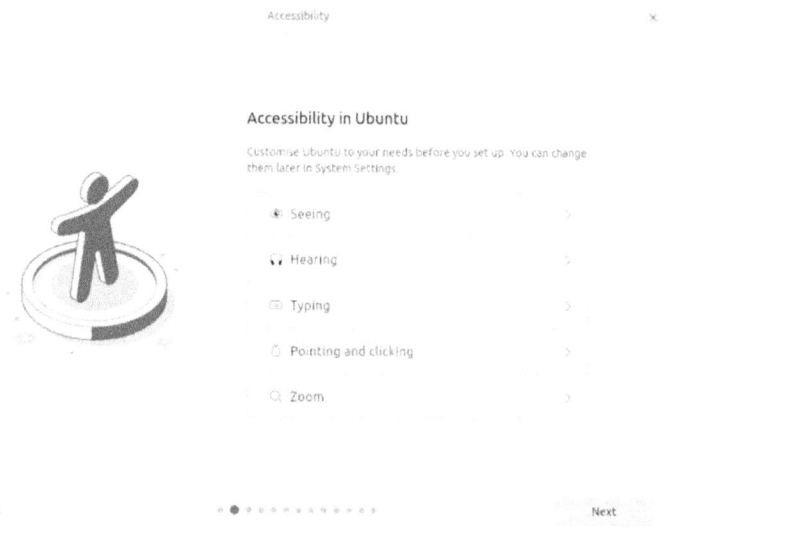

Figure 2-5: Accessibility screen

Keyboard Layout

You are then asked to select a keyboard layout (Keyboard layout screen). Keyboard entries are selected in the "Select your keyboard layout" scroll box. A default is already selected, such as English (US) (see Figure 2-6). If the selection is not correct, you can choose another keyboard in the scroll box.

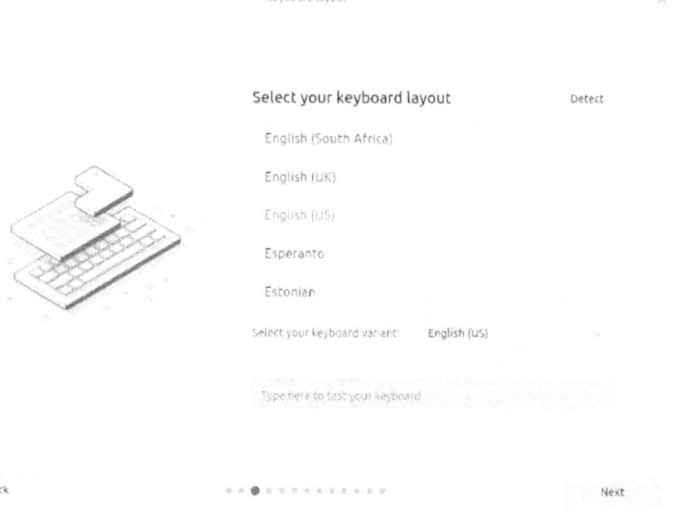

Figure 2-6: Keyboard Layout

The Detect button tries to detect the keyboard using your input. A series of dialogs opens, prompting you to press keys and asking you if certain keys are present on your keyboard. When the dialogs finish, the detected keyboard is then selected in the "Keyboard layout" scroll box.

To test your keyboard, click on the text box at the bottom of the screen and press keys, "Type here to test your keyboard."

Click the Next button to continue.

Internet connection

You are then asked to select the internet connection you want to use (see Figure 2-7). You can choose from wired, Wi-Fi, hidden Wi-Fi, and no connection. The internet connection is used to download and install updates during installation. The options will expand when clicked to prompt you for any required network configuration such selecting a Wi-Fi connection or hidden network.

Figure 2-7: Internet connection

Try or install Ubuntu (direct install only)

If you installed directly, instead of installing by clicking an install icon on the live DVD/USB desktop, you are then asked if you want to install or try Ubuntu (see Figure 2-8). The "Install Ubuntu" option is selected initially. To continue with the installation click the Next button. If you click the "Try Ubuntu" option, the Next button is changed to a Close button. Click on the Close button to end the installation and display the Ubuntu live session desktop. Even if you just opt to try Ubuntu, you can still later perform an installation from the Live USB/DVD. To install, click the "Install Ubuntu" icon on the desktop or on the dock (the Ubuntu icon at the top) (see Figure 2-3). The Install window opens to the Welcome screen for choosing your language.

Chapter 2: Installation 55

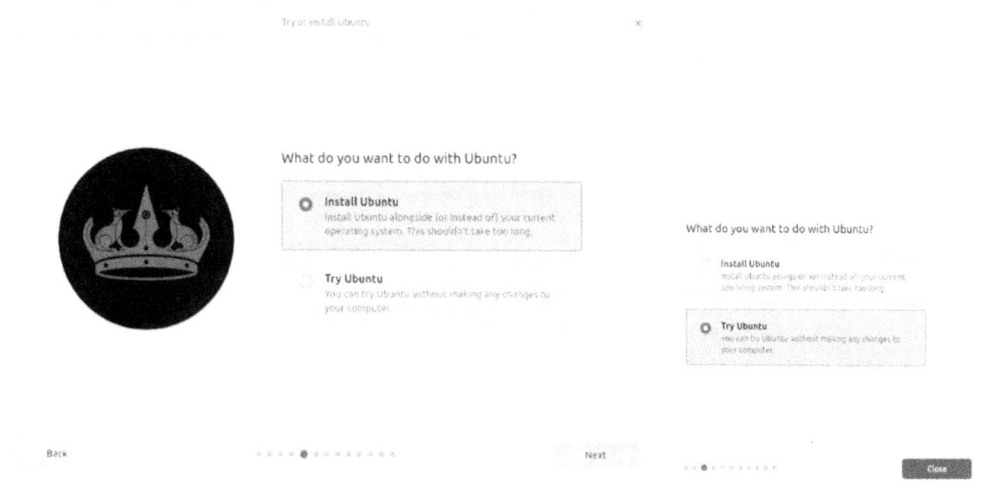

Figure 2-8: Try or install Ubuntu

Type of Installation, Interactive or Automated Install

You are then asked to select either an interactive or automated installation (see Figure 2-9). Most users will only need the interactive installation, which is selected by default. You can just click the Next button to continue to the next screen. The Automated option is reserved for administrators making multiple installations using an **autoinstall.yaml** script. Upon choosing this option, you are prompted to enter the script URL and to validate it.

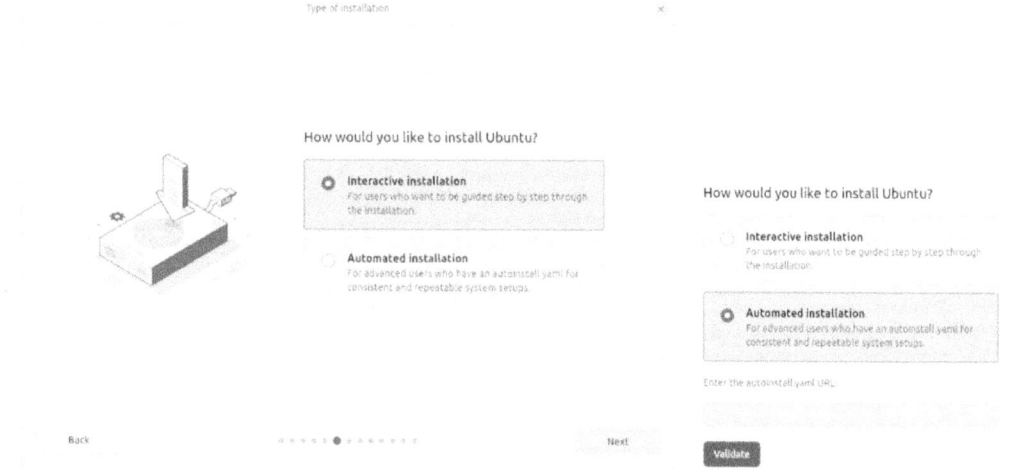

Figure 2-9: Type of Installation, interactive or automatic

Applications: Default and Extended selections

The Applications dialog lets you choose a Default selection or Extended selection (see Figure 2-10). The Default selection will install the operating system along with a very few applications. You can then later install the additional applications you want with the App Center. The Extended selection includes an extensive set of popular Office, graphic, music, and video applications, such as LibreOffice, the Gnome Videos video player, the Rhythmbox music player, and the Shotwell image application. Click the Next button to continue.

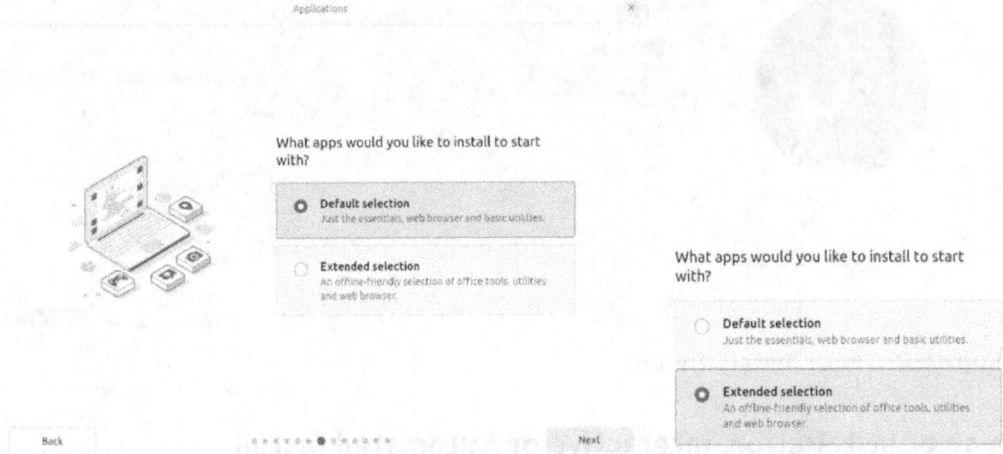

Figure 2-10: Applications, Default and Extended software selections

Optimize your computer: proprietary software

The "Optimize your computer" will install third party applications and codecs (non-open source) (see Figure 2-11). If you have an Nvidia graphics card, you should check the "Install third-party software for graphics and Wi-Fi hardware" option. This option will detect your Nvidia card and download and install the appropriate proprietary Nvidia driver.

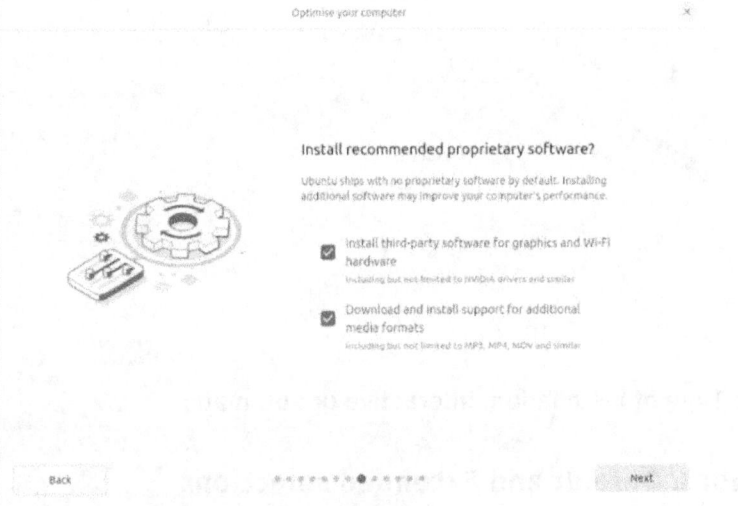

Figure 2-11: Recommended proprietary software

The "Download and install support for additional media formats" option installs additional proprietary and third-party open source codecs for various sound and video media such as MP3, MP4, mkv, and avi, installing packages such as xvidcore, gstreamer-ugly, and gstreamer-bad.

Click the Next button to continue.

Your system detects your hardware, providing any configuration specifications that may be required.

Disk setup

You are now asked to designate the Linux partitions and hard disk configurations you want to use on your hard drives. Ubuntu provides automatic partitioning that covers most situations, like using a blank or new hard drive and overwriting old partitions on a hard drive you no longer want. Ubuntu can also repartition a system with an operating system that uses all of the hard drive, but with unused space within it. In this case, the install procedure reduces the space used by the original operating system and installs Ubuntu on the new free space. A default partition layout sets up a root partition of type **ext4** (Linux native) for the kernel and applications (the swap partition has been replaced by a swap file in the root folder).

Alternatively, you can configure your hard disk manually (the "Manual installation" option). Ubuntu provides a simple partitioning tool you can use to set up Linux partitions.

For multiple-boot systems using Windows, Ubuntu automatically detects the Windows system.

No partitions will be changed or formatted until you click the "Install Now" button. You can opt out of the installation until then, and your original partitions will remain untouched.

Warning: The "Erase disk and install Ubuntu" option will wipe out any existing partitions on the selected hard drive. If you want to preserve any partitions on that drive, like Windows or other Linux partitions, always choose a different option such as "Install Ubuntu alongside ..." or "Manual installation".

You are given choices, depending on the state of the hard disk you choose. A hard disk could be blank, have an older Ubuntu operating system on it, or have a different operating system, such as Windows, already installed. If an operating system is already installed, it may take up the entire disk or may only use part of the disk, with the remainder available for the Ubuntu installation.

Tip: Some existing Linux systems may use several Linux partitions. Some of these may be used for just the system software, such as the boot and root partitions. These can be formatted. Others may have extensive user files, such as a **/home** partition that normally holds user home folders and all the files they have created. You should *not* format such partitions.

No detected operating systems

If no operating systems are detected on the hard drive, which is the case with a drive with only data files or a blank hard drive, the options displayed on the "Disk setup" dialog are (see Figure 2-12):

```
Erase disk and install Ubuntu
Manual installation
```

If you choose "Erase disk and install Ubuntu", your hard drive is automatically partitioned creating a primary partition for your entire file system (a root file system). The "Advanced features" button opens a dialog where you can choose LVM and ZFS disk formats with or without encryption. Alternatively you can specify partitions manually (Manual installation).

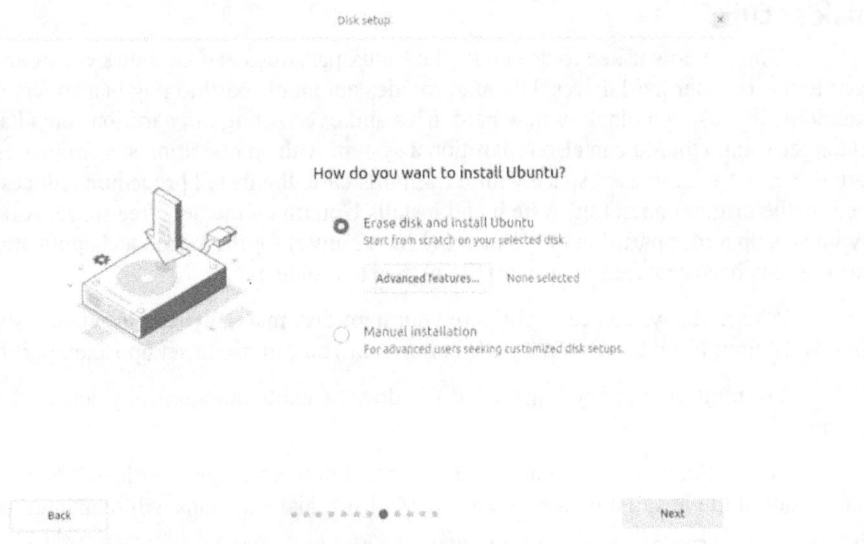

Figure 2-12: Disk setup, No detected operating systems

Advanced Features: LVM, Encryption, and ZFS

Should you want to use LVM or ZFS for your partitions, or either with disk encryption, click the "Erase disk and install Ubuntu" entry to activate the "Advanced features" button. Then click the "Advanced features" button to open a dialog showing options for LVM, LVM and encryption, ZFS, ZFS and encryption, and hardware-backed full disk encryption (see Figure 2-13). Hardware-backed (full disk) encryption uses a TPM (Trusted Platform Module) controller on your motherboard to physically encrypt your hard drive. Keep in mind that ZFS, ZFS with encryption, and hardware-backed (full disk) encryption are all experimental.

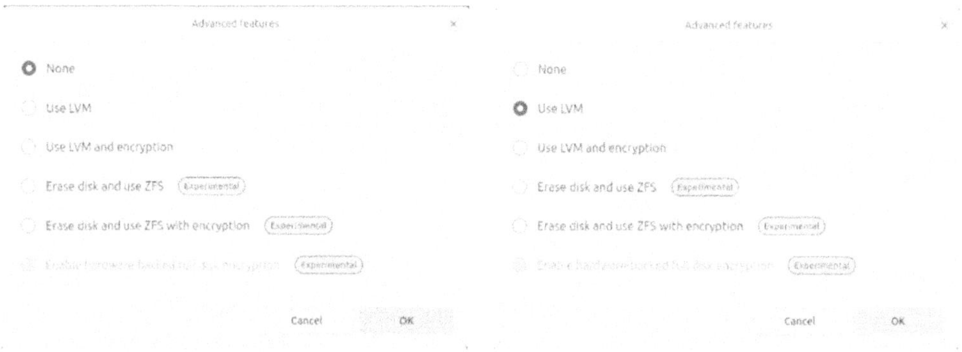

Figure 2-13: Advanced features

There is a None option in case you decided not use LVM or ZFS. Once you have made your selection click the OK button. The "Disk setup" screen will then show your selection, next to the "Advanced features" button. For LVM it will display "LVM selected" (see Figure 2-14).

Figure 2-14: LVM selection

ZFS will perform automatic snapshots of your system, letting you restore your system to a previous state. It will add a History entry to your Grub boot menu that you can use to restore your system to a selected state. Both LVM and ZFS are covered in more detail in Chapter 13.

With the "Use LVM " option, LVM partitions are set up using physical and logical volumes, which can be added to and replaced easily. An LVM physical volume is set up, which contains two LVM logical volumes, one for the swap space and one for the root. After you have installed your system, you can manage your LVM partitions using the LVM commands (see Chapter 13). The default LVM partitions are shown here with **pvscan** (physical volumes), **vgscan** (volume group), and **lvscan** (logical volume) operations. There is one volume group, **vgubuntu**, with two logical volumes, **root** and **swap_1**. The physical LVM partition is named **lvm2**. Two physical partitions are created on your system, an EFI boot partition and the LVM physical partition.

```
$ sudo pvscan
  PV /dev/mapper/sda2   VG vgubuntu         lvm2 [<464.54 GiB / 0    free]
  Total: 1 [<464.54 GiB] / in use: 1 [<464.54 GiB] / in no VG: 0 [0    ]
$ sudo vgscan
  Found volume group "vgubuntu" using metadata type lvm2
$ sudo lvscan
  ACTIVE              '/dev/vgubuntu/root' [463.58 GiB] inherit
  ACTIVE              '/dev/vgubuntu/swap_1' [980.00 MiB] inherit
```

Encrypt the disk

The "Use LVM and encryption" option on the "Advanced Features" dialog lets you encrypt your entire system with a password (see Figure 2-15). This is the tradition passphrase encryption. Not the newer hardware-backed (full-dick TPM) encryption.

Figure 2-15: LVM with encryption

You cannot access your system without that password. The encryption option will destroy any existing partitions if there are any, creating new partitions. Your hard drive will then have only your new Ubuntu system on it. On the "Disk passphrase" screen that follows you are prompted to enter a security key (passphrase) (see Figure 2-16).

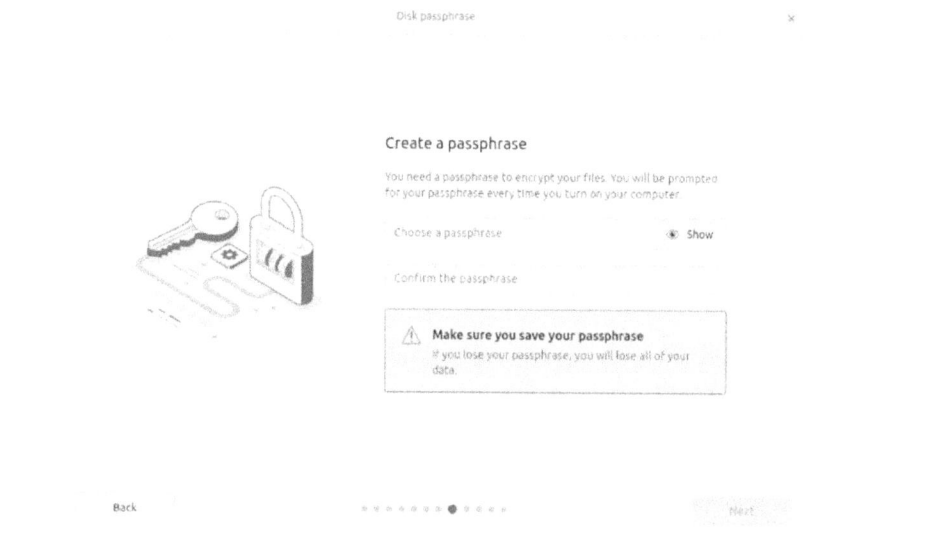

Figure 2-16: Security key for encrypted system

After installation, whenever you start up your system, you are prompted to enter that security key (see Figure 2-17).

 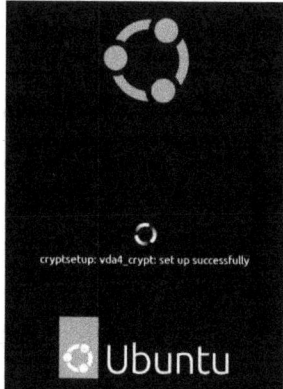

Figure 2-17: Security key login

Detected Ubuntu operating system

If you have another Ubuntu operating system on your disk, you will have the option to erase the Ubuntu system and replace it with Ubuntu 24.04 LTS. If the installed Ubuntu system is version 23.10, then you are also given the option to upgrade your system, preserving your personal files and installed software. You are also given the option to erase the installed operating system, and install the new system.

If the current system has enough unused space, you are also given an install alongside option, resizing the disk to free up space, and installing 24.04 LTS in added partitions on the free space. This will keep your original Linux system, as well as install the new one.

The message displayed on the "Disk setup" dialog is something like this:

"This computer currently has Ubuntu 23.10 on it. What would you like to do?"

You are given three choices. The Upgrade Ubuntu option is selected by default.

If you choose to Erase Ubuntu 23.10 and reinstall, you can also choose the options to encrypt the drive and to use LVM partitions.

```
Upgrade Ubuntu 23.10 to Ubuntu 24.04
Erase Ubuntu 23.10 and reinstall
Manual partitioning
```

On systems that also have Windows installed alongside Ubuntu, you are given the same options, but with an added option to erase everything including your Windows system. You are warned that both Windows and Ubuntu are installed on your system. Should you choose to erase Ubuntu and reinstall (the first entry), your Windows system will be preserved.

Detected other operating systems with free space

If you have another operating system on your disk that has been allocated use of part of the disk, you will have an option beginning with "Install Ubuntu alongside" with the name of the installed operating system listed. Keep in mind that LVM installations, like Fedora Linux, are not detected. To preserve an LVM installation you should choose the "Manual partitioning" option and configure the disk manually.

In this example, you are given three choices. Should you choose to Replace, then the disk encryption and LVM options become active. However, with the Replace option, your Windows system will be overwritten and erased.

```
Install Ubuntu alongside Microsoft Windows
Replace Microsoft Windows with Ubuntu
Manual partitioning
```

Detected another operating system using entire disk (resize)

If you have another operating system on your disk that has been allocated use of the entire disk, you will have an option beginning with "Install Ubuntu alongside" with the name of the installed operating system listed. This option is selected initially. The option is designed for use on hard disks with no unallocated free space but with a large amount of unused space on an existing partition. This is the case for a system where a partition has already been allocated the entire disk. This option will perform a resize of the existing partition, reducing that partition, preserving the data on it, and then creating an Ubuntu partition on that free space. Be warned that this could be a very time-consuming operation. If the original operating system was used heavily, the disk could be fragmented, with files stored all over the hard disk. In this case, the files have to be moved to one area of the hard disk, freeing up continuous space on the remaining area. If the original operating system was used very lightly, then there may be unused continuous space already on the hard drive. In this case, re-partitioning would be quick.

On the "Install alongside" dialog two partitions are displayed, the original showing the new size it will have after the resize, and the new partition for Ubuntu 24.04 LTS formed from the unused space. The size is automatically determined. You can adjust the size if you want by clicking on the space between the partitions to display a space icon, which you can drag left, or right to change the proportional sizes of the partitions.

Upon clicking the Install Now button, a dialog will prompt you with the warning that the resize cannot be undone, and that it may take a long time. Click Next to perform the resize, or click Go Back to return to the "Disk setup" screen. The time it will take depends on the amount of fragmentation on the disk.

Manual installation

All install situations will include a "Manual installation" option to let you partition the hard drive manually (see Figure 2-18). The "Manual installation" option starts up the partitioner, which will let you create, edit, and delete partitions. You can set your own size and type for your partitions. Use this option to preserve or reuse any existing partitions. When you have finished making your changes, click the Next button to continue. At this point, your partitions are changed and software is installed, while you continue with the remaining install configuration for time zone and user account creation.

The "Manual partitioning" screen displays the partitions on your current hard disk, and lists options for creating your Linux partitions. A graphical bar at the top shows the current state of your hard disk or a selected partition or disk, along with their sizes and labels.

A boot loader menu at the bottom of the screen provides a list of hard drives where you can install the boot loader. Your first hard drive is selected by default. If you have several hard drives on your system, you can choose the one on which to install the boot loader. Systems with only one hard drive, such as laptops, have only one hard drive entry.

The partitioner interface lists any existing partitions (see Figure 2-19). Each partition device name and label will be displayed. Unused space will be labeled as free space. Each hard disk is labeled by its device name, such as **sda** for the first Serial ATA device, along with the partition type and size. At the bottom of the screen are actions you can perform on partitions and free space. To the right are the "New partition table" and Revert buttons for the entire disk. To the left are add, delete, and edit buttons for partitions (+, -, and Change). Your current hard disks and their partitions are listed in the main scrollable pane, with headings for Device, Type, Mount point, Format, and Size, as well as the name of an operating system (System) installed on the partition, should there be one.

Creating new partitions on a blank hard drive manually

To create partitions on a blank hard drive manually, choose "Manual installation" (see Figure 2-18) and click Next. The partitioner interface starts up with the "Manual partitioning" screen, listing any existing partitions (see Figure 2-19). For a blank hard drive, the hard drive only, is listed in the main pane.

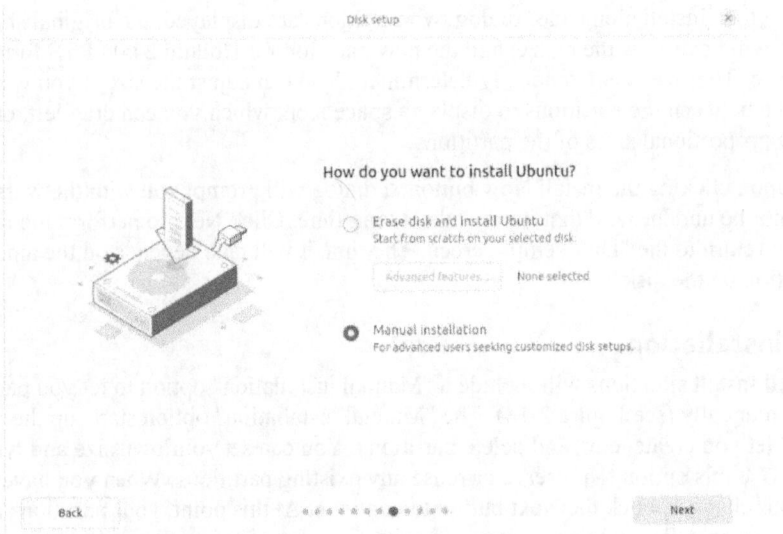

Figure 2-18: Manual Installation (manual partitioning)

For a new blank hard drive, you first create the partition table by clicking the New Partition Table button (see Figure 2-19). This displays a warning that it will erase any data on the drive. Click Next (see Figure 2-20). The warning dialog is there in case you accidentally click the New Partition Table button on a drive that has partitions you want to preserve. In this case, you can click Cancel and no new partition table is created.

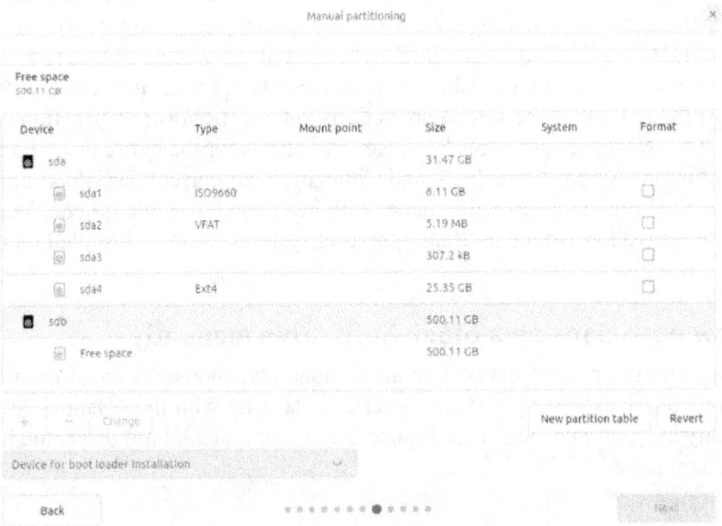

Figure 2-19: Manually partitioning a new hard drive

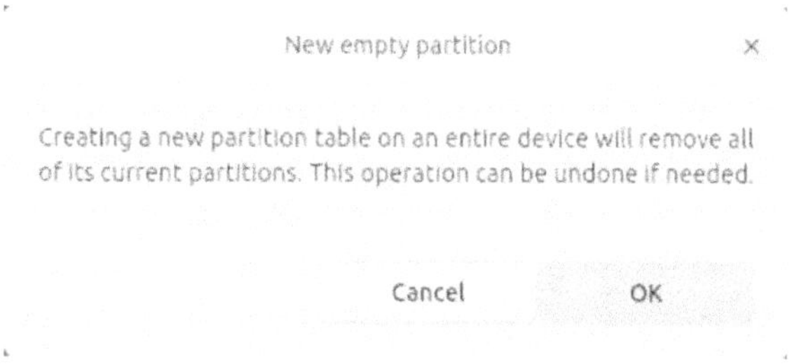

Figure 2-20: Create a new partition table on a blank hard drive

Figure 2-21: Select free space on a blank hard drive

Once the new partition table is set up, the free space entry appears and a graphical bar at the top shows the free space (see Figure 2-21). If your system already has an operating system installed that takes up only part of the disk, you do not need to create a new partition table. Your free space is already listed.

For Ubuntu Linux, you will have to create at least one partition, a Linux root partition, where your system will be installed. If your computer also supports EFI boot, as most do, you will also have to have a boot partition of type EFI System Partition. The EFI boot partition is created for you automatically (see Figure 2-22). You do not have to create it. You can create other partitions if you wish. The swap partition is no longer needed. A swap file is used instead (**/swapfile**). You can, though, if you want, still set up and use a swap partition.

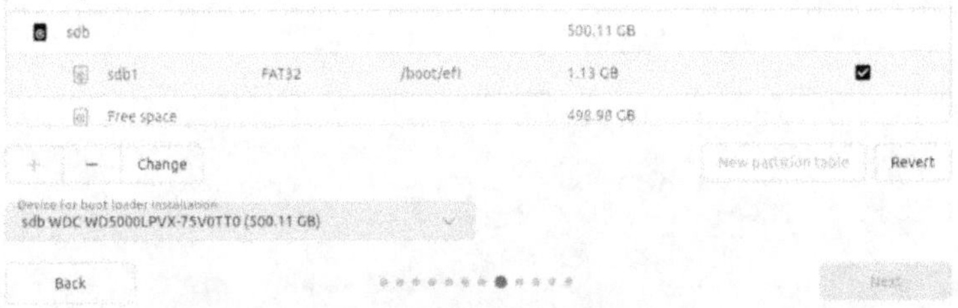

Part 1: Getting Started

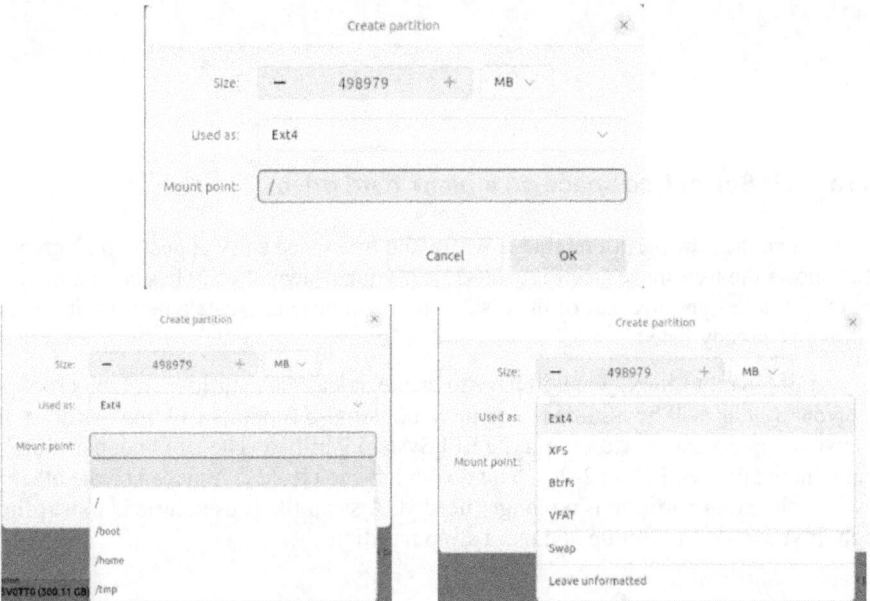

Figure 2-22: Automatically created EFI boot partition

To create a new partition, select the free space entry for the hard disk and click the + button. This opens a Create Partition dialog where you can choose the size of your partition, the file system type (Use as), and the mount point. Do this for each partition. The EFI and swap partitions have no mount point. You only set the size.

The Create Partition dialog displays entries for the size in megabytes, the file system type (Use as), and the Mount point. For the file system type, the "Leave unformated" partition entry is initially selected. Choose a partition type from the drop-down menu. Select Ext4 for the root partition.

For the root partition, from the "Mount point" drop down menu choose the mount point /, which is the root directory (see Figure 2-23). This is where your system will be installed. The size of the partition is specified in megabytes. It will be set to the remaining space. If you want to also set up additional partitions, such as a partition for the **/home** folder, reduce the size to allow space for those partitions.

Figure 2-23: Create a new root partition

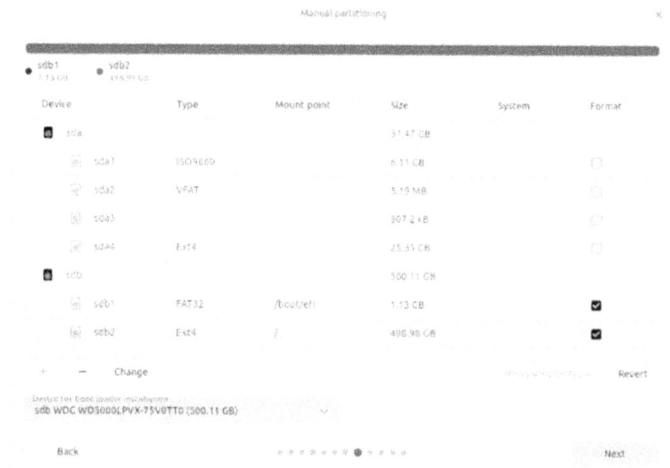

Figure 2-24: Manual partitions

If you make a mistake, you can edit a partition by selecting it and clicking the Change button. This opens an Edit partitions window where you can make changes. You can also delete a partition, returning its space to free space, and then create a new one. Select the partition and click the - button (delete). The partition is not actually deleted at this point. No changes are made at all until you start installing Ubuntu. The "Revert" button is always available to undo all the possible changes you specified so far, and start over from the original state of the hard disk. Click the Next button to continue (see Figure 2-24). You are then asked to perform the actual partition changes.

Ready to install

When you have finished setting up your partitions, the "Ready to install" dialog displays your partitions and install options you have chosen (Review your choices) (see Figure 2-25). Click the "Install" button to perform the partitioning, formatting, and installation.

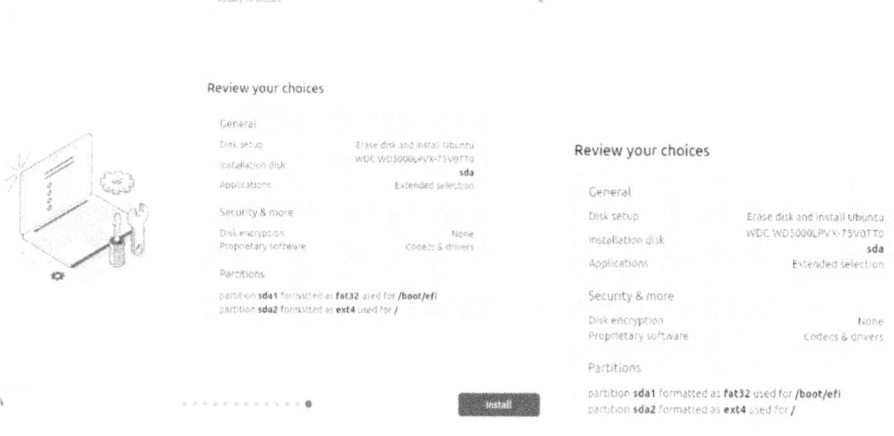

Figure 2-25: Ready to install

Select your timezone

On the "Select your timezone" screen, you can set the time zone by using a map to specify your location (see Figure 2-26). The Time Zone tool uses a map feature that displays the entire earth, with sections for each time zone. Click on your general location, and the entire time zone for your part of the world will be highlighted in green. The major city closest to your location will be labeled with its current time. The selected city will appear in the text box located below the map. You can also select your time zone entering the city in the text box. As you type in the city name, a pop-up menu appears showing progressively limited choices. The corresponding time zone will be highlighted on the map. Click the Next button to continue.

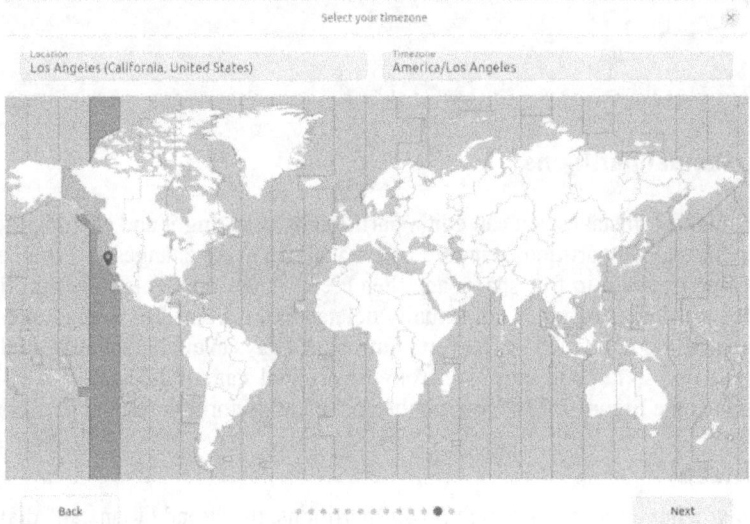

Figure 2-26: Select your timezone

Create your account

On the "Create your account" screen you enter your name, your user login name, and password (see Figure 2-27). When you enter your name, a username will be generated for you using your first name, and a computer name will be entered using your first name and your computer's make and model name. You can change these names if you want. The name for the computer is the computer's network host name. The user you are creating will have administrative access, allowing you to change your system configuration, add new users and printers, and install software. When you enter your password a Strength notice is displayed indicating whether it is too short, weak, fair, or good. For a good password include numbers and uppercase characters. Click the Next button to continue.

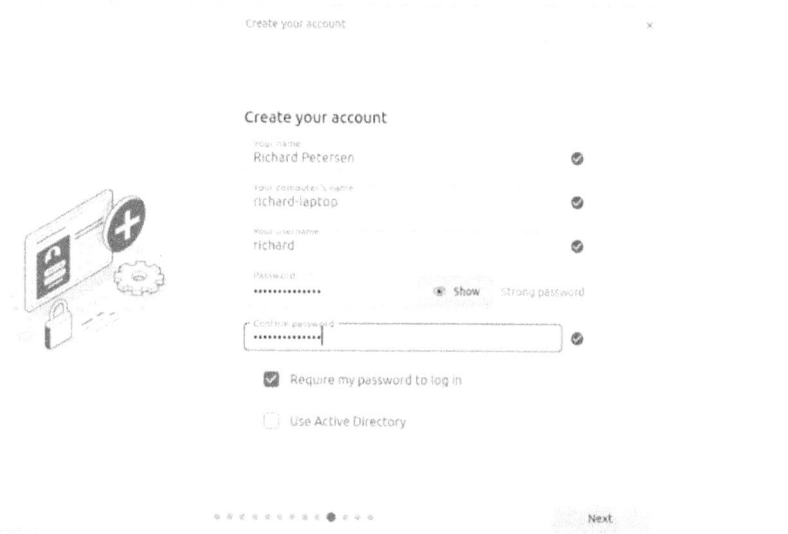

Figure 2-27: Create your account

At the bottom of the screen, you have the options: "Require my password to log in" and "Use Active Directory." Leave the "Require my password to log in" option unchecked to have your system login automatically to your account when you start up, instead of stopping at the login screen. If you check the "Require my password to log in" box, the login process provides a standard login screen where you have to select your user name and enter your password.

Install Progress

Your installation continues with a slide show of Ubuntu 24.04 LTS features such as Web browsers, social services, the App Center, and photo editing (see Figure 2-28). A progress bar at the bottom of the dialog shows the progress of the install process. You can click on the arrow and pause buttons to the left of the progress bar to move through the slide show manually. Click the terminal button to the right of the progress bar to open a terminal section that displays the install operations as they occur.

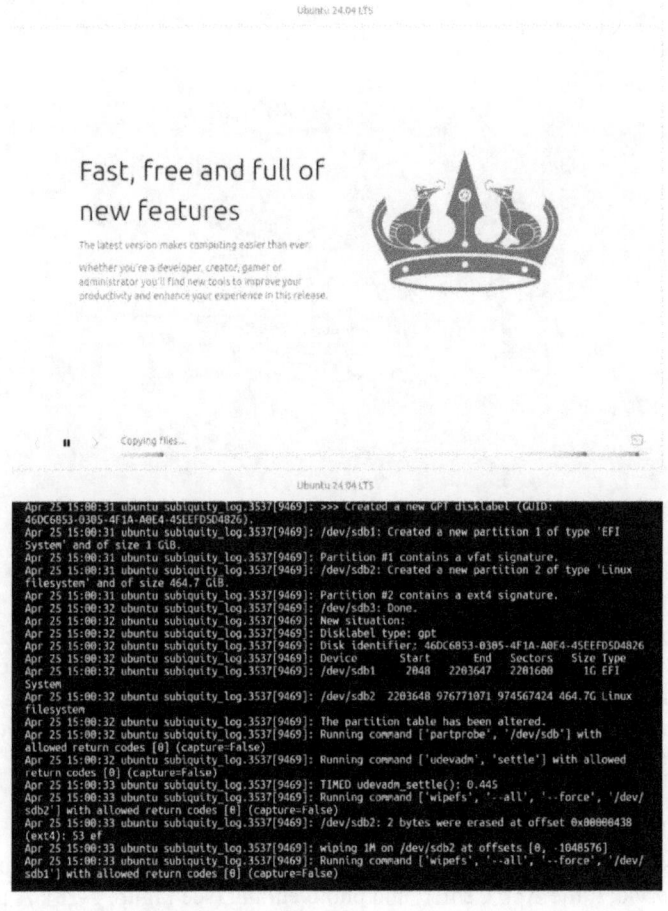

Figure 2-28: Install progress slide show

Once finished, the Installation Complete dialog appears (see Figure 2-29). Click the Restart Now button to restart and reboot to the new installation. If you installed from the Live USB/DVD session, the Continue Testing button lets you return to that session, if you want.

A message will appear prompting you to remove the USB/DVD disk, and then press ENTER.

Figure 2-29: Installation completed

After starting Ubuntu for the first time, you will be prompted to install the updates that were downloaded during the installation process.

Upgrading

You can upgrade a current Ubuntu system to the next release using the APT package manager or the Ubuntu Desktop USB/DVD. Upgrading is a simple matter of updating software to the new release versions, along with updating your GRUB configuration. Check the following site for upgrade details:

https://help.ubuntu.com/community/DiscoUpgrades

You can only upgrade to Ubuntu 24.04 LTS from Ubuntu 23.10 or from 22.04. Be sure you have first performed any needed updates for your Ubuntu system. It must be completely up to date before you perform an upgrade to Ubuntu 24.04.

You cannot upgrade from Ubuntu 23.04, or earlier to 24.04 directly. To upgrade from an earlier release other than 23.10 or 22.04, first, upgrade sequentially up to one of those.

Upgrade over a network from Ubuntu 20.04 and 23.10

To upgrade your system using your Internet connection, you can use Software Updater. The upgrade will be performed by downloading the latest package versions from the Ubuntu repository, directly. When a new release becomes available, Software Updater will display a message notifying you of the new release (provided it is configured to do so).

Be sure to first enable distribution notification for long term support versions. On the Software Updater dialog, click the Settings button on the lower left to open the Software & Updates dialog at the Updates tab. You can also open the Software & Updates application directly and select the Updates tab. On the last menu "Notify me of a new Ubuntu version," choose the "For any new versions" for Ubuntu 23.10, and "For long-term support versions" for Ubuntu 20.04.

An Upgrade button will be displayed next to the message should you decide to upgrade your system to that release (see Figure 2-30). If you want to stay with your installed release, for now, you just click the OK button. Should you want to upgrade to the new release, in this case, Ubuntu 24.04 LTS, you click the Upgrade button to start the upgrade. A Welcome dialog is displayed with links for information about the release. Click the Upgrade button on this dialog to begin the upgrade. Be sure first to update all your current software. An upgrade should be performed from the most recent versions of your current release's software packages. Ubuntu will also periodically display a message asking you to upgrade, displaying buttons to not upgrade, upgrade later, or upgrade now.

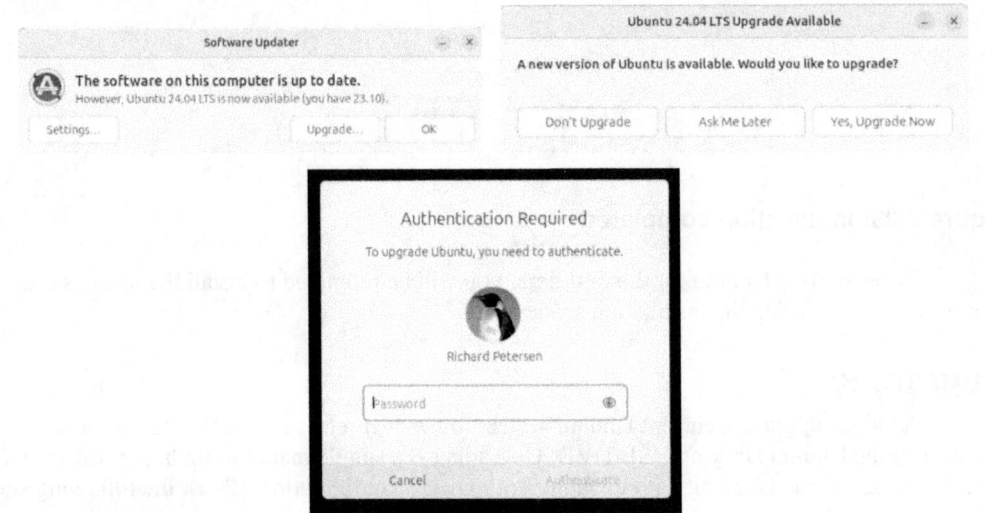

Figure 2-30: Upgrade message and authentication

You can also start the software updater directly for the distribution upgrade by entering the following on a command line (the **-d** option performs a distribution upgrade). Use either a terminal window or press ALT-F2 to open a Run Application window.

```
sudo update-manager -d
```

When you choose to upgrade, an authentication dialog first prompts you for your password. Then a Distribution Upgrade dialog opens showing the progress of the upgrade. The upgrade procedure will first prepare the upgrade, detecting the collection of software packages that have to be downloaded. A dialog will notify you of software packages for which support has ended (older deprecated software). Then a dialog will then open asking if you want to start the upgrade, displaying both a Cancel and Start Upgrade button. You can still cancel the upgrade at this time and nothing will be changed on your system (click the Cancel button). To continue with the Upgrade, click the Start Upgrade button.

The Distribution Upgrade dialog is again displayed (see Figure 2-31). Packages are downloaded (Getting new packages), and then installed on your system (Installing the upgrades). The download process can take some time depending on the speed of your Internet connection.

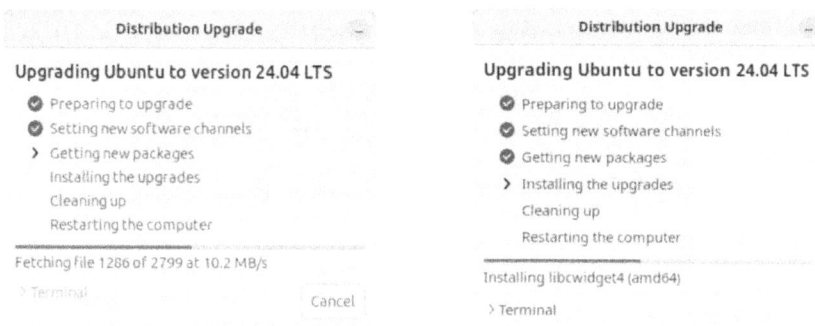

Figure 2-31: Distribution Upgrade dialog

If the download is taking too long, you can click the Cancel button and run the upgrade later. A dialog is displayed telling you that the download will continue later from where it left off.

To start the upgrade again, first start Software Updater, click the Upgrade button, and proceed through the initial steps again, though this time will be much faster (Release notes, Preparing to upgrade, Setting new software channels). The Getting new packages stage will continue with next package.

Depending on the packages you are upgrading, you may have to enter configuration information through the terminal interface. Click the terminal arrow to open the terminal interface and respond to any prompts that may occur.

Once the upgrade is completed, a completion message is displayed. Reboot to start your system with the new release and its kernel.

Upgrading to a new release with apt-get

You can also use the **apt-get** command in a terminal window or on a command line interface to upgrade your system. To upgrade to an entirely new release, use the **dist-upgrade** option. A **dist-upgrade** would install a new release, preserving your original configuration and data. This option will also remove obsolete software packages.

```
sudo apt-get update
sudo apt-get dist-upgrade
```

Recovery, rescue, and boot loader re-install

Ubuntu provides the means to start up systems that have failed for some reason. A system that may boot but fails to start up, can be started in a recovery mode, already set up for you as an entry on your boot loader menu.

Recovery Mode (Advanced Options menu)

If for some reason your system is not able to start up, it may be due to conflicting configurations, libraries, or applications. On the GRUB menu first, choose the "Advanced options for Ubuntu" to open the advanced options menu(see Figure 2-32). Then select the recovery mode entry, the Ubuntu kernel entry with the (recovery mode) label attached to the end. This starts up a menu where you can use the arrow and ENTER keys to select from several recovery options (see

Figure 2-33). These include resume, clean, dpkg, grub, network, and root. Short descriptions for each item are displayed on the menu.

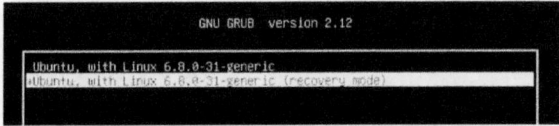

Figure 2-32: Grub advanced options menu with recovery kernels

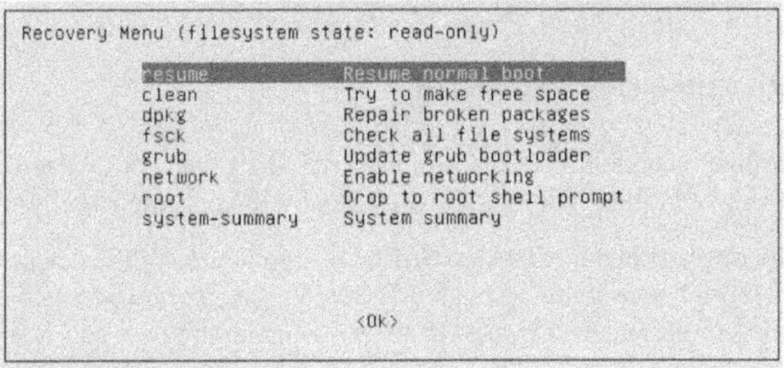

Figure 2-33: Recovery options

The root option starts up Ubuntu as the root user with a command line shell prompt. In this case, you can boot your Linux system in a recovery mode and then edit configuration files with a text editor such as Vi, remove the suspect libraries, or reinstall damaged software with **apt-get**.

The resume entry will start up Ubuntu normally to your desktop.

The **grub** entry will update the grub boot loader. With GRUB2 your hard drive is re-scanned, detecting your installed operating systems and Ubuntu kernels, and implementing any GRUB configuration changes you may have made without updating GRUB.

To rescue a broken system, choose the **root** entry. Your broken system will be mounted and made accessible with a command line interface. You can then use command line operations and editors to fix configuration files.

Re-Installing the Boot Loader

If you have a multiple-boot system, that runs both Windows and Linux on the same machine, you may run into a situation where you have to reinstall your GRUB boot loader. This problem occurs if your Windows system completely crashes beyond repair and you have to install a new version of Windows, if you added Windows to your machine after having installed Linux, or if you upgraded to a new version of Windows. A Windows installation will automatically overwrite your boot loader.

You can reinstall your boot loader manually, using your Ubuntu Desktop USB/DVD live session. The procedure is more complicated, as you have to mount your Ubuntu system. On the Ubuntu Desktop USB/DVD Live session, you can use GParted to find out what partition your Ubuntu system uses. In a terminal window, create a directory on which to mount the system.

```
sudo mkdir myubuntu
```

Then mount it, making sure you have the correct file system type and partition name (usually **/dev/sda5** on dual boot systems).

```
sudo mount -t ext4 /dev/sda5 myubuntu
```

Then use **grub-install** and the device name of your first partition to install the boot loader, with the **--root-directory** option to specify the directory where you mounted your Ubuntu file system. The **--root-directory** option requires a full path name, which for the Ubuntu Desktop USB/DVD would be **/home/ubuntu** for the home directory. Using the **myubuntu** directory for this example, the full path name of the Ubuntu file system would be **/home/ubuntu/myubuntu**. You would then enter the following **grub-install** command.

```
sudo grub-install --root-directory=/home/ubuntu/myubuntu /dev/sda
```

This will re-install your current GRUB boot loader. You can then reboot, and the GRUB boot loader will start up.

ubuntu

3. Usage Basics: Login, Desktop, Network, and Help

Accessing your Ubuntu System

Display Manager

Ubuntu Desktop (GNOME)

Network Connections: wired and wireless

Ubuntu Settings (GNOME)

Help Resources (Ubuntu Desktop Guide)

Command Line Interface

Terminal Window

Using Linux has become an almost intuitive process, with easy-to-use interfaces, featuring graphical logins and desktops. Even the standard Linux command line interface is user-friendly with editable commands, history lists, and cursor-based tools. To start using Ubuntu, you have to know how to access your system and, once you are on the system, how to execute commands and run applications. Access is supported through a graphical login.

Linux is noted for providing easy access to extensive help documentation. It is easy to obtain information quickly about any Linux command and utility while logged into the system. You can access an online manual that describes each command, or obtain help that provides explanations that are more detailed. Your desktop provides help systems with easy access to desktop, system, and application help files.

Accessing Your Ubuntu System

You access your Ubuntu system using the GRUB bootloader to first start Ubuntu, and then use the display manager to log in to your account. From the desktop System menu (top right) you can shut down, restart, or suspend your system. It is also possible to access Ubuntu using a command line interface only, bypassing the desktop interface and its required graphical support.

GRUB Boot Loader

When your system starts, the GRUB boot loader will quickly select your default operating system and start up its login screen. If you have just installed Ubuntu, the default operating system will be Ubuntu.

If you have installed more than one operating system, the GRUB menu is displayed for several seconds at startup, before loading the default operating system automatically. To display the GRUB menu should you have only your Ubuntu system installed, press the SHIFT key at start up. Once displayed, press the ESC key to have GRUB wait until you have made a selection. Your GRUB menu is displayed as shown in Figure 3-1. The Advanced options entry allows you to start Ubuntu in recovery mode or choose a previously installed kernel to use.

The GRUB menu lists Ubuntu along with any other operating systems installed on your hard drive, such as Windows or other versions of Linux. Use the arrow keys to move to the entry you want and press ENTER

For graphical installations, some displays may have difficulty running the graphical startup display. If you have this problem, you can edit your Linux GRUB entry and remove the **splash** term at the end of the **linux** line. Press the **e** key to edit a GRUB entry (see Figure 3-2).

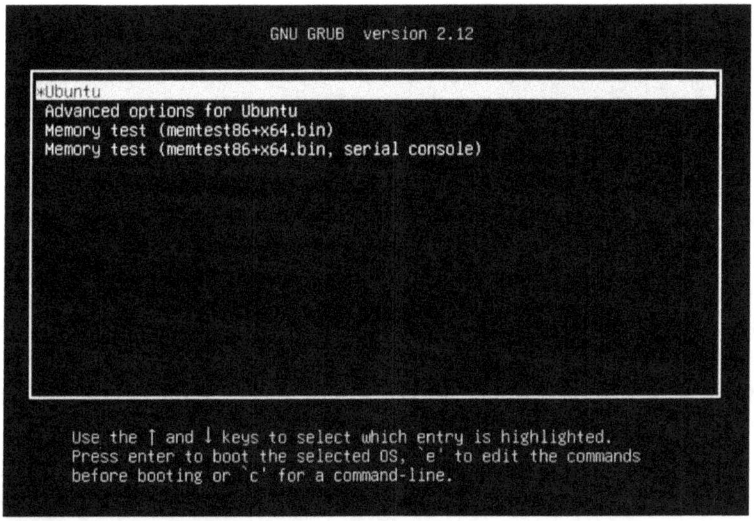

Figure 3-1: Ubuntu GRUB menu

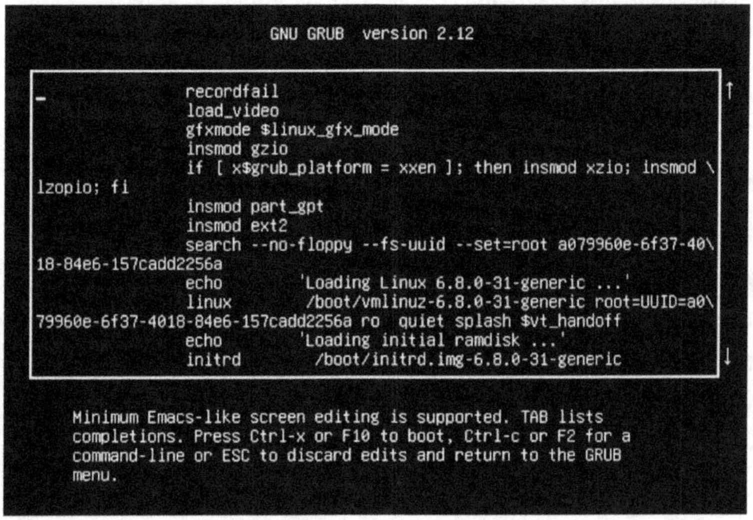

Figure 3-2: Editing a GRUB menu item

To change a particular line, use the up and down arrow keys to move to the line. You can use the left and right arrow keys to move along the line. The Backspace key will delete characters and typing will insert characters. The editing changes are temporary. Permanent changes can only be made by directly editing the GRUB configuration **/etc/default/grub** file, and then running the following command:

```
sudo update-grub
```

When your Ubuntu operating system starts up, an Ubuntu logo appears during the startup. You can press the ESC key to see the startup messages instead. Ubuntu uses Plymouth with its kernel modesetting ability to display a startup animation. The Plymouth Ubuntu logo theme is used by default.

The GNOME Display Manager: GDM

The graphical login interface displays a list of usernames. When you click a username, a login screen replaces the listing of users, displaying the selected user and a text box in which you then enter your password. Upon pressing ENTER, you log in and your desktop starts up.

Graphical logins are handled by the GNOME Display Manager (GDM). The GDM manages the login interface, in addition to authenticating a user password and username, and then starts up a selected desktop. From the GDM, you can shift to the command-line interface with CTRL+ALT+F2, and then shift back to the GDM with CTRL+ALT+F1. The keys F2 through F6 provide different command-line terminals, as in CTRL+ALT+F3 for the third command-line terminal.

When the GDM starts up, it shows a listing of users (see Figure 3-3). A System menu at the top right of the screen displays entries for sound adjustment, screen brightness (for laptops), the battery status (if a laptop), and a power button. Click the power button to display a Power Off menu with entries for Suspend, Restart, and Power Off. Clicking the Power Off entry displays the Power Off dialog with options to Power Off and Cancel. The System menu also shows Quick Settings buttons for networking (Wired, Wi-Fi, Bluetooth, and Airplane Mode), power mode, and buttons for several desktop settings such as night lighting, style, and keyboard.

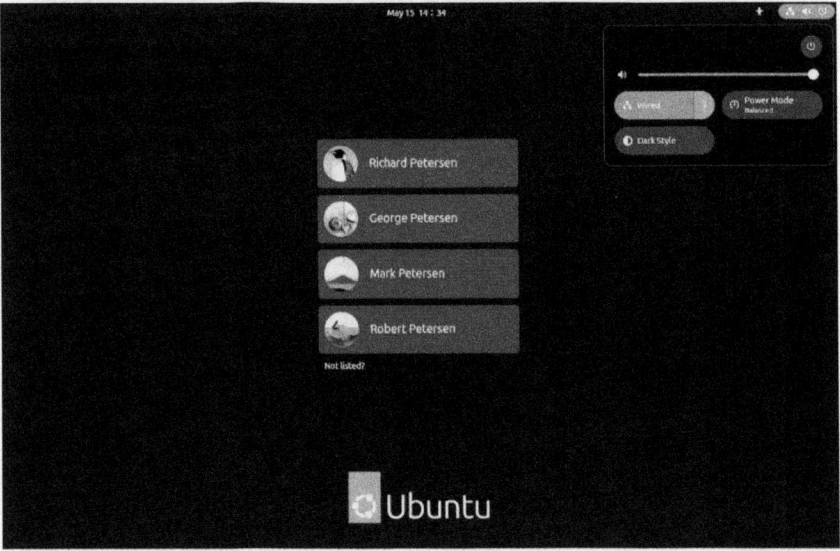

Figure 3-3: The GDM user listing

At the top center of the screen is the date (day of the week) and time. Clicking on the time displays the calendar with the full date specified, and the notifications menu if allowed.

Next to the System menu button is an accessibility button, which displays a menu of switches that let you turn on accessibility tools and such features as the onscreen keyboard, enhanced contrast, and the screen magnifier.

To log in, click a username from the list of users. You are then prompted to enter the user's password (see Figure 3-4). A login screen replaces the user list, showing the username you selected and a Password text box in which you can enter the user's password. By default, the password you enter is hidden. Should you want to display the text of your password, you can click the eye button located to the right in the password text box. Click the eye button again to hide the password. Once you enter the password, press Enter. Your desktop starts up.

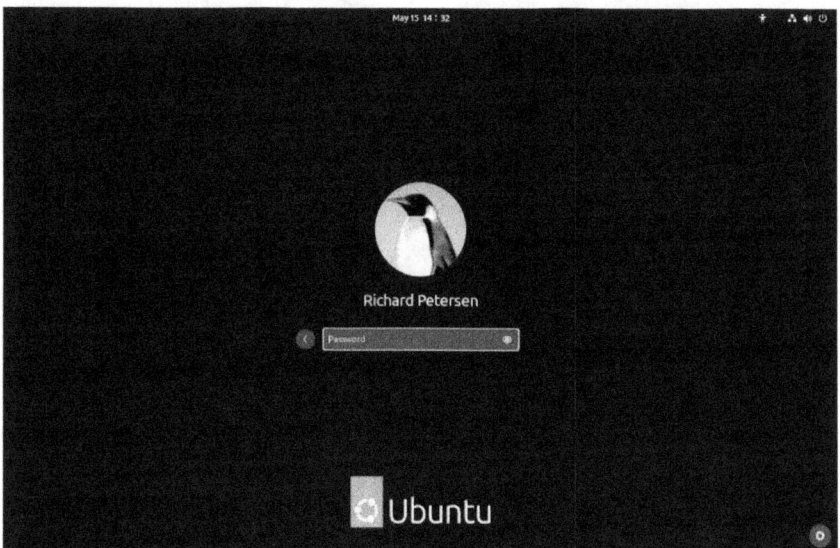

Figure 3-4: GDM login

If the name of a user you want to log in as is not listed, click the "Not listed?" entry at the end of the list, to open a text box, which prompts you first for a username, and then a password.

On the login screen, there is a session button (gear icon) located at the right bottom corner. You can click this button to display a menu listing other installed desktops or the same desktop using a different display server. When you installed the Ubuntu desktop, two display servers were installed, X11 and Wayland. On the session menu you can choose Ubuntu (the Wayland display server and the default) or "Ubuntu on X.org", which uses the older X.org display server.

The session menu will also show other installed desktops you could use instead of Ubuntu (GNOME). Though GNOME is the primary desktop for Ubuntu, it is possible to install and use other desktops, known as Ubuntu Flavors, such as Kubuntu (Plasma, KDE), Xubuntu (Xfce session), and Ubuntu MATE (MATE). These are available on the Ubuntu repository (see Figure 3-5).

Ubuntu uses the systemd login manager, logind. You can configure login manager options with the **/etc/systemd/logind.conf** file. You can set options such as the number of terminals, the idle action, and hardware key operations, such as the power key. Check the **logind.conf** man page for details.

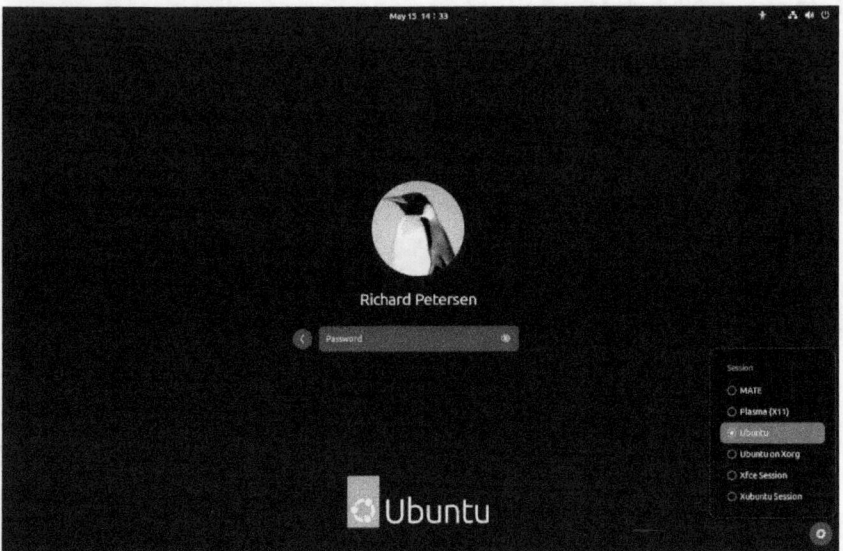

Figure 3-5: GDM Session menu

The System menu

Once logged in, the System menu button is displayed on the right side of the top bar of the desktop (see Figure 3-6). The button will display emblems for network, sound, and power. Clicking the button displays the System menu. At the top, it has buttons for the battery service indicator (battery image), taking a screenshot (camera image), opening Settings (gear image), activating the lock screen (lock image), and displaying the Power Off menu (power button image). The battery service indicator shows the current charge of the battery. Clicking on it opens the Setting Power tab showing the battery level. The Power Off menu lists Suspend, Restart, Power Off, Switch User (if you have more than one), and Logout entries.

Below these buttons are sliding bars for sound and brightness, which you can adjust the volume and brightness. If your display does not support brightness adjustments, only the sound slider is shown.

Below the sliders, a set of Quick Settings buttons lets you quickly activate or deactivate different services and devices. These will be different depending on your computer's capabilities. The network devices are listed first. Most will have either a Wired or Wi-Fi button or both, depending on the kind of network connections supported. If you have Bluetooth, a Bluetooth button is displayed. You can turn a device or service on or off by clicking its button. Activated buttons have a highlighted solid color, whereas deactivated ones are grayed out (dark for the dark style). In addition, the Wi-Fi button will also display your currently selected Wi-Fi connection, the Bluetooth button will show the number of selected Bluetooth devices, and the Power Mode button displays your current power mode (the default is Balanced). An unselected Power Mode button, does not turn off the power mode, it just uses the default power mode, Balanced. Clicking it will select a different power mode such as power saver. Clicking it again will deselect the power mode button, returning you to the Balanced power mode.

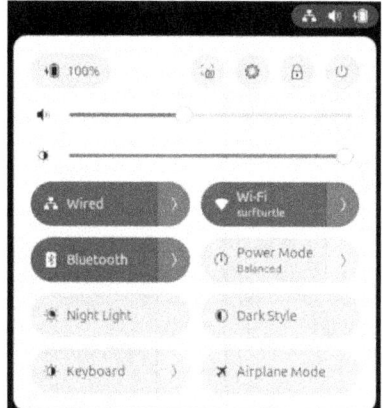 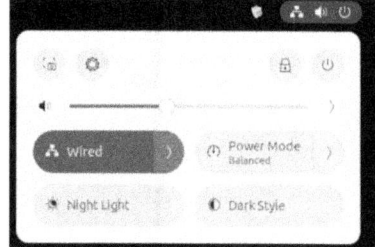

Figure 3-6: System menu

If a device or service can be further configured, its button will have a menu button on its right side indicated by a right arrow, as is the case for Wired, Wi-Fi, Bluetooth, Power Mode, and Keyboard. Clicking on the menu button opens a small dialog where you can select settings. The Wired, Wi-Fi, Bluetooth, and Power Mode buttons will include a link in their menus to their appropriate Settings dialog, allowing you to perform a detailed configuration. The Wired dialog has a Wired Settings link to open the Settings Network tab, and the Power Mode dialog has a Power Settings link to open the Settings Power tab. The Wi-Fi button's dialog has an All Networks link that opens the Settings Wi-Fi tab.

Some button menus let you make simple setting selections, such as the Power Mode button's dialog that lets you choose Performance, Balanced, Power Saver power modes. The Bluetooth button's menu list your available Bluetooth devices. Wi-Fi shows your Wi-Fi connections.

Other buttons just turn a service on or off, such as the Night Light button that turns on night lighting for the display, the Dark Style that switches between the desktop dark and light styles, and Airplane Mode that turns airplane mode on and off. These have no menu buttons on button's right side.

You can also set the power profile from the System menu. You can choose from three profile modes: Performance, Balanced, and Power Saver. Balanced is the default and balances power use and performance. Performance gives priority to CPU performance. Power Saver reduces performance to save power, especially for display operations. Click on the Power Mode button on the System menu to turn the power mode on an off. On the Power Mode button, the current power mode is shown. Click on the Power Mode button's menu button (right arrow on the right side of the button) to display the Power Mode menu where you can choose the profile mode you want (see Figure 3-7). The current power mode has a check mark next to it. To access the Settings Power tab for more detailed power configuration, click the Power Settings link at the bottom of the menu.

84 Part 1: Getting Started

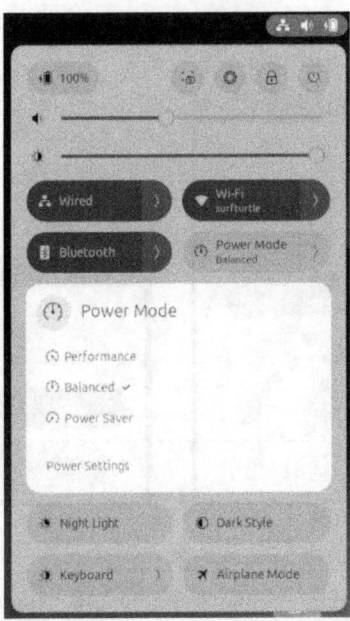

Figure 3-7: System menu power profile modes

On systems that are not laptops, there will be no brightness slider or Battery entry on the System menu. If the system also has no wireless device, the Wi-Fi entry will also be missing.

Lock Screen

You can choose to lock your screen and suspend your system by clicking the Lock button on the top right of the System menu. The screen will go blank. Moving the mouse shows the time and date briefly (see Figure 3-8). To start up again, press any key and your Login screen appears with a password text box. Enter your password to start up your desktop session again. The password you enter is hidden. Should you want to display the text of your password, you can click the eye button located to the right in the password text box. Click the eye button again to hide the password.

Figure 3-8: Lock Screen

Logging Out and Switching Users

If you want to exit your desktop and return to the GDM login screen, or switch to a different user, you click the power button on the top right of the System menu to open the Power Off menu with entries for Suspend, Restart, Power Off, Log Out, and Switch User (see Figure 3-9). If you have only one user configured for your system, then the Switch User entry does not appear. Click the Switch User entry to log out and display the GDM with its list of users you can log into.

Figure 3-9: Power Off menu with Log Out entry

Click the Log Out entry to display a dialog that shows buttons for Cancel and Log Out (see Figure 3-10). Then click the Log Out button to log out of your account, returning to the login screen, where you can log in again as a different user or shut down the system. A countdown will commence in the dialog, showing how much time you have left before it performs the logout automatically.

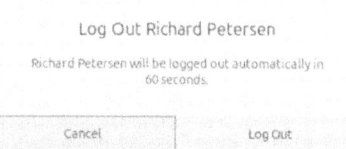

Figure 3-10: Log Out dialog

The Switch User entry switches out from the current user and runs the GDM to display a list of users you can log in as. Click the name to open a password prompt and display a session button. You can then log in as that user. The sessions of users already logged will continue with the same open windows and applications that were running when the user switched off. You can switch back and forth between logged-in users, with all users retaining their session from where they left off. When you switch off from a user, that user's running programs will continue in the background.

Poweroff

From the login screen, you can poweroff (shut down) the system using the System menu on either the login screen or the desktop. Click the power button on the top right of the System menu to open the Power Off menu with entries for Suspend, Restart, Power Off, and Log Out. Click the Power Off" entry to display a Power Off dialog with options to Cancel or Power Off (see Figure 3-11). A countdown will commence in the dialog, showing how much time you have left before it performs the shutdown automatically. You can also just press the power button on your computer to display the Power Off dialog.

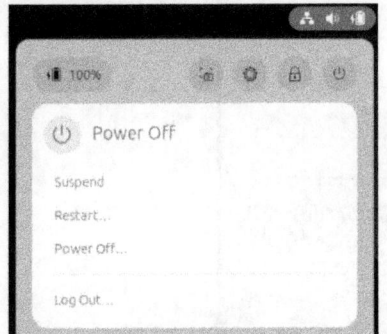
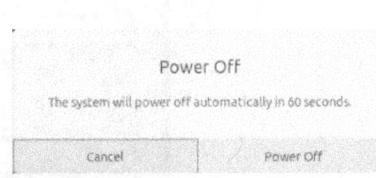

Figure 3-11: Power Off menu and Power Off dialog

Should your display freeze or become corrupted, one safe way to shut down and restart is to press a command line interface key (like CTRL-ALT-F2) to revert to the command line interface, and then press CTRL-ALT-DEL to restart. You can also log in on the command line interface (terminal) and then enter the **sudo poweroff** command.

On the desktop, you can also shut down your system from a terminal window, using the **poweroff** command with the **sudo** command. You will be prompted to enter your password.

```
sudo poweroff
```

To perform a reboot from a terminal window, you can use the **reboot** command.

```
sudo reboot
```

Accessing Linux from the Command Line Interface

You can access the command-line interface by pressing CTRL-ALT-F2 at any time (CTRL-ALT-F1 returns to the graphics interface, login screen). For the command line interface, you are initially given a login prompt. The login prompt is preceded by the hostname you gave your system. In this example, the hostname is **richard-desktop**. When you finish using Linux, you log out with the **logout** command. Linux then displays the same login prompt, waiting for you or another user to log in again. This is the equivalent of the login window provided by the GDM display manager. You can then log in to another account.

Once you log in as a user, you can enter and execute commands. To log in, enter your username and your password. If you make a mistake, you can erase characters with the **backspace** key. In the next example, the user enters the username **richard** and is then prompted to enter the password:

```
Ubuntu 24.04 LTS richard-desktop tty3

richard-desktop login: richard
Password:
```

When you type in your password, it does not appear on the screen. This is to protect your password from being seen by others. If you enter either the username or the password incorrectly, the system will respond with the error message "Login incorrect" and will ask for your username again, starting the login process over. You can then re-enter your username and password.

Once you enter your username and password, you are logged in to the system and the command line prompt is displayed, waiting for you to enter a command. The command line prompt is a dollar sign ($). On Ubuntu, your prompt is preceded by the hostname and the folder you are in. The home folder is indicated by a tilde (~).

```
richard@richard-desktop:~$
richard@richard-desktop:~$ cd Pictures
richard@richard-desktop:~/Pictures$
```

To end your session, issue the **logout** or **exit** command. This returns you to the login prompt, and Linux waits for another user to log in.

```
richard@richard-desktop:~$ logout
```

To shut down your system from the command line, you can use the **poweroff** command with the **sudo** command. You will be prompted to enter your password.

```
sudo poweroff
```

To perform a reboot from the terminal window, you can use the **reboot** command.

```
sudo reboot
```

If you want a time delay on the shutdown, you would use the **shutdown** command with **-h** and the time options with administrative access (**sudo** command). This command will log you out and shut down the system after 5 minutes.

```
richard@richard-desktop:~$ sudo shutdown -h +5
```

The Ubuntu Desktop

The Ubuntu 24.04 LTS desktop uses the Ubuntu GNOME interface. Ubuntu uses the Ubuntu Yaru theme for its interface with the Ubuntu screen background, and menu icons as its default. You can change themes using the GNOME Tweaks Appearance tab's. The Yaru theme places the window control buttons (close, maximize, and minimize buttons) on the right side of a window header bar (see Figure 3-12). There are three window buttons: an x for close, a dash (-) for minimize, and a square for maximize.

window buttons

Figure 3-12: Window header bar and buttons

Ubuntu (GNOME)

Ubuntu 24.04 LTS uses the GNOME desktop. It provides easy-to-use overviews and menus, along with a flexible file manager and desktop. GNOME is based on the gnome-shell, which is a compositing window manager.

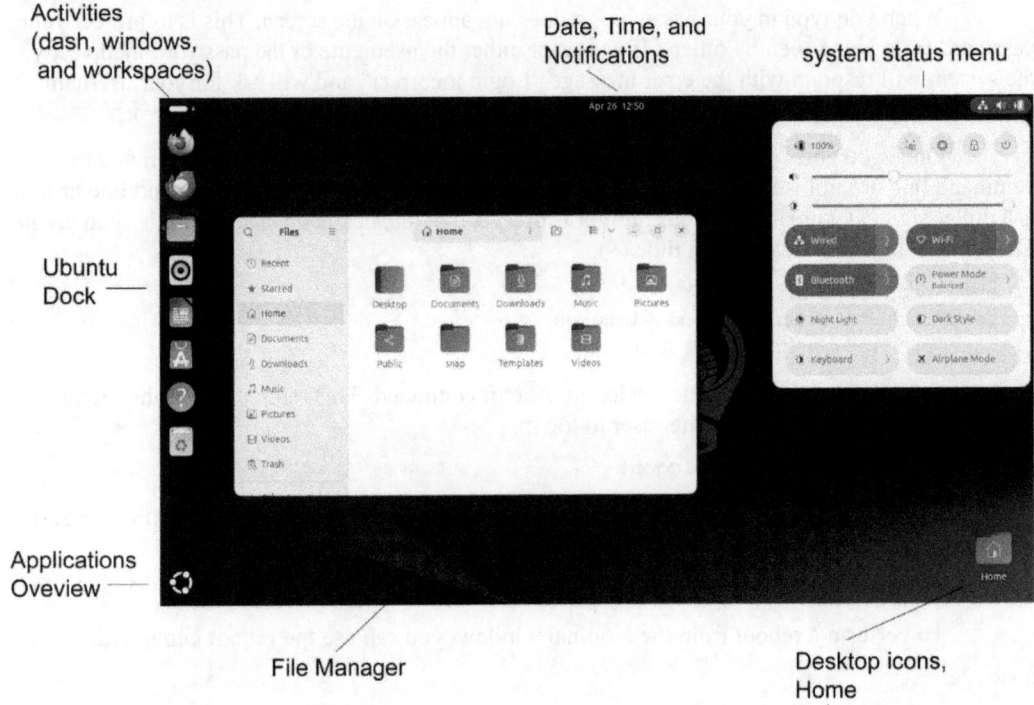

Figure 3-13: The Ubuntu desktop

The Ubuntu desktop displays a top bar and a dock (dash) on the left side, through which you access your applications, windows, and settings (see Figure 3-13). Clicking the System menu button (network, sound, power indicators) at the right side of the top bar displays the System menu, from which you can access the desktop setting, lock the screen, and shut down (Power Off) the system. The dock is a bar on the left side with icons for your favorite applications along with icons for accessing applications. Initially, there are icons for the Firefox web browser, Thunderbird mail, Files (the GNOME file manager), Rhythmbox music application, LibreOffice Writer, the App Center, Ubuntu help, and the Applications overview. The last icon opens an Applications overview that you can use to start other applications. To open an application shown on the dock, click its icon or right-click on the icon and choose New Window from the pop-up menu. You can remove any of the dock icons except the Applications overview icon by right-clicking on the icon and choosing

Unpin. Running applications will also be shown in the dock, which you can pin to the dock if you want by right-clicking and choosing "Pin to Dash." The Ubuntu dock is a GNOME extension implemented by Ubuntu and is a modified version of the GNOME Dock to Dash extension, which places a GNOME dash on the desktop.

You can access open windows and their running applications by using the Activities overview mode. Click the Activities button at the left side of the top bar (or press the Super (Windows) key) (see Figure 3-14). Large thumbnails of open windows are displayed on the windows overview (the desktop workspace area), along with workspaces, if you have more than one. You can use the Search box at the top to locate an application quickly. Part of your next desktop workspace is displayed on the right side. Clicking on that next workspace, moves you to it.

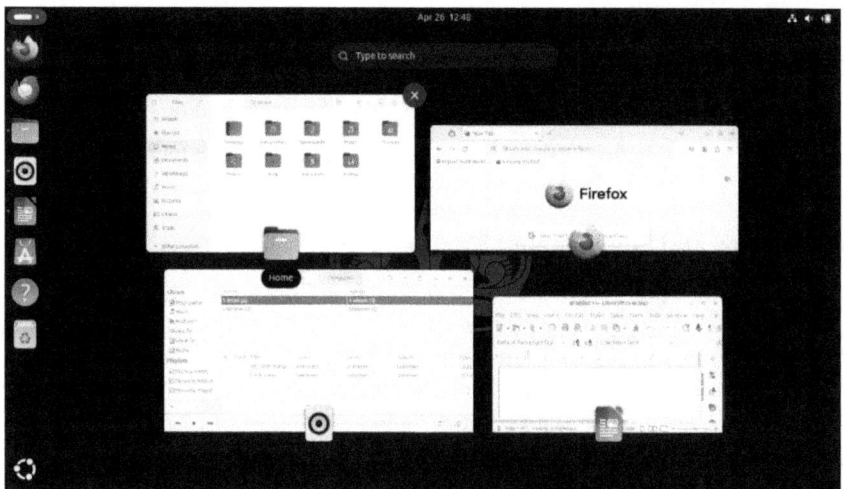

Figure 3-14: Activities overview

You can manually leave the overview at any time by pressing the ESC key, pressing the Super key (Windows key), or by clicking a window thumbnail. While in the Activities overview, the Ubuntu dock is still displayed on the left side of the screen. Clicking on an icon selects the window open with that application or opens a new one, and returns you to the desktop.

You can access windows from the windows overview, which is displayed when you start Activities. The windows overview displays thumbnails of all your open windows. When you pass your mouse over a window thumbnail, a close box appears, at the upper-right corner, with which you can close the window. You can also move the window on the desktop to another workspace.

To see just the windows open for a single application, such as several folders, click the application's icon on the dock to display the windows overview showing all the windows open for that application. Select the one you want.

To move a window on the desktop, click and drag its title bar. To maximize a window, double-click its title bar or drag it to the top bar. To return to normal, double-click the title bar again or drag it away from the top bar. To close a window, click its close box (upper right). To minimize a window, click its minimize button. To maximize a minimized window, click its icon in the dock.

Part 1: Getting Started

The Ubuntu desktop also supports corresponding keyboard operations for desktop tasks, see Table 3-1.

Keypress	Action
SHIFT	Move a file or folder, default
CTRL	Copy a file or folder
CTRL-SHIFT	Create a link for a file or folder
F2	Rename selected file or folder
CTRL-ALT-Arrow (right, left, up, down)	Move to a different desktop
CTRL-w	Close current window
ALT-spacebar	Open window menu for window operations
ALT-F2	Open Run command box
ALT-F1	Open Applications menu
CTRL-F	Find file

Table 3-1: Window and File Manager Keyboard shortcuts

Clicking the Applications icon on the dash or dock (bottom icon) opens the Applications overview listings all your installed applications (see Figure 3-15). Click an application icon to start that application. You can also right-click and choose the New Window entry on the pop-up menu. There is an application folder called Utilities on the applications overview. Utilities lists several tools, such as file roller, backup tool, log viewer, font manager, system monitor, terminal window, and, when installed, GNOME Tweaks.

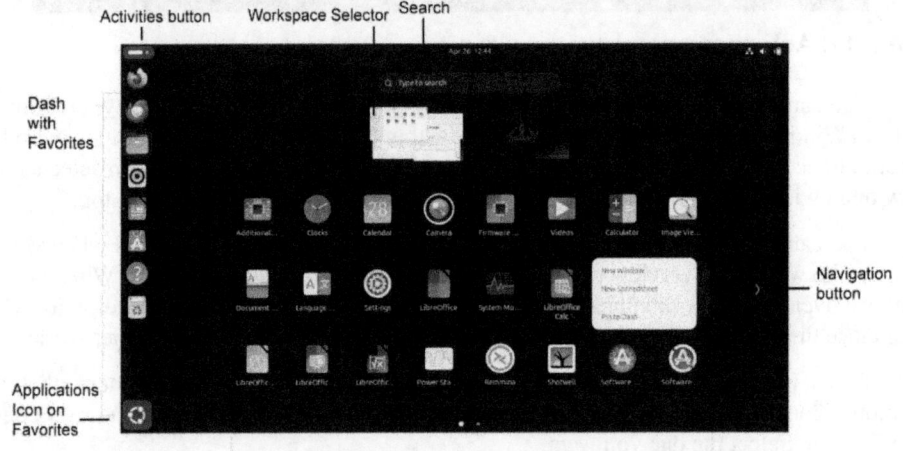

Applications Overview with workspace selector

Figure 3-15: Applications Overview

Files File Manager

You can access your home folder from the Files icon on the dash. A file manager window opens, showing your Home folder (see Figure 3-16). Your Home folder will already have default folders created for commonly used files. These include Documents, Downloads, Music, Pictures, and Videos. Your office applications will automatically save files to the Documents folder by default. Image and photo applications place image files in the Pictures folder. The Desktop folder will hold all files and folders saved to your desktop. When you download a file, it is placed in the Downloads folder.

The file manager window displays several components, including a header bar, which combines the title bar and toolbar, and a sidebar. When you open a new folder, the same window is used to display it, and you can use the forward and back arrows to move through previously opened folders. The header bar displays navigation folder buttons that show your current folder and its parent folders. You can click a parent folder to move to it. The GNOME file manager also supports tabs. You can open several folders in the same file manager window.

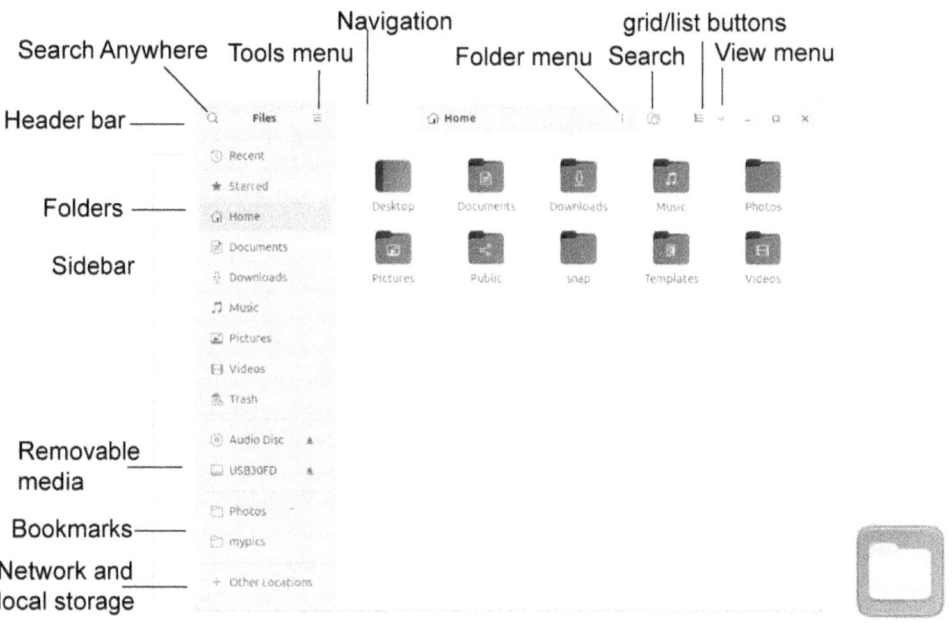

Figure 3-16: Files File manager

You can view a folder's contents as icons or as a detailed list, which you can choose by clicking the grid/list button between the search and view menu buttons on the right side of the toolbar (see Figure 3-17. This button toggles between grid (icon) and list views.

Figure 3-17: File manager grid/list button

There are three menus on the file manager header bar, the folder menu on the navigation button for the current folder, the view menu (down-arrow button) on the right side of the header bar, and tools menu (menu button), on the top right of the sidebar. The sidebar is located on the left side of file manager window (see Figure 3-18).

To the right of the location buttons, is the button for the current folder's folder menu (three vertical dots, ellipses), which you can click to display the folder menu). The menu shows common folder tasks such as creating a new folder (New Folder), open with a different file manager (Open With), and bookmarking the folder (Add to Bookmarks). The Reload button refreshes the display, updating any changes. The Edit Location entry changes the location buttons to an editable location textbox. The Copy Location entry copies the full pathname of the folder, which you can then paste to other documents (CTRL-v). The Properties entry displays the folder's Properties dialog, showing folder information and permissions. You can also open the folder in a terminal window, which is useful for running shell commands on the folder files and subfolders.

To the right of the grid/list button is a button for the View menu (down-arrow). The Views menu has entries for sorting your file manager icons. The sort entries allow you to sort your icons by name (A-Z and Z-A), size, type, and modification date. You can also reverse the order by name and modification date.

The file manager Tools menu (lines button) is located on the sidebar, to the right of the "Files" label. The Tools menu has entries for managing folders and files, as well as entries for configuring the file manager display. There are entries for showing hidden files, adjusting the icon size, and opening a new window or tab. The Keyboard Shortcuts entry displays the list of available shortcut keys, organized by function such as open operations, tabs, navigation, view operations, and edit tasks such as renaming, editing, and copying files.

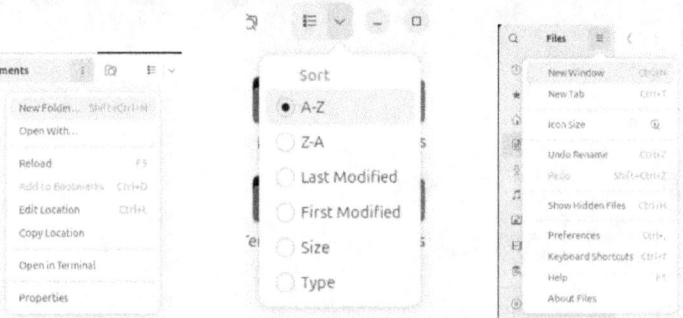

Figure 3-18: File manager folder, view, and tools menus

Ubuntu Customization with GNOME Tweaks: Themes, Icons, Fonts, and Startup Applications

You can perform common desktop customizations using the GNOME Tweaks. Areas to customize include fonts, themes, startup applications, windows, and startup applications. You can access GNOME Tweaks from the Applications overview | Utilities. The GNOME Tweaks has tabs for Fonts, Appearance, Sound, Mouse & Touchpad, Keyboard, Windows, and Startup Applications (see Figure 3-19). GNOME Tweaks is not installed by default. It is available from the App Center as a Debian package.

The Appearance tab lets you set the theme for your icons, cursor, and legacy applications. Ubuntu uses the Yaru theme. Traditionally, GNOME uses the Adwaita Theme with its light and dark variants. As you add other desktops, such as MATE, the available themes increase. There would be many window themes and icons to choose from. On this tab, in the Background section, you can manage your background image, setting the default image for light and dark styles, and different adjustment options such as Zoom, Centered, Stretched, and Wallpaper.

Figure 3-19: GNOME Tweaks - Appearance tab (themes)

Desktop fonts for interface (application or dialog text), documents, and monospace (terminal windows or code) can be changed in the Fonts tab (see Figure 3-20). You can adjust the size of the font or change the font style. Clicking the font name opens a "Pick a Font" dialog from which you can choose a different font. The quality of the text display can be further adjusted with Rendering and Antialiasing options. To simply increase or decrease the size of all fonts on your desktop interface, you can adjust the Scaling Factor.

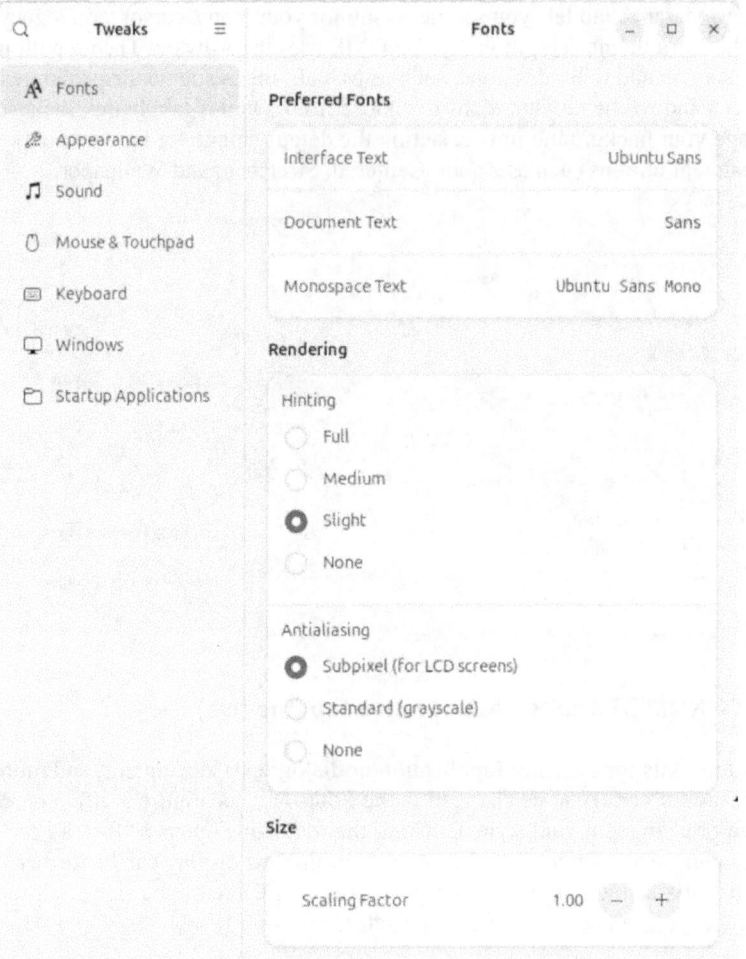

Figure 3-20: GNOME Tweaks - Fonts tab

At times, there may be certain applications that you want started up when you log in, such as the Text Editor, the Firefox web browser, or the Videos movie player. On the Startup Applications tab, you can choose the applications to start up (see Figure 3-21). Click the plus (+) button to open an applications dialog from which you can choose an application. Click the Add button to add the application. Once added, you can later remove the application by clicking its Remove button.

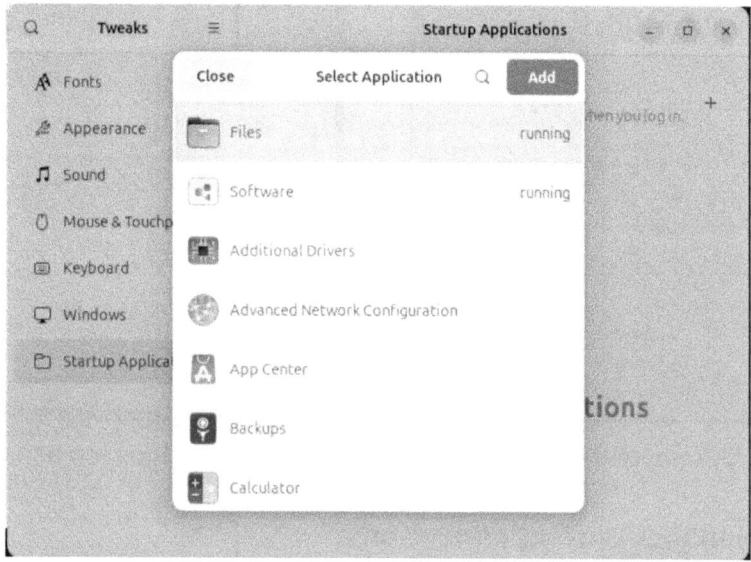

Figure 3-21: GNOME Tweaks - Startup Applications tab

Network Connections

Network connections will be set up for you by NetworkManager, which will detect your network connections automatically, both wired and wireless. NetworkManager provides status information for your connection and allows you to switch easily from one configured connection to another, as needed. For initial configuration, it detects as much information as possible about the new connection.

NetworkManager is user specific. Wired connections will be started automatically. For wireless connections, when a user logs in, NetworkManager selects the connection preferred by that user. From a menu of detected wireless networks, the user can select a wireless connection to use.

NetworkManager displays active network connections in the System menu: the Wired button for the wired connection and the Wi-Fi button for a wireless connection. Each entry will indicate its status, as connected or disconnected. The buttons for these entries will vary according to their connection status: solid (colored) for an active connection and empty (faded) for a disconnected connection (see Figure 3-22). On wired systems that have no wireless devices, there is no Wi-Fi button in the System menu. Clicking all the network buttons, turns networking off, removing the network indicator from the Settings menu button.

96   Part 1: Getting Started

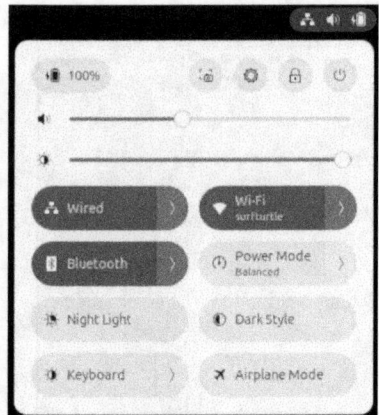 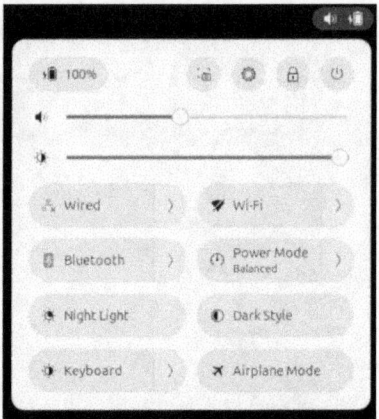

Figure 3-22: System menu with network Quick Settings buttons, on and off

NetworkManager Wired Connections

For computers connected to a wired network, such as an Ethernet connection, NetworkManager automatically detects and establishes the network connection. Most networks use DHCP to provide such network information as an IP address and DNS server. With this kind of connection, NetworkManager can connect automatically to your network whenever you start your system.

NetworkManager Wireless Connections

NetworkManager will scan for wireless connections, checking for Extended Service Set Identifiers (ESSIDs) . If an ESSID identifies a previously used connection, it is selected. If several are found, the recently used one is chosen. If only new connections are available, NetworkManager waits for the user to choose one.

Click the Wi-Fi button's menu link in the System menu to display the Wi-Fi menu showing a list of available Wi-Fi connections you can choose from (see Figure 3-23). Entries display the name of the wireless network and a wave graph showing the strength of its signal. To connect to a network click on an entry. If this is the first time you are trying to connect to that network, an Authentication dialog will prompt you to enter the password or encryption key (see Figure 3-24). The selected Wi-Fi connection will display a checkmark next to its name. Below the list of Wi-Fi connections is an All Networks link you can click to open the Settings Wi-Fi tab.

Chapter 3: Usage Basics 97

Figure 3-23: System Menu Wi-Fi button's menu showing Wi-Fi connections

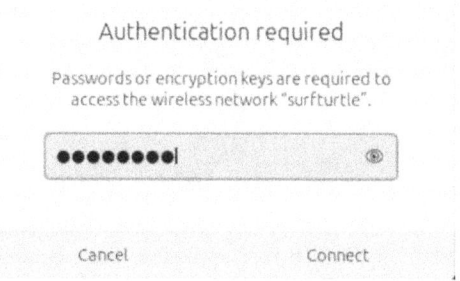

Figure 3-24: Wi-Fi authentication

    The Wi-Fi button on the System menu will also show the name of the connected Wi-Fi network. You can turn off wireless by clicking the Wi-Fi button (see Figure 3-25). When turned off, the button fades. To reactivate your wireless connection, click the Wi-Fi button again.

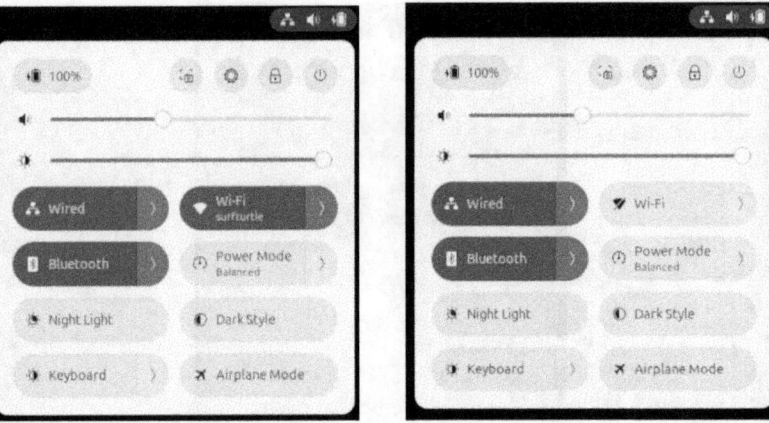

Figure 3-25: System menu with Wi-Fi button on and off

Configuring Network Connections with GNOME Settings

On the GNOME Settings dialog there is a Wi-Fi tab for wireless configuration and a Network tab for wired, VPN, and proxy configurations. Choose the All Networks link from the expanded Wi-Fi button (arrow on right side of the button) in the System menu, or click the Wi-Fi tab in the Settings dialog, to open the Wi-Fi tab (see Figure 3-26). On the Wi-Fi tab, an Airplane Mode switch and a list of visible wireless connections are listed (Visible Networks section). The currently active connection will have a "Connected" label next to its configuration button. At the top of the tab is a Wi-Fi switch for turning wireless on and off. Below the switch are links for dialogs for connections to hidden networks, turning on your computer's Wi-Fi hotspot capability, and listing previously accessed Wi-Fi Networks (Saved Networks). The "Saved Networks" link opens a "Save Wi-Fi Networks" dialog listing your previously accessed Wi-Fi networks, which you can choose to configure or delete (Trash button).

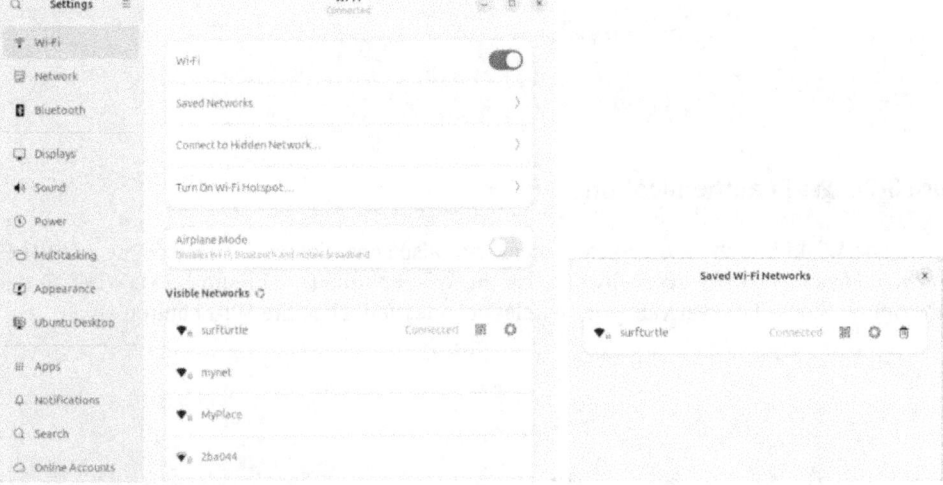

Figure 3-26: Settings Wi-Fi tab

Your current active connection will have a "Connected" label, scan button, and a configuration (gear) button to the right. The scan button displays a Share Network dialog displaying an image to scan to allow quickly sharing your network with yours or other people's devices such as phones and tablets (see Figure 3-27). The network name and password are also shown.

Figure 3-27: Settings Wi-Fi entry with scan button and Scan dialog

Click the configuration button to display a dialog with tabs for managing the connection. The Details tab provides information about the connection (see Figure 3-28). The Security, Identity, IPv4, and IPv6 tabs let you perform a detailed configuration of your connection, as described in Chapter 15. The settings are set to automatic by default. Should you make any changes, click the Apply button to have them take effect. The Details tab has options both for connecting automatically and for providing availability to other users. These are set by default. Should you not want to connect to the wireless network automatically, be sure to uncheck this option. To remove a network's connection information, click the Forget Connection button on the Details tab.

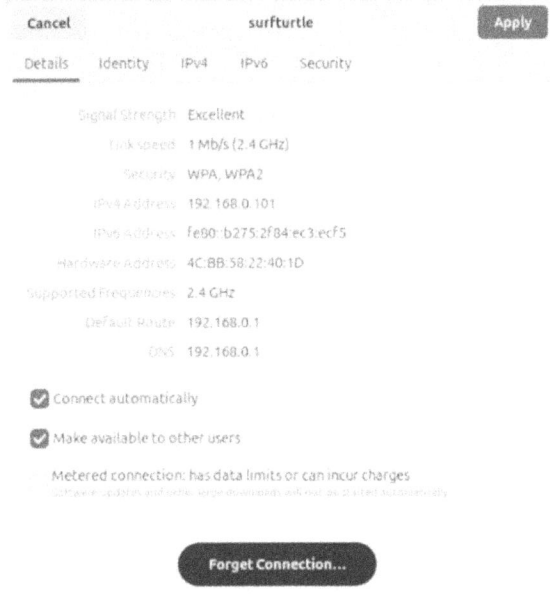

Figure 3-28: Settings Wi-Fi connection - Details tab

For a wired connection, click the Wired Settings entry on the Wired button's menu in the System menu or click the Network tab on GNOME Settings. This will display lists of Wired and VPN connections, as well as an entry for the Network Proxy. The Wired section shows your current wired connections with on and off switches for each. A plus button at the top right of the Wired section lets you add more wired connections. Next to a connection's switch a gear button is displayed (see Figure 3-29). Clicking the gear button opens a configuration dialog for that connection with tabs for Details, Identity, IPv4, IPv6, and Security (see Chapter 15).

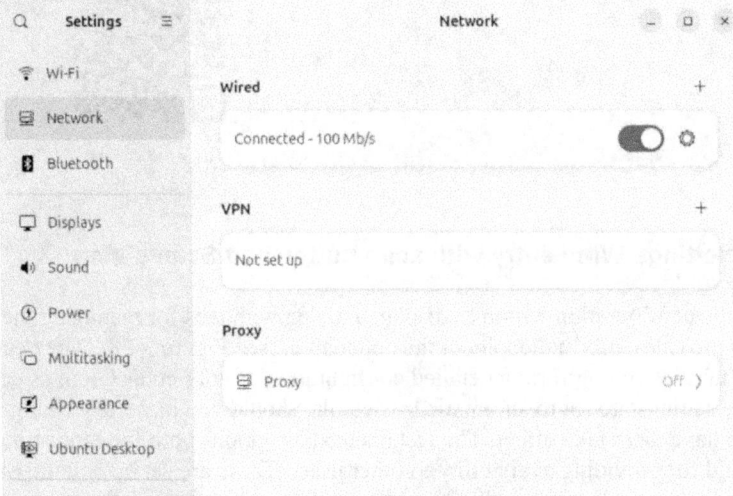

Figure 3-29: Settings Network tab with Wired connection

Clicking on the Network proxy gear button opens a Network Proxy tab with a Network Proxy switch for turning network proxy on and off. The Configuration entry shows a menu to the right with Manual and Automatic options (see Figure 3-30). For the Automatic option, you enter a URL address. The Manual option lets you enter address and port information for the proxy.

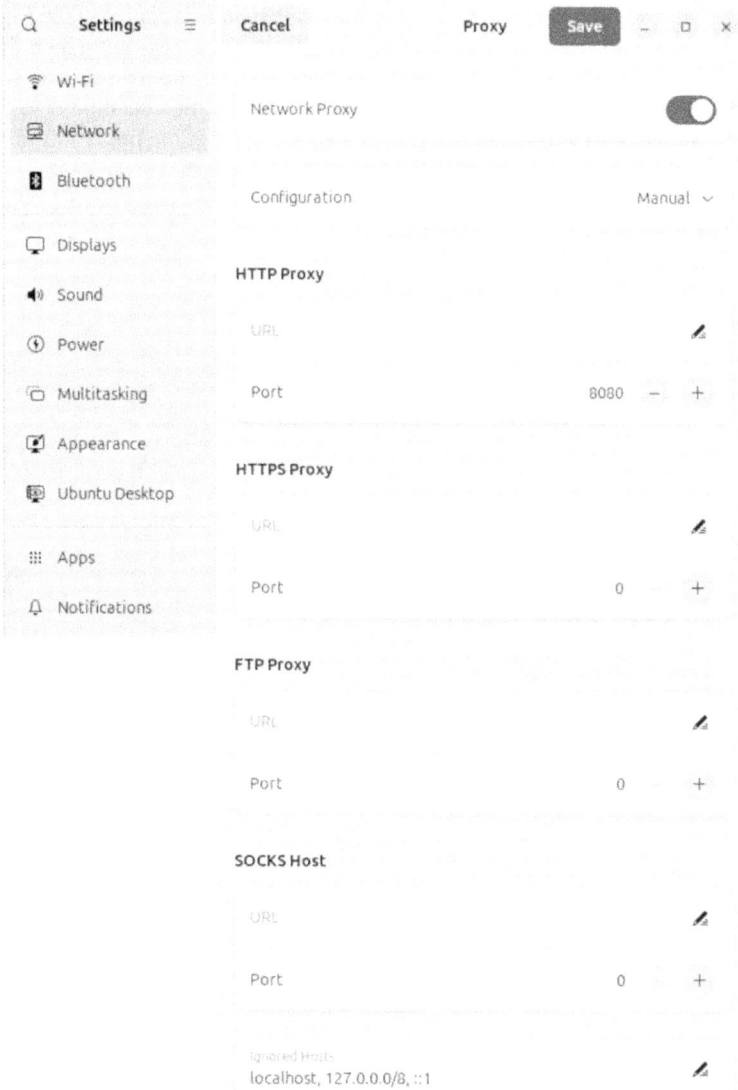

Figure 3-30: Settings Network tab with proxy settings

To add a vpn connection, click the plus (+) button at the top right of the VPN section to open the Add Vpn dialog listing the supported VPN protocols (see Chapter 15). Once a protocol is selected, an appropriate configuration dialog for your VPN network is displayed.

Settings

You can configure desktop settings and perform most administrative tasks using the GNOME configuration tools (see Table 3-2) listed in the Settings application, accessible with the Settings button (gear image) located at the top right of the System menu (see Figure 3-31). Settings displays tabs on a left sidebar for different desktop and system configurations (see Figure 3-32). The tabs are segmented into five groups, beginning with those for networking, then the desktop, application related tabs, devices such as the keyboard and printers, and then several subheadings for accessibility, security, and system management and information which have links to open several tabs. Should you use a link to open a tab, a left arrow is displayed at the upper left of the current tab's header bar. Click on it to return back to the tab with the link you used.

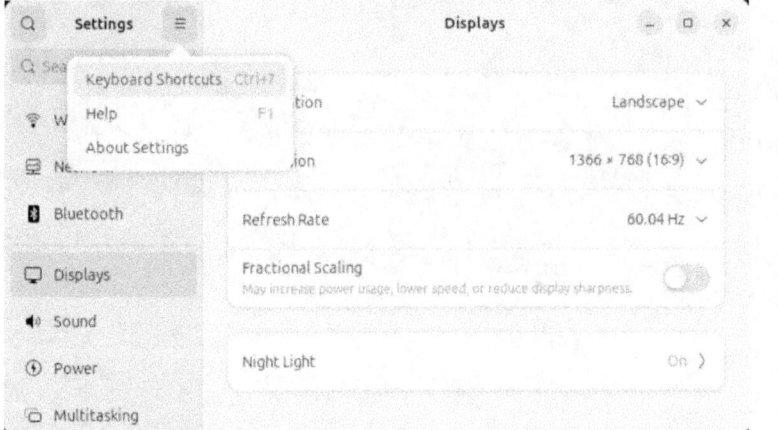

Figure 3-31: Ubuntu (GNOME) Settings

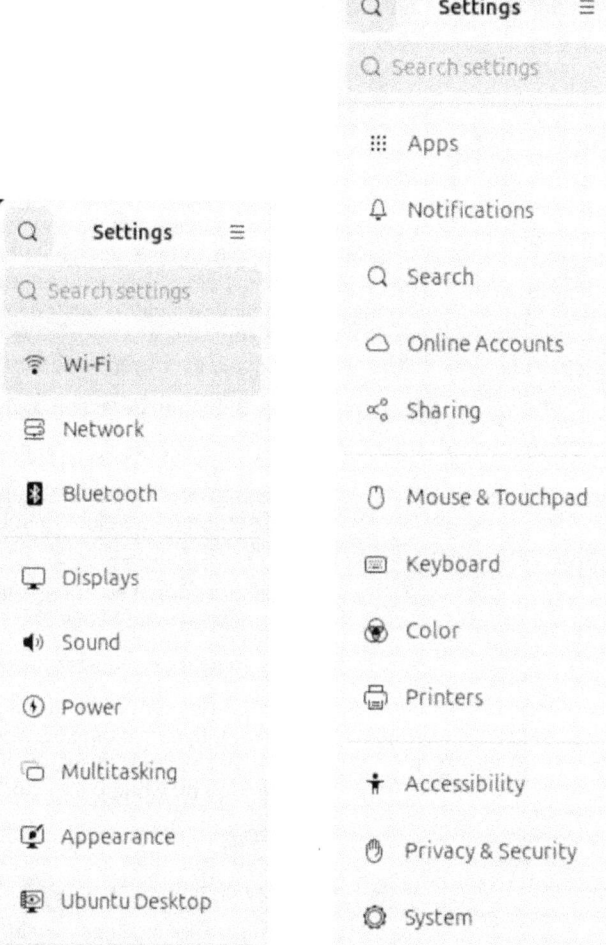

Figure 3-32: Settings Sidebar

Some tabs lists links that you can use to open other tabs or dialogs, such as the System, Privacy & Security, and Accessibility tabs. The links have a right arrow symbol at the end of the link entry. You can click on a link to open the tab or dialog. If the link is to a tab, when the tab opens, a left arrow button appears on the header bar to the left of the tab's name. You click on this button to return to the previous tab. Any tab you link to can, in turn, list links to yet other tabs and dialogs.

Setting	Description
Accessibility	Enables universal access features for the display, keyboard, and mouse. Displays tabs for Seeing, Hearing, Typing, Pointing and Clicking, and Zoom.
Appearance	Style (light, dark, and color accents) and backgrounds.
Apps	Opens a dialog where you can set permissions for applications such as file types and notifications. Also includes a tab for setting default applications such as your Web browser and image viewer, as well as setting default applications for removable media.
Bluetooth	Sets Bluetooth detection and configuration
Color	Sets the color profile for a device.
Displays	Changes your screen resolution, refresh rate, and screen orientation for your connected displays.
Keyboard	Configures input sources, alternate character keys, and shortcut keys.
Mouse & Touchpad	Sets mouse and touchpad configuration
Multitasking	Turn on hot corner, screen edge window resizing, dynamic or fixed workspaces, show workspaces on all displays, and application switching on workspaces and monitors.
Network	Turn wired networks on or off. Allows access to an available wired network. Also specifies proxy configuration, if needed.
Notifications	Turns on notifications for different applications
Online Accounts	Configures online accounts for use by e-mail and browser applications
Power	Sets the power saving options and lists battery levels.
Printers	Configure printers and access print queues
Privacy & Security	Turns on privacy and security features. Displays tabs for Connectivity, Screen Lock, Location, File History & Trash, Diagnostics, and Device Security.
Sharing	Turns on sharing for media.
Sound	Configures system levels, output and input sound devices, and sound effects.
Search	Specifies the resources and locations searched

	by the GNOME activities overview search box
System	Displays tabs for system information and management: Region & Language, Date & Time, Users, Remote Desktop, Secure Shell, and About. Also includes a link to Software Updates for updating your system.
Ubuntu Desktop	Set desktop icon, dock configuration, and enhanced tiling.
Wi-Fi	Configure and manage wireless networks.

Table 3-2: Settings

Accessibility (Universal Access)

The Accessibility tab in Settings lets you configure alternative access to your interface for your display, keyboard, and mouse. Five links open tabs to set the display (Seeing), sound (Hearing), Typing, mouse features (Pointing and clicking), and zooming enhancements (Zoom). A switch at the top lets you choose whether to always display the accessibility menu on the top bar (see Figure 3-33).

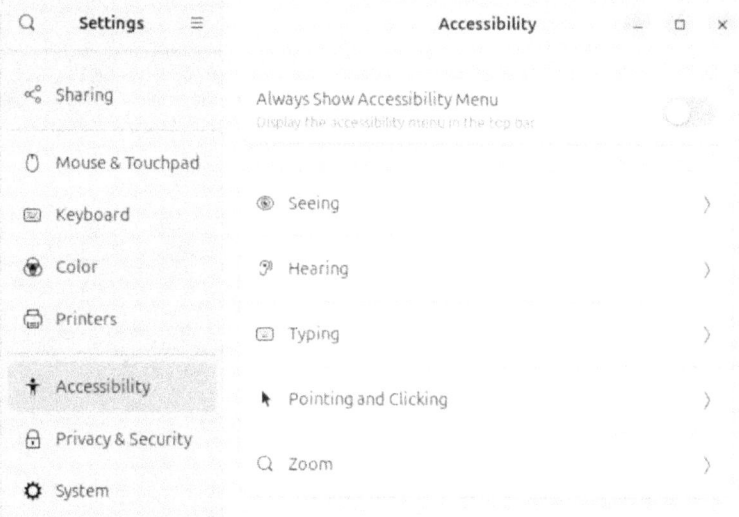

Figure 3-33: Accessibility

The Seeing tab adjusts the contrast and text size, whether to allow sounds for keys, use of the screen reader, whether to show scrollbars, reduce animation to reduce motion, and to use shapes instead of just color for states (see Figure 3-34).

Hearing uses visual cues for alert sounds (Visual Alerts section), and will allow you to increase the volume above normal (Overamplification).

Typing allows you to enable the screen keyboard with keyboard repeat keys and cursor blinking options (Text Cursor section). The Typing Assist section has options to enable repeat keys, sticky keys, slow keys, and bounce keys.

Pointing and Clicking lets you use the keyboard for mouse operations, adjust the double-click delay, and to visually indicate the mouse location by press the CTRL key on the left side of your keyboard. You can also set the delay for displaying the right click effect such as displaying a context menu. The Click Assist section lets to you simulate a right click by holding down a left click and then releasing it. You can also implement hover clicks.

The Zoom tab has sections for Magnifier, Crosshairs, and Color Filters. In the Magnifier section you can set the zoom factor, whether to magnify the full screen or just where the pointer moves (Magnifier View), move beyond the screen edges (Extend Outside Screen Edges), select all or part of the screen such as top, bottom, left, or right halves (Screen Area), and, when moving the mouse, to have the magnifier move with the contents, remain centered, or push contents around. The Crosshairs section lets you use the crosshairs of two lines to mark the location of the mouse. You can adjust the thickness of the lines and whether to cover the entire screen or just part of it. You can also change the color of the lines. The Color Filters section lets you adjust the brightness, contrast, and color intensity of the magnified region. You can also invert the colors if you want.

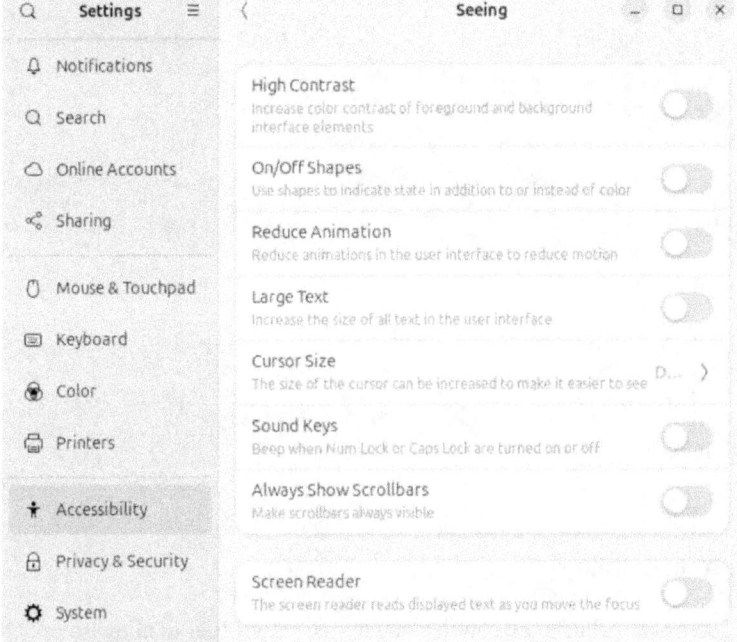

Figure 3-34: Accessibility - Seeing

Appearance

The Appearance dialog lets you set options for the desktop style and the background (see Figure 3-35). The Style section lets you choose either a light or dark theme (Light is the default). You can also choose an accent color from the Color buttons.

Chapter 3: Usage Basics   **107**

In the Background section, you can set your background for the desktop.. The current background is shown and icons of installed backgrounds are displayed. Click on an image to make it your current background. The background on your display is updated immediately. The background image you choose for your desktop also becomes the background image of the login screen. A blurred version of the new background image becomes the background for the lock screen.

To add your own image, click the Add Picture link, at the top right of the Background section, to open a dialog listing the images in your Pictures folder. You can select images from other folders. Once you make your selection, click the Open button at the upper right. You then return to the main Background dialog, showing your new background. An x is displayed on the icons of the images you add, allowing you to remove the image.

Install the **gnome-backgrounds** package to add a collection of GNOME backgrounds. They will appear automatically in the Settings Background tab. You can download more GNOME backgrounds (wallpapers) from **https://www.gnome-look.org/**.

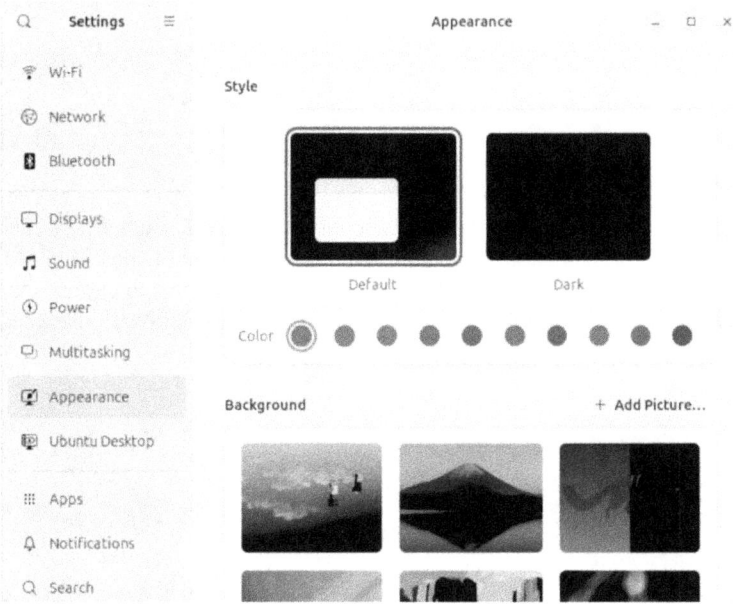

Figure 3-35: Appearance

Apps

On the Apps tab you can set default applications for different tasks and removable media such as the Web browser or video player, as well as configure permissions for resources for your installed applications. The Apps tab lists a link for default applications (Default Apps) and then links for each application installed on your system (see Figure 3-36). Click on a link to open its tab.

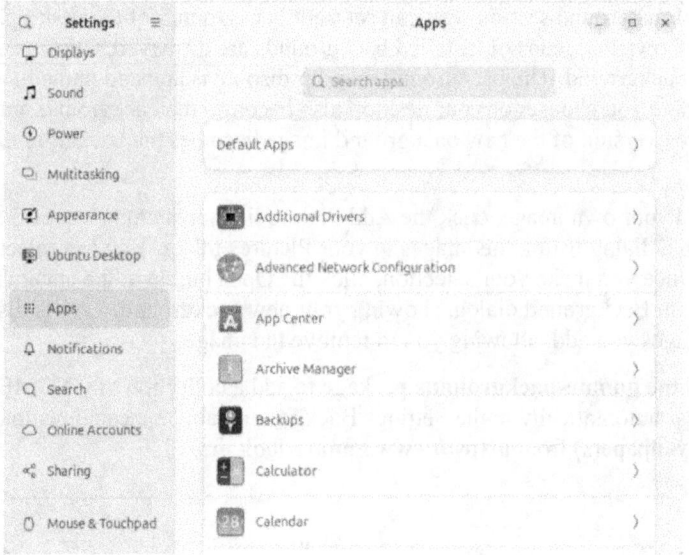

Figure 3-36: Apps

Default Apps

The Default Apps tab has two sections: Default Apps and Removable Media. In the Default Apps section you can set default applications for basic types of files: Web, Mail, Calendar, Music, Video, and Photos (see Figure 3-37). Use the drop-down menus to choose installed alternatives, such as Evolution instead of Thunderbird for Mail, or Shotwell instead of Image Viewer for Photos.

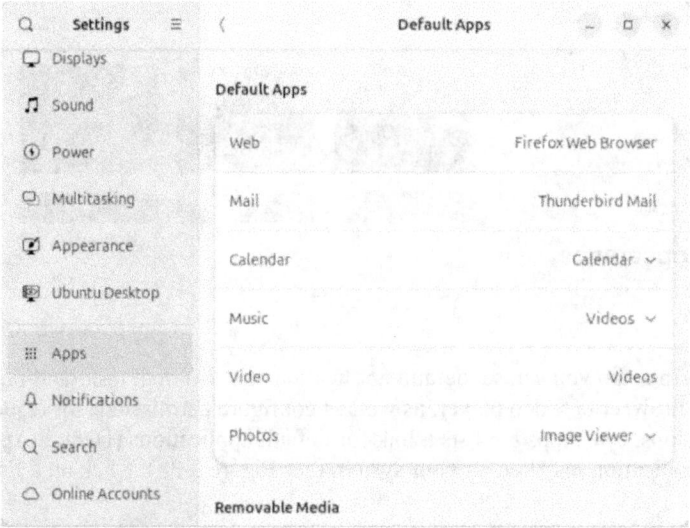

Figure 3-37: Default Applications

Removable Media

Ubuntu supports removable devices and media, such as digital cameras, USB drives, card readers, DVD discs, and external hard drives. These devices are handled automatically with device interfaces set up for them when needed. Removable storage devices and media will appear in the file manager sidebar and on the Ubuntu dock. For example, when you connect a USB drive to your system, it will be detected and can be displayed as a storage device with its own file system by the file manager. An icon for it is also displayed on the Ubuntu dock, which you can click to open a file manager window for it.

Removable devices and media, such as USB drives and DVD/CD discs, can be ejected using Eject buttons on the file manager sidebar. Just click the Eject button, and the media is ejected or unmounted. You can also right-click the device entry in the file manager sidebar or on icon for the device on the Ubuntu dock and, from a pop-up menu, choose the Eject entry. Be sure always to click the Eject button for device entry before removing a drive, such as a USB drive or removable disk drive. Removing the drive before clicking eject can result in incomplete write operations on the disk.

The Removable Media section on the Default Apps tab lets you specify default actions for CD Audio, DVD Video, Music Player, Photos, and Software media (see Figure 3-38) You can select from drop-down menus, the application to use for the different media. Possible options derived from installed applications are listed on the menu for the appropriate media, such as Rhythmbox for CD Audio discs and Videos for DVD-Video. Photos can be opened with the Shotwell photo manager.

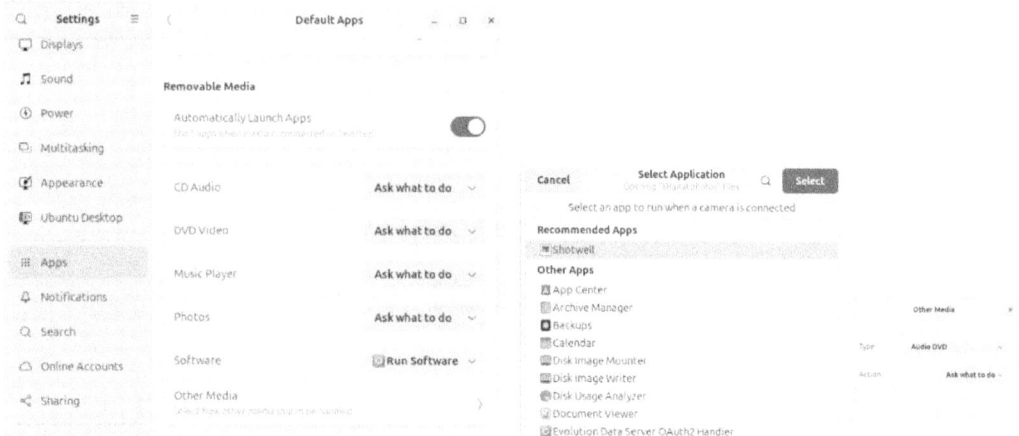

Figure 3-38: Removable Media defaults

These menus also include options for Ask What To Do, Do Nothing, Open Folder, and Other app. The Open Folder option will open a window displaying the files on the disc. Initially, the Ask What To Do option is set for all entries. The "Other app" option opens a dialog listing other installed apps you may want to use instead. The Recommended Apps section list appropriate applications and the Other Apps section lists all other installed applications.

The Other Media link at the bottom of the Removable Media section, opens a dialog that lets you set up an association for less used media such as Blu-Ray discs and Audio DVD.

When you insert removable media, such as a CD audio disc, its associated application is automatically started, unless you change that preference. If you want to turn off this feature for a particular kind of media, you can select the Do Nothing entry. If you want to be prompted for options, use the Ask What To Do entry. Then, when you insert a disc, a dialog with a menu for possible actions is displayed. From this menu, you can select another application or select the Do Nothing or Open Folder options.

You can turn the automatic startup off for all media by clicking the "Automatically Launch Apps" switch at the beginning of the Removable Media section in the Default Apps tab.

App Permissions, Associations (file and link types), and Storage

Clicking on an application link in the Apps tab opens the tab for that application, showing the application name and icon at the top with Open and "Apps Details" buttons . The Open button opens the application and the Apps Details button opens the App Center, where you can locate an application's entry to find out more about it.

The Permissions section then lists possible supported permissions for the selected application. Applications can be either sandboxed or not sandboxed. Applications installed with Snap are sandboxed, whereas those installed from APT repositories are not sandboxed. Those include common GNOME applications such as Image Viewer, Videos, and LibreOffice. Those that are not sandboxed have a highlighted notice a the top of their tab, "App is not sandboxed". These usually only support a permission for Notifications (see Figure 3-39). Only a few, such as Files, Passwords, and Terminal, have the Search permission.

Figure 3-39: Apps - permissions (not sandboxed)

For sandboxed applications (Snap), you can set an extensive set of permissions for resources such as notifications, search, sound, disk space, as well as the file types and links that an application can open. The Firefox Web Browser is an example of an sandboxed application with an extensive number of permissions, such as playing audio, camera support, printing files, accessing persons or system files, accessing removable devices, and accessing your home folder (see Figure 3-40).

Chapter 3: Usage Basics   111

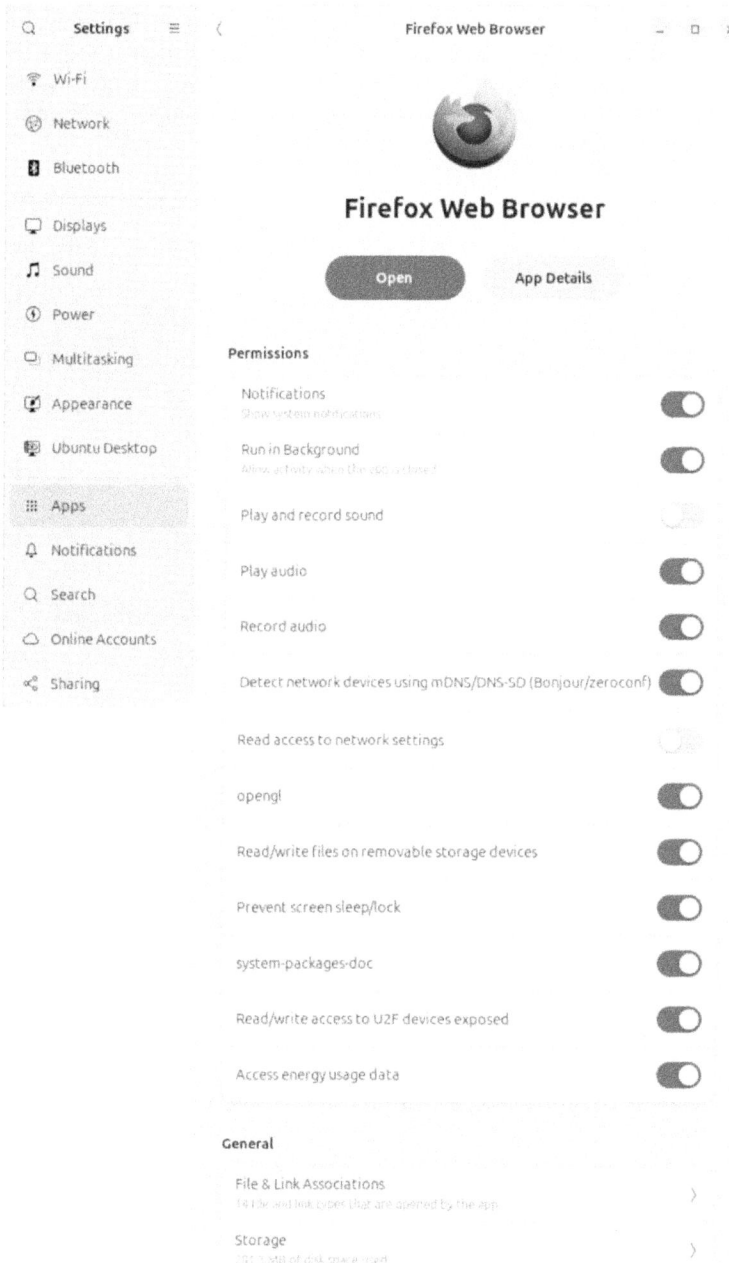

Figure 3-40: Apps - Permissions (sandboxed apps)

There is also a General section with links for file and link associations and storage. Selecting the "File & Link Associations" link opens a dialog with sections for File Types and Link Type (see Figure 3-41). For Firefox there are file types for Web files (HTML, XML, and XHTML),

112 Part 1: Getting Started

image files (JPEG, PNG, and GIF), and Web video. The Link Types section show different Web protocols (types of Web pages) that Firefox supports, such as http://, https://, ftp://, and chrome://. A trash icon to the right of each entry lets you remove it as a file type or type of Web link supported by the application. A Reset button at the bottom of the dialog lets you restore all file types or links you have removed.

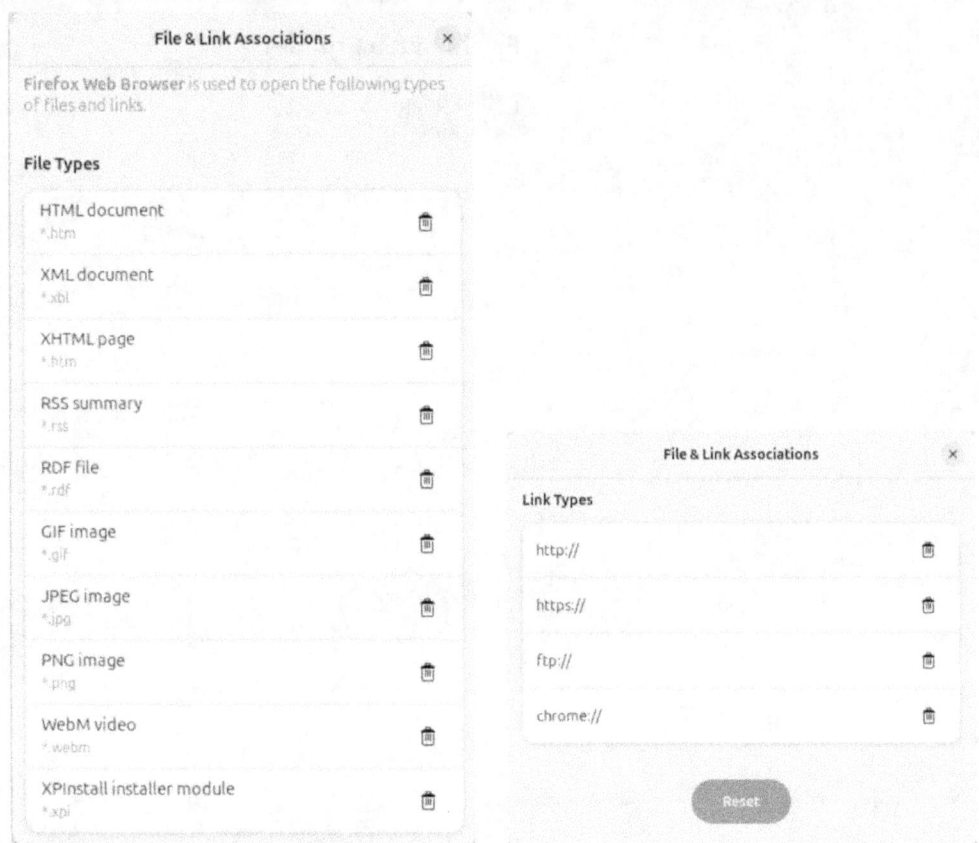

Figure 3-41: Apps - File Type and Link Types

The Storage link opens a dialog that shows how much storage the application is using, with entries for App, Data, Cache, and Total. A "Clear Cache" button at the bottom lets you clear the cache (see Figure 3-42).

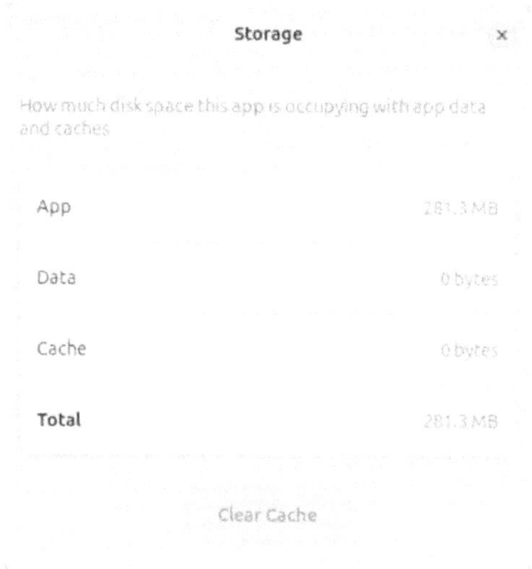

Figure 3-42: Apps - Storage

Color Profiles (GNOME Color Manager)

You can manage the color for different devices by using the Settings Color tab. The Color tab lists devices for which you can set color profiles. Click a device to display buttons at the bottom of the screen for Add profile and Calibrate. Your monitor will have a profile set up automatically. Click the Add Profile button to open the Add Profile dialog from which you can choose a color profile. Click the Add button to add the profile. Available profiles include Adobe RGB, Wide Gamut RGB, and sRGB. You can also import a profile from an ICC profile file of your own.

When you click on a profile entry, its Profiles are listed (see Figure 3-43). Click on a profile to display buttons to Set for all users, Remove profile, and View details. Click the View details button for the color profile information.

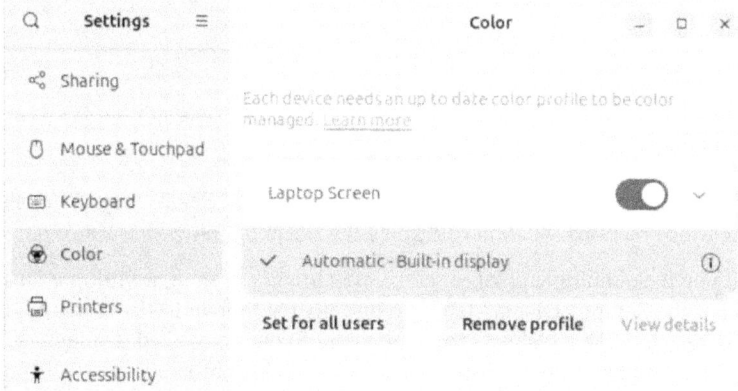

Figure 3-43: Color management dialog

Displays (Resolution, Rotation, Scaling, and Night Light)

The display drivers for Linux used on Ubuntu support user-level resolution and orientation changes. Any user can specify a resolution or orientation, without affecting the settings of other users. The Settings Displays dialog provides a simple interface for setting rotation, resolution, and selecting added monitors, allowing for cloned or extended displays across several connected monitors. Menus let you configure the orientation, resolution, and refresh rate (see Figure 3-44). Should you make changes, an Apply button will appear in the titlebar which you can click. For changes to resolution, the new resolution is displayed with a dialog asking if you want to keep the new display settings. The Revert Settings button returns to the previous resolution and the Keep Changes button keeps the new one.

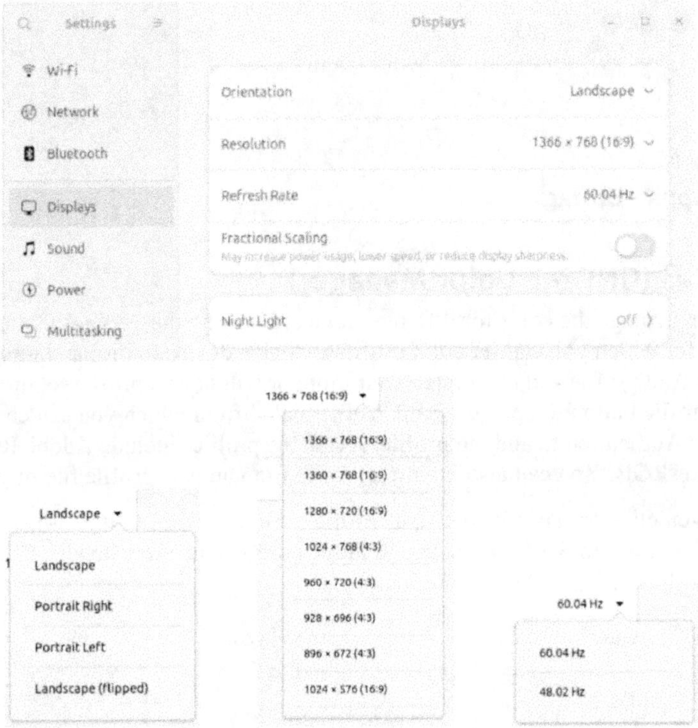

Figure 3-44: Displays

The display server supports scaling using the Fractional Scale entry. To enable scaling, turn on the switch for Fractional Scaling to display the Scale option with a list of possible scales.

Should you have multiple displays connected to your system, a Multiple Displays entry is shown at the top of the Settings Display tab with buttons for Join and Mirror (see Figure 3-45). If the Join button is selected, the tab show icons for each of your connected displays, with a solid bar across the top of the selected primary display. Each display is numbered starting from 1. Click on a display icon to make it the primary display. Below the display icons are links for each display. Click on a link to open the configuration tab for that display. You can also choose to have a display adjusted for TV using the "Adjust for TV" switch.

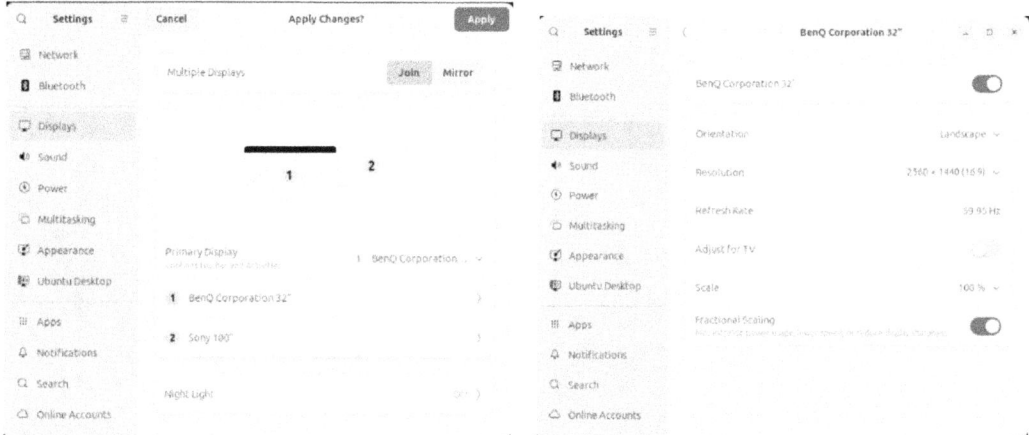

Figure 3-45: Displays - scaling and multiple displays (join)

Should you want to mirror your display instead, showing the same screen on a different display, you can click on the Mirror button to show just the basic configuration options for the primary display (see Figure 3-46). The display icons and the links for the different displays are not shown.

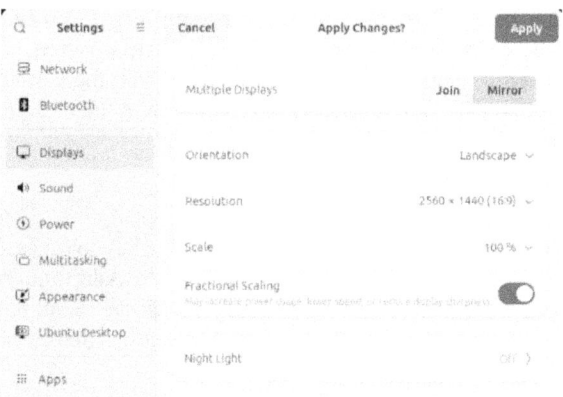

Figure 3-46: Displays - multiple displays (mirror)

The Night Light feature lets you adjust the color temperature of your display to show a warmer image (see Figure 3-47). A warmer color temperature at night helps to reduces eye strain. Click the Night Light link at the bottom of the Displays tab to open the Night Light tab. The Night Light switch lets you turn the Night light on or off. Use the items in the Schedule menu to choose an automatic or manual schedule. The Sunset to Sunrise entry operates from 8 PM to 6 AM. The Manual entry lets you set your own time period. A slider bar at the bottom of the dialog lets you adjust color temperature.

116 Part 1: Getting Started

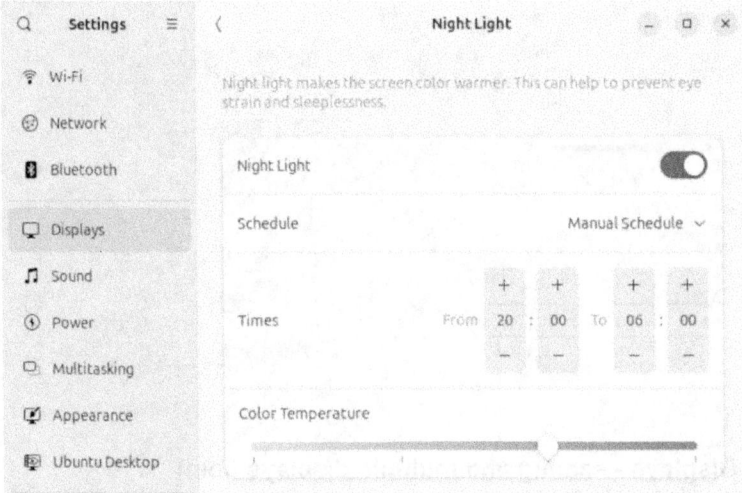

Figure 3-47: Displays - Night Light

Two display servers are available for Ubuntu, X.org and Wayland. The newer Wayland display server is the default, except for systems using the Nvidia proprietary video driver. You can find out more about Wayland at **https://wayland.freedesktop.org/**. You can still use the older X.org displays server. You can find out more about X.org at **https://www.x.org/wiki**. On the login screen you can choose whether to use the Wayland display server, the Ubuntu entry, or the X.org display server, the "Ubuntu on X.org entry. Click the gear icon at the bottom right of the login screen to display these display server options (see Figure 3-5).

Keyboard

The Keyboard tab lets you set the input source for the keyboard (see Figure 3-48). The current input language source is listed and selected. Click the "+ Add Input source" link to open a dialog listing other language sources, which you can add. Click the menu button (vertical ellipses) and select "View Keyboard Layout" to see the keyboard layout of your currently selected input source.

The Input Source Switching section has switches that let you choose whether to allow different sources for each window or use the same source for all windows.

The Special Character Entry section lets you select alternate character keys and compose keys to add more characters than are on your keyboard.

In the Keyboard Shortcuts section, click the "View and Customize Shortcuts" to open the Keyboard Shortcuts dialog. You can assign keys to perform such tasks as starting the web browser or moving a window. The Keyboard Shortcuts dialog list links to tabs for different categories such as Navigation, Sound and media, and Accessibility. The Reset All button at the bottom of the dialog resets the shortcuts to their default value. To perform a search on the shortcuts, use the search text box at the top of the dialog.

Click on a category link to open a tab listing all the shortcuts for that category. To change a shortcut, click on its entry. When the Set Shortcut dialog appears, type the keys for the shortcut, usually three. The keys appear on the next dialog with a Set button in the upper right corner. The changed entry then appears on that category tab with a delete button you can click to remove your shortcut setting.

The Custom Shortcuts link at the end of the category list on the Keyboard Shortcuts dialog, lets you create custom shortcuts. Click on it to open an Custom Shortcut dialog with an Add Shortcut button. Click on this button to open the Add Custom Shortcut dialog, where you enter the name and command before setting the shortcut. The Add Custom Shortcut dialog then opens where you enter the shortcut keys and add the shortcut.

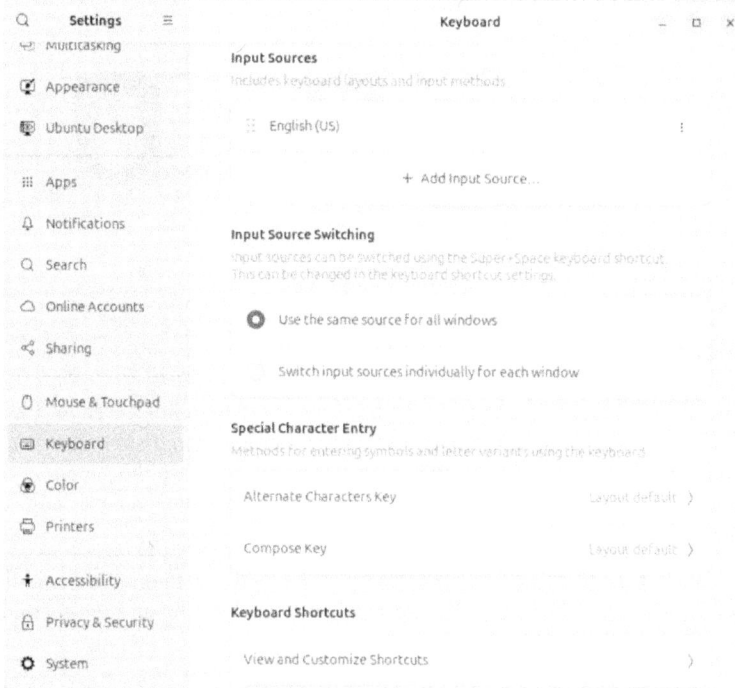

Figure 3-48: Keyboard

Mouse and Touchpad

The Mouse & Touchpad tab is the primary tool for configuring your mouse and touchpad. At the bottom of the tab there are tabs for Mouse and Touchpad. Clicking the Mouse tab displays the Mouse options (see Figure 3-49). Mouse preferences allow you to choose the primary button (left or right), the mouse's speed and acceleration, hand orientation, and scroll direction. A "Test Settings" button at the bottom of the tab lets you check clicks, double-clicks, and scrolling.

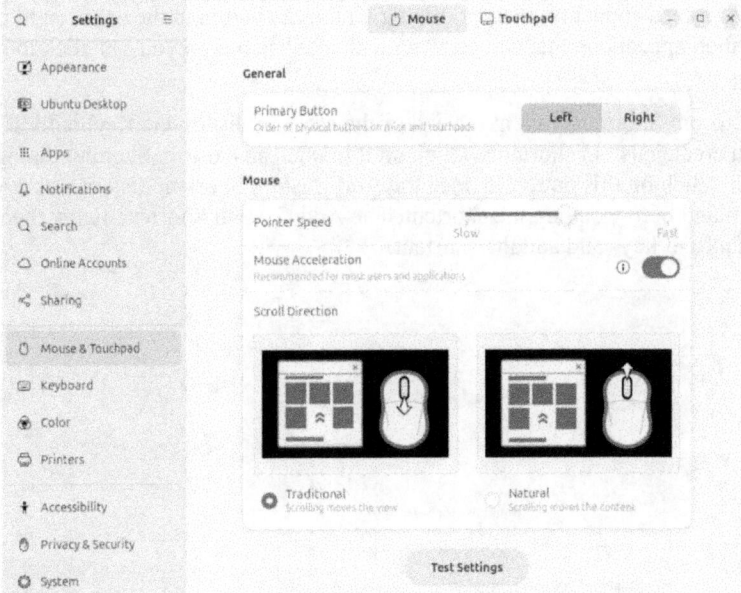

Figure 3-49: Mouse

Click the Touchpad tab at the top of the tab for the touchpad preferences (see Figure 3-50). For laptops, you can configure your touchpad, enabling touchpad and disabling it when typing. You can turn the touchpad on or off. In the Clicking section you can choose the secondary click and a quick click. In the scrolling section you can choose how to scroll (two finger or edge) and how to do scroll directions (view or content).

The GNOME Tweak's Mouse & Touchpad tab has options to enable a middle-click paste for the mouse. For the touchpad you can disable touchpad acceleration and the secondary click.

Chapter 3: Usage Basics   **119**

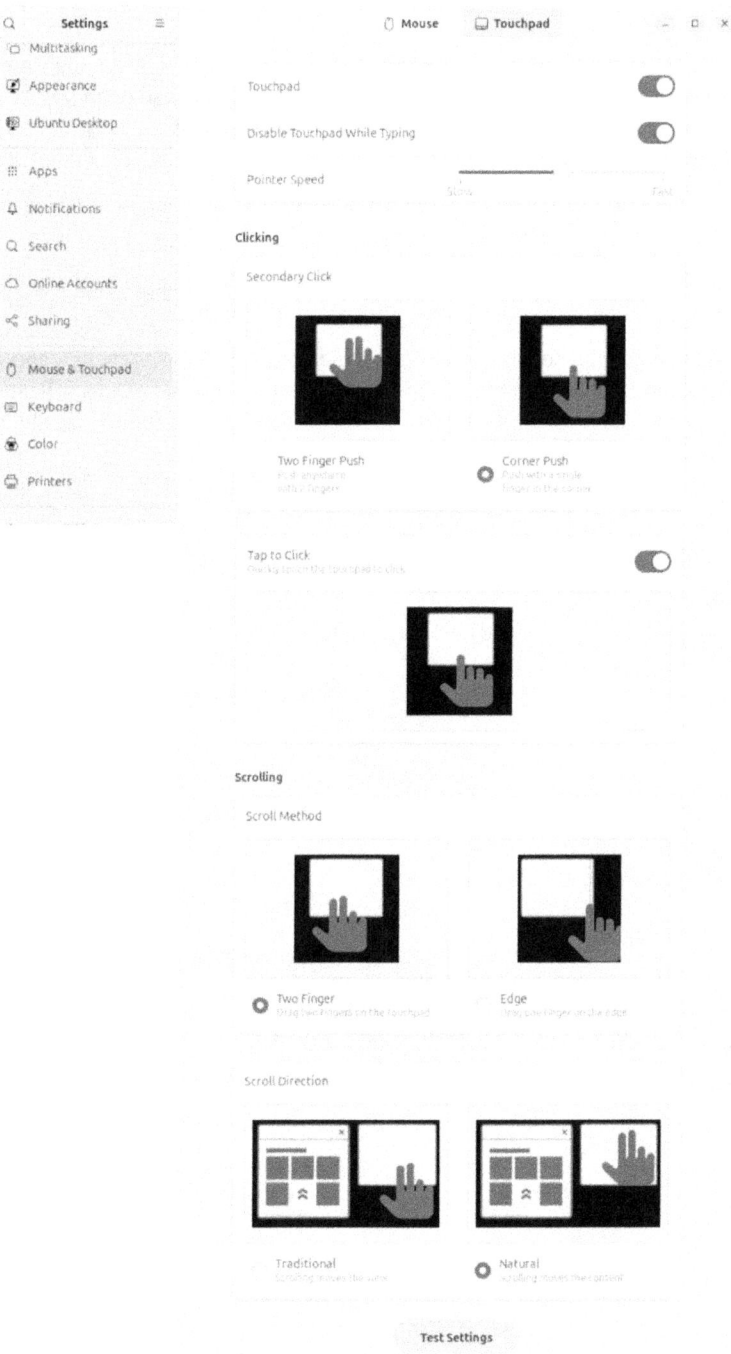

Figure 3-50: Touchpad

Multitasking

Multitasking lets you set various desktop components and features (see Figure 3-51). In the General section you can turn on the Hot Corner function, which will open the Activities overview whenever you move your mouse to the upper left corner of the screen. The Active Screen Edges option lets you resize a window by moving it to the top, right, or left side of the screen.

In the Workspace section you can choose whether to use dynamic or fixed workspaces. If you choose fixed, you can set the number of workspaces.

In the Multi-Monitor section, for systems with multiple displays, you can choose whether to show your workspaces on just your primary display, or on all displays.

In the App Switching section, when using the Meta-Tab keys to switch applications, you can choose to limit application switching to just the current workspace or to applications on other workspaces. Should you have multiple monitors, you can limit switching to just the monitor you are on.

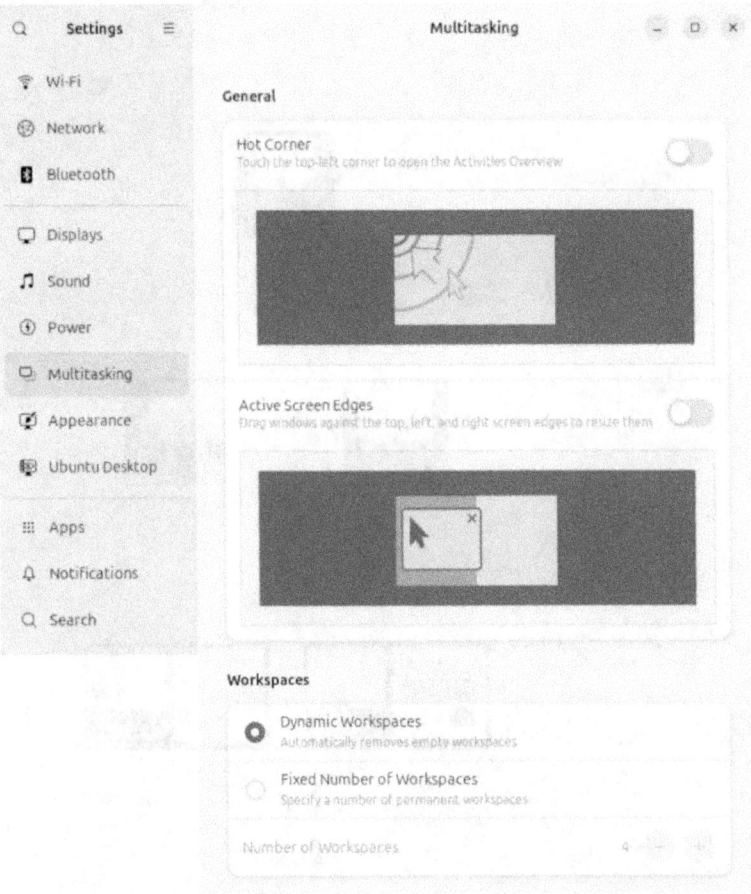

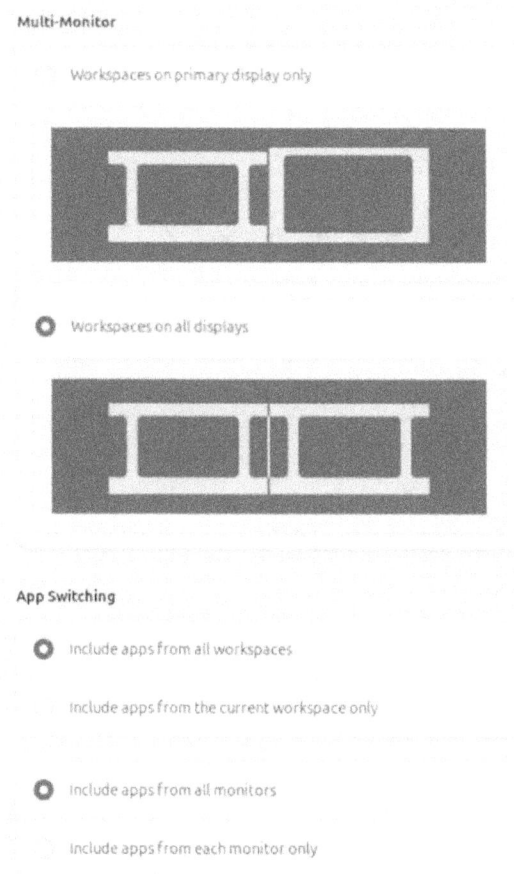

Figure 3-51: Multitasking

Notifications

The Notifications dialog lets you configure notifications for different applications (see Figure 3-52). You also have the options to show pop-up banners at the top of the screen or show notices on the lock screen. The Do Not Disturb option is turned off by default, allowing the display of pop-up banners at the top of the screen, as is done when you remove removable media (USB drives). You can also set the Do Not Disturb option on the desktop notifications section of the clock/calendar on the desktop top bar.

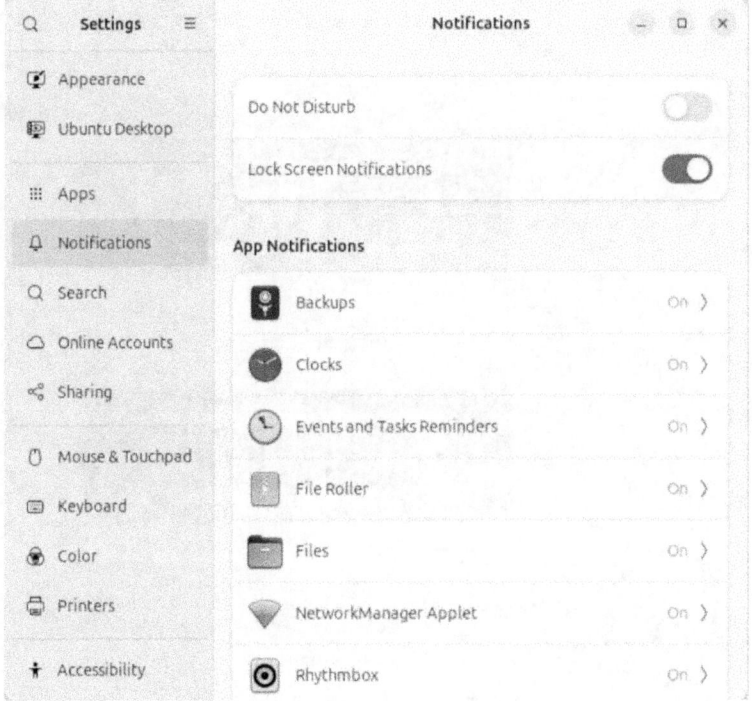

Figure 3-52: Notifications dialog

The App Notifications section lists applications that support notifications. Click an application to display a dialog from which you can turn notifications for the application on or off, as well as set options such as sound alerts, pop-up notifications, and lock screen notification (see Figure 3-53).

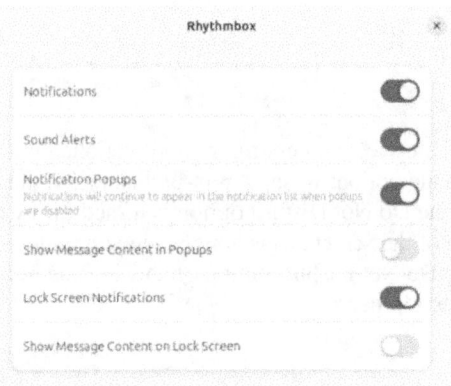

Figure 3-53: Notification settings for an application

Search

The Settings Search tab allows system applications to provide search results (see Figure 3-54). The App Search switch turns this feature on and off. The Search Locations link opens the Search Locations dialog, which specifies locations that can be searched by the applications.

In the Search Results section, a listing of system applications that provide search results is displayed. You can turn the search option on or off for an application by clicking on the application entry. Search results from applications are displayed in the order of the applications listed. The vertical ellipses menu to the right of each application entry lets you move an application up or down in the list.

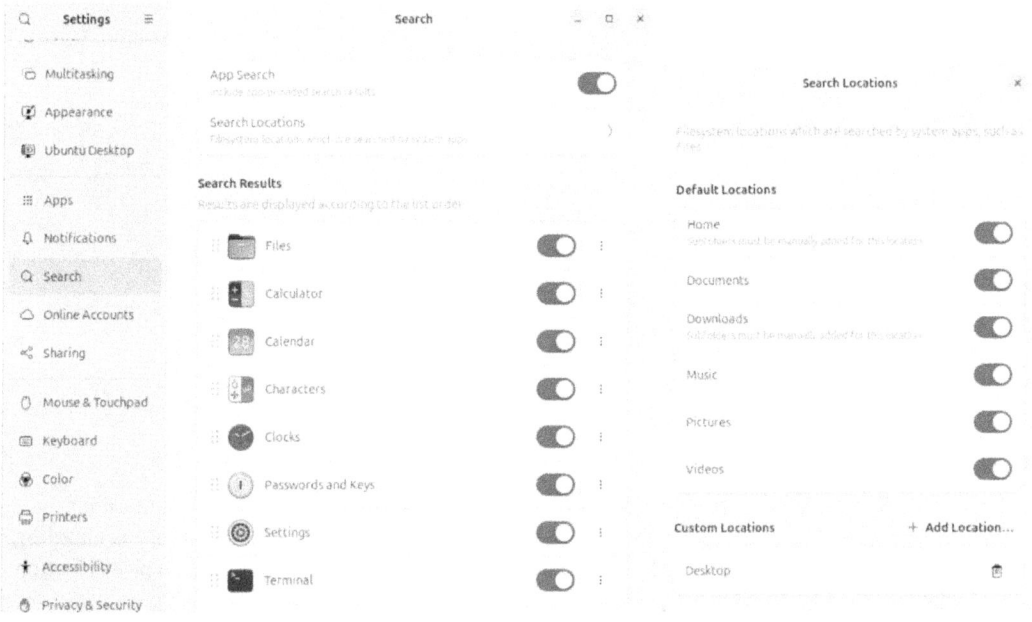

Figure 3-54: Search

Online Accounts

You can configure your online accounts using the Settings Online Accounts tab (see Figure 3-56). Click on an entry to start the sign-in procedure. You are prompted to sign in using your e-mail and password. Access is provided to Google, Facebook, Flickr, Microsoft, Microsoft Exchange, Microsoft Onedrive (Microsoft 365), Nextcloud, Foursquare, and Pocket. Once access is granted, you will see an entry for the service. Clicking on the service shows the different kinds of applications that it can be used for it such as mail, calendar, contacts, chat, and documents. Switches that you can use to turn access on and off are provided.

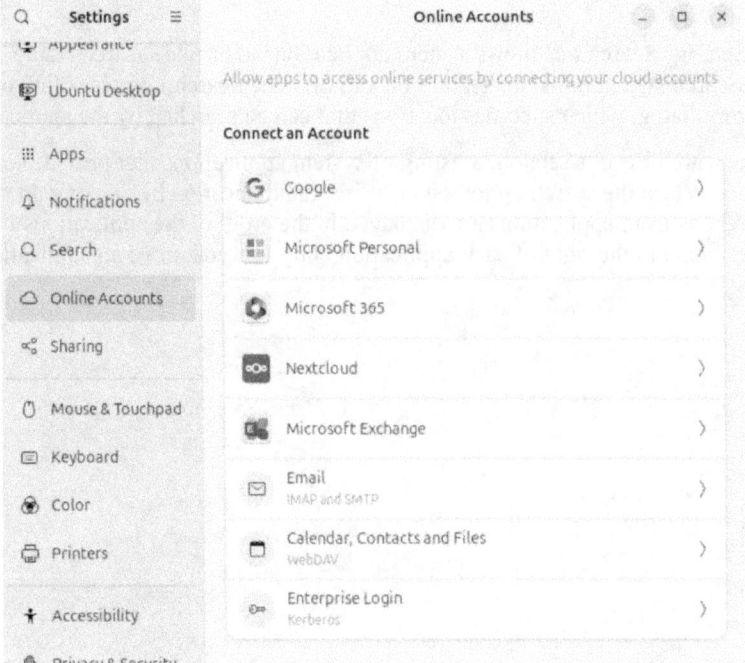

Figure 3-56: Online Accounts

Power

For systems with battery power sources such as laptops, the System menu button on the right side of the top bar displays a battery, showing the remaining power. If the battery is charging a lightning emblem is displayed next to it (see Figure 3-57). On the System menu, a power button is displayed on the top left side, showing the current strength of the battery. Clicking on the power button opens the Settings Power tab.

Figure 3-57: System menu button with battery indicator and System menu with Battery button

The Power Mode quick settings button on the System menu shows your current power mode (see Figure 3-58). There are three power modes available: Performance, Balanced, and Power Saver. Some laptops may only have two settings: Balanced and Power Saver. The Power Mode button displays the power mode currently in use. The default is Balanced. When the Power Mode button is unselected (grayed out), it will use the Balanced power mode. Clicking it, automatically selects the next power mode, such as Power Saver. Clicking it again to unselect it, returns you to the default, the Balanced power mode.

Clicking the Power Mode button's menu button (right arrow) displays the Power Mode menu, which lets you choose from the power modes available: Performance, Balanced, and Power Saver. There is a checkmark next to the current power mode. The Power Settings entry in this menu opens the Settings Power tab.

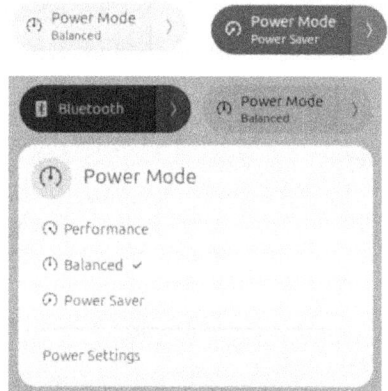

Figure 3-58: System menu Quick Settings Power Mode button and menu

The GNOME Power manager is configured with the Settings Power tab (see Figure 3-59). It is organized into five sections: Battery Level, Connected Devices, Power Mode, Power Saving, and General. On laptops, the Battery Level shows the battery charge and remaining time. The Connected Devices section shows the strength of any remote devices, such as a wireless mouse. The Power Mode lets you choose between the three power profile modes: Performance, Balanced, and Power Saver (Balanced is the default). In the Power Saving section, you can set power saving features for your monitor. When inactive for a period of time, you can choose to turn off the screen (Screen Blank), as well as dim it whenever it is inactive (Dim Screen). The Automatic Power Saver switch changes the Power Mode to Power Saver when the battery is low. Clicking on the Automatic Suspend link opens the Automatic Suspend dialog where you can set time delays for when the system is on battery power or plugged in. You can turn off either option. On battery power the default is 15 minutes, and when plugged in, the default is one hour. In the General section, you can configure your computer's power button to power off (the default), suspend, or do nothing. For systems using a battery such as laptops, you can choose to show the remaining battery percentage on the System menu button on the top bar.

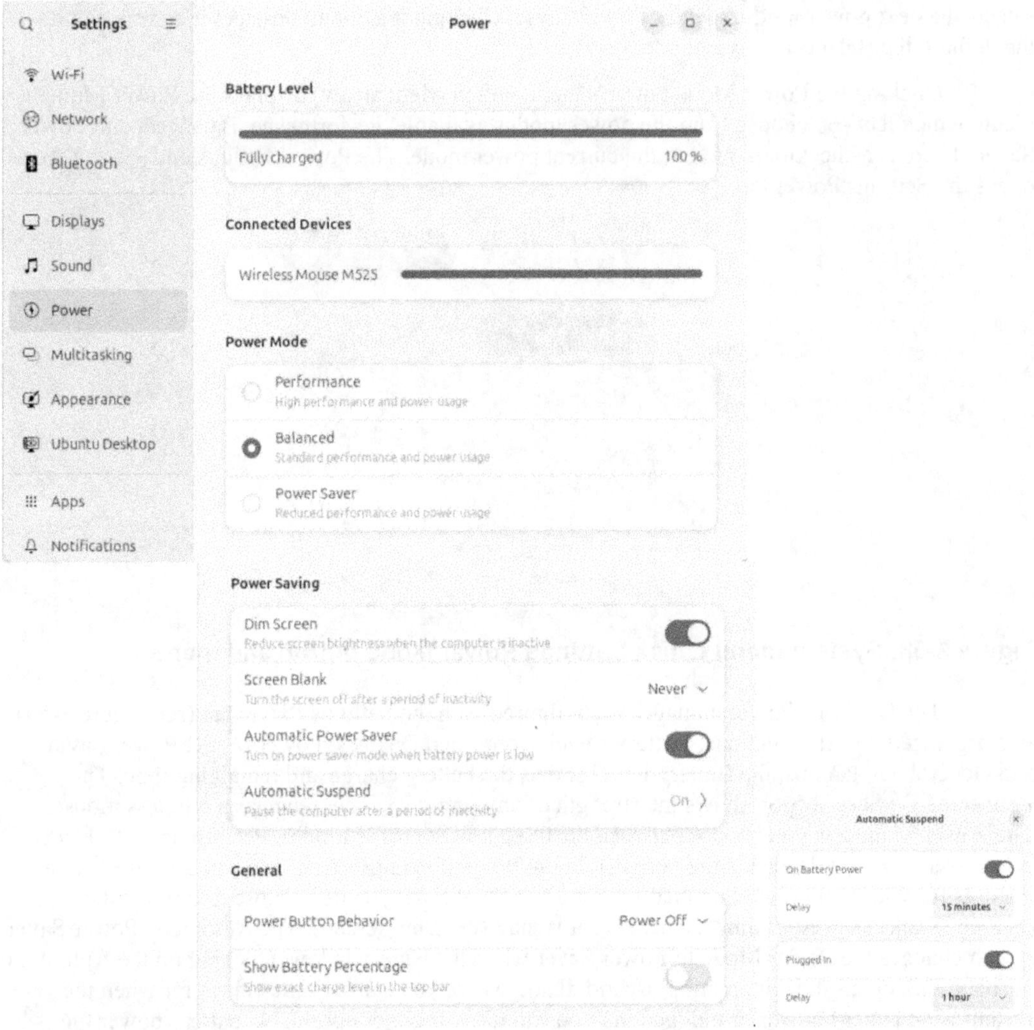

Figure 3-59: Power

       To see how your laptop or desktop is performing with power, you can use Power statistics. This is accessible from the Applications Overview as Power Statistics. The Power Statistics window will display a sidebar listing your different power devices (see Figure 3-60). A right pane will show tabs with power use information for a selected device. The Laptop battery device will display three tabs: Details, History, and Statistics. The History tab will show your recent use, with graph options (Graph type menu) for Time to empty (time left), Time to full (recharging), Charge, and Rate. The Statistics tab can show charge and discharge graphs.

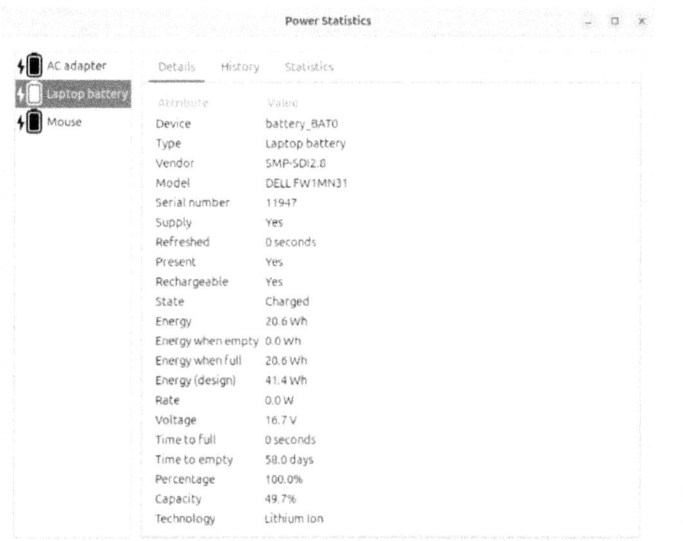

Figure 3-60: Power Statistics

powertop and tuned

For more refined power management you can use the **powertop** and tuned tools. The **powertop** tool runs in a terminal window as the administrative user. It will detect and display information about the use of the CPU by running applications and connected devices. Recommendations are listed on how to configure the power usage. To display a listing of the **powertop** results including recommendations, add the **-d** option.

```
sudo powertop -d
```

For automatic tuning of hard disk and network devices you can use tuned (**tuned**, **tune-gtk**, and **tuned-utils** packages). The tuned daemon monitors your system and tunes the settings dynamically. You can use tuned's **diskdevstat** and **netdevstat** tools to monitor your hard disk and network devices.

Privacy & Security

The Privacy & Security tab allows you to turn on or off privacy features, such as the screen lock, managing history logs, location support, and the purging of trash and temporary files (see Figure 3-70). Clicking on the Privacy & Security tab in Settings opens a set of links to tabs for Connectivity, Screen Lock, Location Services, File History & Trash, Diagnostics, and Device Security. The Connectivity tab turns on connectivity checking for you network connections (see Figure 3-71). It is on by default. The Location Services tab allows your geographical location to be determined. It is turned off by default. The Permitted Apps section lists sandboxed (Snap) Apps that have been given location access. Diagnostics lets you choose whether to send error reports to Canonical, and if so, to do it automatically or manually. Device Security displays hardware security checks, whether secure boot is on, and any security events.

128 Part 1: Getting Started

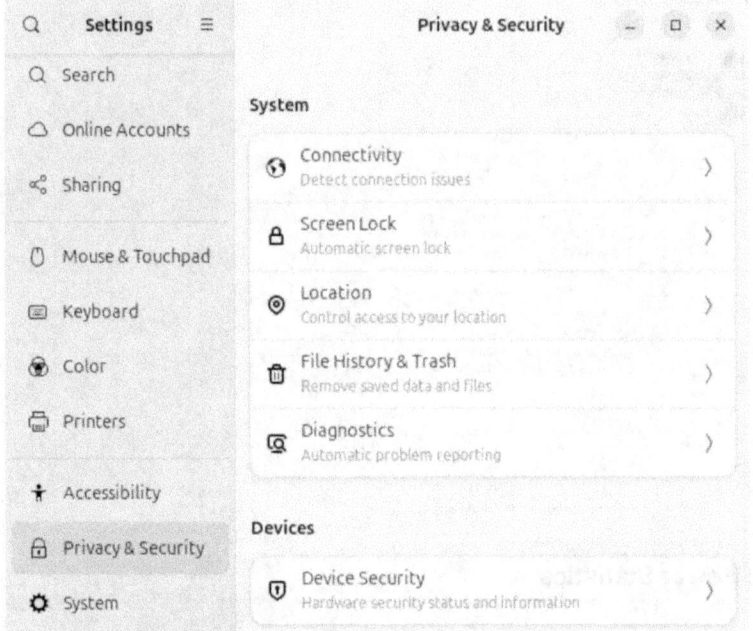

Figure 3-70: Privacy & Security

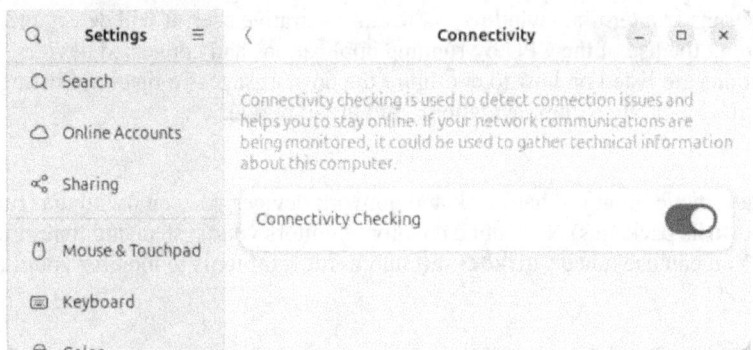

Figure 3-71: Privacy & Security - Connectivity

On the Screen Lock tab you can turn automatic screen lock on or off, lock the screen on a suspension, set it to turn on after a period of idle time, and allow or deny notifications on the Screen Lock screen (see Figure 3-72). Automatic Screen Lock is turned on by default, which activates the Automatic Screen Lock Delay where you choose the time delay for locking the screen.

Chapter 3: Usage Basics   **129**

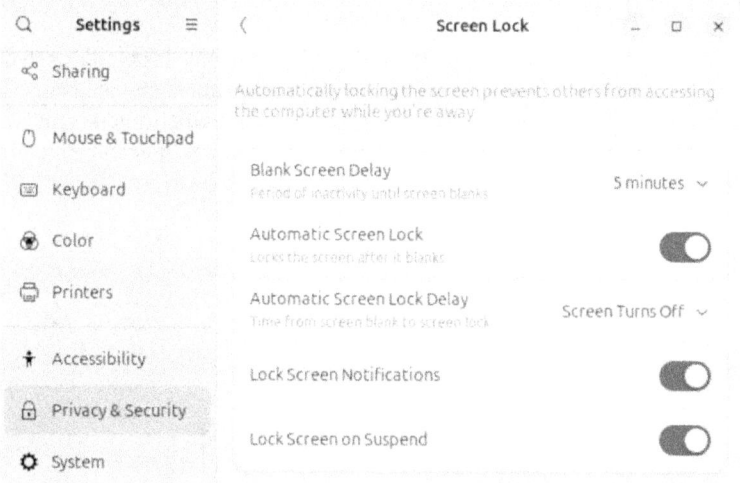

Figure 3-72: Privacy & Security - Screen Lock configuration

The File History & Trash tab lets you turn usage history on or off and set how long to keep it. The entry also has a button that allows you to clear recent history (see Figure 3-73). You can also configure the behavior of your trash folder, with options to automatically empty trash and remove temporary files. You can also set a time limit for deleting files in the trash. These options are turned off by default. There are also buttons that allow you to empty trash and delete temporary files immediately.

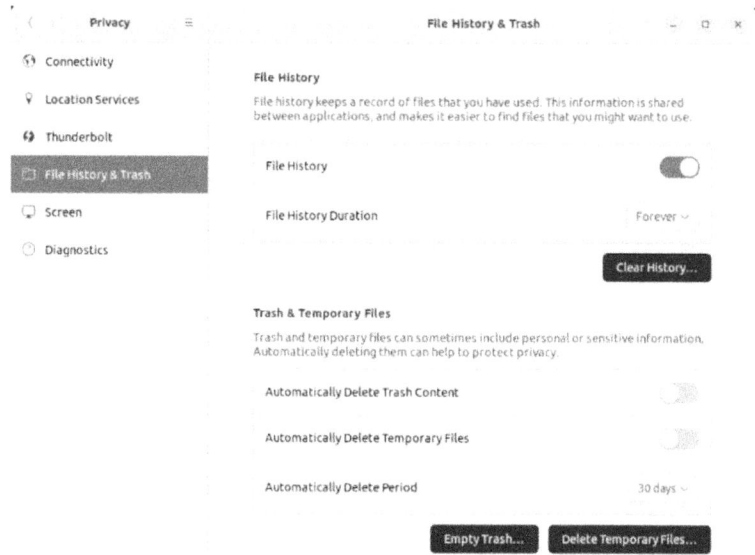

Figure 3-73: Privacy & Security - File History & Trash

Sharing

On the Sharing tab you can change the name of your device, as well as select media folders to share over a network (see Figure 3-74). There is an editable Device Name for your system and a link to open the Media Sharing dialog for sharing media folders. Click on the Device Name entry to change the name of your system. The system name will become an editable text box, letting you change it.

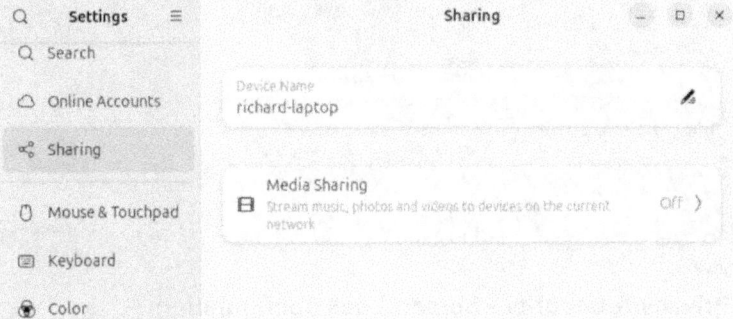

Figure 3-74: Sharing

Media Sharing lets you specify what folders to share over a network and the connection to use. Clicking on the Media Sharing link opens the Media Sharing dialog (see Figure 3-75). Your Music, Videos, and Pictures folders are already selected. Click the plus button to open a "Choose a Folder" dialog to select more. To remove a folder, click the trash icon to its right. You can turn off all media sharing by clicking the Media Sharing switch at the top. Should you have more than one network, you can choose which ones to use. You can also turn a network on or off.

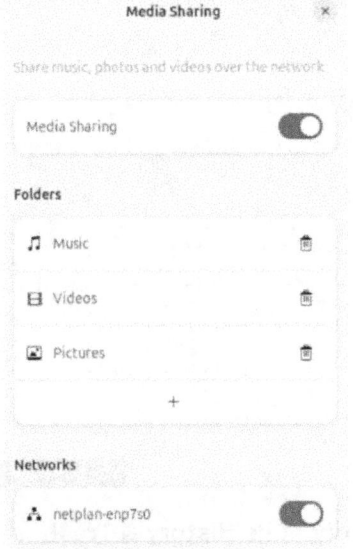

Figure 3-75: Sharing - Media Sharing dialog

System

The System tab list links to tabs for system configuration and information: Regions & Language, Date & Time, Users, Remote Desktop, Secure Shell, and About (see Figure 3-76). A link at the bottom, Software Updates, opens the Software Updater to check for and install updates.

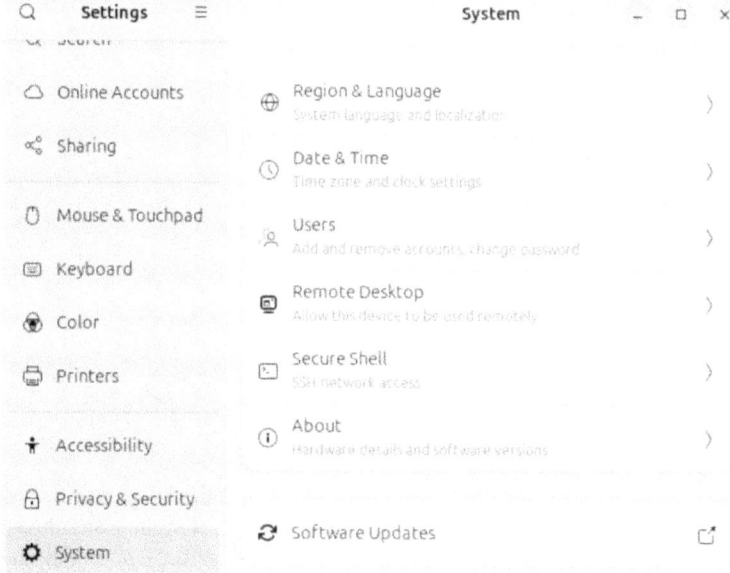

Figure 3-76: System

Regions & Language

The Region & Language Settings tab lets you manage languages on your system, set regional formats, select a language version, and specify formats to use for dates, times, and numbers (see Figure 3-77). The Region and Language tab has two sections: System and Your Account. The System section has a Manage Installed Languages link that opens the Language Support dialog where you can install and remove languages and specify regional formats system wide. The Your Account section has two links for Language and Formats. With these you can personalize your language and format.

132   Part 1: Getting Started

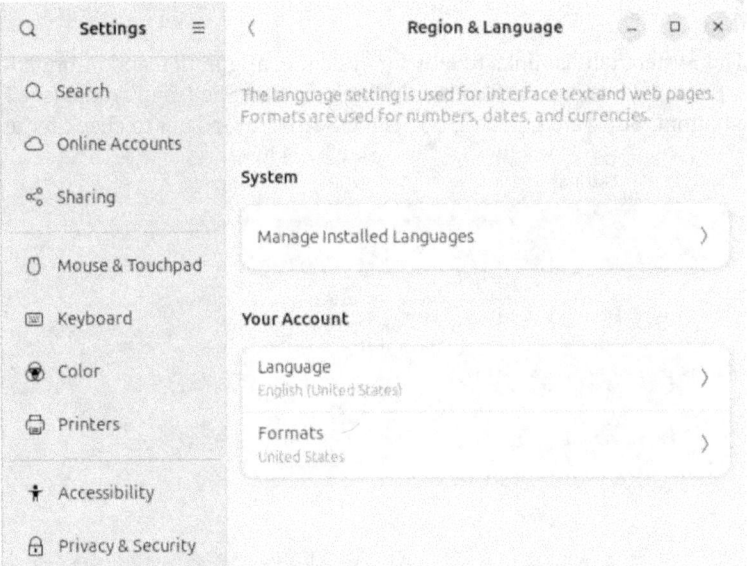

Figure 3-77: System - Region & Language

Clicking on the Manage Installed Languages link opens the Language Support dialog (see Figure 3-78), which as two tabs: Language and Regional Formats. On the Language tab your installed languages are listed. To apply a language system wide, select it and click the Apply System-Wide button. To install or remove a language, click the Install/Remove Languages button to open the Installed Languages dialog. Click the checkbox of the language you want to add, and then click the Apply button. To remove a language, you would click the checkbox to uncheck it.

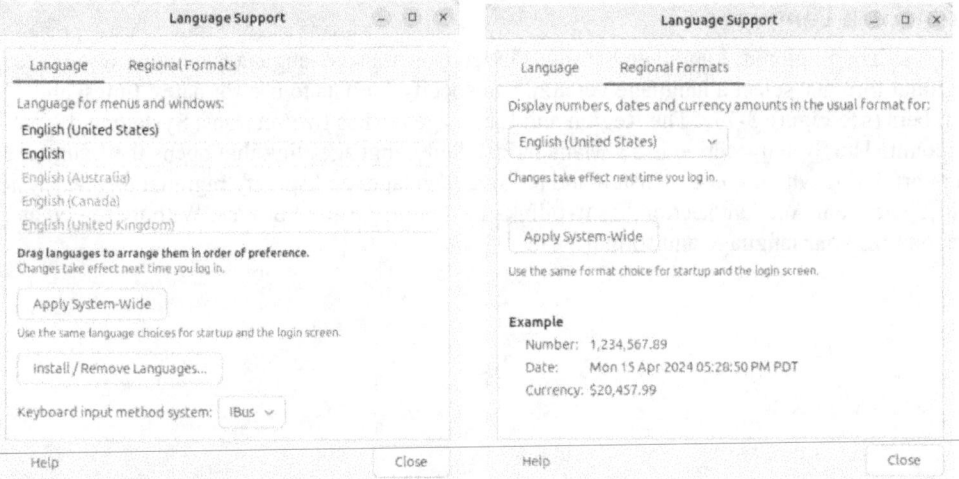

Figure 3-78: Region & Language - Language Support

The "Keyboard input method system" lets you choose IBus, Xim, or none. These input methods are helpful for more symbols that do easily not conform to keys, such as Japanese and Korean. IBus is the recommended input method or Ubuntu.

On the Regional Formats tab you can choose the format for numbers, dates, and currency. Click the Apply System-Wide button to apply it throughout on your system. Examples are shown of your selected format.

On the Region & Language tab, in the Your Account section, clicking on the Language link opens the Select Language dialog (see Figure 3-79), where you can choose from different variations of your language, such as English in the United States or English in Canada. To change to another variation, select it and then click the Select button on the right side of the dialog's header bar.

Clicking on the Formats link in the Your Account section opens the Formats dialog, where you can choose formats (dates, times, numbers, measurements, and paper) associated with your language variations, such as formats for the United Kingdom and the United States. In the All Formats section, you can choose from any format such as Singapore and Denmark. Click the Done button on the right side of the header bar when you have finished making your selection.

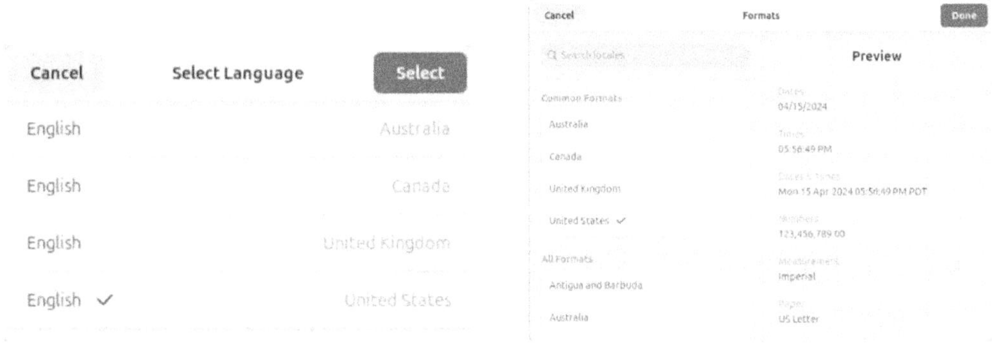

Figure 3-79: Region & Language - Your Account Language and Formats

Date & Time

Date & Time options are set using the Date & Time tab in Setting's System tab. The Date & Time tab lets you set the time, the time zone, and the time format, as well as how the time and date are shown on the top bar (Clock & Calendar section). The time and the time zone are configured for automatic settings using Internet time servers (see Figure 3-80). The time format can be 24-hour or AM/PM. The time zone or the time and date can be set manually by turning off it's Automatic switches. Turning off the Automatic Date & Time switch makes the Date & Time link active, and turning off the Automatic Time Zone switch makes the Time Zone link active. In the Clock & Calendar section, you can use the listed options to adjust the top bar time display. There are options to show the date, weekday, seconds, and week number.

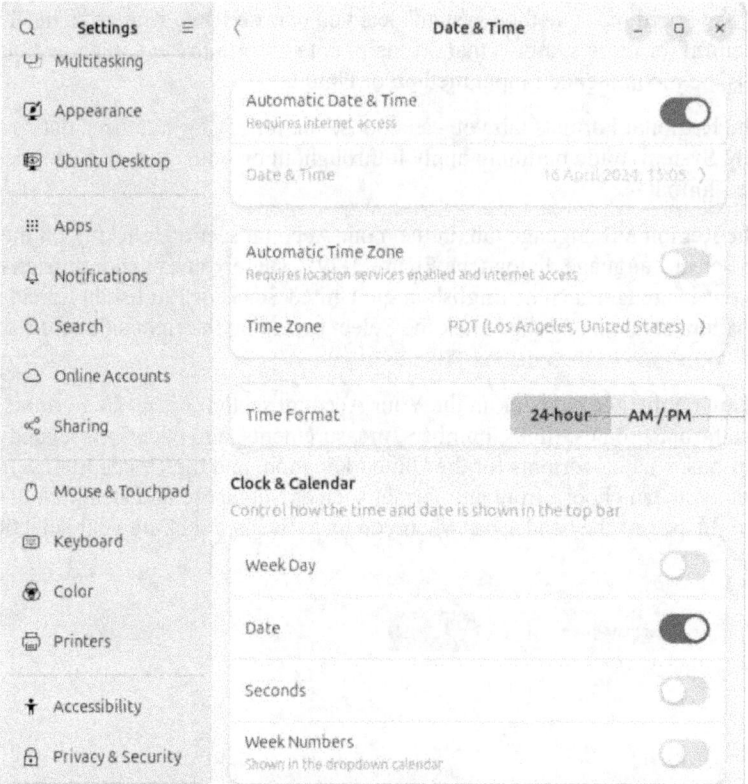

Figure 3-80: System - Date & Time Settings dialog

With the Automatic Date & Time switch turned off, The Date & Time entry is no longer faded, and you can click it to open a dialog with settings for the hour, minutes, day, and year, with a menu for the month (see Figure 3-81). You can use the plus (+) and minus (-) buttons to sequentially change the values.

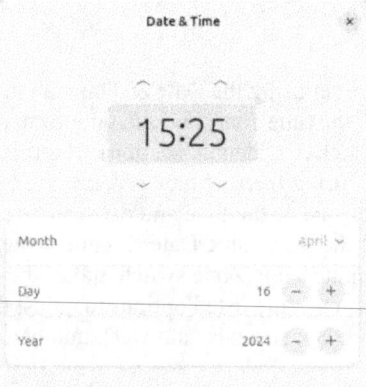

Figure 3-81: Date & Time manual settings

With the Automatic Time Zone switch turned off, the Time Zone is no longer faded, and you can click it to open a dialog with a list of major cities by which you can select a time zone. There is also a search box for quickly locating a city (see Figure 3-82). Click the city entry you want to change the zone to.

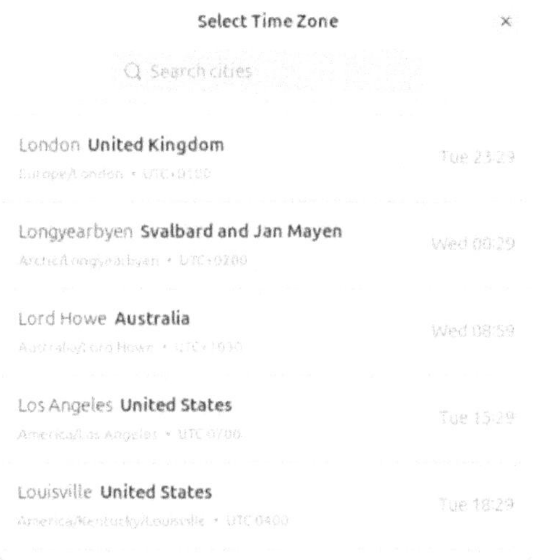

Figure 3-82: Time Zone dialog

The Date & Time calendar and menu are located on the top bar at the center of your desktop (see Figure 3-83). The dialog displays the current time and day of the week but can be modified to display 24-hour or AM/PM time. The calendar shows the current date, but you can move to different months and years using the month scroll arrows at the top of the calendar.

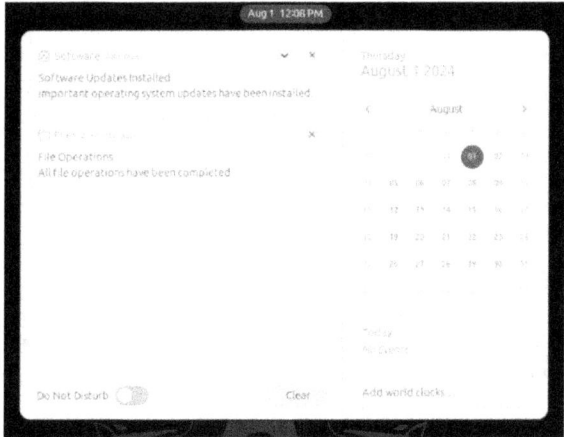

Figure 3-83: Date & Time dialog on the top bar of your desktop

You can also set the system time manually using the **date** command. The **date** command has several options for adjusting both the displaying and setting of the date and time. Check the **date** man page for a detailed list, **man date**. You can set the time with the **--set** option and a string specifying the date. You use human readable terms for the time string, such as Mon or Monday for the day and Jul or July for the month. Hour, minute, and second can be represented by numbers separated by colons. The following sets the date to July 9, 8:15 AM 2024.

```
sudo date --set='Tuesday July 9 08:15 2024'
```

To just set the time you would enter something like:

```
sudo date --set='12:15:43'
```

Users

The Users tab lets you manage your users, adding new ones and modifying current ones. The Users tab is initially locked. Click the Unlock button to gain access (see Figure 3-84). The user for your primary account is shown (the one you set up during installation). Click the Add User button to add more users. New users will appear as links at the bottom of the tab. See Chapter 14 form more information about the Users tab.

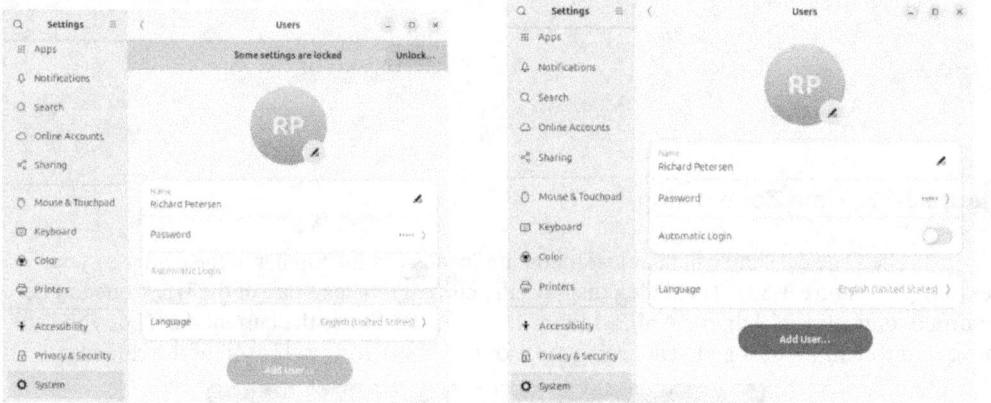

Figure 3-84: System - Users

Remote Desktop

The Remote Desktop tab has two tabs, Desktop Sharing and Remote Login. On the Desktop Sharing tab you can enable remote desktop access, allowing your desktop to be accessed by other computers. On the Remote Login tab you can enable remote login to your account using Remote Desktop Protocol (RDP).

Clicking on the Remote Desktop tab lets you turn on remote desktop sharing and enable remote control. In the "How to Connect" section you provide connection information (device name and address). In the Login Details section you specify your user name and password. (see Figure 3-85).

Should you want to access another desktop remotely you would use the Remmina Remote Desktop Client, accessible from the Applications Overview as Remmina.

Chapter 3: Usage Basics   **137**

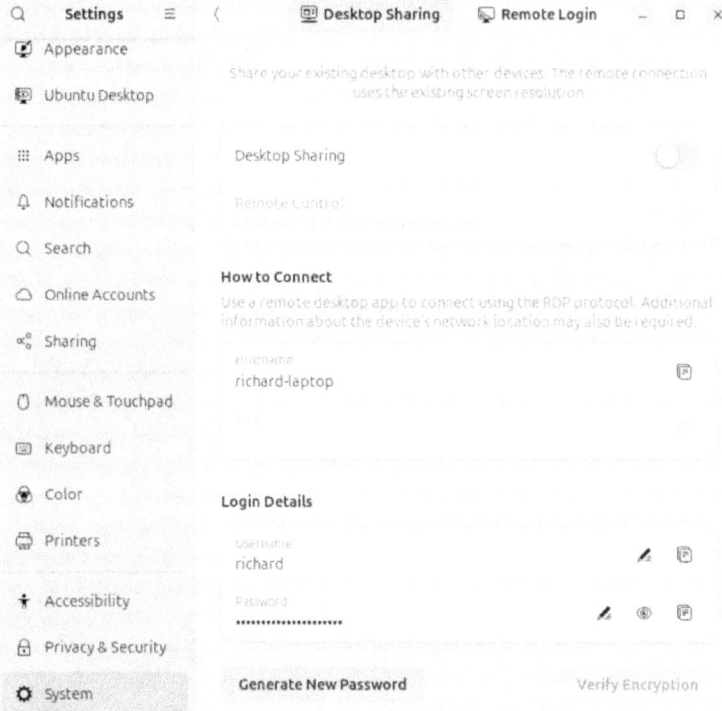

Figure 3-85: System - Remote Desktop - Desktop Sharing

Clicking on the Remote Login tab opens the Remote Login dialog where you can turn on remote login. In the "How to Connect" section you provide connection information (device name and address). In the Login Details section you specify your user name and password (see Figure 3-86). Buttons at the bottom let you generate a strong password and to verify encryption, displaying an encryption fingerprint. Initially the dialog is locked. Click the Unlock button to open an authentication dialog where you enter your password.

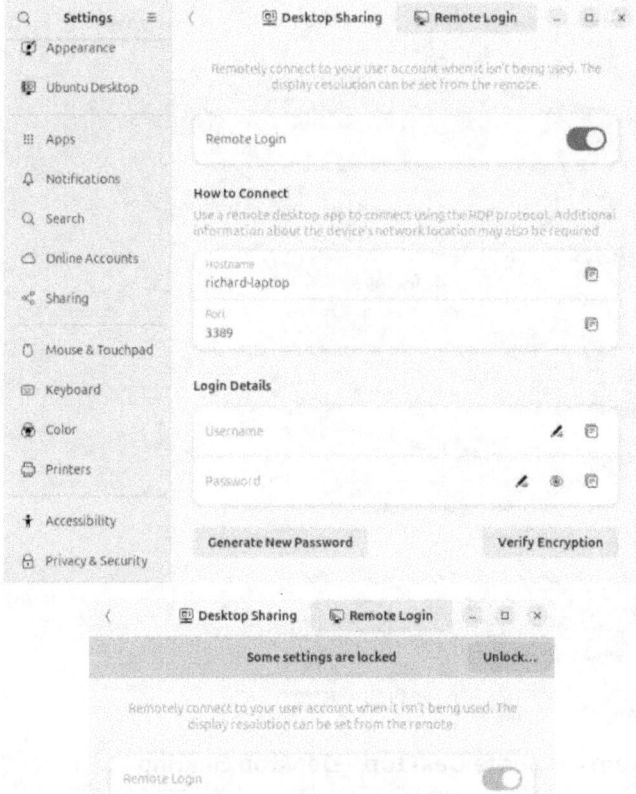

Figure 3-86: System - Remote Desktop - Remote Login

Secure Shell

The Secure Shell tab on the System tab opens a dialog where you can turn on the Secure Shell (SSH). To turn on the Secure Shell you are first prompted for authentication (your password). Your SSH login command is also listed, beginning with the **ssh** command and followed by your host name (see Figure 3-87).

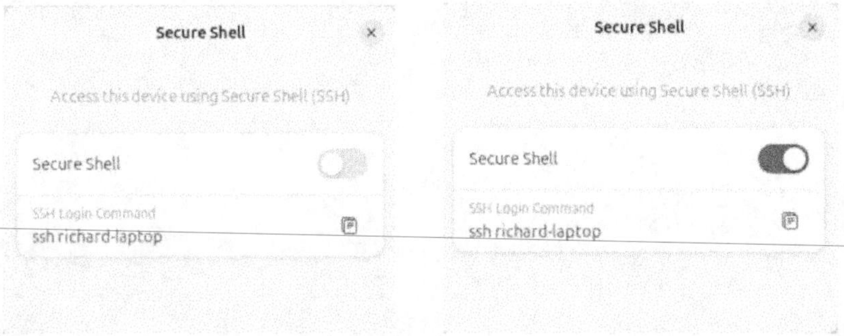

Figure 3-87: System - Secure Shell

About (System Information)

Clicking on the About link displays the About tab showing system information, displaying your hostname (Device name), the name of your operating system, your hardware model, processor, memory, and disk capacity (see Figure 3-88). The Device Name entry showing your host name is an editable textbox you can click on to change your host name.

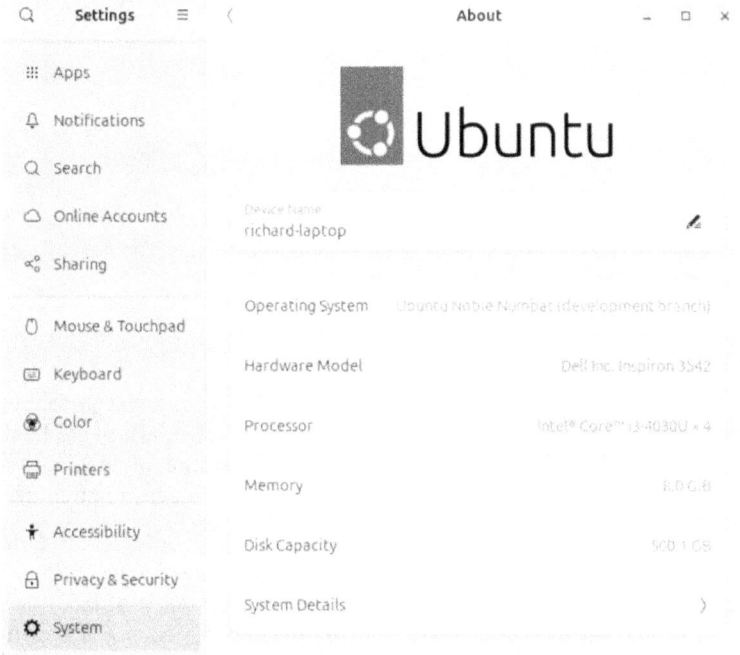

Figure 3-88: System - About

Clicking on the System Details link at the bottom, opens the System Details dialog, which lists hardware and software information (see Figure 3-89). The Hardware Information section provides the same details as on the About tab, but also includes additional hardware such as your graphics card. The Software Information section provides the firmware version, the operating system name, the operating system type (64 or 32 bit), the GNOME version on your system, the windowing system in use (X11 or Wayland), and the Linux kernel version in use.

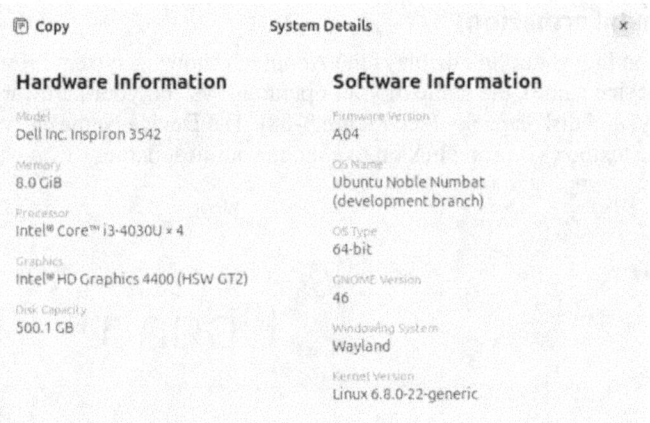

Figure 3-89: System - About - System Details

Ubuntu Desktop: Icons, Dock, and Tiling

On the Ubuntu Desktop tab you can configure the display of icons on the desktop, the behavior and appearance of the dock, and tiling support (see Figure 3-90). In the Desktop Icons section you can choose the size (Small, Normal, Large, Tiny), position of new icons on the screen (Bottom Right is the default), and whether to show your personal folder (home folder).

The Dock section lets you configure your dock. You can choose to auto-hide the dock. The Panel Mode option (the default) displays the dock so that it takes up the entire side of the screen. Turning this off reduces the dock to just the length of the number of icons in it. The Icon Size entry has a slider you can use to customize the size of the dock icons. For systems with multiple displays, the "Show on" menu lets you choose whether to show the dock on just your primary display or on all your displays, if you have more than one. The "Position on Screen" menu lets you choose what side of the screen you want the dock located: Left, Bottom, or Right. Left is the default. You cannot place it at the top.

The Enhanced Tiling section, the Tiling Popup switch and the Tile Groups switch turned on together will display an icon bar of open applications on the other side when you tile the screen. Passing your mouse over an application icon in that icon bar displays icons for that application's open windows. You can then select a window to display on the other tile.

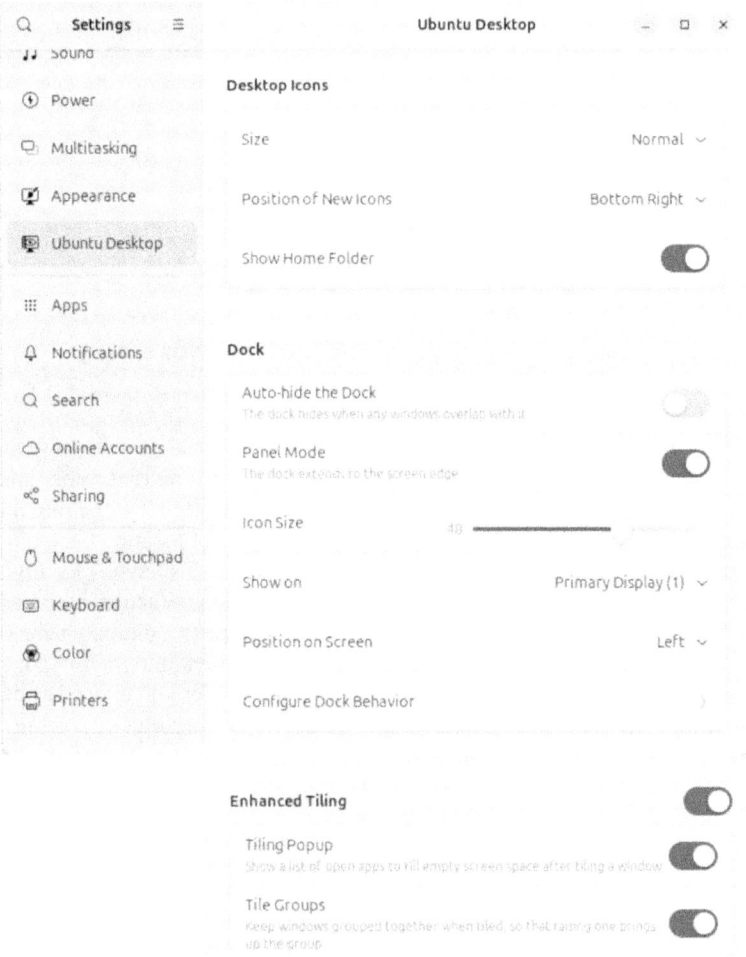

Figure 3-90: Ubuntu Desktop

You can also configure the dock to display unmounted and network file systems, as well as the trash. Click on the "Configure Dock Behavior" link to open a Dock dialog with the options to show volumes and devices (see Figure 3-91). There are checkboxes for unmounted volumes and network volumes. A "Show Trash" switch at the bottom displays the Trash icon on your dock.

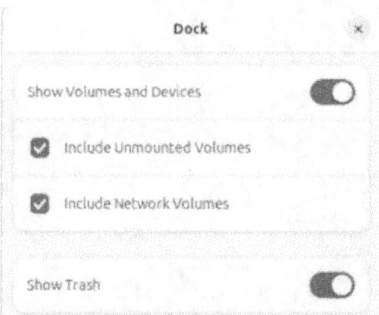

Figure 3-91: Ubuntu Desktop - Configure Desktop Behavior dialog

File Manager Search

The file manager provides a search tool for searching your current folder and subfolders. You can access the file manager search from any file manager window by clicking the Search button on the toolbar (Folder with looking glass on the right side of location bar) to open a Search box. Enter the pattern to search and press ENTER. The results are displayed (see Figure 3-92). Click the menu button to the right to add file-type (What) and date (When) search parameters, or to search file text or just the file name. Selecting the When entry opens a dialog where you can specify the recency of the document's last use or modification, by day, week, month, or year. A calendar button to the right of the text box for the date opens a calendar to let you choose a specific date. The What entry displays a menu with different file categories such as music, Documents, folders, picture, and PDF.

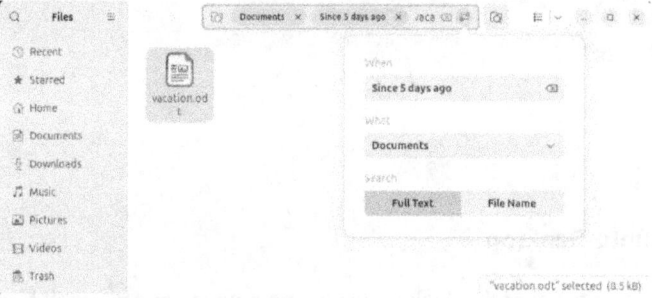

Figure 3-92: Gnome File Manager Search

Accessing File Systems and Devices

When you attach an external storage device such as a USB or CD/DVD-ROM drive, it will be mounted automatically, and you will be prompted to open it in a file manager window. Be sure to unmount (Eject) a drive before removing it, so that data will be written.

Your file systems and removable media appear as entries in the file manager sidebar (see Figure 3-93). External devices such as USB drives are mounted automatically and have Eject buttons next to their entries. Internal hard drive partitions, such as Windows file systems, are not mounted automatically. Double-click the hard drive partition entry to mount them. An Eject button then appears next to the hard drive entry. You are also prompted to open the drive's file system in a new file manager window.

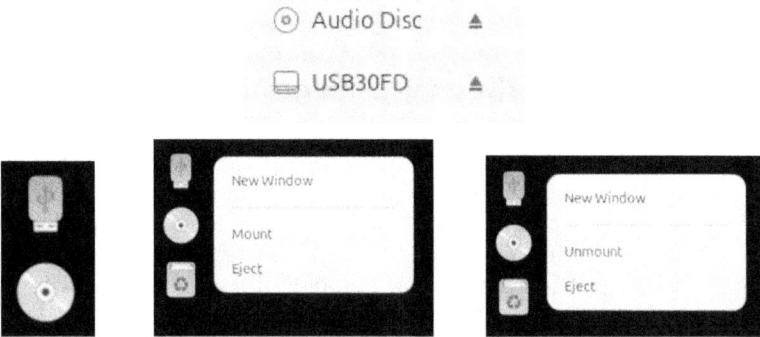

Figure 3-93: Devices sidebar in the file manager window and icons on the dock

Removable media also appears on the Ubuntu dock as an icon. Click on it to open it in a file manager window. Right-click on the icon to display options, such as Mount or Unmount, Eject, and New Window.

When you unmount or eject file systems on removable media, a notification will appear briefly on the top bar(see Figure 3-94).

Figure 3-94: Removable Devices notifications

If you have already configured associated applications for video and audio DVD/CDs, or disks with images, sound, or video files, the disk will be opened with the appropriate application, such as Shotwell for images, Rhythmbox for audio, and Videos for DVD/video. If you have not yet configured these associations, you will be prompted to specify which application you want to open it with.

To see network resources, click the Other Locations entry in the file manager sidebar. This network window will list your connected network Linux computers. Opening these networks displays the shares they provide, such as shared folders that you can have access to. Drag-and-drop operations are supported for all shared folders, letting you copy files and folders between a shared folder on another computer with a folder on your system. Opening a network resource may require you to login to access the resource.

Accessing Archives from GNOME: File Roller

Ubuntu supports the access of archives directly from GNOME using File Roller. You can select the archive file, then right-click and select File Roller to open the archive. The archive contents are listed by File Roller. You can extract or display the contents.

You can also use File Roller to open ISO image files as archives. You can then browse and extract the contents of the ISO image. Right-click on a ISO image file (**.iso** extension) and select "Open with" and then choose "File Roller" on the Open File dialog. The ISO image file is opened as an archive in File Roller.

Mounting ISO Disk Image files: Disk Image Mounter

You can use the GNOME Disk Utility's Disk Image Mounter to mount any ISO disk image file as a file system, accessible with the file manager. Right-click on the ISO image file (**.iso** extension) and choose "Open with Disk Image Mounter" from the menu. The ISO image is then mounted as a file system. An icon from the ISO image in displayed on the dock. Right-click on it and select New Window to open the image file with a file manager window. An entry for it will also appear on the file manager sidebar. It will be read-only. The ISO image will also appear in the Other Locations folder in the "On This Device" section. To unmount the disk image, click the eject button on a file manager sidebar, or right-click on the sidebar entry or the image file's Ubuntu dock icon, and then choose Unmount. An unmount notification will briefly appear on the desktop.

File Manager CD/DVD Creator interface

Using the GNOME file manager to burn data to a DVD or CD is a simple matter of dragging files to an open blank CD or DVD. When you insert a blank DVD/CD disc, a file manager window will open for it with "Blank DVD Disc" as its folder name. To burn files, just drag them to that window. The files are immediately written to the disc (see Figure 3-95). Eject it as you would any disc. You can insert the disk later and add more files if you want.

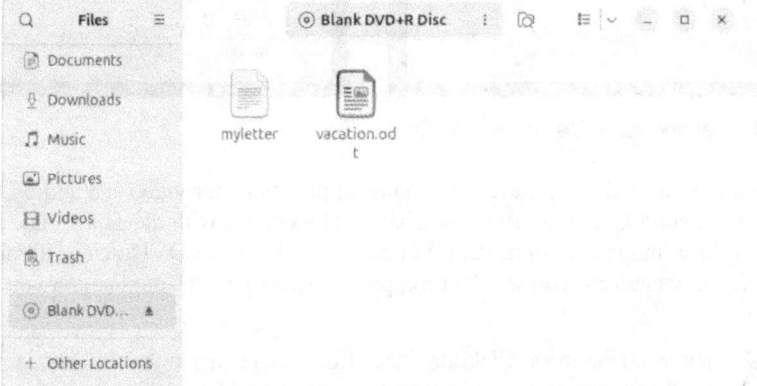

Figure 3-95: File manager window, writing to blank DVD disc

ISO Image File Writing with Disk Utility and Brasero

The GNOME Disk Utility supports burning ISO images to either a USB drive or a DVD drive. Right-click on the ISO image file and choose "Open with" Then select "Disk Image Writer" on the Open File dialog. If "Disk Image Writer" is already the default application for ISO image files, you can just double-click the ISO image file in a file manager window. The GNOME Disks utility will then open and display a Restore Disk image dialog with the destination set to None. Use the Destination menu to carefully select the USB drive or DVD drive you want to write the image to (see Figure 3-96), Then click the Start Restoring button. You are then asked to confirm the write operation. Click Restore to have Disk Utility write the image to the drive.

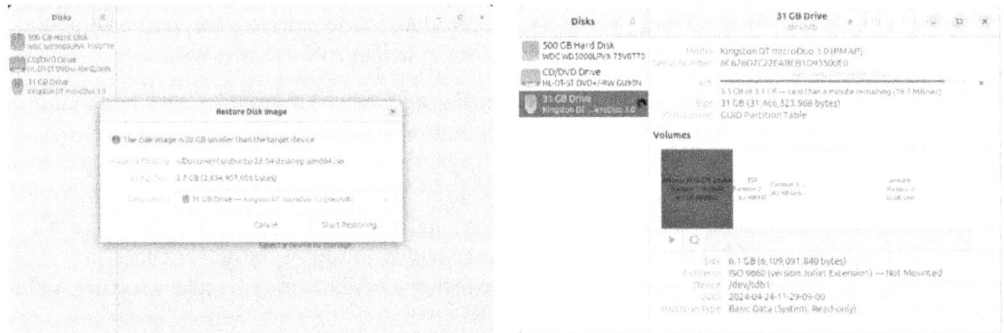

Figure 3-96: Disk Writer, writing ISO image to USB drive.

You can also still use the older Brasero CD/DVD burner to write an ISO image file to a DVD disc (not a USB drive). Brasero is not installed by default and is no longer supported by Ubuntu (Universe repository). Once installed you can selected it as one of the options on the File Roller dialog (right-click on the ISO file and choose Open with Other Application). This opens the Image Burning Setup dialog, which prompts you to burn the image. Be sure first to insert a blank CD or DVD into your CD/DVD burner.

Startup Applications Preferences

On the Startup Applications Preferences dialog, you can select additional programs you want started automatically (accessible from the Applications overview as Startup Applications). Some are selected automatically (see Figure 3-97). Uncheck an entry if you no longer want it to start up automatically. To add an application not listed, click the Add button and enter the application name and program (use Browse to select a program, usually in **/usr/bin**).

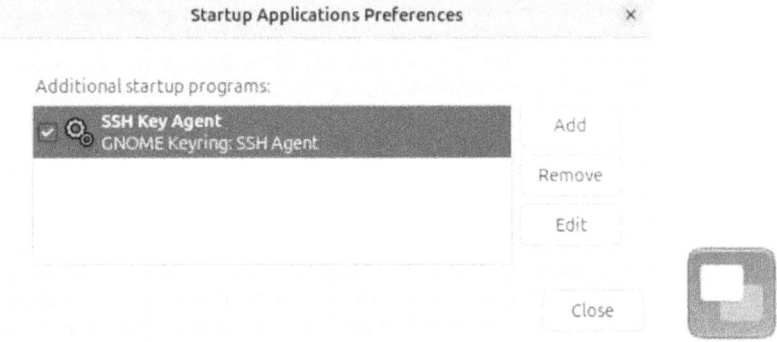

Figure 3-97: Startup Applications Preferences

Display Configuration and Additional Drivers

The graphics interface for your desktop display is implemented by the X Window System. The version used on Ubuntu is X.org (**x.org**). X.org provides its own drivers for various graphics cards and monitors. You can find out more about X.org at **https://www.x.org/wiki/**.

Your display is detected automatically, configuring both your graphics card and monitor. Normally you should not need to perform any configuration yourself. However, if you have a graphics card that uses Graphics processors from a major Graphics vendor like NVIDIA, you have the option of using their driver, instead of the open source X drivers installed with Ubuntu. Some graphics cards may work better with the vendor driver, and provide access to more of the card's features. The open source AMD driver is **xserver-xorg-video-amdgpu** for newer cards and **xserver-xorg-video-radeon** for older ones. The open source NVidia driver is **xserver-xorg-video-nouveau**.

Should your system require an Nvidia proprietary driver, the appropriate driver for your detected graphics card will be installed and enabled during installation, if you checked the "Install third-party software for graphics and Wi-Fi hardware and additional media formats" option on the "Updates and other software" install screen.

You can also manually select a proprietary drivers to use. Open the Software & Updates application (Applications overview) and click on the Additional Drivers tab to list available drivers (see Figure 3-98). Select the driver entry you want and then click on the Apply Changes button to use download and install the driver. The drivers are part of the restricted repository, supported by the vendor but not by Ubuntu. They are not open source, but proprietary.

Once installed, an examination of the Additional Drivers tab on Software & Updates will show the selected driver in use. Should you want to use the original driver, click the Revert button. The open source Xorg driver will be automatically selected and used. For NVIDIA cards, the Nouveau open source drivers are used, which provides some acceleration support. You can switch to another driver by selecting it and clicking the Apply Changes button.

Figure 3-98: Hardware Drivers: Software & Updates, Additional Drivers tab

When you install a new kernel, compatible kernel drivers for your proprietary graphics driver are generated automatically for you by the DKMS (Dynamic Kernel Module Support) utility.

The graphic vendors also have their own Linux-based configuration tools, which are installed with the driver. The NVIDIA configuration tool is in the **nvidia-settings** package. Once installed, you will see NVIDIA Server Settings in the Applications overview. This interface provides NVIDIA vendor access to many of the features of NVIDIA graphics cards like color corrections, video brightness and contrast, and thermal monitoring. You can also set the screen resolution and color depth.

For AMD you would use the open source drivers, Xorg amdgpu, radeon, or ati. For AMD video cards with GCN 1.2 capability and above (series 300 and above), it is recommended that you use the amdgpu AMD open source driver, **xserver-xorg-video-amdgpu**.

If you have problems with the vendor driver, you can always switch back to the original (Revert button). Your original Xorg open source driver will be used instead. The change-over will be automatic.

If the problem is more severe, with the display not working, you can use the GRUB menu on startup to select the recovery kernel. Your system will be started without the vendor graphics driver. You can use the "drop to shell" option to enter the command line mode. From there you can use the **apt** command-line APT tool to remove the graphics driver. The NVIDIA drivers have the prefix **nvidia**. In the following example, the asterisk will match on all the **nvidia** packages.

```
sudo apt remove nvidia*
```

Help Resources

A great deal of support documentation is already installed on your system and is accessible from online sources. Table 1-3 lists Help tools and resources accessible on your Ubuntu Linux system. Both the GNOME and KDE desktops feature Help systems that use a browser-like interface to display help files.

If you need to ask a question, you can access the Ubuntu help support at **https://answers.launchpad.net**. and at **https://askubuntu.com**. Here you can submit your question, and check answered questions about Ubuntu.

Ubuntu Desktop Guide

To access the Ubuntu Desktop Guide, click the Help icon (question mark) on the Ubuntu dock or on the applications overview's Utilities application folder. The Guide displays several links covering Ubuntu topics (see Figure 3-99). Topics covered include the desktop, networking, drivers, video, and system settings.

You can use the right and left arrows to move through the previous documentation you displayed. You can also search for topics. Click on the search button on the right side of the toolbar to open a search box. As you enter a search term possible results are displayed. You can also add bookmarks for documents and search results by clicking the Bookmarks button on the right side of the toolbar to open the bookmark menu with an "Add Bookmark" button. You can also quickly access a bookmarked page from the bookmark menu (Bookmark button).

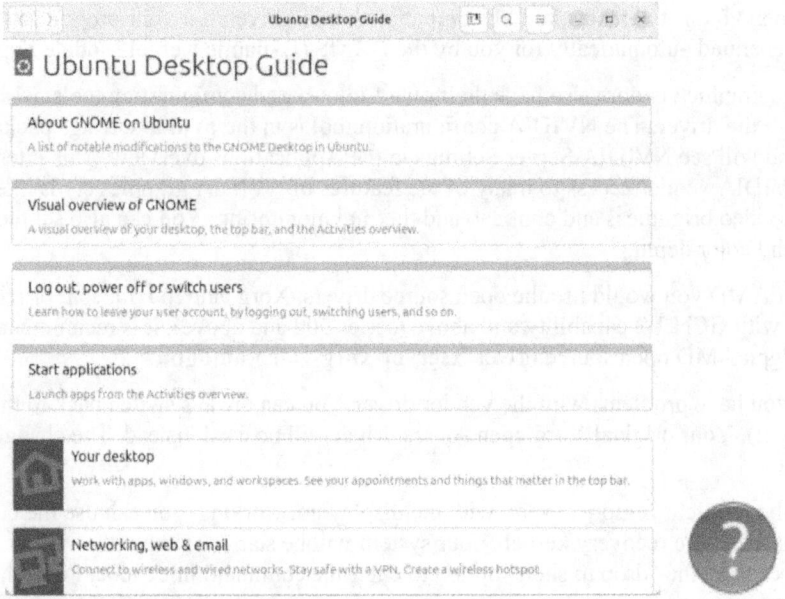

Figure 3-99: Ubuntu Desktop Guide

The pages are organized more like frequently asked questions documents, with more detailed headings designed to provide a clearer understanding of what the document is about (see Figure 3-100). The 'Sound and media" link opens a page with entries like "Why won't DVDs play" and "I can't play the songs I bought."

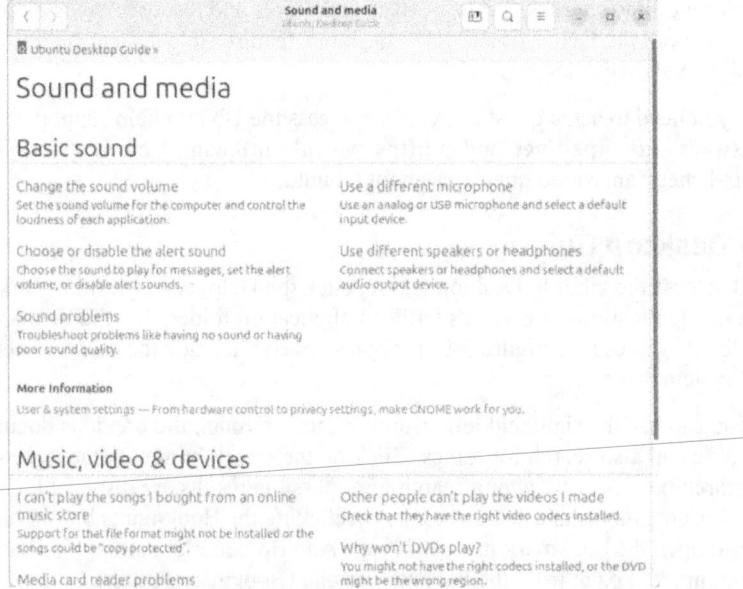

Figure 3-100: Ubuntu Desktop Guide topics

Help documents will include helpful links (see Figure 3-101). At the bottom of most pages, a More Information section will have links for more detailed information.

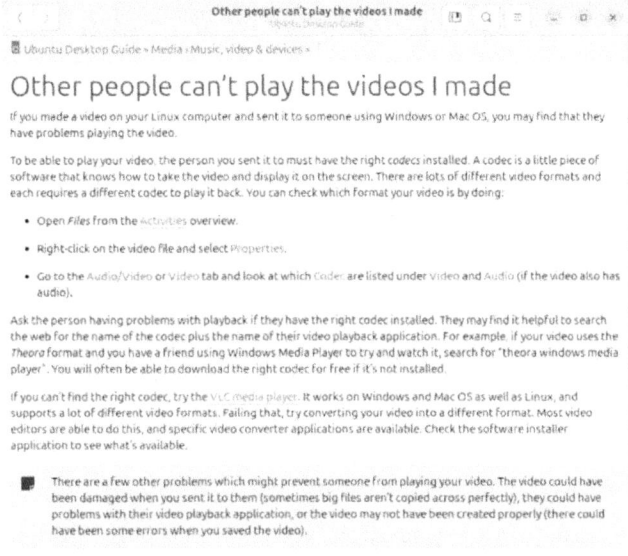

Figure 3-101: Ubuntu Desktop Guide page

If you want to see the application help documents available, choose All Help from the Help menu on the right side of its toolbar. You will see application manuals installed applications such as the Shotwell, Videos movie player, and Rhythmbox (see Figure 3-102).

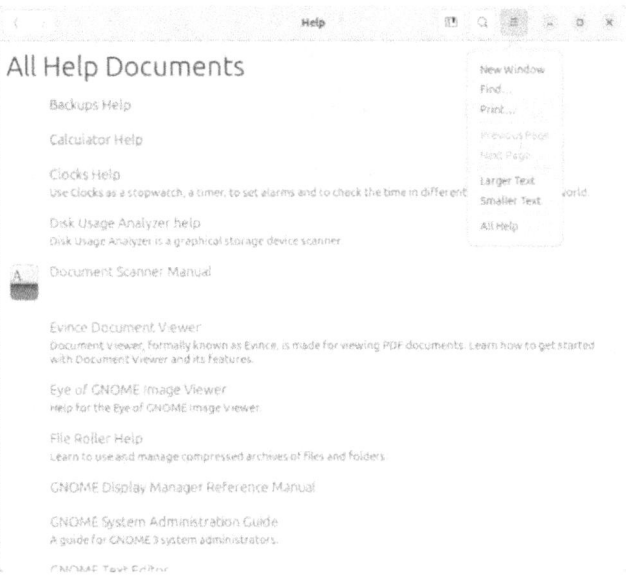

Figure 3-102: Ubuntu Help, All Documents

Context-Sensitive Help

Desktops such as GNOME and KDE, along with applications, provide context-sensitive help. Each KDE and GNOME application features detailed manuals that are displayed using their respective Help browsers. In addition, system administrative tools feature detailed explanations for each task.

Application Documentation

On your system, the **/usr/share/doc** folder contains documentation files installed by each application. Within each folder, you can usually find HOW-TO, README, and INSTALL documents for that application.

The Man Pages

You can access the Man pages, which are manuals for Linux commands, from the command line interface, using the **man** command. In a terminal window, enter **man** along with the command on which you want information. The following example asks for information on the **ls** command:

```
$ man ls
```

Pressing the SPACEBAR key advances, you to the next page. Pressing the **b** key moves you back a page. When you finish, press the **q** key to quit the Man utility and return to the command line. You activate a search by pressing either the slash (/) or question mark (?) keys. The / key searches forward and the ? key searches backward. When you press the / key, a line opens at the bottom of your screen, where you can enter a text to search for. Press ENTER to activate the search. You can repeat the same search by pressing the **n** key. You need not re-enter the pattern.

The Info Pages

Documentation for GNU applications, such as the gcc compiler and the Emacs editor, also exist as info pages accessible from the GNOME and KDE Help Centers. You can also access this documentation by entering the command **info** in a terminal window. This brings up a special screen listing different GNU applications. The info interface has its own set of commands. You can learn more about it by entering **info info** at the command prompt. Typing **m** opens a line at the bottom of the screen where you can enter the first few letters of the application. Pressing ENTER displays the info file on that application.

Terminal Window

The Terminal window allows you to enter Linux commands on a command line. It is installed by default, and is accessible from the Applications overview as Terminal. Its package name is **gnome-terminal** and it is a GNOME 4.6 application for Ubuntu 24.04.

The terminal window provides you with a shell interface for using shell commands instead of your desktop. The command line is editable, allowing you to use the BACKSPACE key to erase characters on the line. Pressing a key will insert that character. You can use the left and right arrow keys to move anywhere on the line, and then press keys to insert characters, or use backspace to delete characters (see Figure 3-103). Folders, files, and executable files are color-coded: white for files (black if background is white), blue for folders, green for executable files, and aqua for links. Shared folders are displayed with a green background.

You can have several terminal windows open at the same time. On the Ubuntu dock, you can right-click on the terminal icon to list all your open terminal windows and use that list to move to a different one or to close a terminal. The Ubuntu dock menu's Quit entry will close all your open terminal windows.

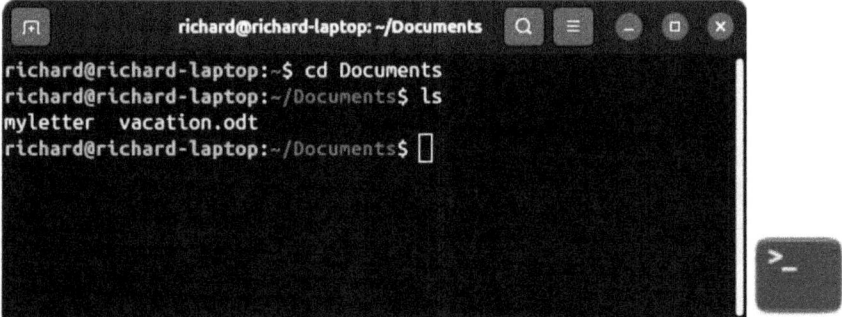

Figure 3-103: Terminal Window

The terminal window menu lets you open a new terminal window and lock the current window to a read only status (see Figure 3-104). Use the Full Screen entry to expand the window and the scaling buttons at the top of the menu to increase or decrease the font size. The Preferences entry opens the terminal window Preferences dialog where you can configure your terminal windows. The Advanced sub-menu lets you reset and clear the window, erasing previously displayed commands. You can also change the size of the terminal window from a set of listed sizes.

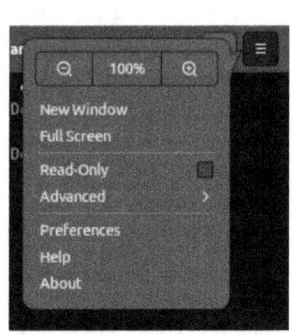
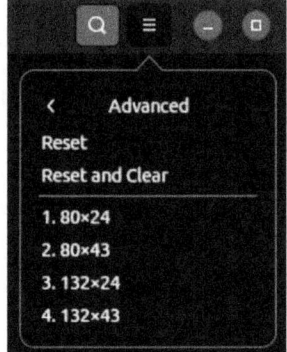

Figure 3-104: Terminal Window menu

The terminal window will remember the previous commands you entered. Use the up and down arrows to have those commands displayed in turn on the command line. Press the ENTER key to re-execute the currently displayed command. You can even edit a previous command before running it, allowing you to execute a modified version of a previous command. This can be helpful if you need to re-execute a complex command with a different argument, or if you mistyped a complex command and want to correct it without having to re-type the entire command. The terminal window will display all your previous interactions and commands for that session. Use the scrollbar to see any previous commands you ran and their displayed results.

To quickly locate either a previous command or message in the terminal window you can use the search dialog (see Figure 3-105). Click on the search button (looking glass button) located on the right side of the terminal window's titlebar. This open a search dialog with options for case, words, regular expressions, and wrap around.

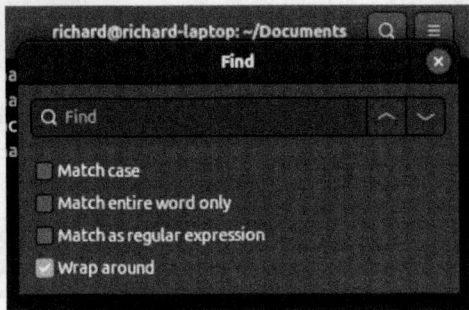

Figure 3-105: Terminal Window Search dialog

You can open as many terminal windows as you want, each working in its own shell. Instead of opening a separate window for each new shell, you can open several shells in the same window, using tabs. Use the keys SHIFT-CTRL-t or click the Tab button on the left side of the terminal window's titlebar (plus symbol) to open a new tab. A tab toolbar opens at the top of the terminal window with the folder name and a close button for each added tab. Each tab runs a separate shell, letting you enter different commands in each (see Figure 3-106). You can right-click on the tab's folder name to display a pop-up menu with options to move to the next or previous tab, close the tab, or detach the tab to a new terminal window. You can move to any tab by clicking on a tab's folder name, selecting its name from the Tabs menu, or pressing the **Ctrl-PageUp** and **Ctrl-PageDown** keys to move through the tabs sequentially. The Tabs menu is the down arrow on the right side of the terminal window and to the right of the tab names. It is displayed if multiple tabs are open.

The terminal window also supports desktop cut/copy and paste operations. You can copy a line from a Web page and then paste it to the terminal window by pressing SHIFT-CTRL-v. The command will appear and then you can press ENTER to execute the command. This is useful for command line operations displayed on an instructional Web page. Instead of typing in a complex command yourself, just select and copy from the Web page directly, and then paste to the Terminal window. You can also perform any edits on the command, if needed, before executing it. Also, should you want to copy a command on the terminal window, select the text with your mouse and then use SHIFT-CTRL-c keys to copy the command. You can select part of a line or multiple lines, as long as they are shown on the terminal window.

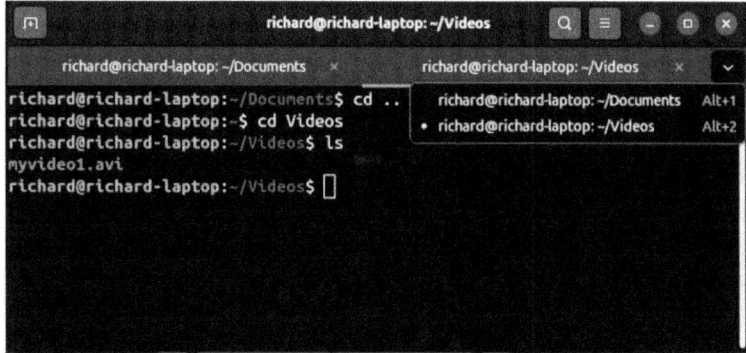

Figure 3-106: Terminal Window with tabs showing tabs menu

You can customize terminal windows using profiles. A default profile is set up already. To customize your terminal window, select Preferences from the terminal window menu. This opens a window for setting your default profile options with option categories on the sidebar for Global and Profiles. In the Profiles section there will be an "Unnamed" profile, the default. Click on the down menu button to the right to open a menu with the options to copy (clone) the profile or change the name. To add another profile, click on the plus button to the right of the "Profiles" heading to open a dialog to create a new profile. For profiles you create you have the added options to delete them and to set one as the default. A selected profile displays tabs for Text, Colors, Scrolling, Command, and Compatibility (see Figure 3-107). On the Text tab, you can select the default size of a terminal window in text rows and columns, as well as the font, spacing, and cursor shape.

Figure 3-107: Terminal Window Profile configuration

Your terminal window will be set up to use a dark background with white text. To change this, you can edit the profile to change the background and text colors on the Colors tab. De-select the "Use colors from system theme" entry. This enables the "Built-in schemes" menu from which you can select a "Black on white" display. Other color combinations are also listed, such as "Black on light yellow" and "Green on black." The Custom option lets you choose your own text and background colors. The colors on your open terminal window will change according to your selection, allowing you to see how the color choices will look. For a transparent background, choose the "Use transparent background" entry and then set the amount of shading (none is completely transparent and full shows no transparency).

The Scrolling tab specifies the number of command lines your terminal history will keep, as well as other scroll options such as whether to display the scrollbar. These are the lines you can move back through and select to re-execute. You can de-select the Limit scrollback option to set this to unlimited to keep all the commands.

To later edit a particular profile, select Preferences from the terminal window menu to open the Preferences window, and then click on the one you want in the Profiles section.

GNOME Console: GNOME 4.2

You can also install the newer GNOME Console application for GNOME 4.6 (see Figure 3-108). Its package name is **gnome-console,** and you can install it from the APT repository.

```
sudo apt install gnome-console
```

GNOME Console is accessible from the Applications overview as Console. It provides a basic terminal window with a search function and tab support. Its menu lets you choose a light or dark theme, or to use the system theme. It also has zoom functions and supports keyboard shortcuts as well as search operations, as well as support for tabs. Its Preferences dialog lets you set the font (the System font is the default) and set the terminal bell as a sound or visual effect.

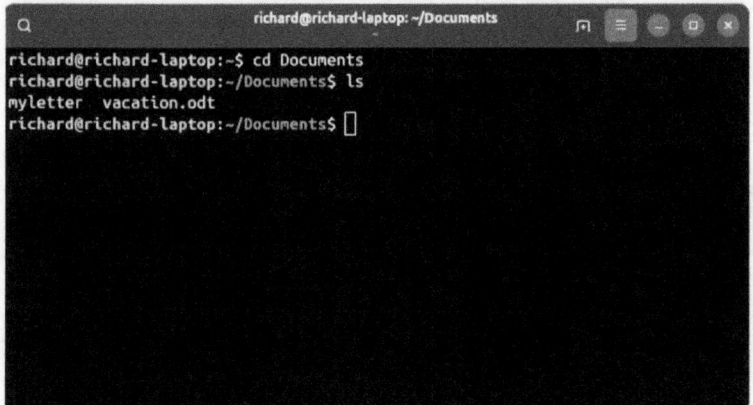
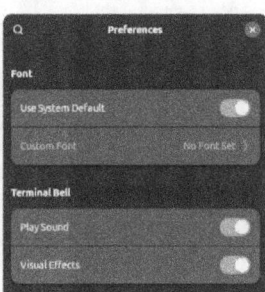

Figure 3-108: GNOME Console

Command Line Interface

When using the command line interface, you are given a simple prompt at which you type in a command. Even when you are using a desktop like GNOME, you sometimes need to execute commands on a command line. You can do so in a terminal window, which is accessed from the

Applications overview. You can keep the terminal window icon on the Dock by right-clicking on it and choosing "Pin to Dash"

Linux commands make extensive use of options and arguments. Be careful to place your arguments and options in their correct order on the command line. The format for a Linux command is the command name followed by options, and then by arguments, as shown here:

```
$ command-name options arguments
```

An option is a one-letter code preceded by one or two hyphens, which modifies the type of action the command takes. Options and arguments may or may not be optional, depending on the command. For example, the **ls** command can take an option, **-s**. The **ls** command displays a listing of files in your folder, and the **-s** option adds the size of each file in blocks. You enter the command and its option on the command line as follows.

```
$ ls -s
```

If you are uncertain what format and options a command uses, you can check the command syntax quickly by displaying its man page. Most commands have a man page. Just enter the **man** command with the command name as an argument.

An argument is data the command may need to execute its task. In many cases, this is a filename. An argument is entered as a word on the command line that appears after any options. For example, to display the contents of a file, you can use the **more** or **less** commands with the file's name as its argument. The **less** or **more** command used with the filename **mydata** would be entered on the command line as follows.

```
$ less mydata
```

The command line is actually a buffer of text you can edit. Before you press ENTER to execute the command, you can edit the command on the command line. The editing capabilities provide a way to correct mistakes you may make when typing a command and its options. The BACKSPACE key lets you erase the character you just typed (the one to the left of the cursor) and the DEL key lets you erase the character the cursor is on. With this character-erasing capability, you can backspace over the entire line if you want, erasing what you entered. CTRL-u erases the whole command line and lets you start over again at the prompt.

You can use the **Up Arrow** key to redisplay your last executed command. You can then re-execute that command, or you can edit it and execute the modified command. This is helpful when you have to repeat certain operations, such as editing the same file. It is also helpful when you have already executed a command you entered incorrectly.

ubuntu

4. Installing and Updating Software: Snap and APT

Installing Software Packages

Ubuntu Package Management Software: Snap and APT

Snap, the **snap** command, and the Snap Store

App Center for Snap

Ubuntu APT Software Repositories

App Center for APT

Gnome Software (APT and Snap)

Synaptic Package Manager

Source code files managed with APT

Managing APT software with apt

Managing APT software with apt-get

Managing non-repository packages with dpkg

Flatpak

Updating Snap packages

Updating Apt packages (Software updater)

Ubuntu software distribution is implemented using the online Ubuntu software repositories, which contain an extensive collection of Ubuntu-compliant software. With the integration of repository access into your Linux system, you can think of that software as an easily installed extension of your current collection. You can add software to your system by accessing software repositories that support Debian packages (DEB) and the Advanced Package Tool (APT), or the newer Snap packages known as **snaps** and the Snap package manager. Software is packaged into DEB or Snap software package files. These files are, in turn, installed and managed by APT or Snap. the App Center provides an easy-to-use front end for installing software with just a click, accessible from the App Center dock icon and from the Applications overview. The App Center supports both Snap and APT (DEB) packages, giving priority to Snap packages.

You can also download source code versions of applications, then compile, and install them on your system. Where this process once was complex, it has been streamlined significantly with the use of configure scripts. Most current source code, including GNU software, is distributed with a configure script, which automatically detects your system configuration and creates a binary file that is compatible with your system.

You can download Linux software from many online sources directly, but it is always advised that you use the Ubuntu prepared package versions if available. Most software for GNOME and KDE have corresponding Ubuntu-compliant packages in the Ubuntu Universe and Multiverse sections. Several proprietary versions of popular software packages, such as Skype, are freely available as Snap packages.

Installing Software Packages: APT and Snap

Installing software is an administrative function performed by a user with administrative access. During the Ubuntu installation, only some of the many applications and utilities available for users on Linux were installed on your system. On Ubuntu, you can install or remove software from your system with the App Center, the Synaptic Package Manager, GNOME Software, or the **snap**, **apt** and **apt-get** commands. Alternatively, you could install software as separate DEB files, or by downloading and compiling its source code.

Ubuntu supports two packages management systems, Snap and DEB (Debian package format). For the older DEB formatted packages, the underlying software management tool is APT. Snap packages (**snaps**) have a different format from DEB, and cannot be managed by APT. Instead they are managed by the Snap package manager, which uses the **snapd** daemon to install, update, and run snap applications. Snap is a completely different package management system, though Snap packages can be installed alongside APT packages, and accessed seamlessly on the Ubuntu desktop.

APT (Advanced Package Tool) is the older tool for installing packages, and is still used for most applications. When you install a DEB package with the App Center or with the **apt install** command, APT will be invoked and will select and download the package automatically from the appropriate online APT managed repository. This will include the entire Ubuntu online repository, including the main, universe, multiverse, and restricted sections.

A DEB software package includes all the files needed for a software application. A Linux software application often consists of several files that must be installed in different folders. The application program itself is placed in a system folder such as **/usr/bin**, online manual files go in another folder, and library files go in yet another folder. When you select an application for installation, APT will install any additional dependent (required) packages. APT also will install all recommended packages by default. Many software applications have additional features that rely on recommended packages.

Snap is the new package format that is replacing much of the DEB package management system on Ubuntu. As noted, the packages are called **snaps**. With the DEB format, as with other Linux pack formats like RPM, the component software files for a software application are installed directly to global system folders such as **/lib**, **/etc**, and **/usr/bin**. In effect, such a package has access to your entire system during installation, posing security risks. In addition, a DEB software package usually has several dependent packages, which also have to be installed. These can be extensive. Under this system, shared libraries, used by different applications can be a problem for developers, as changes in software may have to wait for supporting changes in the shared libraries.

With Snap, the software files for an application are no longer installed in global folders. They are installed in one separate folder, and any dependent software and shared libraries are included as part of the Snap package. In effect, there are no longer any dependencies, and libraries are no longer shared. This makes for more secure and faster updates, though a larger set of installed files. The installation process no longer needs access to your entire system. The entire application is isolated in one location. The problem of a failed update due to broken dependencies is no longer an issue. Applications that used to make use of the same shared library, will now have their own copies of that library. Developers that used to have to wait for changes to be made to a shared library, can now directly just change their own copy.

Keep in mind, that your Ubuntu install USB/DVD will currently install primarily Snap supported software applications, even for those that have corresponding APT packages. The App Center software manager gives priority to Snap packages. It will also display and manage a corresponding APT/DEB version of an application, should there be one. Keep in mind that the Synaptic Package Manager and the **apt** command only manage the APT versions of software applications. For example, there are both APT and Snap packages for Inkscape. The **apt install** command installs the APT version of Inkscape, whereas the App Center would install the Snap version. Should you install both, you will then have two versions of Inkscape on your system.

Should you want to also use the older GNOME Software version of the App Center, you can install it as GNOME Software. This older version of the App Center manages APT supported packages. However, you can install the GNOME Software Snap plugin to let it also manage Snap packages (**gnome-software-plugin-snap**). Should you also want to use Flatpak, there is also a GNOME Software Flatpak plugin (**gnome-software-plugin-flatpak**).

Software Package Types

Ubuntu uses both Snap (snaps) and Debian-compliant software packages (DEB). Snap packages have the extension **.snap** and DEB packages have a **.deb** extension. Other packages, such as those in the form of source code that you need to compile, may come in a variety of compressed archives. These commonly have the extension **.tar.gz**, **.tgz**, or **.tar.bz2**. Packages with the **.rpm** extension are Red Hat Package software packages used on Red Hat, Fedora, SuSE and other Linux distributions that use RPM packages. They are not compatible directly with Ubuntu. You can use the **alien** utility to convert most RPM packages to DEB packages that you can then install on Ubuntu. Table 4-1 lists several common file extensions that you will find for the great variety of Linux software packages available. You can download any Ubuntu-compliant DEB package as well as the original source code package, as single files, directly from **http://packages.ubuntu.com**.

Extension	File
.deb	A Debian/Ubuntu Linux package
.gz	A **gzip**-compressed file (use **gunzip** to decompress)
.bz2	A **bzip2**-compressed file (use **bunzip2** to decompress; also use the **j** option with **tar**, as in **xvjf**)
.tar	A tar archive file (use **tar** with **xvf** to extract)
.tar.gz	A **gzip**-compressed **tar** archive file (use **gunzip** to decompress and **tar** to extract; use the **z** option with **tar**, as in **xvzf**, to both decompress and extract in one step)
.tar.bz2	A **bzip2**-compressed **tar** archive file (extract with **tar -xvzj**)
.tz	A **tar** archive file compressed with the **compress** command
.Z	A file compressed with the **compress** command (use the **decompress** command to decompress)
.bin	A self-extracting software file
.rpm	A software package created with the Red Hat Software Package Manager, used on Fedora, Red Hat, Centos, and SuSE distributions
.snap	A Snap package, replacement for .deb

Table 4-1: Linux Software Package File Extensions

Ubuntu Package Management Software

Software packages can be managed and installed using different package management software tools. The App Center package manager (snap-store) supports both Snap (snaps) and APT (DEB). The **snap** command supports only Snap packages (**snaps**), and all the other package managers support APT. The Software Updater application supports both Snap and APT packages.

APT (Advanced Package Tool) performs the actual software management operations for all applications installed from an APT repository. The Synaptic Package Manager, **dpkg**, **apt**, and **apt-get** are all front-ends for APT, repository files at **/var/cache/apt**. The App Center, though, is also a front-end for Snap and the Snap Store, though it can also manage APT packages.

Snap Snap is the alternative and eventual replacement for APT. Snap packages are downloaded and installed from the Snap Store using the **snapd** daemon. A Snap package, in addition to an application, installs a copy of supporting libraries and configuration files, all located in a separate folder in the **/snap** folder, with user data located in a home folder's **snap** folder. They are not installed on the system globally as APT does. Snap packages and applications are also run and updated by the **snapd** daemon. Each update to a Snap package, has, in turn, a separate revision folder, each with a copy of supporting libraries and configuration files. Updates are easy to perform and require no system-wide updating of supporting libraries. You can easily switch from one revision to another. The App Center, and the **snap** command are front-ends for Snap and the Snap Store. The App Center is a modified version of the **snap-store** application, which manages Snap packages. The App Center can, however, also install and manage DEB packages from APT repositories, though priority is given to Snap packages.

Snap and APT package managers

App Center is the primary desktop interface for locating and installing Ubuntu software. The App Center integrate the snap-store application. The App Center can manage both Snap packages (Snap) and DEB packages (APT). In the App Center, Snap packages are given priority.

Software updater is the Ubuntu graphical front end for updating installed software. It updates APT supported packages and, also, invokes the **snapd** daemon to update Snap packages from the Snap Store.

GNOME Software is the is the older version of the App Center that is based on the GNOME Software application. The basic install supports the APT repositories only (DEB packages). But you can install a Gnome Software plugin for Snap packages, letting you use it to manage Snap packages. You can also install a Flatpak plugin to manage Flatpak packages.

Snap only package managers

snap is the command line command for managing Snap packages (Snap). Packages are installed at **/snap**, with user data in the home folder's **snap** folder.

APT only package managers

Synaptic Package Manager is a Graphical front end for managing DEB packages on APT repositories. It does not support Snap.

Discover Package Manager is the KDE software manager based on the App Center and is a graphical front end for APT.

Muon Package Manager is an older KDE software manager similar to the Synaptic Package Manager and is a graphical front end for APT.

tasksel is a command-line cursor-based tool for selecting package groups and particular servers (front-end for APT). You can run it in a terminal window on a desktop (**sudo tasksel**). Use arrow keys to move to an entry, the spacebar to select, the tab key to move to the OK button. Press ENTER on the OK button to perform your installs.

apt is the primary command line tool for APT, and is used to install, update, and remove software. It is based on **apt-get** and does not have as many options. It uses the APT database, **/var/lib/apt** with repository information at **/var/cache/apt**

apt-get is the older command line tool for APT to install, update, and remove software. It has more options than **apt**. It uses the APT database, **/var/lib/apt** with repository information at **/var/cache/apt**

dpkg is the older command line tool used to install, update, remove, and query DEB software packages. It uses its own database, **/var/lib/dpkg**, Repository files are kept at **/var/cache/apt**, the same as APT.

aptitude is a cursor based front end for **dpkg** and **apt-get**, which uses its own database, **/var/lib/aptitude**.

Snaps Packages

Snaps are designed to provide a universal and independent software repository whose packages will run on any Linux distribution or, even, versions of a Linux distribution. A Snap package can be downloaded and installed on any distribution, including Ubuntu, Fedora, Debian, Centos, Linux Mint, and openSUSE. A Snap package can also run on any version of that distribution. The same Snap package will also run on different Linux releases of a distribution, such as Ubuntu 20.04 and 24.04. Software developers can simply maintain the one Snap package, instead of several for different distributions. This design make it much easier for commercial software companies to provide Linux clients of their proprietary applications. Currently these include Skype, Zoom, and Slack. Such a structure makes updating a simple and fast procedure. Updates are performed automatically within six hours of a revision by the developer by the **snapd** server on your system. You can update manually if you wish or set a different update schedule.

The Snap system is maintained and supported by Ubuntu. An alternative system, called Flatpaks (**https://flatpak.org/**), is an independent project with a similar design.

Check the Snapcraft documentation and tutorials at:

```
https://snapcraft.io/docs
https://snapcraft.io/tutorials
```

It is important to keep in mind the difference between a Snap package and a snap application. Some Snap packages install several applications. Most install only one. There are snap commands that work on packages, such as **install** and **disable**. But there are others that work only on snap applications, such as the **run** command. The Skype package installs only the Skype application, and the name for the package and application are the same. Whereas the Nextcloud service installs several applications, each with a different name such as **nextcloud.apache** for the web server. So for Skype, you can manage both the package and application with the just the name **skype**. But for nextcloud you use the name **nextcloud** to manage the package, but the name of particular nextcloud application to run the application.

```
snap enable nextcloud
snap run nextcloud.apache
```

Managing Snap: App Center and the snap command

The App Center has a Snap backend that integrates Snap packages and allows you to install and remove them. The Synaptic Package Manager and the **apt** command do not support Snap packages. GNOME Software can support Snap packages, if you install its Snap plugin. The easiest way to find and install Snap packages is to use the App Center, which is modified to use the snap-store application (see Figure 4-1). A Channel button is shown on the App Center that lists various Snap tracks with their risk levels. the App Center supports packages both from the Snap Store (**snapcraft.io**) and APT repositories. Many packages, such as those part of the GNOME desktop like Text Editor, will the APT repositories. However, there could be corresponding Snap and Deb packages, as is the case with Inkscape. Should you install the Inkscape Snap package you are installing from the Snap Store (**snapcraft.io**), whereas if you install the Inkscape DEB package you are installing a separate application from the APT Universe repository.

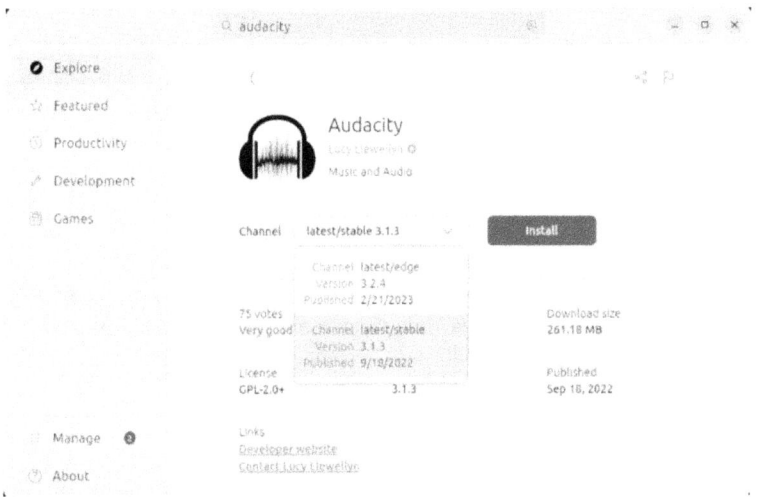

Figure 4-1: App Center - Snap Package

Alternatively, you can simply use the **snap** command in a terminal window to install and manage Snap packages (see Table 4-2). To find a Snap package, use the **snap find** command with the search term (see Figure 4-2).

```
snap find skype
```

You can also search on a search term. The following example searches for FTP clients and servers, and for Web servers.

```
snap find ftp
snap find "web server"
```

Without the search term, a list of popular Snap packages is displayed.

```
snap find
```

Snaps are further organized into sections such as entertainment, games, and productivity. You can see the available sections with the **find --section** command.

```
snap find --section
```

To see available games you would enter the section name preceded by the = sign, as in **--section=games**.

```
snap find --section=games
```

To install a package, use the **snap** command with the **install** option. The following installs the skype Snap package.

```
sudo snap install skype
```

Once installed, the Snap applications installed by the package will appear on the Applications overview, just as any other application.

Use the **remove** command to remove a package completely from your system.

```
sudo snap remove skype
```

Command	Description
find *pattern*	Search for available Snap packages. Without a search term, a list of popular packages is displayed.
find --section	List the available Snap package categories (sections)
find --section=*section-name*	List the Snap packages in a section
refresh	Manually update packages, installing new revisions of installed packages if available. Snaps are automatically updated every six hours by default.
install *snap-package*	Install a Snap package
remove	Remove a Snap package completely
revert [*revision-number*]	Revert to a previous installed revision of a snap. Without a revision number the previous installed revision is used.
disable *snap-package*	Disable a Snap without uninstalling it. The installed snap remains on your system, but is unavailable to users. Will disable all snap applications installed by the package.
enable *snap-package*	Enable a disabled snap, making it available to users again. Will enable all Snap applications installed by the package
list	List your installed Snap packages
list --all	List all your Snap packages along with the revisions for each package, which will also display the revision number of a revision
list --all *snap-package*	List all the revisions for a Snap package, which will also display the revision number for each
connections	List interfaces with their plugs and slots
interface	List available interfaces with a description of each
install channel=*risk-level*	Install a Snap package revision from a specified risk-level (**stable**, **candidate**, **beta**, and **edge**)
info *snap-package*	Display detailed information for an installed Snap package, including all revisions
connect *plug slot*	Manually connect a Snap application (plug) to a system resource (slot)
get	List configuration options for a package you can set if there are any
set	Change configuration options for a package if there are any
unset	Set configuration options to nothing for a package if there are any
run *snap-application*	Run a snap application

Table 4-2: snap commands

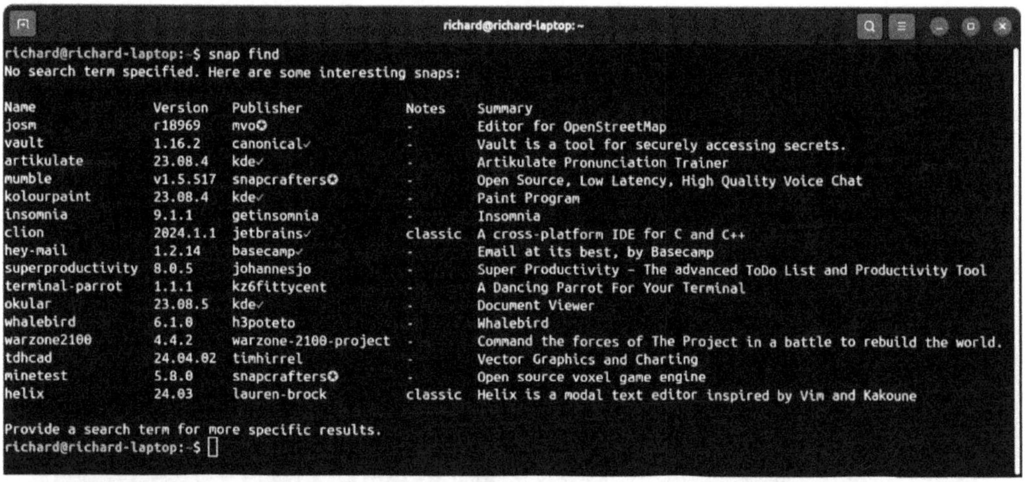

```
richard@richard-laptop:~$ snap find
No search term specified. Here are some interesting snaps:

Name               Version    Publisher              Notes    Summary
josm               r18969     mvo                    -        Editor for OpenStreetMap
vault              1.16.2     canonical✓             -        Vault is a tool for securely accessing secrets.
artikulate         23.08.4    kde✓                   -        Artikulate Pronunciation Trainer
mumble             v1.5.517   snapcrafters           -        Open Source, Low Latency, High Quality Voice Chat
kolourpaint        23.08.4    kde✓                   -        Paint Program
insomnia           9.1.1      getinsomnia            -        Insomnia
clion              2024.1.1   jetbrains✓             classic  A cross-platform IDE for C and C++
hey-mail           1.2.14     basecamp✓              -        Email at its best, by Basecamp
superproductivity  8.0.5      johannesjo             -        Super Productivity - The advanced ToDo List and Productivity Tool
terminal-parrot    1.1.1      kz6fittycent           -        A Dancing Parrot For Your Terminal
okular             23.08.5    kde✓                   -        Document Viewer
whalebird          6.1.0      h3poteto               -        Whalebird
warzone2100        4.4.2      warzone-2100-project   -        Command the forces of The Project in a battle to rebuild the world.
tdhcad             24.04.02   timhirrel              -        Vector Graphics and Charting
minetest           5.8.0      snapcrafters           -        Open source voxel game engine
helix              24.03      lauren-brock           classic  Helix is a modal text editor inspired by Vim and Kakoune

Provide a search term for more specific results.
richard@richard-laptop:~$
```

Figure 4-2: Listing of popular available Snaps: find

With Snap, you have the option of disabling a package, instead of removing it completely. The Snap package remains installed, but is unavailable to any users. Use the **disable** command to disable a package. You can enable a disabled package with the **enable** command. Keep in mind that if the package installed has several applications, all those applications are disabled by the **disable** command. The **enable** command will enable all of them.

```
sudo snap disable skype
sudo snap enable skype
```

Use the **refresh** command to update your Snap packages.

```
sudo Snap refresh skype
```

To see a list of Snap packages already installed, use the **list** command (see Figure 4-3). To include all installed versions of the different packages, add the **--all** option.

```
snap list
snap list --all
```

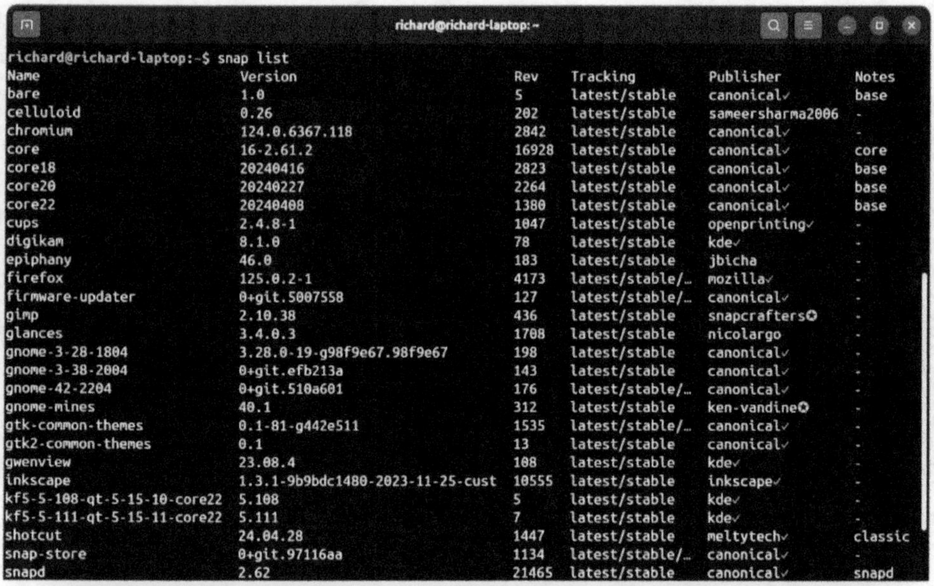

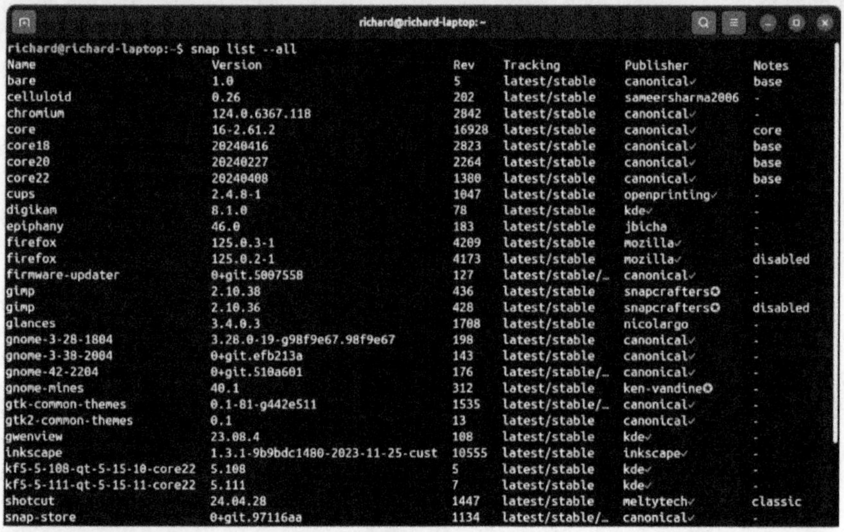

Figure 4-3: Listing of installed snaps: list

To display detailed information about a particular Snap package, you use the **info** command.

```
snap info skype
```

Snap applications are stored as revisions in the **/snap** folder under the package name. Each revision has its own folder, which includes the application executables, as well as all configuration and system support files. In effect, each revision of a Snap application has its own **/etc**, **/usr**, **/bin**, **/lib**, and **/var** folder. A link to the application program currently enabled is held in the **/snap/bin** folder. User data for a Snap application is held in a **snap** folder in your home folder. Systemd support for Snap is provided by the systemd **snapd.service** and **snapd.socket** files.

Should you want to create a Snap package, you can use **snapcraft**, which you can install with the App Center or the **snap install --classic** command.

Snap Channels: tracks and risk levels

Snap packages are managed by channels which organize a package into tracks and risk levels. Developers may also add a branch category for short-term versions of an applications. You will see track and risk-levels listed as possible channel selections in the App Center for a Snap package.

```
track/risk-level
```

The track indicates the revision of a package installed. By default this is **latest**. The risk level indicates the reliability of the software. There are four risk levels: **stable**, **candidate**, **beta**, and **edge**. The **stable** risk level is for reliable software considered ready for mass distribution. The **candidate** risk level is for a version of the application being readied for release but still being tested. The **beta** risk level is for beta versions of applications that may incorporate new features but is considered unstable. The **edge** risk level is for versions that are still under development with ongoing changes that may not always run.

Packages are installed with the latest risk level by default.

```
snap install
```

Should you want to use a different risk level, you can specify it with the appropriate risk level track: **--stable**, **--candidate**, **--beta**, and **--edge**. You can also use the **--channel** option.

```
snap install --candidate
snap install --channel=candidate
```

You can later change the risk level tracked using the **switch** command. This only changes the tracking. It does not install the version for that track. To do that you would have to run the **refresh** command.

```
snap switch --candidate
```

To both perform a switch to a different track and install the version of the applications from that track, you can run the **refresh** command directly.

```
snap refresh --channel=candidate
```

On the App Center, when you display the application page for a Snap package, a Channels menu is displayed on the left side below the application name. Clicking this menu lets you choose from the available versions for this Snap package on different channels, usually stable, beta, and edge (see Figure 4-4). Each version will list the URL, channel, and version. The URL is **snapcraft.io** for the Ubuntu Snap Store. The channel will list the track and risk level, usually **latest/stable** or **latest/beta**. The version shows the version of the software package. The **stable** and **candidate** risk levels usually have the same version, where the **beta** risk level will be different. Some applications will have tracks for special releases, such as the **esr/stable** channel for Firefox's Extended Support Release (**esr**).

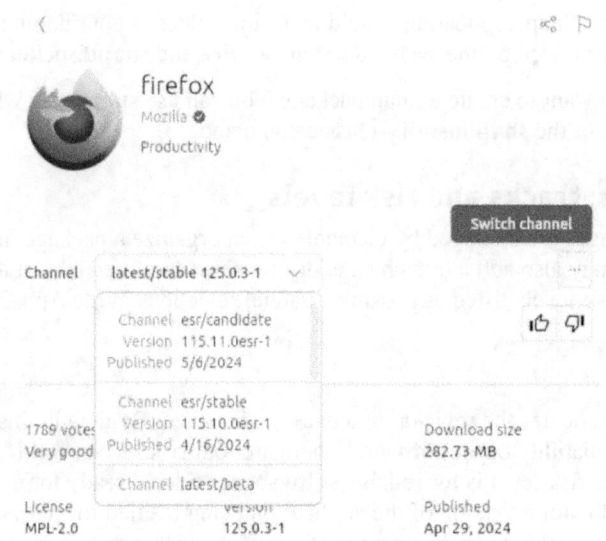

Figure 4-4: App Center - Snap Tracks and Risk Levels

Snap Confinement

Most Snap packages are run using a strict confinement mode, running in isolation with only minimal access to system resources such as networks, system folders, and processes. Some Snap packages are allowed to run in the classic mode, if officially approved, letting them access system resources just as a traditional DEB package can. These packages can only be installed with the **--classic** option. For a package to obtain classic status, it must be carefully examined by Snapcraft for security and stability issues. There is also a **devmode** reserved for developers. To see the confinement mode for a package use the **snap info** command with the **--verbose** option. The **snap list** command, which lists all your Snap packages, will also display each package's confinement mode.

```
snap info --verbose inkscape
```

Access to system resources by a package is setup up by interfaces, which are determined by the developer and implemented when the package is installed. Interfaces usually allow access to resources such as devices. This often includes your home folder, network access, system files, and the display server (Wayland or X11). A Snap package can only access your system through these interfaces. Interfaces consist of plugs and slots. The plug is the package or process that needs the interface (the consumer), and the plug is the service that supports it (the provider). The **snap connections** command will list the interfaces for a package.

```
snap connections inkscape
```

The **snap connections** command with no package as an argument, will list all the packages (plugs) along with the interfaces and slots they use.

```
snap connections
```

A sample of the list is shown here.

```
Interface               Plug                            Slot                    Notes
appstream-metadata      snap-store:appstream-metadata   :appstream-metadata     -
audio-playback          chromium:audio-playback         :audio-playback         -
audio-record            chromium:audio-record           :audio-record           -
avahi-observe           firefox:avahi-observe           :avahi-observe          -
browser-support         chromium:browser-sandbox        :browser-support        -
browser-support         firefox:browser-sandbox         :browser-support        -
camera                  chromium:camera                 :camera                 -
camera                  firefox:camera                  :camera                 -
gsettings               chromium:gsettings              :gsettings              -
gsettings               firefox:gsettings               :gsettings              -
gsettings               inkscape:gsettings              :gsettings              -
gsettings               snap-store:gsettings            :gsettings              -
home                    chromium:home                   :home                   -
home                    firefox:home                    :home                   -
home                    gwenview:home                   :home                   -
home                    inkscape:home                   :home                   -
network                 chromium:network                :network                -
network                 firefox:network                 :network                -
network                 gwenview:network                :network                -
network                 snap-store:network              :network                -
opengl                  chromium:opengl                 :opengl                 -
opengl                  firefox:opengl                  :opengl                 -
opengl                  gwenview:opengl                 :opengl                 -
wayland                 firefox:wayland                 :wayland                -
wayland                 inkscape:wayland                :wayland                -
wayland                 snap-store:wayland              :wayland                -
x11                     chromium:x11                    :x11                    -
x11                     firefox:x11                     :x11                    -
x11                     gwenview:x11                    :x11                    -
x11                     inkscape:x11                    :x11                    -
x11                     snap-store:x11                  :x11                    -
```

The **snap interface** command lists all your interfaces on your system with a description of each.

```
snap interface
```

A sample of the interface list is shown here.

```
Name                    Summary
appstream-metadata      allows access to AppStream metadata
audio-playback          allows audio playback via supporting services
audio-record            allows audio recording via supporting services
avahi-control           allows control over service discovery on a local network
via the mDNS/DNS-SD protocol suite
avahi-observe           allows discovery on a local network via the mDNS/DNS-SD
protocol suite
bluez                   allows operating as the bluez service
browser-support         allows access to various APIs needed by modern web
browsers
camera                  allows access to all cameras
content                 allows sharing code and data with other snaps
cups                    allows access to the CUPS socket for printing
cups-control            allows access to the CUPS control socket
```

```
desktop                     allows access to basic graphical desktop resources
desktop-launch              allows snaps to identify and launch desktop applications
  in (or from) other snaps
desktop-legacy              allows privileged access to desktop legacy methods
fwupd                       allows operating as the fwupd service
gsettings                   allows access to any gsettings item of current user
hardware-observe            allows reading information about system hardware
home                        allows access to non-hidden files in the home directory
joystick                    allows access to joystick devices
login-session-observe       allows reading login and session information
mount-control               allows creating transient and persistent mounts
mount-observe               allows reading mount table and quota information
network                     allows access to the network
network-bind                allows operating as a network service
network-manager-observe     allows observing NetworkManager settings
network-status              allows access to network connectivity status
opengl                      allows access to OpenGL stack
optical-drive               allows access to optical drives
packagekit-control          allows control of the PackageKit service
personal-files              allows access to personal files or directories
pulseaudio                  allows operating as or interacting with the pulseaudio
  service
raw-usb                     allows raw access to all USB devices
removable-media             allows access to mounted removable storage
screen-inhibit-control      allows inhibiting the screen saver
shutdown                    allows shutting down or rebooting the system
snap-themes-control         allows use of snapd's theme installation API
snapd-control               allows communicating with snapd
system-files                allows access to system files or directories
system-packages-doc         allows access to documentation of system packages
u2f-devices                 allows access to u2f devices
udisks2                     allows operating as or interacting with the UDisks2
  service
unity7                      allows interacting with Unity 7 services
upower-observe              allows operating as or reading from the UPower service
wayland                     allows access to compositors supporting wayland protocol
x11                         allows interacting with or running as an X11 server
```

To see the slots and plugs used for an interface, use the **snap interface** command with the name of that interface. The following command lists all the plugs and slots for the network interface.

```
richard@richard-laptop:~$ snap interface network
name:    network
summary: allows access to the network
plugs:
  - chromium
  - digikam
  - gimp
  - firefox
  - gwenview
  - snap-store
slots:
  - snapd
```

You can use the **connect** and **disconnect** commands to manually connect or disconnect an interface for a package. They take as their arguments the plug and slot, with the plug preceded by the package name and a colon. As noted, interfaces for packages are normally set up for you and activated when a package is installed. The following connects the Gwenview image manager to your home folder.

```
sudo snap connect gwenview:home :home
```

Not all interfaces available to an application may be activated when you install it. You can also turn activated interfaces off, denying access for that package to the resource. On the Settings Apps tab, you can easily manage the interfaces for an application by selecting the application in the Apps application's tab. The Permission section lists the permission supported by the application, with switches for each one to turn them on or off. For some permissions there will be a menu instead of a switch to allow you to choose an option. In Figure 4-5, the GIMP application is not allowed to read and write to removeable media, whereas it is allowed access to your network and home folder, as well as to print documents and to run in the background.

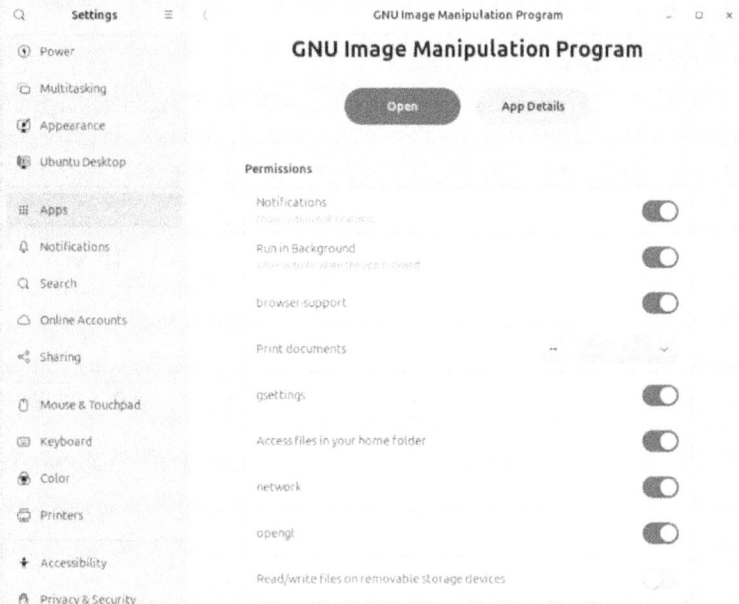

Figure 4-5: Snap application permissions - Settings

You can also check the connections (permissions) allowed using the connections command with the package name, showing the slots and plugs for that package. The following show the GIMP (**gimp**) interfaces. The plug for removable media has no slot, showing that it is disconnected. This permission is turned off.

```
richard@richard-laptop:~$ snap connections gimp
Interface                Plug                     Slot                                Notes
browser-support          gimp:browser-support     :browser-support                    -
content[gnome-3-38-2004] gimp:gnome-3-38-2004     gnome-3-38-2004:gnome-3-38-2004     -
content[gtk-2-engines]   gimp:gtk-2-engines       gtk2-common-themes:gtk-2-engines    -
content[gtk-3-themes]    gimp:gtk-3-themes        gtk-common-themes:gtk-3-themes      -
```

```
content[icon-themes]     gimp:icon-themes         gtk-common-themes:icon-themes    -
content[sound-themes]    gimp:sound-themes        gtk-common-themes:sound-themes   -
cups-control             gimp:cups-control        -                                -
dbus                     -                        gimp:dbus-gimp                   -
desktop                  gimp:desktop             :desktop                         -
desktop-legacy           gimp:desktop-legacy      :desktop-legacy                  -
gsettings                gimp:gsettings           :gsettings                       -
home                     gimp:home                :home                            -
network                  gimp:network             :network                         -
opengl                   gimp:opengl              :opengl                          -
removable-media          gimp:removable-media     -                                -
unity7                   gimp:unity7              :unity7                          -
wayland                  gimp:wayland             :wayland                         -
x11                      gimp:x11                 :x11                             -
```

If your application is not listed in the Settings Apps tab, you can manually set the permission using the **connect** and **disconnect** commands. Use the **snap connect** command to turn on a permission, and the **snap disconnect** command turn it off.

```
snap connect gimp:removable-media  :removable-media
```

Snap Revisions: revert

Snaps are installed as revisions. For any given application, you may have several revisions of an application installed. Each revision is able to run as the application. Priority is given to the current revision, the most recently installed. But you could easily decide to run a previous revision instead. This could happen if a new revision is installed that becomes unstable, or if the changes made to the software have deprecated capabilities you normally use. Major changes to an application are released as a version, which is also considered a revision. Though you could have several revisions for a given version, for most less complex applications you will usually have just the one revision per version.

Whereas a **list** command will display your installed snaps, adding the **--all** option will also display all the revisions of each snap. This operation will display the name, version, revision, tracking, publisher, and notes for each revision.

```
richard@richard-laptop:~$ snap list --all
Name            Version              Rev    Tracking         Publisher     Notes
chromium        81.0.4044.129        1135   latest/stable    canonical✓    disabled
chromium        81.0.4044.138        1143   latest/stable    canonical✓    -
digikam         6.4.0                6      latest/beta      sergiusens    -
dragon          19.04.2              27     latest/stable    kde✓          -
firefox         76.0.1-1             359    latest/stable    mozilla✓      -
gwenview        24.04.0              48     latest/stable    kde✓          -
sensors-unity   18.02                202    latest/stable    paroj         -
skype           8.59.0.77            123    latest/stable    skype✓        disabled,classic
skype           8.60.0.76            128    latest/stable    skype✓        classic
snap-store      3.36.0-80-g208fd61   454    latest/stable/…  canonical✓    -
snap-store      3.36.0-74-ga164ec9   433    latest/stable/…  canonical✓    disabled
snapd           2.44.3               7264   latest/stable    canonical✓    snapd
spectacle       19.04.3              25     latest/stable    kde✓          -
```

Instead of listing all the snaps, you could just list the revisions for a particular snap.

```
richard@richard-laptop:~$ snap list --all skype
Name   Version    Rev  Tracking       Publisher   Notes
skype  8.59.0.77  123  latest/stable  skype✓      disabled,classic
skype  8.60.0.76  128  latest/stable  skype✓      classic
```

The revision number is unique. You could have several revisions with the same version number, but the revision number is the unique identifier for that install. Previous revision can be run using their revision number.

Only one revision of an application can be enabled. This is the one that Snap will run. All other revision of that application are disabled, as shown in the Notes field of the **list --all** output.

You can enable a previous revision, disabling the current one, and thereby letting Snap run it. You do this with the **revert** command and the number of the revision you want to enable. The following example reverts GIMP (**gimp**) to revision 428.

```
sudo snap revert gimp 428
```

If you just want to enable the previous revision, you can leave out the number.

```
sudo snap revert gimp
```

If you decide, after reverting to a previous revision, that you want to return to using the latest revision, run the **revert** command with the revision number of the latest revision.

```
sudo snap revert skype 428
```

You could also just run the **refresh** command on that snap. The latest revision is automatically enabled.

```
sudo snap refresh gimp
```

Keep in mind, that if a new update of a snap is later released, the automatic **refresh** operation, will update the snap to that new revision.

Snap Package Configuration

Some Snap package, such as those for services, may have configuration options you can manage using the **snap get**, **snap set**, and **snap unset** commands. The **snap get** command list configuration options for a snap and their current setting. The **snap set** command can change an option, and the **snap unset** command removes a value. Some Snap packages, such as servers, have options that can be set when the application is started. Each revision will have a configuration that will be applied when that revision is run. Using the **revert** command you could change from using one revision of a server to another, each running separate configurations.

In addition, all snap applications have supporting environment variables. Environment variables will show folders that the snap can access, as well as application information such as the revision and version number. You can see the environment variable for an application by first starting that application's shell with the **run --shell** command.

```
sudo snap run --shell skype
```

Keep in mind that sometimes the package name may not be the same as the application name. A package could install several applications, as is the case with the nextcloud package. To access the Nextcloud web server you would use its application name, **nextcloud.apache**.

```
sudo snap run --shell nextcloud.apache
```

You can then use the shell **env** command to list your environment variables, filtering the output with **grep** and the SNAP pattern to show just the snap related ones.

```
env | grep SNAP
```

The environment variables for the current enabled revision is listed. The folder variables will show the folder of that revision. The SNAP_COMMON and SNAP_USER_DATA variables show the location of the folders that your application can write to.

To leave the shell enter the **exit** command.

Snap and systemd

Snap is managed by the **snapd** daemon, which runs several services. The service files for these are located in the **/lib/systemd/system** folder. Applications installed by a Snap package have access to the application configured by **systemd** using **.mount** files located in the **/etc/systemd/system** folder. The mount file will begin with the term **snap** and have the application name and its revision number. Each revision will have a separate mount file. The mount file for Skype revision 128 is **snap-skype-128.mount**.

/etc/systemd/system/snap-skype-128.mount

```
[Unit]
Description=Mount unit for skype, revision 128
Before=snapd.service

[Mount]
What=/var/lib/snapd/snaps/skype_128.snap
Where=/snap/skype/128
Type=squashfs
Options=nodev,ro,x-gdu.hide
LazyUnmount=yes

[Install]
WantedBy=multi-user.target
```

The file shows the revision number and the location of the revision.

```
Where=/snap/skype/128
```

Snap and Services

Services installed as Snap packages can be managed by **systemctl** commands such as **systemctl start** and **systemctl stop** to start and stop a service. In addition, some Snap packaged services will also provide configuration options you can manage using the snap **get**, **set**, and **unset** commands. There are few services currently available as Snap packages. For most services like the FTP and Web servers, you would still use APT.

Services installed as Snap packages have their systemd service files installed in the **/etc/systemd/system** folder, not in **/lib/systemd/system** as APT services are. All snap installed services are managed through the **snapd** server. The **snapd** server, in turn, has service files for **snapd** in the **/lib/system/system** folder. Furthermore, all the snap installed services have their service files begin with the term **snap**, as in **snap.nextcloud.apache.service** for the Nextcloud web server (part of the **nextcloud** Snap package). You can then use **systemctl** commands to manage the service.

```
systemctl status snap.nextcloud.apache
sudo system restart snap.nextcloud.apache
```

The format of the service file is much the same as other systemd service files, except that execution operation are run by the **snap run** command. The service also requires supporting snap systemd operations such as the **snap-nextcloud** mount and **snapd.apparmor.service**.

/etc/systemd/system/snap.nextcloud.apache.service

```
[Unit]
# Auto-generated, DO NOT EDIT
Description=Service for snap application nextcloud.apache
Requires=snap-nextcloud-20498.mount
Wants=network.target
After=snap-nextcloud-20498.mount network.target snapd.apparmor.service
X-Snappy=yes

[Service]
EnvironmentFile=-/etc/environment
ExecStart=/usr/bin/snap run nextcloud.apache
SyslogIdentifier=nextcloud.apache
Restart=always
WorkingDirectory=/var/snap/nextcloud/20498
ExecStop=/usr/bin/snap run --command=stop nextcloud.apache
TimeoutStopSec=30
Type=simple

[Install]
WantedBy=multi-user.target
```

App Center for Snap

To perform simple installation and removal of software, you can use the App Center, which is the primary supported package manager for Ubuntu (see Figure 4-6). The App Center is modified to use the **snap-store** application, which manages Snap packages. The App Center is designed to be the centralized utility for managing your software. The App Center performs a variety of different software tasks, including installation, removal, updating of software.

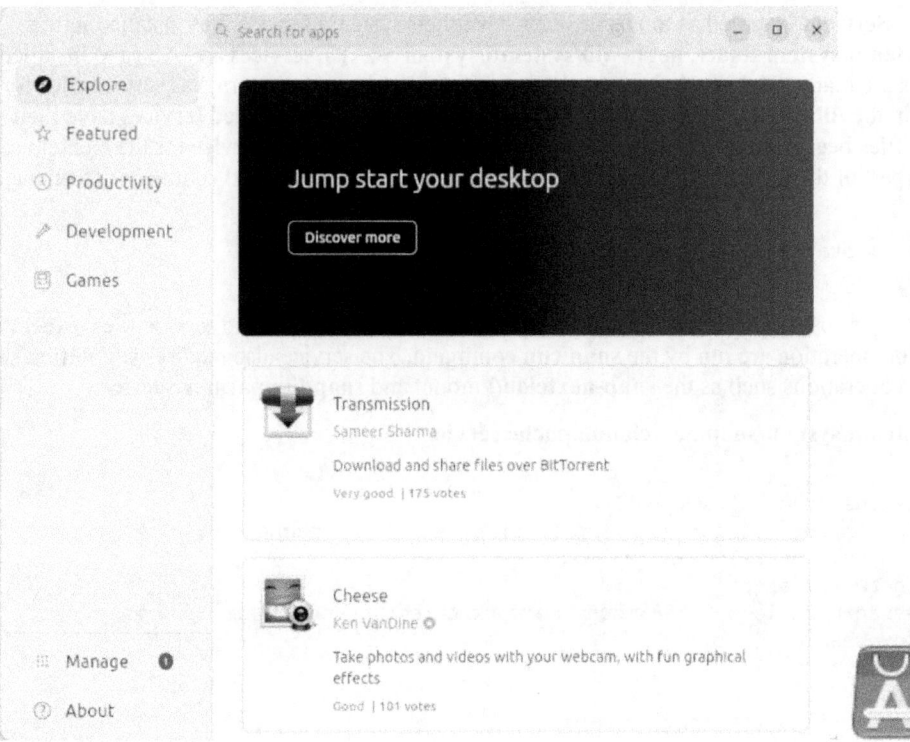

Figure 4-6: App Center

To use the App Center, click the App Center icon on the dock or on the Applications overview. A window opens with a search bar in the header bar and several tab headings in a sidebar. The tabs are Explore, Featured, Productivity, Development, and Games, and, at the bottom, Manage and About.

The Explore tab has sections for the desktop, featured Snap applications, games, developer applications, productivity. Some of these have links to corresponding App Center tabs, such as Feature, Productivity, and Development. All will also list a few popular applications, which you can click on to install directly. Midway through the tab, after games and before developers, there is a Categories section with links to different software categories, such as Art and Design, Music and Audio, Science, Social, and Photo and Video (see Figure 4-7). Click on a link to open a tab listing software in that category.

Chapter 4: Installing and Updating Software   177

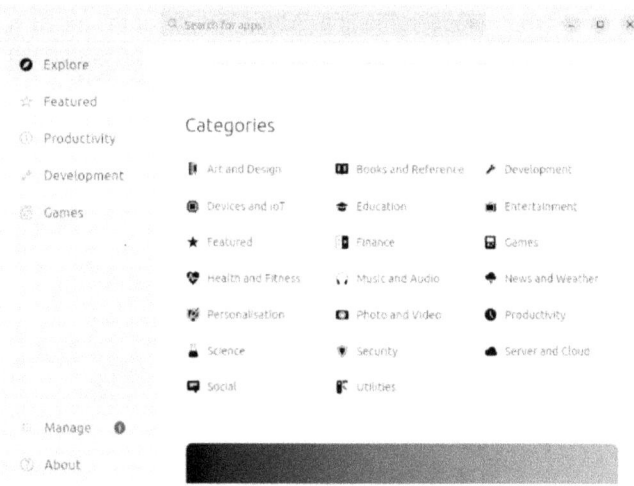

Figure 4-7: App Center Categories

Categories will allow you to further filter the selection a Sort menu, which lets you sort items by name, relevance, or size (Figure 4-8). The applications are listed as icons, which show the application's icon, name, full name, short description, and rating. Packages already installed have a checkmark displayed next to the application's name, just above the description.

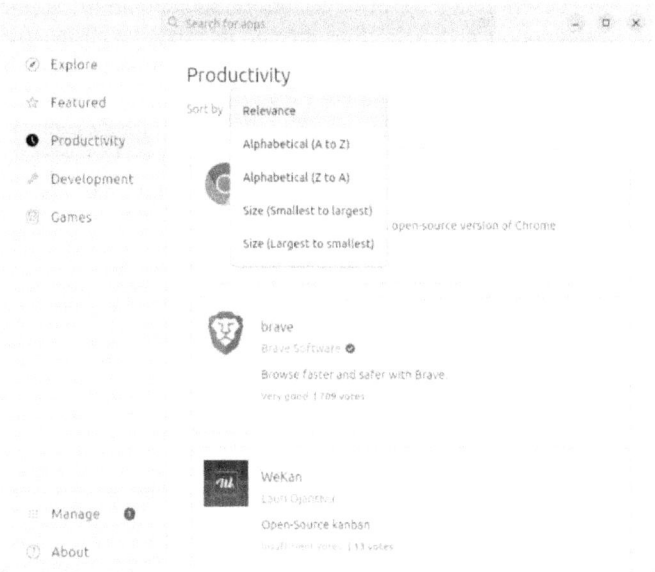

Figure 4-8: App Center category with Sort menu

To search for a package, in the search box on the header bar, enter part of the name or a term to describe the package (see Figure 4-9). Best results are listed in a menu, showing an icon and name for each applications. Applications are organized into a "Snap packages" section and a "Debian packages" section. Click on an entry to open its description page where you can perform

178 Part 1: Getting Started

possible actions such as install, remove, or launch. At the bottom of the menu is a "See all results for" link that will open a tab listing all the applications that match the search pattern. On that tab you can use menus to sort the packages, select either Snap or Debian packages, and choose packages from just a specific category.

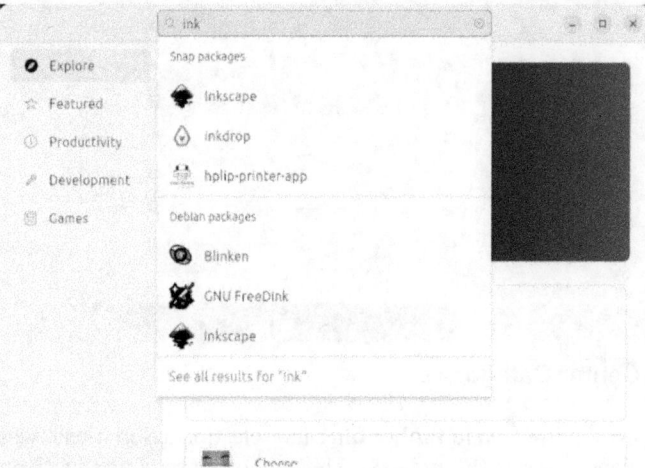

Figure 4-9: App Center, using the search box

The application's description page provides information about the application such as its rating size, version, and date published, as well as links to its related websites (see Figure 4-10). Snap applications show a Channel menu from which you can choose the Snap channel to install the application from such as stable, candidate, and edge (see Figure 4-11). The stable channel is selected by default. Uninstalled software displays an Install button to the right of the Channel menu. Further down the tab is a Gallery section showing a slideshow of images of the application. Below the Gallery is the Description section with a detailed description of the application.

Chapter 4: Installing and Updating Software   179

Figure 4-10: App Center, software descriptor page

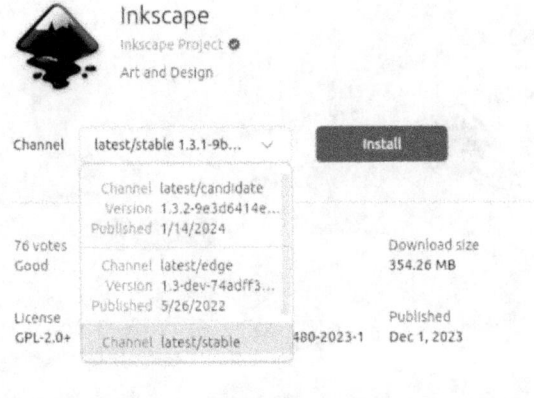

Figure 4-11: App Center, Snap package channels

Click the Install button to install the software. You are first asked to enter your password. As the software is installed, an Installing progress circle appears (see Figure 4-12). When complete, an Open button is displayed to the right, with an ellipses button below it. To later remove the application, if you wish, click on this button to display an Uninstall button, which you can click to uninstall the software (see Figure 4-13). Below the ellipses button are thumbs up and down button you can use to rate the application.

Figure 4-12: App Center, installing applications

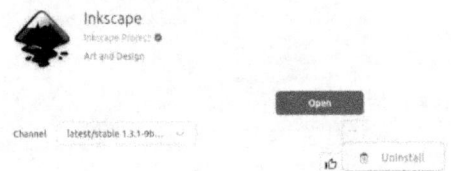

Figure 4-13: App Center, removing applications

The Manage tab lists your installed applications (see Figure 4-14). Those that have to be updated are listed in the "Updates available" section. You can update individual applications (Update button), or click the "Update all" button to update all of them at once. To check for updates, click the "Check for updates" button. An ellipses menu to the right of the Update button display entries for Open and "Show details".

The "Installed and updated" section lists all your installed Snap applications, other than those that need updating. In the search box you can enter patterns to search for applications. You can also search by name (alphabetically), size, and the recency of the last update. A checkbox lets you display Snap system applications, such as the gtk themes or the snapd server.

The application entries show the name, version installed, when last updated, and the size. You can use an Open button to the right to open the application. The ellipses menu displays a menu with a "Show details" entry you can click to open the application's description page.

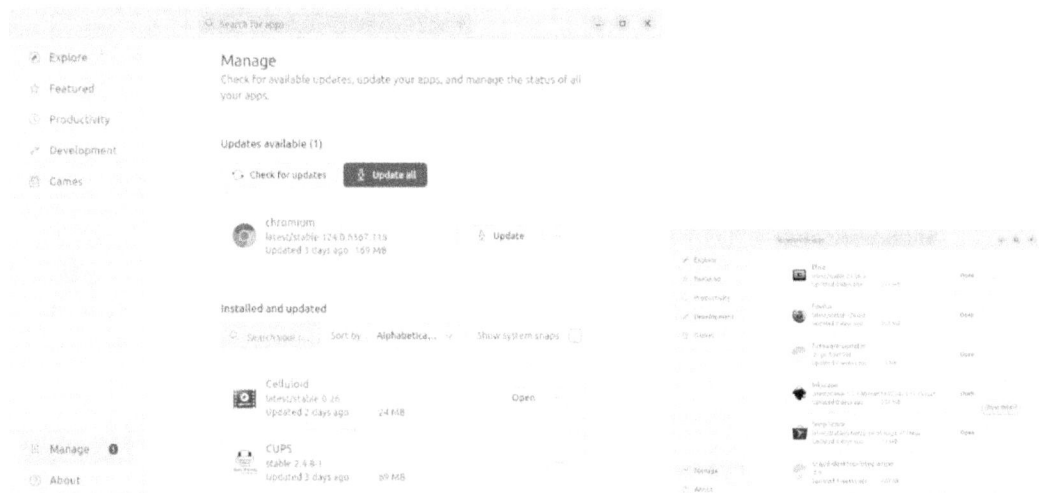

Figure 4-14: App Center, Manage tab

APT: Deb Package Management

As noted previously, Ubuntu also uses Debian packages (DEB) and the Advanced Package Tool (APT) to manage them. The App Center manages both Snap and APT package systems, whereas the Synaptic Package Manager is a front-end for APT and only manages DEB packages. GNOME Software is also a front-end for APT, but can also manage Snap packages. The command-line tools for managing DEB packages with APT are **apt** and **apt-get**.

Ubuntu APT Repositories

For Ubuntu, its APT-based software repository is organized into sections, depending on how the software is supported. Software supported directly is located in the main Ubuntu repository section. Other Linux software that is most likely compatible is placed in the Universe repository section. Many software applications, particularly multimedia applications, have potential licensing conflicts. Such applications are placed in the Multiverse repository section, which is not maintained directly by Ubuntu. Many of the popular multimedia drivers and applications, such as video and digital music, support can be obtained from the Ubuntu Multiverse sections using the same simple APT commands you use for Ubuntu-supported software. Software from the Multiverse and Universe sections are supported by package managers like the App Center and the Synaptic Package Manager, and can be installed just as easily as Ubuntu main section software. Some drivers are entirely proprietary and supplied directly by vendors. This is the case with the NVIDIA vendor-provided drivers. These drivers are placed in a restricted section, noting that there is no open source support.

Four main components or sections make up the Ubuntu APT repository: main, restricted, universe, and multiverse. These components are described in detail at:

https://help.ubuntu.com/community/Repositories/Ubuntu

To see a listing of all packages in the Ubuntu APT repository see:

https://packages.ubuntu.com

To see available repositories and their sections, see the Ubuntu Software tab on Software & Updates, which is accessible from the Applications overview.

APT Repository Components

The following repository components are included in the Ubuntu APT repository:

main: Officially supported Ubuntu software (canonical), such as the GStreamer Good plug-in.

restricted: Software commonly used and required for many applications, but not open source or freely licensed. Because they are not open source, they are not guaranteed to work.

universe: All open source Linux software not directly supported by Ubuntu such as GStreamer Bad plug-ins.

multiverse: Linux software that does not meet licensing requirements and is not considered essential. It is not guaranteed to work. For example, the GStreamer ugly package is in this repository. Check **https://ubuntu.com/licensing**.

APT Repositories

In addition to the Ubuntu APT repository, Ubuntu maintains several other APT repositories used primarily for maintenance and support for existing packages. The updates repository holds updated packages for a release. The security updates repository contains critical security package updates every system will need.

Ubuntu repository: Collection of Ubuntu-compliant software packages for releases organized into main, universe, multiverse, and restricted sections.

Updates: Updates for packages in the main repository, including main, restricted, universe, and multiverse sections.

Backports: Software under development for the next Ubuntu release, but packaged for use in the current one. Not guaranteed or fully tested. Backports access is now enabled by default.

Security updates: Critical security fixes for Ubuntu repository software.

The Backports repository provides un-finalized or development versions for new and current software. They are not guaranteed to work, but may provide needed features.

Note: Though it is possible to add the Debian Linux distribution repository, it is not advisable. Packages are designed for specific distributions. Combining them can lead to irresolvable conflicts.

APT Ubuntu Repository Configuration file: ubuntu.sources and sources.list.d

Ubuntu APT repository configuration is managed by APT using configuration files in the **/etc/apt/sources.list.d** directory. The **/etc/apt/sources.list.d/ubuntu.sources** file holds repository entries. There are two different types of files that can be used to configure repositories, the one-line style format that has a **.list** extension, and the deb822 style format that has a **.sources** extension. Ubuntu now uses a **.sources** file with the deb822 style named **ubuntu.sources**, instead of the **sources.list** file with the One-Line style uses in previous release. The file name is **ubuntu.sources**, which is located in the **/etc/apt/sources.list.d** directory. The **/etc/apt/sources.list** file used in previous release is still present, but is just contains a message referring you to the **/etc/apt/sources.list.d/ubuntu.sources** file.

Both the deb822 style and the one-line style have the same elements in their formats: type, URI, suite, components, and options. The type is the type of repository, either **deb** or **deb-src**. The URI (universal resource identifier) provides the location of the repository, such as an FTP or Web URL. The suite name is a collection of packages in a release. In Ubuntu, it consist of the release name and a qualifier, such as **noble**, **noble-updates**, or **noble-security**. The primary collection normally, for Ubuntu, has no qualifier. It is just the release name, which for Ubuntu 24.04 is **noble**. Ubuntu 22.04 LTS, the previous LTS suite, used **jammy**, **jammy-updates**, and **jammy-security**. The components can be one or more terms that identify a section in that release's repository. There can be more than one term used to specify a component, like **restricted** to specify the restricted component in the Ubuntu APT repository. The Multiverse and Universe sections are referenced as **universe** and **multiverse**.

The URI is the address of the repository, such as **http://us.archive.ubuntu.com/ubuntu**. **jammy** is the name for Ubuntu 22.04, and **noble** is the name for 24.04.

The one-line format places all the information on a single line, with the following format:

```
format    URI    suite    components
```

The entry for the Jammy main, restricted, and universe sections is shown here.

```
deb http://us.archive.ubuntu.com/ubuntu/ jammy  main restricted universe
```

The one-line style requires multiple entries for different suites, such as jammy, jammy-security, and jammy-updates.

A deb822 **.sources** file has a very different format than the older one-line **.list** file. The deb822 style uses a series of stanzas separated by empty lines. Each stanza consists of a series of fields, each on its own line. Commonly used fields are Types, URIs, Suites, and Components. The name of the field is separated by a colon from its values. If the Types, URIs, and Component fields are the same for multiple suites, you would only need one stanza in which the suites are all listed in the Suites field.

The previous one-line style example written in a deb822 style would be:

```
Types: deb
URIs: http://us.archive.ubuntu.com/ubuntu/
Suites: jammy jammy-updates jammy-backports
Components: main restricted universe multiverse
```

In Ubuntu 24.04, **noble**, there is one stanza for the noble, noble-updates, and noble-backports suites.

```
Types: deb
URIs: http://us.archive.ubuntu.com/ubuntu/
Suites: noble noble-updates noble-backports
Components: main restricted universe multiverse
```

As the security suite uses a different URI, it needs a separate stanza.

```
Types: deb
URIs: http://security.ubuntu.com/ubuntu/
Suites: noble-security
Components: main restricted universe multiverse
```

To add source files to your repository configuration, the **deb-src** type is added to the Types field. This is what the Software & Updates Ubuntu Software tab's "Source code" option does.

```
Types: deb deb-src
URIs: http://us.archive.ubuntu.com/ubuntu/
Suites: noble noble-updates noble-backports
Components: main restricted universe multiverse
```

Following the Components field are any options. Ubuntu 24.04 uses the Signed-By option to specify that APT uses the Ubuntu keys in the **ubuntu-archive-keyring.gpg** file to perform verification. Keys for packages are located in the **/usr/share/keyrings** directory.

```
Signed-By: /usr/share/keyrings/ubuntu-archive-keyring.gpg
```

The fields used for Ubuntu 24.04 are Types, URIs, Suites, Components, and Signed-By. The Ubuntu 24.04 **ubuntu.sources** file is shown here.

/etc/apt/sources.list.d/ubuntu.sources

```
Types: deb
URIs: http://us.archive.ubuntu.com/ubuntu/
Suites: noble noble-updates noble-backports
Components: main restricted universe multiverse
Signed-By: /usr/share/keyrings/ubuntu-archive-keyring.gpg

Types: deb
URIs: http://security.ubuntu.com/ubuntu/
Suites: noble-security
Components: main restricted universe multiverse
Signed-By: /usr/share/keyrings/ubuntu-archive-keyring.gpg
```

Most entries can be managed using Software & Updates. Entries can also be managed by editing the **ubuntu.sources** file with Text Editor or with an editor such as **nano**.

```
sudo nano /etc/apt/sources.list.d/ubuntu.sources
```
You could remove a stanza by placing a comment symbol, the #, at the beginning of each line in the stanza. But it is easier to simply add the Enabled field and giving it a **no** value. To re-enable the stanza, change the **no** to **yes**.

```
Enabled: no
```

New APT repositories can be added using the Software & Updates's Other Software tab. You can, though, simply add the repository entries directly. To do this, you do not have to edit the **/etc/apt/sources.list.d/ubuntu.sources** file. Editing such an important file always includes the risk of incorrectly changing the entries. Instead, new repository entries can be placed in a text file with a **.sources** extension with entries in the deb822 style in the **/etc/apt/sources.list.d** folder, which APT will read as if part of the **ubuntu.sources** file.

APT Software Repositories managed with Software & Updates

You can manage your APT repositories with the Software & Updates dialog, allowing you to enable or disable repository sections, as well as add new entries. This dialog edits the **/etc/apt/sources.list.d/ubuntu.sources** file directly. You can access Software & Updates from the Applications overview. You can also access it on the Synaptic Package Manager from the Settings menu as the Repositories entry. The Software & Updates dialog displays seven tabs: Ubuntu Software, Other Software, Updates, Authentication, Additional Drivers, Developer Options, and Ubuntu Pro (see Figure 4-15).

Figure 4-15: Software & Updates - Ubuntu software repository sections

The Ubuntu Software tab lists all the Ubuntu APT repository section entries. These include the main repository, universe, restricted, and multiverse, as well as source code. Those that are enabled will be checked. Initially, all of them, except the source code, will be enabled. You can enable or disable a repository section by checking or un-checking its entry. You can select the repository server to use from the "Download from" drop-down menu.

On the Other Software tab, you can add repositories for third-party APT software (see Figure 4-16). To add a third-party repository manually, click the Add button. This opens a dialog where you are prompted to enter the complete APT entry, but in the older one-line style, starting with the deb type, followed by the URI, suite, and components. The line is place in a **.list** file in the

/etc/apt/sources.list.d and will have a one-line style format. For a Personal Package Archives (PPA) APT repository, you would just enter the ppa: entry. Once entered, click the Add button.

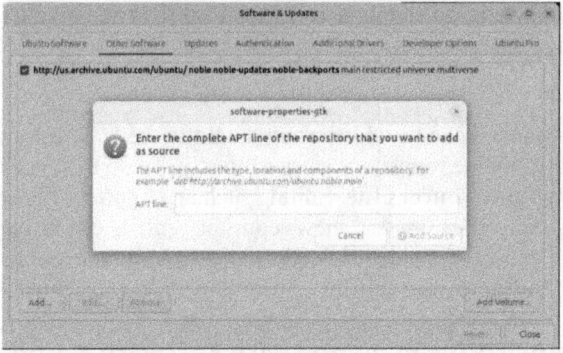

Figure 4-16: Software & Updates - Other Software configuration

The Authentication tab shows the repository software signature keys that are installed on your system (see Figure 4-17). Ubuntu requires a signature key for any package that it installs. Signature keys for all the Ubuntu repositories are installed and are listed on this tab.

Most other third party or customized APT repositories will provide a signature key file for you to download and import. You can add such keys manually from the Authentication tab. Click the "Import Key File" button to open a file browser where you can select the downloaded key file. This procedure is the same as the **apt-key add** operation. Both add keys that APT then uses to verify DEB software packages downloaded from repositories before it installs them.

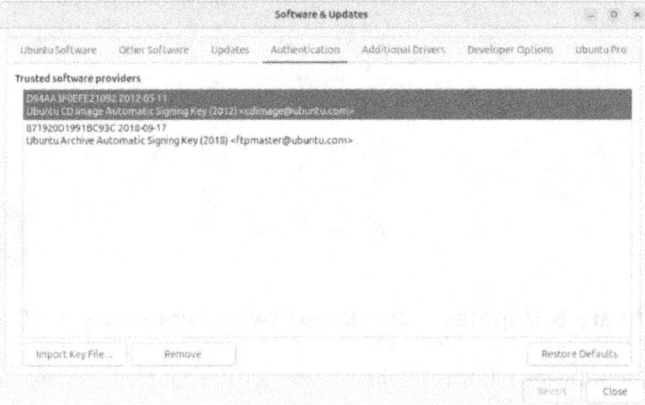

Figure 4-17: Software & Updates - Authentication, package signature keys

On the Developer Options tab, you can click the Pre-released software (noble-proposed) option to choose to receive development updates (see Figure 4-18). These are for testing and may introduce instability.

Figure 4-18: Software & Updates - Developer Options

After you have made changes, click the Close button. If you made any repository changes (Ubuntu Software and Other Software tabs) such as adding or disabling a repository, the Software & Updates tool will notify you that your software package information is out of date, displaying a Reload button. Click the Reload button to make the new repositories or components available on your package managers like the App Center and the Synaptic Package Manager. You also can reload your repository configuration by running the **sudo apt update** command or clicking the Reload button on the Synaptic Package Manager.

App Center for APT (Debian) packages

Though the App Center gives priority to Snap packages, you can also use it to also manage APT packages (see Figure 4-19). APT packages are referred to in the App Center as Debian packages. The categories with which you can browse the App Center, will only display Snap packages. To find and display APT packages, you have to perform a search. The menu of initial results will show a Snap and Debian section showing commonly installed packages. If the packages are only available as Debian packages only the Debian section is shown, and if the packages are only available as Snap packages, only the Snap section is shown. By clicking on the "See all results for" entry at the bottom of the menu, you open a results tab in which you can choose to see Snap or Debian packages. Use the "Filter by" menu to select "Snap packages" or "Debian packages".

188 Part 1: Getting Started

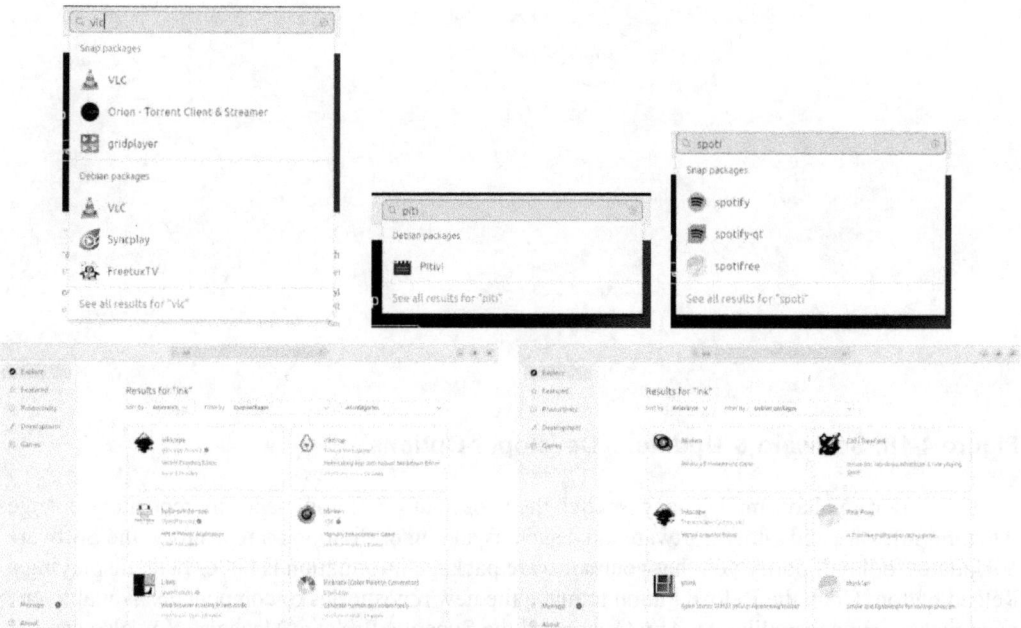

Figure 4-19: App Center, APT (DEB) package

The application page for an APT managed package will display an Install or Uninstall button (see Figure 4-20). It will list the package version, as well as a Gallery of images and a Description. There is no menu.

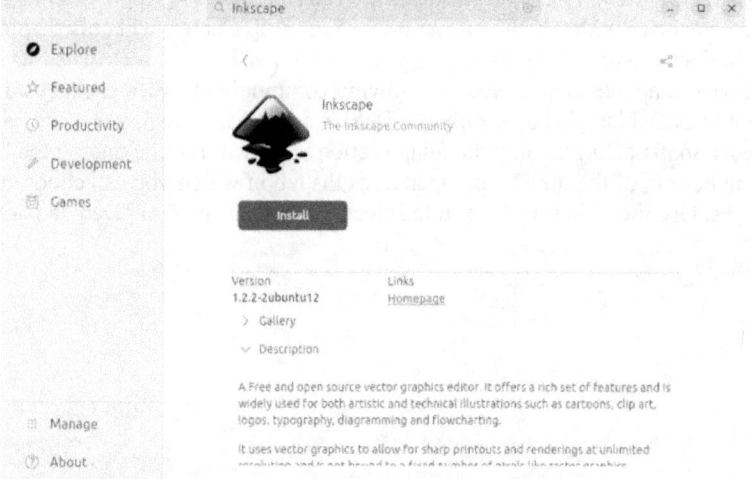

Figure 4-20: App Center, APT (DEB) package application page

If an application has both APT and Snap versions available, and you install both, you can run either of them from the Applications Overview (see Figure 4-21).

Chapter 4: Installing and Updating Software   189

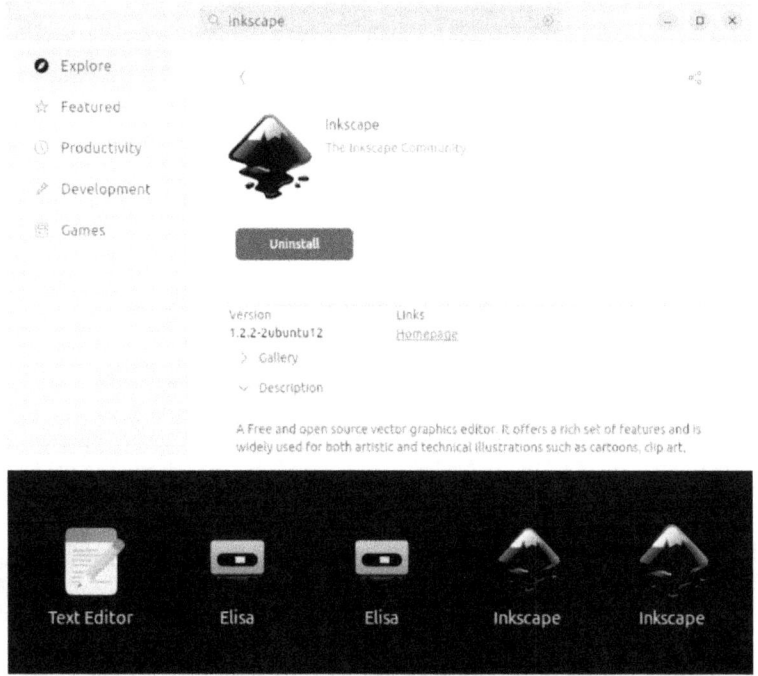

Figure 4-21: App Center, APT and Snap package versions

GNOME Software

You can install the original GNOME Software application using the App Center as a Debian package named Software, or with the Synaptic Package Manager, or the **sudo apt install** command. The name of the GNOME Software package is **gnome-software**.

```
sudo apt install gnome-software
```

Once installed, you can use it to manage Apt packages, and, if you have installed support for it, Flathub packages. The icon for it is labeled Software on the applications overview (see Figure 4-22). GNOME Software also has GNOME Other Categories section for GNOME addons, organized into three categories on the main page: codecs, fonts, and input sources (see Figure 4-23). Categories have a fully functional Show menu with a complete listing of sub-categories.

The GNOME Software Snap plugin is already installed and allows GNOME Software to manage Snap packages. Like the App Center (snap-store), for Snap packages it will display a menu on the right side of the titlebar of snap channels to install. On GNOME Software the menu item for a Snap package is labeled SNAP, whereas the menu item for a Debian package is labeled DEB. In addition, a menu item will indicate whether the package is from the Ubuntu managed repositories, or from another service such as Flathub. A menu item from the Flathub service is labeled FLATPAK.

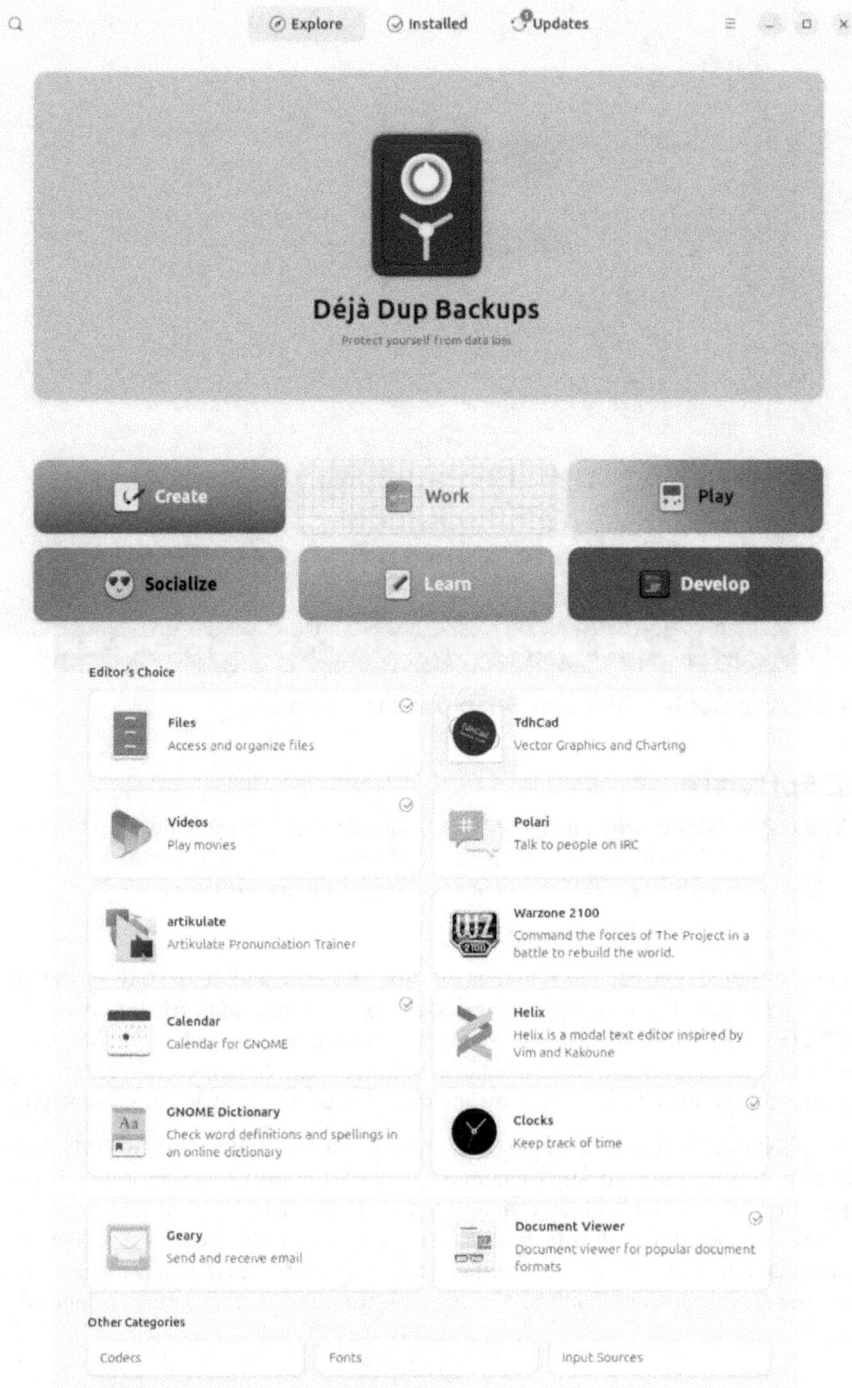

Figure 4-22: GNOME Software

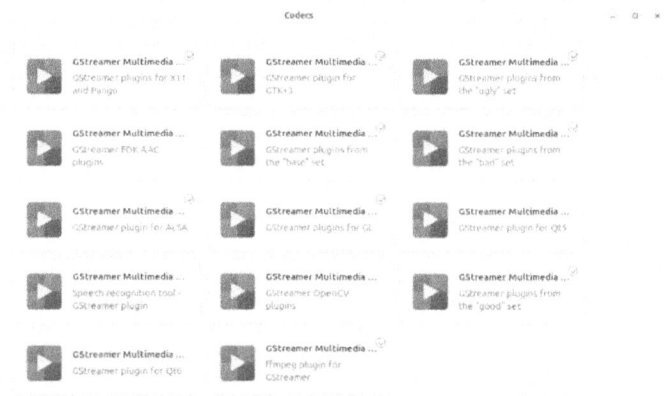

Figure 4-23: GNOME Software Addons for codecs

Synaptic Package Manager: APT only

The Synaptic Package Manager has been replaced by the App Center as the primary package manager. It is not installed by default. Synaptic is no longer supported by Ubuntu, though support is still provided by the Ubuntu community. Packages are listed by name and include supporting packages like libraries and system critical packages. Once installed, you can access the Synaptic Package Manager on the Applications overview. You can install the Synaptic Package Manager from the App Center as a Debian package, or by using the **sudo apt install** command in a terminal window.

```
sudo apt install synaptic
```

The Synaptic Package Manager is a front-end for the APT system and can only access APT repositories. It cannot manage Snap packages. Some packages are available both as Snap and APT packages. Should you install such a Snap package using the App Center and then, again, using the Synaptic Package Manager, you would have two installations of the same software application, one managed by APT and the other by Snap.

Many APT software packages will not be available from the App Center. But you can install them using the Synaptic Package Manager or the **apt** command. Many servers, such as the Vsftpd FTP server and Apache Web server, and desktops, such as Kubuntu and Xfce, are not listed by the App Center, as well as many applications in Universe and Multiverse. You will have to use the Synaptic Packages Manager or the **apt** command to install them.

The Synaptic Package Manager displays three panes: a side pane for listing software categories and buttons, a top pane for listing software packages, and a bottom pane for displaying a selected package's description. When a package is selected, the description pane also displays a Get Screenshot button. Clicking this button will download and display an image of the application if there is one. Click the Get Changelog button to display a window listing the application changes.

Buttons at the lower left of the Synaptic Package Manager window provide options for organizing and refining the list of packages shown (see Figure 4-24). Five options are available: Sections, Status, Origin, Custom Filters, Search results, and Architecture. The dialog pane above the buttons changes depending on which option you choose. Clicking the Sections button will list

192 Part 1: Getting Started

section categories for your software such as Graphics, Communications, and Development. The Status button will list options for installed and not installed software. The Origin button shows entries for different repositories and their sections, as well as those locally installed (manual or disc based installations). Custom filters lets you choose a filter to use for listing packages. You can create your own filter and use it to display selected packages. Search results will list your current and previous searches, letting you move from one to the other.

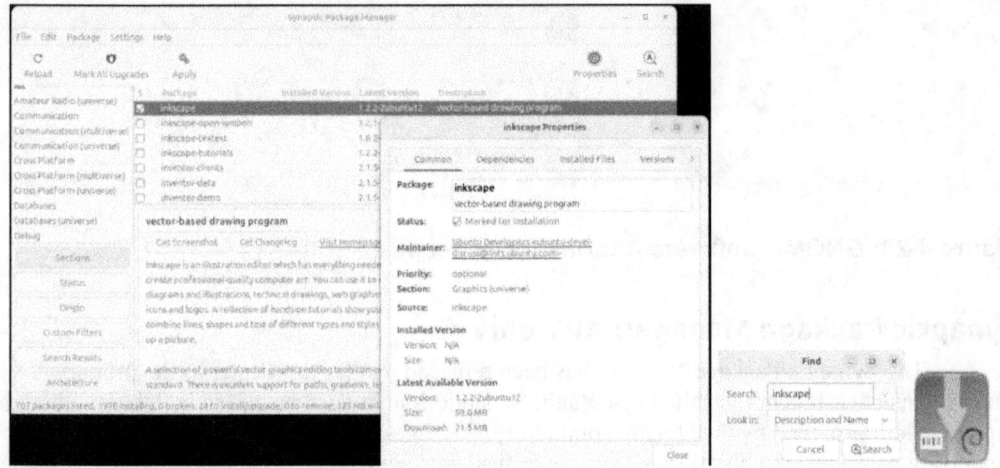

Figure 4-24: Synaptic Package Manager

The Sections option is selected by default (see Figure 4-25). You can choose to list all packages, or refine your listing using categories provided in the pane. The All entry in this pane will list all available packages. Packages are organized into categories such as Cross Platform, Communications, and Editors. Each category is subdivided by multiverse, universe, and restricted software.

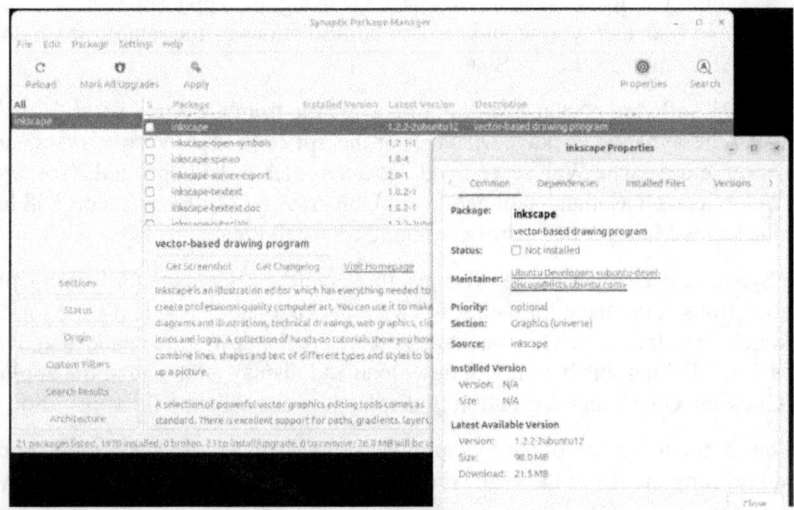

Figure 4-25: Synaptic Package Manager: Sections

To perform a search, you use the Search tool. Click the Search button on the toolbar to open a Search dialog with a text box where you can enter search terms. A pop-up menu lets you specify what features of a package to search such as the "Description and Name" feature. You can search other package features like the Name, the maintainer name (Maintainer), the package version (Version), packages it may depend on (Dependencies), or associated packages (Provided Packages). A list of searches will be displayed in Search Results. You can move back and forth between search results by clicking on the search entries in this listing.

Status entries further refine installed software as manual or as upgradeable (see Figure 4-26). Local software consists of packages you download and install manually.

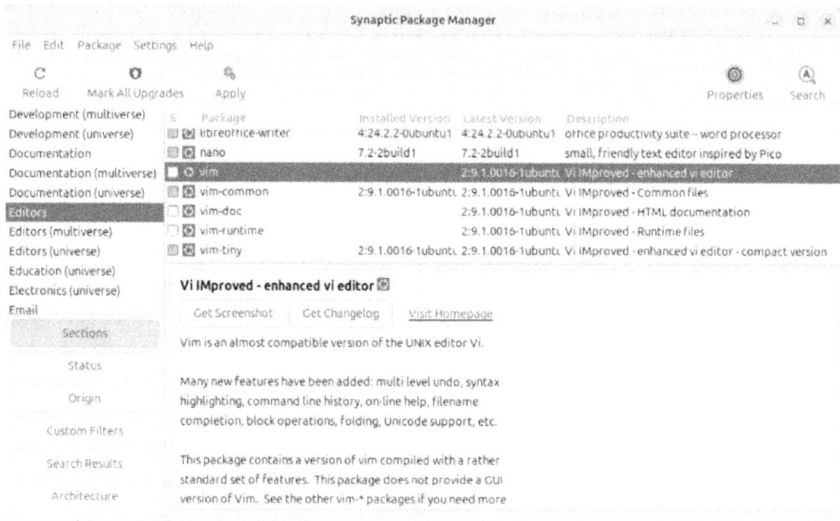

Figure 4-26: Synaptic Package Manager: Status

With the Origin options, Ubuntu-compliant repositories may further refine access according to multiverse, universe, and restricted software. A main section selects Ubuntu-supported software. The Architecture options let you select software compatible with a specified architecture, such as 64-bit or 32-bit.

Properties

To find out information about a package, select the package and click the Properties button. This opens a window with Common, Dependencies, Installed Files, Versions, and Description tabs (see Figure 4-24). The Common tab provides section, versions, and maintainer information. The Installed Files tab show you exactly what files are installed, which is useful for finding the exact location, and names for configuration files, as well as commands. The Description tab displays detailed information about the software. The Dependencies tab shows all dependent software packages needed by this software, usually libraries.

Installing packages

Before installing software, you should press the Reload button to load the most recent package lists from the active repositories

To install a package, single click on its empty checkbox or right-click on its name to display a pop-up menu and select the "Mark for installation" entry. Should any dependent packages exist, a dialog opens listing those packages. Click the Mark button in the dialog to mark those packages for installation. The package entry's checkbox will then be marked in the Synaptic Package Manager window.

Once you have selected the packages you want to install, click the Apply button on the toolbar to begin the installation process. A Summary dialog opens showing all the packages to be installed. You have the option to download the package files only. The number of packages to be installed is listed, along with the size of the download and the amount of disk space used. Click the Apply button on the Summary dialog to download and install the packages. A download window will then appear showing the progress of your package installations. You can choose to show the progress of individual packages, which opens a terminal window listing each package as it is downloaded and installed.

Once downloaded, the dialog name changes to Installing Software. You can choose to have the dialog close automatically when finished. Sometimes installation requires user input to configure the software. You will be prompted to enter the information if necessary.

When you right-click a package name, you also see options for Mark Suggested for Installation or Mark Recommended for Installation. These will mark applications that can enhance your selected software, though they are not essential. If there are no suggested or recommended packages for that application, then these entries will be grayed out.

Certain software, like desktops or office suites that require a significant number of packages, can be selected all at once using metapackages. A metapackage has configuration files that select, download, and configure the range of packages needed for such complex software. For example, the **kubuntu-desktop** meta package will install the entire Kubuntu desktop (Sections | Meta Packages (universe)).

Removing packages

To remove a package, first, locate it. Then right-click it and select the "Mark package for removal" entry. This will leave configuration files untouched. Alternatively, you can mark a package for complete removal, which will also remove any configuration files, "Mark for Complete Removal." Dependent packages will not be removed.

Once you have marked packages for removal, click the Apply button. A summary dialog displays the packages that will be removed. Click Apply to remove them.

The Synaptic Package Manager may not remove dependent packages, especially shared libraries that might be used by other applications. This means that your system could have installed packages that are never being used.

Search filters

You can further refine your search for packages by creating search filters. Select the Settings | Filters menu entry to open the Filters window. The Filters window shows two panes, a filter list on the left, and three tabs on the right: Status, Section, and Properties. To create a new filter, click the New button located just below the filter listing. Click the New Filter 1 entry in the filter list on the left pane. On the Status tab, you can refine your search criteria according to a package's status. You can search only uninstalled packages, include installed packages, include or exclude packages marked for removal, or search for those that are new in the repository. Initially, all criteria are selected. Uncheck those you do not want included in your search. The Section tab lets you include or exclude different repository sections like games, documentation, or administration. If you are looking for a game, you could choose to include just the game section, excluding everything else. On the Properties tab, you can specify patterns to search on package information such as package names, using Boolean operators to refine your search criteria. Package search criteria are entered using the two pop-up menus and the text box at the bottom of the tab, along with AND or OR Boolean operators.

Note: For KDE you can use the Discover Software Center and the Muon package manager to install and update packages (see Chapter 9).

GNOME Software for separate DEB packages

You can also use the GNOME Software (not the App Center) to perform an installation of a single DEB software package. Usually, these packages are downloaded directly from a website and have few or no dependent packages. When you right-click on a deb package, you should see the entry "Open With Software Install." Choose this entry to open GNOME Software, listing the package name, description, details (version number, size, and source), and an Install button.

Source code files

You can install source code files using **apt-get** (not **apt**). Specify the **source** operation with the package name. Packages will be downloaded and extracted.

```
sudo apt-get source mplayer
```

The **--download** option lets you just download the source package without extracting it. The **--compile** option will download, extract, compile, and package the source code into a Debian binary package, ready for installation.

With the **source** operation, no dependent packages will be downloaded. If a software packages requires any dependent packages to run, you would have to download and compile those. To obtain needed dependent files, you use the **build-dep** option. All your dependent files will be located and downloaded for you automatically.

```
sudo apt-get build-dep mplayer
```

Installing from source code requires that supporting development libraries and source code header files be installed. You can do this separately for each major development platform like GNOME, KDE, or the kernel. Alternatively, you can run the APT meta-package **build-essential** for all the Ubuntu development packages. You will have to do this only once.

```
sudo apt-get install build-essential
```

DEB Software Packages

A Debian package will automatically resolve dependencies, installing any other needed packages instead of simply reporting their absence. Packages are named with the software name, the version number, and the **.deb** extension. Check **https://www.debian.org/doc** for more information. The package filename format is as follows:

the package name

version number

distribution label and build number. Packages created specifically for Ubuntu have the ubuntu label here. Attached to it is the build number, the number of times the package was built for Ubuntu.

architecture The type of system on which the package runs, like i386 for Intel 32-bit x86 systems, or amd64 for both Intel and AMD 64-bit systems, x86_64.

package format. This is always **deb**

For example, the package name for 3dchess is 3dchess, with a version and build number 0.8.1-21, and an amd64 architecture for a 64-bit system.

```
3dchess_0.8.1-21ubuntu1_amd64.deb
```

The following package has an Ubuntu label, a package specifically created for Ubuntu that is not the same as the original Debian version (**dfsg**). In the following example, the version and build number is 2:4.15.5 The architecture is amd64 for a 64-bit system.

```
samba_2:4.15.5+dfsg-0ubuntu5_amd64.deb
```

Managing software with apt and apt-get

APT is designed to work with repositories, and will handle any dependencies for you. It uses **dpkg** to install and remove individual packages, but can also determine what dependent packages need to be installed, as well as query and download packages from repositories. Several popular tools for APT let you manage your software easily, like the App Center, the Synaptic Package Manager, GNOME Software, and Aptitude. The App Center, the Synaptic Package Manager, and GNOME Software, rely on a desktop interface like GNOME. If you are using the command line interface, you can use **apt** or **apt-get** to manage packages. Using the **apt** or **apt-get** commands on the command line you can install, update, and remove packages. Check the **apt** and **apt-get** man page for a detailed listing of **apt-get** commands (see Table 4-3). The **apt** command is a new version of **apt-get** with fewer options. For example, the **apt-get** command has the **check** option to check for broken dependencies. Older systems may want to continue using **apt-get**, especially if the command is used in customized system scripts. For basic operations, such as upgrading, installing, or removing packages, you would use **apt** instead.

```
apt-get command package

apt command package
```

The **apt** and **apt-get** commands usually take two arguments: the command to perform and the name of the package. Other APT package tools follow the same format. The command is a term such as **install** for installing packages or **remove** to uninstall a package. You only need to specify the software name, not the package's full filename. APT will determine that. To install the MPlayer package you would use:

```
sudo apt install mplayer
```

To make sure that **apt** or **apt-get** has current repository information, use the **update** command.

```
sudo apt update
```

To remove packages, you use the **remove** command.

```
sudo apt remove mplayer
```

Command	Description
update	Download and resynchronize the package listing of available and updated packages for APT supported repositories. APT repositories updated are those specified in **/etc/apt/sources.list.d/ubuntu.sources**
upgrade	Update packages, install new versions of installed packages if available.
install	Install a specific package, using its package name, not full package filename.
remove	Remove a software package from your system.
source	Download and extract a source code package
check	Check for broken dependencies (**apt-get** command)
clean	Removes the downloaded packages held in the repository cache on your system. Used to free up disk space (**apt-get** command)

Table 4-3: apt-get commands

You can use the **-s** option to check the remove or install first, especially to check whether any dependency problems exist. For remove operations, you can use **-s** to find out first what dependent packages will also be removed.

```
sudo apt-get remove -s mplayer
```

The **apt-get** and **apt** commands can be helpful if your X Windows System server ever fails (your display driver). For example, if you installed a restricted vendor display driver, and then your desktop fails to start, you can start up in the recovery mode, start the root shell, and use **apt** or **apt-get** to remove the restricted display driver. Your former X open source display drivers would be restored automatically. The following would remove the NVIDIA restricted display driver.

```
sudo apt-get remove nvidia*
```

A complete log of all install, remove, and update operations are kept in the **/var/log/dpkg.log** file. You can consult this file to find out exactly what files were installed or removed.

Configuration for APT is held in the **/etc/apt/sources.list.d** folder. Here the **ubuntu.sources** file lists the distribution repositories from where packages are installed. Source lists for additional third-party repositories are also kept in the /**etc/apt/sources.list.d** folder. GPG (GNU Privacy Guard) database files hold validation keys for those repositories. Specific options for **apt-get** can be found in an /**etc/apt/apt.conf** file or in various files located in the /**etc/apt/apt.conf.d** folder.

Updating packages (Upgrading) with apt

The **apt** tool also lets you update your entire system at once. The terms **update** and **upgrade** are used differently from other software tools. In **apt**, the **update** command just updates your package listing, checking for packages that may need to install newer versions, but not installing those versions. Technically, it updates the package list that APT uses to determine what packages need to be updated. The term **upgrade** is used to denote the actual update of a software package. A new version is downloaded and installed. What is referred to as updating by **apt**, other package managers refer to as obtaining the list of software packages to be updated (the reload operation). In **apt**, upgrading is what other package managers refer to as performing updates.

Note: The terms **update** and **upgrade** can be confusing when used with **apt**. The update operation updates the Apt package list only, whereas an upgrade actually downloads and installs updated packages.

Upgrading is a simple matter of using the **upgrade** command. With no package specified, using **apt** with the **upgrade** command will update your entire system. Add the **-u** option to list packages as they are updated. First, make sure your repository information (package list) is up to date with the **update** command, then issue the **upgrade** command.

```
sudo apt update
sudo apt -u upgrade
```

Command Line Search and Information: dpkg-query and apt-cache tools

The **dpkg-query** command lets you list detailed information about your packages. It operates on the command line (terminal window). Use **dpkg-query** with the **-l** option to list all your packages.

```
dpkg-query -l
```

The **dpkg** command can operate as a front end for **dpkg-query**, detecting its options to perform the appropriate task. The preceding command could also be run as:

```
dpkg -l
```

Listing a particular package requires and exact match on the package name unless you use pattern matching operators. The following command lists the **samba** package.

```
dpkg-query -l samba
```

A pattern matching operator, such as *, placed after a pattern will display any packages beginning with the specified pattern. The pattern with its operators needs to be placed in single quotation marks to prevent an attempt by the shell to use the pattern to match on filenames in your current folder. The following example finds all packages beginning with the pattern "samba". This would include packages with names such as **samba-client** and **samba-common**.

```
dpkg-query -l 'samba*'
```

You can further refine the results by using **grep** to perform an additional search. The following operation first outputs all packages beginning with **samba**, and from those results, the **grep** operations lists only those with the pattern "common" in their name, such as **samba-common**.

```
dpkg -l 'samba*' | grep 'common'
```

Use the **-L** option to list the files that a package has installed.

```
dpkg-query -L samba
```

To see the status information about a package, including its dependencies and configuration files, use the **-s** option. Fields will include Status, Section, Architecture, Version, Depends (dependent packages), Suggests, Conflicts (conflicting packages), and Conffiles (configuration files).

```
dpkg-query -s samba
```

The status information will also provide suggested dependencies. These are packages not installed, but likely to be used. For the samba package, the **chrony** time server package is suggested.

```
dpkg-query -s  samba | grep Suggests
```

Use the **-S** option to determine to which package a particular file belongs to.

```
dpkg-query -S  filename
```

You can also obtain information with the **apt-cache** tool. Use the search command with **apt-cache** to perform a search.

```
apt-cache search samba
```

To find dependencies for a particular package, use the **depends** command.

```
apt-cache depends samba
```

To display the package information, use the **show** command.

```
apt-cache show samba
```

Note: If you have installed the Aptitude software manager, you can use the aptitude command with the search and show options to find and display information about packages.

Managing non-repository packages with dpkg

You can use **dpkg** to install a software package you have already downloaded directly, instead of with an APT enabled software tools like **apt-get**, the App Center, or the Synaptic Package Manager. In this case, you are not installing from a repository. Instead, you have manually downloaded the package file from a Web or FTP site to a folder on your system. Such a situation would be rare, reserved for software not available on the Ubuntu repository or any APT enabled repository. Keep in mind that most software is already on your Ubuntu or APT enabled repositories. Check there first for the software package before performing a direct download and installing with **dpkg**. The **dpkg** configuration files are located in the **/etc/dpkg** folder. Configuration is held in the **dpkg.cfg** file. See the **dpkg** man page for a detailed listing of options.

One situation, for which you would use **dpkg**, is for packages you have built yourself, like packages you created when converting a package in another format to a Debian package (DEB). This is the case when converting an RPM package (Red Hat Package Manager) to a Debian package format.

For **dpkg**, you use the **-i** option to install a package and **-r** to remove it.

```
sudo dpkg -i package.deb
```

The major failing for **dpkg** is that it provides no dependency support. It will inform you of needed dependencies, but you will have to install them separately. **dpkg** installs only the specified package. It is useful for packages that have no dependencies.

You use the **-I** option to obtain package information directly from the DEB package file.

```
sudo dpkg -I package.deb
```

To remove a package, you use the **-r** option with the package software name. You do not need version or extension information like **.386** or **.deb**. With **dpkg** when removing a package with dependencies, you first have to remove all its dependencies manually. You will not be able to uninstall the package until you do this. Configuration files are not removed.

```
sudo dpkg -r packagename
```

If you install a package that requires dependencies, and then fail to install these dependencies, your install database will be marked as having broken packages. In this case, APT will not allow new packages to be installed until the broken packages are fixed. You can enter the **apt-get** command with the **-f** and install options to fix all broken packages at once.

```
sudo apt-get -f install
```

Using packages with other software formats

You can convert software packages in other software formats into DEB packages that can then be installed on Ubuntu. To do this you use the **alien** tool, which can convert several different kinds of formats such as RPM and even TGZ (**.tgz**). You use the **--to-deb** option to convert to a DEB package format that Ubuntu can then install. The **--scripts** option attempts also to convert any pre or post install configuration scripts.

```
alien --scripts --to-deb package.rpm
```

Once you have generated the **.deb** package, you can use **dpkg** to install it.

Updating Ubuntu

New updates are continually being prepared for particular software packages as well as system components. These are posted as updates you can download from software repositories and install on your system. These include new versions of applications, servers, and the kernel. Such updates may range from single software packages to whole components. When updates become available, a message appears on your desktop.

Updating Snaps

Snap packages (snaps) are updated automatically by the **snapd** daemon, four times a day (every six hours). You can manually update your snaps with the **snap refresh** command. You can to this for an individual package or for all snaps.

```
sudo snap refresh
sudo snap refresh skype
```

See the Snapcraft update documentation for more details.

```
https://snapcraft.io/docs/keeping-snaps-up-to-date
```

With the **--time** option you can check the time of the last update and when the next one will take place.

```
snap refresh --time
```

To see the list of packages updated with the last refresh, use the **snap changes** command.

```
snap changes
```

The listing will show the number of the package change ID (ID), its status (Status), the time of its revision (Spawn), when it was available (Ready), and a short description of the update including the name of the application affected (Summary).

```
richard@richard-laptop:~$ snap changes
ID   Status  Spawn               Ready               Summary
33   Done    today at 11:37 PDT  today at 11:38 PDT  Auto-refresh snap "skype"
```

To see the changes performed for a particular software package update use the **snap change** command with the change ID of the update.

```
richard@richard-laptop:~$ snap change 33
Status  Spawn               Ready               Summary
Done    today at 11:37 PDT  today at 11:37 PDT  Ensure prerequisites for "skype"
are available
Done    today at 11:37 PDT  today at 11:37 PDT  Download snap "skype" (128) from
channel "latest/stable"
Done    today at 11:37 PDT  today at 11:37 PDT  Fetch and check assertions for
snap "skype" (128)
Done    today at 11:37 PDT  today at 11:37 PDT  Mount snap "skype" (128)
Done    today at 11:37 PDT  today at 11:37 PDT  Run pre-refresh hook of "skype"
snap if present
Done    today at 11:37 PDT  today at 11:37 PDT  Stop snap "skype" services
Done    today at 11:37 PDT  today at 11:37 PDT  Remove aliases for snap "skype"
Done    today at 11:37 PDT  today at 11:37 PDT  Make current revision for snap
"skype" unavailable
Done    today at 11:37 PDT  today at 11:37 PDT  Copy snap "skype" data
Done    today at 11:37 PDT  today at 11:37 PDT  Setup snap "skype" (128) security
profiles
Done    today at 11:37 PDT  today at 11:37 PDT  Make snap "skype" (128) available
to the system
Done    today at 11:37 PDT  today at 11:37 PDT  Automatically connect eligible
plugs and slots of snap "skype"
Done    today at 11:37 PDT  today at 11:38 PDT  Set automatic aliases for snap
"skype"
Done    today at 11:37 PDT  today at 11:38 PDT  Setup snap "skype" aliases
Done    today at 11:37 PDT  today at 11:38 PDT  Run post-refresh hook of "skype"
snap if present
Done    today at 11:37 PDT  today at 11:38 PDT  Start snap "skype" (128) services
Done    today at 11:37 PDT  today at 11:38 PDT  Clean up "skype" (128) install
Done    today at 11:37 PDT  today at 11:38 PDT  Run configure hook of "skype"
snap if present
Done    today at 11:37 PDT  today at 11:38 PDT  Run health check of "skype" snap
```

You can configure snap updates by adjusting the time, suspending updates, and setting a limit on how many package revisions you want to keep. Use the **snap set system** command with various options to configure snap updates. The **refresh.timer** option lets you specify times for updates and how many you want performed. The time is specified by the Snap timer string format (**https://snapcraft.io/docs/timer-string-format**). Use the dash to indicate a range. The following first entry updates only on Monday and Friday. The second entry updates Tuesday through Thursday.

```
sudo snap set system refresh.timer=mon,fri
sudo snap set system refresh.timer=tue-thu
```

Use the **refresh.hold** option to delay updates to a specified time. The **time-metered** option pauses updates, and the **refresh.retrain** option sets the number of stored revisions. The default is 3, and the maximum allowed is 20.

```
sudo snap set system refresh.retrain=4
```

Updating Ubuntu APT software with Software Updater

Updating your APT software on your Ubuntu system is a simple procedure, using Software Updater, which provides a graphical update interface for APT. The Software Updater icon appears on the Dock when updates are available. The Software Updater then displays a simple dialog that shows the amount to be downloaded with "Remind Me Later" and "Install Now" buttons (see Figure 4-27). The Settings button opens the Software & Update dialog to the Updates dialog where you can configure updates (see Figure 4-32). You can also manually update by starting the Software Updater from the Applications overview.

Software Updater will also invoke the **snapd** daemon to update your Snap packages. It does not update them directly. The Software Updater interface only explicitly manages APT packages.

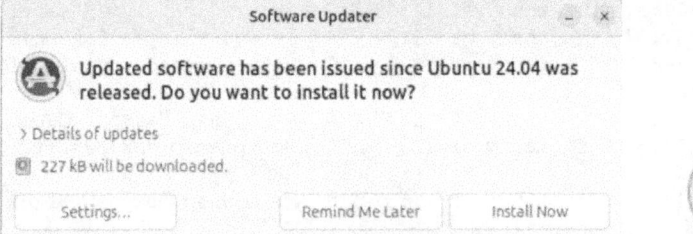

Figure 4-27: Software Updater with selected packages

To see actual packages to be updated, click the "Details of updates" arrow. Packages are organized into application categories such as Ubuntu base for the Ubuntu desktop and Linux OS packages, Firefox for Firefox updates, and LibreOffice for office updates. You can expand these to individual packages. The checkboxes for each entry lets you de-select any particular packages you do not want to update (see Figure 4-28). All the APT-compatible repositories that are configured on your system will be checked for updates.

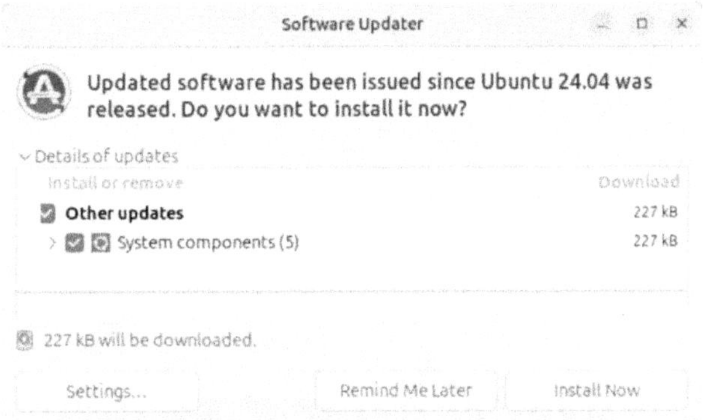

Chapter 4: Installing and Updating Software   **203**

Figure 4-28: Details of updates

To see a detailed description of a particular update, select the update and then click the "Technical description" arrow (see Figure 4-29). The Technical description section displays information about the software, and the Changes and Versions sections lists the changes to be made by the update.

Click the Install Now button to start updating. The packages will be downloaded from their appropriate repository. Once downloaded, the packages are updated.

Figure 4-29: Details of updates, Technical description

When downloading and installing, a dialog appears showing the download and install progress (see Figure 4-30). You can choose to show progress for individual files. A window will open up that lists each file and its progress. Once downloaded, the updates are installed. Click the Details arrow to see install messages for particular software packages.

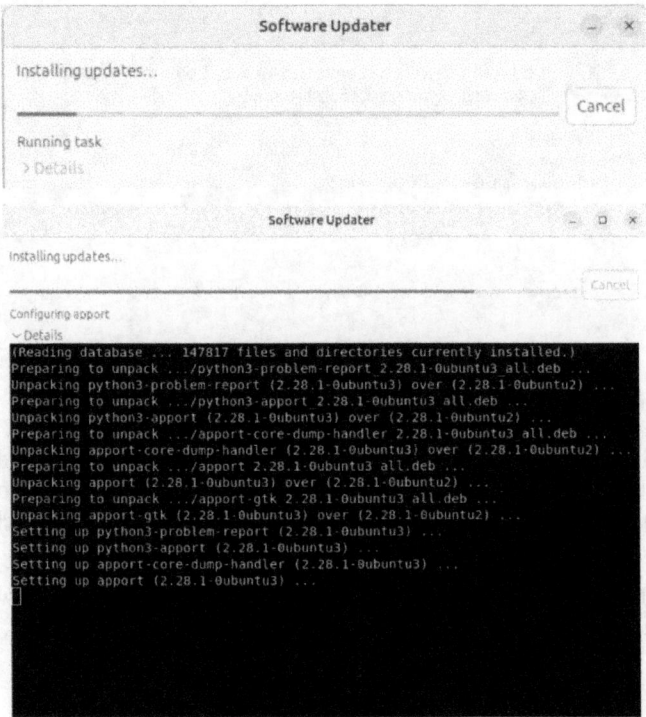

Figure 4-30: Downloading updates

When the update completes, Software updater will display a message saying that your system is up-to-date. If a critical package was installed such as a new kernel, you will be prompted to restart your system. You can restart now or later (see Figure 4-31).

Figure 4-31: Downloaded updates

You can configure Software Updater using the dconf editor. The Software Updater keys are located at apps | update-manager. There are keys to auto-close the install window, check for distribution upgrades, show details and versions, and set the window dimensions.

Configuring Updates with Software & Updates

The Updates tab in Software & Updates lets you configure how updates are managed (see Figure 4-32). Snap packages are updated automatically, which is a feature of the Snap system. You do not configure their updates. For packages that are not installed by Snap, which includes many of the Ubuntu main, universe, and multiverse packages, you can configure updates. Keep in mind that the options listed on this tab have no effect on Snap updates.

Figure 4-32: Software & Updates Update configuration

From the menu labeled "For other packages, subscribe to:" you can choose All updates, security and recommended updates, and security updates only (noble-security). The "All updates" entry is already selected. Your system is already configured to check for updates automatically on a daily basis. For packages not installed by Snap, you can opt not to check for updates by choosing never from the "Automatically check for updates" menu. You also have options for how security updates are handled. You can download and install any security updates automatically, without confirmation. You can download them and install them later. Or you can just be notified of available security updates, and then choose to install them when you want. For all other updates you can adjust when you want to be notified of updates (immediately, weekly, or every two weeks). On this tab, you also can choose what Ubuntu releases to be notified of: the long term support (LTS) releases only, all releases, or none.

The UbuntuPro tab lets you extend Ubuntu security updates for your Main and Universe repository packages to 2034, and it lets you use the Canonical Livepatch service, which allows you to install security updates that do not require a restart immediately (see Figure 4-33). You will need a Canonical account to use it. When turned on, you can click on the Livepatch menu on the top bar to see the current status and access the Livepatch settings directly.

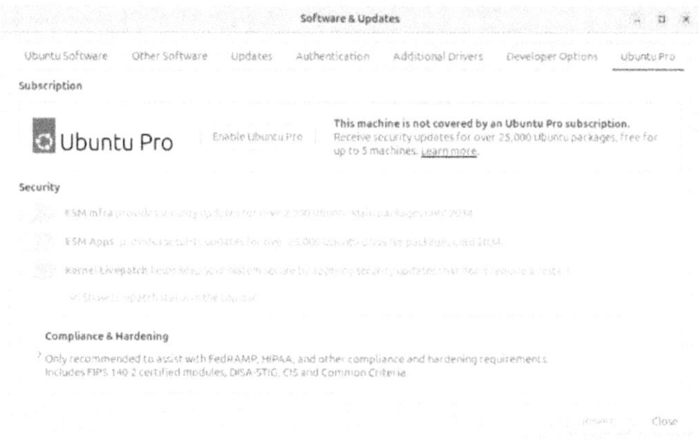

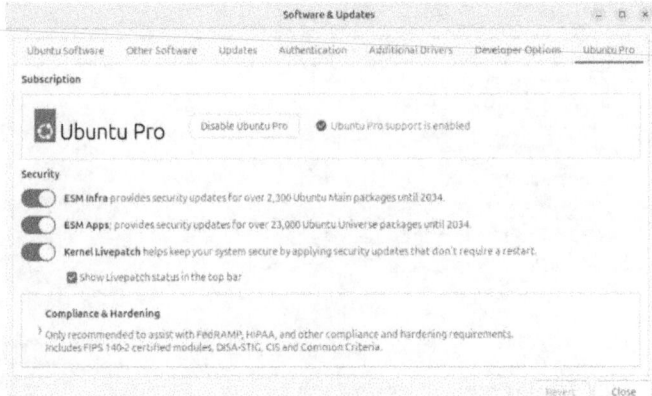

Figure 4-33: Software & Updates - Ubuntu Pro (Livepatch)

Firmware Updater

With the Firmware Updater utility you can update the firmware for your devices directly (see Figure 4-34). A sidebar lists tabs for your hardware firmware. The UEFI entry is your motherboard. You may have others for hard disks and wireless devices. Each tab shows the current version and information about the firmware. The All Versions button shows your current version, with detailed information about the update. A Reinstall button lets you reinstall the update. If there was no update, just the current version information is provided. If previous updates were installed, there will be an "Older Versions" link at the bottom you can click to list the previous updates. They will have a Downgrade button you can click should you need to reinstall a previous version for some reason.

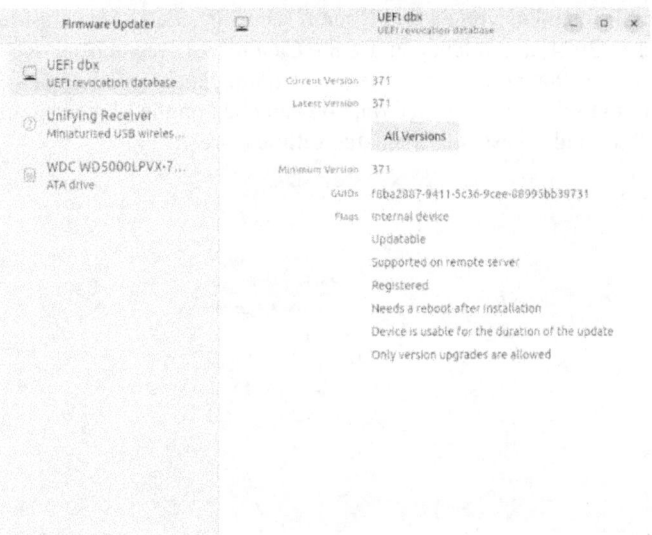

Figure 4-34: Firmware Updater

Flatpak

Flatpak is an open source alternative to Snap. A Flatpak package installs its own set of supporting libraries that can be kept up to date without affecting those on your system, much like Snap does. In effect, Flatpak packages run inside their own environment, separate from your system. These include popular applications such as VLC, Spotify, Bookworm, Krita, Steam, and Blender. These applications are downloaded from the Flathub repository. Some applications, such as Bookworm, are only available as Flatpak packages.

You install the **flatpak** package with the **sudo apt install** command or from the Synaptic Package Manager.

```
sudo apt install flatpak
```

With the GNOME Software Flatpak plugin (**gnome-software-plugin-flatpak**), you can also manage Flatpak packages. You will have to install the plugin. You can install the plugin from the GNOME Software page on Software, or from a terminal window with a shell command. From a terminal window use the following.

```
sudo apt install gnome-software-plugin-flatpak
```

You will also have to add the **flathub** repository.

```
flatpak remote-add flathub https://dl.flathub.org/repo/flathub.flatpakrepo
```

Restart your system to load the repository.

For Flatpak packages, GNOME Software will list the **dl.flathub.org** site as the source on the application description page. Should there also be an APT version of an application available, a Flathub menu is displayed on the right side of the titlebar showing the Flatpak application and the DEB (Ubuntu) application (see Figure 4-35). Choose the one you want to install. Should GNOME Software be configured to support Snap, APT, and Flatpak, applications available on all of them, such as VLC, will list separate entries for each.

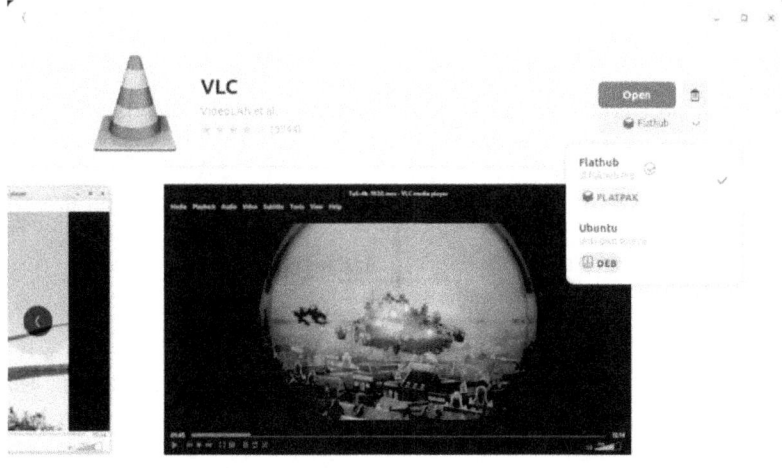

Figure 4-35: GNOME Software Flatpak

Installing and Running Windows Software on Linux: Wine

Wine is a Windows compatibility layer that will allow you to run many Windows applications natively on Linux. The actual Windows operating system is not required. Windows applications will run as if they were Linux applications, able to access the entire Linux file system and use Linux-connected devices. Applications that are heavily driver-dependent, like graphic intensive games, may not run. Others that do not rely on any specialized drivers, may run very well, including Photoshop and Microsoft Office. For some applications, you may also need to copy over specific Windows dynamic link libraries (DLLs) from a working Windows system to your Wine Windows system32 or system folder.

You can install the current version of Wine on your system with the App Center as a Debian package, or the Synaptic Package Manager. The **ttf-mscorefonts-installer** for the Microsoft core fonts will also be installed. You will be prompted to accept the Microsoft end user agreement for using those fonts. Should you have difficulty with it, you can download an older version that may be more compatible from the WineHQ Ubuntu repository. See **https://wiki.winehq.org/Ubuntu** for detailed instructions.

Wine should work on both **.exe** and **.msi** files. You may have to make them executable by checking the file's Properties dialog Permissions tab's Execute checkbox. If an **.msi** file cannot be run, you may have to use the **msiexec** command with the **/a** option.

```
msiexec /a winprogram.msi
```

The Wine applications include Wine configuration (**winecfg**), the Wine software uninstaller, and Wine file browser, as well as Winetricks and notepad. The Winetricks application can be run directly on you Ubuntu desktop and provides an easy way to install compatible Windows applications.

For many windows applications, including **winecfg**, you will need to install the Wine Geckos package. You can download it directly from the WineHQ website at **https://wiki.winehq.org/Gecko**. Once installed you can use the **wine msiexec** command to install it.

```
wine msiexec wine-gecko-2.47.1-x86_64
```

To set up Wine, start the Wine Configuration tool (enter the **sudo winecfg** command in a terminal window) to open a window with tabs for Applications, Libraries (DLL selection), Audio (sound drivers), Drives, Desktop Integration, and Graphics. On the Applications tab, you can select the version of Windows an application is designed for. The Drives tab lists your detected partitions, as well as your Windows-emulated drives, such as drive C. The C: drive is actually just a folder, **.wine/drive_c**, not a partition of a fixed size. Your actual Linux file system will be listed as the Z drive.

```
sudo winecfg
```

Once configured, Wine will set up a **.wine** folder on the user's home folder (the folder is hidden, enable Show Hidden Files in the file manager View menu to display it). Within that folder will be the **drive_c** folder, which functions as the C: drive that holds your Windows system files and program files in the Windows and Program File subfolders. The System and System32 directories are located in the Windows folder. This is where you would place any needed DLL files.

The Program Files folder holds your installed Windows programs, just as they would be installed on a Windows Program Files folder.

You can open a terminal window and run the **wine** command with a Windows application as an argument.

```
$ wine winprogram
```

The following starts the MS Paint application on your Ubuntu desktop using Wine.

```
wine mspaint
```

To run the Windows explorer file manager for your Wine Window files, enter the following.

```
wine explorer
```

The command for the Wine task manager is **taskmgr** and for the registry editor it is **regedit**. The Wine task manager lets you search for and run installed applications.

```
wine taskmgr
wine regedit
```

An easy way to install and manage Window applications on Wine is to use Winetricks. You can start Winetricks directly from the Ubuntu applications overview. A "What do you want to do" dialog lets you choose different task such as install an application or game. To install an application, click the "Install an application" entry and then click the OK button to display a list of possible compatible Windows applications. Some you can download and install directly. A few require an application DVD or CD. Some will require a manual download. Once installed you can then return to the wineprefix dialog. The "Select the default wineprefix" option lets you perform system tasks such as running **winecfg**, the explorer file manager, and install fonts. When Wine installs a Windows application, it may display several install messages. You can turn this off by choosing "Enable silent install" on the "What do you want to do" dialog. The term wineprefix in the Winetricks titebar refers to the folder Wine is installed on.

Alternatively, you can use the commercial Windows compatibility layer called Crossover Office. This is a commercial product tested to run certain applications like Microsoft Office. Check **https://www.codeweavers.com** for more details. Crossover Office is based on Wine, which CodeWeavers supports directly.

Part 2: Applications

Office Suites, Editors, and E-mail
Multimedia and Graphics
Internet Applications

ubuntu

5. Office Suites, Editors, and E-mail

LibreOffice

Calligra

GNOME Office Applications

Running Microsoft Office on Linux

Document Viewers (PostScript, PDF, and DVI)

E-book readers

GNOME Notes, Clocks, and Weather

Editors

Database Management Systems

Mail Clients: Evolution, Thunderbird, Kmail

Command Line Mail Clients

Newsreaders

Several office suites are now available for Ubuntu (see Table 5-1). These include professional-level word processors, presentation managers, drawing tools, and spreadsheets. The freely available versions are described in this chapter. LibreOffice is currently the primary office suite supported by Ubuntu. Calligra is an office suite designed for use with KDE. CodeWeavers CrossOver Office provides reliable support for running Microsoft Office Windows applications directly on Linux. You can also download the Apache OpenOffice suite (originally, Oracle/StarOffice).

Web Site	Description
https://www.libreoffice.org	LibreOffice open source office suite
https://calligra.org	Calligra Suite, for KDE
https://www.codeweavers.com	CrossOver Office (MICROSOFT Office support)
https://www.openoffice.org	Apache OpenOffice
https://www.scribus.net	Scribus desktop publishing tool

Table 5-1: Linux Office Suites

Several database management systems are also available for Linux, which include high-powered, commercial-level database management systems, such as Oracle and IBM's DB2. Most of the database management systems available for Linux are designed to support large relational databases. Ubuntu includes both MySQL and PostgreSQL open source databases in its distribution, which can support smaller databases. Various database management systems available to run under Linux are listed in Table 5-8 later in this chapter.

Linux also provides several text editors that range from simple text editors for simple notes to editors with more complex features such as spell-checkers, buffers, or complex pattern matching. All generate character text files and can be used to edit any Linux text files. Text editors are often used in system administration tasks to change or add entries in Linux configuration files found in the **/etc** folder or a user's initialization or application configuration files located in a user's home folder (dot files). You can also use a text editor to work on source code files for any of the programming languages or shell program scripts.

Ubuntu also supports several E-book readers. Some such as Calibre, Foliate, FBReader run natively on Linux.

Ubuntu provides full scale database management system such as MariaDB and MySQL, as well a smaller database systems such as LibreOffice Base.

Ubuntu also provides a full range of email clients, including Thunderbird, Evolution, and Kmail email applications, along with the command line clients **mailx** and **mutt**. Newsreaders are also provided such as Pan, tin, and slrn, as well as News Transport Agents such as INN, Leafnode, and Papercut.

LibreOffice

LibreOffice is a fully integrated suite of office applications developed as an open source project and freely distributed to all. It is the primary office suite for Ubuntu. LibreOffice applications are accessible from the Applications overview. There is also a default dock item for

LibreOffice Writer. LibreOffice is the open source and freely available office suite derived originally from OpenOffice. LibreOffice is supported by the Document Foundation, which was established after Oracle's acquisition of Sun, the main developer for Open Office. LibreOffice is now the primary open source office software for Linux. Oracle retains control of all the original OpenOffice software and does not cooperate with any LibreOffice development. LibreOffice has replaced OpenOffice as the default Office software for most Linux distributions.

LibreOffice includes word processing, spreadsheet, presentation, and drawing applications (see Table 5-2). Versions of LibreOffice exist for Linux, Windows, and Mac OS. You can obtain information such as online manuals and FAQs as well as current versions from the LibreOffice website at **https://www.libreoffice.org**. The LibreOffice suite of applications is installed as part of the Ubuntu Desktop installation. Ubuntu 24.04 installs LibreOffice 24.2. Check its release notes for more information.

https://wiki.documentfoundation.org/ReleaseNotes/24.2

Application	Description
Calc (Spreadsheet)	LibreOffice spreadsheet
Draw (Drawing)	LibreOffice drawing application
Writer (Word Processing)	LibreOffice word processor
Math (Formula)	LibreOffice mathematical formula composer
Impress (Presentation)	LibreOffice presentation manager
Base (Database)	Database front end for accessing and managing a variety of different databases.

Table 5-2: LibreOffice Applications

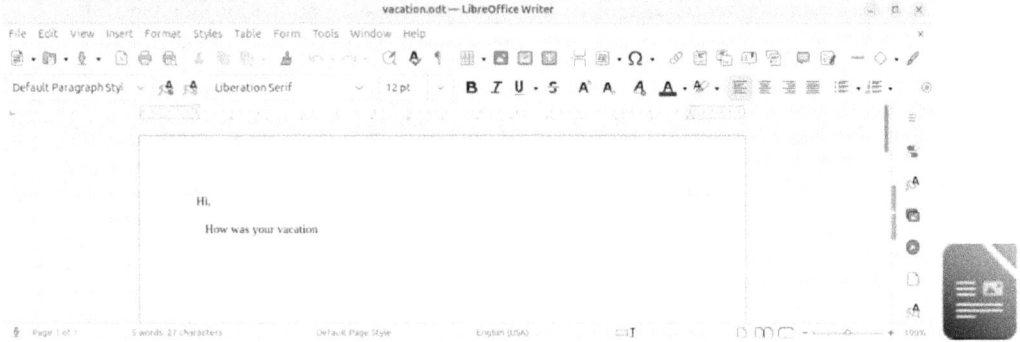

Figure 5-1: LibreOffice Writer word processor

LibreOffice is an integrated suite of applications. You can open the writer, spreadsheet, or presentation application directly. The LibreOffice Writer word processor supports standard word processing features, such as cut and paste, spell-checker, and text formatting, as well as paragraph styles (see Figure 5-1). Context menus let you format text easily. Wizards (Letter, Web page, Fax, and Agenda) let you generate different kinds of documents quickly. You can embed objects within documents, such as using Draw to create figures that you can then drag-and-drop to the Writer document. LibreOffice Writer is compatible with earlier versions of Microsoft Word. It will read and convert Word documents to LibreOffice Writer document, preserving most features including contents, tables, and indexes. LibreOffice Writer documents also can be saved as Word documents.

LibreOffice provides access to many database files. File types supported include ODBC (Open Database Connectivity), JDBC (Java), MySQL, PostgreSQL, and MDB (Microsoft Access) database files. You can also create your own simple databases. Check the LibreOffice Features | Base page (**https://www.libreoffice.org/discover/base/**) for detailed information on drivers and supported databases.

LibreOffice Calc is a professional-level spreadsheet. With LibreOffice Math, you can create formulas that you can embed in a text document. With the presentation manager (Libre Office Impress), you can create images for presentations, such as circles, rectangles, and connecting elements like arrows, as well as vector-based illustrations. Impress supports advanced features such as morphing objects, grouping objects, and defining gradients. LibreOffice Draw is a sophisticated drawing tool that includes 3-D modeling tools. You can create simple or complex images, including animation text aligned on curves. LibreOffice also includes a printer setup tool with which you can select printers, fonts, paper sizes, and page formats.

Scribus is a desktop publishing tool, **https://www.scribus.net**. Scribus is available from the App Center as a Debian package.

Calligra

Calligra is an integrated office suite for the K Desktop Environment (KDE) consisting of several office applications, including a word processor, a spreadsheet, and graphics applications. You can download and install each Calligra application from the App Center as Debian packages. Calligra allows components from any one application to be used in another, letting you embed a spreadsheet from Calligra Sheets or diagrams from Karbon in a Calligra Words document. It also uses the open document format (ODF) for its files, providing cross-application standardization. There is also a Windows version available. You can obtain more information about Calligra from **https://calligra.org**.

Application	Description
Stage	Presentation application
Words	Word processor (desktop publisher)
Sheets	Spreadsheet
Karbon	Vector graphics program
Kexi	Database integration
Plan	Project management and planning
Krita	Paint and image manipulation program
Kontact (separate project)	Contact application including mail, address book, and organizer

Table 5-3: Calligra Applications

Currently, Calligra includes Calligra Sheets, Calligra Flow, Calligra Words, Karbon, Krita, Plan, Calligra Stage, and Kexi (see Table 5-3). The contact application, Kontact, has been spun off as a separate project. Kontact is an integrated contact application including Kmail, Korganizer, Kaddressbook, and Knotes. Calligra Sheets is a spreadsheet, Calligra Stage is a presentation application, Karbon is a vector graphics program, and Calligra Words is a publisher-like word processor. Krita is a paint and image editor. Kexi provides database integration with Calligra applications, currently supporting PostgreSQL and MySQL.

Calligra Sheets is the spreadsheet application, which incorporates the basic operations found in most spreadsheets, with formulas similar to those used in MS Excel. You can also embed charts, pictures, or formulas using Krita and Karbon. With Calligra Stage, you can create presentations consisting of text and graphics modeled using different fonts, orientations, and attributes such as colors. Karbon is a vector-based graphics program, much like Adobe Illustrator and LibreOffice Draw. It supports the standard graphic operations such as rotating, scaling, and aligning objects. Calligra Words can best be described as a desktop publisher, with many of the features found in publishing applications. Although it is a fully functional word processor, Calligra Words sets up text in frames that are placed on the page like objects. Frames, like objects in a drawing program, can be moved, resized, and reoriented. You can organize frames into a frame set, having text flow from one to the other.

GNOME Office Applications

There are several GNOME office applications available including AbiWord, Gnumeric, Evince, and Evolution. GNOME office applications are part of Ubuntu and can be downloaded with the App Center as Debian packages. A current listing of common GNOME office applications is shown in Table 5-4. All implement the support for embedding components, ensuring drag-and-drop capability throughout the GNOME interface.

Application	Description
AbiWord	Cross-platform word processor
Gnumeric	Spreadsheet
Evince	Document Viewer
Evolution	Integrated email, calendar, and personal organizer
Dia	Diagram and flow chart editor
GnuCash	Personal finance manager
Glom	Database front end for PostgreSQL database
glabels	Label Designer

Table 5-4: Office Applications for GNOME

AbiWord is an open source word processor that aims to be a complete cross-platform solution, running on Mac, Unix, and Windows, as well as Linux. It is part of a set of desktop productivity applications being developed by the AbiSource project (**https://www.abisource.com**).

Gnumeric is a professional-level GNOME spreadsheet meant to replace commercial spreadsheets. Gnumeric supports standard spreadsheet features, including auto filling and cell formatting, and an extensive number of formats. Gnumeric also supports plug-ins, making it possible to extend and customize its abilities.

Dia is a drawing program designed to create diagrams, such as database, circuit object, flow chart, and network diagrams. You can create elements along with lines and arcs, with different types of endpoints such as arrows or diamonds. Data can be saved in XML format, making it transportable to other applications.

GnuCash (**http://www.gnucash.org**) is a personal finance application for managing accounts, stocks, and expenses.

Running Microsoft Office on Linux: Wine and CrossOver

One of the concerns for new Linux users is what kind of access they will have to their Microsoft Office files, particularly Word files. The Linux operating system and many applications for it are designed to provide seamless access to Microsoft Office files. The major Linux Office suites, including Calligra, LibreOffice, and Oracle Open Office, all read and manage Microsoft Office files. In addition, these office suites are fast approaching the same level of features and support for office tasks as found in Microsoft Office.

Note: You can use your browser to run the Microsoft Office Online version, which runs from a remote Microsoft cloud site.

Wine (Windows Compatibility Layer) allows you to run many Windows applications directly, using a supporting virtual windows API. See the Wine website for a list of supported applications, **https://www.winehq.org**, AppDB tab. Well-written applications may run directly from Wine. Sometimes you will have to have a working Windows system from which you can copy system DLLs needed by particular applications. You can also import Windows fonts by directly copying them to the Wine font folder. Each user can install and run their own version of Wine with its own simulated C: partition on which Windows applications are installed. The simulated drive is installed as **drive_c** in your **.wine** folder. The **.wine** folder is a hidden folder. It is not normally displayed with the **ls** command or the GNOME file manager (Show Hidden Files). You can also use any of your Linux folders for your Windows application data files instead of your simulated C: drive. These are referenced by Windows applications as the **z:** drive.

In a terminal window, using the **wine** command with an install program will automatically install that Windows application on the simulated C: drive. The following example installs Microsoft Office. Though there may be difficulties with the latest Microsoft Office versions and with the 64-bit versions, Office 2002, 2007, 2010, and 2013 32bit versions should work fine (see **https://www.winehq.org**, AppDB tab, search for Office Suites). Applications are rated platinum, gold, silver, bronze, and garbage. Several of the Microsoft Office suites are gold or platinum.

When you insert the Microsoft Office CD, it will be mounted to the **/media**/*username* folder using the disk label as its folder name. Check the **/media** folder under the user's name to see what the actual name is. You then run the **setup.exe** program for Office with wine. Depending on the version of Office you have, there may be further subfolders for the actual Office **setup.exe** program. The following example assumes that the label for Office is OFFICE and that the **setup.exe** program for Office is on the top-level folder of that CD.

```
$ wine /media/richard/OFFICE/setup.exe
```

The install program will start up and you will be prompted to enter your product key. Be sure to use only uppercase as you type. Once installed, choose Applications | Wine | Programs |

Microsoft Office, and then choose the application name to start up. The application should start up normally. The application is referenced by Wine on the user's simulated **c:** drive.

The Windows My Documents folder is set up by Wine to be the user's Ubuntu Documents folder. There you will find any files saved to My Documents.

Wine is constantly being updated to accommodate the latest versions of Windows applications. However, for some applications you may need to copy DLL files from a working Windows system to the Wine Windows folder, **.wine/drive_c/windows**, usually to the **system** or **system32** folders. Though effective, Wine support will not be as stable as Crossover.

CrossOver Office is a commercial product that lets you install and run most Microsoft Office applications. CrossOver Office was developed by CodeWeavers, which also supports Windows web browser plug-ins as well as several popular Windows applications like Adobe Photoshop. CrossOver features both standard and professional versions, providing reliable application support. You can find out more about CrossOver Office at **https://www.codeweavers.com**.

CrossOver can be installed either for private multi-user mode or managed multi-user mode. In private multi-user mode, each user installs Windows software, such as full versions of Office. In managed multi-user mode, the Windows software is installed once and all users share it. Once the software is installed, you will see a Windows Applications menu on the main menu, from which you can start your installed Windows software. The applications will run within a Linux window, but they will appear just as if they were running in Windows.

Also, with VMware, you can run Windows under Linux, allowing you to run Windows applications, including Microsoft Office, on your Linux system. For more information, check the VMware website at **https://www.vmware.com**.

Another option, for users with high-powered computers that support virtualization, is to install the Windows OS on a virtual machine using the Virtual Machine Manager or Boxes. You could then install and run Windows on the virtual machine and install Microsoft Office on it.

Document Viewers, and DVI)

PostScript, PDF, DVI, and E-book viewers are more commonly used with Office applications (see Table 5-5). Evince is the default document viewer for GNOME. It is started automatically whenever you double-click a PDF file on the GNOME desktop. Okular is the default document viewer for KDE. Atril is the MATE desktop document viewer. Okular, Evince, and Atril are PDF viewers and can display both PostScript (**.ps**) and PDF (**.pdf**) files. They include many of the standard Adobe reader features such as zoom, two-page display, and full-screen mode. All these viewers have the ability to print documents. You can install these viewers with the App Center; Evince as a Snap package and Okular and Atril as both Snap and Debian packages. To generate PDF documents you can use LibreOffice Writer or the Scribus desktop publisher (**https://www.scribus.net**).

Linux also supports a professional-level typesetting tool, called TeX, commonly used to compose complex mathematical formulas. TeX generates a DVI document that can be displayed by DVI viewers, several of which are available for Linux. DVI files generated by the TeX document application can be viewed by Evince and Okular.

Viewer	Description
Evince	Document Viewer for PostScript, DVI, and PDF files
Okular	KDE tool for displaying PDF, DVI, and postscript files
Atril	MATE Document Viewer for PostScript, DVI, and PDF files
Scribus	Desktop publisher for generating PDF documents
Simple Scan	GNOME Scanner interface for scanners

Table 5-5: PostScript, PDF, and DVI viewers

Note: To scan documents directly, you can use Simple Scan which you can save as jpeg, png, or PDF files.

E-book Readers: FBReader, Foliate, and Calibre

To read E-books on Ubuntu, you can use Calibre, FBReader, and Foliate (see Table 5-6). FBReader is an open source reader that can read non-DRM E-books, including mobipocket, html, chm, EPUB, text, and rtf. It is available as a Snap or Debian package in the App Center. FBReader opens to the library window, which displays your books, as well as suggested books. Suggested books will have a download button to the right (see Figure 5-2). From the sidebar you can quickly access books by author, recently opened or downloaded, series, network catalogs, and bookmarks. Use the arrow keys on the toolbar to move through pages of books. You can also bookmark a page. You can display the books as covers or in a list. From the menu you can open a selected book, import books, and open the preferences dialog. On the Preferences dialog, you can changes the text font and size, as well as line spacing, colors, and bookmark styles.

Clicking a book entry opens a window for reading the book. Moving the mouse to the right side displays an arrow button for moving to the next page. The arrow buttons on the header bar moves through previously viewed chapters. The contents button opens a dialog listing the table of contents, which you can use to move to different chapters (see Figure 5-3). You can also search for text and bookmark pages. The menu lets you open books, close the current book, or return to the library window, as well as access the Preferences dialog. The toolbar holds operations that move you through the text and configure your reader, adding books and setting interface preferences.

Foliate is a GNOME E-book reader. Install with the App Center either as a Snap or Debian package. It opens to the library view, which lists your books. A sidebar lets you choose different catalogs. You can view your books as a grid or list (menu). Clicking a book opens it for reading. From the reading menu you can set styles, zoom, enable scroll mode, and open the Font & Layout settings dialog, where you can choose the font style and size, layout margins and spacing, and the background color. Click the sidebar icon on the left side of the header bar to return to the library view.

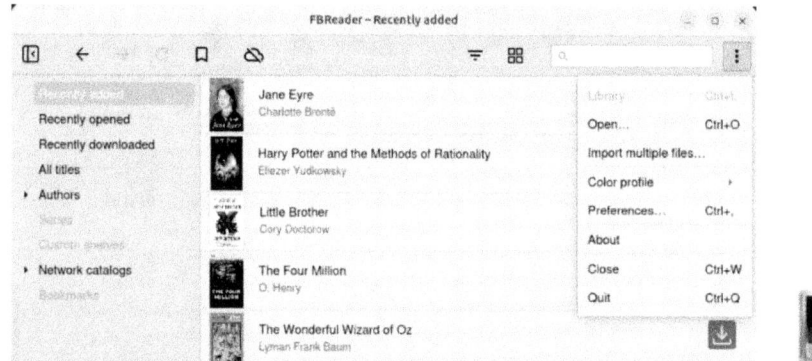

Figure 5-2: FBReader E-book reader - library window

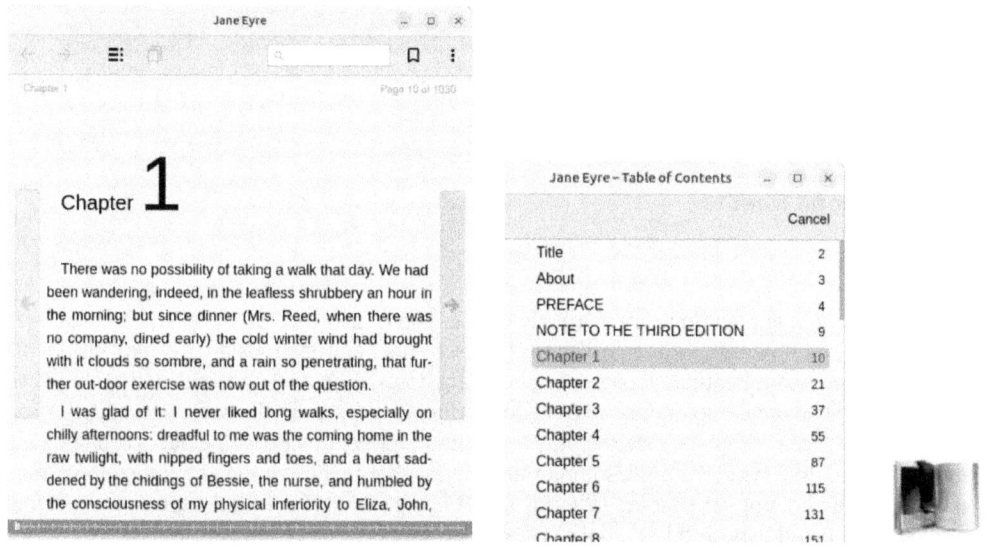

Figure 5-3: FBReader E-book reader - book dialog

Calibre reads PDF, EPUB, Lit (Microsoft), and Mobipocket E-books. It is available on the App Center as a Debian package. Calibre functions as a library for accessing and managing your E-books (see Figure 5-4). Calibre also can convert many document files and E-books to the EPUB format, the open source standard used by Apple (iPad) and Barnes and Noble (Nook). It can take as conversion input text, HTML, TRF, and ODT (LibreOffice), as well as E-books.

222 Part 2: Applications

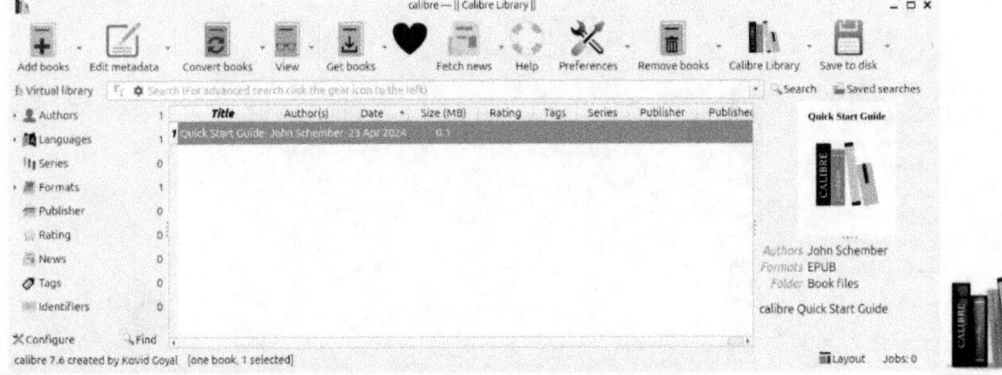

Figure 5-4: Calibre E-book reader, organizer, and converter

Viewer	Description
Calibre	E-book reader and library, also converts various inputs to EPUB E-books.
E-book reader	FBReader E-book reader
Foliate	GNOME E-book reader

Table 5-6: E-book Readers

Notes

Several note applications are available on the App Center as both Snap and Debian packages. The older GNOME Gnote and Notes (Bijiben) note applications are available as Debian packages. The Gnote applications lets you easily create notes, adjusting font size and features (see Figure 5-5). You can create notebooks to hold collection of notes. A toolbar lets you add, rename, configure, an remove notebooks. Use the plus (+) button on the left side of the header to open a tab for adding a note. Preferences provides numerous plugins that features such as print support and underlining. Many are not yet enabled (Plugins tab). On the General and Links tabs choose a font, color scheme, bulleted lists, and URL links. Gnote also supports synchronization of notes using a local folder or online service.

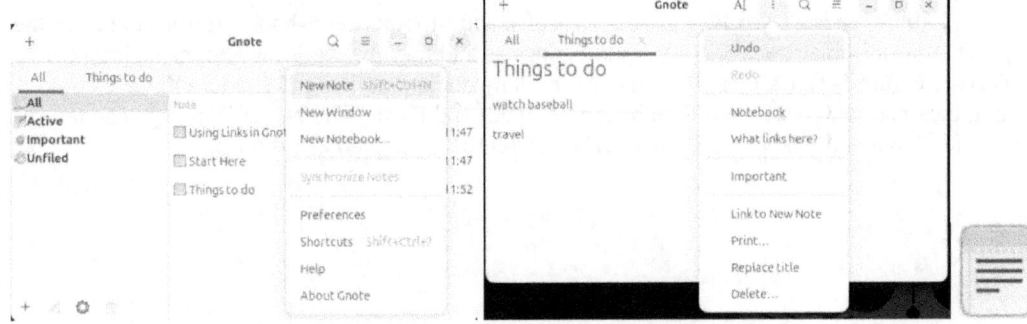

Figure 5-5: Gnote

The GNOME Notes application lets you create and organize simple notes on your desktop. It is available from the App Center as a Debian package named Notes. Its package name is **bijiben** package. The Notes window lists your new and recent notes, showing the note title and the first few lines of text. In the header bar, the search button opens a search box that lets you search for notes. The list button lets you switch between icon and list views. The check button lets you delete or organize your notes. A checkbox is displayed at the right lower corner of the note icons. Clicking on that checkbox opens a taskbar at the bottom with buttons to delete the note, add it to a collection (notebooks), or email it. There is also a color button you can use the background color.

To create a new note, click on the New button on the header bar to open a new text. The first line is the title of your note. Press the ENTER key to move to the next line. A button at the top right opens a dialog that lets you choose the color for a note. The task menu (menu button) provides undo/redo functions, deletion, and email options. You can also add the note to a notebook. You can use notebooks to organize your notes. To delete a note, click on the checkmark button to display a checkbox next to each note. Check the ones you want to delete and click the Done button.

GNOME Clocks and Weather

Two helpful tools are the clocks and weather applications. GNOME Clocks is a Snap package, and GNOME Weather is a Debian package. Clocks has four tabs: World, Alarms, Stopwatch, and Timer. The World tab displays the current time at any city and at your current location (see Figure 5-6). Click the plus button on the left side of the header bar, to open a dialog where you can add a city. To remove a city, click the trash button button the right of an entry. The Alarm tab works as an alarm clock, letting you repeat on a day of the week, set ring and snooze duration, and to name an alarm. The Stopwatch tab operates a stopwatch, letting you mark laps. The timer counts down in time, with quick starts for common durations up to an hour.

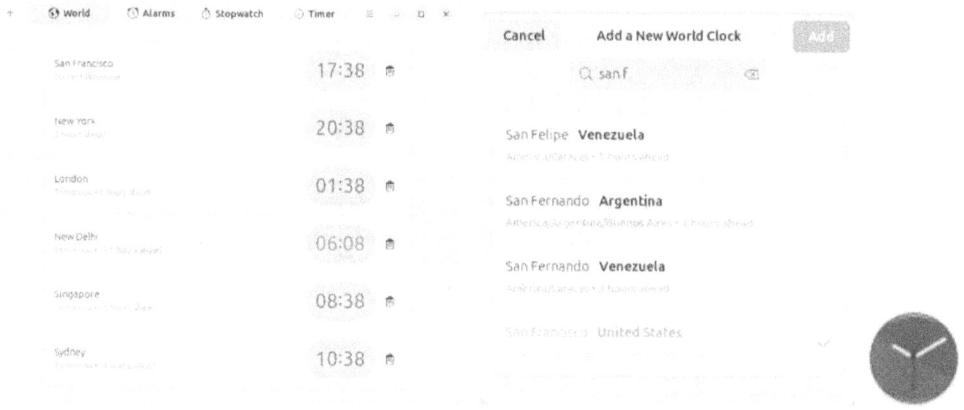

Figure 5-6: GNOME Clocks: World tab

The GNOME weather tool lets you display the weather in any city. Upon opening the Weather application, you are first asked to provide your location. A dialog opens where you can enter the name of your city. A partial entry is matched on, giving you a listing of possible cities. Clicking on a city displays the weather and temperature for that city (see Figure 5-7). There are two tabs, Hourly and Daily. The Hourly tab shows the weather and forecast for the next twelve hours. Clicking on the refresh button on the left side of the header bar will refresh the temperature. The

224 Part 2: Applications

Daily tab shows the forecast for the next week. Each day has a menu you can click to display temperature, humidity, and wind for the night, morning, afternoon, and evening (see Figure 5-8). The Places menu, to the right of the displayed city, shows a list of previous cities you have viewed. The search box lets you find an choose a different city. The menu on the header bar lets you choose Celsius or Fahrenheit measurements.

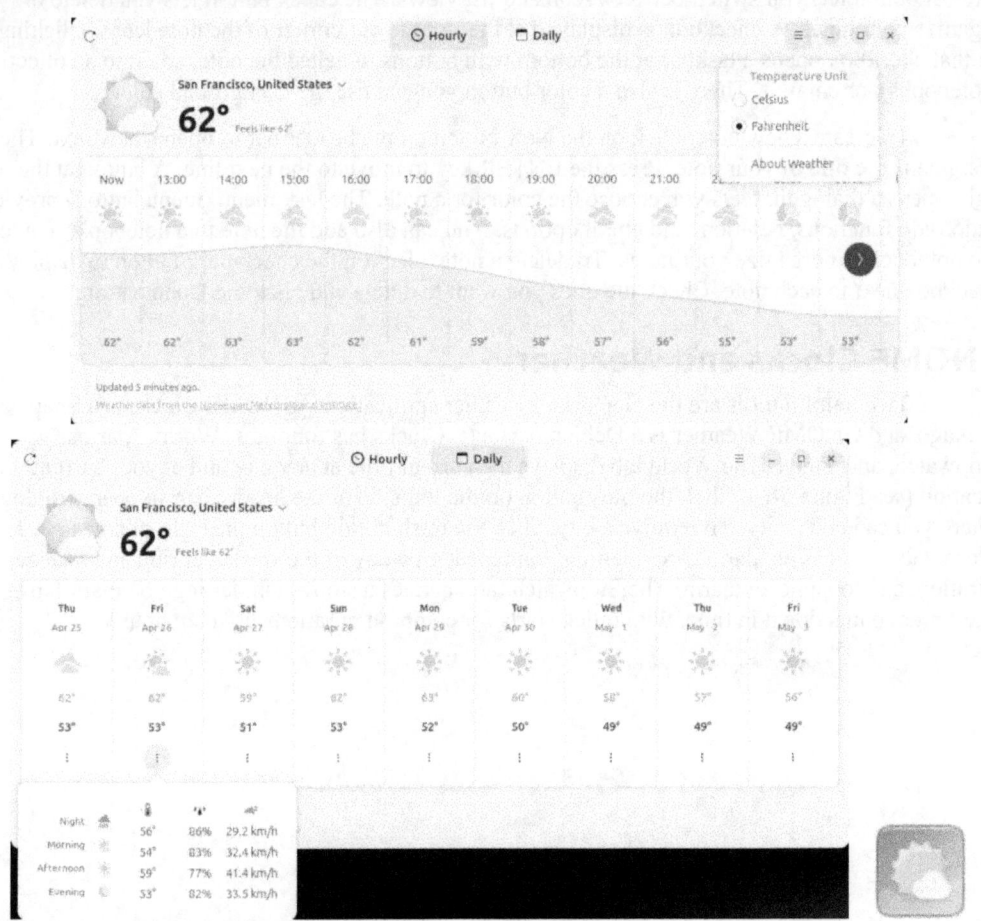

Figure 5-7: GNOME Weather: city with forecast

GNOME Characters and Fonts

The GNOME Characters utility lets you copy a color character image to use in a document. You can choose from several categories (see Figure 5-8). These characters are open source emojis. You can access GNOME Characters from the applications overview Utilities application folder as Characters. Click on the character you want to display. A dialog prompts you to copy the character to the copy the character to the clipboard. In your text editor, you can then paste it as an inline character. The characters include images, as well as math symbols, punctuation, and currencies.

Chapter 5: Office Suites, Editors, and E-mail   **225**

Figure 5-8: GNOME Characters

Fonts provides a simple listing of your installed fonts, showing the font style (see Figure 5-9). You can access Fonts from the applications overview's Utilities application folder. Click on a font image to display examples of the font and an info button at the top right on the title bar, which you can click to display information about the font, including style, type, version, and copyright.

Figure 5-9: Fonts

GNOME Calendar

GNOME Calendar lets you manage a calendar, specifying events (see Figure 5-10) . Events can be imported from Web sources. To add an event, click on a date to open a dialog where you can enter the event name and select a calendar. Click the Edit Details button to display a dialog for setting the time, duration, location, and any notes. Personal and Birthday calendars are already set up. Click the calendar button at the right side of the title bar to open a dialog to let you add new calendars.

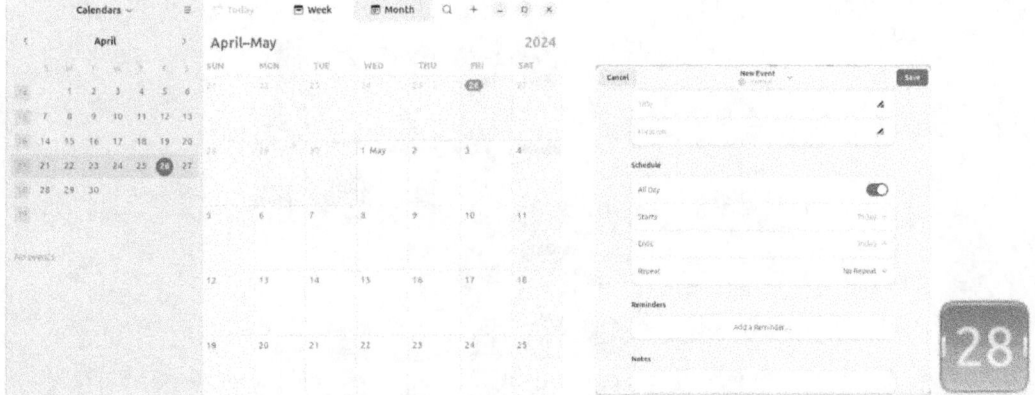

Figure 5-10: GNOME Calendar

Editors

The Ubuntu desktop supports powerful text editors with full mouse support, scroll bars, and menus. These include basic text editors, such as Text Editor and Kate, as well as word processors, such as LibreOffice Word, and Calligra Words. Ubuntu also provides the cursor-based editors Nano, Vim, and Emacs. Nano is a cursor-based editor with an easy-to-use interface supporting menus and mouse selection (if run from a terminal window). Vim is an enhanced version of the Vi text editor used on the Unix system. These editors use simple, cursor-based operations to give you a full-screen format. Table 5-7 lists several desktop editors for Linux. Vi and Emacs have powerful editing features that have been refined over the years. Emacs, in particular, is extensible to a full development environment for programming new applications. Both Vim and Gvim can be run on the desktop with support for mouse, menu, and window operations.

GNOME Text Editors: Text Editor and Gedit

For Ubuntu 20.04, Text Editor is the default text editor (GNOME 4.6), replacing Gedit. You can still install Gedit, if you wish.

GNOME Text Editor

GNOME Text Editor is the new replacement text editor included in the GNOME 4.6 release (see Figure 5-11). It is the default editor and a Snap package. You can install it either as a Snap or Debian package. The name of the application is **gnome-text-editor**.

Text Editor is accessible from the Applications Overview as Text Editor (see Figure 5-11). It supports tabs. From the menu you can choose the light or dark style, or to use the system theme. It also supports find and replace, printing, and keyboard shortcuts. From the configuration menu (gear button) you can activate features such as line numbers, right margin, automatic indentation, tabs, text wrapping, and spell check. The document type entry lets you choose a the Plain Text type (the default) or several programming or scripting type such as C++ or Python. The Text Editor also supports tabs. You can open or start several text files at the same time, and each is placed in a separate tab.

Chapter 5: Office Suites, Editors, and E-mail **227**

The Preferences dialog, accessible from the menu, lets you select a style and font, set the right margin, and to set display features such as an overview map (pages), highlighting the current line, and a grid pattern on the text. To start a new additional text file, click the tab button on the header bar to open a new tab for it. To open an additional existing text file, click the Open button.

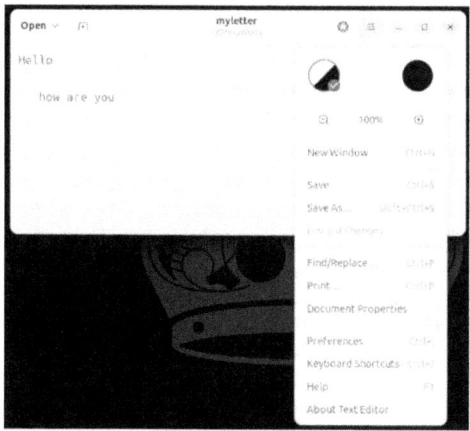
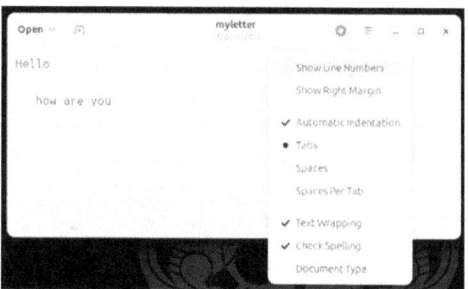

Figure 5-11: GNOME Text Editor

Application	Description
Kate	Text and program editor
Calligra Words	Desktop publisher, part of Calligra Suite
Text Editor	GNOME text editor
Gedit	GNOME legacy text editor
AbiWord	Word processor
OpenWriter	LibreOffice word processor that can edit text files
nano	Easy to use screen-based editor, installed by default
GNU Emacs	Emacs editor with X Window System support
XEmacs	X Window System version of Emacs editor
gvim	Vim version with X Window System support

Table 5-7: Desktop Editors

GNOME Gedit

The Gedit editor is an older text editor for the GNOME desktop. It is available on the App Center as a Debian package. Gedit provides full mouse support, implementing standard desktop operations, such as cut and paste to move text, and click and drag to select and move/copy text (see Figure 5-12) . It supports standard text editing operations such as Find and Replace. The editor is accessible from the Applications overview as **gedit**. You can use Gedit to create and modify your text files, including configuration files. Gedit also provides more advanced features such as print preview and configurable levels of undo/redo operations, and it can read data from pipes. To configure Gedit, select Preferences from the menu to open the Preferences dialog with tabs for View, Editor, Font & Colors, and Plugins. On the Views tab you can configure options such as text wrapping, highlighting, and what features to display such as line numbers and the statusbar. On the Editor tab you can set tab stops and file saving, including autosave. On the Font & Colors tab you can select the font and color scheme. Clicking on the font entry opens the "Pick the editor font" dialog, where you can select the font and the size.

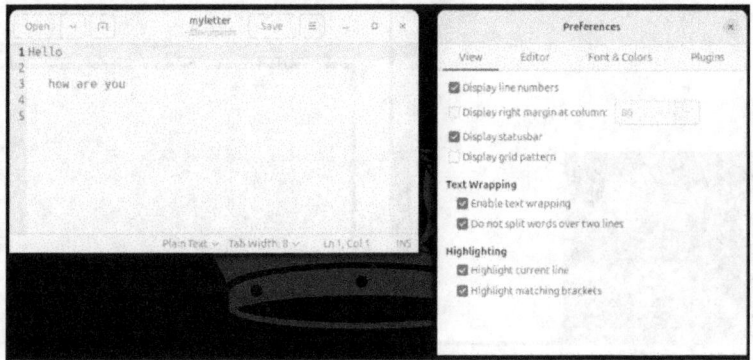

Figure 5-12: GNOME Gedit

Gedit features plug-ins that provide added functionality, including spell checking, document statistics, and sorting. Install **gedit-plugins** for more plugins such as word completion and color schemes. To activate a plugin, select on the Preferences Plugins tab. Plugins are accessible from the Gedit menu and its Tools submenu.

The nano text editor

The nano editor is a simple screen-based editor that lets you visually edit your file, using arrow and page keys to move around the file. You use control keys to perform actions. CTRL-x will exit and prompt you to save the file, CTRL-o will save it. CTRL-k will cut the current line.

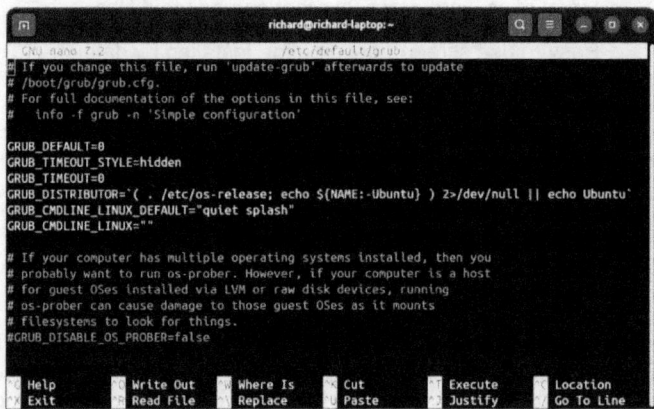

Figure 5-13: Editing with nano

You start nano with the **nano** command entered in a terminal window or on the command line interface. To edit a configuration file, you will need administrative access. Figure 5-13 shows the nano editor being used to edit the GRUB configuration file, **/etc/default/grub**.

```
sudo nano /etc/default/grub
```

KDE Editor: Kate

The KDE editor Kate provides full mouse support, implementing standard GUI operations, such as cut and paste to move text, and click and drag to select and move/copy text. You can install it from the App Center as either a Snap or Debian package. The editor is accessible from the Applications | Utilities menu on the KDE desktop, and from the Applications overview on the Ubuntu desktop. Kate is an advanced editor, with such features as spell checking, font selection, and highlighting. Most commands can be selected using menus. A toolbar of icons for common operations is displayed across the top of the Kate window. A sidebar displays panels for a file list. Kate also supports multiple views of a document, letting you display segments in their own windows, vertically or horizontally. You can also open several documents at the same time, moving among them with the file list. Kate is designed to be a program editor for editing software programming/development-related source code files. Kate can format the syntax for different programming languages, such as C, Perl, Java, and XML.

The Emacs Editor

Emacs can best be described as a working environment featuring an editor, a mailer, a newsreader, and a Lisp interpreter. The editor is tailored for program development, enabling you to format source code according to the programming language you use. GNU Emacs is X Window System capable, enabling GUI features such as menus, scroll bars, and mouse-based editing operations. You can find out more information about Emacs at **https://www.gnu.org/software/emacs/**.

The Emacs editor operates much like a standard word processor. The keys on your keyboard represent input characters. Commands are implemented with special keys, such as control (CTRL) keys and alternate (ALT) keys. There is no special input mode, as in Vi. You type in your text, and if you need to execute an editing command, such as moving the cursor or saving text, you use a CTRL key. You invoke the Emacs editor with the command **emacs**. You can enter the name of the file you want to edit, and if the file does not exist, it is created. In the next example, the user prepares to edit the file **mydata** with Emacs.

```
$ emacs mydata
```

The GNU Emacs editor supports basic desktop editing operations such as selection of text with click-and-drag mouse operations, cut/copy/paste, and a scroll bar for moving through text. The Mode line and Echo areas are displayed at the bottom of the window, where you can enter keyboard commands.

The Vi Editor: Vim and Gvim

The Vim editor is an enhanced version of the Vi editor. It includes all the commands and features of the Vi editor. Vi, which stands for *visual*, remains one of the most widely used editors in Linux. On Ubuntu, a basic version of Vi, called **vim-tiny**, is installed as part of the basic installation. For the full version, install the Vim package from the App Center as a Debian package, or with the **sudo apt install** command.

Keyboard-based editors like Vim and Emacs use a keyboard for two different operations: to specify editing commands and to receive character input. Used for editing commands, certain keys perform deletions, some execute changes, and others perform cursor movement. Used for character input, keys represent characters that can be entered into the file being edited. Usually, these two different functions are divided among different keys on the keyboard. Alphabetic keys are reserved for character input, while function keys and control keys specify editing commands, such as deleting text or moving the cursor. Such editors can rely on the existence of an extended keyboard that includes function and control keys.

Editors in Unix were designed originally to assume a minimal keyboard with alphanumeric characters and some control characters, as well as the ESC and ENTER keys. Instead of dividing the command and input functions among different keys, the Vi editor has three separate modes of operation for the keyboard: command, input modes, and line editing modes. In command mode, all the keys on the keyboard become editing commands; in the input mode, the keys on the keyboard become input characters. Some of the editing commands, such as **a** or **i**, enter the input mode. On typing **i**, you leave the command mode and enter the input mode. Each key now represents a character to be input to the text. Pressing ESC automatically returns you to the command mode, and the keys once again become editor commands. As you edit text, you are constantly moving from the command mode to the input mode and back again. With Vim, you can use the CTRL-o command to jump quickly to the command mode and enter a command, and then automatically return to the input mode. Table 5-8 lists a basic set of Vi commands to get you started.

Command	Description
h	Moves the cursor left one character.
l	Moves the cursor right one character.
k	Moves the cursor up one line.
j	Moves the cursor down one line.
CTRL-F	Moves forward by a screen of text; the next screen of text is displayed.
CTRL-B	Moves backward by a screen of text; the previous screen of text is displayed.
Input	*(All input commands place the user in input; the user leaves input with ESC.)*
a	Enters input after the cursor.
i	Enters input before the cursor.
o	Enters input below the line the cursor is on; inserts a new empty line below the one the cursor is currently on.
Text Selection (Vim)	
v	Visual mode; move the cursor to expand selected text by character. Once selected, press key to execute action: **c** change, **d** delete, **y** copy, **:** line-editing

	command, **J** join lines, **U** uppercase, **u** lowercase.
v	Visual mode; move the cursor to expand selected text by line.
Delete	
x	Deletes the character the cursor is on.
dd	Deletes the line the cursor is on.
Change	*(Except for the replace command, r, all change commands place the user into input after deleting text.)*
cw	Deletes the word the cursor is on and places the user into the input mode.
r	Replaces the character the cursor is on. After pressing **r**, the user enters the replacement character. The change is made without entering input; the user remains in the Vi command mode.
R	First places into input mode, and then overwrites character by character. Appears as an overwrite mode on the screen but actually is in input mode.
Move	Moves text by first deleting it, moving the cursor to the desired place of insertion, and then pressing the **p** command. (When text is deleted, it is automatically held in a special buffer.)
p	Inserts deleted or copied text after the character or line the cursor is on.
P	Inserts deleted or copied text before the character or line the cursor is on.
dw p	Deletes a word, and then moves it to the place you indicate with the cursor (press **p** to insert the word *after* the word the cursor is on).
yy or Y p	Copies the line the cursor is on.
Search	The two search commands open up a line at the bottom of the screen and enable the user to enter a pattern to be searched for; press ENTER after typing in the pattern.
/*pattern*	Searches forward in the text for a pattern.
?*pattern*	Searches backward in the text for a pattern.
n	Repeats the previous search, whether it was forward or backward.
Line Editing Commands	**Effect**
w	Saves file.
q	Quits editor; **q!** quits without saving.

Table 5-8: Vi Editor Commands

Although you can create, save, close, and quit files with the Vi editor, the commands for each are not similar. Saving and quitting a file involves the use of special line editing commands, whereas closing a file is a Vi editing command. Creation of a file is usually specified on the same shell command line that invokes the Vi editor. To edit a file, type **vi** or **vim** and the name of a file on the shell command line. If a file by that name does not exist, the system creates it. In effect, entering the name of a file that does not yet exist instructs the Vi editor to create that file. The following command invokes the Vi editor, working on the file **booklist**. If **booklist** does not yet exist, the Vi editor creates it.

```
$ vim booklist
```

After executing the **vim** command, you enter Vi's command mode. Each key becomes a Vi editing command, and the screen becomes a window onto the text file. Text is displayed screen by screen. The first screen of text is displayed, and the cursor is positioned in the upper-left corner. With a newly created file, there is no text to display. When you first enter the Vi editor, you are in the command mode. To add text, you need to enter the input mode. In the command mode, **a** is the editor command for appending text. Pressing this key places you in the input mode. Now the keyboard operates like a typewriter, and you can input text to the file. If you press ENTER, you merely start a new line of text. With Vim, you can use the arrow keys to move from one part of the entered text to another and work on different parts of the text. After entering text, you can leave the input mode and return to the command mode by pressing ESC. Once finished with the editing session, you exit Vi by typing two capital Zs, ZZ. Hold down the SHIFT key and press **Z** twice. This sequence first saves the file and then exits the Vi editor, returning you to the Linux shell. To save a file while editing, you use the line editing command **w**, which writes a file to the disk. **w** is equivalent to the Save command found in other word processors. You first type a colon to access the line editing mode, and then type **w** and press ENTER, **:w**.

You can use the **:q** command to quit an editing session. Unlike the **ZZ** command, the **:q** command does not perform any save operation before it quits. In this respect, it has one major constraint. If any modifications have been made to your file since the last save operation, the **:q** command will fail and you will not leave the editor. You can override this restriction by placing a **!** qualifier after the **:q** command. The command **:q!** will quit the Vi editor without saving any modifications made to the file in that session since the last save (the combination **:wq** is the same as ZZ).

To obtain online help, enter the **:help** command. This is a line editing command. Type a colon, enter the word **help** on the line that opens at the bottom of the screen, and then press ENTER. You can add the name of a specific command after the word **help**. Pressing the **F1** key also brings up online help.

As an alternative to using Vim in a command line interface, you can use gvim, which provides X Window System–based menus for basic file, editing, and window operations. Gvim can be installed from the App Center as a Debian package. For the **sudo apt install** command, the package is called the **vim-gui-common** package, which includes several links to Gvim such as **evim**, **gview**, and **gex** (open Ex line editor). To use Gvim, you can enter the **gvim** command at a terminal prompt. The standard Vi interface is shown, but with several menu buttons displayed across the top along with a toolbar with buttons for common commands like search and file saves. All the standard Vi commands work just as described previously. However, you can use your mouse to select items on these menus. You can open and close a file, or open several files using split windows or different windows. The editing menu enables you to cut, copy, and paste text, as well as undo or redo operations. In the editing mode, you can select text with your mouse with a click-and-drag operation, or use the Editing menu to cut or copy and then paste the selected text. Text entry, however, is still performed using the **a**, **i**, or **o** command to enter the input mode. Searches and replacements are supported through a dialog window. There are also buttons on the toolbar for finding next and previous instances. You can also split the view into different windows to display parts of the same file or different files. Use the **:split** command to open a window, and use **:hide** to close the current one. Use CTRL-w with the up and down arrow keys to move between them. On Gvim, you use entries in the Windows menu to manage windows. Configuration preferences can be placed in the user's **.vimrc** file.

Database Management Systems

Several database systems are provided for Ubuntu, including LibreOffice Base, MySQL, SQLite, and PostgreSQL. Ubuntu continues to provide the original MySQL database. In addition, commercial SQL database software is also compatible with Ubuntu. Table 5-9 lists database management systems currently available for Linux. SQLite is a simple and fast database server requiring no configuration and implementing the database on a single disk file. For small, embedded databases you can use Berkeley DB (db4). In addition, Ubuntu also supports document-based non-SQL databases such as MongoDB. MongoDB is a document-based database that can be quickly searched.

SQL Databases (RDBMS)

SQL databases are relational database management systems (RDBMSs) designed for extensive database management tasks. Many of the major SQL databases now have Linux versions, including Oracle and IBM. These are commercial and professional database management systems. Linux has proved itself capable of supporting complex and demanding database management tasks. In addition, many free SQL databases are available for Linux that offer much the same functionality. Several commercial databases also provide free personal versions.

System	Site
LibreOffice	LibreOffice database (Ubuntu repository): https://www.libreoffice.org/discover/base/
PostgreSQL	The PostgreSQL database (Ubuntu repository): https://www.postgresql.org/
MySQL	MySQL database (Ubuntu repository): https://www.mysql.com
SQLite	Simple SQL database: https://www.sqlite.org/index.html
MongoDB	Document-based database: https://www.mongodb.com/
MariaDB	MariaDB database, based on MySQL: https://mariadb.org/

Table 5-9: Database Management Systems for Linux

LibreOffice Base

LibreOffice provides a basic database application, LibreOffice Base, that can access many database files. You can set up and operate a simple database, as well as access and manage files from other database applications. When you start up LibreOffice Base, you will be prompted either to start a new database or connect to an existing one. File types supported include ODBC (Open

Database Connectivity), JDBC (Java), MySQL, PostgreSQL, and MDB (Microsoft Access) database files (install the **unixodbc** and **libmysql-java** packages). You can also create your own simple databases. Check the LibreOffice Base page (**https://www.libreoffice.org/discover/base/**) for detailed information on drivers and supported databases.

MySQL

MySQL, included with Ubuntu, is a true multi-user, multithreaded SQL database server, supported by MySQL AB. MySQL is an open source product available free under the GPL license. You can obtain current information on it from its website, **https://www.mysql.com**. The site includes detailed documentation, including manuals and FAQs. Currently, MySQL is owned by Oracle.

MariaDB

MariaDB is a fully open source derivative of MySQL, developed after MySQL was acquired by Oracle. It is designed to be fully compatible with MySQL databases. Like MySQL, MariaDB is structured on a client/server model with a server daemon filling requests from client programs. MariaDB is designed for speed, reliability, and ease of use. It is meant to be a fast database management system for large databases and, at the same time, a reliable one, suitable for intensive use. To create databases, you use the standard SQL language. Packages to install are **mariadb-client** and **mariadb-server**.

PostgreSQL

PostgreSQL is based on the POSTURES database management system, though it uses SQL as its query language. POSTGRESQL is a next-generation research prototype developed at the University of California, Berkeley. Linux versions of PostgreSQL are included in most distributions, including the Red Hat, Fedora, Debian, and Ubuntu. You can find more information on it from the PostgreSQL website at **https://www.postgresql.org**. PostgreSQL is an open source project, developed under the GPL license.

E-Mail Clients

You can send and receive email messages in a variety of ways, depending on the type of mail client you use. Although all email utilities perform the same basic tasks of receiving and sending messages, they tend to use different interfaces. Some mail clients are designed to operate on a specific desktop interface such as KDE and GNOME. Several older mail clients use a screen-based interface and can be started only from the command line. For Web-based Internet mail services, such as Gmail and Yahoo, you use a Web browser instead of a mail client to access mail accounts provided by those services. Table 5-10 lists several popular Linux mail clients. Mail is transported to and from destinations using mail transport agents like Sendmail, Exim, and Postfix. To send mail over the Internet, Simple Mail Transport Protocol (SMTP) is used.

Mail Client	Description
Kontact	Includes the K Desktop mail client, KMail; integrated mail, address book, and scheduler (KMail, KAddressbook, KOrganizer)
Evolution	Email client, **https://wiki.gnome.org/Apps/Evolution**
Thunderbird	Mozilla mail client and newsreader
Sylpheed	Gtk mail and news client
Claws-mail	Extended version of sylpheed Email client
Mutt	Screen-based mail client
bsd-mailx	Original Unix-based command line mail client
unity mail	GNOME email notification
gnubiff	Email checker and notification tool
newmail	email notification

Table 5-10: Linux Mail Clients

Thunderbird

Thunderbird is a full-featured stand-alone email client provided by the Mozilla project (**https://www.mozilla.org**). It is installed by default along with LibreOffice. Thunderbird is designed to be easy to use, highly customizable, and heavily secure. It features advanced intelligent spam filtering, as well as security features like encryption, digital signatures, and S/MIME. To protect against viruses, email attachments can be examined without being run. Thunderbird supports both Internet Message Access Protocol (IMAP) and the Post Office Protocol (POP). It also functions as a newsreader and features a built-in RSS reader. Thunderbird also supports the use of the Lightweight Directory Access Protocol (LDAP) for address books. Thunderbird is an extensible application, allowing customized modules to be added to enhance its abilities. You can download extensions such as dictionary search and contact sidebars from the website. Thunderbird also supports HTML mail, displaying Web components like URLs in mail messages.

Thunderbird is installed by default. You can access it from the dock. It provides better integration with popular online mail services like Gmail, saved searches, and customized tags for selected messages. You can access Thunderbird from the dock and the Applications overview.

The Thunderbird interface uses a vertical layout, which uses tabs. The first tab lists mail accounts and their mailboxes (see Figure 5-14). The next tab is the message list tab and the third tab shows a selected message's text. On the side is the Spaces toolbar with tabs for Mail (mail accounts), Address Book, Calendar, Tasks, Chat, and, at the bottom, Settings. A search text box in the header lets you search messages. On the right side of the header is the Thunderbird menu from which you can create new accounts and messages, change the display layout, access settings, select add-ons and themes, and access tools. From the Tools submenu you can search messages, set message filters, access the download manager, and manage security keys. The Views submenu lets you choose what toolbars to display (Menu, Spaces, and Status), as well as customize them. You can also choose the Thunderbird layout: Classic, Wide, and Vertical. Vertical, which uses tabs, is the default.

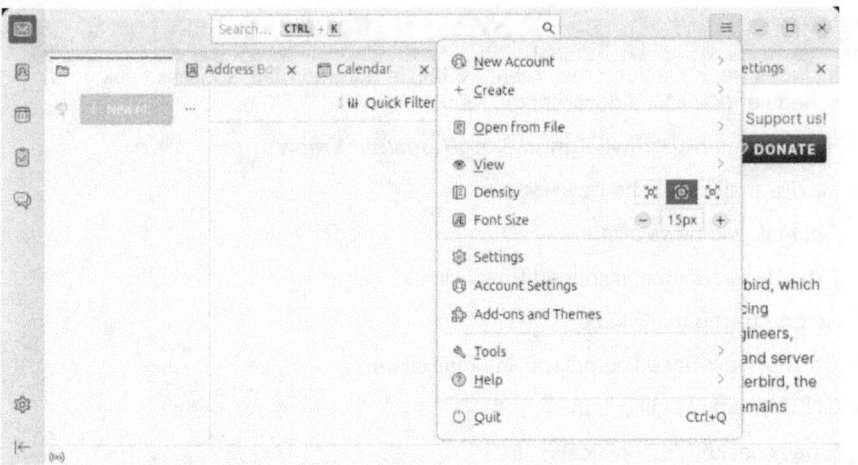

Figure 5-14: Thunderbird Email client

The message list tab has a menu located to the right of the Quick Filter button that lets you sort messages by a specific field ("Sort by" submenu), and whether to view them as a table or as cards. Selecting Threaded will gather the messages into respective threads with replies grouped together. Thunderbird supports a variety of quick display filters (Quick Filter button), such as displaying only messages from people included in your address book (contact) and display messages with attached files (Attachment). Search and sorting capabilities also include filters that can match selected patterns in any field, including subject, date, or the message body.

To compose a message, click the New Message button at the top of the mail account tab (first tab) to open the Write window. Basic editing tools are provided.

When you first start up Thunderbird, The Account Setup tab opens, which prompts you to create an email account. You can add more email accounts or modify current ones by selecting New Account from the Thunderbird menu and then choosing Existing Email Account to add an email account you already have. The first page of the Account Setup tab prompts you to enter your name, email address, and password. Thunderbird then attempts to detect and configure your email account automatically. Popular email services such as Gmail (Google) and Yahoo will be detected and their incoming and outgoing mail servers configured automatically. You can also just choose to abandon the email setup by clicking the Start Over link. If the account detection fails, you will be prompted to enter the username and password, along with the names of the incoming and outgoing mail servers for that account. For a more detailed configuration, click the Configure Manually link where you can specify the security protocol like SSL/TSL.

To edit an email account, select the Account Settings menu entry from the Thunderbird menu to open the Account Settings tab. You will see an entry for your mail account, with tabs for Server Settings, Copies & Folders, Composition & Addressing, Synchronization & Storage, and Return Receipt. The Server Settings tab has entries for your server name, port, username, security settings, and server such as how often to check for messages.

To remove an account, open the Account Actions menu in the email account's Account Settings tab and select Remove Account.

Thunderbird provides an address book where you can enter complete contact information, including email addresses, street addresses, phone numbers, and notes. Select Address Book from the Spaces toolbar (sidebar) Address Book button to display the Address Book tab. A button bar at the top of the tab shows buttons for "New Address Book", "New Contact", "New List", and Import. There are three panes: one for the address books available, another listing the contacts for the selected address book, and one to display the address information of a selected contact, such as the email address, street addresses, and phone. Only fields with values are displayed. To modify or add to the contact, click the Edit button. To create a new entry in an address book, click the New Contact button to open a tab with numerous textboxes for entries such as First Name, Email Address, Addresses, Phone Numbers, and Notes. To create email mailing lists, you click the New List button to open the New Mailing List dialog where you specify the name of the list and enter the email addresses.

Once you have set up your address book, you can use its addresses when creating mail messages. On the Write window, when you start to enter an email address in the To text box, the address will auto-complete to the corresponding address in your address book. Alternatively, you can open the address book and drag-and-drop addresses to an address box in the message window.

Evolution

Evolution is the primary mail client for the GNOME desktop. It is available on the App Center as a Debian package. Though designed for GNOME, it will work equally well on KDE. Evolution is an integrated mail client, calendar, and address book. It supports numerous protocols (SMTP, POP, and IMAP). With Evolution, you can create multiple mail accounts on different servers, including those that use different protocols such as POP or IMAP. You can also decrypt Pretty Good Privacy (PGP) or GNU Privacy Guard (GPG) encrypted messages. Messages are indexed for easy searching. As an added feature, you can display Web calendars within evolution. See the Evolution website for resources and documentation links.

```
https://wiki.gnome.org/Apps/Evolution
```

The Evolution mailer provides a simple desktop interface, with a toolbar for commonly used commands and a sidebar for shortcuts. A set of buttons on the lower left allows you to access other operations, such as the calendar and contacts. The main screen is divided into two panes, one for listing the mail headers and the other for displaying the currently selected message (see Figure 5-15). You can click any header label to sort your headers by that category. Evolution also supports the use of virtual folders that can be created by the user to hold mail that meets specified criteria. Incoming mail can be automatically distributed to a virtual folder.

With evolution, you can also create search folders to organize access to your messages. A search folder is not an actual folder. It simply collects links to messages based on certain search criteria. Using search folders, you can quickly display messages on a topic, or subject, or from a specific user. In effect, it performs an automatic search on messages as they arrive. To set up a search folder, select Search Folders in the Edit submenu (Edit | Search Folders) to open the Search Folders dialog, and click Add to then open the Add Rule dialog. Here you can add criteria for searches and the folders to search. You can also right-click a message header that meets criteria you want searched and select Create Rule from Message, and then select one of the Search Rule entries.

238 Part 2: Applications

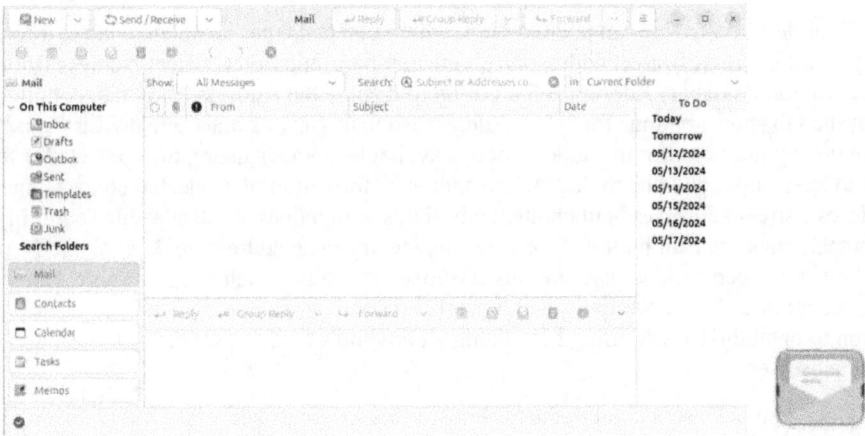

Figure 5-15: Evolution Email client

To configure Evolution, select Preferences from the Edit submenu (Edit | Preferences). On the Evolution Preferences window, a sidebar shows icons for mail accounts, contacts, mail preferences, composition preference, calendar and tasks, and certificates. The Mail accounts tab displays a list of current accounts. An Add button lets you add new accounts, and the Edit button allows you to change current accounts. When editing an account, the Account Editor displays tabs for Identity, Receiving email (your incoming mail server), sending email (outgoing mail server), and security (encryption and digital signatures) among others. Mail Preferences lets you configure how Evolution displays and manages messages. The Mail Preferences Automatic Contacts tab is where you can specify whether the addresses of mail you have replied to should be added automatically to the Evolution Contacts list. Composer Preferences lets you set up composition features like signatures, formatting, and spell-checking. Calendar and Tasks lets you configure your calendar, specifying a type zone, work days, display options, and publishing.

Numerous plugins are available to extend Evolution's capabilities. Most are installed and enabled for you automatically, including the SpamAssassin plug-in for handling junk mail. To manage your plug-ins, select the Plugins entry in the Edit menu (Edit | Plugin) to open the Plugin Manager, with plug-ins listed in a left scroll window and configuration tabs located for a selected plug-in on the right side.

Evolution also supports filters. You can use filters to direct some messages automatically to certain folders, instead of having all incoming messages placed in the inbox folder. To create a filter, you can select the Message Filters entry in the Edit menu (Edit | Message Filters) and click Add to open the Add Rule window. You can also right-click the header of a message whose heading meets your criteria, like a subject or sender, and select Create Rule from Message and select a Filter entry for sender, subject, or recipient. On the Add Rule window, you can add other criteria and specify the action to take, like moving the message to a particular folder. You can also add other actions, like assigning a score, changing the color, copying the message, or deleting it.

A user's email messages, addresses, and configuration information are kept in files located in the **.evolution** folder within the user's home folder. Backing up this information is as simple as making a copy of that folder. Messages for the different mailboxes are kept in a **mail** subfolder. If you are migrating to a new system, you can just copy the folder from the older system. To back up the mail for any given mail account, just copy the **mail** subfolder for that account. You can also backup the address book, calendar, memos, and tasks subfolders.

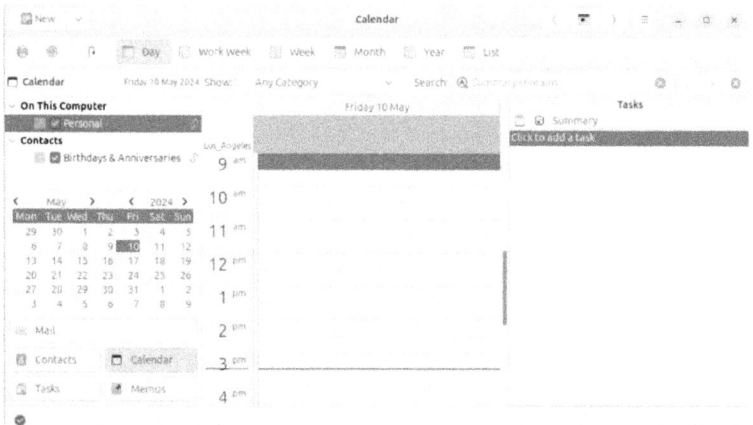

Figure 5-16: Evolution Calendar

Evolution also supports contact operations like calendars, contact lists, and memos. On the left side pane, the bottom section displays buttons for these different functions: Mail, Contacts, Calendars, Tasks, and Memos. To see and manage your contacts, click the Contacts button on the left sidebar. The Calendar displays a browsable calendar on the left pane to move easily to a specific date (see Figure 5-16). The right pane shows a daily calendar page by the hour with sections for tasks and memos. You can set up several calendars, which you can access at the top of the right pane. A personal calendar is set up for you already. To add a new calendar, select Calendar from the New menu to open a New Calendar dialog where you can choose the type and name.

Note: Other GNOME mail clients include sylpheed and Claws-mail (both are on the Ubuntu Universe repository). Sylpheed is a mail and news client with an interface similar to Windows mail clients. Claws-mail is an extended version of Sylpheed with many additional features (**https://www.claws-mail.org/**). You can install them from the App Center as Debian packages.

The KDE Mail Client: KMail

The KDE mail client, KMail, provides a full-featured desktop interface for composing, sending, and receiving email messages. KMail is part of the KDE Personal Information Management suite (KDE-PIM) which also includes an address book (KAddressBook), an organizer and scheduler (KOrganizer), and a note writer (KNotes). All these components are also directly integrated on the desktop into Kontact. You can start up KMail directly or as part of the Kontact applications (Mail). KMail is installed as part of the KDE desktop, but you can also install it on the Ubuntu Desktop with the App Center as a Debian package, or with the **sudo apt install** command.

The KMail window displays three panes for folders, headers, and messages. The lower-left pane displays your mail folders: an inbox folder for received mail, an outbox folder for mail you have composed but have not sent yet, and a sent-mail folder for messages you have previously sent.

You can create your own mail folders and save selected messages in them. You can designate certain folders as favorite folders and have them listed in the Favorite Folders pane (right-click on the Favorite Folders pane and select Add Favorite Folder to choose a folder).

Command Line Mail Clients

Several mail clients use a simple command line interface. They can be run without any other kind of support, such as the X Window System, desktops, or cursor support. They are simple and easy to use, and include an extensive set of features and options. Two of the more widely used mail clients of this type are Mail and Mutt. Mail is the mailx mail client that was developed for UNIX. It is considered a default mail client that can be found on most UNIX and Linux systems. Mutt is a cursor-based client that can be run from the command line.

Mutt

Mutt has an easy-to-use cursor-based interface with an extensive set of features. You can find more information about Mutt from the Mutt website, **http://www.mutt.org**. The Mutt manual is located in the **/usr/doc** folder under Mutt. To use Mutt, enter the **mutt** command in a terminal window or on the command line. Install the **mutt** package with the **sudo apt install** command.

Mail

What is known now as the Mail utility was originally created for BSD Unix and called, simply, mail. Later versions of Unix System V adopted the BSD mail utility and renamed it mailx. Now, it is simply referred to as Mail. Mail functions as a default mail client on most Unix and Linux systems. It is not installed by default on Ubuntu. Install the **bsd-mailx** package with the **sudo apt install** command.

To send a message with Mail, type **mail** on the command line along with the address of the person to whom you are sending the message. Press ENTER and you are prompted for a subject. Enter the subject of the message and press ENTER again. At this point, you are placed in input mode. Anything you type is considered the contents of the message. Pressing ENTER adds a new line to the text. When you finish typing your message, press CTRL-d on a line of its own to end the message. You will then be prompted to enter a user to whom to send a carbon copy of the message (cc). If you do not want to send a carbon copy, just press ENTER. You will then see EOT (end-of-transmission) displayed after you press CTRL-d.

You can send a message to several users at the same time by listing those users' addresses as arguments on the command line following the **mail** command. In the next example, the user sends the same message to both **chris** and **aleina**.

```
$ mail chris aleina
```

To receive mail, you first enter the **mail** command and press **enter**. This invokes a Mail shell with its own prompt and mail commands. A list of message headers is displayed. Header information is arranged into fields beginning with the status of the message and the message number. The status of a message is indicated by a single uppercase letter, usually N for new or U for unread. A message number, used for easy reference to your messages, follows the status field. The next field is the address of the sender, followed by the date and time the message was received, and then the number of lines and characters in the message. The last field contains the subject the sender gave for the message. After the headers, the Mail shell displays its prompt, an ampersand

(&). At the Mail prompt, you enter commands that operate on the messages. An example of a Mail header and prompt follows:

```
$ mail
Mail version 8.2 01/15/2001. Type ? for help.
"/var/spool/mail/larisa": 3 messages 1 new 2 unread
 1 chris@turtle.mytrek. Thu Jun  7 14:17 22/554 "trip"
>U 2 aleina@turtle.mytrek Thu Jun  7 14:18 22/525 "party"
 U 3 dylan@turtle.mytrek. Thu Jun  7 14:18 22/528 "newsletter"
& q
```

Mail references messages either through a message list or through the current message marker (>). The greater-than sign (>) is placed before a message considered the current message. The current message is referenced by default when no message number is included with a Mail command. You can also reference messages using a message list consisting of several message numbers.

You use the **R** and **r** commands to reply to a message you have received. The **R** command entered with a message number generates a header for sending a message and then places you into input mode to type the message. The **q** command quits Mail. When you quit, messages you have already read are placed in a file called **mbox** in your home folder. Instead of saving messages in the **mbox** file, you can use the **s** command to save a message explicitly to a file of your choice. Mail has its own initialization file, called **.mailrc**, which is executed each time Mail is invoked, either for sending or receiving messages. Within it, you can define Mail options and create Mail aliases.

Notifications of Received Mail

As your mail messages are received, they are automatically placed in your mailbox file, but you are not automatically notified when you receive a message. You can use a mail client to retrieve any new messages, or you can use a mail monitor tool to tell you when new mail has arrived in your inbox. Several mail notification tools are also available, such as **gnubiff**, **unity-mail**, **gnome-shell-mailnag**, **evolution-plugins**, and **birdtray** (Thunderbird notifications). The **gnubiff** tool will notify you of any POP3 or IMAP mail arrivals.

For command line interfaces, you can use the biff utility, which notifies you immediately when a message is received. biff automatically displays the header and beginning lines of messages as they are received. To turn on biff, you enter **biff y** on the command line. To turn it off, you enter **biff n**. To find out if biff is turned on, enter **biff** alone.

Accessing Mail on Remote Mail Servers

Most new mail clients are equipped to access mail accounts on remote servers. Mail clients, such as Evolution, KMail, Sylpheed, and Thunderbird, enable you to set up a mailbox for such an account and access a mail server to check for and download received mail. You must specify what protocol a mail server uses. This is usually either the Post Office Protocol (POP) or the IMAP protocol (IMAP). Using a mail server address, you can access your account with your username and password.

For email clients such as **mail** and **mutt** that do not provide mail server access, you can use Fetchmail to have mail from those accounts sent directly to the inbox maintained by your Linux system for your Linux account. All your mail, whether from other users on your Linux system or from remote mail accounts, will appear in your local inbox. Fetchmail checks for mail on remote mail servers and downloads it to your local inbox, where it appears as newly received mail. Enter **fetchmail** on the command line with the mail server address and any needed options. The mail protocol is indicated with the **-p** option and the mail server type, usually POP3. If your email username is different from your Linux login name, you use the **-u** option and the email name. Once you execute the **fetchmail** command, you are prompted for a password. The syntax for the **fetchmail** command for a POP3 mail server is shown here.

```
fetchmail -p POP3 -u username mail-server
```

You will see messages telling you if mail is there and, if so, how many messages are being downloaded. You can then use a mail client to read the messages from your inbox. You can run Fetchmail in daemon mode to have it check automatically for mail. You have to include an option specifying the interval in seconds for checking mail.

```
fetchmail -d 1200
```

To have fetchmail run automatically you can set the START DAEMON option to yes in the **/etc/default/fetchmail** file. Edit the file with the **sudo nano** command or the Text Editor.

You can specify options such as the server type, username, and password in a **.fetchmailrc** file in your home folder. You can also include entries for other mail servers and accounts you may have. Once Fetchmail is configured, you can enter **fetchmail** with no arguments. It will read entries from your **.fetchmailrc** file. You can also make entries directly in the **.fetchmailrc** file. An entry in the **.fetchmailrc** file for a particular mail account consists of several fields and their values: poll, protocol, username, and password. The poll field refers to the mail server name. You can also specify your password, instead of having to enter it each time Fetchmail accesses the mail server.

Mailing Lists

Users on mailing lists automatically receive messages and articles sent to the lists. Mailing lists work much like a mail alias, broadcasting messages to all users on the list. Mailing lists were designed to serve specialized groups of people. Numerous mailing lists, as well as other subjects, are available for Linux. By convention, to subscribe to a list, you send a request to the mailing list address with a **-request** term added to its username. For example, to subscribe to **gnome-list@gnome.org**, you send a request to **gnome-list-request@gnome.org**.

You can use the Mailman application to manage your mailing lists automatically. Mailman is the GNU mailing list manager, included with Ubuntu (**http://www.list.org**).

MIME: /etc/mime.types

MIME (Multipurpose Internet Mail Extensions) is used to enable mail clients to send and receive multimedia files and files using different character sets such as those for different languages. Multimedia files can be images, sound clips, or even video. Mail clients that support MIME can send binary files automatically as attachments to messages. MIME-capable mail clients maintain a file called **mailcap** that maps different types of MIME messages to applications on your system that can view or display them. For example, an image file will be mapped to an application that can display images. Your mail clients can then run that program to display the image message. A sound file will be mapped to an application that can play sound files. Most mail clients have MIME capabilities built in and use their own version of the **mailcap** file. Others use a program called metamail that adds MIME support. MIME is used not only in mail clients. Both the KDE and GNOME file managers use MIME to map a file to a particular application so that you can launch the application directly from the file.

Applications are associated with binary files by means of the **mailcap** and **mime.types** files. The **mime.types** file defines different MIME types, associating a MIME type with a certain application. The **mailcap** file then associates each MIME type with a specified application. Your system maintains its own MIME types file, usually **/etc/mime.types**.

Entries in the MIME types file associate a MIME type and possible subtype of an application with a set of possible file extensions used for files that run on a given kind of application. The MIME type is usually further qualified by a subtype, separated from the major type by a slash. For example, a MIME type image can have several subtypes such as jpeg, gif, or tiff. A sample MIME type entry defining a MIME type for JPEG files are shown here. The MIME type is image/jpeg, and the list of possible file extensions is "jpeg jpg jpe":

```
image/jpeg      jpeg jpg jpe
```

The applications specified will depend on those available on your particular system. The application is specified as part of the application type. In many cases, X Window System–based programs are specified. Comments are indicated with a **#**. The following entries associate **odt** files with the LibreOffice writer and **qtl** files with the QuickTime player.

```
application/vnd.oasis.opendocument.text    odt
application/x-quicktimeplayer              qtl
```

Though you can create your own MIME types, a standard set already is in use. The types text, image, audio, video, application, multipart, and message, along with their subtypes, have already been defined for your system. You will find that commonly used file extensions such as **.tif** and **.jpg** for TIFF and JPEG image files are already associated with a MIME type and an application. Though you can easily change the associated application, it is best to keep the MIME types already installed. The current official MIME types are listed at the IANA website (**https://www.iana.org/assignments/media-types/media-types.xhtml**) under the name Media Types, provided as part of their Assignment Services.

S/MIME and OpenPGP/MIME are authentication protocols for signing and encrypting mail messages. S/MIME was originally developed by the RSA Data Security. OpenPGP is an open standard based on the PGP/MIME protocol developed by the PGP (Pretty Good Privacy) group. Clients like Evolution can use OpenPGP/MIME to authenticate messages.

Usenet News

Usenet is an open mail system on which users post messages that include news, discussions, and opinions. It operates like a mailbox to which any user on your Linux system can read or send messages. Users' messages are incorporated into Usenet files, which are distributed to any system signed up to receive them. Certain Usenet sites perform organizational and distribution operations for Usenet, receiving messages from other sites and organizing them into Usenet files, which are then broadcast to many other sites. Such sites are called backbone sites, and they operate like publishers, receiving articles and organizing them into different groups.

To access Usenet news, you need access to a news server, which receives the daily Usenet newsfeeds and makes them accessible to other systems. Your network may have a system that operates as a news server. There are also many commercial servers you can access for a fee. To read Usenet articles, you use a newsreader, a client program that connects to a news server and accesses the articles. On the Internet and in TCP/IP networks, news servers communicate with newsreaders using the Network News Transfer Protocol (NNTP) and are often referred to as NNTP news servers. You can also create your own news server on your Linux system to run a local Usenet news service or to download and maintain the full set of Usenet articles. News transport agent applications can be set up to create such a server.

Usenet files were originally designed to function like journals. Messages contained in the files are referred to as articles. A user could write an article, post it in Usenet, and have it immediately distributed to other systems. Usenet files themselves were organized as journal publications. Because journals are designed to address specific groups, Usenet files are organized according to groups called newsgroups. When a user posts an article, it is assigned to a specific newsgroup. You can also create articles of your own, which you can then add to a newsgroup for others to read. Linux has newsgroups on various topics. Some are for discussion, and others are sources of information about recent developments. On some, you can ask for help for specific problems. A selection of some of the popular Linux newsgroups is provided here:

Newsgroup	Topic
comp.os.linux.announce	Announcements of Linux developments
comp.os.linux.admin	System administration questions
comp.os.linux.misc	Special questions and issues
comp.os.linux.setup	Installation problems
comp.os.linux.help	Questions and answers for particular problems
linux.help	Obtain help for Linux problems

Newsreaders

You read Usenet articles with a newsreader, such as Pan and tin, which enable you to select a specific newsgroup and then read the articles in it. A newsreader operates like a user interface, letting you browse through and select available articles for reading, saving, or printing. Most newsreaders employ a retrieval feature called threads that pulls together articles on the same discussion or topic. Several popular newsreaders are listed in Table 5-11.

Most newsreaders can read Usenet news provided on remote news servers that use the NNTP protocol. Desktop newsreaders, such as Pan, have you specify the Internet address for the remote news server in their own configuration settings. Shell-based newsreaders such as **tin**, obtain the news server's Internet address from the NNTPSERVER shell variable, configured in the **.profile** file.

```
NNTPSERVER=news.domain.com
export NNTPSERVER
```

Newsreader	Description
Pan	GNOME Desktop newsreader
Thunderbird	Mail client with newsreader capabilities (X based)
Sylpheed	GNOME Windows-like newsreader
Slrn	Newsreader (cursor based)
Emacs	Emacs editor, mail client, and newsreader (cursor based)
tin	Newsreader (command line interface)
trn4	Newsreader (command line interface)
SABnzbd+	Binary only NZB based news grabber

Table 5-11: Linux Newsreaders

Binary Newsreaders and Grabbers

A binary newsreader can convert text messages to binary equivalents, like those found in **alt.binaries** newsgroups. There are some news grabbers, applications designed only to download binaries. The binaries are normally encoded with RAR compression, which have an **.rar** extension. To decode them you first have to install the **unrar-free** (free version) or **unrar** packages (proprietary version). The **ubuntu-restricted-extras** package will install the **unrar** proprietary version for you. Binaries normally consist of several **rar** archive files, some of which may be incomplete. To repair them you can use Par2 recovery program. Install the **par2** or **parchive** package. A binary should have its own set of par2 files also listed on the news server that you can download and use to repair any incomplete **rar** files. The principle works much the same as RAID arrays using parity information to reconstruct damaged data.

The SABnzbd+ nzb grabber application works using NZB files to locate and download binaries. You first have to obtain the NZB file to use. But if you can obtain an NZB file, then NZB is by far the easiest to use. It works through you Web browser. Simply add an NZB file. Configuration is detailed letting you specify folders, server, notifications, and download scheduling. You can install SABnzbd+ from the App Center either as a Snap or Debian package.

slrn

The **slrn** newsreader is cursor-based. Commands are displayed across the top of the screen and can be executed using the listed keys. Different types of screens exist for the newsgroup list, article list, and article content, each with its own set of commands. An initial screen lists your subscribed newsgroups with commands for posting, listing, and subscribing to your newsgroups. When you start slrn for the first time, you may have to create a **.jnewsrc** file in your home folder. Use the following command: **slrn -f .jnewsrc -create**. Also, you will have to set the **NNTPSERVER** variable in your **.profile** file and make sure it is exported. You can install slrn with the **sudo apt install** command.

The slrn newsreader features a utility called **slrnpull** that you can use to download articles in specified newsgroups automatically. This allows you to view your selected newsgroups offline. The slrnpull utility was designed as a simple single-user version of Leafnode; it will access a news server and download its designated newsgroups, making them available through slrn whenever the user chooses to examine them. Newsgroup articles are downloaded to the **SLRNPULL_ROOT** folder. On Ubuntu, this is **/var/spool/slrnpull**. The selected newsgroups to be downloaded are entered in the **slrnpull.conf** configuration file placed in the **SLRNPULL_ROOT** folder. In this file, you can specify how many articles to download for each group and when they should expire. To use **slrn** with **slrnpull**, you will have to configure the **.slrnrc** file to reference the **slrnpull** folders where newsgroup files are kept.

News Transport Agents

Usenet news is provided over the Internet as a daily newsfeed of articles and postings for thousands of newsgroups. This newsfeed is sent to sites that can then provide access to the news for other systems through newsreaders. These sites operate as news servers. The newsreaders used to access them are their clients. The news server software called news transport agents, provide newsreaders with news, enabling you to read newsgroups and post articles. For Linux, several popular news transport agents are INN, Leafnode, Papercut, and sn. Both Papercut and Leafnode are small and simple, and useful for small networks. INN is more powerful and complex, designed with large systems in mind (see **https://www.isc.org/** for more details).

Daily news feeds on Usenet are often large and consume much of a news server's resources in both time and memory. For this reason, you may not want to set up your own Linux system to receive such newsfeeds. If you are operating in a network of Linux systems, you can designate one of them as the news server and install the news transport agent on it to receive and manage the Usenet newsfeeds. Users on other systems on your network can then access that news server with their own newsreaders. If your network already has a news server, you need not install a news transport agent at all. You only have to use your newsreaders to access that server remotely.

You can also use news transport agents to run local versions of news for only the users on your system or your local network. To do this, install INN, Leafnode, or Papercut configure them just to manage local newsgroups. Users on your system could then post articles and read local news.

ubuntu

6. Graphics and Multimedia

- Graphics Applications
- Multimedia
- Music Applications
- Video Applications
- Sound Configuration

Ubuntu includes a wide range of graphics and multimedia applications, including simple image viewers such as the Eye of GNOME, sophisticated image manipulation programs like GIMP, music, music players such as Rhythmbox, and video players like Videos. Several helpful Linux multimedia sites are listed in Table 6-1. There is strong support for graphics and multimedia tasks from image management, video and DVD, to sound and music editing (see Tables 6-1, 6-4 and 6-5). Most are available on Ubuntu's multiverse and universe repositories. In addition, the Ubuntu Studio project has collected popular multimedia development software into several collections for audio, video, and graphics.

Projects and Sites	Description
Advanced Linux Sound Architecture (ALSA)	The Advanced Linux Sound Architecture (ALSA) project for current sound drivers: www.alsaproject.org
Open Sound System	Open Sound System, drives for older devices: www.opensound.com
PulseAudio	PulseAudio sound interface, now the default for Ubuntu. https://www.freedesktop.org/wiki/Software/PulseAudio/
Phoronix	Site for the latest news and reviews of Linux hardware compatibility, including graphics cards. https://www.phoronix.com
Ubuntu Studio	Ubuntu Studio multimedia development applications and desktop, audio, video, and graphics collection installed from ubuntustudio meta packages, Meta Packages (universe) https://ubuntustudio.org

Table 6-1: Linux and Ubuntu Multimedia Sites

Support for many popular multimedia operations, specifically MP3, DVD, and DivX, are part of the main Ubuntu repository because of licensing and other restrictions. These are provided on the Ubuntu multiverse and universe repositories. Precompiled packages for many popular media applications and libraries, such as VideoLan, Celluloid, and XviD, are also available on the Ubuntu multiverse and universe repositories.

Graphics Applications

The GNOME and KDE desktops support an impressive number of graphics applications, including image viewers, screen grabbers, photo managers, image editors, and paint tools. Table 6-2 lists some popular graphics tools for Linux.

Tools	Description
Shotwell	GNOME digital camera application and image and video library manager (https://wiki.gnome.org/Apps/Shotwell)
GNOME Snapshot (Camera)	GNOME Webcam application for taking pictures and videos
ubuntustudio-graphics	Ubuntu Studio meta package (Meta Packages (universe)), includes a collection of graphics applications. Use Synaptic Package Manager.
Digikam	Digital photo management tool, works with both GNOME and KDE (https://www.digikam.org/)
KDE	
Gwenview	Image browser and viewer (default for KDE)
ShowFoto	Simple image viewer, works with digiKam
Spectacle	Screen grabber
KolourPaint	Paint program
Krita	Image editor (https://krita.org/en/)
GNOME	
Eye of Gnome	GNOME Image Viewer (eog package)
GIMP	GNU Image Manipulation Program (https://www.gimp.org/)
Inkscape	GNOME Vector graphics application (https://inkscape.org/en/)
gpaint	GNOME paint program
Blender	3d modeling, rendering, and animation
LibreOffice Draw	LibreOffice Draw program
X Window System	
Xpaint	Paint program
Xfig	Drawing program
ImageMagick	Image format conversion and editing tool

Table 6-2: Graphics Tools for Linux

Photo Management: Shotwell, Photos, and Camera (Snapshot)

Shotwell provides an easy and powerful way to manage, display, and import, and publish your photos and images (**https://wiki.gnome.org/Apps/Shotwell**). It is the default photo manager for Ubuntu 24.04 LTS. See the Shotwell user manual for full details (Help | Contents menu and at **http://yorba.org/shotwell/help/**). Shotwell is accessible as the Shotwell Photo Manager from the Applications overview. Shotwell also supports video files.

You can import folders from cameras or folders (see Figure 6-1). Your Pictures folder is the default library folder, whose photos are imported automatically. Adding an image file to the Pictures folder also imports it to Shotwell. Photo thumbnails are displayed in the right pane. The

View menu lets you control the thumbnail display, allowing you to sort photos, zoom, show photo filenames (Titles), or select by rating or event. You can adjust the size of the displayed thumbnails using a slider bar in the toolbar located at the bottom right of the Shotwell window. The small figure button to the left of the slider reduces thumbnails to their smallest size, and the large figure button to the right of the slider expands them to the largest size.

Figure 6-1: Shotwell Photo Management

To see a full-screen slide show of the photos, choose the Slideshow entry in the View menu. The slide show starts automatically. During the slideshow, moving your mouse to the center bottom of the screen displays slideshow controls for pausing and stepping through photos. The Settings button opens a dialog where you can set the display time. To end the slide show and return to the desktop, click the full-screen button. The slideshow buttons are shown here.

Photos are organized automatically by the time they were taken. Dates are listed under the Events entry in the left sidebar, arranged by year, month, and date. To name a photo, right-click on it and choose Edit Title to open a dialog where you can enter the name. You can also tag photos placing them in groups, making them easier to access. To tag a photo, right-click it and choose Add Tags to open a dialog where you can enter a tag name. The tag will show up as a label for the photo. You can access photos by tags using the Tags entries in the left sidebar. For each photo, you can also set a rating indicated by five stars or less.

To search for photos, click the Find button to open a search bar, which displays a text box for entering the search pattern. Buttons to the left let you refine the search by image type, photos or videos, flagged files, and ratings.

You can perform complex edits either within the Shotwell window or in full screen. To edit a photo within the Shotwell window, double-click its image to display the edit toolbar, which hold Rotate, Crop, Straighten, Red-eye, Adjust, and Enhance buttons. For full-screen edits, select the photo and then choose View | Fullscreen (F11) to open the photo in the Shotwell photo editor (see Figure 6-2). Move your mouse to the bottom of the screen to display edit toolbar (Rotate, Crop, Straighten, Red-eye, Adjust, and Enhance buttons). You can also zoom in or out from the photo using the slider bar. The Crop button opens an adjustable border, with a menu for choosing the display proportions you may want such as HD video or postcard. The Adjust button opens a dialog for refined changes such as exposure, saturation, tint, temperature, shadows, and highlights. Edits are stored in a Shotwell database; they are not made to the original photo. To revert to the original photo, right-click and choose "Revert to Original" or choose that entry from the Photos menu.

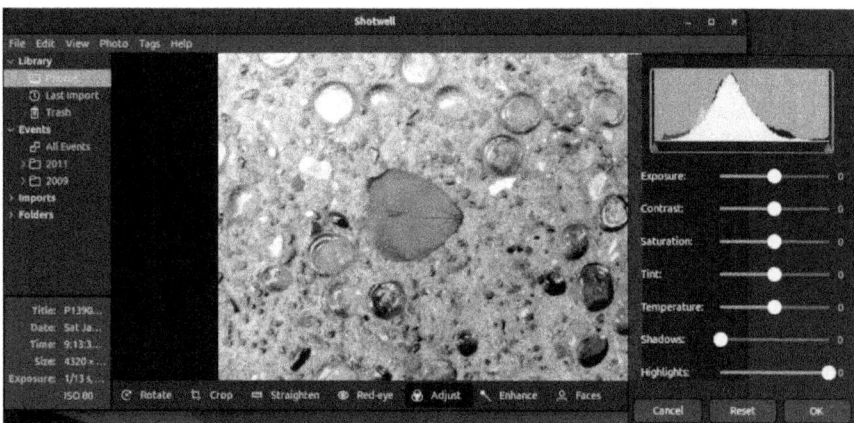

Figure 6-2: Shotwell Photo Editing

Note: You can also set Shotwell display features using the dconf editor's Shotwell keys located at org | yorba | shotwell.

DigiKam (**https://www.digiKam.org**) is a KDE photo manager with many of the same features as Shotwell. DigiKam is accessible from the Applications overview. A side panel allows easy access by album, date, tags, or previous searches (see Figure 6-3). The program also provides image-editing capabilities, with numerous effects. The digiKam configuration (Settings menu) provides extensive options, including image editing, digital camera support, and interface configuration. You can install DigiKam from the App Center as a Snap package.

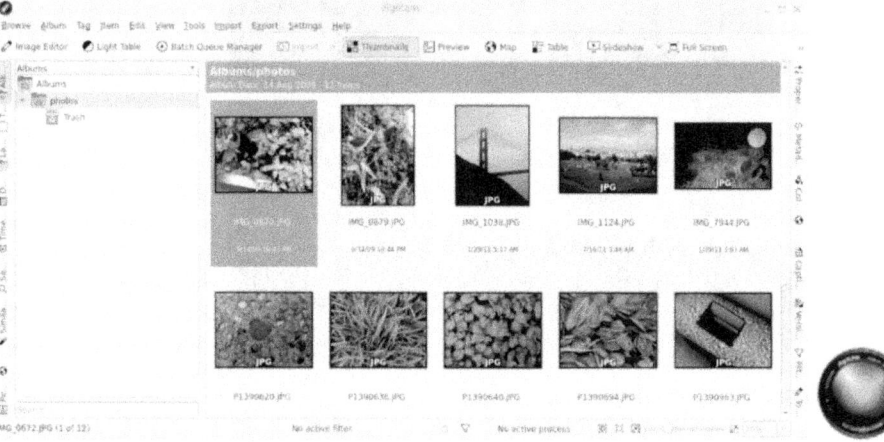

Figure 6-3: digiKam Photo Manager

Tip: The Windows version of Photoshop is supported by Wine. You can install Photoshop CS on Ubuntu using Wine. Once started, Photoshop will operate like any Linux desktop application.

Camera (GNOME Snapshot) is a Webcam picture-taking and video-recording tool, replacing Cheese (which you can still install if you want) . It is available as a Debian package. With Camera, you can snap pictures from your Webcam and then open them with an image viewer such as Shotwell and Image Viewer to apply effects. On the bottom right, Select the Photo button (the default) to snap photos and the Video button to record video. A photo button is displayed to the left of the main button showing your recent photo. Click on it to display the photo gallery, with navigation buttons on the bottom left for moving through your photos. The ellipses button at the top right lists options to delete the photo or copy it. Click the link button on the bottom right to open an Open With dialog showing graphic applications such as Shotwell and Image Viewer that you can open the photo with. Click the return button (left-arrow) at the top left to return to the Camera window.

GNOME Graphics Applications

GNOME features several powerful and easy-to-use graphics applications. The Eye of GNOME is the GNOME image viewer. It is installed by default and is accessible as "Image Viewer" on the Applications overview's Utilities application folder. The image viewer provides basic image display operations such as enlargement, full-screen display, rotation, and slide shows (see Figure 6-4). The image Gallery (icon list of images at the bottom of the screen), the Statusbar (bottom bar with size and position of selected photo), and Side Pane (properties of a selected image) are configured for display from entries in the Show submenu. Most preferences can be set using the preferences dialog (Preferences entry in the menu). User interface preferences, such as trash confirmations and the gallery position, can be set using the dconf editor's eog keys at org | gnome | eog | ui.

Figure 6-4: Image Viewer (Eye of Gnome)

The gThumb application is an image viewer and browser that lets you browse images using thumbnails and organize them into catalogs for easy reference. You can install gThumb from the App Center as either a Snap or Debian package.

Note: GNOME Photos has be deprecated from Ubuntu 24.04 due to stability issues.

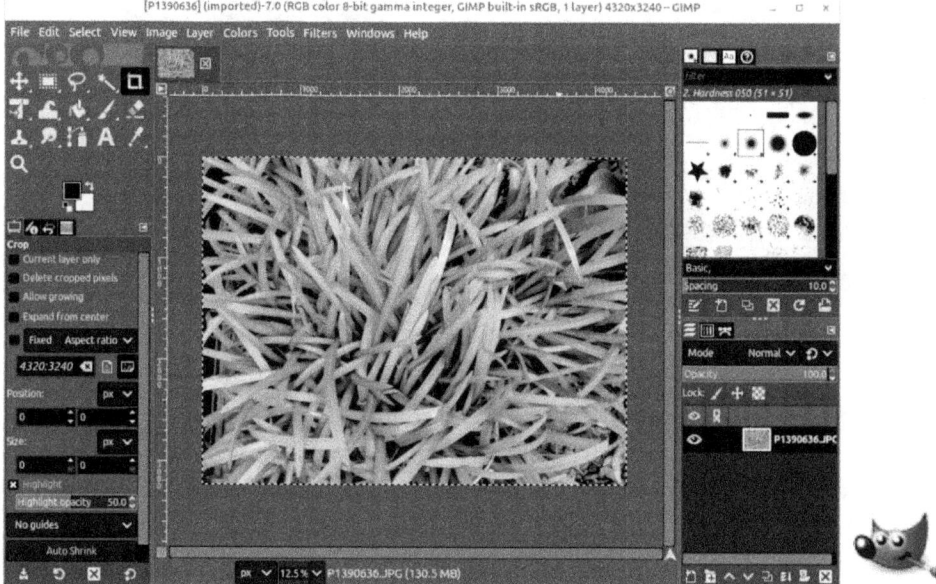

Figure 6-5: GIMP

GIMP is the GNU Image Manipulation Program, a sophisticated image application much like Adobe Photoshop (see Figure 6-5). You can use GIMP for such tasks as photo retouching, image composition, and image authoring. It supports features such as layers, channels, blends, and gradients. GIMP makes effective use of the GTK+ widget set. GIMP is accessible as the GIMP Image Editor. You can find out more about GIMP from its website at **https://www.gimp.org**. GIMP is freely distributed under the GNU Public License. You can install GIMP from the App Center as either a Snap or Debian package.

Inkscape is a vector graphics application for SVG (Scalable Vector Graphics) images (see Figure 6-6). Inkscape is accessible as Inkscape Image Editor on the Applications overview. It features abilities similar to professional level vector graphics. The SVG format allows easy generation of images for Web use as well as complex art. Though its native format is SVG, it can also export to the Portable Network Graphics (PNG) format. It features layers and easy object creation, including stars and spirals. A color bar lets you quickly change color fills. You can install Inkscape from the App Center as either a Snap or Debian package.

254 Part 2: Applications

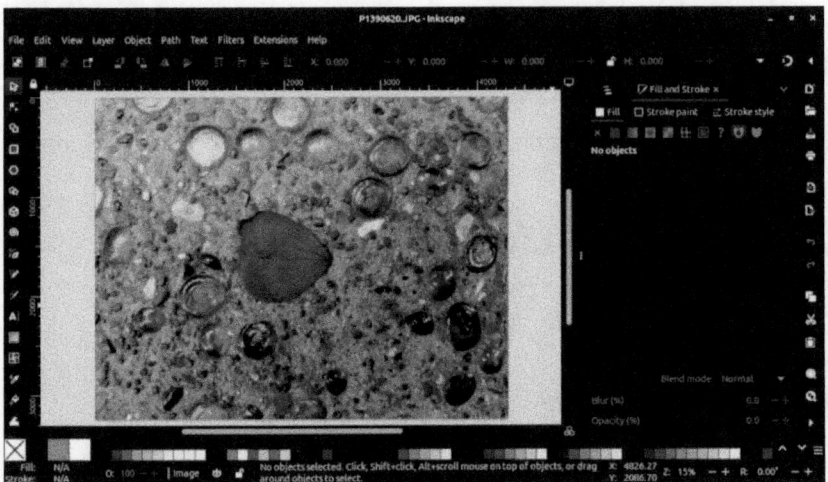

Figure 6-6: Inkscape

KDE Graphics Applications

The KDE desktop features the same variety of graphics applications found on the GNOME desktop. Many are available from the Ubuntu main repository. Most do not require a full installation of the KDE desktop. The Spectacle program is a simple screenshot application for KDE. Gwenview is an easy-to-use image browser and viewer supporting slide shows and numerous image formats. It is the default viewer for KDE, but can also be used on GNOME (see Figure 6-7). Gwenview can share photos with social networking sites directly. KolourPaint is a basic paint program with brushes, shapes, and color effects. Krita is a professional image paint and editing application, with a wide range of features such as the ability to create web images and modify photographs. You can install them on the Ubuntu desktop with the App Center as either a Snap or Debian package. You can also install them with the **sudo apt install** command.

Figure 6-7: Gwenview

X Window System Graphic Programs

X Window System based applications run directly on the underlying X Window System. These applications tend to be simpler, lacking the desktop functionality found in GNOME or KDE applications. Most are available on the Ubuntu Universe repository. Xpaint is a simple paint program that allows you to load graphics or photographs and then create shapes, add text and colors, and use brush tools with various sizes and colors. Xfig is a drawing program. ImageMagick lets you convert images from one format to another. You can install them with the App Center or the **sudo apt install** command.

Multimedia

Many applications are available for both video and sound, including sound editors, MP3 players, and video players (see Tables 6-5 and 6-6). Linux sound applications include mixers, digital audio tools, CD audio players, MP3 players, and network audio support. To use restricted formats such as commercial DVD video and Blu-Ray see the following site.

```
https://help.ubuntu.com/community/RestrictedFormats
```

Note: For games, Ubuntu 24.04 installs by default the **gamemode** daemon, which temporarily optimizes a games uses of system resources such as the CPU.

Multimedia support

A listing of popular multimedia codecs available is shown in Table 6-3. Of particular interest may be the liba52, faad2, and lame codecs for sound decoding, as well as the xvidcore, x264, libdvdcss, vaapi, and libdvbpsi for video decoding.

To install support for most of the commonly used codecs, you can install the Ubuntu restricted packages, **ubuntu-restricted-addons** and **ubuntu-restricted-extras**, which are available from the Synaptic Package Manager (Meta Packages (multiverse) section, ubuntu-restricted-extras and ubuntu-restricted-addons). These packages are meta packages that will download a collection of other packages that provide support for DVD, MP3, MPEG4, DivX, and AC3, as well as Flash (non-free). The **ubuntu-restricted-addons** package will install the GStreamer ugly and bad packages, ffmpeg Chromium codecs and ffmpeg gstreamer plugin, as well as the Gstreamer Video Acceleration API packages (**gstreamer1.0-vaapi**). The **ubuntu-restricted-extras** package will install the Microsoft font collection (**ttf-mscorefonts**), RAR archive extraction (**unrar**), and additional ffmpeg audio codecs (**libavcodec-extra**) .

```
ubuntu-restricted-addons
ubuntu-restricted-extras
```

Many video files require that the Gstreamer ugly and bad packages are installed for them to play. If, when you installed Ubuntu, on the Applications page you did **not** choose "Extended selection", you will have to install the **ubuntu-restricted-addons** package manually with the **sudo apt install** command in a terminal window.

```
sudo apt install ubuntu-restricted-addons
```

The "Extended selection" option only install the **ubuntu-restricted-addons** package. If you also want the **ubuntu-restricted-extras** package, you will also have to install it manually with the **sudo apt install** command in a terminal window.

```
sudo apt install ubuntu-restricted-extras
```

Package	Description
`liba52`	HDTV audio (ATSC A/52, AC3)
`faad`	MPEG2/ 4 AAC audio decoding, high quality (faad2)
`faac`	MPEG2/ 4 AAC sound encoding and decoding
`ffmpeg`	Play, record, convert, stream audio and video. Includes digital streaming server, conversion tool, and media player.
`libavcodec-extra`	FFmpeg libraries, includes encoders and additional formats
`gstreamer1.0-libav`	ffmpeg plug-in for GStreamer
`gstreamer-plugins-bad`	Not fully reliable codecs and tools for GStreamer, some with possible licensing issues
`gstreamer-plugins-ugly`	Reliable video and audio codecs for GStreamer that may have licensing issues
`gstreamer1.0-vaapi`	The Gstreamer Video Acceleration API packages.
`lame`	MP3 playback capability
`libdvbpsi`	MPEG TS stream (DVB and PSI) decoding and encoding capability, VideoLAN project
`libdvdcss (libdvd-pkg)`	DVD commercial decryption, install and configure the **libdvd-pkg** package.
`libmad0`	MPEG1 audio decoding
`libmpeg2`	MPEG video audio decoding (MPEG1/2 audio and video, AC3, IFO, and VOB)
`libquicktime2`	QuickTime playback
`mpeg2dec`	MPEG2 and MPEG1 playback
`x264`	H264/AVC encoding (high definition media)
`libxvidcore4`	OpenDivx codec (DivX and Xvid playback)
`libsmpeg`	Smpeg MPEG 1 video and audio decoder
`libxine2-all-plugins`	Added video/ audio playback plugins for Xine

Table 6-3: Multimedia third-party codecs

If you have installed GNOME Software, this package also installed a codec wizard. The codec wizard will automatically detect whenever you need to install a new multimedia codec. If you try to run a media file for which you do not have the proper codec, the codec wizard will appear, listing the codecs you need to download and install. The packages are installed as Debian packages by GNOME Software, not the App Center. Often there are several choices (see Figure 6-8). The codec wizard will select and let you install these packages, simplifying the process of installing the various multimedia codecs available for Linux. In most cases it simply installs the **ubuntu-restricted-addons** and **ubuntu-restricted-extras** packages.

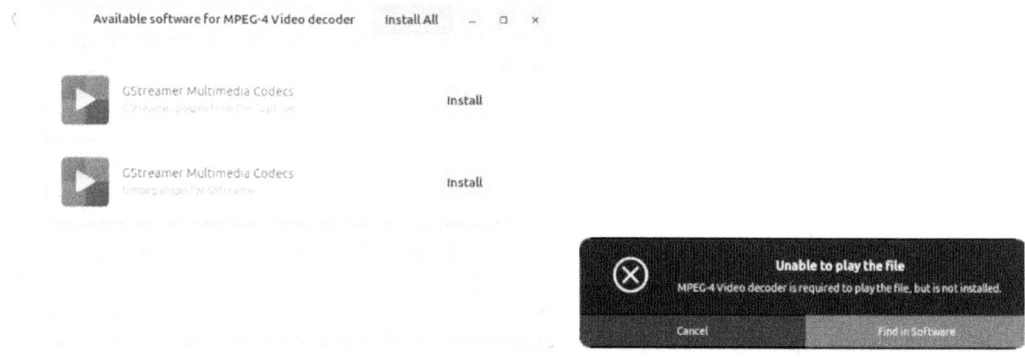

Figure 6-8: GNOME Software's codec wizard

For the Kubuntu desktop, you would also install the KDE version (install with the **sudo apt install command** or the Discover Package Manager).

```
kubuntu-restricted-addons
kubuntu-restricted-extras
```

GStreamer

Many GNOME-based applications make use of GStreamer, a streaming media framework based on graphs and filters (**https://gstreamer.freedesktop.org/**). Using a plug-in structure, GStreamer applications can accommodate a wide variety of media types. For example, the Videos (Totem) video player uses GStreamer to play DVDs, VCDs, and MPEG media, Rhythmbox and Clementine provide integrated music management, and Sound Juicer is an audio CD player.

GStreamer Plug-ins: the Good, the Bad, and the Ugly

Many GNOME multimedia applications like Videos use GStreamer to provide multimedia support. To use such features as DVD-Video and MP3, you have to install GStreamer additional plugins, like those in the Gstreamer ugly collection. You can find more information about GStreamer and its supporting packages at **https://gstreamer.freedesktop.org/**.

GStreamer has four different support packages called the base, the good, the bad, and the ugly. The base package is a set of useful and reliable plug-ins. These are in the Ubuntu main repository. The good package is a set of supported and tested plug-ins that meets all licensing requirements. This is also part of the Ubuntu main repository. The bad package is a set of unsupported plug-ins whose performance is not guaranteed and may crash, but still meet licensing requirements (**ubuntu-restricted-extras** package). The ugly package contains plug-ins that work fine, but may not meet licensing requirements, like DVD support (**ubuntu-restricted-addons** package).

- **The base** Reliable commonly used plug-ins
- **The good** Reliable additional and useful plug-ins
- **The ugly** Reliable but not fully licensed plug-ins (DVD/MP3 support)
- **The bad** Possibly unreliable but useful plug-ins (possible crashes)

Another plug-in for GStreamer that you may want include is **ffmpeg** for Matroska (mkv) and OGG support (**gstreamer1.0-libav** package). The Gstreamer Video Acceleration API packages (**gstreamer1.0-vaapi**) provides hardware video acceleration for gstreamer applications, **https://01.org/linuxmedia/vaapi**.

GStreamer MP3 Compatibility: iPod

Ubuntu provides support for your iPod and iPod Touch from your desktop directly. For your iPod and other MP3 devices to work with GNOME applications like Rhythmbox, you are prompted to install MP3 support for GStreamer the first time you use them (**gstreamer-plugins-ugly** package). MP3 support is not installed initially because of licensing issues.

The **libgpod** library allows player applications like Rhythmbox and Clementine to play songs from your iPod. To synchronize, import, or extract data from your iPod, you can use iPod management software such as **gtkpod** (Universe). For the iPhone, you can use **ifuse**.

Music Applications

Many music applications are currently available for GNOME, including sound editors, MP3 players, and audio players (see Table 6-4). You can use Rhythmbox, GNOME Music, and Sound Juicer to play music from different sources, and the GNOME Sound Recorder to record sound sources. Several applications are also available for KDE, including the media players Clementine and Juk, and a mixer (KMix).

GNOME includes music applications like the Sound Juicer (Audio CD Extractor), GNOME Music, and Rhythmbox. Rhythmbox is the default sound multimedia player, supporting music files, radio streams, video, and podcasts (see Figure 6-9). If you right-click on the Rhythmbox icon on the dock, a menu is displayed with entries to play or stop playing, and to move to the next or previous song or audio source.

The Rhythmbox application window shows buttons in the header for Songs and Categories. The Songs button lists music files, and the Categories button displays them organized into categories. The search (looking glass) lets you search for files. The sidebar shows tabs for your music files (Music), currently queued files (Play Queue, other audio sources (Podcasts, Radio, Libre.fm), and playlists. The bottom of the sidebar displays buttons for managing playlists. Playlists you add also appear as tabs on the sidebar.

To see the list of your music files, click the Music tab on the sidebar. At the bottom of the Rhythmbox window are buttons to play selected songs. A slider shows the progress. Buttons to the right let you repeat your songs and to play in random order. To play a song, click on it and then click on the play button. To remove a music file from Rhythmbox, right click on the file and select Move to Trash. To see information about the song, right click on it and select Properties.

You can create a queue of songs to play by selecting the ones you want and then right-clicking on one to display a menu where you can choose the Add to Queue entry. The Play Queue entry on the sidebar will show the number of songs in the queue. Click on the Play Queue entry to open the Play Queue tab listing the songs. Click on the play button at the bottom of the window to start playing the songs.

To add a new playlist, click on the plus button (+)at the bottom of the sidebar. This will add a new entry to the sidebar for that playlist. To remove the playlist, select it on the sidebar and the click the minus button (-) at the bottom of the sidebar. To add a song to a playlist, right click on the file to display a menu with an "Add to Playlist" entry. Select it to see a list of your playlists and then select the one you want. To remove it from the playlist, right-click on it and choose 'Remove from Playlist" in the menu.

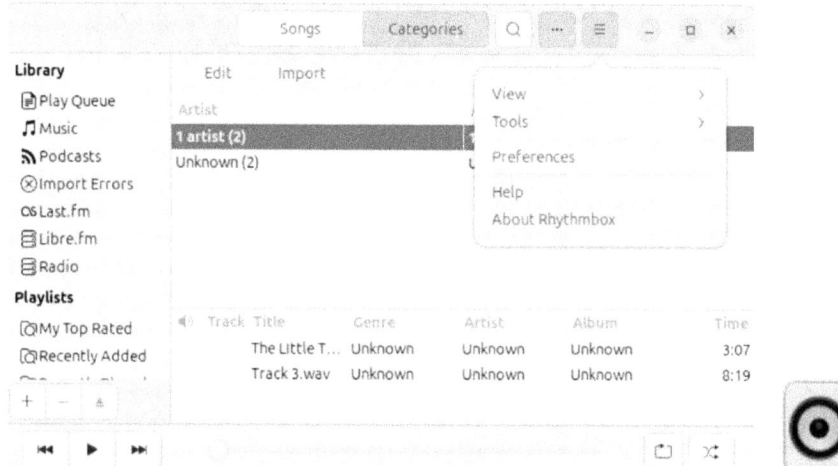

Figure 6-9: Rhythmbox GNOME Multimedia Player

Application	Description
Rhythmbox	Music management (GStreamer), default Music player with iPod support
Clementine	Multimedia audio player based on Amarok (KDE)
Elisa	KDE music player
Sound Juicer	GNOME CD audio ripper (GStreamer)
GNOME Music	GNOME Music player
Audacious	Multimedia player
JuK (Kmix)	KDE5 Music player (jukebox) for managing music collections
Goobox	CD player and ripper
Sound Recorder	GNOME Sound recorder
XMMS2	CD player
ubuntustudio-audio	Ubuntu Studio meta package (Meta Packages (universe)), includes a collection of audio applications. Use Synaptic Package Manager
QMidiRoute	MIDI event router and filter (universe)

Table 6-4: Music players, editors, and rippers

KDE music applications include Elisa, Clementine and Juk. Elisa is a basic music player for KDE with browsing and playlist support (see Figure 6-10). The Clementine music player is based on Amarok and will play on the GNOME desktop. It includes access to Internet sources, local music files, and local devices like Audio CDs. Both Elisa and Clementine are available from the App Center as Snap packages. JuK (Music Jukebox) is the KDE music player for managing music collections.

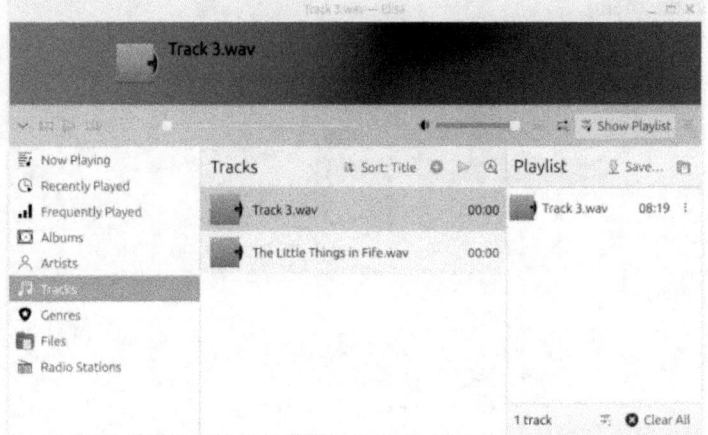

Figure 6-10: Elisa KDE Multimedia Player

GNOME Music is the GNOME Music player with tabs for Albums, Artists, and Playlists (see Figure 6-11). GNOME Music is available from the App Center as a Debian package. GNOME Music accesses sound files in your Music folder. Click on the Playlists tab to display a sidebar with entries such as Favorite Songs, Most Played, and Never Played. The Never Played tab lists all the songs on your Music folder that you have not played yet. You can click on a song to play it. A toolbar opens at the bottom with buttons to control the playback. The button to the right opens a menu with shuffle and repeat options. To add a selected file to a playlist click on the ellipses button on the right side of the song's entry to display a menu with an "Add to Playlist" entry, which opens an "Add to Playlist" dialog listing your playlists. On this dialog you can also create new playlists using the "New Playlist" textbox at the bottom. Your playlists will appear as tabs on the sidebar. Click on one to display the songs in that playlist.

Figure 6-11: GNOME Music

Due to licensing and patent issues, Ubuntu does not install MP3 support by default. MP3 playback capability has been removed from multimedia players like Rhythmbox. Be sure you have install the **gstreamer-plugins-ugly** package to provide MP3 support. As an alternative to MP3, you can use Ogg Vorbis compression for music files.

CD/DVD Burners

Several CD/DVD ripper and writer programs can be used for CD music and MP3 writing (burners and rippers). These include Sound Juicer, Brasero, and K3b (See Table 6-5). GNOME features the CD audio ripper Sound Juicer and Goobox. For burning DVD/CD music and data discs, you can still use the Brasero CD/DVD burner and for KDE you can use K3b.

Brasero, K3b, ogmrip, and dvdauthor can all be used to create DVD-Video discs. OGMrip can rip and encode DVD video. DVD-Video and CD music rippers may require addition codecs installed. You can also use the **mkisofs** (**genisoimage** package), **cdrecord** (**wodim** package), and **cdda2wav** (**icedax** package) command line tools to write DVD/CD discs.

Application	Description
Brasero	Full service CD/DVD burner, for music, video, and data discs (no longer supported)
Sound Juicer (Audio CD Extractor)	GNOME music player and CD burner and ripper (App Center)
Goobox	GNOME CD player and ripper (App Center)
ogmrip	DVD ripping and encoding with DivX support
K3b	KDE CD writing interface
dvdauthor	Tools for creating DVDs

Table 6-5: CD/DVD Burners

Video Applications

Several projects provide TV, video, DivX, DVD, and DVB support for Ubuntu (see Table 6-6). Aside from GStreamer applications, there are also several third-party multimedia applications you may want, also available on the Ubuntu repositories, such as Celluloid, MPlayer and vlc.

Video and DVD Players

Most current DVD and media players are provided on the Ubuntu repositories. The default video player is GNOME Videos. The Videos window displays two tabs: Videos and Channels (see Figure 6-12). The Videos tab lists videos on your system and for those at specific sites on the Internet. The Channels tab list streaming services. Click the plus button at the left side of the header bar to display a menu for adding local or Web videos. For a Web video, you enter the video's Web address.

262 Part 2: Applications

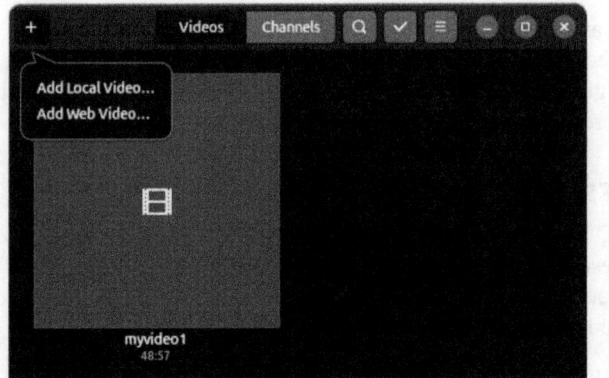

Figure 6-12: GNOME Videos: Videos tab

To Play a video, click on it (see Figure 6-13). For full-screen viewing, click the expand icon on the right side of the header bar. Move the mouse toward the bottom of the dialog to display viewing controls, including pause/play, repeat, sound volume, and skipping to the next or previous video. Click the back button (left side of the header bar) to return to the video listing.

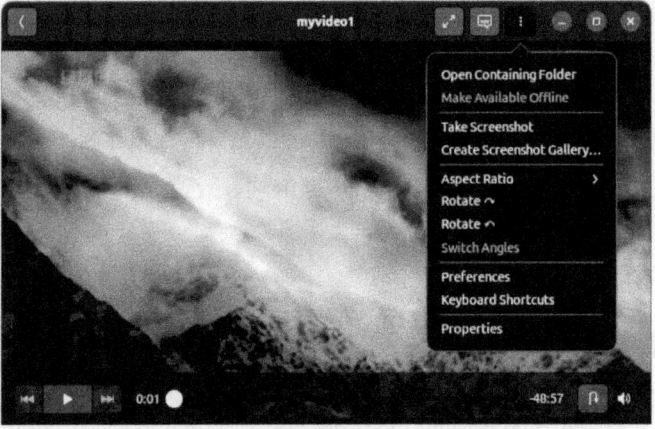

Figure 6-13: GNOME Videos, playing a video

To play several videos in sequence click on the check icon at the right side of the header bar to display checkboxes at the corner of each video icon. Click the checkboxes of the videos you want to see, and then click the Play button on the lower left corner of the dialog. To randomize the sequence, click the Shuffle button instead.

To remove a video, click the check icon at the right side of the header bar to display checkboxes at the corner of each video icon. Click the checkboxes of the videos you want to remove and then click the Delete button on the lower right corner of the dialog.

Clicking on the search icon opens a text box for searching for videos (see Figure 6-14). The resource searched is shown on the right side of the text box. Clicking on the resource name displays a menu with possible resources you can search, including your local system, DLNA connection, and bookmarks.

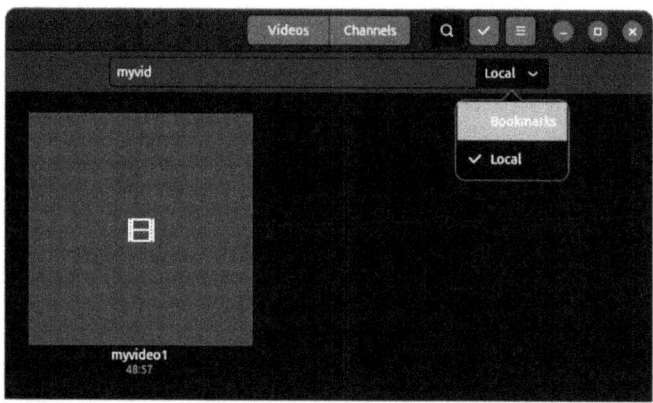

Figure 6-14: GNOME Videos Search

Projects and Players	Sites
Videos	Video and DVD player for GNOME using GStreamer, includes plugins for DVB, YouTube, and MythTV. It is based on the original GNOME Totem video player.
Celluloid	GTK+ frontend for the MPV video player (**https://github.com/celluloid-player/celluloid**)
Dragon Player	Dragon Player video and DVD player for KDE and Ubuntu
VLC Media Player (vlc)	Network multimedia streaming and video player **www.videolan.org**
MPlayer	MPlayer DVD/multimedia player **www.mplayerhq.hu**
MythTV	Home media center with DVD, DVR, and TV capabilities **https://www.mythtv.org**
mpv	Open source video player based on Mplayer
tvtime	TV viewer, **https://tvtime.sourceforge.net**
XviD	Open Source DivX, **https://www.xvid.com**
Kaffeine	An older KDE media player, including HDTV, DVB, DVD, CD, and network streams (Universe repository, install with Synaptic or Discover)
ubuntustudio-video	Ubuntu Studio meta package (Meta Packages (universe)), includes a collection of video applications.
PiTiVi	Video editor
Shotcut	Video editor

Table 6-6: Video and DVD Projects and Applications

Several popular video players available for Ubuntu are listed here:

Dragon Player is a KDE multimedia player, installed with KDE desktop but will play on the GNOME Ubuntu desktop For the KDE players like Dragon Player, be sure to install the **kubuntu-restricted-extras** and **kubuntu-restricted-addons** packages. You can install it from the App Center as a Snap package.

MPlayer is a cross-platform open source alternative to RealPlayer and Windows Media Player (**www.mplayerhq.hu**). MPlayer uses an extensive set of supporting libraries and applications like **lirc**, **lame**, **lzo**, and **aalib**, which are also available on the Ubuntu repository. If you have trouble displaying video, be sure to check the preferences for different video devices and select one that works best (**mplayer** package, Universe repository). Install with the App Center.

mpv is an open source video player based on Mplayer and supports an extensive selection of codecs and formats. Run from the Applications Overview or from a terminal window with the **mpv** command. Install with the App Center as a Debian package.

Videos is the GNOME Video player that uses GStreamer (see Figure 6-14). To expand Videos capabilities, you need to install added GStreamer plug-ins, as discussed previously. You can use the **dconf** editor to modify default settings (org.gnome.Totem) (**totem** package, Ubuntu main repository). Though the name of the application is Videos, the package name is still totem. Videos is available from the App Center as a Snap package.

The **VideoLAN** project (**http://www.videolan.org**) offers network streaming support for most media formats, including MPEG-4 and MPEG-2 (see Figure 6-15). It includes a multimedia player, VLC, which can work on any kind of system (**vlc** package, Universe repository). VLC supports high-def hardware decoding. VideoLAN is available from the App Center as a Snap packages.

Celluloid is a GTK+ frontend for the MPV video player (**https://github.com/celluloid-player/celluloid**) (see Figure 6-16). It provides a basic interface with standard controls and playlist. You can also select video, audio, and subtitle tracks. It is the default video player for Ubuntu MATE. Celluloid is available from the App Center as a Snap package.

Xine is a multipurpose video engine and for Linux/Unix systems that can play video, DVD, and audio discs. Many applications like Videos and Kaffeine use Xine support to playback DVD Video. See **http://xinehq.de** for more information. (**xine** support packages, universe repository). For the Xine user interface, install the **xine-ui** package with the **sudo apt install** command.

Kaffeine is an older KDE multimedia player (video and dvb) (**kaffeine** package, Ubuntu Universe repository, install from the App Center).

Chapter 6: Graphics and Multimedia **265**

Figure 6-15: VLC Video Player (VideoLAN)

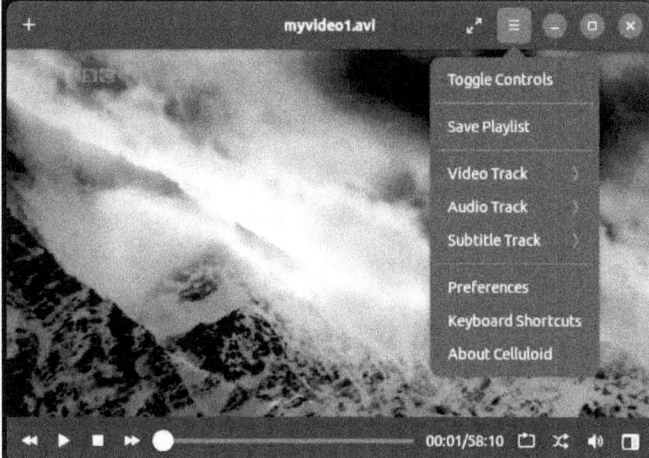

Figure 6-16: Celluloid on Ubuntu

Videos Plugins

The Videos movie player uses plugins to add capabilities like a subtitle downloader. Select Preferences from the Videos top bar menu to open the Preferences dialog. On the General tab click on the Plugins button to open the Configure Plugins window (see Figure 6-17).

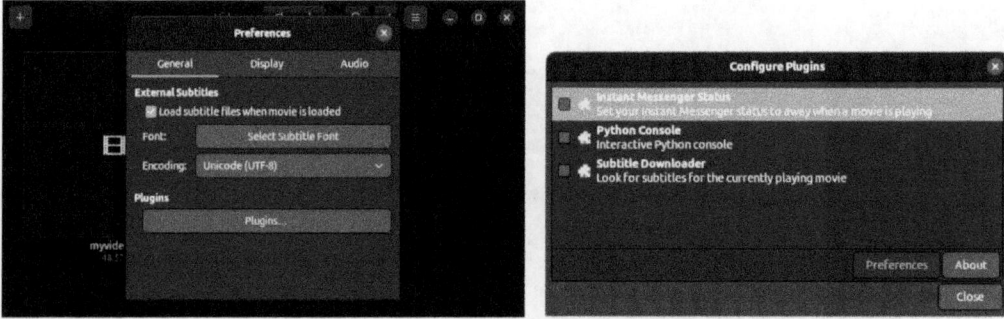

Figure 6-17: Videos (Totem) Movie Player plugins

DVD Video support

Unencrypted DVD Video support is provided by three packages available on the Ubuntu repository: **gstreamer-plugins-ugly**, **libdvdnav4**, and **libdvdread7**. These packages are available on the Ubuntu repository and can be installed with the **sudo apt install** command. With the **libdvdnav4** library, these players feature full DVD menu support. The **libdvdread7** library provides basic DVD interface support, such as reading IFO files.

None of the DVD-Video applications will initially play commercial DVD-Video discs. That requires Content Scrambling System (CSS) decryption for commercial DVDs, which is provided by the **libdvdcss** package. The **libdvdcss** library works around CSS decryption by treating the DVD as a block device, allowing you to use any of the DVD players to play commercial DVDs. It also provides region-free access. See the following page for complete details.

https://help.ubuntu.com/community/RestrictedFormats/PlayingDVDs

The easiest way to install the **libdvdcss** package is to use the **libdvd-pkg** package, which is provided on the Ubuntu repository, multiverse. This package will compile the libdvdcss library, prompting you for the automatic upgrades option. You can install it with the **sudo apt install** command in a terminal window, and then run the **dpkg-reconfigure** command on it. When it installs, it will also install the C++ compiler (**g++** and **gcc**) along with development tools and libraries, if you have not done so already.

```
sudo apt install libdvd-pkg
sudo dpkg-reconfigure libdvd-pkg
```

Alternatively, you can directly download the source code with your Web browser from the VideoLan site.

```
http://download.videolan.org/pub/libdvdcss/
```

PiTiVi and Shotcut Video editors

The PiTiVi Video editor is an open source application that lets you edit your videos. It is accessible from the Applications overview. Pitivi is available from the App Center as a Debian package. Check the PiTiVi website for more details (**http://www.pitivi.org**). You can download a quick-start manual from the Documentation page. Pitivi is a GStreamer application and can work with any video file supported by an installed GStreamer plugins, including the GStreamer Ugly plugin.

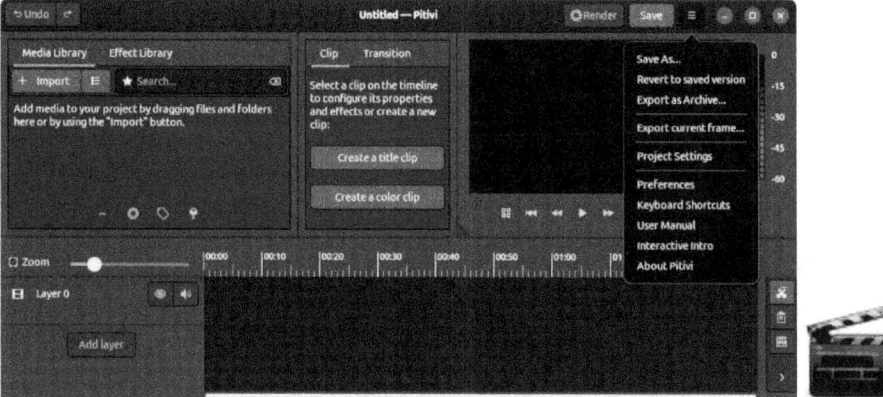

Figure 6-18: Pitivi video editor

The PiTiVi window shows a Clip Library pane on the left, and video playback for a selected video clip on the right (see Figure 6-18). To run a video clip, right click on its icon and select Play Clip. To add a video file to the library, click the Import clips button on the toolbar. You can also drag-and-drop files directly to the Clip Library. The timeline at the bottom of the window displays the video and audio streams for the video clip you are editing, using a rule to shows your position. To edit a video, drag its icon from the Clip Library to the timeline. To trim a video, you pass the mouse over the timeline video and audio streams. Trimming handles will appear that you can use to shorten the video. PiTiVi features ripple editing and rolling editing, splitting, and transitions.

Shotcut is a another open-source video editor that supports numerous video formats (see Figure 6-19). Shotcut is available from the App Center as a Snap or Debian package.

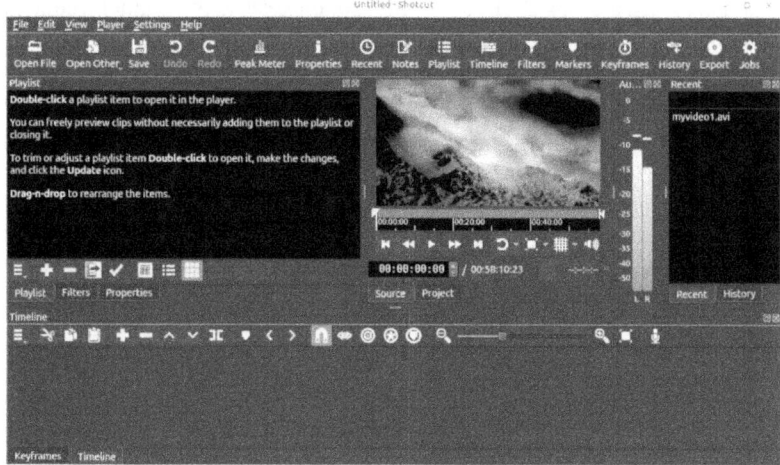

Figure 6-19: Shotcut video editor

TV Players

Some of the TV players available on Ubuntu repositories are listed here:

TV player **tvtime** works with many common video capture cards, relying on drivers developed for TV tuner chips on those cards like the Conexant chips. Check **https://tvtime.sourceforge.net** for more information.

MythTV is a popular video recording and playback application on Linux systems.

Kaffeine is a popular KDE video recording and playback application on Linux systems. It can also play ATSC over the air digital broadcasts.

DVB and HDTV support

For DVB and HDTV reception, you can use most DVB cards as well as many HDTV cards. The DVB kernel driver is loaded automatically. You can use the **lsmod** command to see if your DVB module is loaded.

Be sure you have installed the restricted add-ons and extras packages (**kubuntu-restricted-extras**, **kubuntu-restricted-addons**, **ubuntu-restricted-extras**, and **ubuntu-restricted-addons**), which provide support for appropriate decoders like mpeg2, FFmpeg, and A52 (ac3) (**liba52**, **libxine2-ffmpeg**, **gstreamer1.0-libav**, and **libdvbpsi**). You can use the Synaptic Package Manager to install them.

For DVB broadcasts, some DVB-capable players and tools like Kaffeine , as well as vdr, will tune and record DVB broadcasts in t, s, and c formats. Some applications, like Kaffeine, can scan DVB channels directly. Others may require that you first generate a **channels.conf** file. You can do this with the **w_scan** command (w-scan package). Then copy the generated **channels.conf** file to the appropriate applications folder. Channel scans can be output in vdr, Kaffeine, and Xine formats for use with those applications as well as others like Mplayer and MythTV. The **w_scan** command can also generate **channel.conf** entries for ATSC channels (HDTV), though not all applications can tune ATSC channels (Kaffeine can tune HDTV as well as scan for HDTV channels). You can also use the **dvbscan** tool (**dvb-apps** package) for scanning your channels and the **azap** tool for accessing the signal directly. This tool makes use of channel frequencies kept in the **/usr/share/dvb** folder. There are files for ATSC broadcast as well as cable.

Kaffeine DVB and ATSC tuning

The Kaffeine KDE media player can scan for both DVB and ATSC channels. You will need to have a DVB or ATSC tuner installed on your system. On Kaffeine, from the Television menu choose Configure Television, and on the device tab choose the source such as ATSC. Then from the Television menu, select Channels to open a Channel dialog. Your tuner device is selected on the Search on menu. Click on the Start scan button to begin scanning. Detected channels are listed on the "Scan results" scroll box. Select the ones you want and click Add Selected to place them in the Channels scroll box. Be sure to add the channel you want to watch on the Channel list.

You can use Kaffeine to both tune and record both DVB and ATSC HDTV channels. Kaffeine records an HDTV file as an **m2t** HDV MPEG-2 file, the High Definition Video (HDV) format used for high definition camcorders. The **m2t** files that Kaffeine generates can be played back by most video players, including Videos, Dragon Player, and vlc. To schedule a recording on Kaffeine, click the Television tab or click Digital TV from the Start tab. From the Television menu choose Recording Schedule or click the calendar button in the lower left corner to open the Recording Schedule dialog. Click the New button to open a Schedule Entry dialog where you can name the program, select the channel, set the time and duration, and choose to repeat daily or weekly.

Xvid (DivX) and Matroska (mkv) on Linux

MPEG-4 compressed files provide DVD-quality video with relatively small file sizes. They have become popular for distributing high-quality video files over the Internet. When you first try to play an MPEG-4, the codec wizard will prompt you to install the needed codec packages to play it. Many multimedia applications like VLC already support MPEG-4 files.

MPEG-4 files using the Matroska wrapper, also known by their file extension **mkv**, can be played on most video players including the VideoLan vlc player, Videos, Dragon Player, and Kaffeine. You will need HDTV codecs, like MPEG4 AAC sound codec, installed to play the high definition **mkv** file files. You will need the **ubuntu-restricted-addons** and **ubuntu-restricted-extras** packages installed. For the KDE players be sure to install the **kubuntu-restricted-extras** and **kubuntu-restricted-addons** packages. To manage and create MKV files you can use MakeMKV, MkvToolNix (**mkvtoolnix-gui** package). Install with the App Center.

You use the open source version of DivX known as Xvid to play DivX video (**libxvidcore4** package, Universe repository. Install with the **sudo apt install** command. Most DivX files can be run using XviD. XviD is an entirely independent open source project, but it is compatible with DivX files. You can also download the XviD source code from **https://www.xvid.com**.

Ubuntu Studio

Ubuntu Studio features Linux software for multimedia production, including sound, music, video, and graphics applications. You can install Ubuntu Studio as its own installation (see Chapter 11) or as an added desktop on your Ubuntu desktop install.

You can download the Ubuntu Studio install USB/DVD from **https://ubuntustudio.org**. The install procedure is the same for the Ubuntu desktop.

To add Ubuntu Studio to your current desktop, install the **ubuntustudio-desktop** Meta package, which will install the complete Ubuntu Studio desktop. Use the **sudo apt install** command in a terminal window. You also have to install the Ubuntu Studio software collections including **ubuntustudio-audio, ubuntustudio-graphics,** and **ubuntustudio-video**. Ubuntu studio uses the Ubuntu Studio desktop theme with Ubuntu Studio icons, Applications menu categories, and background image.

Sound

Your sound cards are detected automatically for you when you start up your system, by ALSA, which is invoked by udev when your system starts up. Removable devices, like USB sound devices, are also detected. See Table 6-7 for a listing of sound device and interface tools.

In addition to hardware drivers, sound systems also use sound interfaces to direct encoded sound streams from an application to the hardware drivers and devices. Ubuntu uses the Pipewire server for its sound interface. The ALSA hardware drivers are still used, but the application interface is handled by Pipewire. Pipewire is installed as the default set up for Ubuntu.

As an alternative, you can use the command-line ALSA control tool, **alsamixer** (**alsamixergui** is the desktop version). This will display all connections and allow you to use a keyboard command to select (arrow keys), mute (m key), or set sound levels (Page Up and Down). Press the ESC key to exit. The **amixer** command lets you perform the same tasks for different sound connections from the command line. To actually play and record from the command-line, you can use the **play** and **rec** commands. They are installed as part of the **alsa-utils** package.

Note: Sound devices on Linux are supported by hardware sound drivers. With the Ubuntu kernel, hardware support is implemented by the Advanced Linux Sound Architecture (ALSA) system. You can find more about ALSA at **https://alsa-project.org/**.

Sound tool	Description
alsamixer	ALSA sound connection configuration and volume tool
amixer	ALSA command for sound connection configuration
Settings Sound	GNOME Settings Sound tab, used to select and configure your sound interface
Pipewire	Pipewire sound interface and server. The default for Ubuntu.
PulseAudio	PulseAudio sound interface and server. https://www.freedesktop.org/wiki/Software/PulseAudio/

Table 6-7: Sound device and interface tools

Volume Control

The sliding sound bar on the System also lets you set the sound volume (see Figure 6-20). If you have multiple sound devices, they will be listed, letting you switch between them. To perform volume control for specific devices like a microphone, you use the Settings Sound dialog.

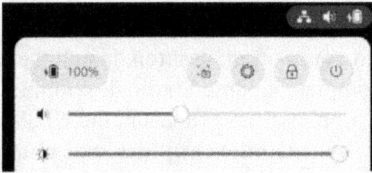

Figure 6-20: System menu Volume Control

Settings Sound

The Pipewire sound server has replace the Pulseaudio sound server in Ubuntu 22.04. You can, if you wish, install the older Pulseaudio sound server, but all future development will use Pipewire.

You configure sound devices and set the volume for input, output, and the system using the Settings Sound dialog. The Sound dialog has been combined into one dialog with three sections: Output, Input, and Sounds (see Figure 6-21). The Sounds section has links to dialogs for the Volume Levels of system sounds and the Alert Sound). In the Output and Input sections you can set sound volumes for different devices. To turn off the sound for a device, click the speaker or microphone button on the left side of the volume slider. This will set the volume to zero. The button is a toggle. To turn on the sound again, click it again. This will return sound level to its previous settings.

On the Output section, you set the input volume for an output device, and configure its balance settings. If you have more than one device, it will be listed in the Output Device menu. Choose the one you want to configure. On the Output Volume slider you can set the sound level for a selected device. For the Balance adjustment, the available settings will change according to the device selected. For a simple Analog Stereo Output, there is only a single Balance setting. The Over-Amplification option lets you raise volume over 100 percent, which may be useful for low powered speakers.

On the Input section, you set the input volume for an input device such as a microphone. When speaking or recording, the input level is displayed. If you have more than one input device, they will be listed in the Input Device menu. Choose the one you want to configure. To turn off the microphone, click the microphone button on the left side of the volume slider. This will set the volume to zero. To turn the microphone back on, click the microphone button again to return to the previous settings.

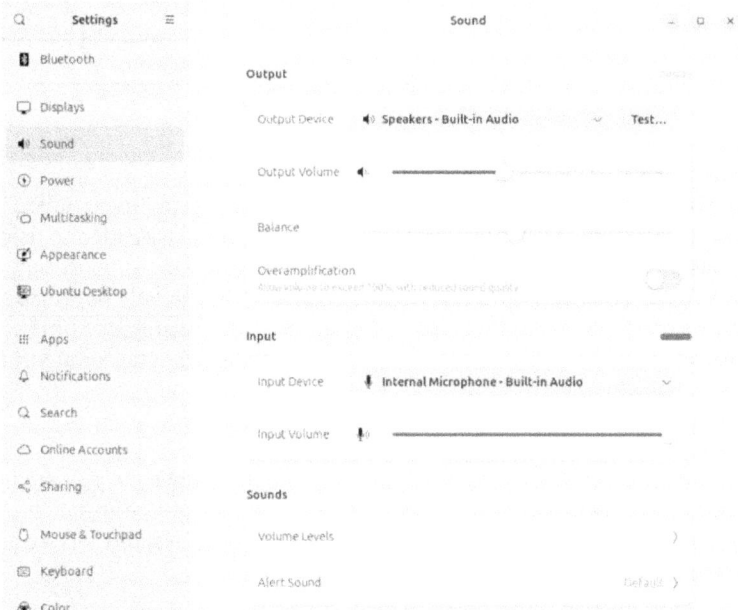

Figure 6-21: Settings Sound tab

Sound devices that support multiple interfaces like analog surround sound 7.1 and digital SPDIF output, may have an extensive list of interface combinations in the Output Device menu. The Output section will then display configuration settings for the selected device. With Analog

Surround 7.1 Output selected, the Output section will show settings for Balance, Fade, and Subwoofer. Configuring digital output for SPDIF (digital) connectors is a simple matter of selecting the digital output entry on the Output Device menu.

In the Sounds section, the Volume Levels link opens a dialog for setting the system sound, and the Alert Sound link open a dialog for selecting the alert sound to use (see Figure 6-22). Volume Levels dialog has a System Sounds sliding bar that sets the volume for system sounds. To turn off system sound, click the music button on the left side of the System Sounds volume slider. This will set the volume to zero. To turn the system sounds back on, simply click the music button again, returning the sound levels to their previous settings. The Alert Sound dialog lets you select an alert sound, such as Click or Hum. Use the Volume Levels' System Sounds to set the volume for your sound alerts.

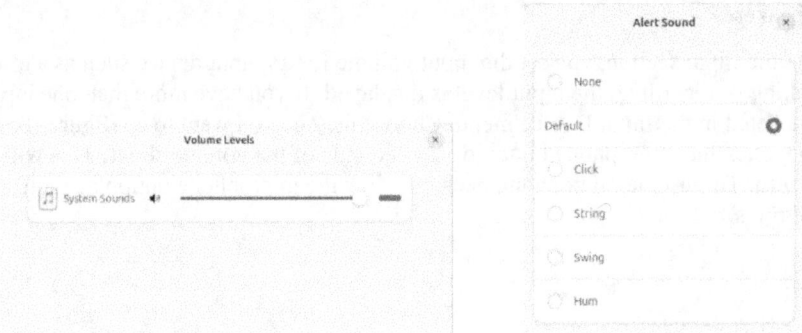

Figure 6-22: Volume Levels and Alert Sound dialogs

PulseAudio server and applications

You could also install the older Pulseaudio server if you wish. Some older GNOME applications may still use Pulseaudio, though eventually they should transition to using Pipewire. If you decide to install the Pulseaudio server, then the Pipewire desktop support applications will be removed. The Pipewire server and libraries remain installed. You can only have one sound server interfacing with your desktop, either Pipewire or Pulseaudio. Specifically, the **pipewire-audio** and **pipewire-alsa** packages are removed. You can install Pulseaudio using the **sudo apt install** command in a terminal window.

```
sudo apt install pulseaudio
```

Should you decide to change back to Pipewire, simply remove the pulseaudio package. The **pipewire-audio** and **pipewire-alsa** packages will be automatically re-installed. All the Pulseaudio applications and libraries are removed, including the pulseaudio service and socket files in **/lib/systemd/user**.

```
sudo apt remove pulseaudio
```

PulseAudio is cross-platform sound server, allowing you to modify the sound level for different audio streams separately. See **https://www.freedesktop.org/wiki/Software/PulseAudio/** for documentation and help. PulseAudio offers complete control over all your sound streams, letting you combine sound devices and direct the stream anywhere on your network. PulseAudio is not confined to a single system. It is network capable, letting you direct sound from one PC to another.

For additional configuration abilities, you can also install the PulseAudio applications. They begin with the prefix **pa** in the package name. PulseAudio applications are accessible from the Applications overview.

PulseAudio Volume Control, **pavucontrol**

PulseAudio Volume Meter, **pavumeter**

PulseAudio Preferences, **paprefs**

You can use the PulseAudio Volume Control application (**pavucontrol**) to set the sound levels for different playback applications and sound devices (PulseAudio Volume Control on the Applications overview). The PulseAudio Volume Control applications will show tabs for Playback, Recording, Output Devices, Input Devices, and Configuration. The Playback tab shows all the applications currently using PulseAudio. You can adjust the volume for each application separately. You can use the Output tab panel to set the volume control at the source and select different output devices, such as Headphones. The volume for input and recording devices are set on the Recording and Input Devices tabs. The Configuration tab lets you choose different device profiles, such as selecting Digital output or Surround Sound.

Sound tool	Description
pacat	Play, record, and configure a raw audio stream
pacmd	Generates a shell for entering configuration commands
pactl	Control a PulseAudio server, changing input and output sources and providing information about the server.
padsp	PulseAudio wrapper for OSS sound applications
pamon	Link to pacat
paplay	Playback audio. The -d option specifies the output device, the -s option specifies the server, and the --volume option sets the volume (link to pacat)
parec	Record and audio stream (link to pacat)
parecord	Record and audio stream (link to pacat)
pasuspender	Suspend a PulseAudio server
pax11publish	Access PulseAudio server credentials

Table 6-8: PulseAudio commands (command-line)

You can also use the PulseAudio Volume control to direct different applications (streams) to different outputs (devices). For example, you could have two sound sources running, one for video and another for music. The video could be directed through one device to headphones, and the music through another device to speakers, or even to another PC. To redirect an application to a different device, right-click its name in the Playback tab. A pop-up menu will list the available devices and let you select the one you want to use.

The PulseAudio Volume Meter application will show the volumes of your devices.

To configure network access, you use the PulseAudio Preferences application (**paref**). Here you can permit network access, configure the PulseAudio network server, and enable multicast and simultaneous output. Simultaneous output creates a virtual output device to the same hardware device. This lets you channel two sources onto the same output. With PulseAudio Volume Control, you could then channel playback streams to the same output device, but using a virtual device as the output for one. This lets you change the output volume for each stream independently. You could have music and voice directed to the same hardware device, using a virtual device for music and the standard device for voice. You can then reduce the music stream, or raise the voice stream.

In addition, there are PulseAudio command-line tools available as shown in Table 6-8. Install the **pulseaudio-utils** package.

ubuntu

7. Internet Applications

Web Browsers: Firefox, GNOME Web, Chromium, Links
BitTorrent: Transmission
Java for Linux
Network File Transfer: FTP
FTP Clients
Instant Messenger
VoIP: Skype
GNOME Maps

Ubuntu provides powerful Web and FTP clients for accessing the Internet. Some of these applications are installed automatically and are ready to use when you first start up your Ubuntu system. Ubuntu also includes full Java development support. Web and FTP clients connect to sites that run servers, using Web pages and FTP files to provide services to users.

On your Ubuntu system, you can choose from several Web browsers, including Firefox, Web (Epiphany), Chromium, and Links. Firefox, Chromium, and Web are desktop browsers that provide full picture, sound, and video display capabilities. The Links browser is a line-mode browser that displays only lines of text.

Web browsers and FTP clients are commonly used to conduct secure transactions, such as logging into remote sites, ordering items, or transferring files. Such operations are currently secured by encryption methods provided by the Transport Layer Security (TLS) and its older Secure Sockets Layer (SSL) protocols. If you use a browser for secure transactions, it should be TLS/SSL enabled. Most browsers include TLS/SSL support. Ubuntu distributions include SSL (OpenSSL) as part of a standard installation.

URL Addresses

An Internet resource is accessed using a Universal Resource Locator (URL). A URL is composed of three elements: the transfer protocol, the hostname, and the pathname. The transfer protocol and the hostname are separated by a colon and two slashes, **://**. The pathname begins with a single slash:

```
transfer-protocol://host-name/path-name
```

The transfer protocol is usually HTTP (Hypertext Transfer Protocol), indicating a Web page. Other possible values for transfer protocols are **ftp** and **file**. As their names suggest, **ftp** initiates FTP sessions, whereas **file** displays a local file on your own system, such as a text or HTML file. The hostname is the computer on which a particular website is located. You can think of this as the address of the website. By convention, many hostnames begin with **www**, though not necessarily. In the next example, the URL locates a Web page called **guides.html** on the **http://tldp.org** website:

```
http://tldp.org/guides.html
```

If you do not want to access a particular Web page, you can leave the file reference out, and then you access the website's home page automatically. To access a website directly, use its hostname. If no home page is specified for a website, the file **index.html** in the top folder is used as the home page. In the next example, the user brings up the GNOME home page:

```
https://www.gnome.org/
```

Most Web sites use the protocol (Hypertext Transfer Protocol Secure), as shown in the previous example. This protocol uses Transport Layer Security (TLS) encryption for security. For these sites you use the **https://** designation as show in the previous example. TLS is based on the older Secure Sockets Layer (SSL) security.

The resource file's extension indicates the type of action to be taken on it. A picture has a **.gif** or **.jpeg** extension and is converted for display. A sound file has an **.au** or **.wav** extension and is played. The following URL references a **.gif** file. Instead of displaying a Web page, your browser invokes a graphics viewer to display the picture.

Web Browsers

Popular browsers for Ubuntu include Firefox (Mozilla), Chromium (Google), Epiphany, and Links (see Table 7-1). Firefox is the default Web browser used on most Linux distributions, including Ubuntu. Web is the GNOME Web browser (formerly known as Epiphany). Chromium is the open source version of the Google Web browser. Links and Lynx are text based browsers with no graphics capabilities, but in every other respect, they are fully functional Web browsers.

Web Site	Description
Firefox	The Mozilla project Firefox Web browser, Ubuntu desktop default browser https://www.mozilla.org
Web	GNOME Web browser (formerly called Epiphany) https://wiki.gnome.org/Apps/Web
Chromium	Open source version of Google Chrome Web browser http://www.chromium.org
lynx	Text-based command-line Web browser (Ubuntu supported)
Links and Links2	Text-based command-line Web browser (Ubuntu supported), Link2 also provides a graphical interface.

Table 7-1: Web browsers

The Firefox Web Browser

The Mozilla project is an open source project based on the original Netscape browser code that provides a development framework for web-based applications, primarily the web browser and e-mail client. The Mozilla project site is **https://www.mozilla.org**, and the site commonly used for plug-in and extension development is **https://www.mozdev.org**. You can also sign up for a Firefox account which can then make your bookmarks available to the Firefox browsers on all your devices. So you can save a bookmark on one of your Firefox browsers, and have it available on the Firefox browsers on all your devices.

Ubuntu uses Firefox as its primary browser (see Figure 7-1). Firefox is installed by default with icons on the dock and the Applications overview. Firefox is no longer available on the Apt (DEB) repositories. It is now installed and maintained from the Snap repository.

When opened, Firefox displays the first tab. Firefox is designed to display tabs, each of which can display a complete Web page, including the Firefox toolbar and sidebar. The tab title is shown at the top, and next to it is a plus button (+) you can click to add a new tab. You can also press CTRL+t. You can easily switch from one page to another by clicking its tab. You can re-arrange tabs by clicking and holding on a tab title and moving it to the right or left.

Within a tab, a navigation toolbar is displayed at the top, with an address bar (text box) for entering a URL address and a series of navigation buttons for accessing web pages. On the left side of the toolbar are the Next and Previous buttons for paging through previously accessed web pages, followed by a cancel button for loading a page (X) which becomes a refresh button when the page is fully displayed.

278 Part 2: Applications

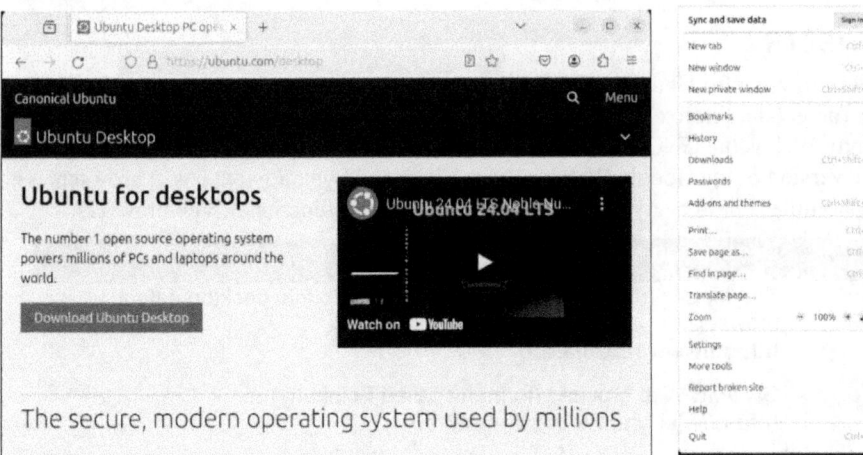

Figure 7-1: Firefox Web Browser

When you enter a web page name in the address bar, Firefox performs a dynamic search on previously accessed pages and displays the pages in a drop-down menu, which you can choose from. Within the address bar to the right is a button for marking the page as a bookmark (star). Should the page support it, additional buttons are displayed such as a reader view to display just the text of the page.

Firefox provides a search bar (text box) for searching the Web, selected sites, or particular items. To the right of the address bar are buttons for saving to Pocket and the Firefox menu. The menu displays entries for accessing your bookmarks, history, and downloads.

To add a bookmark for a page, click the bookmark button on the right side of the address bar (the star button). This displays an New Bookmark dialog with a pop-up menus for folders and tags. The Folder menu is set to the Other Bookmarks folder by default. You can also select the Bookmarks Toolbar or the Bookmarks Menu. The Bookmark Toolbar displays bookmark buttons at the top of the browser. You can manage bookmarks by selecting Bookmarks from the Firefox menu to display the Bookmarks menu. From this menu select the "Manage bookmarks" entry to open the Library dialog at the Bookmarks tab.

To search a current page for certain text, enter CTRL+f. This opens a search toolbar at the bottom of Firefox from which you can enter a search term. You have search options to highlight found entries or to match character case. The Next and Previous buttons let you move to the next found pattern.

When you download a file using Firefox, the download is managed by the Download Manager. You can download several files at once. Progress is displayed download button on the toolbar, which you can click to see your downloads. You can cancel a download at any time or just pause a download, resuming it later.

Selecting History on the Settings menu (accessible from the toolbar) displays the History menu, showing a list of your recently accessed Web pages from which you can select one to view. You can also see recently closed tabs and Firefox windows. To clear your recent history, chose the "Clear Recent History" entry. The "Manage history" option at the bottom opens the Library dialog as the History tab, letting you edit, access, bookmark, or remove previous pages.

The Firefox menu (right-side of the window) lets you perform Web page tasks such as zooming, opening new windows, printing and saving a page, and performing searches on a page. There are also administrative options such as Settings (preferences), Passwords, Add-ons and themes (Add-on Manager), as well as submenus for History and Bookmarks.

You can access the Settings page (about:preferences) from the menu as Settings. The account icon (person image) on the toolbar opens the Settings page to the Sync tab. On the Settings page you can set your privacy and search options, as well as setting your home page, language, fonts, download location (see Figure 7-2). On the Settings Search tab you can choose your default search engine, which includes Google, Bing, Amazon, DuckDuckGo, Twitter, Wikipedia, and eBay.

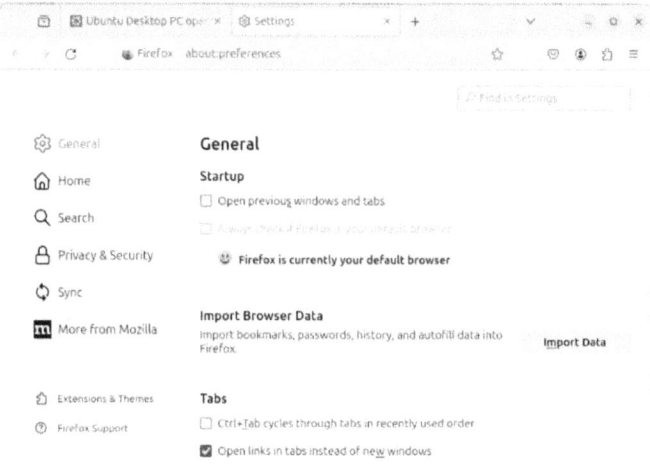

Figure 7-2: Firefox Settings

The Extensions button on the toolbar (jigsaw piece) opens the Add-ons Manager window with tabs for Extensions, Themes, Plugins, and Languages (see Figure 7-3). Click the one you want to open a brief description and display the Add to Firefox button, which you click to open a download and install dialog. The Extensions tab lists Extensions you have installed and recommended Extensions. Installed Extensions display a switch you can use to turn it on or off. Click on the ellipses button (three dots) to display a menu to remove, report, or manage an extension. The manages entry shows permissions and information about the Extension. On the Plugins tab, you can disable or enable embedded applications, such as iTunes, QuickTime, and Skype. An ellipses menu lists options for Always Activate, Never Activate, and manage. The Themes tab lets you choose a theme.

Part 2: Applications

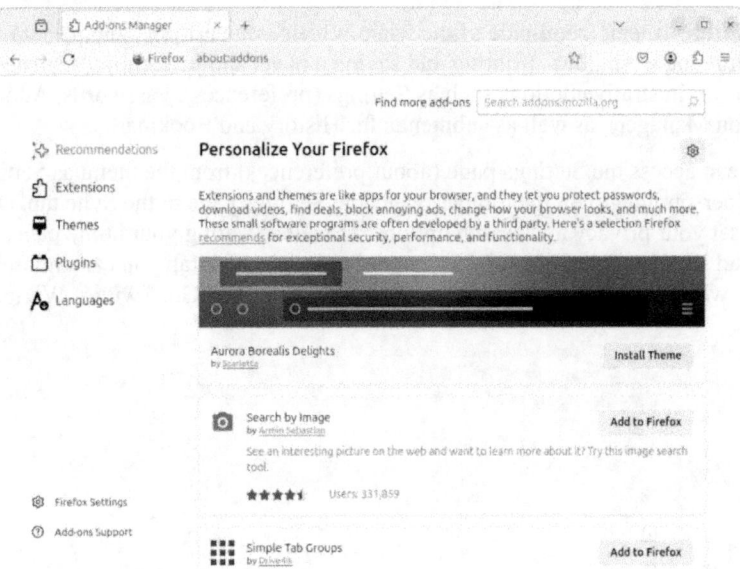

Figure 7-3: Firefox Add-ons Management

Firefox also supports profiles. You can set up different Firefox configurations, each with preferences and bookmarks. This is useful for computers like laptops that connect to different networks or are used for different purposes. You can select and create profiles by starting up the profile manager. Enter the **firefox** command in a terminal window with the **-P** option.

```
firefox -P
```

A default profile is already set up. You can create a new profile, which runs the profile wizard to prompt you for the profile name and folder to use. Select a profile to use and click Start Firefox. The last profile you used will be used again the next time you start Firefox. You have the option to prompt for the profile to use at startup, otherwise run the **firefox -P** command again to change your profile.

GNOME Web (Epiphany)

GNOME Web, formerly known as Epiphany, is a GNOME web browser with a simple interface designed to be fast (see Figure 7-4). You can find out more about Epiphany at **https://wiki.gnome.org/Apps/Web**. Web works well as a simple browser with a clean interface. It is also integrated with the desktop, featuring a download applet that will continue after closing Web. Web also supports tabbed panels for multiple web site access. Its menu (click the menu button at the top right) lists options such as New Window, New Incognito Window, the import and export of bookmarks, History, and Preferences, as well as buttons for page-specific operations such as tabs, print, save, zooming, and find. Within the address box, to the right, is a button (star icon) to bookmark the page. On the right of the header bar are buttons to display tabs and your bookmarks. On the left side are buttons to refresh the page and start a new tab. You can install GNOME Web using App Center (search under "GNOME Web") as a Snap package. Once installed, you can access it as Web.

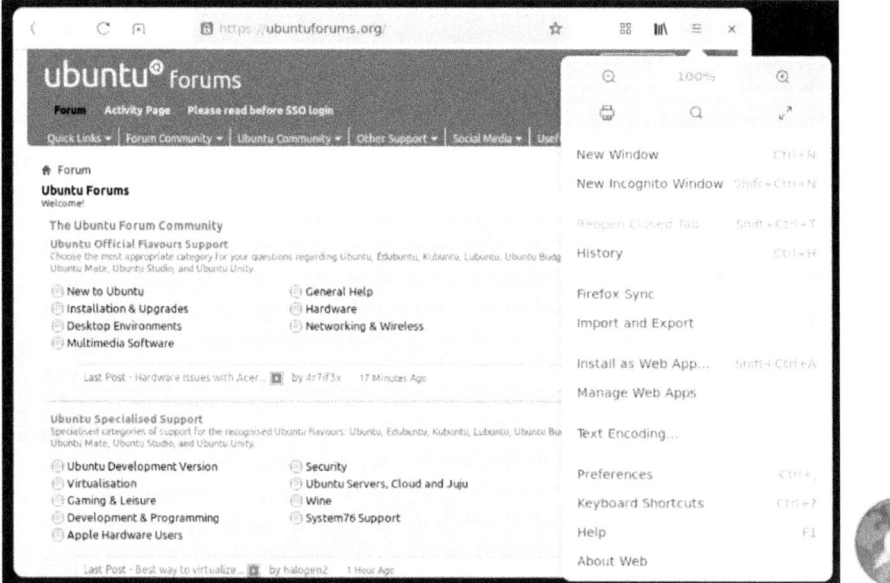

Figure 7-4: Web (Epiphany) Web browser

Chromium

Google's Chromium web browser (**https://www.chromium.org**) provides easy and very secure access to the Web with full Google integration. You can install it using the App Center as a Snap package. You can access Chromium from the Applications overview as Chromium Web Browser. You are first prompted to enter your Google account e-mail and password so that your online preferences and bookmarks can be used, but you can pass.

On Chromium, primacy is afforded to tabs. At the top of the Chromium window are your tabs for open web pages, with a square image button at the end of the tabs for opening a new tab (see Figure 7-3). Chromium features a simple toolbar with navigation buttons and a bookmark button (star icon). To close a tab, click the close button to the right of the tab title.

To the left of the close box on the header, a menu button displays a drop-down menu for menu items for browser operations such as new tabs, print, zoom, history, bookmarks, and downloads. To configure Chromium, select Preferences from this menu to open the Chromium Preferences tab. Here you can set your home page, default search service, and themes. Click the Advanced on the sidebar to expand the Settings dialog to let you manage passwords, languages, downloads, printing, and accessibility.

When you open a new tab, a thumbnail listing of recently closed and most visited sites is displayed, as well as bookmarked sites. Clicking a thumbnail moves you to that site.

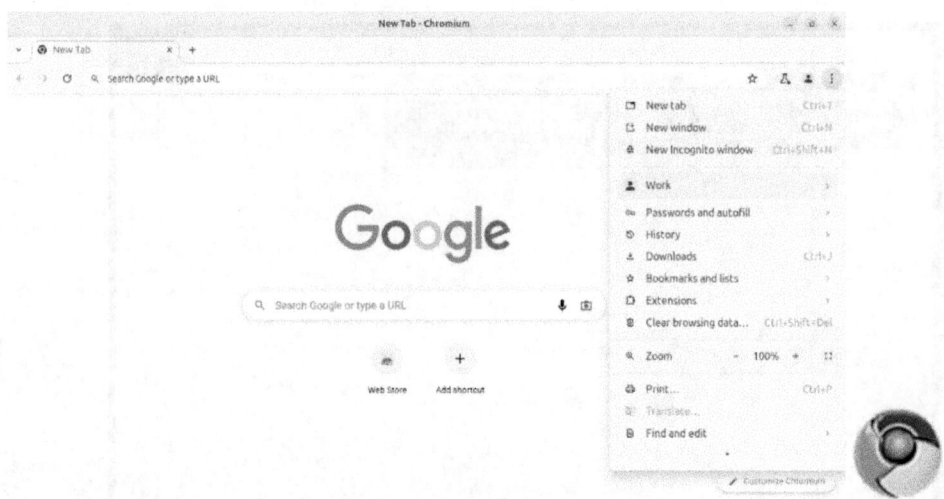

Figure 7-5: Chromium Web Browser (Google Chrome)

Links and Lynx: Line-Mode Browsers

Linux features line-mode browsers such as Links and Lynx, which you can use from a command line interface. You can install Links with the App Center as a Snap package, and Lynx with **sudo apt install** command. On these browsers, a Web page is displayed as text only. A text page can contain links to other Internet resources but does not display graphics, video, or sound. Except for the display limitations, Links and Lynx are fully functional Web browsers. You can also use them to download files or access local pages. All information on the Web is still accessible to you. Because they do not require as much overhead as desktop-based browsers, they can operate much faster, quickly displaying Web page text. To start the Lynx browser, use the **lynx** command, and to start Links use the **links** command. Use the ESC key to display the menu. The Links2 application (**links2**) also provides a graphical interface you can access from the desktop.

Java for Linux

To develop Java applications, use Java tools, and run many Java products, you use the Java 2 Software Development Kit (SDK) and the Java Runtime Environment (JRE). The SDK is a superset of the JRE, adding development tools like compilers and debuggers. Together with other technologies like the Java API, they make up the Java Platform, Standard Edition.

Oracle has open sourced Java as the OpenJDK project and supports and distributes Linux versions. The JRE subset can be installed as OpenJRE. They are directly supported by Ubuntu as packages on the Snap and APT Ubuntu repositories. The Snap repository provides OpenJDK-22. The APT repository provides OpenJDK-21 (**openjdk-21-jdk** package), along with previous versions should you need them (8, 11, and 17). You can install the APT versions with the **sudo apt install** command. , OpenJDK installs both the JRE and the Java development tools. Java packages and applications are listed in Table 7-2.

Application	Description
Java Development Kit, OpenJDK	An open source Java development environment with a compiler, interpreters, debugger, and more (include the JRE), **http://openjdk.java.net**. Included on the Ubuntu Snap repository, OpenJDK-22. On the APT repository, **openjdk-21-jdk** package
Java Runtime Environment, OpenJRE	An open source Java runtime environment, including the Java virtual machine, included with the OpenJDK package
Java Platform Standard Edition (JSE)	Complete Java collection, including JRE, JDK, and API, **http://www.oracle.com/technetwork/java/javase/downloads/index.html**

Table 7-2: Java Packages and Java Web Applications

BitTorrent Clients (transmission)

GNOME and KDE provide effective BitTorrent clients. With BitTorrent, you can download large files quickly in a shared distributed download operation where several users participate in downloading different parts of a file, sending their parts of the download to other participants, known as peers. Instead of everyone trying to access a few central servers, all peers participating in the BitTorrent operation become sources for the file being downloaded. Certain peers function as seeders, those who have already downloaded the file, but continue to send parts to those who need them.

For Ubuntu you can install the GNOME BitTorrent client, Transmission, from the App Center as a Snap package. It is then accessible from the Applications overview. For Kubuntu, you can use the Ktorrent BitTorrent client. To perform a BitTorrent download you need the BitTorrent file for the file you want to download. The BitTorrent file for the Ubuntu Desktop USB/DVD iso image is **ubuntu-24.04-desktop-amd64.iso.torrent**. You can download the file from the **https://ubuntu.com/download/alternative-downloads** site. When you double-click the file it will open it directly with Transmission.

Figure 7-6: Transmission BitTorrent client

Transmission can handle several torrents at once. On the toolbar are buttons for starting, pausing, and removing a download. The Open button can be used to load a BitTorrent file (**.torrent**), setting up a download. You also can drag-and-drop a torrent file to the Transmission window. When you first open a torrent file, the Torrent Options window opens where you can specify the destination folder and the priority. The option to start the download automatically is selected by default. Figure 7-6 shows the Transmission window with two BitTorrent operations set up, both of which are active. A progress bar shows how much of the file has been downloaded.

You could set up Transmission to manage several BitTorrent operations, of which only a few may be active, others paused, and still others that have finished but continue to function as seeders. From the first Show menu, you can select All, Active, Downloading, Seeding, Paused, and Finished torrents. You can also choose those verifying and those that have errors. From the second menu, you can choose Trackers.

To remove a torrent, right-click on it and select Remove. Choose Delete Files and Remove to remove what you have downloaded so far.

To see more information about a torrent, select it and then click the Properties button (see Figure 7-7). This opens a Properties window with tabs for Information, Peers, Tracker, Files, and Options. On the Information tab, the Activity section shows statistics like the progress, times, and errors, and the Details section shows the origin, comment, and locations of the download folder. Peers show all the peers participating in the download. Tracker displays the location of the tracker, the server that manages the torrent operation. Files shows the progress of the file download (a torrent could download more than one file). The Options tab lets you set bandwidth and connection parameters, limiting the download or upload, and the number of peers.

Figure 7-7: Transmission BitTorrent client properties

FTP Clients

With File Transfer Protocol (FTP) clients, you can connect to a corresponding FTP site and download files from it. These sites feature anonymous logins that let any user access their files. Basic FTP client capabilities are incorporated into the Files (GNOME), Dolphin (KDE), and Caja (MATE) file managers. You can use a file manager window to access an FTP site and drag files to local folders to download them. Effective FTP clients are also now incorporated into most Web browsers, making Web browsers the primary downloading tool. Firefox, in particular, has strong FTP download capabilities.

Although file managers and Web browsers provide effective access to public (anonymous login) sites, to access private sites, you may need a stand-alone FTP client like curl, wget, Filezilla, gFTP, lftp, or **ftp**. These clients let you enter usernames and passwords with which you can access a private FTP site. The stand-alone clients are also useful for large downloads from public FTP sites, especially those with little or no Web display support. Popular Linux FTP clients are listed in Table 7-4.

Network File Transfer: FTP

With File Transfer Protocol (FTP) clients, you can transfer extremely large files directly from one site to another (see Table 7-3). FTP can handle both text and binary files. FTP performs a remote login to another account on another system connected to you on a network. Once logged into that other system, you can transfer files to and from it. To log in, you need to know the login name and password for the account on the remote system. Many sites on the Internet allow public access using FTP. Such sites serve as depositories for large files anyone can access and download. These sites are often referred to as FTP sites, and in many cases, their Internet addresses begin with the term ftp, such as **ftp.gnome.org**. These public sites allow anonymous FTP login from any user. You can then transfer files from that site to your own system.

FTP Clients	Description
Caja	MATE file manager
Dolphin	KDE file manager
Files	GNOME file manager (nautilus)
gFTP	GNOME FTP client, **gftp** package
ftp	Command line FTP client
lftp	Command line FTP client capable of multiple connections
curl	Internet transfer client (FTP and HTTP)
Filezilla	Linux version of the open source Filezilla ftp client (Universe repository)

Table 7-3: Linux FTP Clients

Several FTP protocols are available for accessing sites that support them. The original FTP protocol is used for most anonymous sites. FTP transmissions can also be encrypted using SSH2, the SFTP protocol. More secure connections may use FTPS for TLS/SSL encryption. Some sites support a simplified version of FTP called File Service Protocol, FSP. FTP clients may support different protocols like gFTP for FSP and Filezilla for TLS/SSL. Most clients support both FTP and SSH2.

Web Browser-Based FTP

You can access an FTP site and download files from it with any Web browser. Browsers are useful for locating individual files, though not for downloading a large set of files. A Web browser is effective for checking out an FTP site to see what files are listed there. When you access an FTP site with a Web browser, the entire list of files in a folder is listed as a Web page. You can move to a subfolder by clicking its entry. You can easily browse through an FTP site to download files. To download a file, click the download link. This will start the transfer operation, opening a dialog showing the download. The default name is the same as on the remote system. On many browsers, you can manage your downloads with a download manager, which will let you cancel a download operation in progress or remove other downloads requested. The manager will show the time remaining, the speed, and the amount transferred for the current download.

GNOME Desktop FTP

The easiest way to download files from an FTP site is to use the built-in FTP capabilities of the GNOME file manager, GNOME Files. On GNOME, the desktop file manager has a built-in FTP capability much like the KDE file manager. The FTP operation has been seamlessly integrated into standard desktop file operations. Downloading files from an FTP site is as simple as dragging files from one folder window to another, where one of the folders happens to be located on a remote FTP site. Use the GNOME file manager (GNOME Files) to access a remote FTP site, listing files in the remote folder, just as local files are (see Figure 7-8). In a file manager's Location bar (**Ctrl-l**), enter the FTP site's URL using the prefix **ftp://** and press ENTER. A dialog opens prompting you to specify how you want to connect. You can connect anonymously for a public FTP site, or connect as a user supplying your username and password (private site). You can also choose to remember the password.

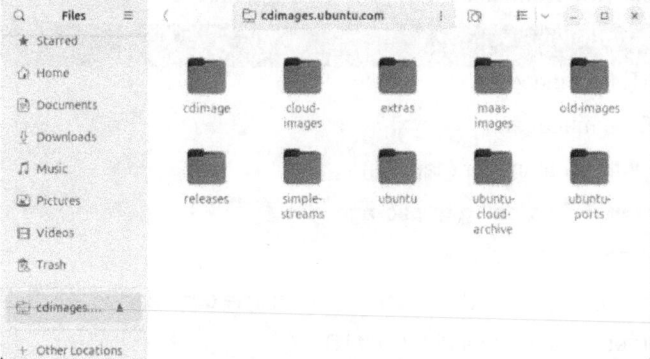

Figure 7-8: GNOME FTP access with the file manager

Folders on the FTP site will be displayed, and you can drag files to a local folder to download them. You can navigate through the folders as you would with any file manager folder, opening folders or returning to the parent folder. To download a file, just drag it from the FTP window to a local folder window. To upload a file, drag it from your local folder to the window for the open FTP folder. Your file will be uploaded to that FTP site (if you have permission to do so). You can also delete files on the site's folders if allowed.

You can also use the Connect bar in the file manager (see Figure 7-9) to connect, which remembers your previous FTP connections. To access the Connect bar, click on the "Other Locations" entry in any file manager sidebar. The Connect bar is displayed at the bottom of the file manager window. It shows a text box for the server address, a menu button to display previous addresses, and a Connect button. Enter the remote server address. The address is remembered and added to the previous servers list. Then click the Connect button. A dialog opens letting you specify an Anonymous login or to enter a username and password. Click the Connect button to access the site.

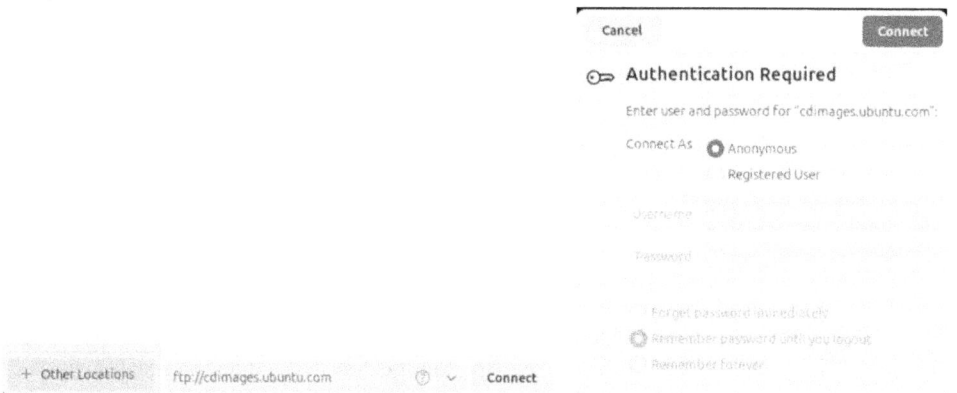

Figure 7-9: GNOME FTP access with the file manager Other Locations Connect bar

The top folder of the remote FTP site will be displayed in a file manager window. Use the file manager to progress through the remote FTP site's folder tree until you find the file you want. Then, open another window for the local folder to which you want the remote files copied. In the window showing the FTP files, select those you want to download. Then click and drag those files to the window for the local folder. As files are downloaded, a Copying entry is shown at the bottom of both file manager sidebars for each window showing a progress circle for the download. Clicking on it displays a progress bar displaying the name of the file and amount to download and time remaining (see Figure 7-10).

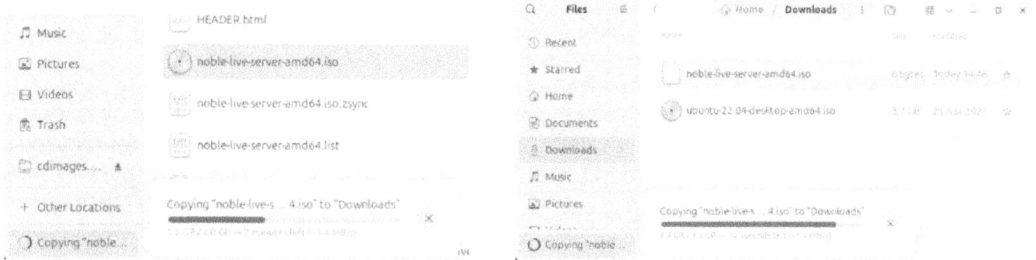

Figure 7-10: GNOME FTP file download

The file manager window's sidebar will list an entry for the FTP site accessed. An eject button is shown to the right of the FTP site's name. To disconnect from the site, click this button. The FTP entry will disappear along with the FTP sites icons and file listings.

FileZilla

FileZilla is an open source FTP client originally implemented on Windows systems (**https://filezilla-project.org/**). Use the App Center to install it as a Debian package. Once installed, you can access it from the Applications overview. The interface displays a left and right pane for local and remote folders. You can navigate through folder trees, with the files of a selected folder displayed below. To download a file, right-click on a file in the Remote site pane (right) and select Download. To upload, right-click on the file in the Local site pane (left) and select Upload. Text boxes at the top let you specify the host, username, password, and port. A Quick connect menu will connect to a preconfigured site.

To configure a remote site connection, use the Site Manager (File | Site Manager). In the Site Manager window, click on the New Site button to create a new site connection. Four configuration tabs become active: General, Advanced, Transfer settings, and Charset. On the General tab, you can specify the host, user, password, and account. The server type menu lets you specify a particular FTP protocol like SFTP for SSH encrypted transmissions or FTPS for TLS/SSL encryption.

gFTP

The gFTP program is an older GNOME FTP client designed to let you make standard FTP file transfers. The package name for gFTP is **gftp**, and it is located in the Universe repository. You can install it from the App Center as a Debian package.

The gFTP window consists of several panes. The top-left pane lists files in your local folder, and the top-right pane lists your remote folder. Subfolders have folder icons preceding their names. The parent folder can be referenced by the double period entry (**..**) with an up arrow at the top of each list. Double-click a folder entry to access it. The pathnames for all folders are displayed in boxes above each pane. A drop down menu to the far right lets you specify the FTP protocol to use such as FTP for a standard transmission, SSH2 for SSH encrypted connections, and FSP for File Service Protocol transmissions. Two buttons between the panes are used for transferring files. The left arrow button, <-, downloads selected files in the remote folder, and the right arrow button, ->, uploads files from the local folder. Menus across the top of the window can be used to manage your transfers.

wget

The wget tool lets you access Web and FTP sites for particular folders and files. Folders can be recursively downloaded, letting you copy an entire website. The **wget** command takes as its option the URL for the file or folder you want. Helpful options include **-q** for quiet, **-r** for recursive (folders), **-b** to download in the background, and **-c** to continue downloading an interrupted file. One drawback is that your URL reference can be very complex. You have to know the URL already. You cannot interactively locate an item as you would with an FTP client. The following would download the Ubuntu Install DVD in the background.

```
wget -b ftp://releases.ubuntu.com/noble/ubuntu-24.04-desktop-amd64.iso
```

curl

The **curl** Internet client operates much like **wget**, but with much more flexibility. With curl, you can specify multiple URLs on its command line. You can also use braces to specify multiple matching URLs, like different websites with the same domain name. You can list the different website host names within braces, followed by their domain name (or vice versa). You can also use brackets to specify a range of multiple items. This can be very useful for downloading archived files that have the same root name with varying extensions. **curl** can download using any protocol, and will try to intelligently guess the protocol to use if none is provided. Check the **curl** man page for more information.

ftp

The **ftp** client uses a command line interface, and it has an extensive set of commands and options you can use to manage your FTP transfers. It is the original FTP client used on Unix and Linux systems. See the **ftp** man page for more details. Alternatively, you can use **sftp** for more secure access. The **sftp** client has the same commands as **ftp** but provides SSH (Secure SHell) encryption.

You start the **ftp** client by entering the command **ftp** at a shell prompt. If you want to connect to a specific site, you can include the name of that site on the command line after the **ftp** keyword. Otherwise, you need to connect to the remote system with the ftp command **open**. You are then prompted for the name of the remote system with the prompt "(to)". When you enter the remote system name, ftp connects you to the system and then prompts you for a login name. After entering the login name, you are prompted for the password. In the next example, the user connects to the remote system **garnet**, and logs in to the **robert** account:

```
$ ftp
ftp> open
(to) garnet
Connected to garnet.berkeley.edu.
220 garnet.berkeley.edu FTP server ready.
Name (garnet.berkeley.edu:root): robert
password required
Password:
user robert logged in
ftp>
```

Once logged in, you can execute Linux commands on either the remote system or your local system. You execute a command on your local system in ftp by preceding the command with an exclamation point. Any Linux commands without an exclamation point are executed on the remote system. One exception exists to this rule. Whereas you can change folders on the remote system with the **cd** command, to change folders on your local system, you need to use a special ftp command called **lcd** (local **cd**). In the next example, the first command lists files in the remote system, while the second command lists files in the local system:

```
ftp> ls
ftp> lcd
```

The ftp program provides a basic set of commands for managing files and folders on your remote site, provided you have the permission to do so. You can use **mkdir** to create a remote folder, and **rmdir** to remove one. Use the **delete** command to erase a remote file. With the **rename** command, you can change the names of files. You close your connection to a system with the **close** command. You can then open another connection if you want. To end the ftp session, use the **quit** or **bye** command.

```
ftp> close
ftp> bye
Good-bye
$
```

To transfer files to and from the remote system, use the **get** and **put** commands. The **get** command receives files from the remote system to your local system, and the **put** command sends files from your local system to the remote system. In a sense, your local system gets files from the remote folder and puts files to the remote folder. In the next example, the file **weather** is sent from the local system to the remote system using the **put** command:

```
ftp> put weather
PORT command successful.
ASCII data connection
ASCII Transfer complete.
ftp>
```

lftp

The **lftp** program is an enhanced FTP client with advanced features such as the abilities to download mirror sites and to run several FTP operations in the background at the same time. You can install it with the **sudo apt install** command in a terminal window.

It uses a command set similar to that for the ftp client. You use **get** and **mget** commands to download files, with the **-o** option to specify local locations for them. Use **lcd** and **cd** to change local and remote folders.

When you connect to a site, you can queue commands with the **queue** command, setting up a list of FTP operations to perform. With this feature, you could queue several download operations to a site. The queue can be reordered and entries deleted if you wish. You can also connect to several sites and set up a queue for each one. The **mirror** command lets you maintain a local version of a mirror site. You can download an entire site or just update newer files, as well as remove files no longer present on the mirror.

You can tailor **lftp** with options set in the **.lftprc** file. System-wide settings are placed in the **/etc/lftp.conf** file. Here, you can set features like the prompt to use and your anonymous password. The **.lftp** folder holds support files for command history, logs, bookmarks, and startup commands. The **lftp** program also supports the **.netrc** file, checking it for login information.

Social Networking

Ubuntu provides integrated social networking support for IM (Instant Messenger) and VoIP (Voice over Internet). User can communicate directly with other users on your network (see Table 7-1). Most of these applications are not supported by Ubuntu and are not installed by default. You can install them from the App Center or the Synaptic Package Manager.

Instant Messenger

Instant messenger (IM) clients allow users on the same IM service to communicate across the Internet (see Table 7-4). Currently, some of the major IM services are AIM (AOL), Microsoft Network (MSN), Yahoo, ICQ, and Jabber. Some use an XML protocol called XMPP, Extensible Messaging and Presence Protocol.

Clients	Description
Skype	VoIP application (Partner repository)
Slack	Slack group messenger
Pidgin	Older instant messenger client used in previous releases and still available.
Jabber	Jabber IM (XMPP)
Finch	Command line cursor-based IM client
Konversation	KDE IRC client

Table 7-4: Instant Messenger, Talk, and VoIP Clients

Pidgin

Pidgin is an older IM client that works with most IM protocols. It is still available on the Universe repository, and can be installed with the App Center as a Debian package. Pidgin will be accessible from the Applications overview. Pidgin will open a Buddy List window with menus for Buddies, Accounts, Tools, and Help. Use the Buddies menu to send a message or join a chat. The Accounts menu lets you configure and add accounts. The Tools menu provides configuration features, such as preferences, plugin selection, privacy options, and sound.

The first time you start Pidgin, the Add Account window is displayed with Basic, Advanced, and Proxy tabs for setting up an account. Later you can edit the account by selecting it in the Accounts window (Accounts | Manage) and clicking the Modify button. Pidgin is not supported by Online Accounts.

To create a new account, select Manage Accounts from the Accounts menu (Accounts | Manage). This opens the Accounts dialog, which lists your current accounts. Click the Add button to open the Add Account dialog with a Basic, Advanced, and Proxy tabs. On the Basic panel, you choose the protocol from a pop-up menu that shows items such as AIM, Bonjour, Yahoo, and IRC, and then enter the appropriate account information. You can also select a buddy icon to use for the account. On the Advanced tab, you specify the server and network connection settings. Many protocols will have a server entered already.

To configure your setup, select Preferences from the Tools menu (Tools | Preferences) to open the Preferences dialog where you can set options for logging, sounds, themes, and the interface display. You can find out more about Pidgin at **http://pidgin.im**. Pidgin is a GNOME front end that used the libpurple library for actual IM tasks (formerly libgaim). The libpurple library is used by many different IM applications.

VoIP Applications

Ubuntu provides the popular VoIP application Skype, which is proprietary (available on the App Center, Snap repository).

Skype

Skype is part of the Snap repository. You can install Skype as a Snap packages from the App Center. Once installed, you can access Skype from the Applications overview. The interface is similar to the Windows version. A Skype panel icon will appear on the panel, once you start Skype.

You can use it to access Skype throughout your session. Click to open Skype and right-click to display a menu from which you can change your status and sign out. The panel icon changes according to your status.

Also, the **pidgin-skype** package provides a Skype plugin, which will let you use Ubuntu applications like Pidgin, Finch, and Empathy to operate through Skype connections.

GNOME Maps

GNOME Maps is a GNOME map utility that provides both street and satellite maps. It can also detect your current location (see Figure 7-11). Use the zoom buttons or mouse scroll button to zoom in and out. To search for a location, enter the name in the search box, and options will be listed. To see your current location, click the Geolocation button on the left side of the header bar. To trace routes click the route planner button to the right side to open a dialog where you can enter the source and destination locations. You can install GNOME Maps from the Ubuntu Apps Center as a Debian package.

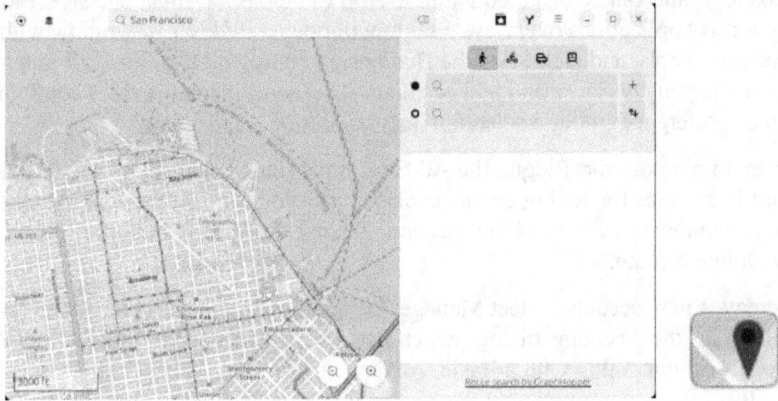

Figure 7-11: GNOME Maps

Part 3: Desktops

Ubuntu Desktop
Kubuntu
Ubuntu MATE
Ubuntu Flavors
The Shell

ubuntu

8. Ubuntu Desktop

Ubuntu GNOME
Favorites/Dock
System Menu
Activities
Applications Overview
Windows
Workspaces
Files File Manager

The Ubuntu 24.04 desktop is based on GNOME. As discussed in Chapter 3, check the Ubuntu Desktop Guide for a help and documentation. The Ubuntu GNOME desktop uses the GNOME Files file manager, as well as GNOME desktop configuration tools (see Chapter 3).

GNOME

The GNU Network Object Model Environment, also known as GNOME, is a powerful and easy-to-use environment consisting primarily of a panel, a desktop, and a set of desktop tools with which program interfaces can be constructed. GNOME is designed to provide a flexible platform for the development of powerful applications. Currently, GNOME is supported by several distributions and is the primary interface for the Ubuntu Desktop. GNOME is free and released under the GNU Public License. GTK+ is the widget set used for GNOME applications. The GTK+ widget set is entirely free under the Lesser General Public License (LGPL). The LGPL enables developers to use the widget set with proprietary software, as well as free software (the GPL is restricted to free software).

For detailed documentation, check the GNOME documentation site at **https://help.gnome.org**. Documentation is organized by users, administrators, and developers. "GNOME Help" provides a complete tutorial on desktop use. For administrators, the "GNOME System Administration Guide" details how administrators can manage user desktops. Table 8-1 offers a listing of useful GNOME sites.

Web Site	Description
https://www.gnome.org	Official GNOME website
https://help.gnome.org	GNOME documentation website for users, administrators, and developers
https://wiki.gnome.org/Personalization	Desktop themes and background art
https://wiki.gnome.org/Apps	GNOME software applications, applets, and tools
https://developer.gnome.org/	GNOME developer's site

Table 8-1: GNOME Resources

GNOME releases new versions on a frequent schedule. The Ubuntu 24.04 uses GNOME 46.0. Key changes with GNOME 46.0 are described in detail at the following:

```
https://release.gnome.org/46/
```

The Ubuntu GNOME Desktop

GNOME is based on the gnome-shell, which is a compositing window manager (see Figure 8-1). The key components of the gnome-shell are a top bar, an Activities overview, the Ubuntu Dock, clock and calendar, Applications overview, and a notifications feature. The top bar has a dialog for the date and time (calendar) with notifications, and a System menu for sound volume, network connections, power information, and user tasks such as accessing settings and logging out. The Activities overview lets you quickly access favorite applications, locate applications, select windows, and change workspaces. The notification system notifies you of recent events, such as updates and recently attached devices. The Applications overview lets you find and start applications.

Figure 8-1: Ubuntu Desktop

You can configure desktop settings and perform most administrative tasks using the GNOME configuration tools (see Table 8-1) listed in the GNOME Settings dialog, accessible from the System menu (see Figure 8-25). In addition, the GNOME Tweaks application lets you customize your desktop, windows, the top bar, selecting desktop fonts, and changing the appearance (themes and backgrounds).

Top Bar

The screen displays a top bar, with buttons for the Activities overview and the System menu. Clicking the System menu button (network, sound, and power emblems) at the right of the top bar displays the System menu with buttons to set the sound level, screen brightness (laptop), wired and wireless connections, Bluetooth, and a power button to logout, shut down, or lock the screen (see Figure 8-1). There are also buttons for Settings, lock screen, screen shot, power mode, lighting, style, keyboard, and airplane mode. The center of the top bar has a button to display your clock and calendar, which will also display your notifications. To the left is the Activities button, which you click on to open the Activities overview. The Activities button is also a dynamic workspace indicator, displaying dots of your open workspaces and highlighting the one you are currently working on. You can also use the dynamic workspace indicator to switch between your workspaces by hovering the mouse over the indicator and then using your scroll wheel to move between workspaces.

System Menu

The System menu button (network, sound, and power emblems) is displayed on the right side of the top bar (see Figure 8-2). Clicking the button displays the System menu. At the top, it has buttons for the battery service indicator (battery image), taking a screenshot (camera image), opening Settings (gear image), activating the lock screen (lock image), and displaying the Power Off menu (power button image). The battery service indicator shows the current charge of the battery. Clicking on it opens the Setting Power tab showing the battery level. The Power Off menu lists Suspend, Restart, Power Off, Switch User (if you have more than one), and Logout entries.

Below these buttons are sliding bars for sound and brightness, which you can adjust the volume and brightness . If your display does not support brightness adjustments, only the sound slider is shown.

Below the sliders, a set of Quick Settings buttons lets you quickly activate or deactivate different services and devices. These will be different depending on your computer's capabilities. The network devices are listed first. Most will have either a Wired or Wi-Fi button or both, depending on the kind of network connections supported. If you have Bluetooth, a Bluetooth button is displayed. You can turn a device or service on or off by clicking its button. Activated buttons have a highlighted solid color, whereas deactivated ones are grayed out (dark for the dark style). In addition, the Wi-Fi button will also display your currently selected Wi-Fi connection, the Bluetooth button will show the number of selected Bluetooth devices, and the Power Mode button displays your current power mode (the default is Balanced). An unselected Power Mode button, does not turn off the power mode, it just uses the default power mode, Balanced. Clicking it will select a different power mode such as power saver. Clicking it again will deselect the power mode button, returning you to the Balanced power mode.

If a device or service can be further configured, its button will have a menu button on its right side indicated by a right arrow, as is the case for Wired, Wi-Fi, Bluetooth, Power Mode, and Keyboard. Clicking on the menu button opens a small dialog where you can select settings. The Wired, Wi-Fi, Bluetooth, and Power Mode buttons will include a link in their menus to their appropriate Settings dialog, allowing you to perform a detailed configuration. The Wired dialog has a Wired Settings link to open the Settings Network tab, and the Power Mode dialog has a Power Settings link to open the Settings Power tab. The Wi-Fi button's dialog has an All Networks link that opens the Settings Wi-Fi tab.

Some button dialogs let you make simple setting selections, such as the Power Mode button's menu that lets you choose Performance, Balanced, Power Saver power modes. The Bluetooth button's menu list your available Bluetooth devices. Wi-Fi shows your Wi-Fi connections.

Other buttons just turn a service on or off, such as the Night Light button that turns on night lighting for the display, the Dark Style that switches between the desktop dark and light styles, and Airplane Mode that turns airplane mode on and off. These have no menu buttons on button's right side.

Chapter 8: Ubuntu Desktop **299**

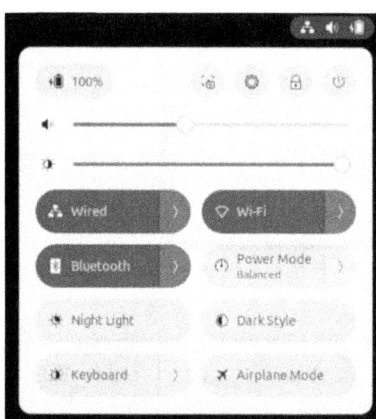 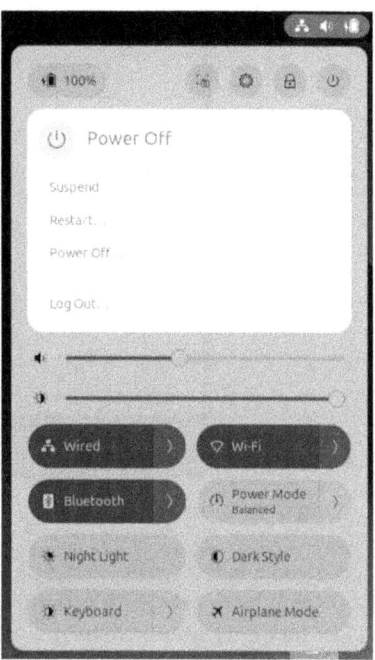

Figure 8-2: System menu

On systems that are not laptops, there will be no brightness slider or Battery button on the System menu. If the system has no wireless device, the Wi-Fi entry will also be missing. A system of this kind will only have a sound slider and a Wired, Power Mode, Night Light, Style, and Keyboard button.

To log out, you click the Power button to display the Power Off menu to show Log Out, Switch User, Suspend, and Power Off entries. The Log Out returns you to the login screen, where you can log in as another user. The Switch User entry is not shown unless your system has more than one user configured. To switch to another user, click the Switch User entry to display the login screen. You can then log in as another user. When you log out or choose Switch User, you can then select the original user. When you log back in, your session is restored.

Desktop menu and Desktop folder

Right-clicking anywhere on the desktop background displays the desktop menu with entries for the Desktop folder and the access to Settings Appearance and Displays dialogs (see Figure 8-3). You can use this menu to create a new folder directly on the desktop, as well as open the Desktop folder with the file manager or a terminal window (Show desktop in Files). Items you place on the desktop are located in your home folder's Desktop folder. Adding a file or folder directly to your Desktop folder displays it on your desktop. The "Change Background" entry open Settings at the Appearance dialog where you can choose a new background, and the "Display Settings" entry opens Settings at the Displays dialog where you can configure your monitor.

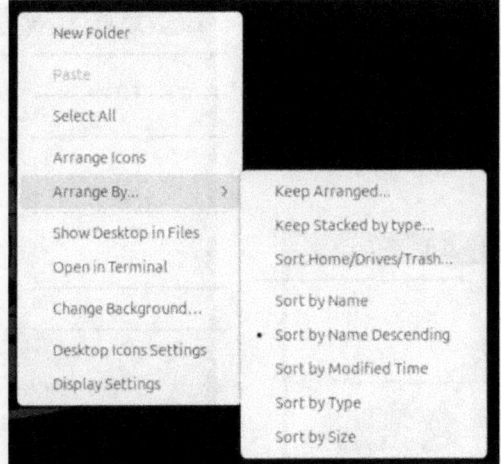

Figure 8-3: Desktop Menu

Should you create a folder on the desktop using the desktop menu, the folder is displayed on the desktop (see Figure 8-4). Its location is your home folder's Desktop folder. You can right-click on a folder on the desktop to display a menu with tasks you can perform on that folder.

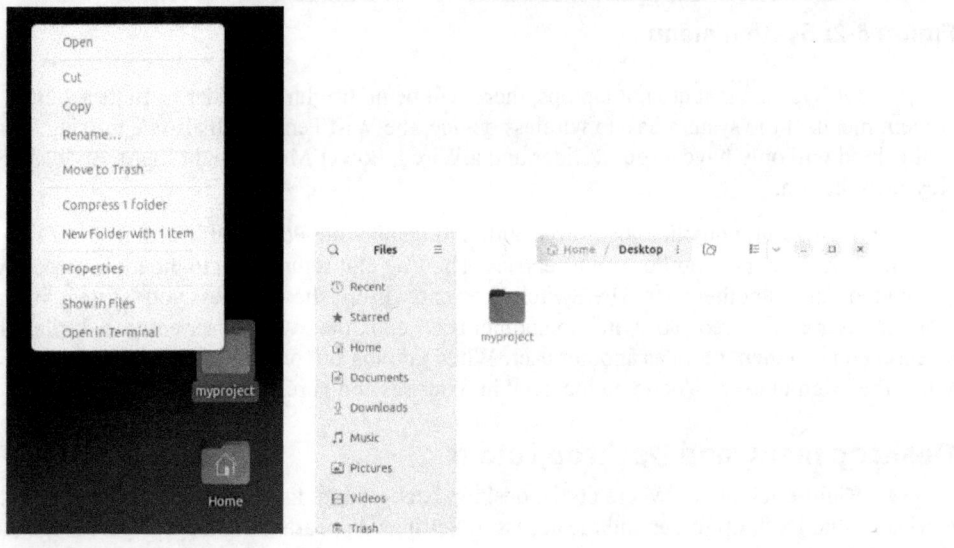

Figure 8-4: Desktop folder

Activities Overview

To access applications and windows, you use the Activities overview mode. Click the Activities button at the left side of the top bar or press the SUPER (Windows) key. The Activities overview mode consists of thumbnails of open windows, and workspace thumbnails (see Figure 8-5). You can use the search box at the top center to locate applications and files.

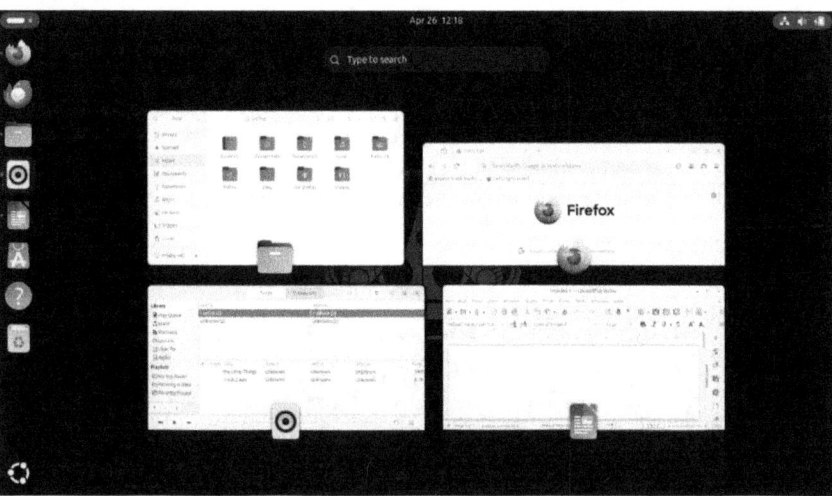

Figure 8-5: Activities Overview

Another way to quickly access the Activities overview is to enable the Hot Corner option in the Settings Multitasking tab (see Figure 8-6). Instead of clicking on the Activities button, just move your mouse to that upper left corner. The Activities overview is then displayed.

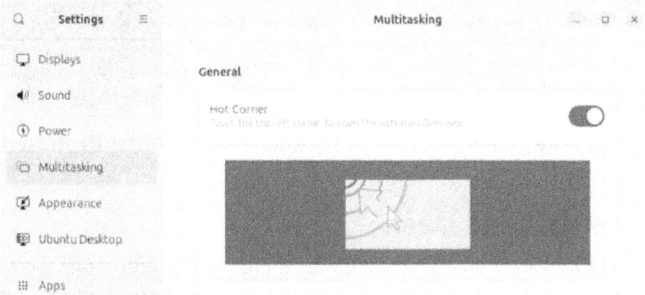

Figure 8-6: Settings Multitasking tab Hot Corner option

Partially hidden thumbnails of your adjacent desktops workspace are displayed on either side, to the right and left of you current workspace. Ubuntu is initially configured for dynamic, not fixed, workspaces. It shows only your current workspace and an empty one to the right. When you first use another empty workspace, it becomes activated, with another empty one generated to its right. Moving your mouse to the right side moves you to the adjacent workspace, making it your current workspace. To move a window from your current workspace to an adjacent workspace, click and drag it to the right or left side of the screen showing part of the adjacent workspace.

The first time you move to the empty adjacent workspace on the right, that workspace becomes activated and you now have multiple workspaces. Whenever you have multiple workspaces, a workspace selector is displayed at the top of the screen showing thumbnails of your workspaces (see Figure 8-7). You can use the workspace selector to move directly from one workspace to another, as well as move windows displayed in the thumbnails from to another workspace. To move to another workspace, just click on the workspace want. To move a window, click and drag it to another workspace thumbnail.

You can configure your workspaces to be fixed instead of dynamic, setting up a limited number of workspaces. In this case, the workspace thumbnail list is always displayed, letting you move to whatever workspace you want with just a click. Fixed and dynamic workspaces are configured in the Settings Multitasking tab in the Workspaces section.

You can manually leave the Activities overview mode at any time by pressing the ESC key, the SUPER key, or clicking the activities button on the left side of the top bar.

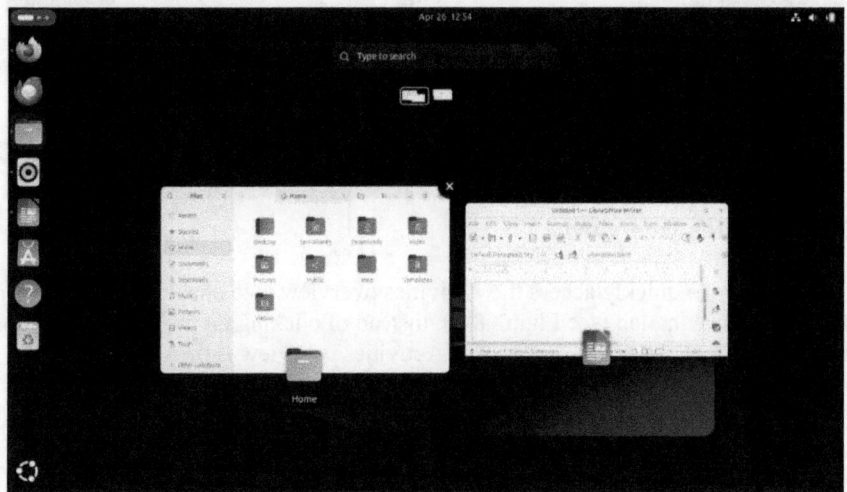

Figure 8-7: Activities Overview with workspace selector (multiple workspaces)

Ubuntu Dock and GNOME Dash

The Ubuntu dock is a bar on the left side of the desktop with icons for your favorite applications (see Figure 8-8). It is displayed on the desktop and Activities and Applications overviews. The Ubuntu dock is a GNOME extension implemented by Ubuntu and is a modified version of the GNOME Dock to Dash extension, which places the GNOME dash on the desktop. Initially, there are icons for the Firefox web browser, Thunderbird mail, Files (the GNOME file manager), Rhythmbox music application, LibreOffice Writer, the App Center, GNOME help, the Trash folder, and the Applications overview. To open an application from the dock, click its icon, or right-click and choose New Window from the pop-up menu.

On the Activities overview click-and-drag the icon to the windows thumbnail area or to a workspace thumbnail at the top. Clicking on the dock icon for an application with an open window, brings that window to the forefront. If you want, you can change this action to a minimize operation instead. In that case clicking the icon would minimize the open window. To do so you have to change the default action using **gsettings** or the **deconf** editor. The setting to change is org.gnome.shell.extensions.dash-to-dock's click action option.

```
gsettings set org.gnome.shell.extensions.dash-to-dock click-action 'minimize'
```

Favorites are always displayed on the dock. When you run other applications, they are also placed on the dock during the time they are running. To add a running application to the dock as a favorite, right-click the icon on the dock and choose Pin to Dash. You can later remove an application as a favorite by choosing Unpin. You can also add any application to the dock from the Applications overview, by clicking-and-dragging its icon to the dock, or by right-clicking the icon and choosing Pin to Dash from the menu (see Figure 8-8).

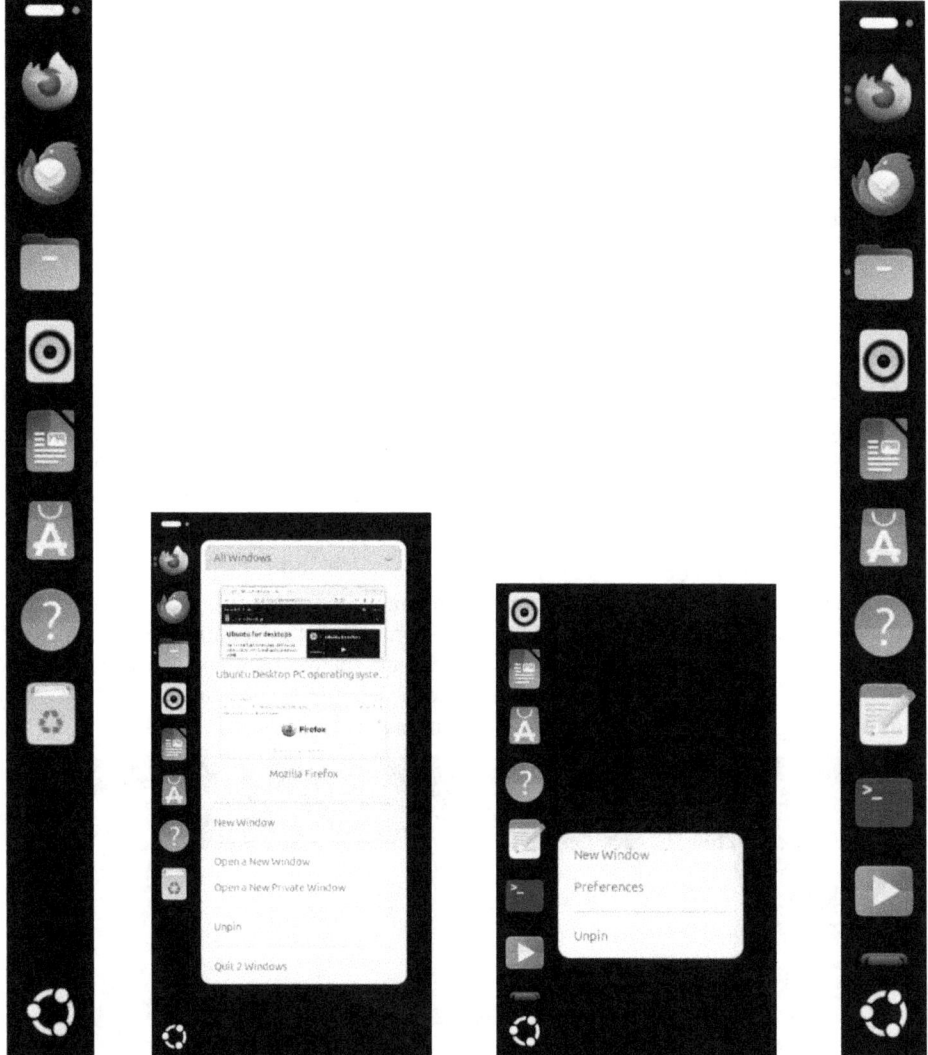

Figure 8-8: Dock/Dash with favorites and running applications

You can configure the Ubuntu dock using the Settings Ubuntu Desktop tab's Dock section (see Figure 8-9). Here you can adjust the size of the icons, the location of the dock on the screen (left, right, bottom), and whether to hide the dock when not in use (Auto-hide). The "Configure dock behavior" entry opens a dialog with options to include unmounted and network file systems, and whether to show the trash.

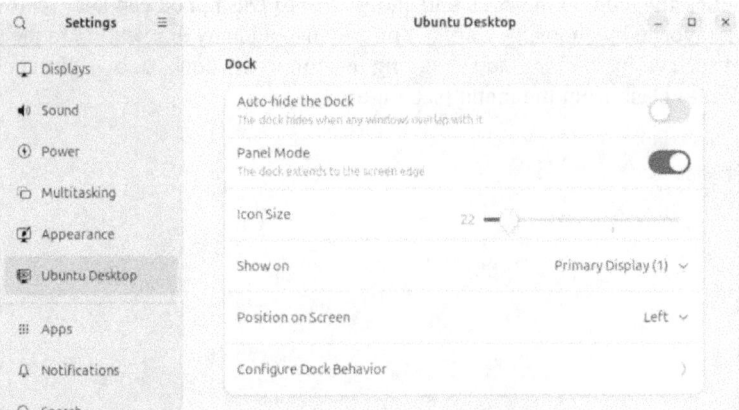

Figure 8-9: Dock Configuration on Settings Appearance

Window Thumbnails

To see just the windows open for a single application, such as several folders, first click on one of the application's windows to make it the primary window, and then click the application's icon on the dock to display the windows overview showing all the windows open for that application. Select the one you want.

You can access all open windows using the window thumbnails on the Activities overview. Thumbnails are displayed of all your open windows in the current workspace (see Figure 8-10). To select a window, move your mouse over the window's thumbnail. The selected window also shows an x (close) button at the top right of the window's thumbnail, which you can use to close the window directly. To access the window, move your mouse over it and click. This displays the window, exiting the Activities overview and returning to the desktop.

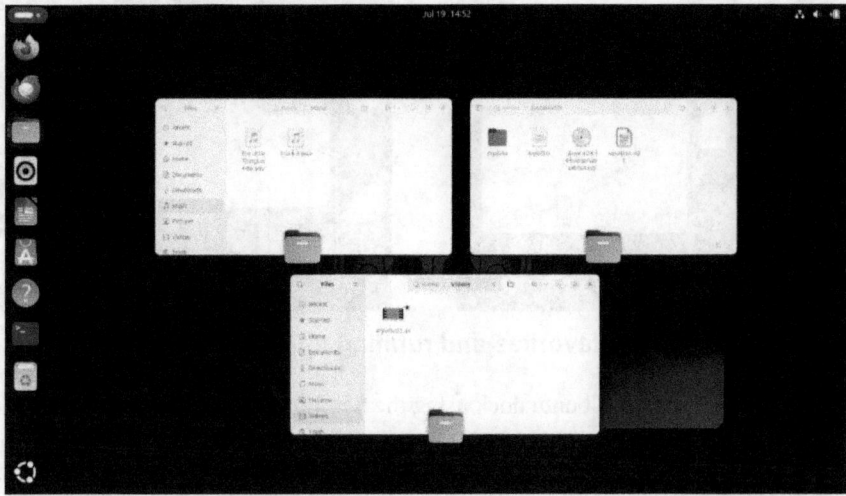

Chapter 8: Ubuntu Desktop 305

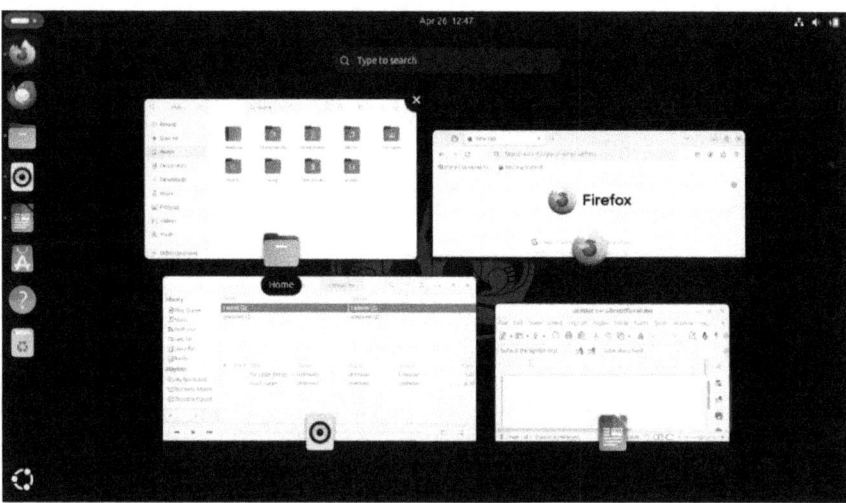

Figure 8-10: Window thumbnails (Activities and single click on application dock icon)

The windows displayed are those for the current workspace. To see windows for another workspace, you can use the scroll button on your mouse to scroll through workspaces, as well as use the CTRL-ALT LEFT and right arrow keys. To move to just the next or previous workspace you can click on the part of the workspace displayed on the left and right sides of the screen. As you move to a different workspace, the windows on that workspace are displayed (see Figure 8-11). You can also move windows or applications directly to an adjoining workspace by clicking and dragging it to the right and left side of the screen, which then switches you to the adjoining workspace. Your window is now placed on that workspace.

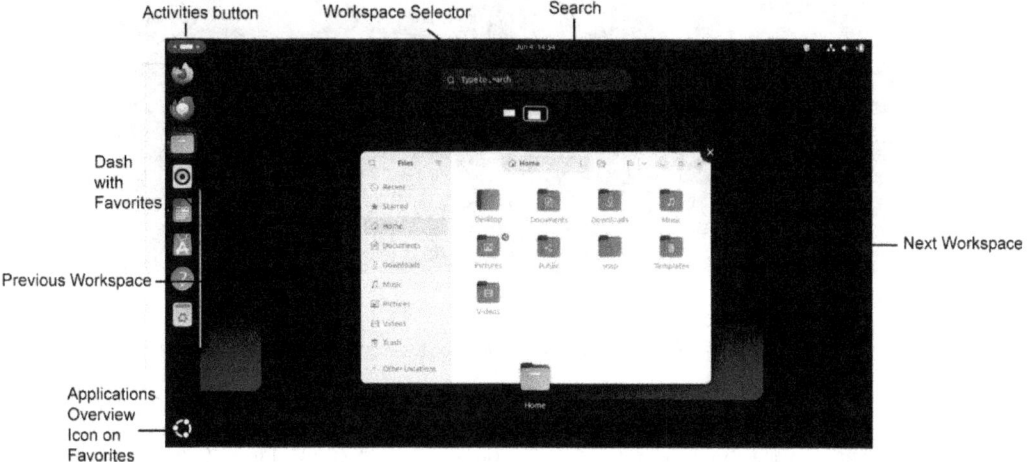

Activities Overview with workspace selector

Figure 8-11: Workspace thumbnails with workspace selector

Whenever you have multiple workspaces, a workspace selector is displayed at the top of the screen showing thumbnails of your workspaces. You can use the workspace selector to move directly from one workspace to another, as well as move windows displayed in the thumbnails to other workspaces. To move a window from one workspace to another, click and drag it to another workspace thumbnail in the workspace selector.

Applications Overview

Clicking the Applications icon (last icon, grid button) on the dash opens the Applications overview, from which you can locate and open applications. Icons for installed applications are displayed (see Figure 8-12). A pager consisting of buttons, located on the bottom of the screen, lets you move quickly through the list of applications. There is a special application folder called Utilities. Clicking on its icon opens another, smaller overview, showing system tool applications, such as Logs, Tweaks, and Backups. Click an application icon to open it and exit the overview. Should you return to the overview mode, you will see its window in the overview. The super key (Windows key) with the **a** key (SUPER+a) will switch from the desktop to the Applications overview. Pressing it again switches to the Activities overview and the window thumbnails.

The top of the Applications overview shows the workspace selector that contains thumbnails of your workspaces. You can switch to another workspace directly by clicking its thumbnail.

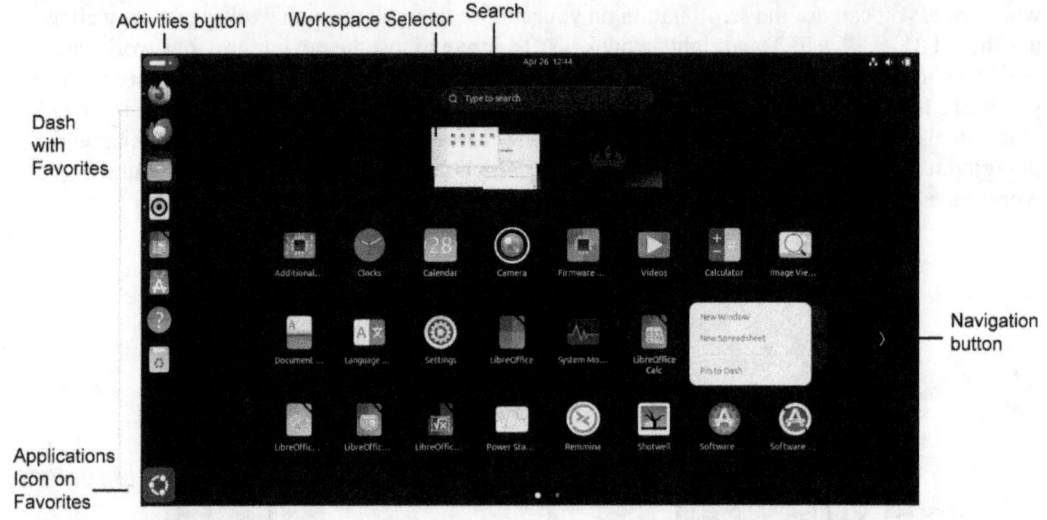

Applications Overview with workspace selector

Figure 8-12: Applications overview

To add an application as a favorite on the dock, you can simply drag its icon from the Applications overview to the dock directly.

Overview Application Folders

You can organize the overview icons into application folders, much in the same way as your phone. Decide on two icons you want to group into a folder, and then drag one icon on top of the other. A new application folder is automatically created for them, placing both within the new application folder. You can then add more icons to the folder.

The name given to the folder will be based on the category of the icon you dragged the other icon to. Clicking on the folder open a dialog displaying the icons and an edit button on the top right. Click on the edit button to change the folder's name.

To remove an icon from a folder, open the folder and drag the icon outside the folder dialog. Removing all the icons from the folder will also remove the folder.

In Figure 8-13, the Image Viewer icon is dragged to the Shotwell icon, creating a new application folder that is named Graphics. If the icons have unrelated categories, the folder is labeled Unknown. In Figure 8-14 the Calendar icon is combined with the Clocks icon to create an Unknown folder. This folder is then opened and its name edited and changed to Time and Date (see Figure 8-14).

For the LibreOffice applications, a LibreOffice folder is set up, which includes LibreOffice, LibreOffice Calc, LibreOffice Draw, LibreOffice Math, and LibreOffice Impress icons (see Figure 8-15).

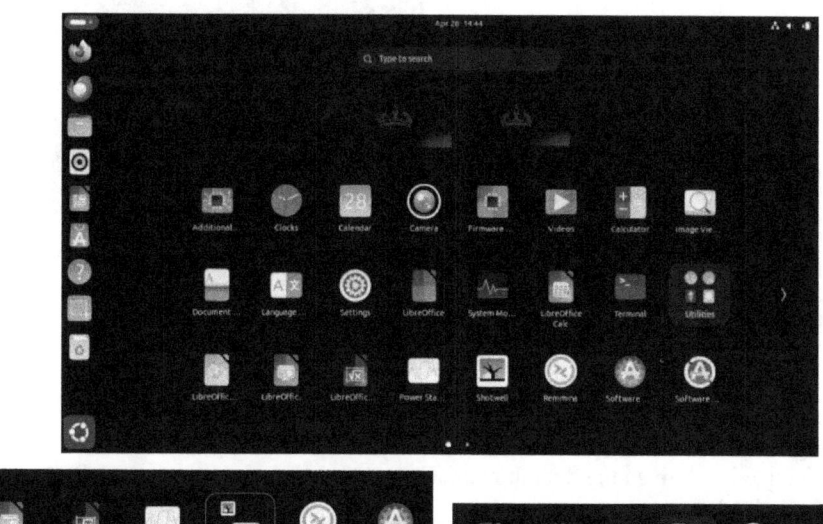

Figure 8-13: Creating Overview Application Folders

308 Part 3: Desktops

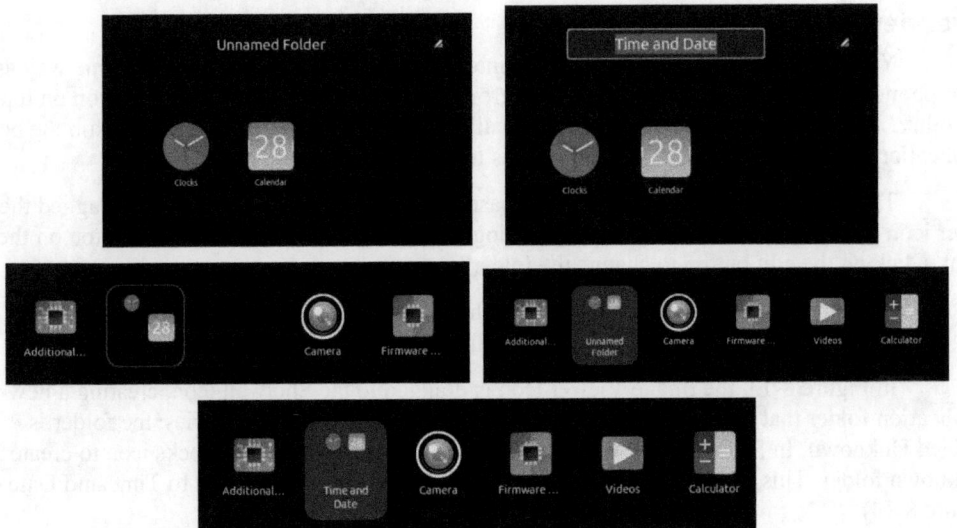

Figure 8-14: Changing Overview Application Folder Names

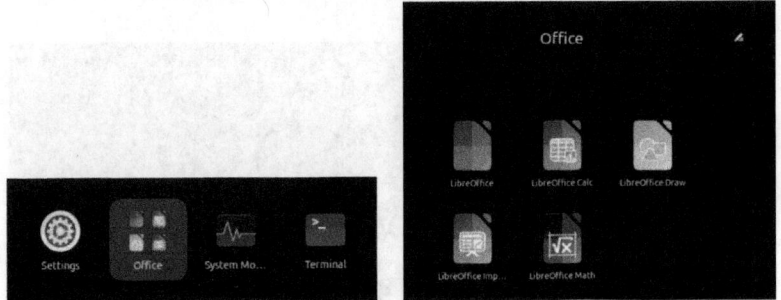

Figure 8-15: Adding Icons to an Overview Application Folder

You can make as many application folders as you want. In Figure 8-16, a Game folder is created by dragging the Mahjongg icon to the Mines icon. The new application folder is automatically created and given the default name Games, as Mines is a game. AisleRiot and Sudoku are then added to it.

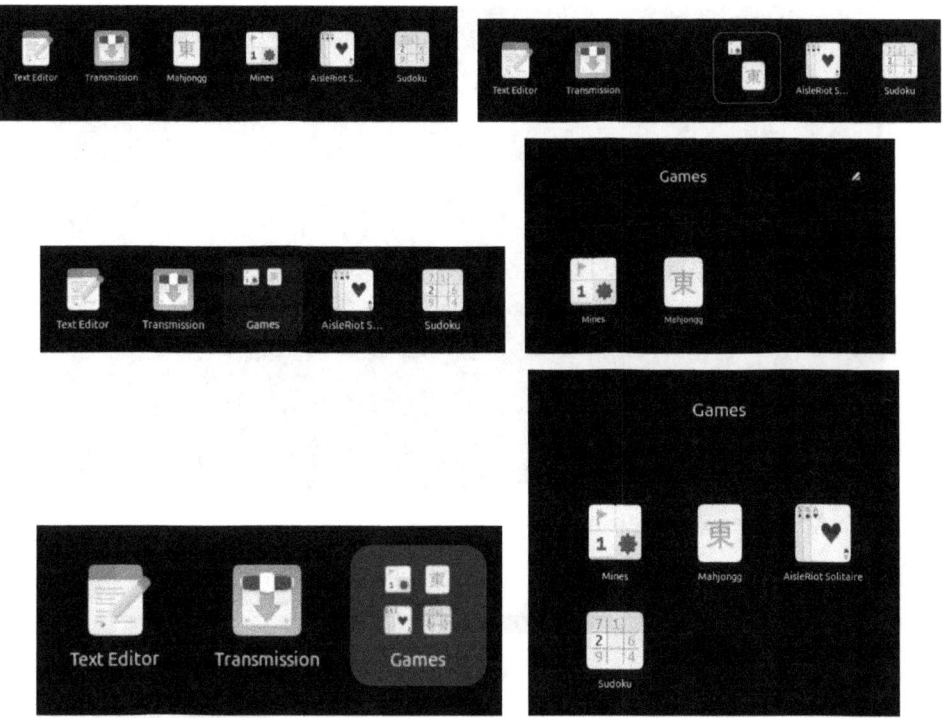

Figure 8-16: Overview Application Folders

Activities Search

The Activities search will search applications and files. Should you know the name of the application you want, you can simply start typing, and the matching results are displayed (see Figure 8-17). Your search term is entered in the search box as you type. The results dynamically narrow the more you type. The first application is selected automatically. If this is the one you want, just press ENTER to start it. Results will also show Settings tools as well as folders and files.

The search box for the Activities overview can be configured from the Settings Search tab (see Figure 8-18). Here, you can turn search on or off and specify which applications are to support searches. By default, these include Calendar, the Files file manager, Passwords and Keys, and terminal. You can also configure search permissions for applications using the Settings Application dialogs. Other GNOME applications are added automatically when installed such as GNOME Notes, Photos, Documents, and Weather. You can change the priority of the applications searched by moving them up or down in the list.

310 Part 3: Desktops

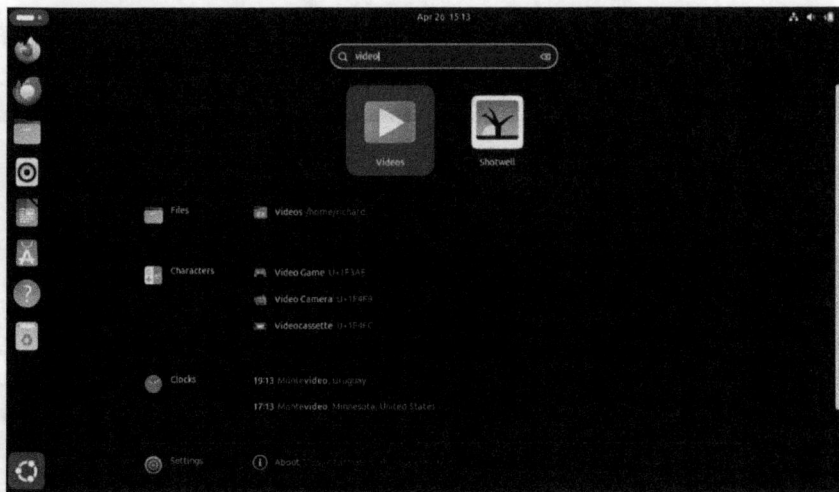

Figure 8-17: Activities - search box

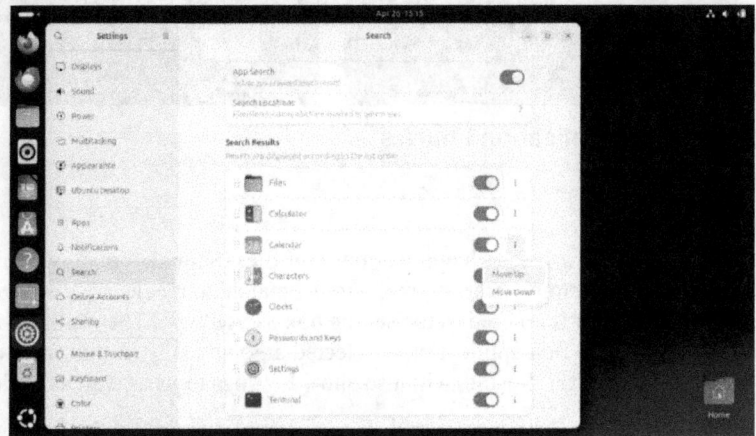

Figure 8-18: Activities - Search configuration

Managing Windows

You can select the color accents of your windows using the Settings Appearance tab (see Figure 8-19). In the Style section, you can choose either a light or dark theme (Light is the default). You can also choose an accent color from the Color buttons. Clicking on an button changes the colors for your desktop immediately.

Chapter 8: Ubuntu Desktop **311**

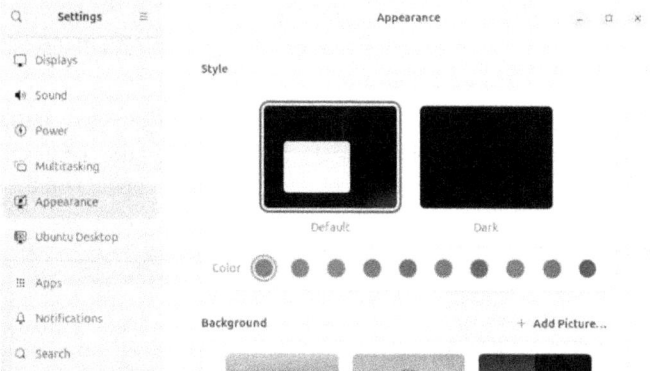

Figure 8-19: Window colors, Settings | Appearance

The title bar and the toolbar for GNOME windows are combined into a single header bar, as shown in the following for the file manager.

The minimize and maximize buttons are shown on the right side of the header bar by default. The display and placement of these buttons can be configured by the GNOME Tweaks' Window tab's Titlebar Buttons section. The maximize operations can also be carried out by a dragging operation or by double-clicking the header bar. To maximize a window, double-click its header bar or drag the header bar to the top edge of the screen. To return a window to its normal size, drag the title away from the top edge of the screen. You can also use a window's menu entries to maximize or minimize it. Right-click the header bar or press ALT+spacebar to display the window menu. The option to resize an application window by dragging to the top, right, or left edge is set in the Settings Multitasking tab as Active Screen Edges (see Figure 8-20). Turning this option off no longer resizes the window when you move it to the top, right, or left edge of the screen.

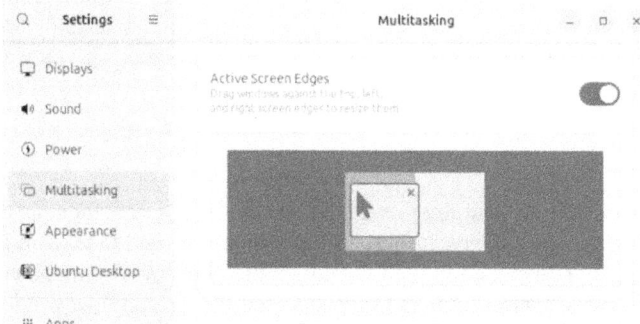

Figure 8-20: Settings Multitasking Active Screen Edges option

For each favorite or open application on the dock, an application menu is provided. Right-click on the dock icon to display this menu, which will show an "All windows" entry, a "New window" entry, "Remove from Favorites", and a Quit entry. Also any task for that application will also be listed such as "Open a New Private Window" for Firefox. The menu will also show a Quit entry. If multiple windows are open for an application, the Quit entry will also show the number of windows it will close, such as "Quit 3 Windows."

Clicking on the "All windows" entry displays a submenu showing thumbnails for all the open windows for that application (see Figure 8-21). Move through the list to select a window you want to either switch to that window or to close it. A close button appears on the currently selected thumbnail.

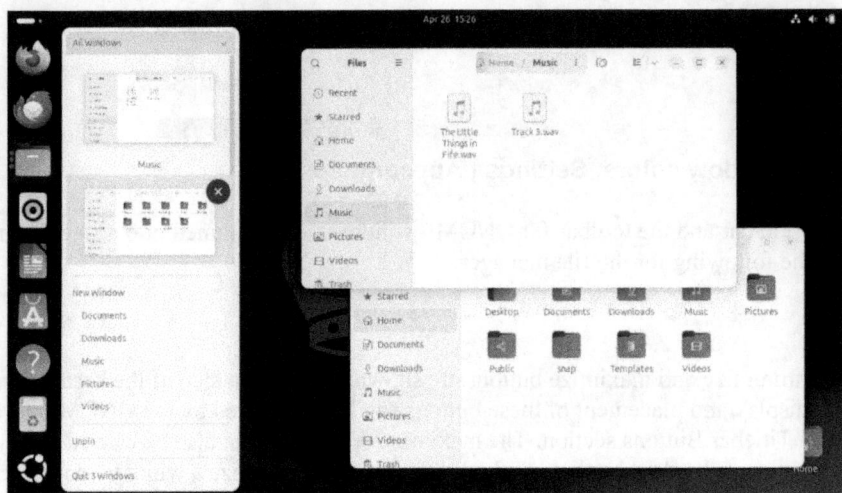

Figure 8-21: Favorites window thumbnails

To minimize an open window so that it no longer displays on the desktop, click the minimize button on the header bar or right-click the header bar to display the window menu and choose minimize. This will hide the window. You can then display the window later, using the window's thumbnails on the activities overview (Activities button). If the application for a minimized window is shown on the dock, you can display that minimized window again by using that dock icon's menu "All windows" entry. Right-click on the dock icon and click on the "All windows" entry to display all the open windows. Find the minimized one you want, and then click on it to re-display that window.

To close a window, click its close box or right-click on its titlebar and choose "Close" from the menu.

To tile a window, click-and-drag its header bar to the left or right edge of the screen. When your mouse reaches the edge of the screen, the window is tiled to take up that half of the screen (see Figure 8-22). You can do the same with another window for the other edge, showing two windows side by side. Quarter tiling is also supported. You can drag a window to the corner of the screen to take up just that quarter. Tiling works or any corner, letting you tile four windows at the same time.

Chapter 8: Ubuntu Desktop **313**

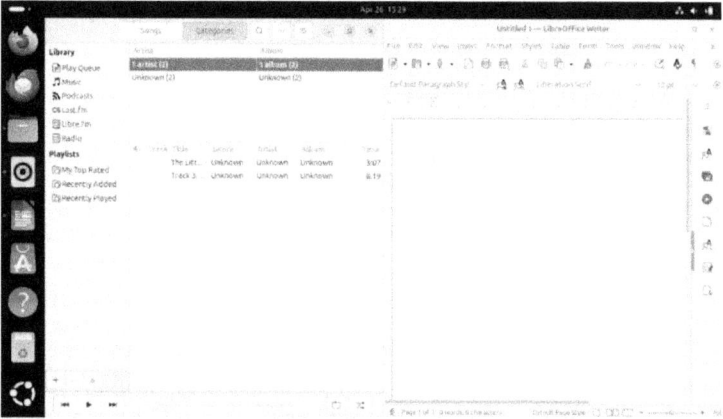

Figure 8-22: Window Tiling

Ubuntu 24.04 enables enhanced tiling. You can check the settings on the Settings Ubuntu Desktop tab, in the Enhanced Tiling section (see Figure 8-23). With the Tiling Popup option, when you tile a window, the other side displays a list of open apps you can choose from for that other side (see Figure 8-24). The Tile Groups option groups tiled windows. When raising one, the other is also raised.

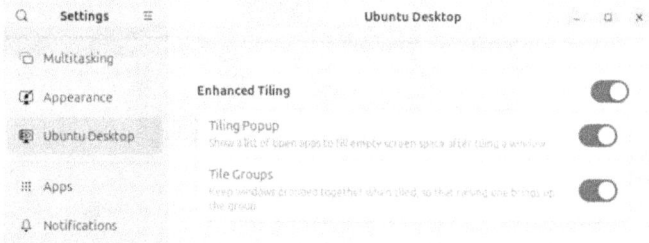

Figure 8-23: Enhanced Tiling option in Settings Ubuntu Desktop

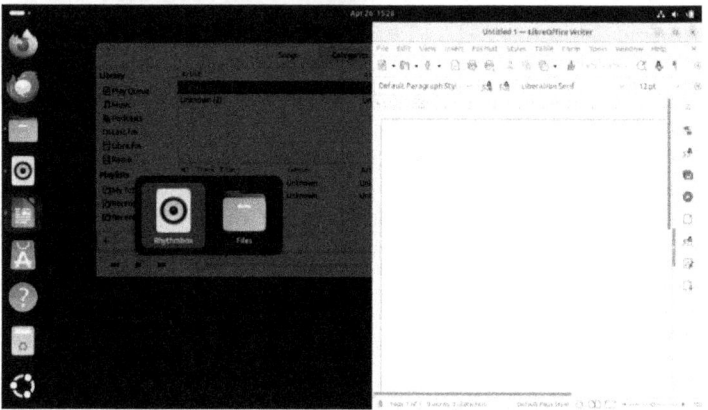

Figure 8-24: Tiling Popup option showing apps to tile

To resize a window, move the mouse to the edge or corner or the window until it changes to an edge or corner mouse, then click-and-drag.

The scrollbar to the right also features fine scrolling. When scrolling through a large number of items, you can fine scroll to slow the scrolling when you reach a point to search. To activate fine scrolling, click and hold the scrollbar handle, or press the SHIFT key while scrolling.

You can use the Window Switcher on the desktop to search open windows. Press the ALT+TAB keys to display an icon bar of open windows on the current workspace (see Figure 8-25). While holding down the ALT key, press the TAB key to move through the list of windows. Instead of continuing to press the TAB keys to move through the list of windows, you can use the forward and back arrow keys while holding the ALT key down. To move through the applications directly use the SUPER key (Windows key) and the TAB key, SUPER-TAB. Open windows are grouped by application and displayed as a list below the selected application. This is helpful if you have many windows open that use a many of the same applications. For those applications with multiple open windows, press the tilde (~) key (above the TAB key) to move through a list of the open windows.

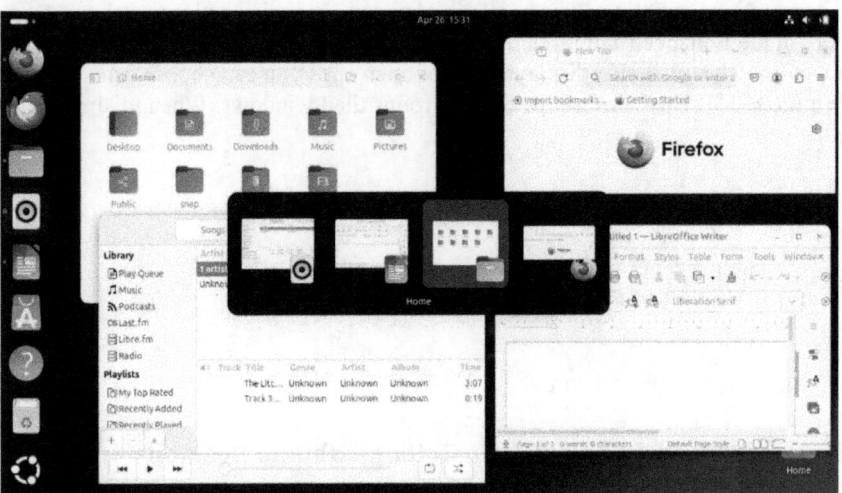

Figure 8-25: Window Switcher (ALT+TAB)

On the GNOME Tweaks Windows tab, you can configure certain windows' actions and components. Attached Modal Dialogs will attach a dialog that an application opens to the application's window (see Figure 8-26). You can use the switch to turn this feature off, allowing you to move a modal dialog away from the application window. The Titlebar buttons section lets you configure actions on the title bar, such as double-click to maximize and secondary-click to display the menu. There are also switches to display the Maximize and Minimize buttons on the title bar, and buttons to position them on the right or left side.

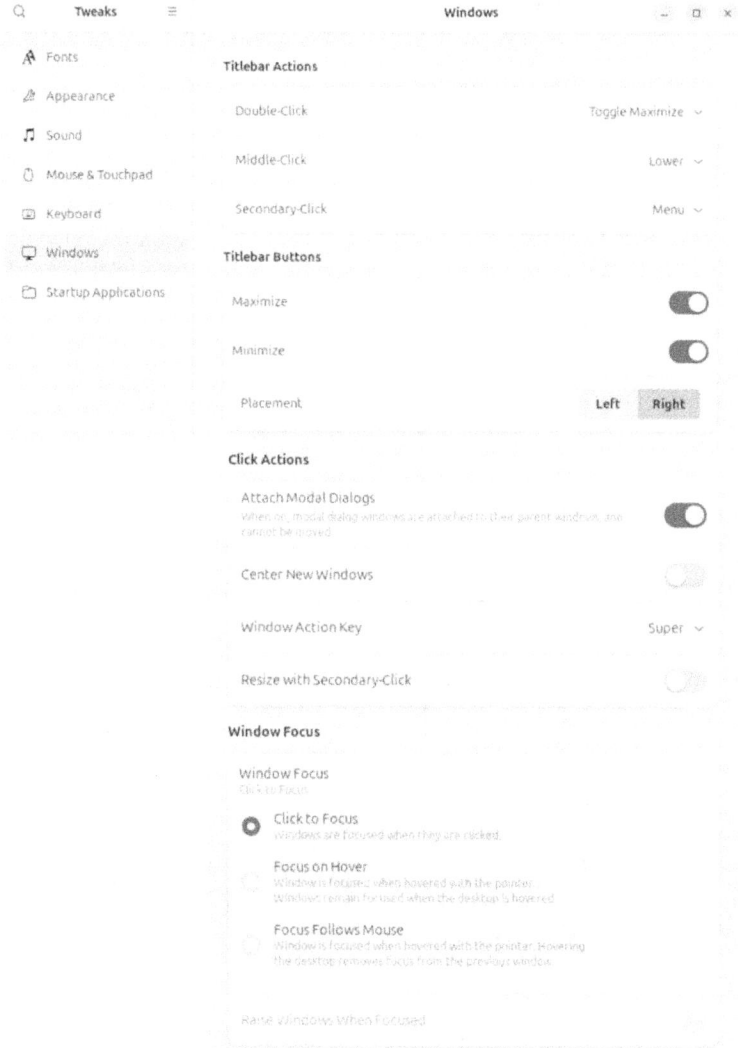

Figure 8-26: GNOME Tweaks, Windows configuration

Workspaces

You can organize your windows into different workspaces. The number of workspaces you have and the one you are using are shown on the Activities button on the upper left corner of the screen (see Figure 8-27). The Activities button is also a dynamic workspace indicator. You can use the dynamic workspace indicator to switch between your workspaces by hovering the mouse over the indicator and then using your scroll wheel to move between workspaces.

Figure 8-27: Activities button showing number of workspaces and the current one used

Workspaces are accessed using the Workspace selector in either the Activities or Applications overview. Workspaces can be either dynamic or fixed. As installed, Ubuntu is configured to use dynamic workspaces. You can use the Settings Multitasking tab to change workspaces from dynamic to fixed, letting you specify a fixed number of workspaces (see Figure 8-28).

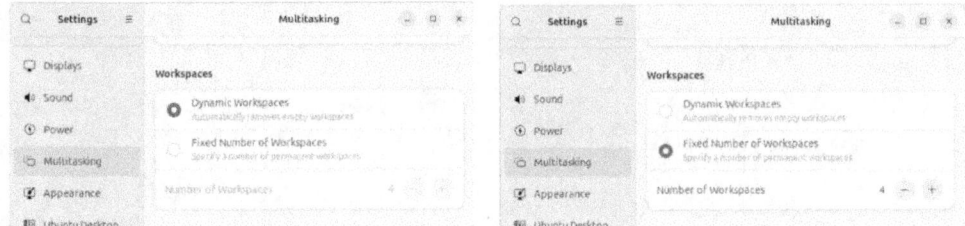

Figure 8-28: Settings Multitasking tab Dynamic and Fixed workspaces

With dynamic workspaces, any empty workspaces (those without open windows) are automatically removed. A new empty workspace is always generated to the right of the last workspace. If you are using only one workspace, that workspace will have an one empty workspace to the right. With fixed workspaces you can have empty workspaces (see Figure 8-29). The Activities overview with dynamic and fixed workspaces is shown in Figure 8-30.

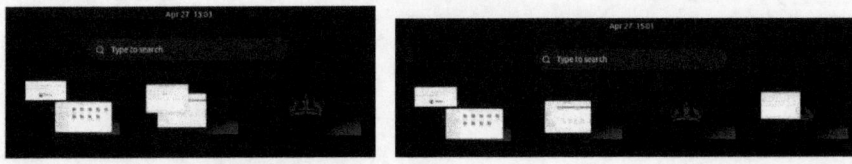

Figure 8-28: Workspaces, dynamic and fixed.

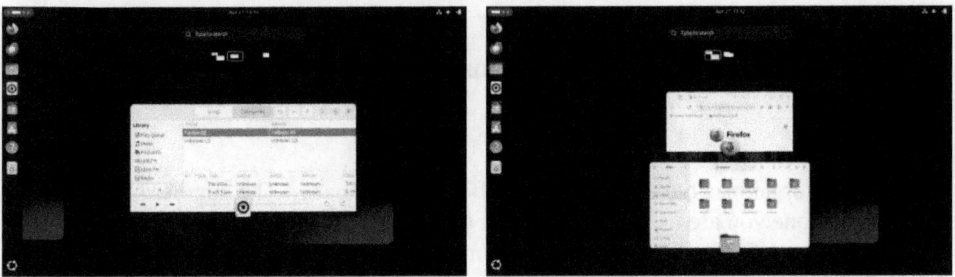

Figure 8-30: Workspaces on the activities overview, dynamic and fixed

Should you be using multiple monitors, on the Settings Multitasking tab you can specify whether the workspaces should be on the primary display or on all displays (see Figure 8-31).

Chapter 8: Ubuntu Desktop **317**

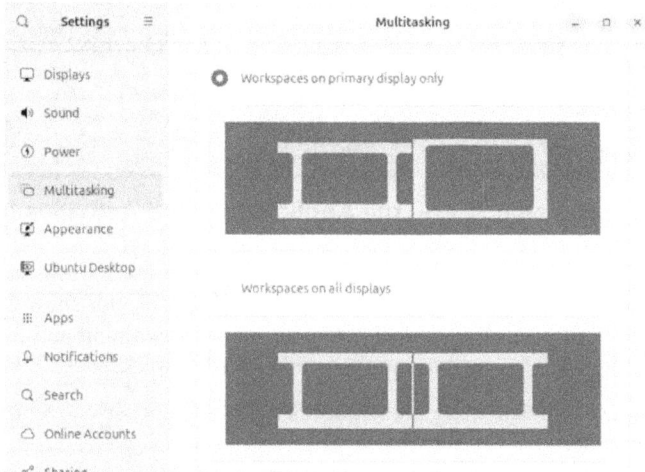

Figure 8-31: Settings Multitasking - workspaces on multiple monitors

You can choose which workspace to use with the workspace selector. This is an thumbnail bar at the top of the Activities and Applications overviews. To move to a workspace click on its thumbnail in the workspace selector (see Figure 8-32). You can also use CTRL+ALT with the right and left arrow keys to move to the next or previous workspaces, as well as use the scroll wheel on your mouse. For dynamic workspaces, if you use only one workspace, then the workspace selector is not shown. If you start using another workspace, the workspace selector is then displayed. For fixed workspaces, the workspace selector is always shown, displaying thumbnails for all you workspaces, even the empty ones.

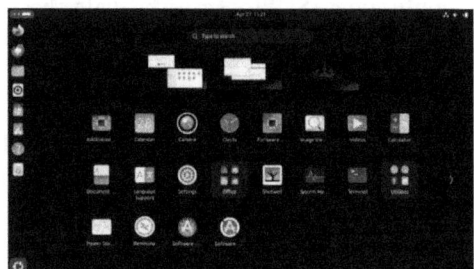 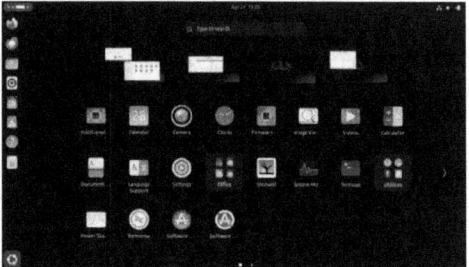

Figure 8-32: Workspace selector on the Applications overview - dynamic and fixed

The workspace selector appears differently in the Activities and Application overviews. On the Application overview it appears as large thumbnails, and on the Activities overview it appears and small thumbnails (see Figure 8-33). Even though the thumbnails on the Activities overview are small, you can still move open windows between the thumbnails, changing their workspace.

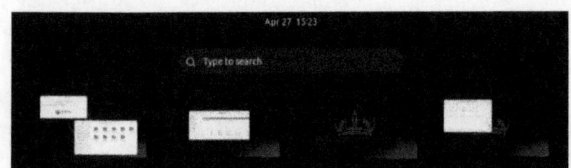 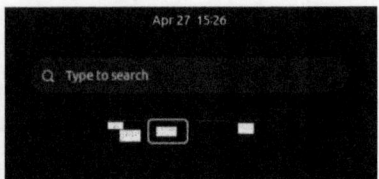

Figure 8-33: Workspace selector on the Applications and Activities overviews

You can also move an open window in a workspace to another workspace using the workspace selector. The workspace thumbnails in the workspace selector show thumbnails of your open windows in that workspace. You can click and drag a window thumbnail to any other workspace thumbnail in the selector, moving the window to that workspace.

You can move a window using the window's menu and choose Move to Workspace Down or Move to Workspace Up.

On the Activities overview, you can move an open window to an adjacent workspace by clicking and dragging it to the part of the adjacent workspace showing on either side of the screen. You can also use CTRL+ALT+SHIFT and the up or down arrow keys to move the window to the next workspace. Continue pressing the arrow to move it further should you have several workspaces.

Notifications and Message dialog

Notifications, such as software updates and removable device removal, are displayed in the message area on the left side of the clock/calendar dialog (see Figure 8-34). Click on the clock/calendar button on the center of the top panel to display your notifications. You can also press the super key with the **m** key to display your notifications (SUPER+m). The dialog has a "Do not Disturb" switch at the bottom, which you can flip to turn off notification pop-ups such as those for newly removed devices. Notifications will still be listed in the clock/calendar dialog. A Clear button lets you delete all the displayed notifications.

Notifications display a header showing the application it came from. To the right, a close button is shown that you click the remove the notification. If there are several notifications from the same application, an expansion button is shown that you can use to hide or display those notifications or display additional controls.

Notifications provide enhanced features, not just message texts. For some applications, controls are shown you can use directly to control tasks, such as those for Rhythmbox and Videos.

Chapter 8: Ubuntu Desktop **319**

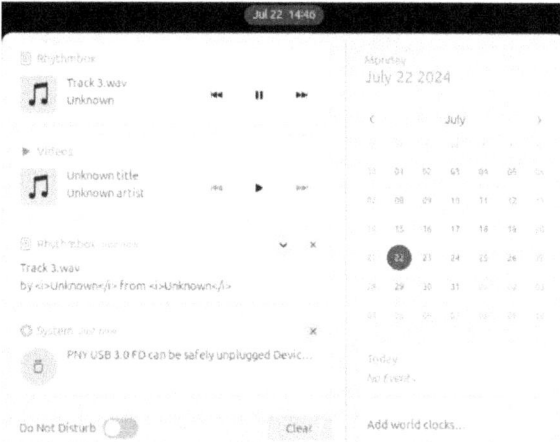

Figure 8-34: Notifications

Desktop Customization with GNOME Tweaks: Themes, Icons, Fonts, and Startup Applications

You can perform common desktop customizations using GNOME Tweaks. Areas to customize include the fonts, themes, startup applications, window behavior, sound, keyboard, and mouse. You can access GNOME Tweaks from the Applications overview Utilities application folder, once installed. GNOME Tweaks has tabs for Appearance, Fonts, Sound, Mouse & Touchpad, Keyboard, Windows, and Startup Applications (see Figure 8-35).

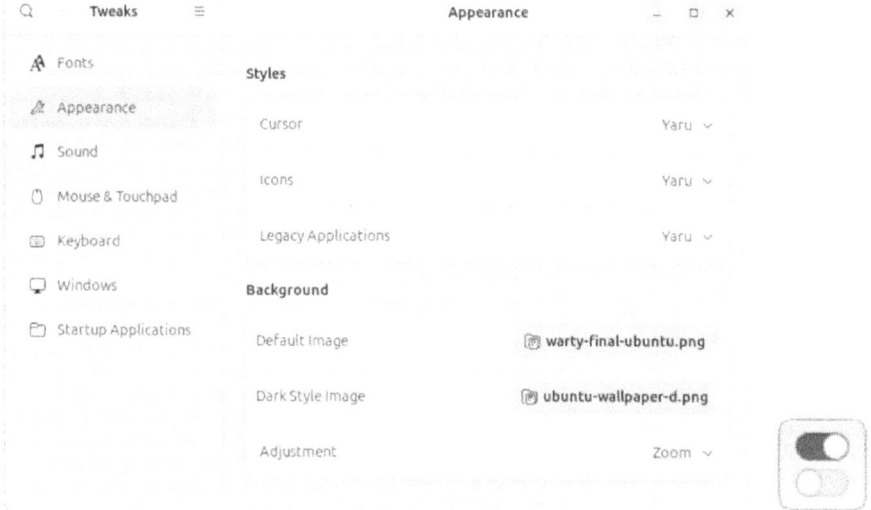

Figure 8-35: GNOME Tweaks Tool - Appearance tab (themes)

The Appearance tab lets you set the theme for your windows, icons, and cursor. Ubuntu uses the Yaru theme as its default. GNOME traditionally uses the Adwaita Theme, with its light and dark variant.

Desktop fonts for window titles, interface (application or dialog text), documents, and monospace (terminal windows or code) can be changed in the Fonts tab. You can adjust the size of the font or change the font style. Clicking the font name opens a "Pick a Font" dialog from which you can choose a different font. The quality of text display can be further adjusted with Hinting and Antialiasing options. To simply increase or decrease the size of all fonts on your desktop interface, you can adjust the Scaling Factor.

At times, there may be certain applications that you want started up when you log in, such as Text Editor, the Firefox web browser, or the Videos movie player. On the Startup Applications tab, you can choose the applications to start up. Click the plus (+) button to open an applications dialog from which you can choose an application to start up. Once added, you can later remove the application by clicking its Remove button.

Desktop Customization: manually placing application launchers on the Desktop

To place an application launcher directly on desktop, as you could with older versions of GNOME, you would copy the application's launcher file to your Desktop folder, and then make that copy launchable. The launcher files for applications are located in the **/usr/share/applications** folder and have the extension **.desktop**. You can open this folder using your file manager and clicking the Other Locations entry in the sidebar, and then clicking on the Ubuntu icon. Access the **/usr/share/applications** folder (see Figure 8-36). Then open another file manager window and click the Desktop entry in the sidebar. Find the application launcher you want to copy in the Applications folder, and then click and drag it, while holding the CTRL key, to the Desktop folder. The launcher file will appear on your desktop as a file. Right-click it and select the "Allow Launching" entry (see Figure 8-37). The launcher file will be displayed as its application icon on the desktop, which you can double-click to start that application.

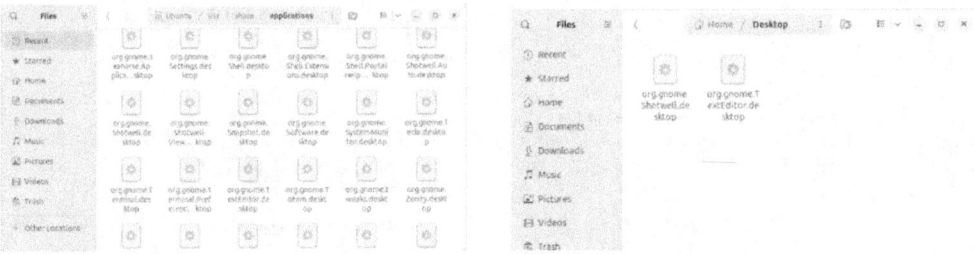

Figure 8-36: Accessing and copying application launchers

Chapter 8: Ubuntu Desktop **321**

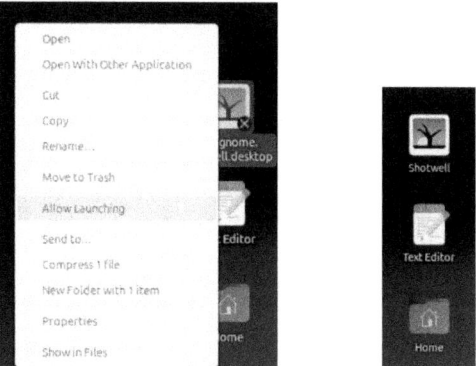

Figure 8-37: Application Launchers on the Desktop

GNOME Help Browser

The GNOME Help browser provides a browser-like interface for displaying the GNOME Desktop Help and documentation for the Ubuntu desktop and various GNOME applications, such as System Monitor, Software Updater, Rhythmbox, and Text Editor. You can access it from the dock (question mark icon) or from the Applications overview Utilities folder (see Figure 8-38). It features a toolbar that enables you to move through the list of previously viewed documents. You can even bookmark specific items. You can search for topics using the search box, with results displayed in the drop-down menu. Initially, the Ubuntu Desktop manual is displayed. To see other help pages and manuals, choose All Help from the menu next to the close box (see Figure 8-39).

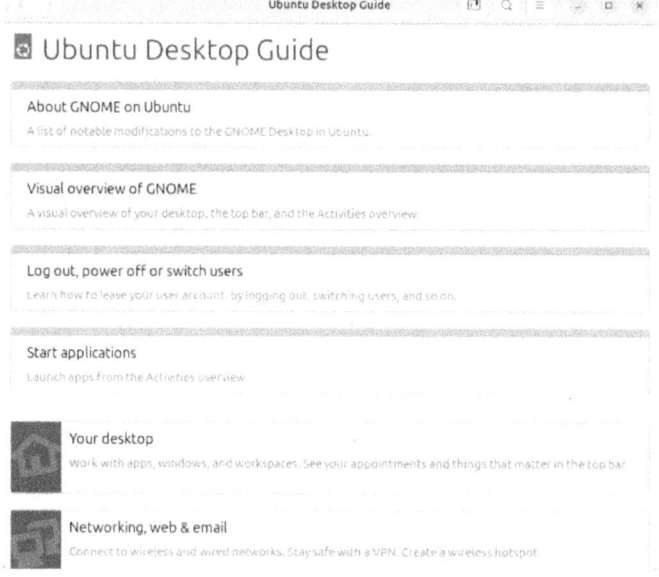

Figure 8-38: GNOME Help browser - Ubuntu Desktop Guide

322   Part 3: Desktops

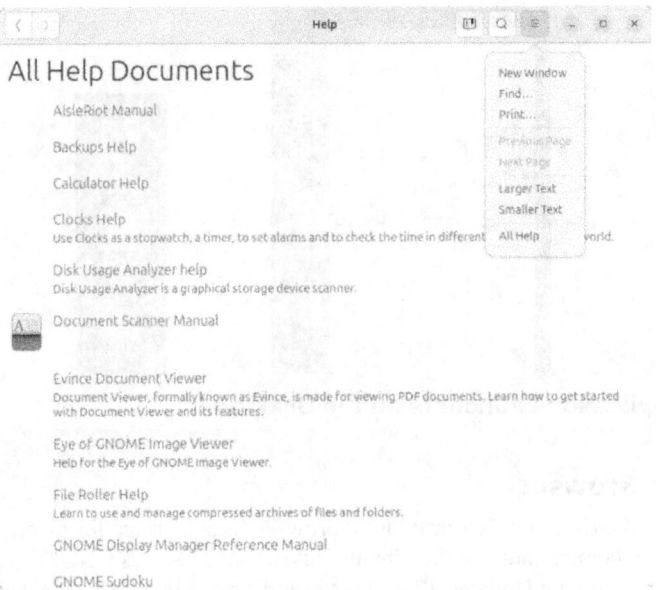

Figure 8-39: GNOME Help - All Documents

The Files File Manager

The Files file manager supports the standard features for copying, removing, and deleting items as well as setting permissions and displaying items. The name used for the file manager is Files, but the actual program name is still nautilus.

Home Folder Subfolders

Files uses the Common User Directory Structure (xdg-user-dirs at **http://freedesktop.org**) to set up subfolders in the user home folder (directory). Folders include Documents, Music, Pictures, Downloads, and Videos. These localized user folders are used as defaults by many desktop applications. Users can change their folder names or place them within each other. For example, Music can be moved into Videos or Documents into Pictures. Local configuration is held in the **.config/user-dirs.dirs** file. System-wide defaults are set up in the **/etc/xdg/user-dirs.defaults** file. You can edit the local configuration using a text editor and change the folders for the current ones.

File Manager Windows

When you click the Files icon on the dock, a file manager window opens showing your home folder. The file manager window displays several components, including a toolbar and a sidebar (see Figure 8-40). The sidebar displays folder, device, bookmark, and network items showing your removable file systems and the default home folders. The main pane (to the right) displays the icons, or lists files and subfolders in the current folder.

When you select a file, a status section at the bottom right of the window displays the name of the file and its size. Selecting several files displays the number of files selected and their

Chapter 8: Ubuntu Desktop **323**

total size. When you select a folder, a status section shows the name of the folder and the number of items in the folder. Selecting several folders displays the number of folders selected and the total number of folders and files in all the selected folders.

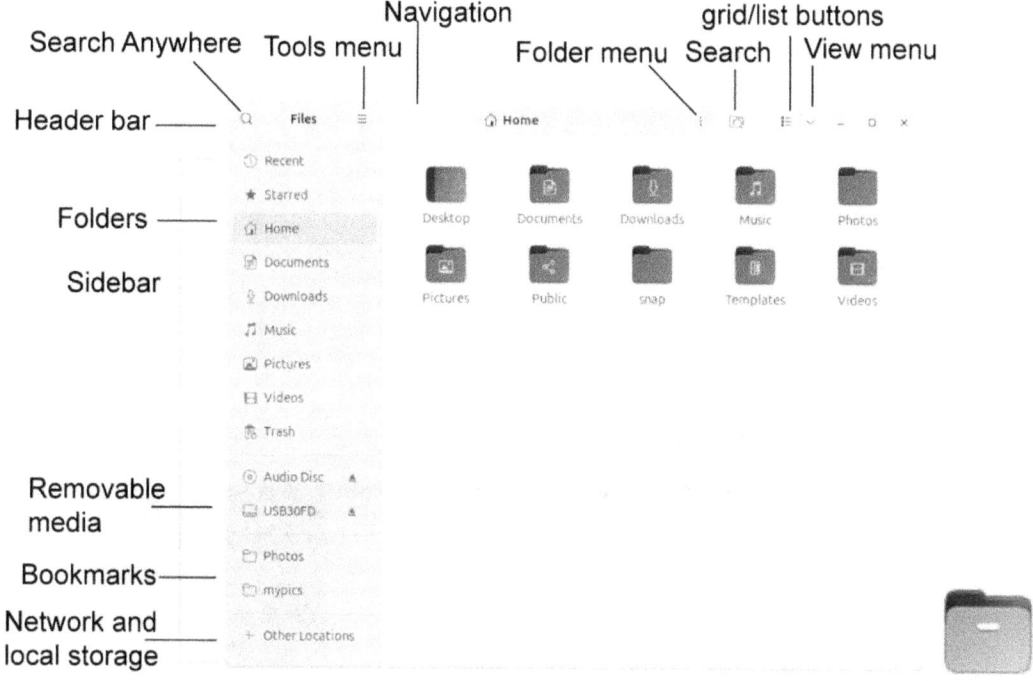

Figure 8-40: File manager with sidebar

When you open a new folder, the same window is used to display it, and you can use the forward and back arrows to move through previously opened folders (top left). As you open subfolders, the main toolbar displays buttons for your current folder and its parent folders, as shown here:

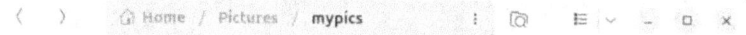

You can click a folder button to move to it directly. You can also display a location URL text box instead of buttons, from which you can enter the location of a folder, either on your system or on a remote one. Press CTRL+L to display the text box. Press the ESC key to revert back to the folder location buttons.

To the right of the location buttons, is the button for the current folder's folder menu (three vertical dots, ellipses), which you can click to display the folder menu (see Figure 8-41) (see Table 8-2). The menu shows common folder tasks such as creating a new folder (New Folder), open with a different file manager (Open With), and bookmarking the folder (Add to Bookmarks). The Reload button refreshes the display, updating any changes. You may need to do this for folders connected to remote sites, where changes have been made on the remote site, but may not show up on your folder. The Edit Location entry changes the location buttons to an editable location textbox. The Copy Location entry copies the full pathname of the folder, which you can then paste to other documents (CTRL-v). The Properties entry displays the folder's Properties dialog, showing folder information and permissions. You can also open the folder in a terminal window, which is useful for running shell commands on the folder files and subfolders or running shell scripts from that folder (see Figure 8-42).

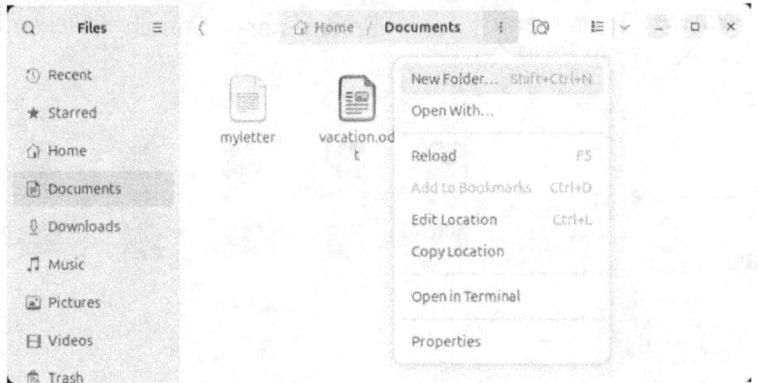

Figure 8-41: File manager folder menu

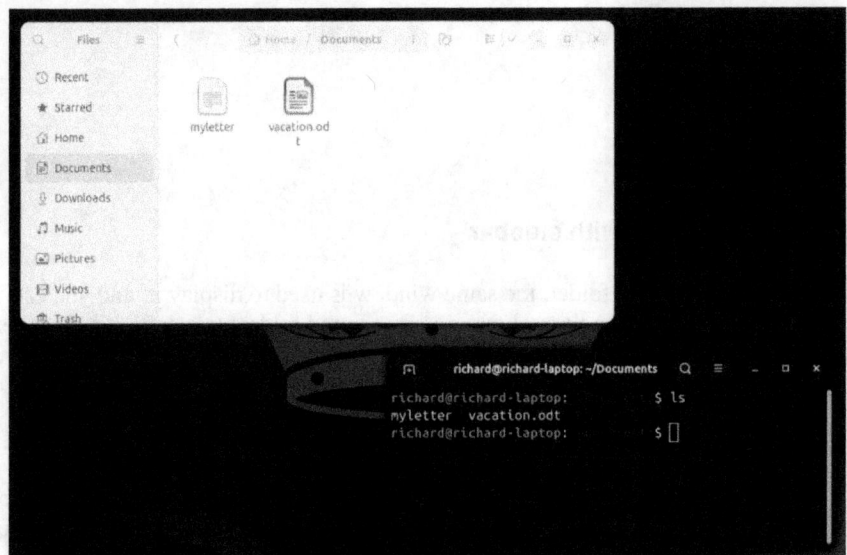

Figure 8-42: File manager folder menu - Open in Terminal

You can right-click anywhere on the empty space on the main pane of a file manager window to display a pop-up menu with entries to create a new folder, select all icons in the folder, open the current folder in a terminal window with a command line prompt, and open the folder's properties dialog (see Table 8-3). If you have copied or cut a file or folder in another folder, a Paste entry will be displayed, which you can click to copy or move the file or folder here. A right-click on the icon for any of the subfolders in the current folder displays a folder menu for operations on that subfolder.

When you create a folder, a New Folder dialog is displayed with a text box where you enter the name of the new folder (see Figure 8-43).

Figure 8-43: File manager New Folder

Menu Item	Description
New Folder	Creates a new subfolder in the current folder
Open With	Open with a different application
Reload	Re-display the file manager icons
Add to Bookmarks	Bookmark this folder and display an entry for it on the sidebar
Edit Location	Display the folder's location text box
Copy Location	Copy the full pathname of the current folder to paste in other documents
Open in Terminal	Open a terminal window at the current folder
Properties	Opens the Properties dialog for the folder

Table 8-2: File Manager Folder Menu

Menu Item	Description
New Folder	Creates a new subfolder in the current folder
Open With	Open with a different file manager application
Paste	If you have copied or cut a file or folder in another folder, the Paste entry will copy or move the file or folder here
Select All	Select all folders and files in the current folder
Open in Terminal	Open a terminal window at the current folder
Properties	Opens the Properties dialog for the folder

Table 8-3: File Manager Pop-up Menu

File Manager adaptive feature for narrow widths

The file manager window can adapt to a narrow width, by adjusting its layout. The file manager sidebar is not displayed, and the icon sort, navigation operations, and icon display, become buttons on a bottom bar of the file manager window (see Figure 8-44). The right side of the bottom bar displays the icon display button and the icon sort menu (see figure 8-45). The left side

326 Part 3: Desktops

shows navigation button for previous and next folders you have accessed with this window. To display the sidebar, click the sidebar button on the left side of the file manager window's header bar (see Figure 8-46). If you increase the width of the window enough, the original file manager layout is shown.

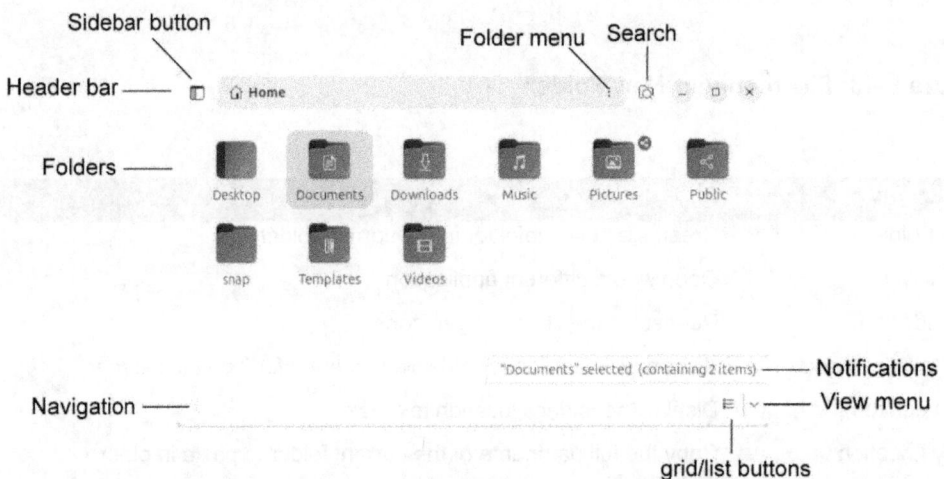

Figure 8-44: File manager adaptive narrow width, notifications and no sidebar

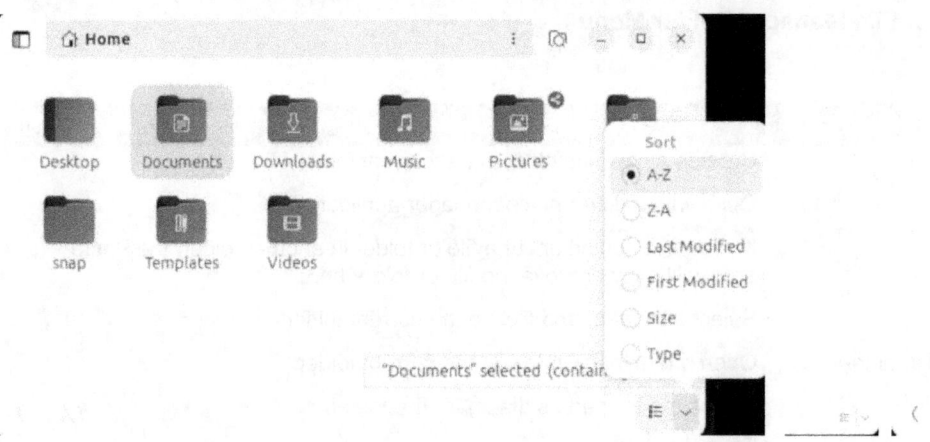

Figure 8-45: File manager adaptive narrow width, sort menu and navigation

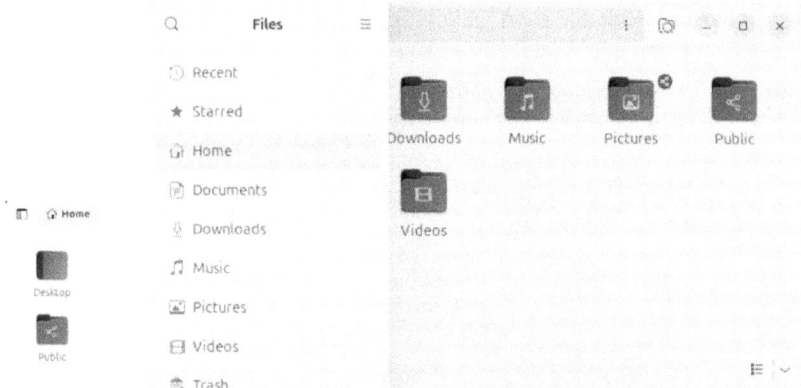

Figure 8-46: File manager adaptive narrow width, displayed sidebar

File Manager Sidebar and Tools menu

The file manager sidebar shows file system locations that you can access such as folders, devices, bookmarks, and network folders (See Figure 8-47). The Recent folder holds links to your recently used files. Selecting the Other Locations entry opens a folder with an Ubuntu icon in the "On This Device" section which you can open to place you at the top of the file system, letting you move to any accessible part of it. Should you bookmark a folder (Add to Bookmarks entry in the folder menu), the bookmark will appear on the sidebar. To remove or rename a bookmark, right-click its entry on the sidebar and choose Remove or Rename from the pop-up menu. The bookmark's name changes, but not the original folder name.

You can also mark a file or folder as a favorite and have them displayed in the Starred folder. Right-click on the file and choose Star from the pop-up menu. To see your favorites, click the Starred entry on the sidebar.

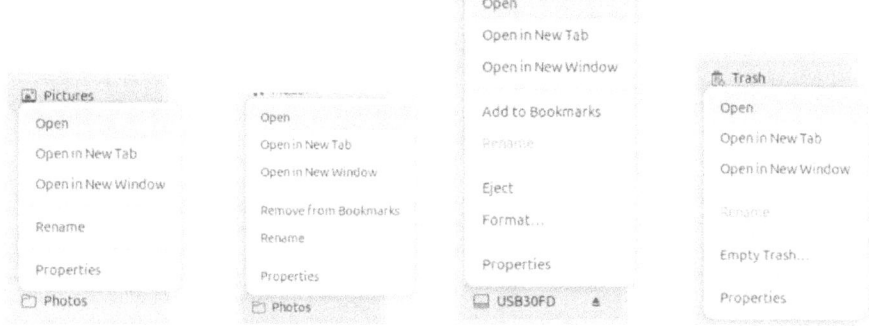

Figure 8-47: File manager sidebar menus

The file manager Tools menu (lines button) is located on the sidebar, to the right of the "Files" label (see Figure 8-48) (see Table 8-4). The Tools menu has entries for managing folders and files, as well as entries for configuring the file manager display. There are entries for showing hidden files, adjusting the icon size, and opening a new window or tab. The Keyboard Shortcuts

328 Part 3: Desktops

entry displays the list of available shortcut keys, organized by function such as open operations, tabs, navigation, view operations, and edit tasks such as renaming, editing, and copying files.

Menu Item	Description
New Folder	Creates a new subfolder in the current folder
New Tab	Creates a new tab
Icon Size (Zoom In and Zoom out buttons)	Enlarge icon size or reduce icon sizes in the folder
Undo Move	Undo move of files or folders
Redo	Redo the move of files and folders
Show Hidden Files	Shows administrative dot files
Preferences	Open the Files file manager Preferences dialog
Keyboard Shortcuts	Display a dialog listing keyboard shortcuts
Help	Open GNOME desktop help
About Files	Display the about dialog for Files, showing the version and a link to its Web site.

Table 8-4: File Manager Sidebar Tools Menu

The Preferences entry opens the Files Preferences dialog where you can configure your file manager interface such as specifying the open action, specifying the date and time format (simple or detailed), and adding file or folder information to the captions of icons in the grid view.

Icon Size entry has zoom in and zoom out buttons. The zoom in button (+ button) enlarges your view of the window, making icons bigger. The zoom out button (- button) reduces your view, making them smaller. You can also use the CTRL++ and CTRL+- keys to zoom in and out.

Figure 8-48: File manager sidebar Tools menu

Tabs

The GNOME file manager supports tabs with which you can open several folders in the same file manager window. To open a tab, click the New Tab entry button in the Tools menu (see Figure 8-48) or press CTRL+t. You can use the Tabs buttons to move from one tab to another, or to rearrange tabs. You can also use the CTRL+PageUp and CTRL+PageDown keys to move from one tab to another. Use the SHIFT+CTRL+PageUp and SHIFT+CTRL+PageDown keys to rearrange the tabs. To close a tab, click its close (x) button on the right side of the tab (see Figure 8-49), or press CTRL+w. Tabs are detachable. You can drag a tab out to open a separate window.

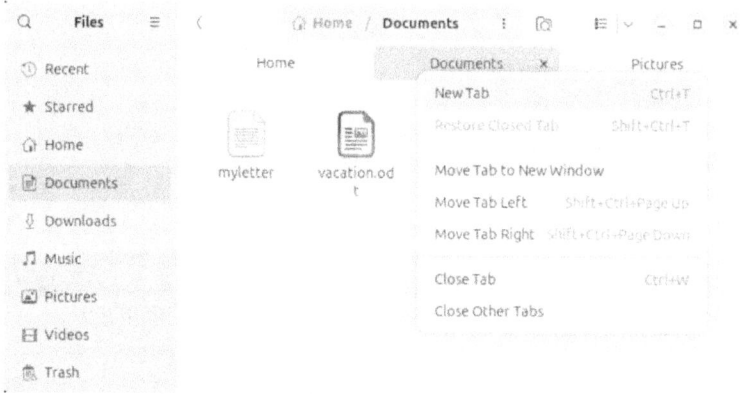

Figure 8-49: File manager window with tabs

Displaying and Managing Files and Folders

You can view a folder's contents as icons or as a detailed list, which you can choose by clicking the grid/list button between the search and view menu buttons on the right side of the toolbar as shown here. This button toggles between grid (icon) and list views.

Use the CTRL key to change views quickly: CTRL+1 for list and CTRL+2 for grid (icons). The list view provides the name, size, date, and favorite status. Buttons are displayed for each field across the top of the main pane. You can use these buttons to sort the list according to that field. For example, to sort the files by date, click the Modified button; to sort by size, click Size. Click again to alternate between ascending and descending order. To display the context menu in the list view, right click on the empty space to the left or right of the list entries.

Certain types of file icons display previews of their contents. For example, the icons for image files display a thumbnail of the image.

To the right of the grid/list button is a button for the View menu (down-arrow). The Views menu has entries for d sorting your file manager icons (see Table 8-5) (see Figure 8-50). The sort entries allow you to sort your icons by name (A-Z and Z-A), size, type, and modification date. You can also reverse the order by name and modification date.

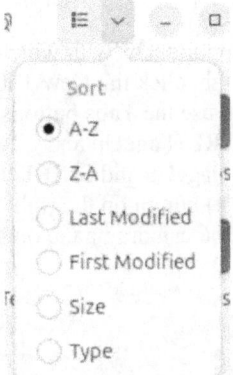

Figure 8-50: File manager View and Tools menus

Menu Item	Description
Undo	Undo the previous operation
Redo	Redo an undo operation
A-Z	Sort in alphabetic order
Z-A	Sort in reverse alphabetic order
Last Modified	Sort by last modified date
First Modified	Sort by recent modified date
Size	Sort by file size
Type	Sort by file type
Reload	Refreshes file and folder list

Table 8-5: File Manager View Menu

Navigating in the File Manager

The file manager operates similarly to a web browser, using the same window to display opened folders. It maintains a list of previously viewed folders, and you can move back and forth through that list using the toolbar buttons. The left arrow button moves you to the previously displayed folder, and the right arrow button moves you to the next displayed folder. Use the sidebar to access your storage devices (USB, DVD/CD, and attached hard drives), as well as mounted network folders. You can also access your home folders, trash, and recent files. As noted, the Computer icon on the Other Locations folder opens your root (top) system folder.

To open a subfolder, you can double-click its icon or right-click the icon and select Open from the menu (see Table 8-6). To open the folder in a new tab, select Open in New Tab.

You can open any folder or file system listed in the sidebar by clicking it. You can also right-click an entry to display a menu with entries to Open in a New Tab and Open in a New

Window (see Table 8-7). The menu for the Trash entry lets you empty the trash. You can also remove and rename the bookmarks.

Entries for removable devices in the sidebar, such as USB drives, also have eject buttons and a menu item for Eject. Internal hard drives have an Unmount option instead.

Menu Item	Description
Open	Opens the file with its associated application. Folders are opened in the file manager. Associated applications are listed.
Open With *application*	Open a file with the default application
Open With	Open a file with a different application
Cut, Copy	Cuts or copies the selected file or folder
Move To	Moves a file to another folder
Copy To	Copies a file to another folder
Rename (F2)	Renames the file
Compress	Archives the file with zip, tar.xz, or 7z formats
Email	E-mails the file
Move To Trash	Moves a file to the Trash folder, where you can later delete it
Open in Terminal	Open a folder in a terminal window
Sharing Options	Open the sharing dialog for a folder. Displayed only if you have installed the **nautilus-share** package.
Properties	Displays the Properties dialog

Table 8-6: The File and Folder Pop-up Menu

Menu Item	Description
Open	Opens the file with its associated application. Folders are opened in the file manager. Associated applications are listed.
Open in a New Tab	Opens a folder in a new tab in the same window
Open in a New Window	Opens a folder in a separate window, accessible from the toolbar with a right-click
Remove	Removes the bookmark from the sidebar
Rename	Renames the bookmark
Properties	Open the folder's properties dialog

Table 8-7: The File Manager Sidebar Pop-up Menu

Managing Files and Folders

As a GNOME-compliant file manager, Files supports desktop drag-and-drop operations for copying and moving files. To move a file or folder, drag-and-drop from one folder to another.

The move operation is the default drag-and-drop operation in GNOME. To copy a file to a new location, press the CTRL key as you drag-and-drop.

You can also perform remove, rename, and copy operations on a file by right-clicking its icon and selecting the action you want from the pop-up menu that appears (see Table 8-5). For example, to remove an item, right-click it and select the Move To Trash entry from the menu. This places it in the Trash folder, where you can later delete it.

Renaming Files

To rename a file, you can either right-click the file's icon and select the Rename entry from the pop-up menu or click its icon and press the F2 function key. A dialog is displayed with the current name in a small text box (see Figure 8-51). You can overwrite the old one or edit the current name by clicking a position in the name to insert text, as well as by using the Backspace key to delete characters. When renaming a file, be sure to click the Rename button once you have entered the new name. You can also rename a file by entering a new name in its Properties dialog box.

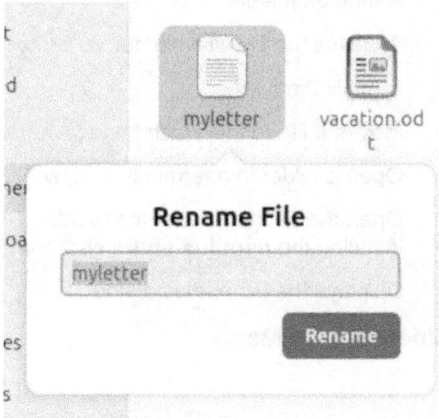

Figure 8-51: File manager Rename dialog

You can also change several filenames at once by selecting the files and then right-clicking and choosing Rename. A dialog opens listing the selected files and a text box for specifying the new names (see Figure 8-52). You can add to the name (Rename using a template) or choose the "Find and replace text" option to change a common part of the names. For the template option, clicking the Add button lets you choose from a list of possible automatic number formats to add. The template is displayed in brackets in the text box. The Original File Name entry adds the original file name specifier to the text box, should you remove it. Once you have selected a template, an Automatic Number Order menu is displayed with options for sorting the renamed files (ascending, descending, first or last modified.

Chapter 8: Ubuntu Desktop **333**

Figure 8-52: File manager - Renaming several files at once - template

The "Find and replace text" option lets you replace a common part of the names (see Figure 8-53). This could even be the file type if you wish. The selected parts of the files to be changed will be highlighted. Should you want to undo the changes, press CTRL-Z in the file manager window.

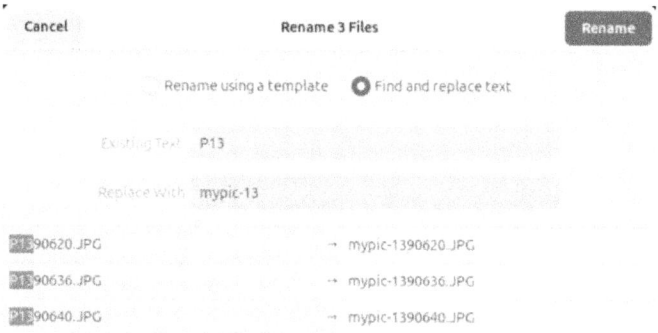

Figure 8-53: File manager - Renaming several files at once - Find and Replace

Compress and Archive Files

You can also compress and archive files and folders (see Figure 8-54). Select the files or folders to compress and archive, right-click and choose the Compress option. A Create Compressed Archive dialog opens where you can specify the name of the compressed archive and the archive format. Choose the format of the archive from the menu to the right of the name (zip, tar, and 7z).

334   Part 3: Desktops

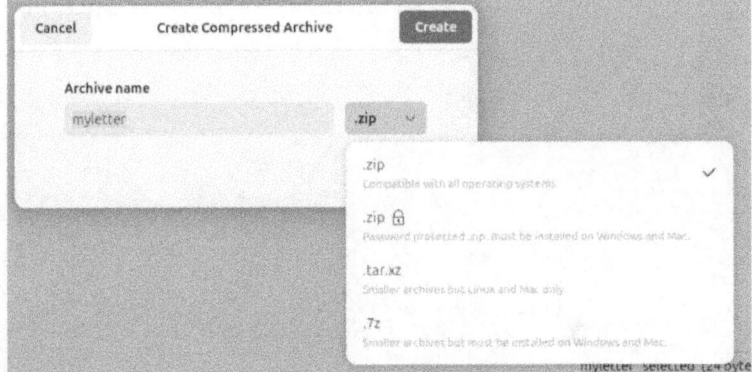

Figure 8-54: File manager - Compress and Archive dialogs

Copying Files

To copy a file to a new location, press the CTRL key as you drag-and-drop. When copying a large file or many files, a button is displayed at the bottom of the sidebar to the left showing a circle chart and the progress of the copy operation (see Figure 8-55). Clicking on the button displays a notification showing the progress of the copy operation, with an x to the right that you can click to cancel the copy. When the copy process for a file is completed, the x becomes a checkmark. When the entire copy process is completed for all files, the button shows a full circle.

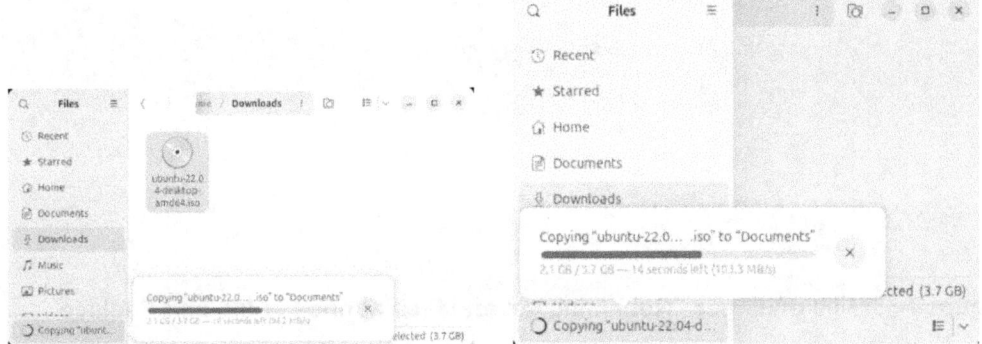

Figure 8-55: File manager - Copying files

Grouping Files

You can select a group of files and folders by clicking the first item and then holding down the SHIFT key while clicking the last item, or by clicking and dragging the mouse across items you want to select. To select separated items, hold the CTRL key down as you click the individual icons. If you want to select all the items in the folder, right-click on the current folder's empty space to display the folder's pop-up menu and choose the Select All entry. You can also just press CTRL+a. You can then copy, move, or delete several files at once.

Opening Applications and Files MIME Types

You can start any application in the file manager by double-clicking either the application or a data file used for that application. If you want to open the file with a specific application, you can right-click the file and select the Open With entry to display the Open File dialog (se Figure 8-56). Several entries will be displayed for default, recommended applications (if any), and all other applications. The default is in the Default App section, recommended similar applications are listed in the Recommended Apps section, and all other applications are listed in the Other Apps section. Select the application you wish to open the file with and click the Open button on the top right of the dialog.

To change or set the default application to use for a certain type of file, you select a different application in the Recommended Apps or Other Apps sections, and then click on the "Always use for this file type" switch at the bottom of the dialog.

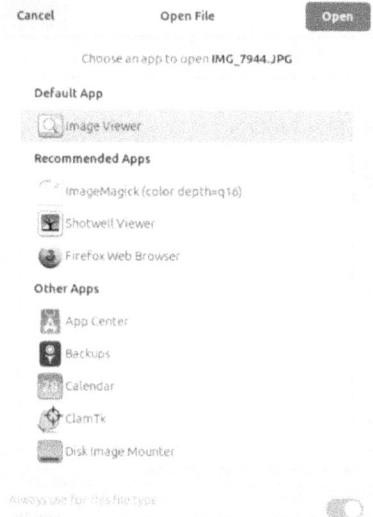

Figure 8-56: File manager - Open File dialog (Open With)

File and Folder Properties

In a file's Properties dialog, you can view detailed information on a file and set options and permissions (see Figure 8-57). Right-click on the file and choose Properties from the menu. A file's Properties dialog will include a link to a Permissions dialog, as well as a link, if applicable, to a dialog with information about a file such as image or audio specifications. The Properties dialog shows the parent folder of the file, along with the date and time it was last accessed, modified, and when it was created. The file's icon is displayed at the top, with a text box showing the file's name. You can edit the filename in the Name text box. Below the textbox is the file type and its size. You can click the star in the upper left corner to add the file to your Starred folder. Text files will display an "Executable as Program" switch at the bottom, which you can click to make the file executable (see Figure 8-58). Use this for text files that are shell scripts. This has the effect of setting the execute permission.

336 Part 3: Desktops

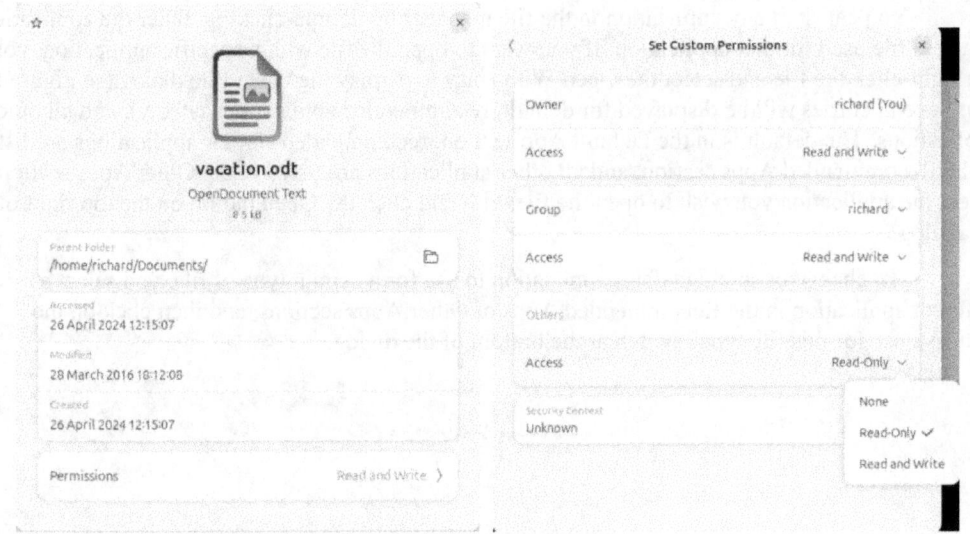

Figure 8-57: File properties and permissions

Figure 8-58: File properties and permissions for executable file

The Permissions dialog for files shows the read, write, and execute permissions for owner, group, and others, as set for this file. You can change any of the permissions here, provided the file belongs to you. You configure access for the owner, the group, and others, using drop-down menus. You can set owner permissions as Read Only or Read and Write. For group and others, you can also set the None option, denying access. Clicking the group name displays a menu listing different groups, allowing you to select one to change the file's group.

Certain kind of files will have an additional dialog, providing information about the file. For example, an audio file will have an Audio Properties dialog listing the type of audio file and any other information, such as the duration and the codec used. An image file will have an Image Properties dialog listing the resolution and type of image. A video file will contain an Audio and Video Properties dialog showing the type of video file, along with compression and resolution information.

The Permissions dialog for folders operates much the same way, with Access menus for Owner, Group, and Others. The Access menu controls access to the folder with options for None, List files only, Access files, and Create and delete Files. These correspond to the read and execute permissions given to files. To set the permissions for all the files in the folder accordingly (not just the folder), click the "Change Permissions for Enclosed Files" button to open a dialog where you can specify the owner, group, and others permissions for files and folders in the folder.

File Manager Preferences

You can set preferences for your file manager in the Preferences dialog, accessible by selecting the Preferences item in any file manager window's Tools menu to open the Preferences dialog (see Figure 8-59). The Preferences dialog has four sections: General, Optional Context Menu Actions, Performance, Date and Time Format, and Grid View Captions. In the General section you can choose to sort folders before files are displayed and whether to open items with a double-click (the default) or a single click. You can also choose to have the list view display an expandable tree, showing files and subfolders within an expanded folder.

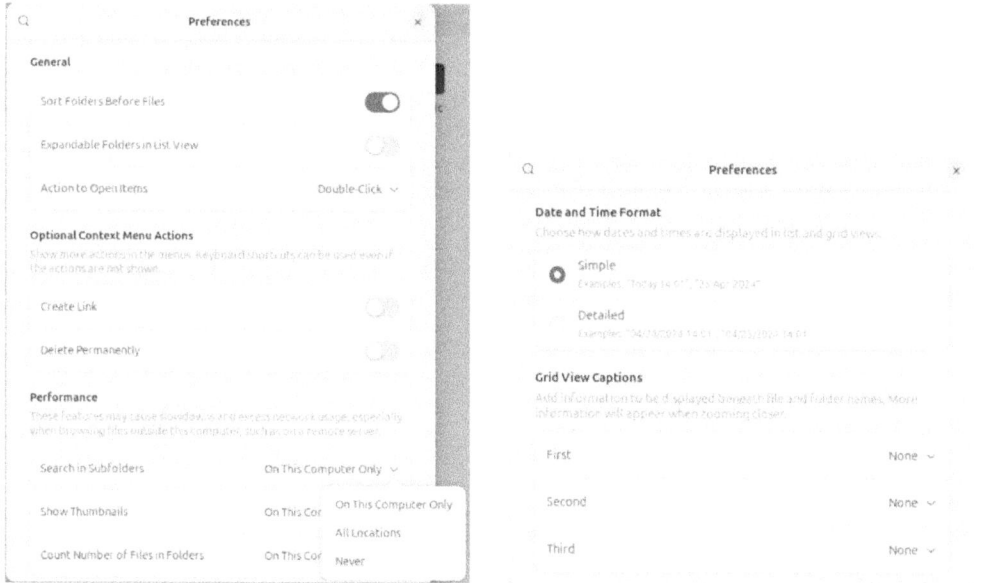

Figure 8-59: File manager Preferences

For the Context Menu you can add entries to the context menu for a file or folder to create a link (Create Link) and delete a file or folder permanently (Delete Permanently), instead of sending it to the trash.

In the Performance section, you can choose whether to limit searches to your local computer, to display as a file's icon a thumbnail of that file's content, and whether to show the number of files in a folder on the file manager window.

In the Date and Time Format section you can specify either a simple format or a detailed one.

In the Grid View Captions section, you can choose what information you want displayed in an icon caption, such as the size or modification date. You can choose up to three items to display.

File Manager Search

Three primary search tools are available for your GNOME desktop: the GNOME dash search, the GNOME Search Anywhere search, and the GNOME file manager search. The GNOME Search Anywhere will search your all your folders and subfolders, as well as any locations listed in the Settings Search tab's Search Locations dialog. A few local ones on your account are listed, but you can add others, including any folders on your system that you have access to. The Gnome file manager search will only search the current folder and its subfolders. To perform a Search Anywhere search, click the Search Anywhere button (looking glass image) on the top left side of the file manager sidebar.

With GNOME file manager, you enter a pattern to search. You can further refine your search by specifying dates and file types. Click the Search button (folder icon with embedded looking glass) on the toolbar the right of the folder menu (ellipses) to open a Search box. Enter the pattern to search, then press Enter. The results are displayed (see Figure 8-60). Click the menu button to the right to add the file-type (What) and date (When) search parameters, to search file text, or just the file name. Selecting the When entry opens a dialog where you can specify the recency of the document's last use or modification, by day, week, month, or year. A calendar button to the right of the text box for the date opens a calendar to let you choose a specific date. The What entry displays a menu with different file categories such as music, Documents, folders, pictures, and PDF.

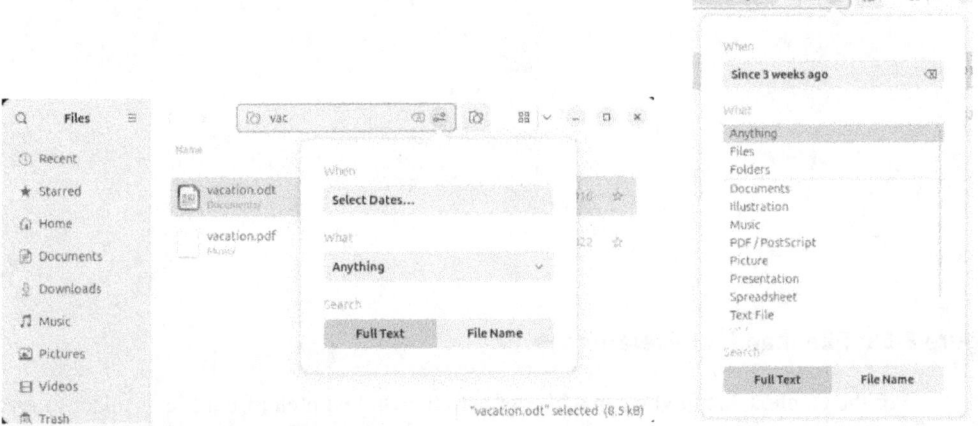

Figure 8-60: File manager search

Chapter 8: Ubuntu Desktop 339

If the file search has no results, a button is displayed for the Search Everywhere search (see Figure 8-61). You can click it to perform a search on all your folders and subfolders, as well as any locations specified in the Settings Search tab's Search Locations dialog. The search box will show a looking glass icon on the left indicating a Search Anywhere search, instead of a folder icon with an embedded looking glass that indicates local file manager searches.

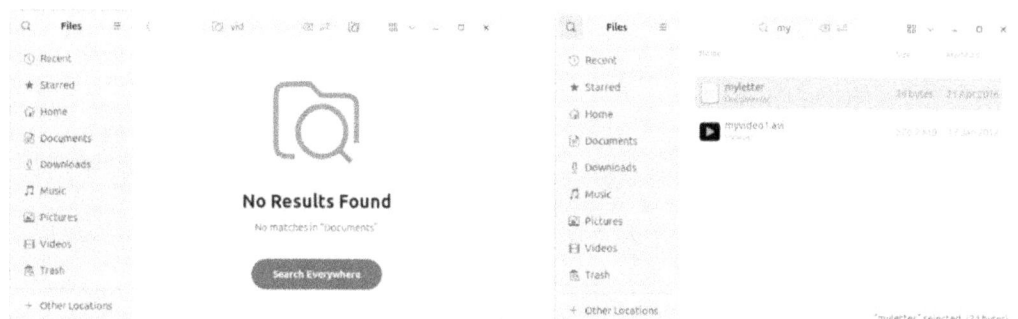

Figure 8-61: File manager search with no results

In the file manager window, you can directly access Search Everywhere by clicking on the looking glass button located on the top left side of the sidebar (see Figure 8-62). The Search Locations dialog in Settings | Search specifies locations that are searched by Search Anywhere, which is a feature in current system Apps, including the Files file manager.

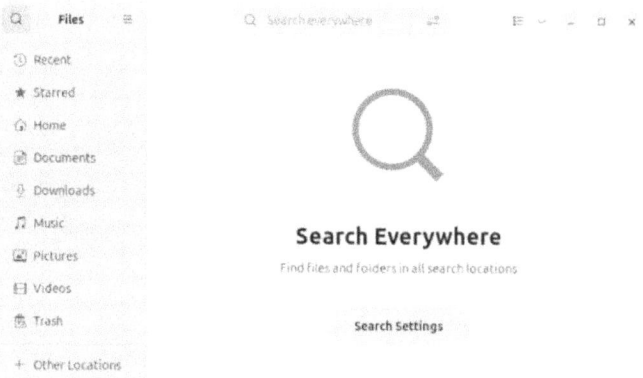

Figure 8-62: File manager sidebar Search Everywhere search

9. Kubuntu (KDE Plasma)

The KDE Plasma Desktop
Application Menus
Plasma
Widgets
Activities
Desktop Effects
KDE File Manager: Dolphin
Discover Package Manager
KDE System Settings

Plasma is the desktop developed and distributed by KDE (the K Desktop Environment). It is often referred to as simply the KDE desktop. Plasma includes the standard desktop features, such as a window manager and a file manager, as well as an extensive set of applications that cover most Linux tasks. The KDE Plasma version of Ubuntu is called Kubuntu and is available as a separate desktop USB/DVD, and as the **kubuntu-desktop** meta-package on the APT repository (Synaptic Package Manager or **apt** command). The KDE Plasma desktop is developed and distributed by the KDE Project. KDE is open source software provided under a GNU Public License and is available free of charge along with its source code. KDE development is managed by the KDE Core Team. Kubuntu uses the stable version of KDE at the time of the Kubuntu release. It will be less recent than the current KDE release. The KDE Plasma version used in Kubuntu 24.04 is 5.27, whereas the KDE Plasma version is 6.1.

The KDE software development and distribution is organized into three projects: Plasma, Gear (formerly Applications), and Frameworks. KDE Gear provide numerous applications written specifically for KDE Plasma that are accessible from the desktop. These include editors, photo and image applications, sound and video players, and office applications. Some applications have the letter *K* as part of their name, for example, Kate. On a system administration level, KDE provides several tools for managing your system, such as the Discover Software Manager, and the KDE System Monitor. KDE applications also feature a built-in Help application. See **https://apps.kde.org//** Applications tab for a list and descriptions of current applications. The KDE Gear version used in Kubuntu 24.04 is 23, whereas the current KDE Gear version is 24.

KDE Frameworks provides support libraries designed to work with the Qt libraries that KDE Plasma and Applications depend on. Frameworks is designed to be cross-platform, enabling any KDE Application to run on systems that support the Qt libraries. Frameworks can be used as a basis for any custom operating system, such as Lubuntu. KDE Framework packages have the prefix **kf5**, such as the **kf5-filesystem** that provides support for the KDE filesystem. Development for Plasma, Frameworks, and Applications proceed at different paces. The KDE Frameworks version used in Kubuntu 24.04 is 5.115, whereas the KDE Plasma version is 6.3.

Web Site	Description
https://www.kde.org	KDE website
https://www.kubuntu.org	Kubuntu site
https://www.kde.org/applications/	KDE Applications website
https://www.qt.io/	Site for the Qt company
https://store.kde.org	KDE desktop themes
https://mail.kde.org/mailman/listinfo/	KDE mailing lists
https://www.kde.org/plasma-desktop	KDE Plasma desktop website
https://docs.kde.org	KDE documentation site

Table 9-1: KDE Web Sites

KDE, initiated by Matthias Ettrich in October 1996, is designed to run on any Unix implementation, including Linux, Solaris, HP-UX, and FreeBSD. The official KDE website is **https://www.kde.org**, which provides news updates, download links, and documentation. Detailed documentation for the KDE desktop and its applications is available at **https://docs.kde.org**.

Several KDE mailing lists are available for users and developers, including announcements, administration, and other topics. Development support and documentation can be obtained at the KDE Techbase site at **https://techbase.kde.org**. Most applications are available on the Ubuntu repositories and can be installed directly from Discover Software, the Synaptic Package Manager, and the **sudo apt install** command. Various KDE websites are listed in Table 9-1. KDE uses as its library of GUI tools the Qt library, currently developed and supported by the QT company, owned by Digia (**https://www.qt.io**). It provides the Qt libraries as Open Source software that is freely distributable, though a commercial license is also available.

KDE Plasma 5 and Kubuntu 24.04 LTS

The KDE Plasma 5 release is a major reworking of the KDE desktop. KDE Plasma 5.27.11 is included with the Kubuntu 24.04 LTS distribution. Check the Kubuntu and KDE sites for detailed information on KDE 5.

```
https://www.kde.org/announcements/plasma5.0/
```

For features added with KDE Plasma 5.27, check:

```
https://kde.org/announcements/plasma/5/5.27.0/
```

KDE development is organized into a plasma, frameworks, and applications releases. The plasma release covers the desktop interface (the Plasma desktop shell), and the applications release covers KDE applications. Plasma has containments and plasmoids (also called widgets). Plasmoids operate similar to applets, small applications running on the desktop or panel. Plasmoids operate within containments. There are two Plasma containments, the panel and the desktop. In this sense, the desktop and the panel are features of an underlying Plasma operation. They are not separate programs. Each has their own set of widgets. Kubuntu also supports Activities, multiple plasma desktop containments, each with their own set of active widgets and open windows.

The Kubuntu edition of Ubuntu installs KDE as the primary desktop from the Kubuntu install disc. Kubuntu 24.04 LTS officially supports and installs KDE Plasma 5.27.11. The latest features included with Kubuntu 24.04 LTS are discussed at:

```
https://kubuntu.org/news/kubuntu-24-04-lts-noble-numbat-released/
```

Kubuntu 24.04 LTS also uses KDE Gear 23.08, check:

```
https://kde.org/announcements/gear/23.08.0/
```

Installing Kubuntu

You can download the Kubuntu Desktop discs from the Kubuntu site at:

```
http://kubuntu.org/
```

You can also obtain the ISO image for Kubuntu from:

```
https://kubuntu.org/getkubuntu/
```

If you are installing Kubuntu from the Kubuntu USB/DVD, you will follow the similar steps as those used for the Ubuntu Desktop USB/DVD: Language and Internet connection selection, and option to try or install Kubuntu, Welcome (language selection), Location (time zone and date), Keyboard, Customize (full, normal, minimal software collections (Installation Mode), along with updates and third party packages), Partitions (automatic or manual), Users (your name, login name, password, host name, automatic login option), Summary (review of selected location, keyboard, and partitions), Install, and Finish (All Done screen with restart option). The artwork will be different, but the tasks will be the same.

You can also add Kubuntu as a desktop to an Ubuntu desktop installation. KDE includes numerous packages. Instead of trying to install each one, you should install KDE using its Debian meta package, **kubuntu-desktop**. Use the **sudo apt install** command in a terminal window. You will be prompted to keep the GDM display manager for logins, though you can change to SDDM, the Simple Desktop Display Manager. Once installed, KDE will then become an option you can select from the Sessions menu on the Login screen as "Plasma."

```
sudo apt install kubuntu-desktop
```

Note: Kubuntu has its own restricted packages, kubuntu-restricted-extras and kubuntu-restricted-addons, for multimedia codecs.

SDDM

Kubuntu uses the Simple Desktop Display Manager (SDDM) to manage logins. A login greeter is displayed at the center of the screen where you can select a user icon and enter a password (see Figure 9-1). A user list of user icons is shown that you can choose from. Sleep, Restart, Shut Down, and Other buttons are displayed below the login button. Use the Other button to login as a user not displayed in the user list. Click the "Virtual Keyboard" link in the lower left corner to display a virtual keyboard.

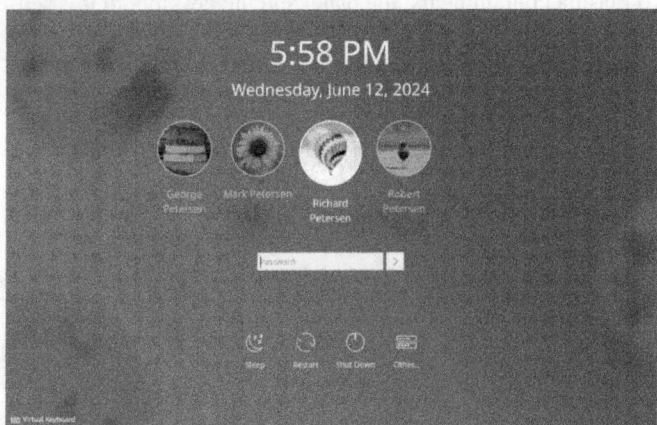
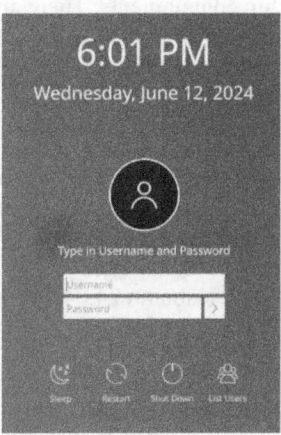

Figure 9-1: SDDM Display Manager, login screen

Upon choosing a user icon and entering the password, press ENTER or clicking the login button (right arrow symbol) at the right end of the password text box. Your KDE session then starts up.

If you have more than one desktop installed on your system, such as MATE or LXDE, then a Desktop Sessions menu appears in the bottom left of the screen (see Figure 9-2). Click on it to display available desktops you can choose. The name for KDE is "Plasma", which is displayed as one of the menu items. You can use it to return to using the KDE desktop.

Chapter 9: Kubuntu (KDE)   **345**

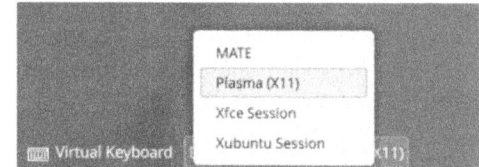

Figure 9-2: SDDM Display Manager, Desktop Session menu

You can change the theme of the login greeter using the Login Screen (SDDM) tab in the Startup and Shutdown dialog (System Settings | Startup and Shutdown in the Workspace section). The theme section lists available themes. Currently, only Breeze is listed. To change the background image, click on a theme to display it in the Customize section to the right. Then click on the Background icon and choose the "Load from file" option from the pop-up menu. On the Advanced tab, you can choose the default user, the desktop for your session, and whether to automatically log in. You can also manually configure SDDM using the **/etc/sddm.conf** file, which lists your default user and desktop (Session).

The Plasma Desktop

One of KDE's aims is to provide users with a consistent integrated desktop (see Figure 9-3). Plasma provides its own window manager (KWM), file manager (Dolphin), program manager, and desktop and panel (Plasma). You can run any X Window System or Wayland compliant application, such as Firefox, in Plasma, as well as any GNOME application. Kubuntu still uses the X.org server as its default. Though you can choose to try the Wayland server, it is not supported.

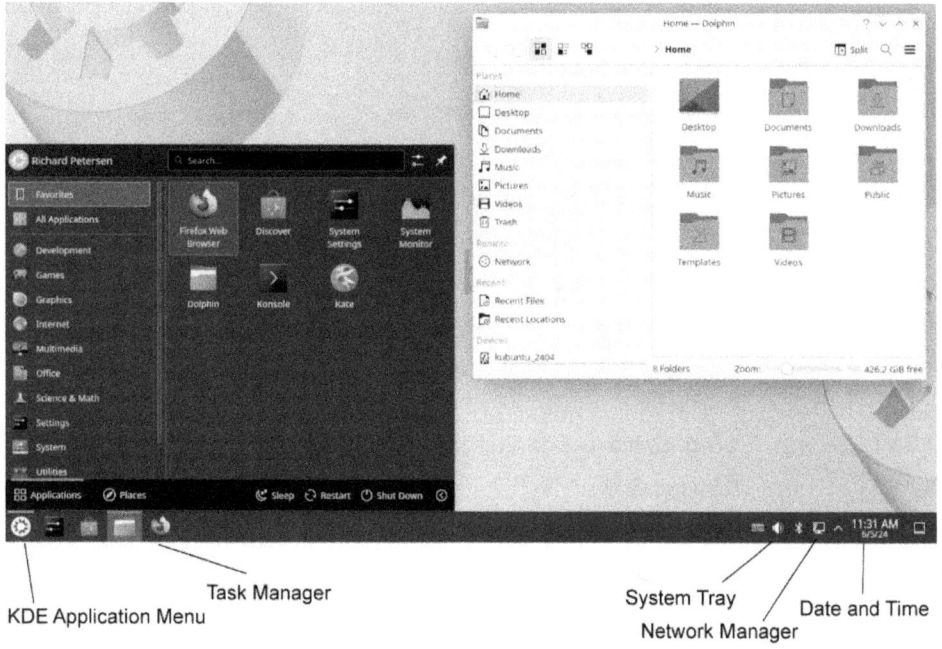

Figure 9-3: The KDE desktop

In turn, you can also run any KDE application, including the Dolphin file manager in GNOME. The Plasma 5 desktop features the Plasma desktop shell with new panel, menu, widgets, and activities. Keyboard shortcuts are provided for many desktop operations, as well as plasmoid (widget) tasks (see Table 9-2).

To configure your desktop, you use the System Settings dialog (Favorites | System Settings), which lists tabs for dialogs such as Global Theme, Font, Icons, Application Style, Workspace behavior, Search, Window Management, Driver Manager, and Bluetooth. Workspace Theme lets you choose desktop, cursor, and splash themes. Workspace behavior is where you can set desktop effects and virtual desktops. Windows Management controls window display features like window switchers and title bar actions.

The desktop supports drag-and-drop and copy-and-paste operations. With the copy-and-paste operation, you can copy text from one application to another. You can even copy and paste from a Konsole terminal window.

Keys	Description
ALT-F1	Application menu
ALT-F2	KRunner, command execution, entry can be any search string for a relevant operation, including bookmarks and contacts, not just applications.
up/down arrows	Move among entries in menus, including Application and menus
left/right arrows	Move to submenus menus, including Application and Quick Access submenus menus
ENTER	Select a menu entry, including an Application or QuickAccess
PageUp, PageDown	Scroll up fast
ALT-F4	Close current window
ALT-F3	Window menu for current window
CTRL-ALT-F6	Command Line Interface
CTRL-ALT-F8	Return to desktop from command line interface
CTRL-r	Remove a selected widget
CTRL-s	Open a selected widget configuration's settings
CTRL-a	Open the Add Widgets window to add a widget to the desktop
CTRL-l	Lock your widgets to prevent removal, adding new ones or changing settings
AT-TAB	Cover Switch or Box Switch for open windows
META-F8	Desktop Grid
CTRL-F9	Present Windows Current Desktop
CTRL-F10	Present Windows All Desktops

Figure 9-3: KDE Keyboard Shortcuts

The KDE Help Center

The KDE Help Center provides a browser-like interface for accessing and displaying both KDE Help files and Linux Man and info files (see Figure 9-4). The same documentation is available at **https://docs.kde.org**. You can start the Help Center from the Applications menu, the Help entry. The Help window displays a sidebar that holds two tabs, one listing contents and one providing a glossary. The main pane displays the currently selected document. A help tree on the contents tab in the sidebar lets you choose the kind of Help documents you want to access. Here you can choose KDE fundamentals (overview of the KDE desktop), the Plasma Manual (KDE manual pages), info documents (Browse info Pages), or application manuals (Application Manuals). Online Help provides links to KDE websites such as the KDE user forum and the KDE tech base sites. Click the "Table of Contents" button on the toolbar to open a listing of all KDE help documents, which you can browse through and click on to open.

A navigation toolbar enables you to move through previously viewed documents. KDE Help documents contain links you can click to access other documents. The Back and Forward buttons move you through the list of previously viewed documents. The KDE Help system provides an effective search tool for searching for patterns in a Help document. Click the Find button on the toolbar or choose the Find entry from the Edit menu, to open a search box at the bottom of the Help window where you can enter a pattern to search on the current open help document. The Options menu lets you refine your search with regular expressions, case sensitive queries, and whole words-only matches.

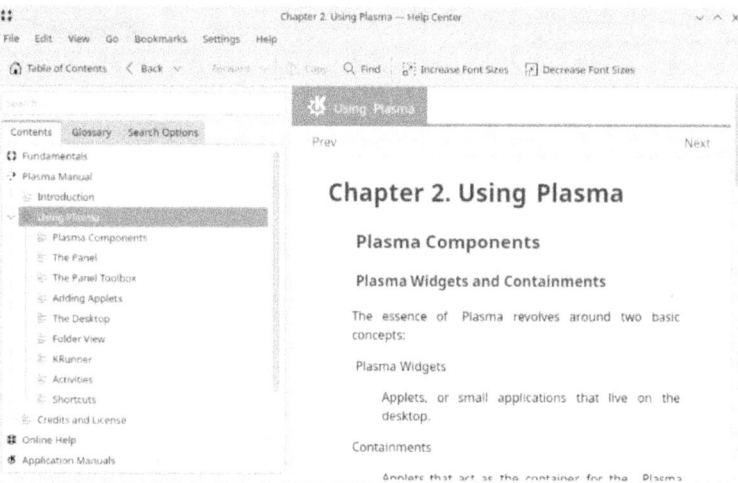

Figure 9-4: KDE Help Center

Desktop Menu and Display Configuration

Right-clicking anywhere on the desktop background displays the desktop menu with options to configure the desktop and display, sort icons on your desktop, add widgets and panels, refresh the desktop, and enter edit mode for the desktop and panel (see Figure 9-5) .

Part 3: Desktops

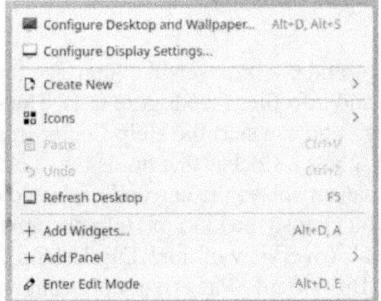

Figure 9-5: Desktop Menu

Should you want to configure your display settings, choose Configure Display Settings from the desktop menu to open the System Settings Display and Monitor dialog (see Figure 9-6). The dialog has four tabs: Display Configuration, Compositor, Gamma, and Night color. On the Display Configuration tab you can set the resolution, orientation, and refresh rate, as well as the scale. On the Gamma tab you can set the gamma, and color saturations (red, green, and blue). On the Night Color tab you can set the night color temperature and the activation time.

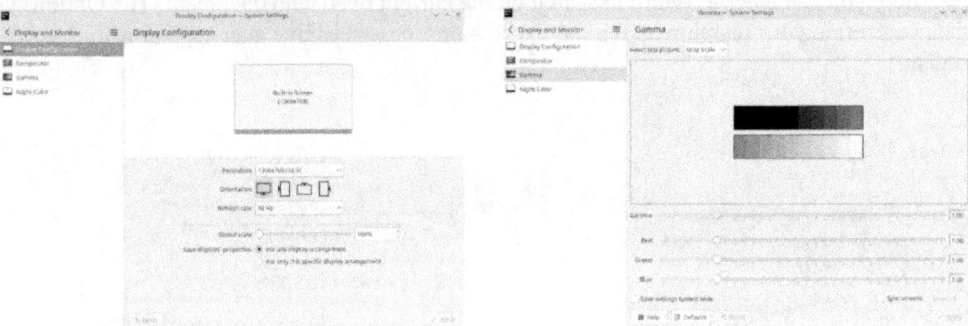

Figure 9-6: Display Settings

Edit Mode

In Edit Mode, you can modify widgets on both the desktop and panel. On the panel you can move and remove widgets (see Figure 9-7). On the desktop, you can hover your mouse over a widget to display its sidebar, allowing you to move, configure, or remove the widget. You can enter edit mode either from the desktop menu or from the panel menu, Enter Edit Mode. In edit mode a button bar at the top of the screen has buttons to open the System Settings dialogs for the desktop and wallpaper, the global theme selection, and the display settings. You can also open the Widgets dialog where you can add widgets to the desktop.

Chapter 9: Kubuntu (KDE) 349

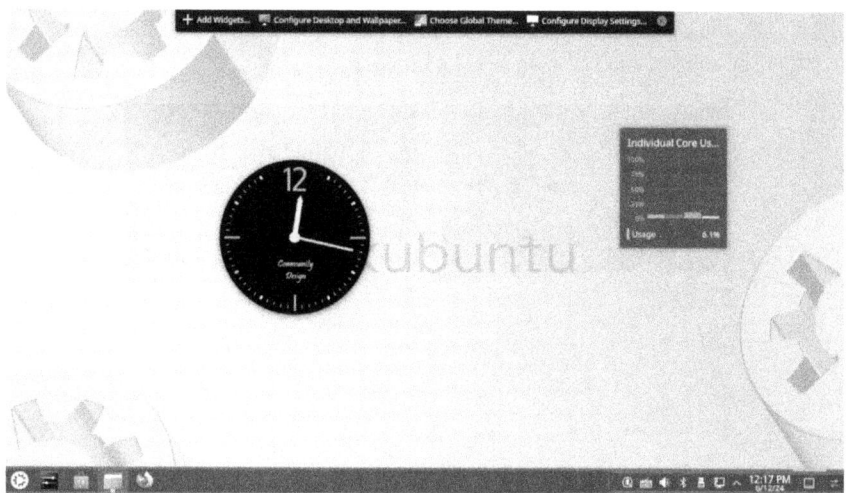

Figure 9-7: Edit Mode

Desktop Backgrounds (Wallpaper)

The background (wallpaper) is set from the desktop menu directly. Right-click on the desktop to display the desktop menu and then select Configure Desktop and Wallpaper to open the Desktop Settings dialog (see Figure 9-8). The background is called wallpaper in KDE and can be changed in the Wallpaper tab. You can select other wallpapers from the wallpaper icons listed or select your own image by clicking the Open button.

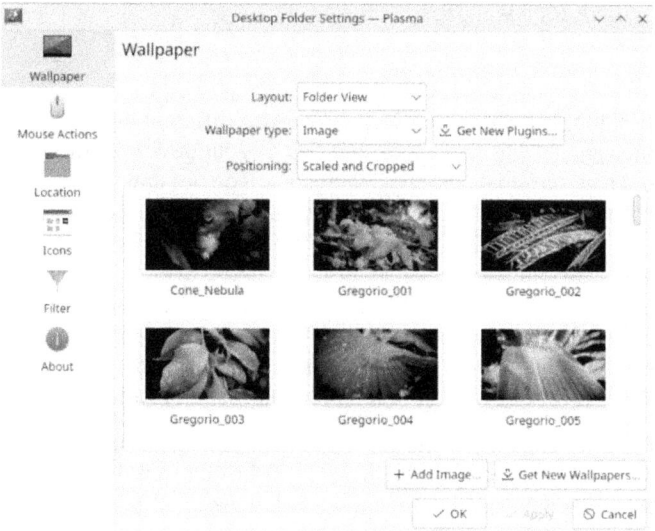

Figure 9-8: Desktop Settings, wallpaper

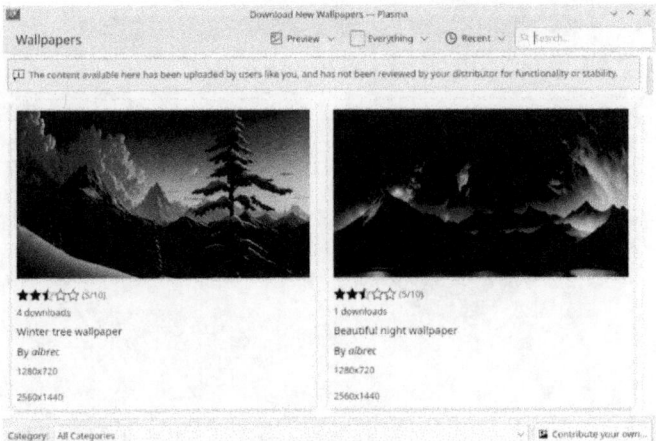

Figure 9-9: Desktop Settings, Get New Wallpapers

You can add more wallpaper by clicking the "Get New Wallpaper" button to open a "Wallpapers" dialog, which lists and downloads wallpaper posted on the **https://store.kde.org** site (see Figure 9-9). Each wallpaper entry shows an image, description, and rating. Buttons on the header bar of the dialog let you view the entries in details (list) or icon mode. You can use menus at the bottom of the dialog to refine the wallpaper listing by category), installed, newest, rating, and popularity (most downloads). Pass your mouse over the icon of the wallpaper you want, to display Install and Details buttons. Click the Install button to download the wallpaper and add it to your Desktop Setting's Wallpaper tab. The wallpaper is downloaded and the Install button changes to Uninstall. To remove a wallpaper, you can select installed wallpapers to find the entry quickly. You can also search by pattern for a wallpaper.

Themes

For your desktop, you can also select a variety of different themes, icons, and window decorations. A theme changes the entire look and feel of your desktop, affecting the appearance of desktop elements, such as scrollbars, buttons, and icons. Themes and window decorations are provided for workspaces. Access the System Settings dialog from any of the Application menus' Settings submenu. On the System Settings dialog, click the Global Theme entry in the "Appearance" section. The Global Theme tab lets you choose overall look and feel, cursor themes, and a splash screen (startup) themes. The Plasma Style dialog lists plasma style themes. Click the Get New Global Themes button to open a Global Themes dialog, listing desktop themes from **https://store.kde.org** (see Figure 9-10). Pass your mouse over the theme you want, to display the Install button. Click the theme's Install button to download and install the theme.

For window decorations, you use the Application Style dialog, Window Decorations tab, where you can select window decoration themes. Click the Get New Window Decorations button to download new decorations. Icons styles are chosen using the Icons tab where you can choose the icon set to use, and even download new sets (Get New Icons).

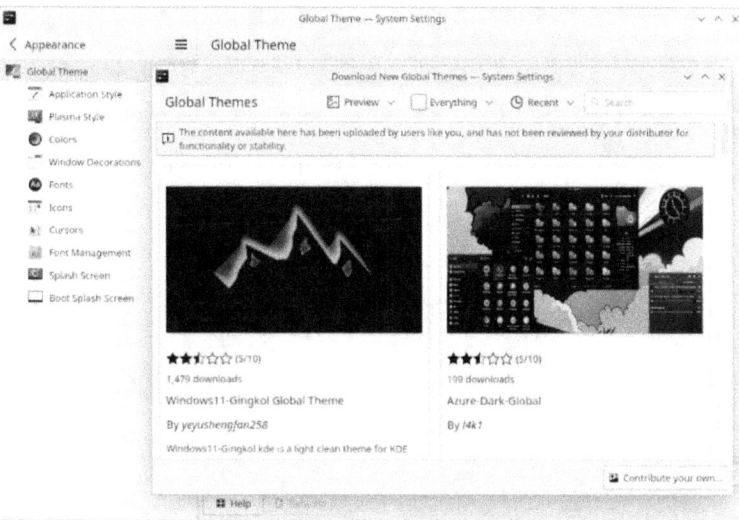

Figure 9-10: System Settings | Appearance | Global Theme | Get New Themes

Leave KDE

You can right-click anywhere on the desktop and select the Leave entry from the pop-up menu, to open a leave dialog with the Log Out button selected (see Figure 9-11). Buttons to the left let you choose between the sleep, restart, and shutdown operations.

Figure 9-11: Log Out dialog

If you just want to lock your desktop, you can select the Lock entry from the desktop pop-up menu, and your screen saver will appear. To access a locked desktop, click on the screen and a box appears prompting you for your login password. When you enter the password, your desktop re-appears.

To shut down your system, you use the KDE Applications menus. KDE uses the Application menus as its main menu, accessible by clicking on the KDE icon on the left side of the panel. The Application menus replace the older Kickoff menus used in older releases. You use an Application menu to leave the KDE desktop. There are three Application menus you can use: Application Launcher, Application Menu, and Application Dashboard. The leave options are displayed differently on each Application menu.

352 Part 3: Desktops

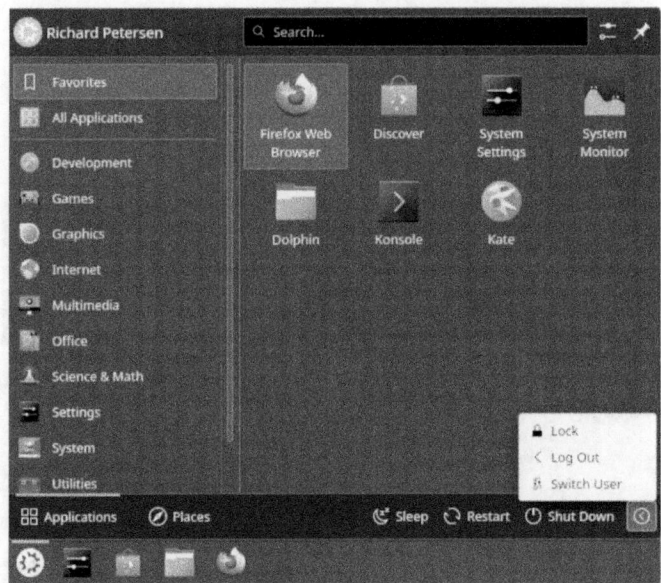

Figure 9-12: Application Launcher leave buttons

For the Application Launcher (the default), there are there are Sleep, Restart, Shut Down, and leave buttons on the lower right of the Application Launcher dialog (see Figure 9-12). The leave button has a left-arrow image. Clicking on the leave button displays a menu for Lock, Log Out, and Switch User.

If you are using the Application Menu, click the Power Session entry on the KDE Application Menu (see Figure 9-13) to display a submenu with entries to lock, log out, switch user, sleep, restart, and shut down.

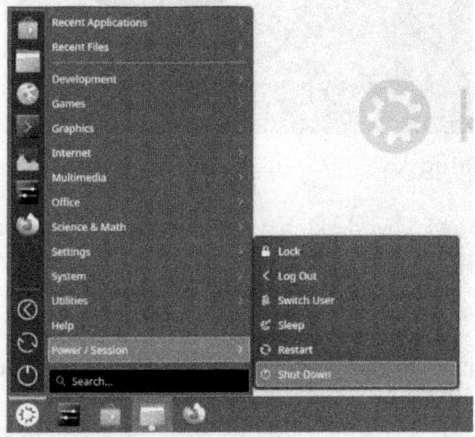

Figure 9-13: Application Menu Power/Session menu

If you are using the Application Dashboard for your main menu, instead of the Application Launcher, you can click the logout, shut down, and restart buttons on the lower left. For a complete selection choose the Power/Session category on the right (see Figure 9-14).

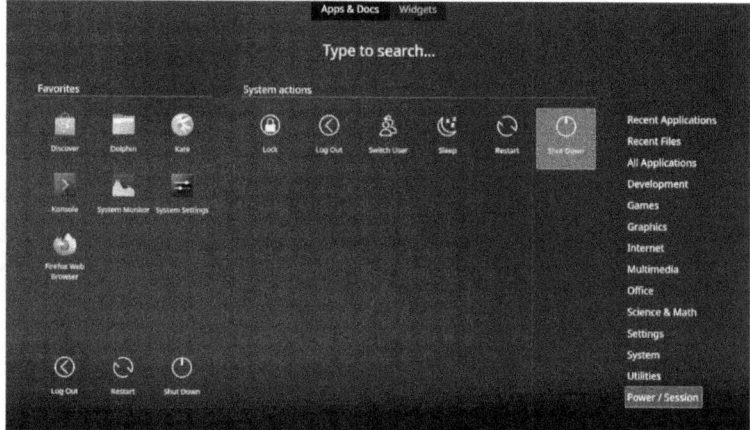

Figure 9-14: Application Dashboard Power/Session

The Shut Down entry will display the Leave dialog with the Shut Down button selected (see Figure 9-15). The Log Out option displays the same dialog with the Log Out button selected. The Switch User option displays a dialog showing a user list to choose from. Should the user you want not be listed, you can click the Other button at the bottom of the list to open a dialog where you can enter the username along with the password. Click the List Users button at the bottom to return to the user list.

Figure 9-15: Shut Down dialog

The Main Menu - Application Menus

The KDE main menu is now provided by the Application Menus, of which there are three: Application Launcher, Application Menu, and Application Dashboard. They replace the older Kickoff menu, which is no longer used. You can switch between the three by right-clicking on the KDE main menu icon on the left side of the panel and choosing Show Alternatives from the pop-up menu (see Figure 9-16). This displays the list of the Application menus, with the one in use highlighted. Click on the one you want to use and click the Switch button shown below the list.

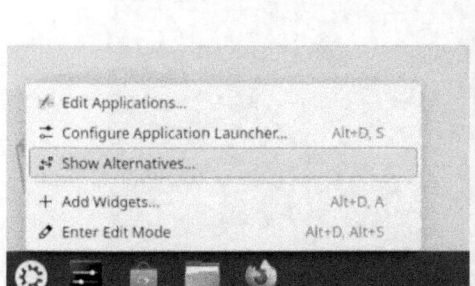 

Figure 9-16: Application menu alternatives

Application Launcher

The Application Launcher is the default used for the main menu (see Figure 9-17). The sidebar has tabs for displaying either Application categories or Places, which includes locations of frequently used applications. Click the button at the bottom of the sidebar for the one you want. Initially the Applications tab is displayed. On the bottom right are the sleep, restart, and shut down buttons along with a leave button for a pop-up menu listing lock, logout, and switch user. The top bar of the dialog shows the user icon, the user name, a search box for searching for applications and locations, an Application Launcher configuration button, and a toggle pin to let you keep the menu open. Clicking on the user icon opens the System Settings User dialog at that user's entry, where you can make user configuration changes.

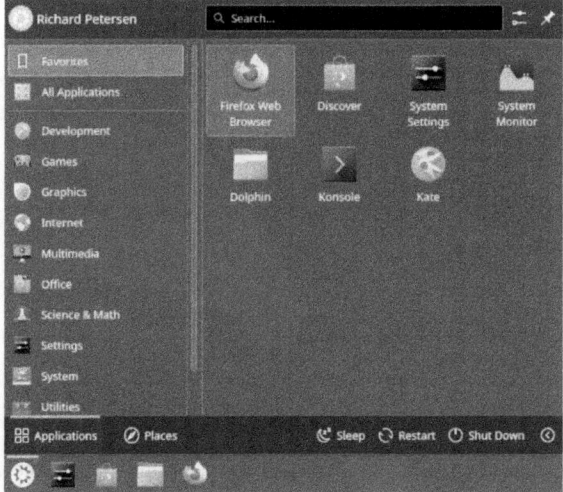

Figure 9-17: Application Launcher

The Applications tab on the sidebar lists entries for common categories such as Office, Multimedia, and Graphics (see Figure 9-18). Icons for applications in a selected category are shown on the right side. Click on an application icon to start it. The Favorites category lists commonly used applications. The All Applications entry lists all your applications organized under alphabetic headings (see Figure 9-15). In addition to the software categories, there are three administration categories: Settings, System, and Utilities. Settings holds the System Settings icon for configuring your desktop. System has administration tools such as the Discover software manager, the Konsole terminal window, the KSystemLog log manager, and the System Monitor. The Utilities entry list helpful system tools such as the Ark archiver, Kate text editor, the Spectacle screenshot tool, and the Kcalc calculator.

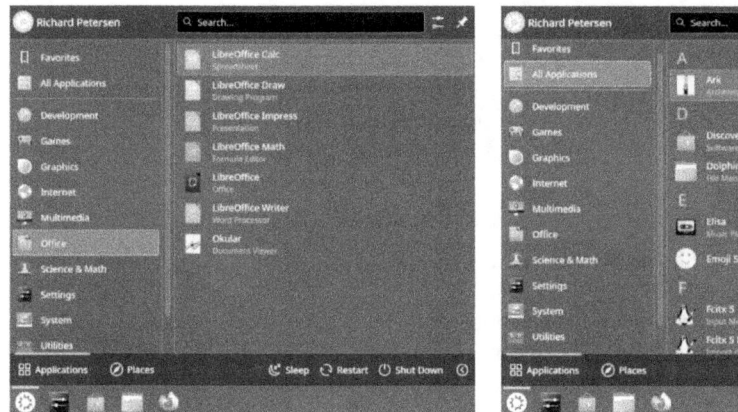

Figure 9-18: Application Launcher Applications

The Places tab on the sidebar lists entries for Computer, History, and Frequently used (see Figure 9-19). The Computer entry displays items in sections: Applications, Places, Remote, Recent, and Searched For. The Applications section lists a few helpful system tools such as the Discover software manager and the System Settings desktop configuration tool. The Places section lists all your default home folders such as Documents and Pictures. The Remote section has an entry for Network, which opens a file manager folder with icons for all your network devices and shares (Bluetooth and Samba). The Recent and Searched For sections have entries for open a file manager window at the Recent or Searched For tabs.

Figure 9-19: Application Launcher Places

To configure the Application Launcher click on the configure button at the top right to open the Application Launcher Settings dialog (see Figure 9-20). Here you can choose an icon to use for the Application Launcher on the panel. You can choose whether to display favorite and application icons in a list or a grid. The "Configure enabled search plugins" button opens the System Settings Search dialog where you can select and configured search plugins.

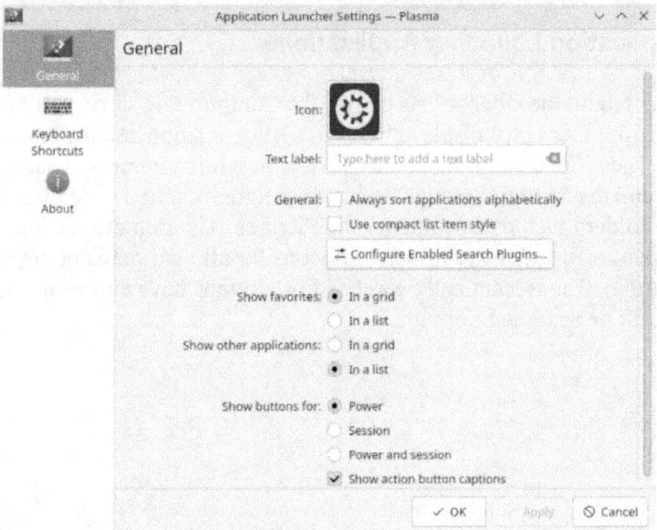

Figure 9-20: Application Launcher Settings

You can choose to show buttons for the power, session, or power and session (see Figure 9-21). Power is the default and shows Sleep, Restart, and Shut Down buttons with a leave menu. Session shows only Lock, Logout, and Switch User buttons along with a power button in place of the leave menu. Power and Session displays buttons for all options: Lock, Log Out, Switch User, Sleep, Restart, and Shut Down.

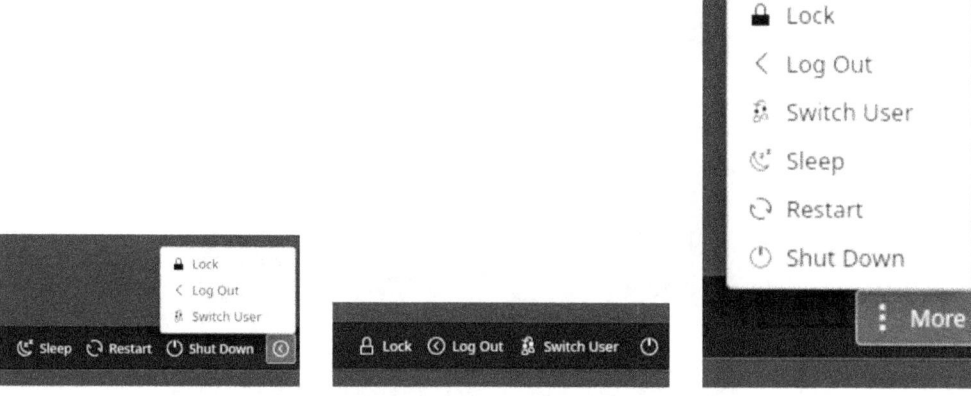

Figure 9-21: Application Launcher Power and Session buttons

Application Menu

The Application Menu implements a traditional menu, with a main menu listing categories, each with submenus for application (see Figure 9-22). There are categories such as System for system configuration dialogs and Utilities for system tools. Office lists the LibreOffice applications, and Graphics the KDE graphic applications. Recently accessed applications are listed under Recent Applications, and recent files used are under Recent files. The Power/Session category lists exit operations such as Shut Down and Log Out. A sidebar shows icons for common applications such as Firefox, the Discover software manager, System Settings, System Monitor, Dolphin file manager, the Konsole terminal window, and the Kate text editor. There are also buttons for Log Out, Reset, and Shut Down. A search box at the bottom of the menu lets you search for applications. Dialogs open with headings for Applications and for System Settings, listing matches found for the search pattern.

358 Part 3: Desktops

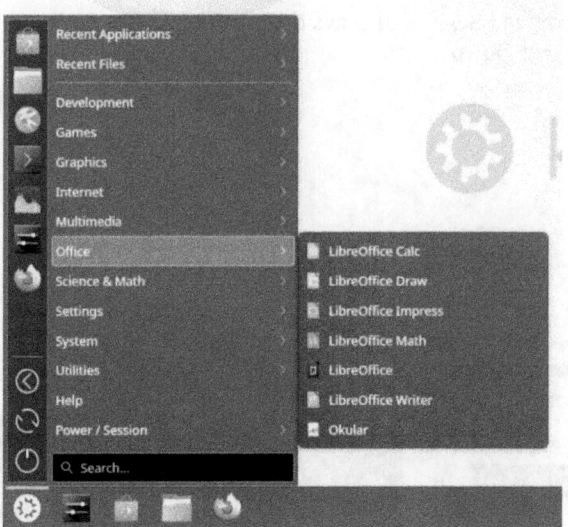

Figure 9-22: Application Menu

To configure the Application Menu, right-click on the main menu icon on the panel and choose "Configure Application Menu" to open the Application Menu Settings dialog (see Figure 9-23). You can choose to show applications by their name or description, or both. The behavior of the menus can be adjusted to list alphabetically and remove any subcategories in the submenus. You can choose where to show the Recent applications, Recent files, or Recent contacts categories. Recent can be defined as either recently used or often used. Search can be expanded to include bookmarks, files, and emails. Search results can be listed at the bottom or top.

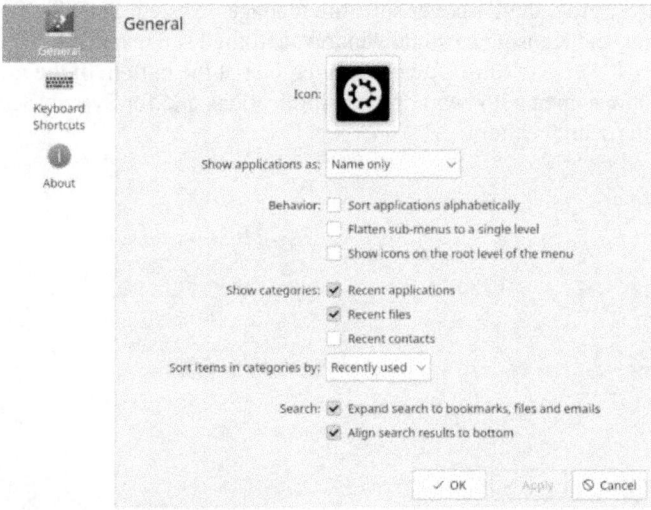

Figure 9-23: Application Menu Settings

Application Dashboard

The Applications Dashboard displays menu entries on a full-screen dashboard, showing sections for applications, favorites, logout/shutdown options, and categories (see Figure 9-24). Press the ESC key to leave the dashboard without making a selection. You can add an application to the Favorites section by right-clicking on the application's icon and selecting Pin to Dash. To remove an application from the Favorites section, right-click on it and select Remove from Favorites. The Applications section shows categories to the right and the icons for a selected category to the left. There are also categories for recent applications and documents. The Power/Session category lists the complete set of leave options, including lock, sleep, and switch user. The All Applications category lists all your applications under alphabetic headings (see Figure 9-25).

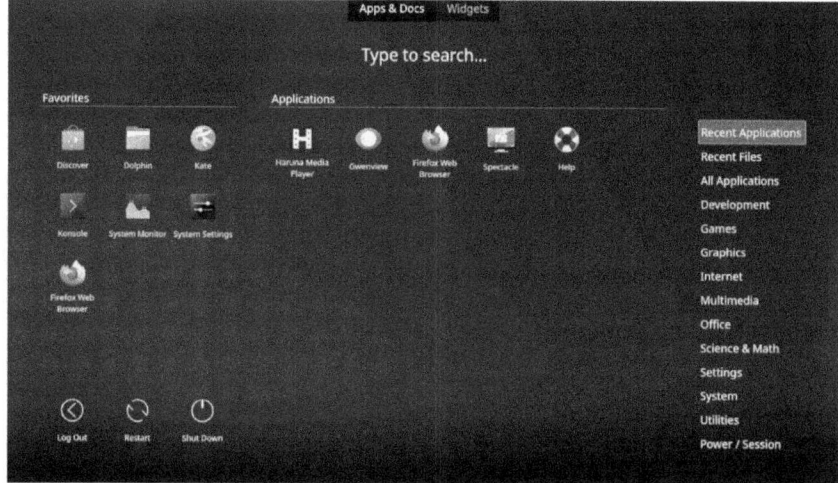

Figure 9-24: Application Dashboard

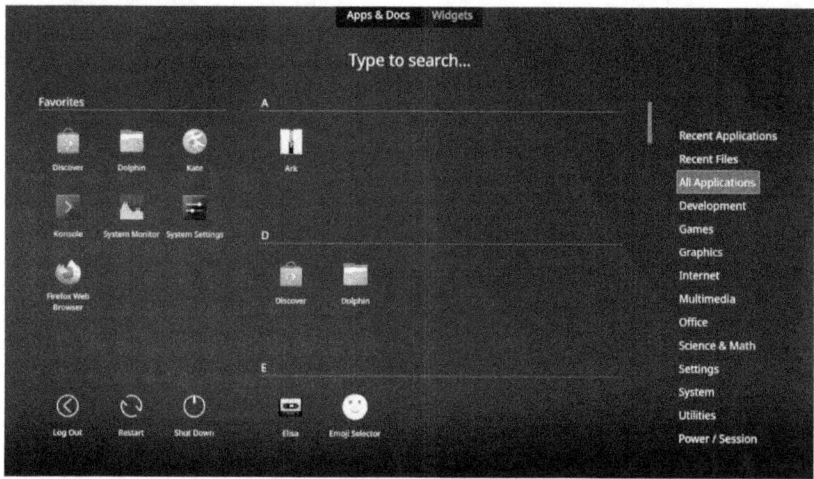

Figure 9-25: Application Dashboard - All Applications

To configure the Application Dashboard, right-click on the main menu icon on the panel and choose "Configure Application Dashboard" to open the Application Dashboard Settings dialog (see Figure 9-26. You can choose to show applications by their name or description, or both. The behavior of the menus can be adjusted to list alphabetically. You can choose where to show the Recent applications, Recent files, or Recent contacts categories. Recent can be defined as either recently used or often used. Search can be expanded to include bookmarks, files, and emails.

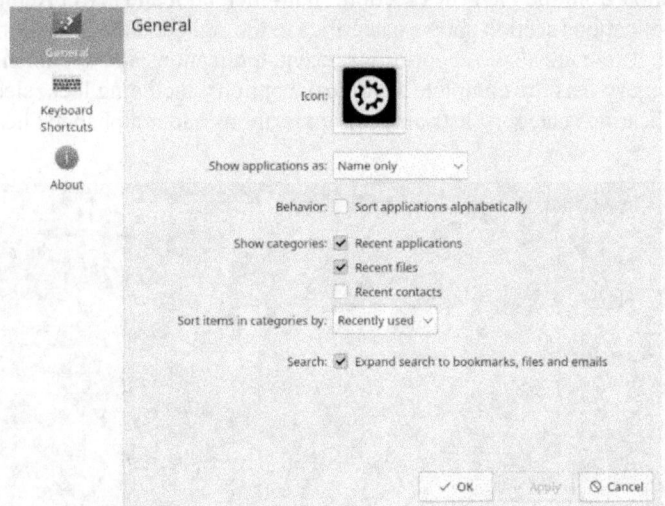

Figure 9-26: Application Dashboard Settings

KRunner

For fast access to applications, bookmarks, contacts, and other desktop items, you can use KRunner. The KRunner widget operates as a search tool for applications and other items such as bookmarks. To find an application, enter a search pattern and a listing of matching applications is displayed. Click on an application entry to start the application. You can also place an icon (application launcher) for an entry on the desktop by simply clicking and dragging its entry from the list to the desktop. For applications where you know the name, part of the name, or just its basic topic, KRunner is a fast way to access the application. To start KRunner, press ALT-F2 or ALT-SPACE. Enter the pattern for the application you want to search for and press enter. The pattern "software" or "package" would display an entry for Discover Software. Entering the pattern "office" displays entries for all the LibreOffice applications, as well as additional office applications you can install (see Figure 9-27).

Clicking the settings button at the left opens the Configure Search dialog, which lists plugins for searching applications, widgets, and bookmarks, as well as providing capabilities such a running shell commands, opening files, and spell checking. The Clear History button deletes earlier search results. You can also configure KRunner search using System Settings | Search | KRunner (Workspace section).

Chapter 9: Kubuntu (KDE) **361**

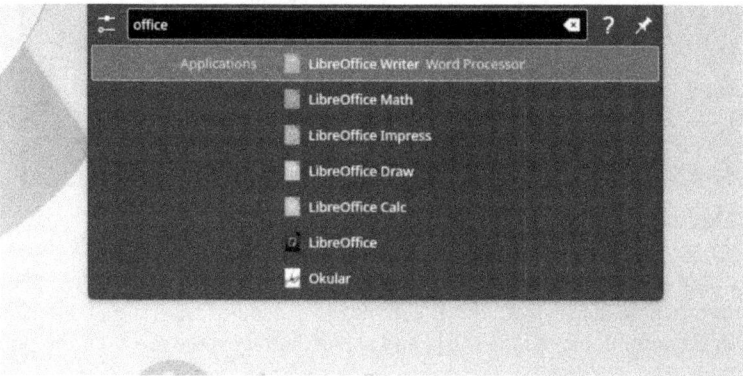

Figure 9-27: KRunner application search

Removable Devices: Device Notifier

Installed on the system tray to the right is the Device Notifier. Removable devices are not displayed as icons on your desktop. Instead, to open the devices, you use the Device Notifier. Click on the Device Notifier icon in the panel to open its dialog (see Figure 9-28). The device is unmounted initially with an mount button displayed. Click on this button to mount the device. An eject button is then displayed which you can later use to unmount and eject the device. Clicking on the eject button for a DVD/CD disc will physically eject it. For a USB drive, the drive will be unmounted and prepared for removal. You can then safely remove the USB drive. The Device Notifier is displayed on the system tray only if at least one removable device is attached.

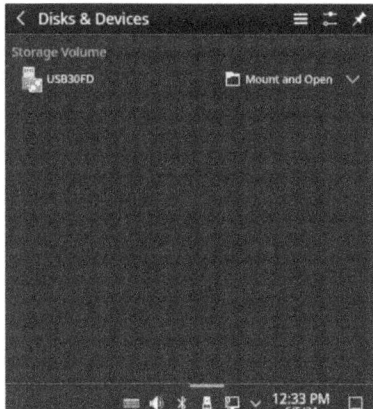

Figure 9-28: Device Notifier

The first time you attach a device to your system, it is not mounted. To open a device, click on its entry in the Device Notifier to display a menu of the actions you can use to open the device, such as the file manager or image viewer applications (see Figure 9-29). Click on the action you want to open the device with. The next time you attach a devices, it will be mounted automatically.

362 Part 3: Desktops

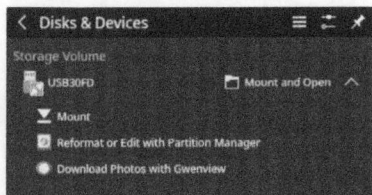 

Figure 9-29: Device Notifier menu and its panel icon

Removable media are also displayed on the File manager window's side pane. You can choose to eject removable media from the file manager instead of from the Device Notifier by right-clicking on the removable media entry, and select "Safely remove" from the popup menu.

KDE Network Connections: NetworkManager

On KDE, the NetworkManager plasma widget provides panel access for NetworkManager. This is the same NetworkManager application but adapted to the KDE interface. The widget icon image changes for wireless only and wired connections. Clicking on the widget icon in the panel opens a dialog listing your current available wireless and wired connections. When you pass the mouse over an active connection, a Disconnect button appears (see Figure 9-30). For entries not connected, Connect buttons are displayed. Clicking on a connected entry opens tabs for Speed and Details (see Figure 9-31). Networks you have connected to are listed in the Active connections section and the Available connections section list networks you have not connected to. These will include available Wi-Fi networks. To connect to a Wi-Fi network, click on the network's Connect button to open a textbox where you enter the passcode. The connected Wi-Fi network is then listed as an active connection.

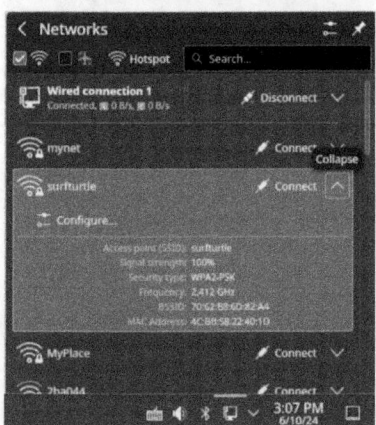 

Figure 9-30: NetworkManager connections and panel icons:

 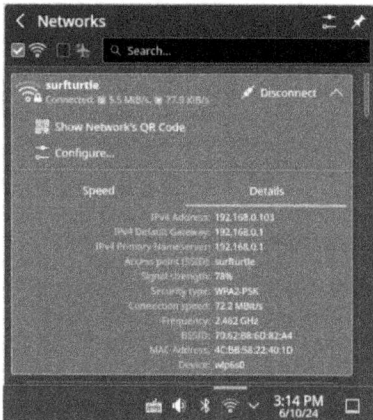

Figure 9-31: KDE NetworkManager connection information - speed and details:

The toolbar at the top of the network plasma widget has buttons for wireless and airplane mode connections (shown below). Checkboxes next to each connection icon show if it is enabled. Clicking on the checkbox for a connection will enable or disable the connection. Disabled connections have an empty checkbox and a red icon.

You can use the "Connection editor" to configure your established connections. Either click the settings button on the right side of the toolbar at the top of the network dialog or right-click on the network dialog to display a menu where you can choose "Configure Network Connections." The Connection editor then opens, which lists your connections (see Figure 9-32). Select a connection in the sidebar with tabs for General, Wired, Security, and IPv tabs for a wired or wireless connections as described in Chapter 15. To add a new connection manually, click the Add button at the bottom of the sidebar to display a dialog listing different connection types.

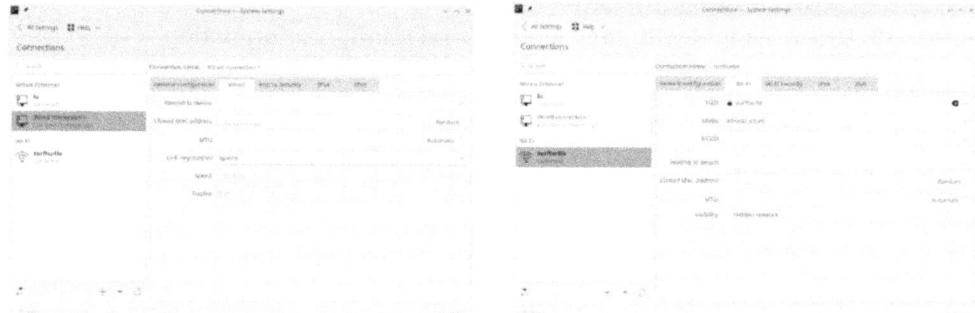

Figure 9-32: KDE connection editor and KDE NetworkManager

Desktop Widgets (Plasmoids)

The KDE desktop features the Plasma desktop that supports plasmoids. Plasmoids are integrated into the desktop on the same level as windows and icons. Just as a desktop can display windows, it can also display plasmoids. Plasmoids can take on desktop operations, running essential operations, even replacing, to a limited extent, the need for file manager windows. The name for plasmoids used on the desktop is widgets.

Managing desktop widgets

When you either long click (click and hold for several seconds) your mouse on a widget its sidebar is displayed with buttons for rotating, configure, and removing the widget (see Figure 9-18), as well as a grid for resizing the widget. Click and drag buttons on the grid to change the widget size. Clicking the configure button opens that widget's settings dialog (see Figure 9-33). You can also display the sidebar by entering Edit Mode by selecting Enter Edit Mode from the desktop or panel menus and then hovering your mouse over the widget.

To move a widget, long click on it to display its sidebar and while holding the click, drag the icon to the position you want. In Edit Mode, you can hover over the widget to display the sidebar and then click and drag the widget.

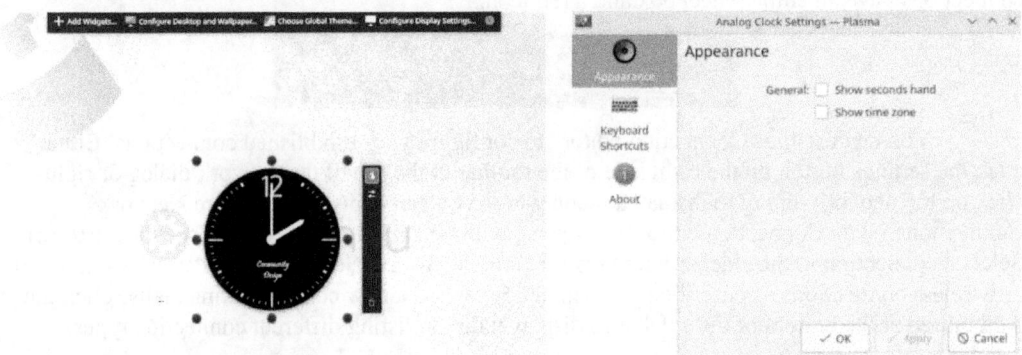

Figure 9-33: Clock Widget with task sidebar and configuration dialog

To add a widget to the desktop, right-click anywhere on the desktop and select Add Widgets from the pop-up menu. This opens the Widgets dialog at the left side of the desktop that lists widgets you can add (see Figure 9-34). Clicking on the Categories button (top-right) opens a pop-up menu with different widget categories like Date and Time, Online Services, and Graphics. Double-click or drag a widget to the desktop to add it to the desktop. You can enter a pattern to search for a widget using the search box located at the top of the dialog.

Chapter 9: Kubuntu (KDE) **365**

Figure 9-34: Adding a widget - Widgets dialog

To remove a widget, long click on the widget to display its toolbar, and then click on the red Remove button (trash icon) at the bottom of the toolbar. In Edit Mode, you can hover over the widget to display the sidebar and then click its remove button. When you remove a widget, a notification message is displayed with an Undo button, as shown here. Clicking on the Undo button will restore the widget.

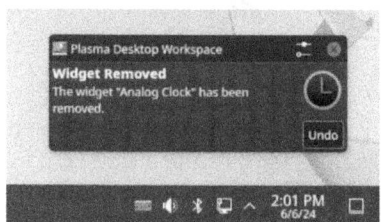

Figure 9-35 shows the folder view, digital clock, sticky notes, calculator, hard disk activity, and individidual cores widgets. The desktop folder widget is just a folder widget set initially to the desktop folder.

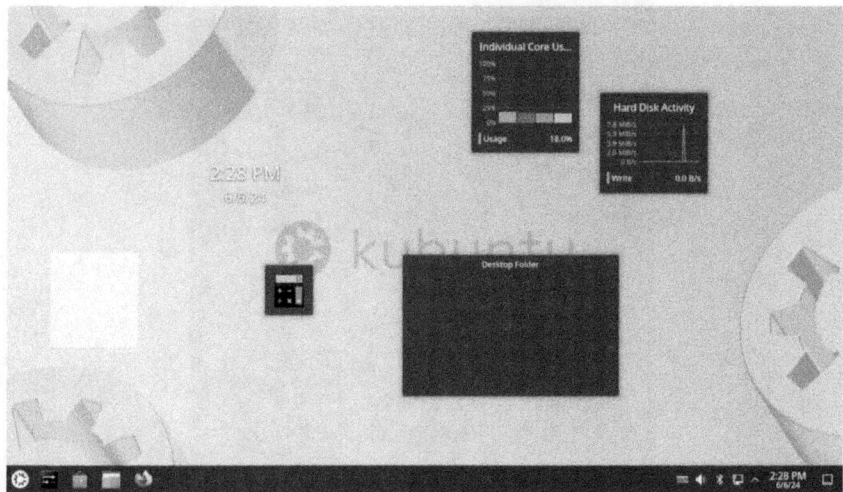

Figure 9-35: Folder View, Calculator, Digital Clock, Individual Cores Usage, Hard Disk Activity, and Sticky Notes widgets:

Folder and Icon Widgets

You can place access to any folders on the desktop by simply dragging their icons from a file manager window to the desktop (see Figure 9-36). A small menu will appear that includes options for the Icon and Folder widgets. The Folder option sets up a Folder widget for the folder showing icons for subfolders and files. The Icon entry creates an Icon widget.

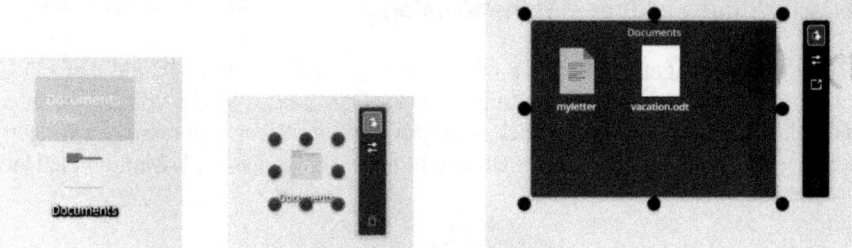

Figure 9-36: Folder and Icon widgets:

For any Folder widget, you can use that widget's settings dialog to change the folder it references. A Folder widget has options for showing the desktop folder, a folder on your Places list, or a specific folder. You can also specify a title. You can easily create a Folder widget for your home folder.

Activities

KDE is designed to support multiple activities. Activities are different plasma containments, each with its set of widgets. An activity is not the same as virtual desktop. Virtual desktops affect space, displaying additional desktops. An activity has its own set of widgets (widgets) and windows, displaying a different set of widgets and windows for each activity. In effect, each activity has a different desktop and set of virtual desktops. Technically, each activity is a Plasma containment that has its own collection of widgets and windows. You can switch to a different activity (containment) and display a different collection of widgets and windows on your desktop.

An activity is often tailored for a certain task. You could have one activity for office work, another for news, and yet another for media. Each activity could have its own set of appropriate widgets, like clock, calculator, notes, and folder widgets for an office activity. A media activity might have a Media Player widget and media applications open.

Multiple activities are managed using the Activities Switcher. Initially your system is set up with just one activity, the default activity. With just this one activity, the Activities Switcher remain inactive and you will not be able to access it. To access the Activities Switcher, you can use the keyboard sequence ALT-D-A (hold the ALT key down and then press first the **d** key and then the **a** key. You also can add an Activities Switcher widget to the desktop or panel. These include Activities, Activity Bar, and Activity Pager. Once you add a new activity, giving you more than one, a "Show Activity Switcher" entry appears in the desktop menu, which you can also use to access the Activities Switcher (see Figure 9-37).

Figure 9-37: Activities menu entry and the Activities widget

Files and folders can be attached to an activity, displaying them only on that activity. Right-click on the folder or file icon in the File Manager, and choose the Activities submenu to choose an activity. Windows are set by default to display on the activity they are opened on. The window switcher is configured to work only on the current activity. The setting is configured in the Window Management dialog (Workspace section of the System settings dialog). On the Task Switcher tab, the 'Filter windows by" section has Activities checked and "Current activity" selected.

To add an activity, click the Activity Switcher widget on the desktop or the "Show Activity Switcher" entry on the desktop menu to display the Activities Manager listing your activities on the left side of the screen (see Figure 9-38). A default activity icon for your desktop will already be displayed. Click the "Create activity" button (plus button) at the bottom of the Activities Manager to add a new activity. A "Create a new activity" window opens with entries for the name and description (see Figure 9-39). Click on the Icon image to open a dialog where you can choose an icon for your activity. You can choose not to track usage and to set up a keyboard shortcut for the activity. Click the Create button to add the new activity. An activity entry then appears on the Activities Manager. To switch to another activity, click its icon in the Activities Manager.

368 Part 3: Desktops

Figure 9-38: Activities Manager

Moving the mouse over an activity icon displays Configure and Stop buttons. The Configure button opens the "Activity settings" dialog for that activity, which is the same as the create dialog, with Name, description, and icon settings. The Stop button deactivates the activity and places it at the bottom of the Activity Manager under the "Stopped activities" heading. To start a stopped activity, simply click its icon in the "Stopped activities" list.

To remove an activity, first stop it, then move your mouse over the activity icon in the Stopped activities section (see Figure 9-40). A remove button (trash icon) appears to the right of the activity entry. Click it to remove the activity. You are prompted to confirm the deletion.

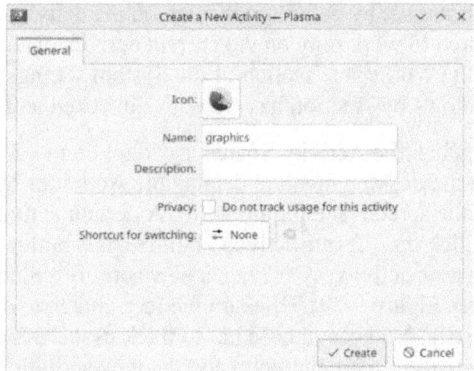

Figure 9-39: Create an activity

To add widgets to an activity, first, click the activity to make it the current activity, and then click the Add Widgets button to display the Widgets dialog. Widgets you add are placed in the current activity.

You can quickly switch from one activity to another using the META-TAB to move forward through your list of activities. Continually pressing the META-TAB key moves you through the list. The Activities Switcher is displayed, showing the one currently selected. Alternatively, first, display the Activities Manager by choosing "Show Activities Switcher" from the desktop menu (right-click on desktop) or the Activities widget button on the desktop or panel (if installed). Then click on the activity you want. The new Activity becomes your desktop (see Figure 9-41). If you have installed an Activity Switcher widget such as the Activity Bar or Activity Pager, you can also use that to switch between activities. To change to another activity, you can use the META-TAB keys to move through the list or open the Activities Manager again (desktop menu or Activities widget) and click the activity icon you want. Your original desktop is the first icon (Default).

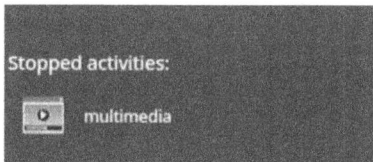

Figure 9-40: stop Activity icons

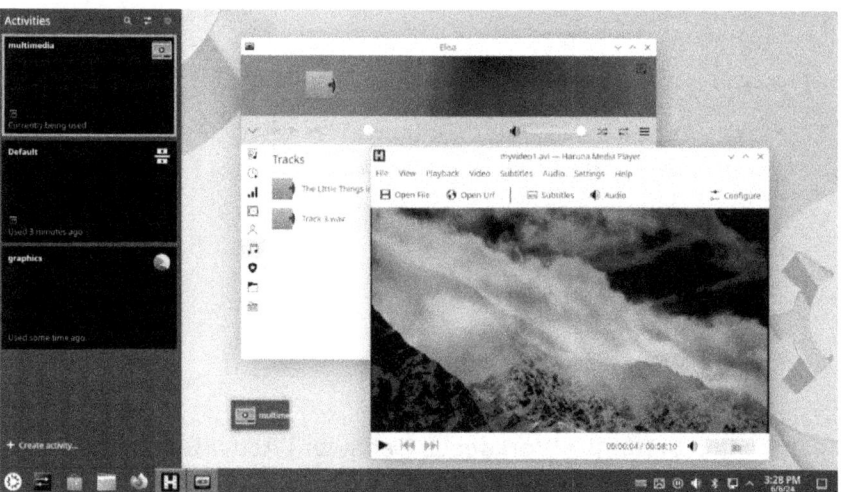

Figure 9-41: Activity Manager and screen of selected activity

An window opened in an activity is shown only in that activity. Should you want a window shown on other activities, you can right-click on the window's header bar to display the window's menu and select the "Show in Activities" entry to display a submenu that lists all your activities, with the current activity with the window selected (see Figure 9-42). Check the activities you want the window displayed in. You can also choose to move the window to another activity.

Keep in mind that the "Show in Activities" entry only appears if you have more than one activity. Should you only have the default activity, the entry is not shown.

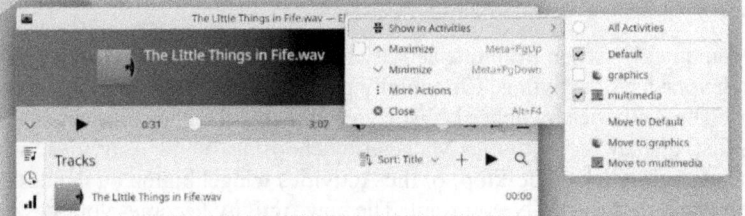

Figure 9-42: Window Activity menu

You can configure the activities with the System Setting | Workspace Behavior | Activities dialog. You can access it quickly from the configure button at the top right of the Activities Switcher. The Activities settings dialog has two tabs, Activities and Switching (see Figure 9-43). The Activities tab lists all your current activities and allows you to create new ones (Create New button at the bottom). You can easily access an activities configuration dialog, or delete the activity. The Switching tab shows the keys for switching activities (META+TAB for forward and META+SHIFT+TAB for reverse). You can add alternates if you wish.

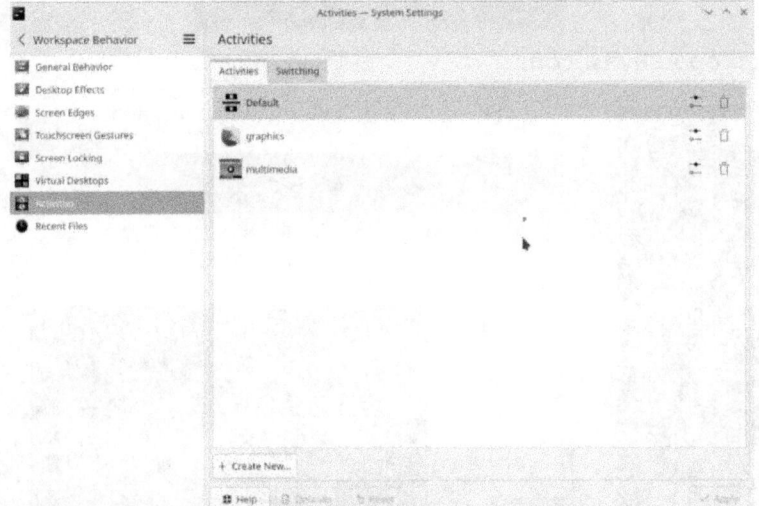

Figure 9-43: System Settings | Workspace Behavior | Activities

Activity Switcher Widgets for the Desktop and Panel

To move easily between activities, you can add the Activity Switcher widgets to either the desktop or to the panel. Both desktop and panel Activity Switcher widgets appear and operate the same with the same configuration dialogs. There are three desktop and panel widgets: the Activities button, the Activity Pager, and the Activity Bar (see Figure 9-44).

Chapter 9: Kubuntu (KDE) **371**

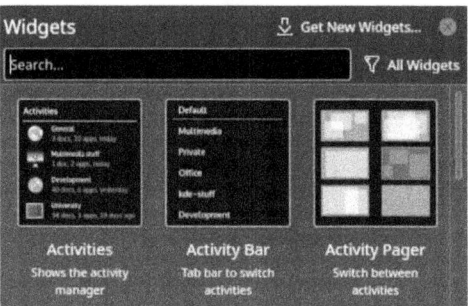

Figure 9-44: Activity Switcher Widgets for Desktop and Panel

The Activities widget is a simple button that appears on the desktop or panel that will display the Activities Switcher when clicked (see Figure 9-45). You can then use the Activities Switcher to change to another activity or just display the Activity Switcher and manage your activities. You can configure the button to show either a generic image or the name of the current activity.

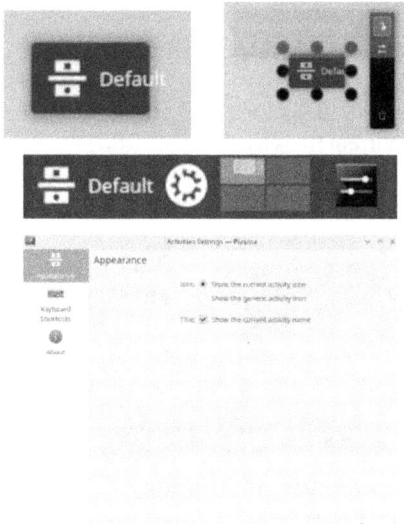

Figure 9-45: Activities button for desktop and panel

The Activity Pager operate like the workspace pager. Each activities is a square on the pager that you can click to move to that Activity (see Figure 9-46). Unlike the Activities widget, it does not display the Activities Switcher (except briefly as you move to another activity). The Activity Pager Settings dialog has a general and Keyboard shortcuts tab for configuring the pager. You can configure the pager to show the activity number or name. You could show the bare desktop upon clicking the current activity is you want. You can choose between a horizontal, vertical, or the default square layouts for the pager. You can also choose to show the outlines of open windows on the activities.

372 Part 3: Desktops

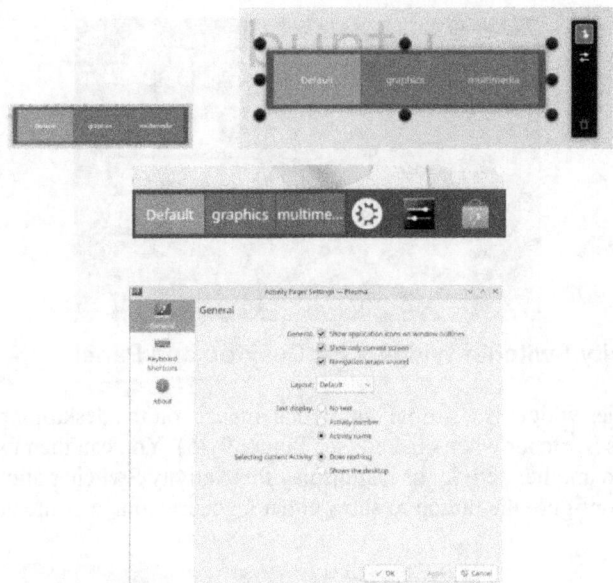

Figure 9-46: Activity Pager for the desktop and panel

The Activity Bar displays buttons for each activity. Click on one to move to a different activity (see Figure 9-47). The current activity has a blue line above. There is no configuration dialog for the activity bar. Like the Activity Pager widget, it does not display the Activities Switcher (except briefly as you move to another activity).

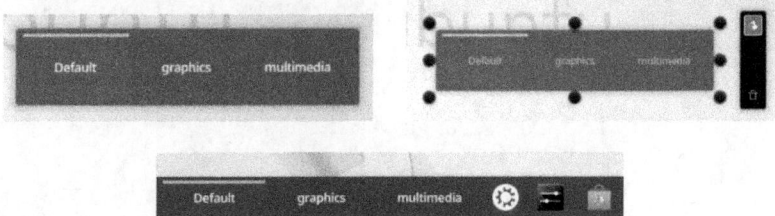

Figure 9-47: Activity Bar for desktop and panel

The desktop activity widgets only appear on the activity they were created on, whereas the panel activity widgets appear on the panel for on each activity.

Should you right click on either a desktop or panel activity widget, a menu will display an entry for Show Alternatives (see Figure 9-48). This will display a menu showing the three Activity Switcher widgets. Selecting a different activity widget displays that widget in place of the current one. The other widgets do not have to be first installed.

Figure 9-48: Activity Switcher widget alternatives selection

KDE Windows

A KDE window has the same functionality you find in other window managers and desktops. You can re-size the window by clicking and dragging any of its corners or sides. A click-and-drag operation on a side extends the window in that dimension, whereas a corner extends both height and width at the same time. Within the window, menus, icons, and toolbars for the particular application are displayed.

The top of the window has a title bar showing the name of the window, the program name in the case of applications, and the current folder name for the file manager windows. The active window has the title bar highlighted. To move the window, click the title bar and drag it where you want. Right-clicking the window title bar displays a pop-up menu with entries for window operations, such as minimize, maximize, and moving the window to a different desktop or activity. The More Actions submenu includes closing or resizing the window, the shade option to roll up the window to the title bar, and full screen.

You can configure the appearance and operation of a window by selecting "Configure Window Manager" from the More Actions submenu in the Window menu (right-click the title bar). Here you can set appearance (Window Decoration), button and key operations (Window Actions), the focus policy, such as a mouse-click on the window or just passing the mouse over it (Window Focus Behavior), and how the window is displayed when moving it (Window Movement). All these features can be configured also using the System Setting's Window Behavior tool in the Workspace section.

To the right of the title bar are three small buttons for minimizing, maximizing, or closing the window (down, up, and x symbols). You can switch to a window at any time by clicking its task manager button. You can also maximize a window by dragging it to the top edge of the screen.

From the keyboard, you can use the ALT-TAB key combination to display a list of current open windows. Holding down the ALT key and sequentially pressing TAB moves you through the list.

A window can be displayed as a tile on one-half of the screen. Another tile can be set up for a different window on the other side of the screen, allowing you to display two windows side by side on the full screen (see Figure 9-49). You can tile a window by dragging it to the side of the screen (over the side edge to the middle of the window). A tile outline will appear. Add a second tile by moving a window to the other side edge. You can add more windows to a tile by moving them to that edge. Clicking on a window's task manager button will display it on its tile.

The same process works for corners. You can tile a window to a corner by moving it to that corner. You can then have four tiled windows open at each corner. You could even have several windows open on the same corner, displaying the one you want by clicking its task manager button.

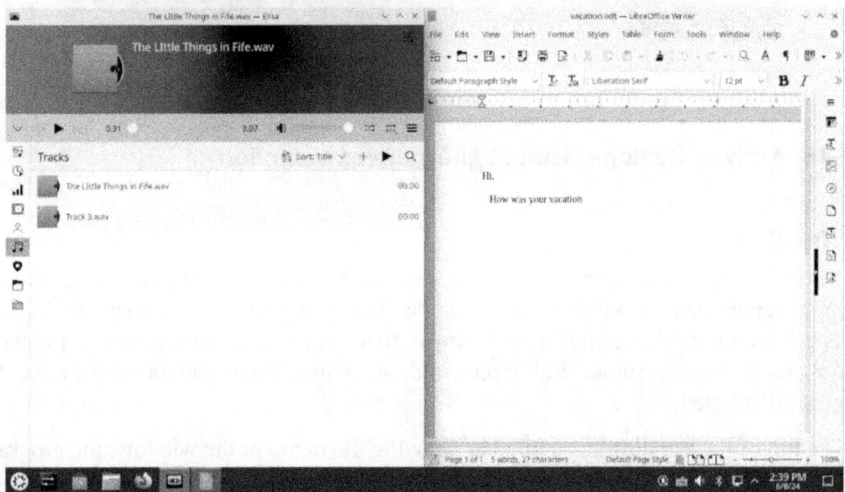

Figure 9-49: Window tiles

Task Managers

KDE proves three different task managers that you can use to manage your open windows: the Icon-only Task Manager (the default), Task Manager, and Window list. The Icon-only Task Manager is a new task manager with enhanced capabilities. Task Manager is the older version used in previous KDE releases, along with Window list. The Icon-only Task Manager is the default, but you can choose one of the other options by right-clicking on an empty space on the panel and selecting "Show Alternatives" to display the Alternative Widgets dialog (see Figure 9-50). Click on the one you want and then click on Switch.

Figure 9-50: Choosing a task manager from panel menu

Both the Icon-only Task Manager and the Task Manager show the same menus when you right-click on an application or widget icon on the panel. The menus applications display a menu with common window operations such as move to a different desktop or selecting which activities it is to be shown on (see Figure 9-51). A More submenu displays standard window operations such as move, resize, minimize, maximize. Application specific operations are shown at the top of the menu such as the "Open a New Private Window" for Firefox, and a Places section for the home folders such as Documents and Music.

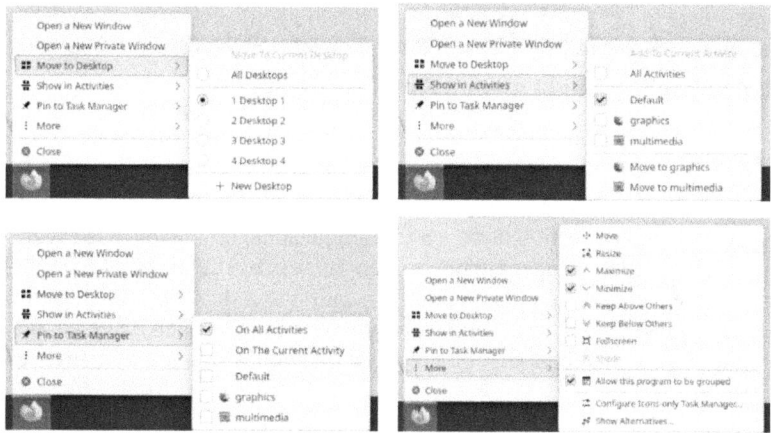

Figure 9-51: Application panel menus

Application specific operations are shown at the top of the menu such as the "Open a New Private Window" for Firefox, and, for the Dolphin file manager, a Places section for the home folders such as Documents and Music (see Figure 9-52). A "more Places" entry such as "5 more Places", when clicked, expands the menu to include all the primary home folders and submenus for Remote (Network), Recent (Recent Files and Recent Locations). Multimedia applications will show media controls such as play, pause, and stop.

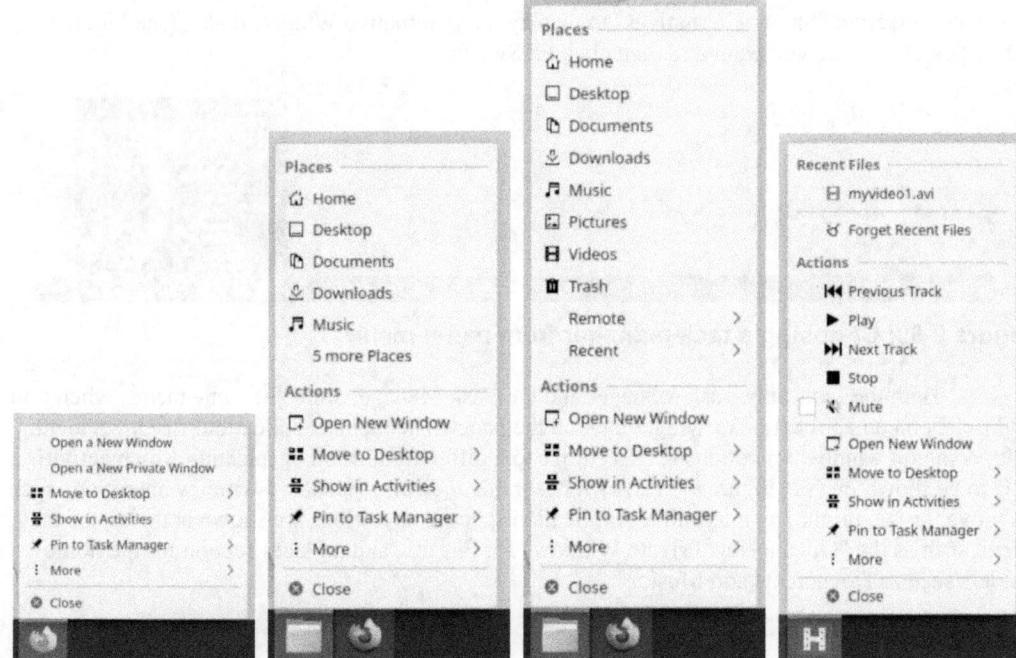

Figure 9-52: Application panel menus Application section

Icon-only Task Manager

The Icon-only Task Manager is the task manager used for the KDE desktop. It reduces all the open windows that an application has open to a single application icon (see Figure 9-53). Should you have several file manager windows open, these are referenced by a single file manager application icon in the panel, with a plus sign underneath it to indicate multiple open windows by that application. If you were to have several web browser windows open, there would only be a single web browser icon with a plus sign on the panel that you would use to reference them.

Figure 9-53: Icon-only Task Manager, application icons

Passing your mouse over an Icon-only Task Manager application icon automatically displays a thumbnail bar above the icon showing thumbnails of all the application's open windows (see Figure 9-54). The thumbnails of those windows currently displayed on the desktop will show contents of those displayed window. Those windows that are minimized will only show the application's icon. To select or to maximize a minimized window, click on its thumbnail.

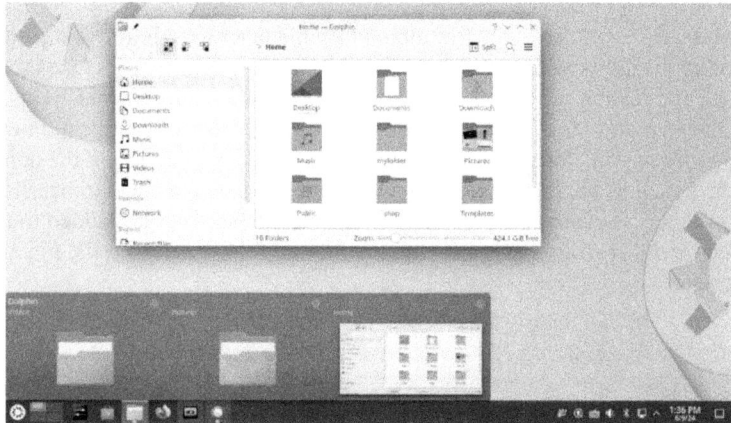

Figure 9-54: Icon-only Task Manager, application thumbnails for open windows

Should you then move your mouse over the thumbnail of a minimized window, the window it references is shown as it would appear maximized on your desktop (see Figure 9-55). Clicking on it maximizes the window. This is how you maximize a window that has been minimized on the Icon-only Task Manager. When you minimize a window, it disappears from the desktop. There will be an application icon on the panel for the application that the window was using. To maximize the window again, pass your mouse over its application icon on the panel to display the thumbnail bar of all the windows open with that application. Click on the one you want to maximize.

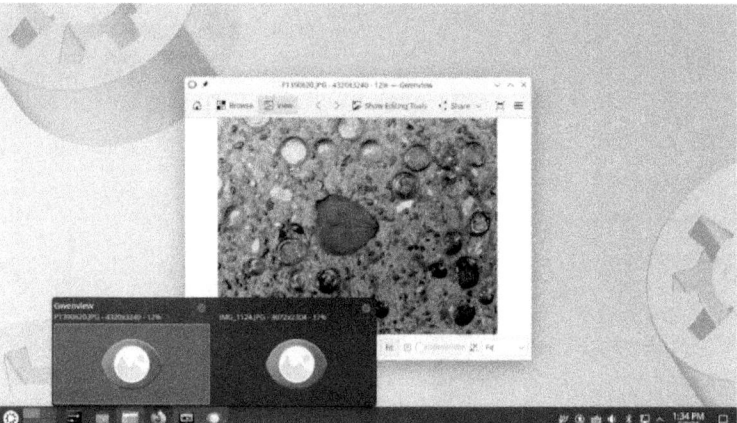

Figure 9-55: Icon-only Task Manager, maximizing a minimized window using thumbnails

The Icon-only Task Manager reduces the task manager to a small list of application icons. To maximize a minimized window, it helps to keep in mind the application it was using. By passing your mouse over all the application icons in the task manager, you can quickly display the thumbnails of all your open windows, one application at a time.

Task Manager

Task Manager is similar to the traditional task manager used in previous releases. Icons are displayed for applications added to the panel and have no open windows, ones that are not running. When an application opens a window, its application icon disappears and is replaced by a button for that open window. Each open window, whether for the same application or a different one, has a button. When you close all the open windows for an application, if the application has been added to the panel, its application icon is again displayed on the panel, otherwise it disappears. Figure 9-56 shows the Task Manager panel application icons (applications added to the panel) with no open windows, and then with buttons for open windows for the Dolphin file manager and Firefox web browser.

Figure 9-56: Task Manager panel applications with unopened and opened windows

The task manager shows buttons for the different programs you are running or windows you have open (see Figure 9-57). This is essentially a docking mechanism that lets you change to a window or application by clicking its button. When you minimize a window, it is reduced to its task manager button. You can then restore the window by clicking its task manager button. A live thumbnail of a window on the task manager is displayed as your mouse passes over its task manager button, showing its name, desktop, and image. Music and video players will show basic multimedia controls, such as pause, stop, and play on the thumbnail. All thumbnails will feature a red close button (x) in the upper right corner that you can use to close the window.

Figure 9-57: Task Manager

Window List

Window List is a stripped down version of the task manager, displaying a menu of opened windows you can select to access. The entire task manager is reduced to a single window list icon. The icon shows the name of the current active window. Clicking on the icon displays the menu of open windows, with a description of the content opened (see Figure 9-58). Both displayed and minimized windows are listed. Click on an entry to access it.

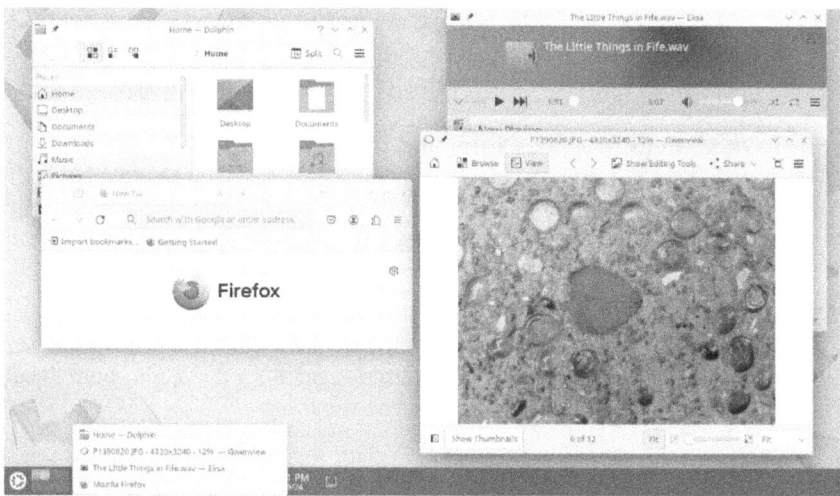

Figure 9-58: Window List

Applications

You can start an application in KDE in several ways. If an entry for it is in the Applications menu, you can select that entry to start the application. You can right-click on any application entry in the Applications menu to display a pop-up menu with "Add to Panel (Widgets)", "Add to Desktop", and "Pin to Task Manager" entries. Select one to add a shortcut icon for the application to the desktop, the panel, or the task manager. You can then start an application by double-clicking its desktop icon, or single-clicking its panel or task manager icon.

The applications will appear differently in the Icon-only Task Manager (the default) and the Task Manager (similar to the one used in older releases). The Icon-only Task Manager only displays the application icons (see Figure 9-59). Applications with open windows have a plus sign underneath their icons, and passing your mouse over it displays an thumbnail bar showing all the open windows for that application.

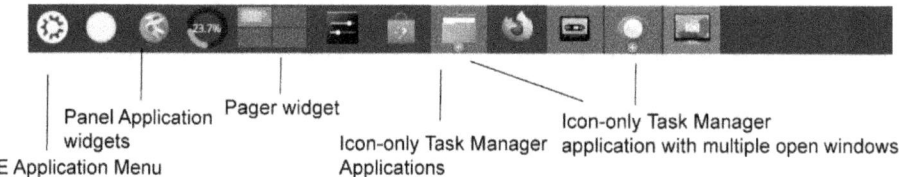

Figure 9-59: Icon-only Task Manager Applications

The Task Manager show icons for applications with no open windows. For applications with open windows, it shows buttons for each open window instead of the application icon. In Figure 9-60, the Kate, Memory Usage, and Weather Report applications have been added to the panel as widgets (Add to Panel), appearing as icons next to the Pager widget. The Konsole, LibreOffice Writer, and VLC media player applications have been added to the Task Manager (Pin to Task Manager), appearing just before the Task manager window buttons.

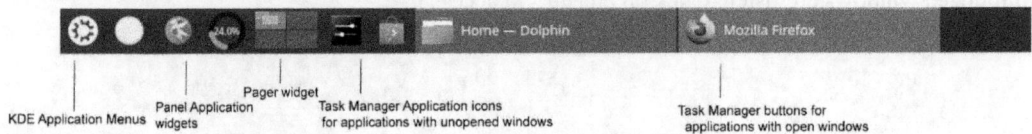

Figure 9-60: Task Manager Applications and opened buttons

An application icon on the desktop is implemented as a desktop widget. Performing a long click on the application icon on the desktop displays a sidebar with the icon for the widget settings. This opens a Settings window that allows you to specify a keyboard shortcut.

You can also run an application by right-clicking on the desktop and selecting the Show KRunner (or press Alt-F2 or Alt-space) which will display the KRunner tool consisting of a box to enter a single command. You need only enter a pattern to search for the application. Results will be displayed in the KRunner window. Choose the one you want.

Virtual Desktops: Pager and Overview

KDE supports virtual desktops, extending the desktop area on which you can work. They function the same as workspaces on GNOME (Ubuntu and MATE). You could have a Web browser running on one desktop and be using a text editor in another. KDE can support up to 16 virtual desktops. To use virtual desktops, you use the Pager widget on your panel or desktop, or the Overview Effect.

Pagers

When a pager is added to the panel, it will have just one desktop. The pager on the panel is not shown if it has only one desktop. This is the case for your initial default panel. The pager is there, but not visible until you add more desktops.

To add desktops to the pager, use the System Settings Workspace Behavior tab's Virtual Desktops configuration tab (System Settings | Workspace Behavior | Virtual Desktops). Once you have added the desktops, the pager will appear on the panel, next to the Applications menu.

To configure the rows, name, and the number of desktops, select the Configure Virtual Desktops entry in the pop-up menu to open the Virtual Desktops dialog, which displays entries for your active desktops (see Figure 9-61). Click the Add button to add a desktop and the Rows button to add the number of rows you want them organized into. To delete a desktop, move the mouse over the desktop entry to display edit and x buttons. Click the x button to delete the desktop. You can change any of the desktop names by moving the mouse over the entry and click the edit button (pencil) and then entering a new name. Click the Apply button to make the changes.

You can also access the Virtual Desktops dialog by right-clicking on the Desktop Pager widget and, from the menu, select Configure Virtual Desktops. If you just want to add a desktop, right-click on the Desktop Pager widget and click the Add Virtual Desktop entry.

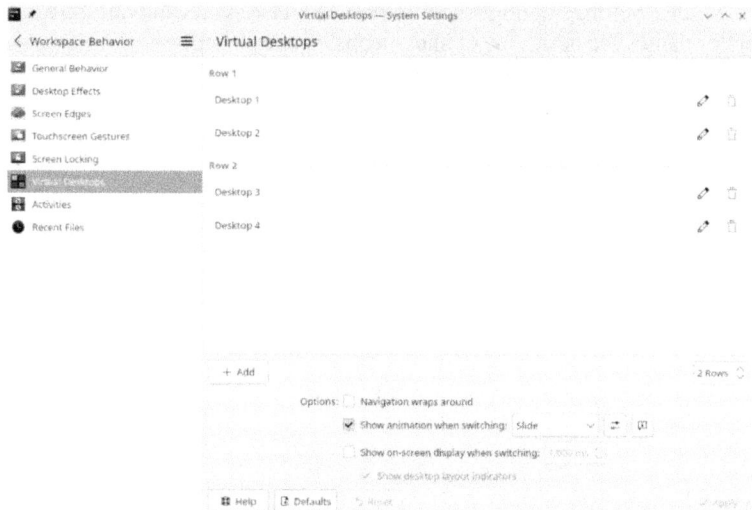

Figure 9-61: Virtual Desktops configuration with System Settings and the Pager widget

You can also add additional pagers to the panel or desktop. On the panel, you can use edit mode (right-click on panel and choose Enter Edit Mode) to move it to the location you want on the panel.

Figure 9-62: Pager Panel and Desktop widgets

The Pager represents your virtual desktops as miniature screens showing small squares for each desktop. It works much like the GNOME Workspace Switcher (see Figure 9-62). To move from one desktop to another, click the square for the destination desktop. The selected desktop will be highlighted. Just passing your mouse over a desktop image on the Pager will open a message displaying the desktop number along with the windows open on that desktop.

If you want to move a window to a different desktop, first open the window's menu by right-clicking the window's title bar. Then select the Move To Desktop entry, which lists the available desktops. Choose the one you want.

You can also configure KDE so that if you move the mouse over the edge of a desktop screen, it automatically moves to the adjoining desktop. You need to imagine the desktops arranged next to each. You enable this feature by enabling the "Switch desktop on edge" feature in the

System Settings | Workspace Behavior | Screen Edges tab. This feature will also allow you to move windows over the edge to an adjoining desktop.

To change how the pager displays desktops, right-click on the pager and choose Configure Pager to open the Pager Settings dialog (see Figure 9-63). Here you can configure the pager to display numbers or names for desktops, or show icons of open windows.

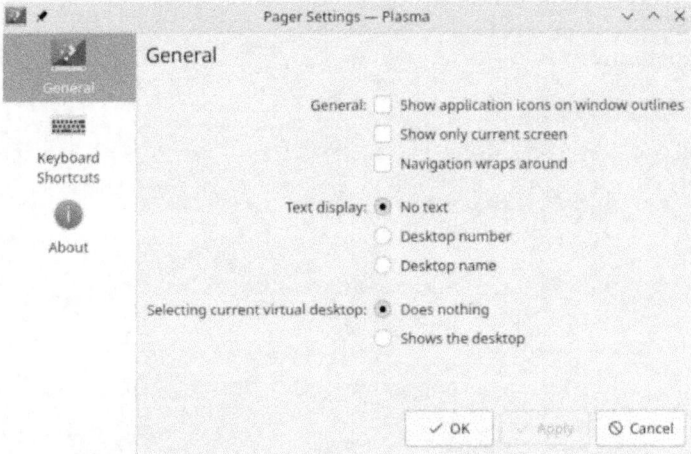

Figure 9-63: Pager Widget Settings:

Tip: Use **Ctrl** key in combination with a function key to switch to a specific desktop: for example, **Ctrl-f1** switches to the first desktop and **Ctrl-f3** to the third desktop.

Overview Effect

The Overview effect also accesses and manages your virtual desktops. You can access the Overview effect from your keyboard by pressing the Meta (Windows key) and the **w** key, META-W (see Figure 9-64).

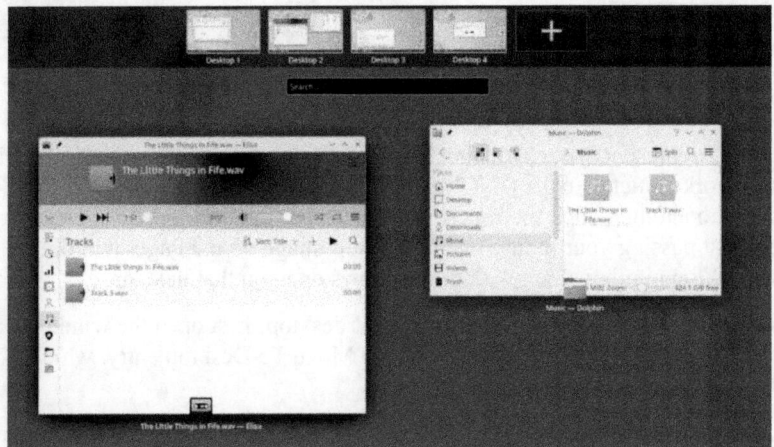

Figure 9-64: Overview effect

This displays a screen with a thumbnail bar of your virtual desktops at the top of the screen (see Figure 9-65). Your current desktop is outlined in blue. To move to a different desktop, click on the desktop's thumbnail. The Overview effect closes and you are placed in the selected desktop.

Figure 9-65: Overview effect virtual desktops

Using the thumbnail bar, you can easily add and remove desktops (see Figure 9-66). You can add more desktops by clicking on the large plus button on the right side of the thumbnail bar. Hovering your mouse over a desktop's thumbnail displays a trash icon in its upper right corner that you can click to remove the desktop.

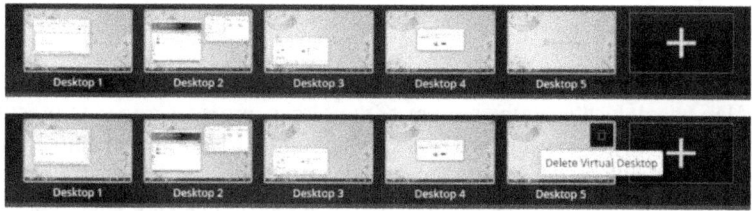

Figure 9-66: Overview effect managing desktops

You can return to the current desktop at any time by clicking anywhere on the screen, which closes the Overview effect.

The Overview effect also shows the windows open on the current desktop. To move a window to a different desktop, drag and drop it to the thumbnail of the desktop you want it moved to. You are also moved to that desktop, still within the Overview effect screen.

Hovering your mouse over a window displays a close box (red x), which you can use to close a window.

The Overview effects screen also provides a Krunner text box you can use to search from and start applications. Once you start an application from Krunner, you return to the current desktop.

The Overview effect is enabled and configured on the System Settings | Workspace behavior | Desktop Effects tab, in the Window Management section (see Figure 67). Click on its configuration button to open the Overview dialog where you can set the key to use to open the Overview effect, the layout mode for the displayed windows (closest or natural), and whether to blur the background. Click the Default button to return to the defaults (Natural layout and META-W key).

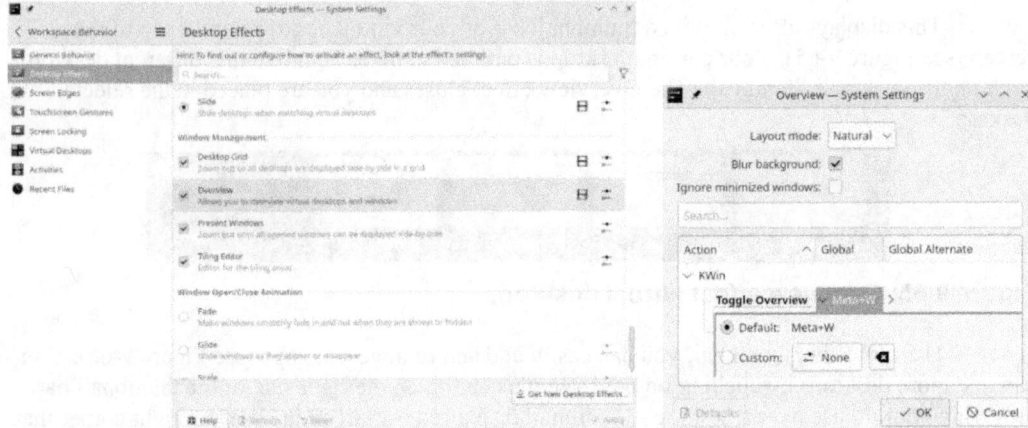

Figure 9-67: Overview effect configuration on System Settings

KDE Panel

The KDE panel, located at the bottom of the screen, provides access to most KDE functions (see Figure 9-68). The panel is a specially configured Plasma containment, just like the desktop. The panel can include icons for menus, folder windows, specific programs, and virtual desktops. These are widgets that are configured for use on the panel. At the left end of the panel is a button for the Application menus.

To add an application to the panel, right-click on its entry in any of the Application menus to open a pop-up menu and select Add to Panel.

As noted in the previous section on task managers, there are three different task managers on for the panel: the new Icon-only Task Manager, Task Manager (similar to the one use in previous releases), and Window List. Both the Icon-only Task Manager and Task Manager look the same when you have no windows open. Figure 9-68 shows the Icon-only task manager with a single window open for the Dolphin file manager as shown by its thumbnail. Figure 9-69 shows the Task Manager with a button for the open Dolphin file manager window.

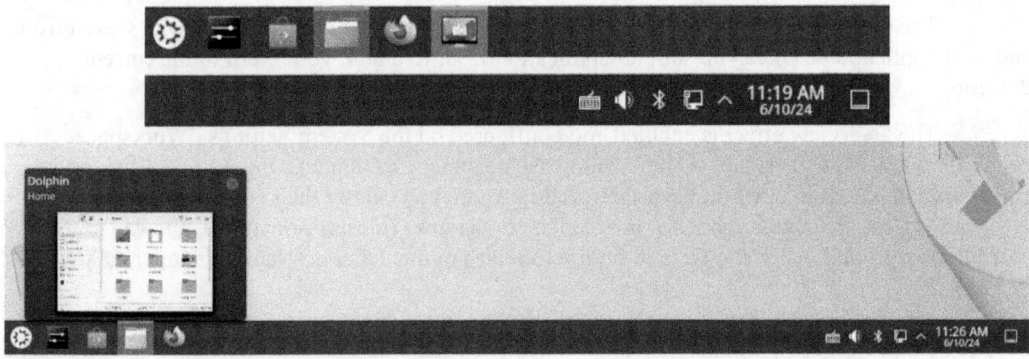

Figure 9-68: KDE panel with Icon-only Task Manager and open window

Figure 9-69: KDE panel with Task Manager and open window

KDE Panel Widgets

The Plasma panel supports several kinds of Windows and Tasks widgets, including the Task Manager and system tray. To the right of the system tray is the digital clock. To add a widget to the panel, right-click on the panel, or on any panel widget, to open a pop-up menu and select the Add Widgets entry (see Figure 9-70). This opens the Widgets dialog that lists widgets you can add to the panel (see Figure 9-71). A search box at the top of the dialog lets you search for widgets. A drop-down menu to the right of the search box lets you choose different widget categories like Date and Time, Online Services, and Graphics. You add a widget just as you add a desktop widget, click on the widget to want. An icon for the widget is shown on the left side of the panel. In Figure 9-72, the weather report, Kate sessions launcher, and the memory usage widget has been added to the panel. Clicking on a widget displays information the widget provides.

Another way to open the Widgets dialog is to right-click on the panel and choose "Enter Edit Mode" to open the configuration panel, and then click the Add Widgets button on the top left side of the desktop.

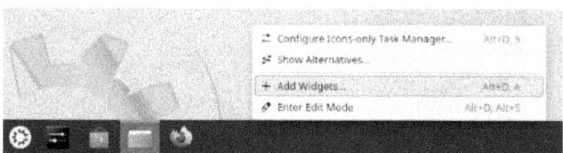

Figure 9-70: KDE Add Widgets option on panel

386 Part 3: Desktops

Figure 9-71: KDE Add Widgets dialog for panel

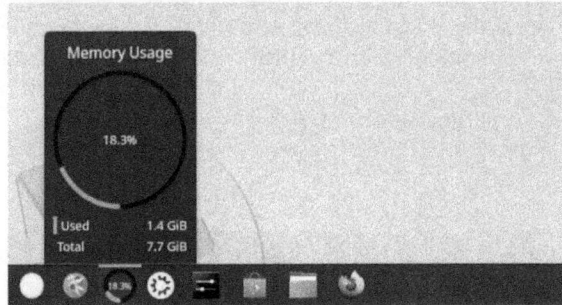

Figure 9-72: Displaying panel widget information

To remove a widget, you have to enter edit mode (right-click on the panel and choose Enter Edit Mode from the menu). In edit mode, when you pass your mouse over a widget, a menu is displayed showing a Remove option (see Figure 9-73). You can also right click on the widget to display a menu with a Remove option.

Figure 9-73: Removing a widget from the panel in edit mode

KDE System Tray

The system tray holds widgets for desktop operations like update notifier, the clipboard, Bluetooth, device notifier, sound settings, media player (if a multimedia player is active), and NetworkManager, as shown here.

The pop-up menu (arrow icon) on the right side of the system tray display widgets that are not in use, or not often used (see Figure 9-74). The Battery and Brightness entry displays a dialog to see battery charges and set screen brightness .

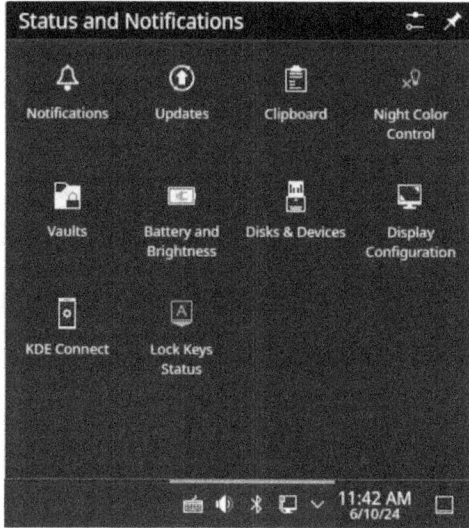

Figure 9-74: System Tray

To configure the system tray, right-click on the system tray menu (arrow icon) and choose Configure System Tray to open the System Tray Settings dialog at the Entries tab, where you can decide what items to always show, hide until needed, hide always, or disable (see Figure 9-75). The entries are organized into Application Status, Hardware Control, System Services, and Miscellaneous. You can also add keyboard shortcuts for the entry. Click on its keyboard shortcut button to change the button to Input from None, then press the keys you want associated with the entry. The keys will appear on the button. If the keys you chose are already in use, you are notified to choose a different set of keys. When you click the Apply button your changes are made and any additional items you want shown are displayed.

388 Part 3: Desktops

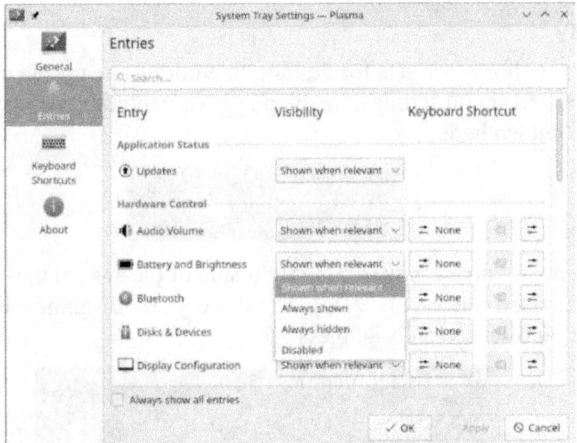

Figure 9-75: KDE panel system tray settings

KDE Panel Configuration

To configure a panel, changing its position, size, and display features, select the Enter Edit Mode entry in the panel menu (right-click on the panel to display the menu). This will open an additional configuration panel with buttons for adding widgets, moving the panel, changing its size, and a More Settings menu for setting visibility and alignment features. Figure 9-76 shows the configuration panel as it will appear on your desktop. Figure 9-77 provides a more detailed description, including the More Settings menu entries.

With the configuration panel activated, you can also move widgets around the panel. Clicking on a widget will overlay a movement icon, letting you then move the widget icon to a different location on the panel.

As you move your mouse over a widget in the panel, a pop-up dialog opens showing the widget's name, a settings button, and a delete button. To remove the widget from the panel, click its delete button.

Figure 9-76: KDE Panel Configuration, Edit Mode

The lower part of the configuration panel is used for panel position settings. On the left side is a slider for positioning the panel on the edge of the screen. On the right side are two sliders for the minimum (bottom) and maximum (top) size of the panel.

The top part of the panel has buttons for changing the location and the size of the panel. The Screen Edge button lets you move the panel to another side of the screen (left, right, top, bottom). Just click and drag. The height button lets you change the panel size, larger or smaller. The Add Widgets button will open the Add Widgets dialog, letting you add new widgets to the panel. The Add Spacer button adds a spacer to separate widgets. Right-click on the spacer to set the flexible size option or to remove the spacer.

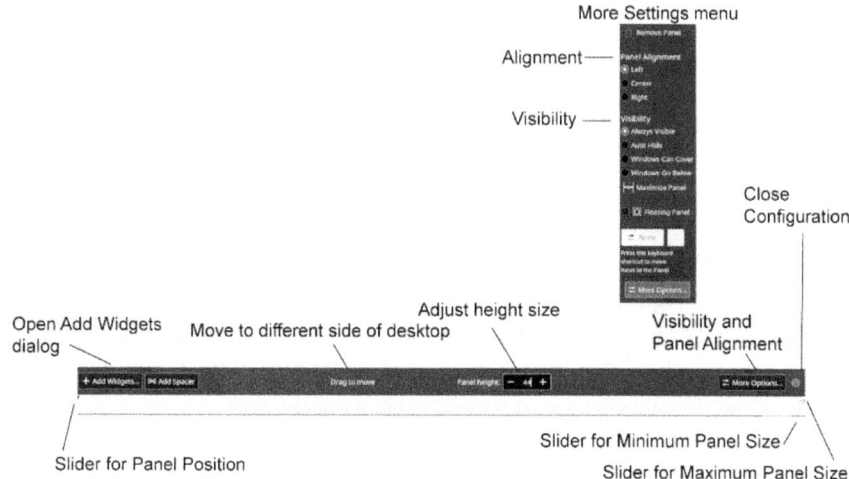

Figure 9-77: KDE Panel Configuration details and display features

The More Setting menu lets you set Visibility and Alignment features. You can choose an AutoHide setting that will hide the panel until you move the mouse to its location. The "Windows can cover" option lets a window overlap the panel. For smaller panels, you can align to the right, left, or center of the screen edge. The More Settings menu also has an entry to remove the panel. Use this entry to delete a panel you no longer want.

When you are finished with the configuration, click the red x icon the upper right side.

Desktop Effects

Desktop effects can be enabled on the System Settings Desktop Effects tab in the Workspace Behavior dialog in the Workspace section (System Settings | Workspace Behavior). For virtual desktop switching you can choose Slide, Fade, and Scale (see Figure 9-78). The more dramatic effects are found in the Windows Management section. Desktop Effects requires the support of a capable graphics chip (GPU). You may have to install a proprietary graphics driver (System Settings | Driver Manager).

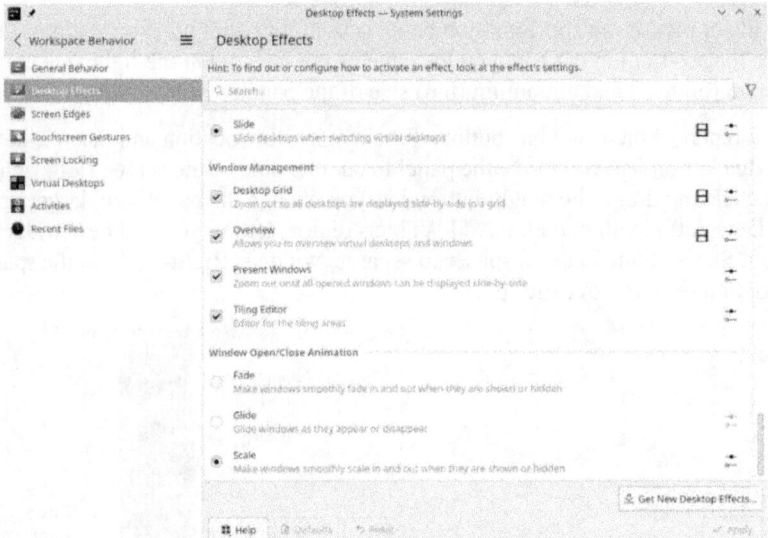

Figure 9-78: Desktop Effects selection

Key	Operation
ALT-TAB	Cover Switch, Thumbnail, or Breeze for open windows
CTRL-F8	Desktop Grid (use mouse to select a desktop)
CTRL-F9	Present Windows Current Desktop
CTRL-F10	Present Windows All Desktops

Table 9-3: KWin desktop effects keyboard shortcuts

Several Windows effects are selected by default, depending on whether your graphics card can support them. A check box is filled next to active effects. If there is a dialog icon to the right of the effects entry, it means the effect can be configured. Click on the icon to open its configuration dialog. Figure 9-79 shows the configuration dialog for the Desktop Grid effect. For several effects, you use certain keys to start them. The more commonly used effects are Cover Switch, Desktop Grid, Present Windows, and Desktop Cube. The keys for these effects are listed in Table 9-3.

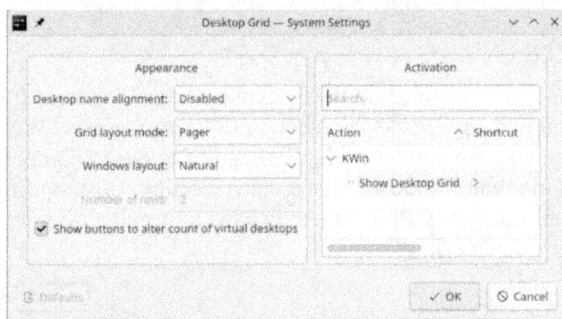

Figure 9-79: Desktop Effects configuration

Window switching using ALT-TAB is controlled on the Window Management dialog's Task Switcher tab, not from Workspace behavior's Desktop Effects tab (see Figure 9-80). In the Visualization section, you can choose the window switching effect you want to use from the drop-down menu. These include Breeze, Thumbnails, Grid, Cover Switch, and Flip Switch, as well as smaller effects such as informative, compact, text icons, and small icons. The ALT-TAB keys implement the effect you have chosen. Continually pressing the Tab key while holding down the Alt key moves you through the windows. Thumbnails displays windows in a boxed dialog (see Figure 9-81, whereas Cover Switch arranges windows stacked to the sides, and Flip Switch arranges the windows to one side. The default is Breeze, which arranges the window images to the left side of the screen (see Figure 9-82).

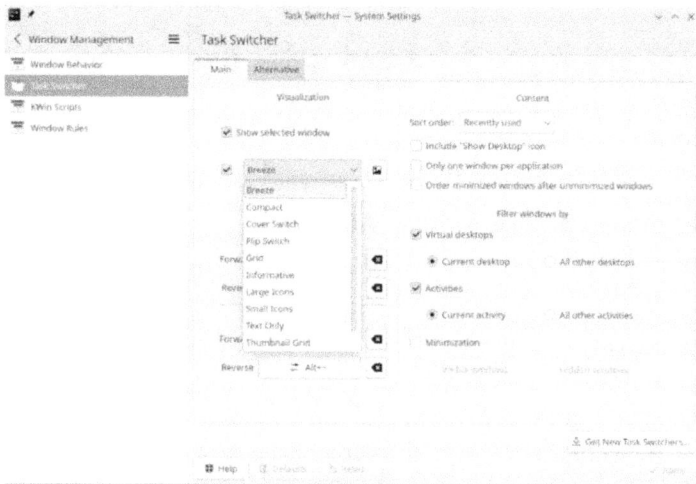

Figure 9-80: Window Management | Task Switcher

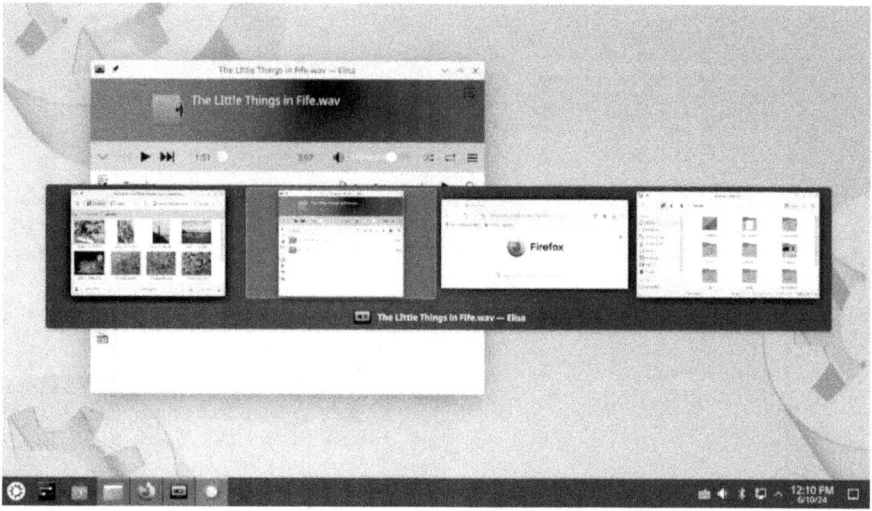

Figure 9-81: Thumbnail Switch - ALT-TAB

392 Part 3: Desktops

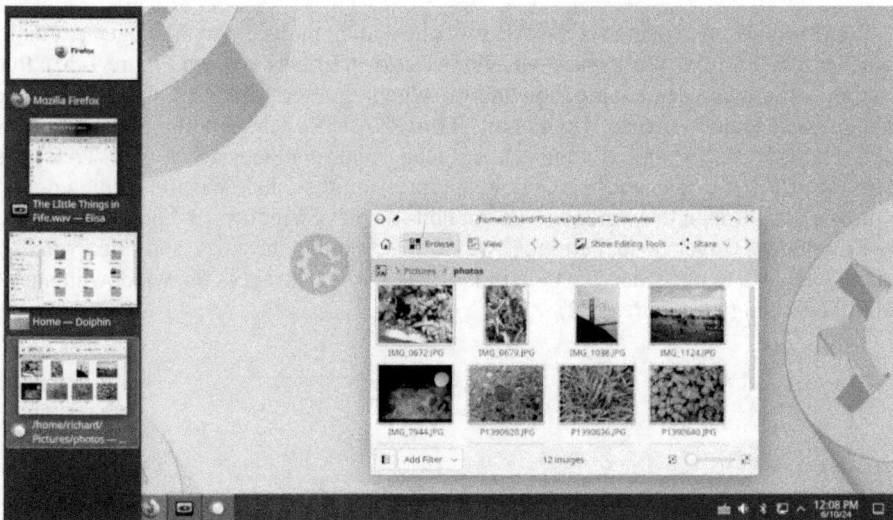

Figure 9-82: Thumbnail Breeze Switch - ALT-TAB

The Present Windows effect displays images of the open windows on your screen with the selected one highlighted (see Figure 9-83). You can use your mouse to select another. This provides an easy way to browse your open windows. You use CTRL-F9 to display windows on your current virtual desktop statically and use the arrow key to move between them. Use CTRL-F10 to display all your open windows across all your desktops. Press the ESC key to return to the desktop.

Desktop Grid will show a grid of all your virtual desktops (META-F8), letting you see all your virtual desktops on the screen at once (see Figure 9-84). You can then move windows and open applications between desktops. Clicking on a desktop makes it the current one. The plus and minus keys allow you to add or remove virtual desktops.

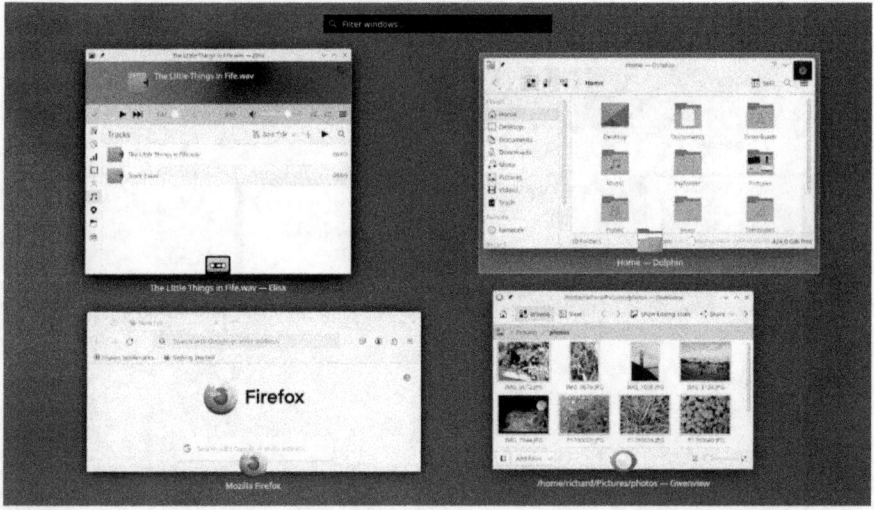

Figure 9-83: Present Windows (Windows effects) CTRL-F9 and CTRL-F10

Chapter 9: Kubuntu (KDE) **393**

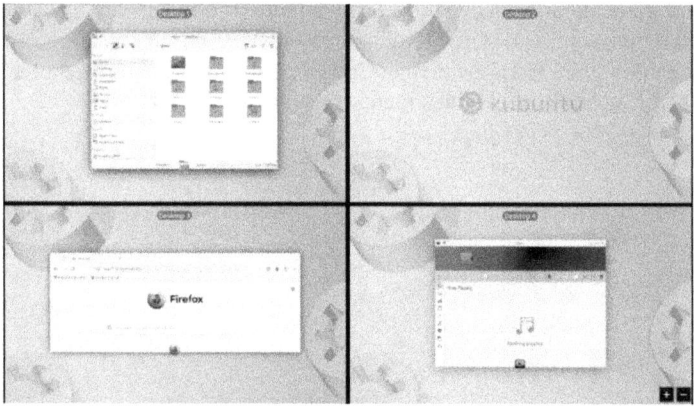

Figure 9-84: Desktop Grid - META-F8

KDE File Manager: Dolphin

Dolphin is KDE's dedicated file manager (see Figure 9-85). A navigation bar shows the current folder either in a browser or edit mode. In the browse mode it shows icons for the path of your current folder, and in the edit mode, it shows the path name in a text-editable box. You can use either to move to different folders and their subfolders. Click to the right of the folder buttons to use the edit mode. Clicking on the checkmark at the end of the editable text box returns you to the browser mode. If you are using the menubar, you can also choose View | Location Bar | Editable Location.

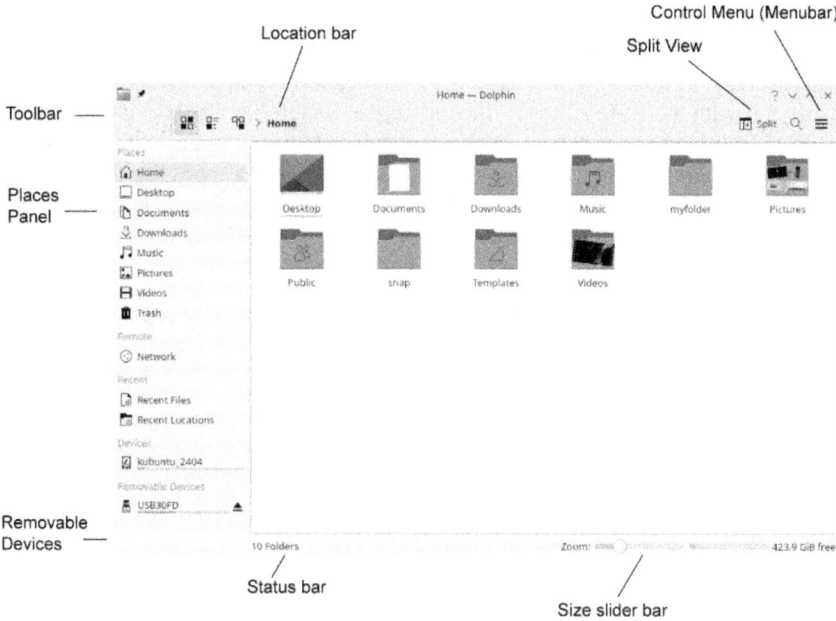

Figure 9-85: The KDE file manager (Dolphin)

394 Part 3: Desktops

The Dolphin menubar has been hidden by default. The menus are displayed when clicking the Control button on the right end of the toolbar (see Figure 9-86). You can redisplay the menubar by choosing "Show Menubar" from the menu (**Ctrl-m**). You can hide the menubar again by choosing Show Menubar from the Settings menu (or pressing **Ctrl-m**).

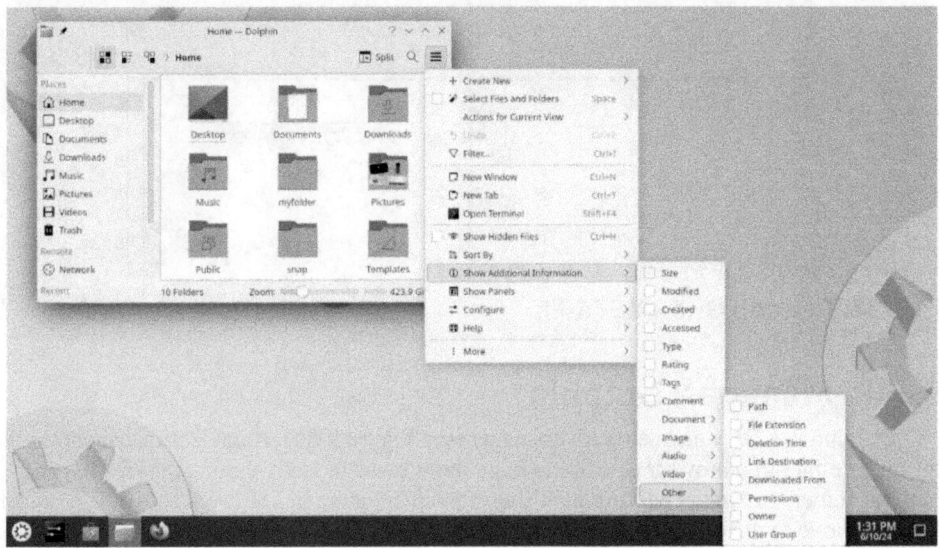

Figure 9-86: The KDE file manager menus

You can open a file either by double-clicking it or by right-clicking it, and choosing the "Open With" entry to list applications to open it with. If you want to just select the file or folder, just single-click it. A double-click will open the file. If the file is a program, that program starts up. If it is a data file, such as a text file, the associated application is run using that data file. Clicking a text file displays it with the Kate editor while clicking an image file displays it with the Gwenview image viewer. If Dolphin cannot determine the application to use, it opens a dialog box prompting you to enter the application name. Also, if the application you want is not listed in the "Open With" menu, you can choose "Other Application" to open this same dialog. You can choose from a list of installed applications or search for an application. You can also click the folder button by the search box to use a folder tree to locate the application program you want.

Dolphin can display panels to either side (Dolphin refers to these as panels, though they operate more like stand-alone tabs). The Places panel will show icons for often-used folders like Home, Network, and Trash, as well as removable devices. To add a folder to the Places panel, just drag it there.

The files and folders listed in a folder can be viewed in several different ways using the icons on the left side of the toolbar. If you are using the menubar, you also can choose an option from the View | View Mode submenu. Files and folders can be displayed as icons, a detailed list, and as columns. See Table 9-4 for keyboard shortcuts.

The "Show Additional Information" submenu in the menu lets you display additional information about files such as the size, date, type, and comments (if you are using the menubar, you can choose it on the View menu). Type specific information can also be displayed such as album, track, and duration for audio files, and word and line counts for documents. You can also display the full path, permissions, and group information (Other submenu).

Keys	Description
ALT-LEFT ARROW, ALT-RIGHT ARROW	Backward and Forward in History
ALT-UP ARROW	One folder up
ENTER	Open a file/folder
LEFT/RIGHT/UP/DOWN ARROWS	Move among the icons
PAGE UP, PAGE DOWN	Scroll fast
CTRL-C	Copy selected file to clipboard
CTRL-V	Paste files from clipboard to current folder
CTRL-S	Select files by pattern
CTRL-L	URI text box location bar
CTRL-F	Find files
CTRL-Q	Close window

Table 9-4: KDE File Manager Keyboard Shortcuts

You can display additional panels by selecting them from the Show Panels submenu in the menu (if you are using the menubar, choose it from the View menu). The Information panel displays detailed information about a selected file or folder, and the Folders panel displays a folder tree for the file system. The panels are detachable from the file manager window (see Figure 9-87). Be sure to choose "Unlock Panels" in the Show Panels menu to make them detachable.

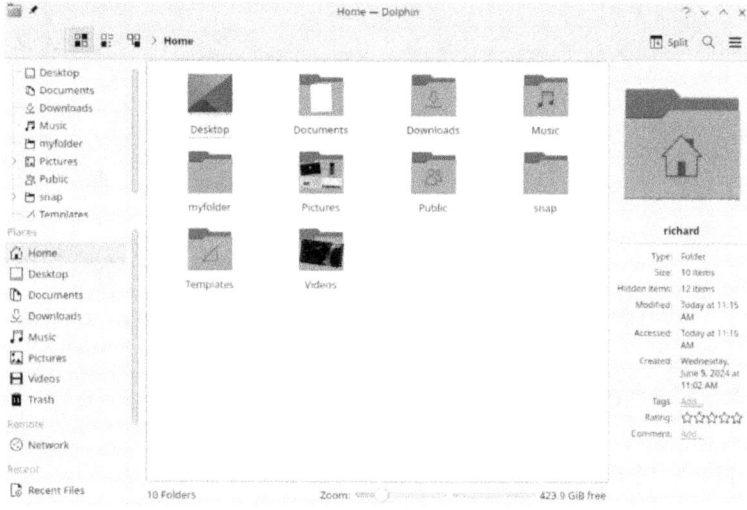

Figure 9-87: The KDE file manager with panels

The Places panel makes use of file metadata to provide easy access to files by category and date. The Places panel has five sections: Places, Remote, Recent, Search For, and Devices. The Places section holds your home folder, the Desktop folder, and the trash. The Devices section holds your attached devices, including removable devices. The Recent section lets you display files and folders you accessed fairly recently (see Figure 9-88). The Search For section lets you display files of specified types: documents, images, audio files, and videos. The Remote section holds a Network entry that lists your network devices.

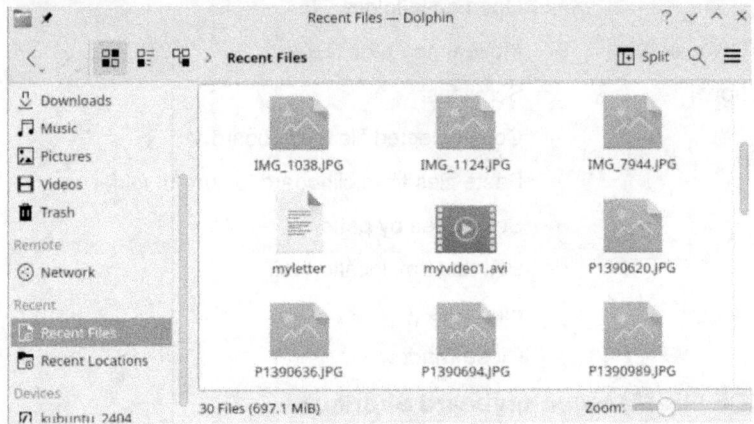

Figure 9-88: The KDE file manager panel Recent

Dolphin supports split views, where you can open two different folders in the same window. Click the Split button in the toolbar. You can then drag folder and files from one folder to the other (see Figure 9-89).

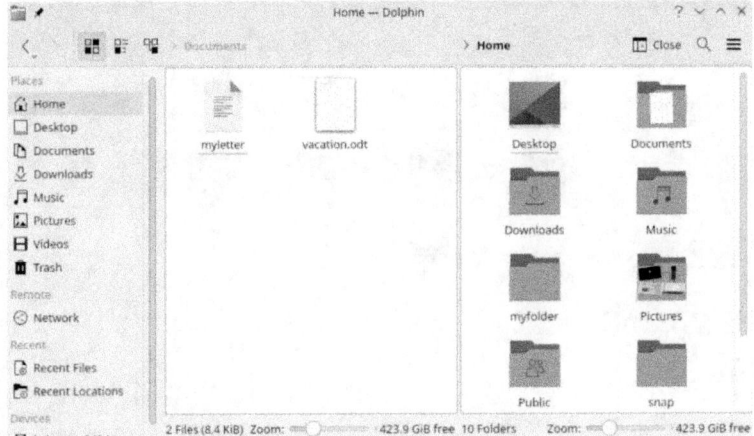

Figure 9-89: The KDE file manager with split views

Dolphin also supports file sharing with Samba. To share a folder, right-click on the folder icon and choose Properties to open the Properties dialog. Then on the Share tab, you can choose to share the folder with Samba (Microsoft Windows). You can also set permissions for users: Read

Only, Full Control, and Deny (See Figure 9-90). For the Everyone entry, you would usually set the permission to Read Only.

Figure 9-90: The KDE file manager share dialog for folders

If the Samba service is not yet installed, this tab will show a button, which you can click to install it. Should it fail to install, open the Konsole terminal window and issue the following command.

```
sudo apt install samba
```

You are then prompted to create a Samba user password, which you use to access shares (see Figure 9-91). You will also have to enter the password of an administrative user to create the Samba password.

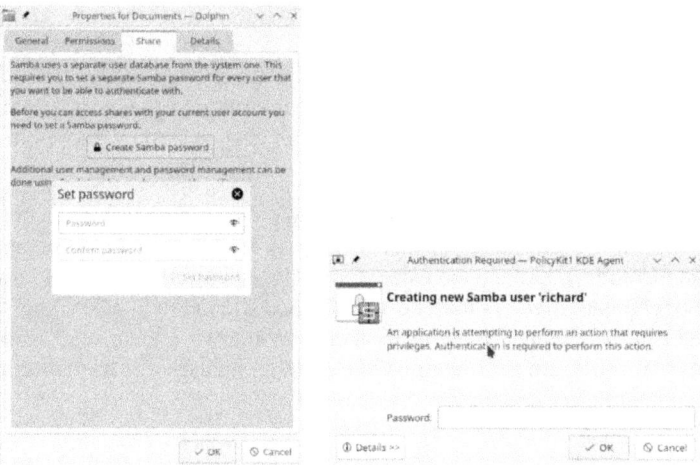

Figure 9-91: The KDE file manager Samba password creation

398 Part 3: Desktops

To configure Dolphin, click Configure Dolphin from the Control menu to open the Dolphin Preferences dialog with tabs for General, Startup, View Modes, Navigation, Context Menu, Trash, and User Feedback (see Figure 9-92). If you are using the menubar, you can select Configure Dolphin from the Settings menu.

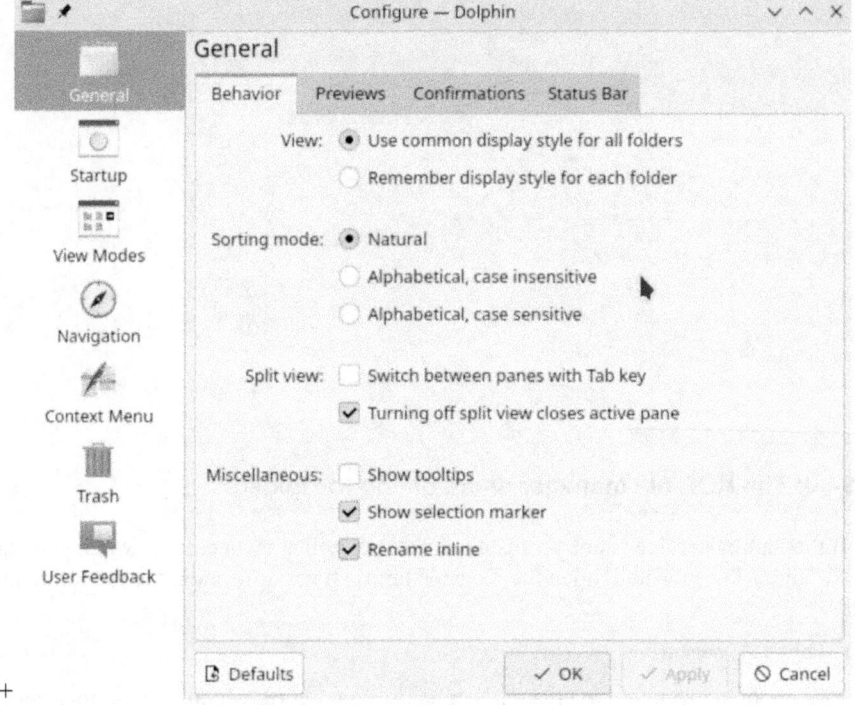

Figure 9-92: Dolphin file manager configuration

The General tab has sub-tabs for Behavior, Previews, Confirmations, and Status Bar. The Behavior tab is where you can enable tool tips and show selection markers. Preview lets you choose which type of files to preview. The image, jpeg, and PDF types are already selected. On Confirmations, you can require confirmation prompts for emptying the trash, moving files to the trash, or closing multiple tabs. On the Status tab, you can choose to show the zoom slider and the amount of free storage.

On the Startup tab, you can specify features like the split view and the default folder to start up with. On the View Modes tab, you can set display features for the different display modes (Icons, Details, and Column), like the icon size, font type, and arrangement. The Navigation tab sets features like opening archives as folders. The Context Menu tab is where you specify services to be shown in the context menu such as "open in New Window", Delete, and "Run in Konsole." The Trash tab lets you configure trash settings like deleting items in the trash after a specified time and setting the maximum size of the trash.

Navigating Folders

Within a file manager window, a double-click on a folder icon moves to that folder and displays its file and sub-folder icons. To move back up to the parent folder, you click the back arrow button located on the left end of the navigation toolbar. A double-click on a folder icon moves you down the folder tree, one folder at a time. By clicking the back arrow button, you move up the tree.

The Navigation bar can display either the folder path for the current folder or an location box where you can enter in a pathname. For the folder path, you can click on any displayed folder name to move you quickly to an upper-level folder.

The location box can be opened in editable mode, or in replacement mode. The replacement mode selects the path for you to let you press the delete key to remove it entirely so that you can type in another path.

To use the location box, click to the right of the folder path. The Location box is opened in edit mode. If you are using the menubar, you can select Show Full Location in the View | Location Bar | Editable location menu item. The navigation bar changes to an editable textbox where you can edit a path name. To change back to the folder path, click the check mark to the right of the text box. You can also press F6 to display the location box in edit mode. To open the location box in replacement mode, you press CTRL-L. If you are using the menubar, you can choose Show Full Location in the View | Location Bar | Replace location menu item. Both F6 and CTRL-L will toggle between the folder path and location box.

Like a Web browser, the file manager remembers the previous folder it has displayed. You can use the back and forward arrow buttons to move through this list of prior folders. You can also use several keyboard shortcuts to perform such operations, like **Alt-back-arrow** to move up a folder, and the arrow keys to move to different icons.

Copy, Move, Delete, Rename, and Link Operations

To perform an operation on a file or folder, you first have to select it by clicking the file's icon or listing. To select more than one file, hold down the CTRL key while you click the files you want. You can also use the keyboard arrow keys to move from one file icon to another.

To copy and move files, you can use the standard drag-and-drop method with your mouse. To copy a file, you locate it by using the file manager. Open another file manager window to the folder to which you want the file copied. Then drag-and-drop the file icon to that window. A pop-up menu appears with selections for Move Here, Copy Here, or Link Here. Choose Copy Here. To move a file to another folder, follow the same procedure, but select Move Here from the pop-up menu. To copy or move a folder, use the same procedure as for files. All the folder's files and subfolders are also copied or moved. Instead of having to select from a pop-up menu, you can use the corresponding keys: **Ctrl** for copy, **Shift** for move, and **Ctrl-Shift** for link.

To rename a file, Click its icon and then click the icon's name or press F2. You can also right-click the icon and select Rename from the pop-up menu. A text box appears around the name and you can enter a new name or edit the current one.

You can delete a file by placing it in the Trash folder to delete later. To place a file in the Trash folder, drag-and-drop it to the Trash icon on the Dolphin Places panel, or right-click the file and choose "Move To Trash" from the pop-up menu. You can later open the Trash folder and delete the files. To delete all the files in the Trash folder, right-click the Trash icon in Dolphin file manager Places panel, and select Empty Trash from the pop-up menu. To restore files in the Trash bin, open the Trash window and right click on the file to restore and select Restore.

Each file or folder has properties associated with it that include permissions, the filename, and its folder. To display the Properties dialog for a given file, right-click the file's icon and select the Properties entry. On the General tab, you see the name of the file displayed. To change the filename, replace the name there with a new one. Permissions are set on the Permissions tab. Here, you can set read, write, and execute permissions for user, group, or other access to the file. The Group entry enables you to change the group for a file. The Checksums tab lets you check the validity of a downloaded file by checking its checksum to make sure it was downloaded correctly. The Details tab show information about the file such as size, modification time, and type.

Search Bar and Filter Bar

The Dolphin search tool provides a simplified search bar for files and folders. KDE also supports a filter bar to search files and folders in the current folder. For quick access to basic categories and recent use you can use the Dolphin file manager Places panel's Recent and Search For entries, as noted previously.

Search Bar

To search for files, click the Find button on the icon bar to open the search bar, which displays a search text box (CTRL-f). The search bar displays a search text box where you enter the pattern of the file or folder you are searching for. Click the red x button to the left to close the find bar, and use the black x button in the text box to clear the search pattern.

Buttons below the search box provide options to qualify the search. The Filename button (the default) searches on the filename. The Content button will search the contents of text files for the pattern. The "From Here" button searches from the current folder, and the "Your files" button searches from the user's home folders (see Figure 9-93). The "More Search Tools" button displays a menu of other search tools you can use.

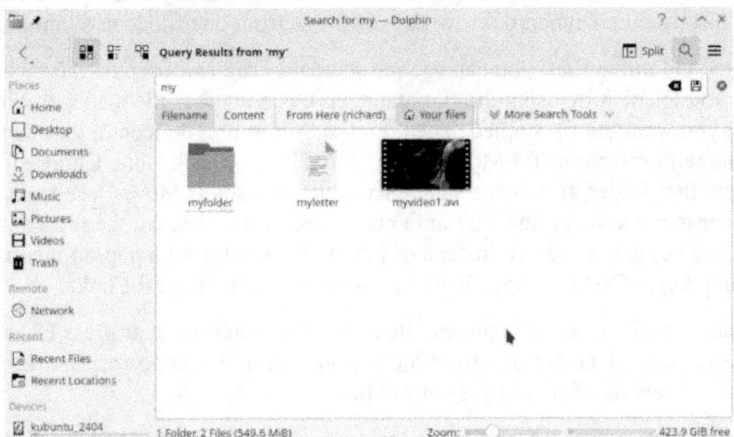

Figure 9-93: The KDE Search Bar

The search results are displayed in the main pane. You can double-click a file to have it open with its appropriate application. Text files are displayed by the Kate text editor, images by Gwenview, and applications are run. When you are finished searching, click the Search close button.

The search operation makes use of the KDE implementation of Baloo desktop search. To configure desktop search, choose System Settings | Workspace | Search | File Search tab. On the File Search tab, you can enable or disable file searching, and choose folders not to search. You can also enable file content indexing.

Filter Bar

For a quick search of the current folder, you can activate the Filter bar by choosing Filter entry on the menu or by pressing CTRL-i (if you are using the menubar, you can choose it from the Tools menu) This opens a Filter search box at the bottom of the window. Enter a pattern, and only those file and folder names containing that pattern are displayed. Click the x button at the right of the Filter box to clear it (see Figure 9-94).

Figure 9-94: The KDE Filter Bar

FTP

On the KDE Desktop, the desktop file manager Dolphin has built-in FTP capability. The FTP operation has been seamlessly integrated into standard desktop file operations. Downloading files from an FTP site is as simple as copying files by dragging them from one folder window to another, with one of the folders located on a remote FTP site. To download files from an FTP site, you open a window to access that site, entering the URL for the FTP site in the window's location box. Use the **ftp://** protocol for FTP access. Once connected, open the folder you want, and then open another window for the local folder to which you want the remote files copied. In the window showing the FTP files, select the ones you want to download. Then click-and-drag those files to the window for the local folder. A pop-up menu appears with choices for Copy, Link, or Move. Select Copy. The selected files are then downloaded. Another window opens, showing the download progress and displaying the name of each file in turn, along with a bar indicating the percentage downloaded so far.

KDE Configuration: KDE System Settings

With the Plasma configuration tools, you can configure your desktop and system, changing the way it is displayed and the features it supports. The configuration dialogs are accessed on the System Settings. On Plasma, you can access System Settings from the System Settings entry in the Computer or Favorites menus, or from Applications | Settings | System Settings.

The System Settings window can be displayed either with the icon view or sidebar view. Use the Configure dialog | General tab to choose the view you want. You can access the Configure dialog from the menu on the sidebar view (upper left corner) or the Configure button on the icon view (top toolbar). The sidebar view is the current default (see Figure 9-95).

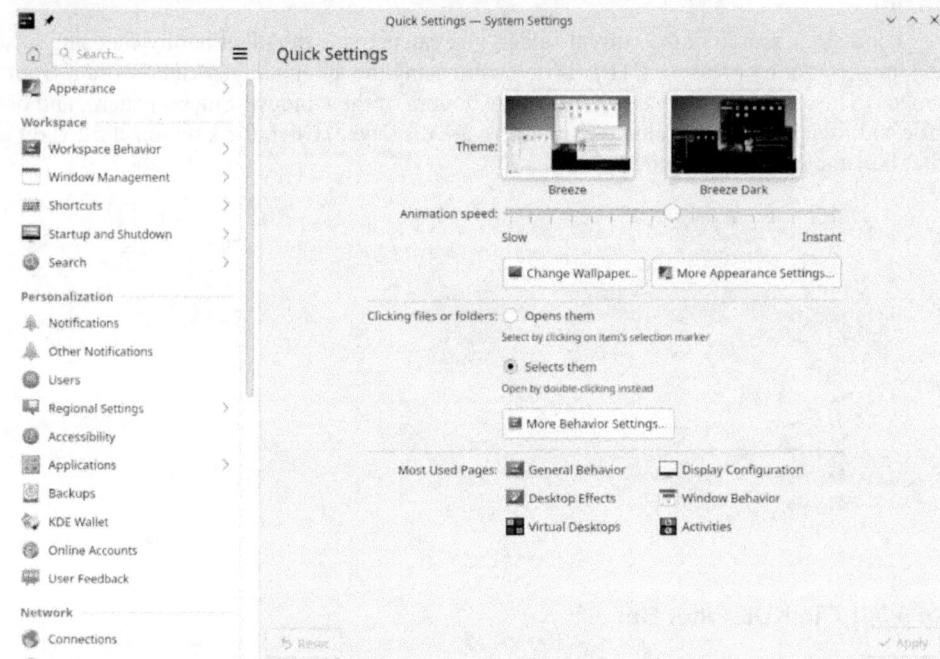

Figure 9-95: Plasma System Settings - Sidebar view

The sidebar organizes settings into several sections (see Figure 96). The Appearance section lets you set the desktop theme, manage fonts, choose icon sets, and select application and window styles (see Figure 9-97). The Workspace section lets you set desktop effects, virtual desktops, window actions, startup applications, and desktop search. The Network section holds icons for configuring networking preferences, Bluetooth connections, and sharing. Personalization lets you perform administrative tasks such as user management, the date and time, notifications, online accounts, and file/application associations. Hardware lets you set the printer configuration, power management, multimedia devices (sound), your display resolution, and to manage drivers.

Note: On KDE, use the System Settings Online Accounts to set up access to your online services, where you can add and configure online accounts such as Google.

Chapter 9: Kubuntu (KDE)   403

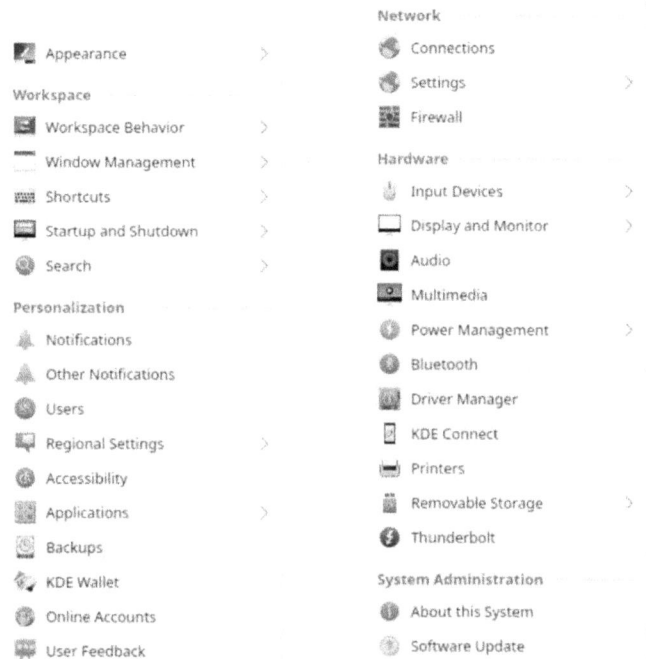

Figure 9-96: Plasma System Settings - Sidebar icon list

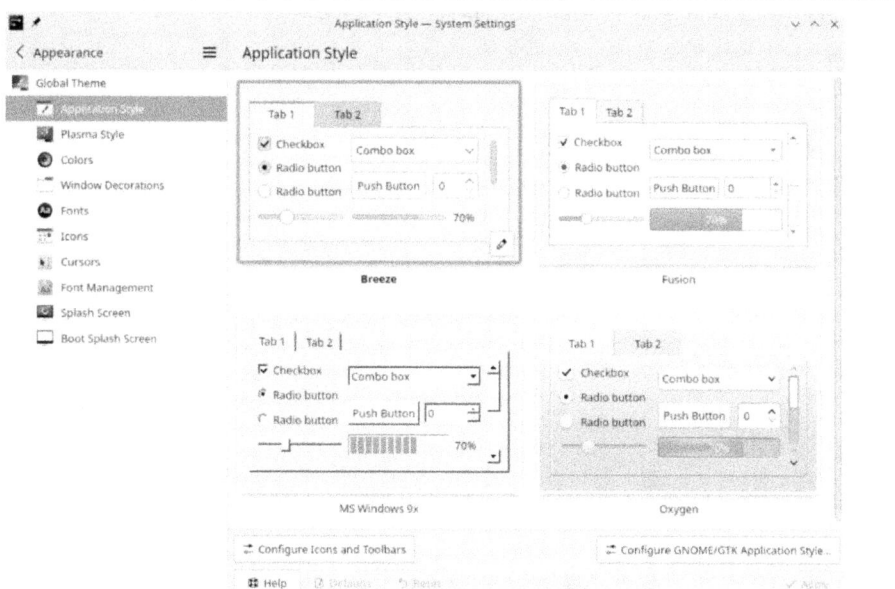

Figure 9-97: KDE System Settings | Appearance | Global Theme | Application Style

User management is provided by Kuser, accessible from System Settings | Account Details (Personalization section), User Manager tab (see Figure 9-98).

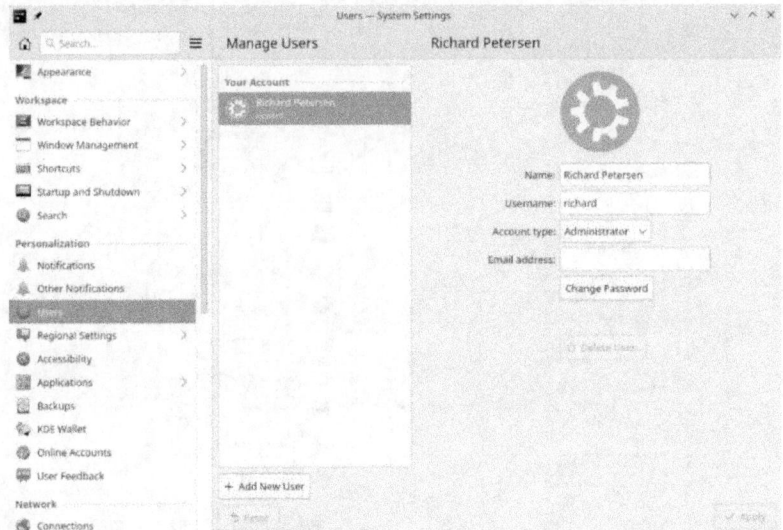

Figure 9-98: KDE System Settings | Users

The icon view was the default in previous releases. With the icon view, System Settings shows a display of icons arranged in several sections: Appearance, Workspace, Personalization, Network, Hardware, and System Administration (see Figure 9-99).

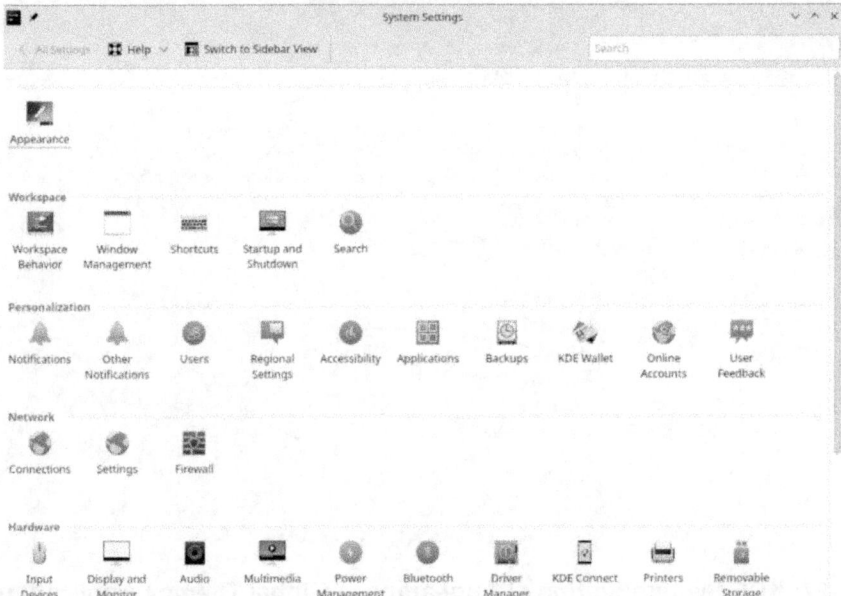

Figure 9-99: Plasma System Settings - Icon view

Click an entry to display a new icon list in the sidebar with configuration entries for that category. Some entries, such as Color and Global Theme, will have no added configuration entries. Selecting an entry shows the configuration settings on the right pane (see Figure 9-100).

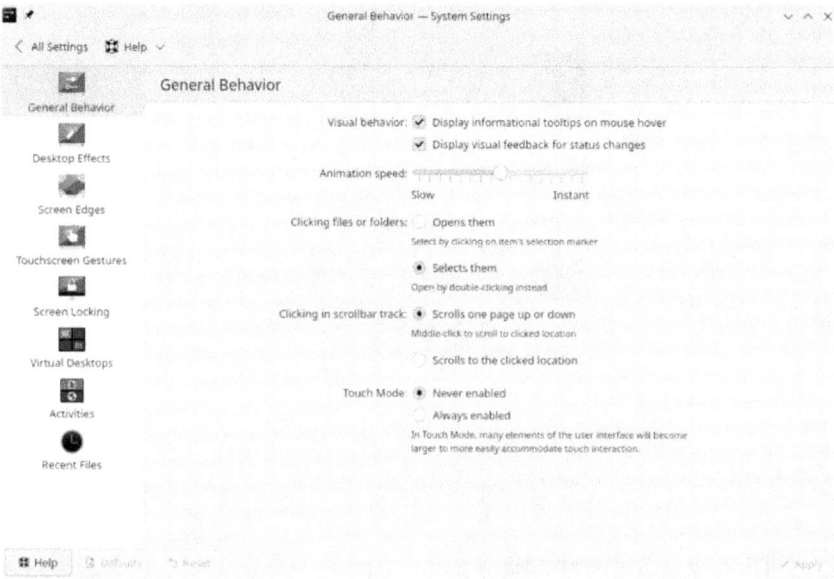

Figure 9-100: Plasma System Settings - Icon view (Workspace Behavior)

Plasma Software Management: Discover

Discover is Plasma's software manager. It uses a simple interface to let you quickly locate and install software. Applications can be easily removed with a click. With Discover, you can also install Plasma (KDE) desktop add-ons, including widgets for the desktop and panel. Discover shows a sidebar on the left and a list of applications to the right (see Figure 9-101). You use the Discover sidebar to locate software packages. Clicking on a package entry expands it to a software description with an Install button (installed packages have a Remove button) (see Figure 9-102). A Sources menu, next to the Install menu, lets you choose whether to install from an APT repository such as ubuntu-noble-universe, or from the Snap repository.

The Applications entry expands to software categories on the sidebar, which, when selected, will display a list of available and installed packages in the right pane. The Installed entry lists all your installed packages with a Remove button for easy deletion. You can also use the Search box at the top of the sidebar to locate a package. The Settings entry lists your repositories, which you can enable or disable.

The Plasma Addons entry on the sidebar provides an extensive set of addons to different parts of the Plasma desktop. There are categories for fonts, themes, icons, window effects, window switching, and wallpapers, among others. You use the Plasma Widgets entry to manage your desktop and panel widgets.

406 Part 3: Desktops

The Application Addons entry lists addons for particular applications, such as calendar events for Korganizer.

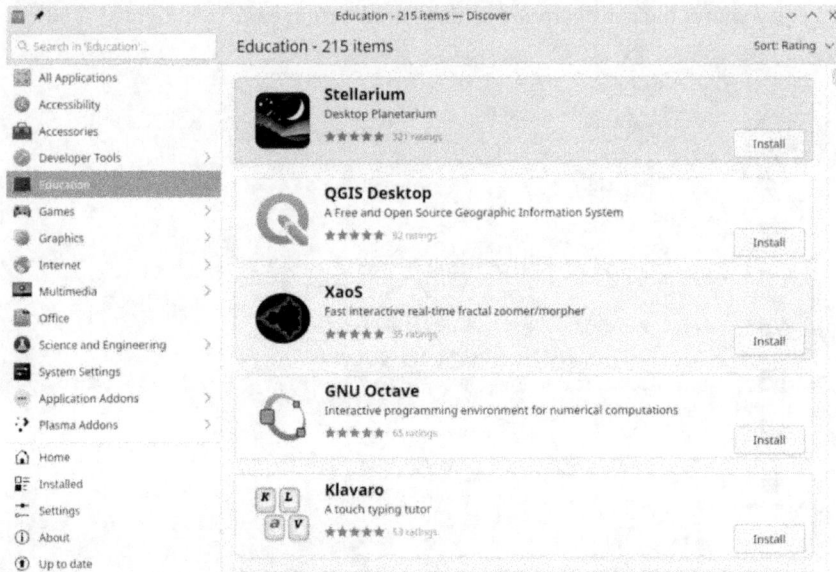

Figure 9-101: Discover Software Manager

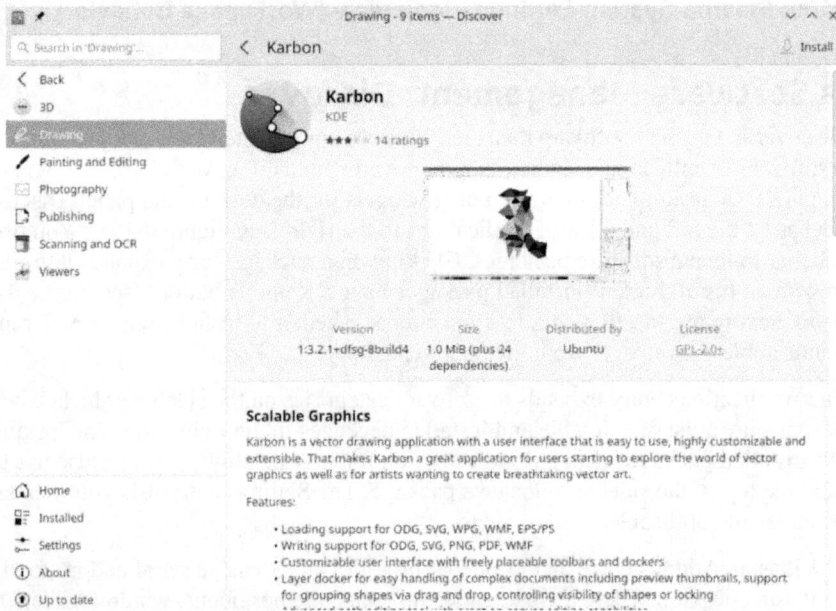

Figure 9-102: Discover Software Manager - Application Description

ubuntu

10. Ubuntu MATE

- MATE Desktop
- Windows
- Workspaces
- MATE Menu
- MATE Panel
- Applets
- The Caja File Manager
- Preferences (desktop configuration)

The MATE desktop is a simplified and easy to use desktop derived from the GNOME 2.4 desktop. MATE's official file manager is Caja. Those familiar with GNOME 2 will find similar features. The Ubuntu MATE desktop use the MATE desktop with Ubuntu software repositories. The MATE version of Ubuntu is called Ubuntu MATE and is available as a separate Desktop USB/DVD, and as the **ubuntu-mate-desktop** meta-package on the APT repository (Synaptic Package Manager or **sudo install apt** command in a terminal window). The version of MATE used for 24.04 is MATE 1.26.2. It uses several different applications from Ubuntu, such as the Ayatana Indicator applet, the Celluloid video player, and the Webcamoid webcam application. Ubuntu MATE is an official Ubuntu Flavour, supported by Ubuntu. The Ubuntu MATE website is:

https://ubuntu-mate.org

Key changes with Ubuntu MATE 24.04 include:

For software management, the App Center replaces Software Boutique.

The Ubuntu Mate Welcome application is retired and no longer available.

For more information check the Ubuntu MATE release notes at:

https://ubuntu-mate.org/blog/ubuntu-mate-noble-numbat-release-notes/

Ubuntu MATE Help and Documentation

The Ubuntu MATE Guide provides detailed documentation on using MATE (see Figure 10-1) . It is accessible from the Accessories menu and from the system menu (power button) as MATE Help. The "All Help" option on the MATE Guide menu displays a lists of documentation for applications.

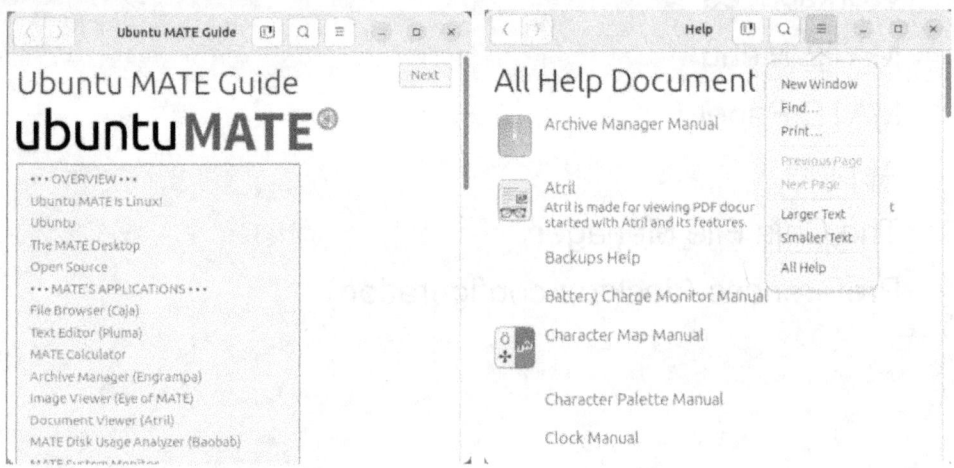

Figure 10-1: Ubuntu MATE Guide

You should also check the online Ubuntu MATE Guide at:

https://guide.ubuntu-mate.org/

It provides a detailed description of all the Ubuntu Mate desktop features, with examples.

For information about Ubuntu, check the Ubuntu documentation site at:
https://help.ubuntu.com

You can access it from the System menu's (power button on right side of the top panel) Ubuntu Help entry.

MATE Applications

MATE features several applications. The applications are on the Ubuntu repository and can be installed on Ubuntu, but are promoted to default status on Ubuntu Mate. For example, Ubuntu uses Videos as its primary video player, whereas Ubuntu MATE uses Celluloid. In place of the GNOME Snapshot web cam (Camera), MATE uses Webcamoid. For a text editor, MATE uses Pluma, instead of Text Editor. MATE also has versions of system tools and utilities that operate in a similar way to their corresponding Ubuntu versions such as the Engrampa Archive Manager, Eye of MATE Image Viewer, MATE Dictionary, MATE terminal, the Mate User Manager, and the MATE System Monitor.

Webcamoid is a cross-platform basic webcam picture and video capture application available for Linux, MACOS, and Windows (see Figure 10-2). It is based on the Qt library used by KDE. A simple dock at the bottom of the Webcamoid window lets you run and configure your webcam. Click the Play button to turn the webcam on or off. There are buttons to configure sources, sound, and effects. When running you can take a photo and record the session. The Preferences dialog lets you add a webcam, enable advanced effects, select video and audio libraries to use, add plugins. The Webcamoid configuration settings are located in your home folder in the **.config/Webcamoid** folder.

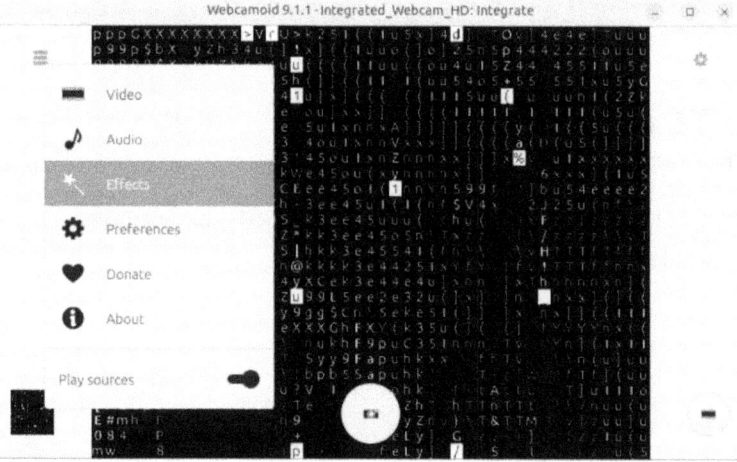

Figure 10-2: Webcamoid webcam application

Webcamoid provides virtual camera support allowing other applications to interface with it. Linux applications are supported, including Gstreamer, as well as commercial application such as Firefox web browser and Skype. See the Webcamoid web site for more details:
https://webcamoid.github.io/.

Celluloid is a GTK+ frontend for the MPV video player formerly known as GNOME MPV (**https://github.com/celluloid-player/celluloid**). It provides a basic interface with standard controls and playlist (see Figure 10-3). You can also select video, audio, and subtitle tracks. The Preferences dialog has four tabs: Interface, Config Files, Miscellaneous, and Plugins. On the Interface tab you can configure the application with features such as the dark theme, floating controls, and cursor autohide. Config Files lets you load an MPV configuration file containing additional MPV option. A list of available MPV options are described in the MPV manual, **https://mpv.io/manual/stable/#synopsis**. Should you have user scripts for configuration, you can load them on the on Miscellaneous tab. The configuration file for Celluloid is **/etc/mpv/mpv.conf**.

Figure 10-3: Celluloid on MATE

The MATE Desktop

The MATE desktop is designed to be simple, with a top and bottom panel and desktop icons (see Figure 10-4). The top panel at the top of the screen holds menus, program launchers, applet icons, and indicators. You can display the panel horizontally or vertically, and have it automatically hide to show you a full screen.

Chapter 10: Ubuntu MATE **411**

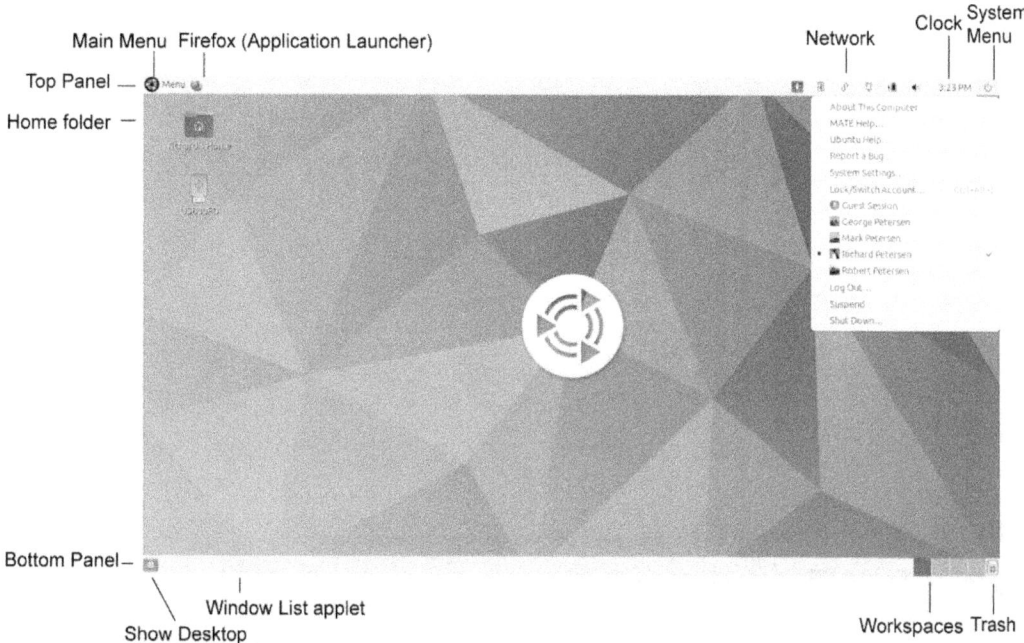

Figure 10-4: MATE desktop and panel

On the left side of the top panel is the button for the main menu. With this menu, you can access places and applications. On the right side of the panel is the Indicator Applet Complete that includes buttons for system tools such as Accessibility, Bluetooth, NetworkManager, notifications, battery, sound volume, the time and date, and the system menu (power button). On the bottom panel to the left is the Show Desktop button, which hides your open windows, followed by the Window List applet, which shows buttons for open windows. On the right side is the workspace switcher and the trash.

On the right side of the top panel is the system menu (power button) with entries for opening the Control Center (System Settings), switching users, locking the screen, and performing log out, suspend, and shut down operations (see Figure 10-5). The Lock/Switch Account entry displays the lock screen that has a button for Switch User. This starts the login manager and displays a list of users you can login as. Below the Lock/Switch Account entry is a list of favorite users you can directly switch to. There are also entries to access the MATE Desktop User Guide (MATE Help) and the Ubuntu Documentation web site which has a link to the installation guide (Ubuntu Help). The "About this Computer" entry opens the System Monitor at the System tab showing information about your Ubuntu version, your computer hardware, and available disk space.

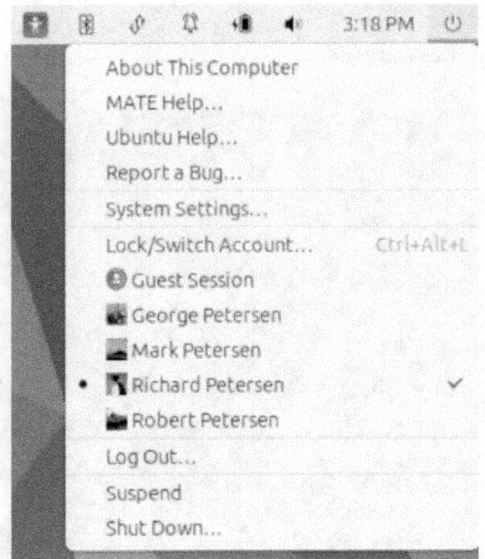

Figure 10-5: MATE system menu

The remainder of the screen is the desktop, where you can place folders, files, and application launchers. You can use a click-and-drag operation to move a file from one window to another or to the desktop. A drag-and-drop with the CTRL key held down will copy a file. A drag-and-drop operation with both the CTRL and SHIFT keys held down (CTRL-SHIFT) creates a link on the desktop to that folder or file. Your home folder is accessed from the Home Folder icon on the desktop. Double clicking it opens a file manager window for your home folder. A right-click anywhere on the desktop displays a desktop menu with which you can align your desktop icons, change the background, and create new folders.

To quit the desktop, you click the system menu the right side of the top panel and select the Shut Down entry. This opens a menu with options to Log Out, Suspend, and Shut Down.

Indicator Applet Configuration

MATE uses the Ayatana Indicators applet, a cross-platform compatible version of the Ubuntu Indicators. There are three possible indicator applets: Indicator Applet, Indicator Applet Appmenu, and Indicator Applet Complete. They are used for various desktop layouts that Ubuntu MATE supports. For the Ubuntu MATE default layout (Familiar), the Indicator Applet Complete is used, though you can add the others if you want to. The Indicator Applet Complete includes indicators for accessibility, Bluetooth, network connections, notifications, battery, sound, time and date, and system (power button). The Indicator Applet is the same, but without the Time and Date indicator.

Figure 10-6: Indicator Applet Complete

You can configure the indicator applet (top right panel) with the Control Center Indicator dialog. Open the Control Center and click on the Indicators icon in the Look and Feel section to open the Ayatana Indicators Settings dialog (see Figure 10-7). The dialog has tabs for Session (System Menu), Date and Time, Sound, Power, Messages, Bluetooth, Notifications, and Keyboard. A button at the bottom of each tab lets you enable the indicator on login. On the Sessions tab you can set options for the System Menu such as showing the user name on the panel, removing log out or restart entries, or removing the list of users from the menu.

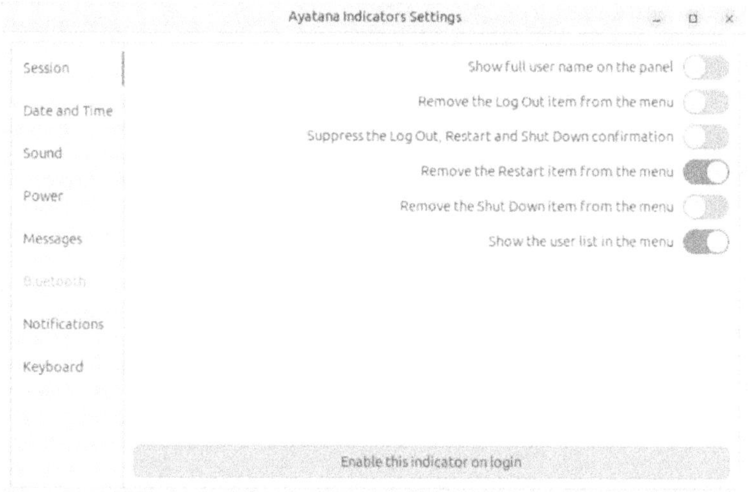

Figure 10-7: MATE Indicator Applet Configuration - Sessions (System Menu)

For Date and Time you can choose to show the year, month, weekdays, and seconds on the panel, as well as the calendar, calendar week numbers, and events in the menu (see Figure 10-8).

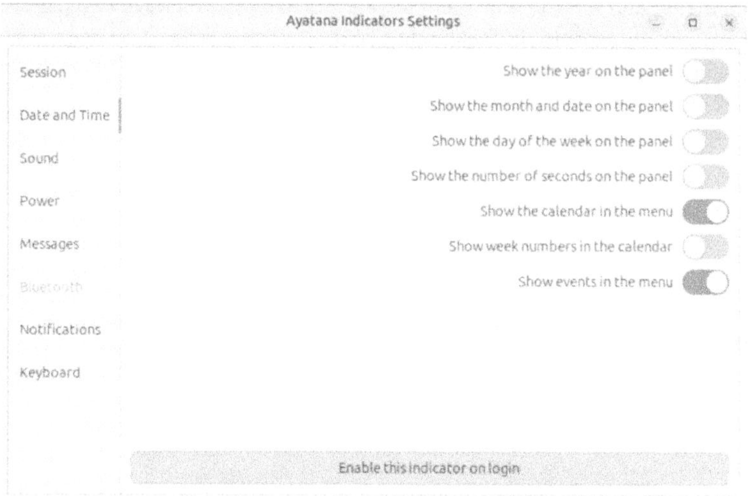

Figure 10-8: MATE Indicator Applet Configuration - Date and Time

Sound has an option to allow the volume to go above 100%. For Power you can show the percentage left on a battery as well as the time. For Notifications you can choose the maximum number of items to show (see Figure 10-9). You can also choose what applications not to display in the indicator messages menu. The Spotify, NetworkManager and MATE Tweak applications are already chosen. To add more, right-click on the cursor in the text box below the list to display a menu of possible applications to choose from. Once chosen, click the Add button.

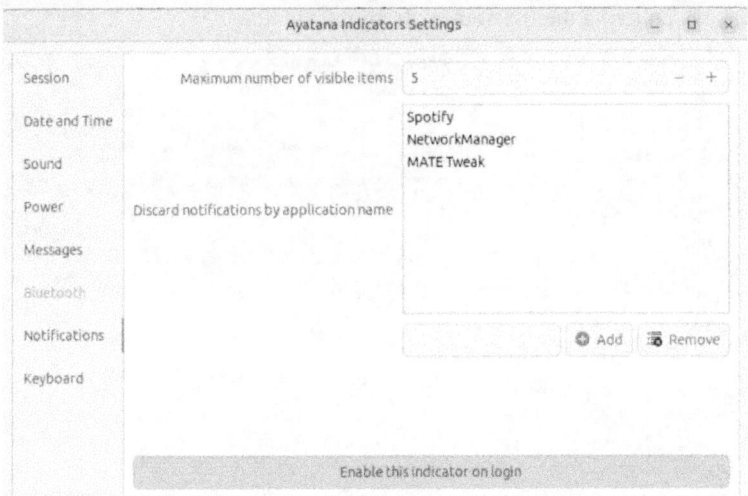

Figure 10-9: MATE Indicator Applet Configuration - Notifications

MATE Components

From a user's point of view, the desktop interface has four components: the desktop, the panels, the main menu, and the file manager (see Figure 10-10). You have two panels displayed, used for menus, application icons, and managing your windows. When you open a window, a corresponding button for it will be displayed in the lower panel, which you can use to minimize and restore the window.

Chapter 10: Ubuntu MATE **415**

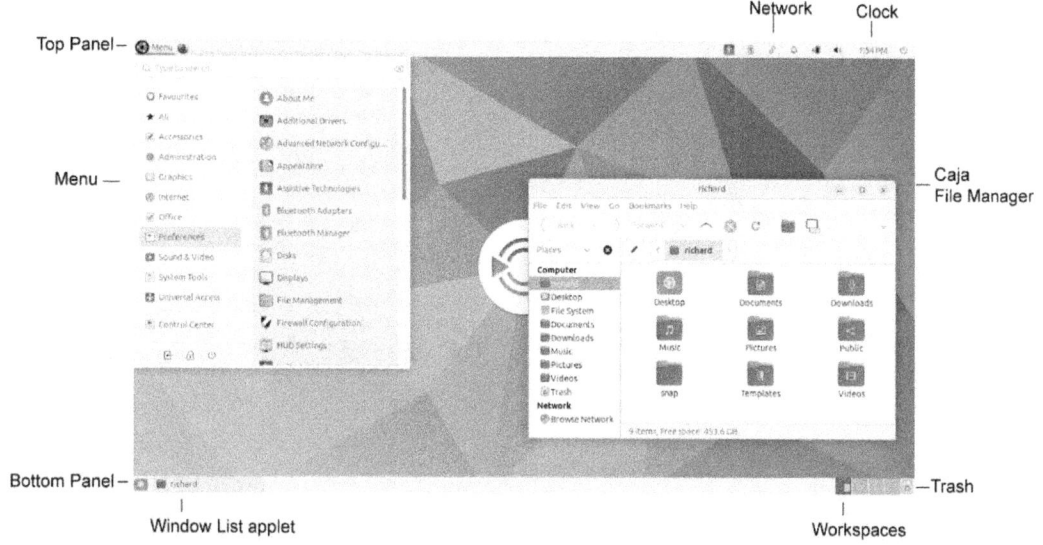

Figure 10-10: MATE with Brisk Menu and Caja file manager

To start a program, you can select its entry from the main menu. You can also click its application icon in the panel (if one is present) or drag-and-drop data files to its icon. To add an icon for an application to the desktop, right-click on its entry in the main menu and select "Add to desktop". You can also click the ALT-F2 keys to open the Run Applications dialog which lists available applications (see Figure 10-15). A search box at the top of the dialog lets you search for an application. There are options you can select to run in a terminal window, "Run in a terminal", and to select a file to open with the application, "Run with file…".

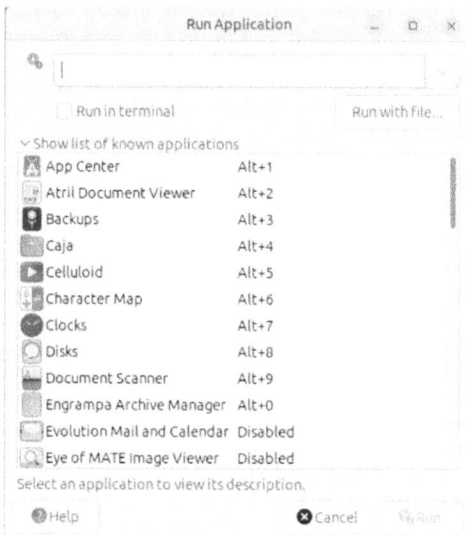

Figure 10-11: Run Application dialog, Alt-F2

You can also quickly access a menu of applications on the desktop with the ALT-F1 keys (see Figure 10-12). Click anywhere on the desktop and press ALT-F2 to display a menu of application categories which expand to submenus of applications when you pass your mouse over them. Click on the application you want to start.

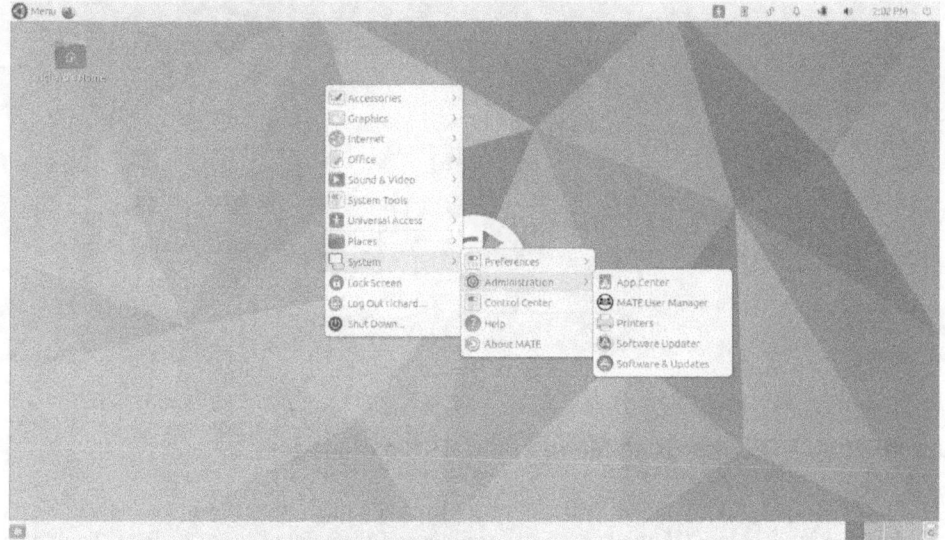

Figure 10-12: Application desktop menu, Alt-F1

Drag-and-Drop Files to the Desktop

Any icon for an item that you drag-and-drop from a file manager window to the desktop also appears on the desktop. However, the default drag-and-drop operation is a move operation. If you select a file in your file manager window and drag it to the desktop, you are actually moving the file from its current folder to the desktop folder, which is located in your home folder and holds all items on the desktop. The desktop folder is named **Desktop**. In the case of dragging folders to the desktop, the entire folder and its subfolders will be moved to the Desktop folder.

To remove an icon from the desktop, you right-click and choose "Move to Trash." If you choose to display the trash icon on the desktop, you can simply drag-and-drop it in the trash.

You can copy a file to your desktop by pressing the CTRL key and then clicking and dragging it from a file manager window to your desktop. You will see the mouse icon change to hand with a small + symbol, indicating that you are creating a copy, instead of moving the original.

You can also create a link on the desktop to any file. There are two ways to create a link. While holding down the Ctrl and Shift keys, CTRL-SHIFT, drag the file to where you want the link created. A copy of the icon then appears with a small arrow in the right corner indicating it is a link. You can click this link to start the program, open the file, or open the folder, depending on the type of file to which you linked. Alternatively, first click and drag the file out of the window, and after moving the file but before releasing the mouse button, press the ALT key. This will display a pop-up menu with selections for Move Here, Copy Here, and Link Here. Select the Link Here option to create a link.

The drag-and-drop file operation works on virtual desktops provided by the Workspace Switcher. The Workspace Switcher creates icons for each virtual desktop in the panel, along with task buttons for any applications open on them.

MATE Tweak

You can configure desktop and window display settings using the MATE Tweak dialog, which you can access from the Preferences menu, or from the Control Center (see Figure 10-13). The MATE Tweak dialog has three tabs: Desktop, Panel, and Windows. The Desktop tab lets you choose which system icons to display on the desktop. The Computer and Home folder icons are initially selected, along with Mounted volumes for external file systems such as USB drives or external hard drives that you attach. You can also choose to display the Computer, Network, and Trash icons. The first option lets you disable this feature, hiding all the desktop icons.

Figure 10-13: MATE Tweak

The Panel tab lets you configure your panel, choosing from a panel layout style, possible features for the panel chosen (Panel Menu Features), and added panel features such as using a dock, displaying a keyboard LED, and choosing the size of icons in the panel.

On Windows tab, you can turn off compositing by changing the window manager. Change the location of the minimize, maximize, and close buttons from the right side of the title bar to the left side. You can also enable or disable window features such as window snapping and animations, as well as select the font you want to use for windows.

Applications on the Desktop

In some cases, you will want to create another way on the desktop to access a file without moving it from its original folder. You can do this either by using an application launcher icon or by creating a link to the original program. Application launcher icons are the components used in menus and panels to display and access applications. To place an application icon on your desktop for an entry in the menus, you can simply drag-and-drop the application entry from the menu to the desktop, or right-click and select "Add to desktop."

For applications that are not on a menu, you can either create an application launcher button or create a direct link for it. To create an application launcher, right-click the desktop background to display the desktop menu, and then select the "Create Launcher" entry. To create a simple link, click-and-drag a program's icon while holding the Ctrl-Shift keys down to the desktop.

The Desktop Menu

You can right-click anywhere on the empty desktop to display the desktop menu that includes entries for common tasks, such as creating an application launcher, creating a new folder, or organizing the icon display (see Figure 10-14). Keep in mind that the Create Folder entry creates a new folder on your desktop, specifically in your Desktop folder (**Desktop**), not your home folder. The entries for this menu are listed in Table 10-1.

Menu Item	Description
Create Folder	Creates a new folder on your desktop, within your DESKTOP folder.
Create Launcher	Creates a new desktop icon for an application.
Create Document	Creates files using installed templates or a simple text file
Revert to Previous Version	Restore files from backup
Open in Terminal	Open Desktop folder in a terminal window
Keep Aligned	Aligns your desktop icons.
Organize Desktop by Name	Arranges your desktop icons.
Lock Icons Position	Fix icons at current positions.
Cut, Copy, Paste	Cuts, copies, or pastes files, letting you move or copy files between folders.
Change Desktop Background	Opens a Background Preferences dialog to let you select a new background for your desktop.

Table 10-1: The MATE Desktop Menu

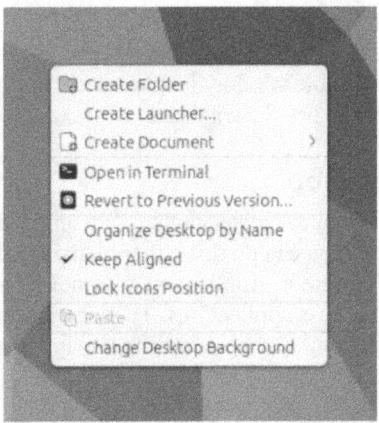

Figure 10-14: MATE Desktop Menu

Windows

You can resize a window by clicking any of its sides or corners and dragging. You can move the window with a click-and-drag operation on its title bar. You can also ALT-click and drag anywhere on the window. The upper-right corner of a window shows the Minimize, Maximize, and Close buttons (minus, square, and x buttons). Clicking the Minimize button no longer displays the window on the desktop. A button for it remains on the bottom panel (the Window list applet) that you can click to restore it. The panel button for a window works like a display toggle. If the window is displayed when you click the panel button, it will no longer be shown. If not displayed, it will then be shown. Right-click anywhere on the title bar to display a window menu with entries for window operations (see Figure 10-15). The options include workspace entries to move the window to another workspace (virtual desktop) or make visible on all workspaces, which displays the window no matter to what workspace you move.

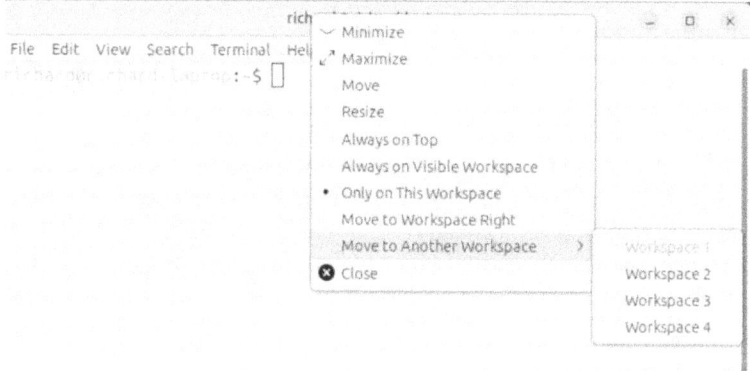

Figure 10-15: MATE window and window menu

You can quickly move between windows by pressing the Alt-Tab keys. A window switcher bar opens displaying thumbnails of open windows (see Figure 10-16). Continue pressing the Alt-Tab keys to move through them. To enable thumbnails, be sure that the "Enable software compositing window manager" option is selected on the Windows Preferences dialog's General tab (Preferences | Windows). You also have the option to disable thumbnails for the switcher, displaying only small icons for the open windows.

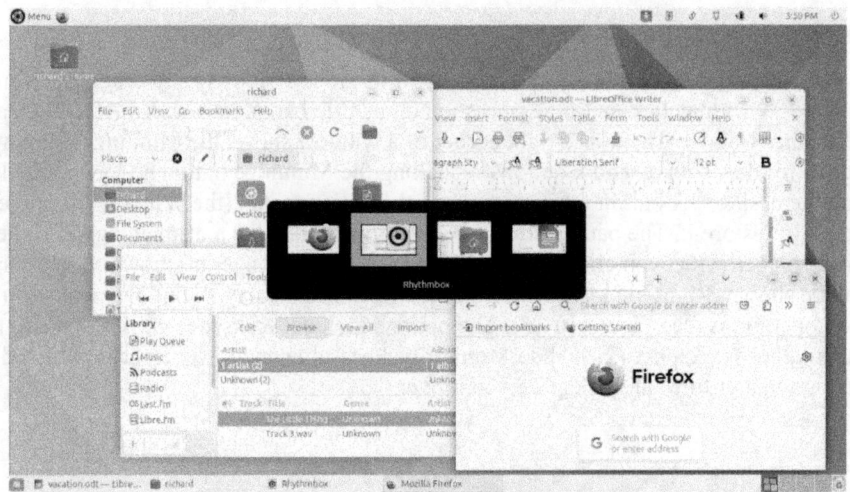

Figure 10-16: Switching Windows with thumbnails (Alt-Tab)

You can configure window behavior using the Window Preferences dialog's Behavior tab accessible from the Preference menu and the Control Center. You choose features such as to select windows by moving the mouse over them and use the Super key instead of the Alt key to move a window. From a menu, you can choose the action to perform when the title bar is double-clicked. The default is maximize, but other options include to roll up the window and minimize it.

On the Placement tab, you can choose to center new windows and to enable window snapping (side by side tiling).

Window List

The Window List applet on the left side of the bottom panel shows currently opened windows (see Figure 10-17). The Window List arranges opened windows in a series of buttons, one for each window. A window can include applications such as a Web browser or a file manager window displaying a folder. You can move from one displayed window to another by clicking its button. When you minimize a window, you can later restore it by clicking its entry in the Window List. Hovering your mouse over a window button displays a thumbnail of the window, showing you the application opened and its content.

Right clicking a window's Window List button opens a menu that lets you Minimize or Unminimize, Move, Resize, Maximize, or Close the window, and move the window to another workspace. The Minimize operation will reduce the window to its Window List entry. Right clicking the entry will display the menu with an Unminimize option instead of a Minimize one, which you can then use to redisplay the window. The Close entry will close the window, ending its application. There are also entries for moving the window to another workspace.

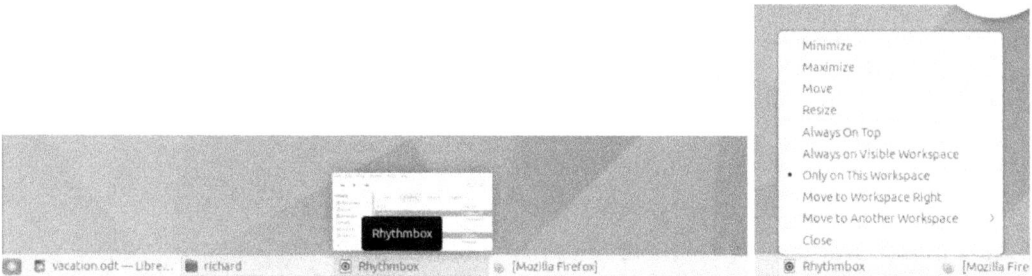

Figure 10-17: Window List applet

The Window List applet is represented by a small bar at the beginning of the window list applet. To configure the Window List applet, right-click on this area and select the Preferences entry to open the Window List Preferences dialog (see Figure 10-18). Here, you can set features such as whether to group windows on the panel, whether to show all open windows or those from just the current workspace, and which workspace to restore windows to.

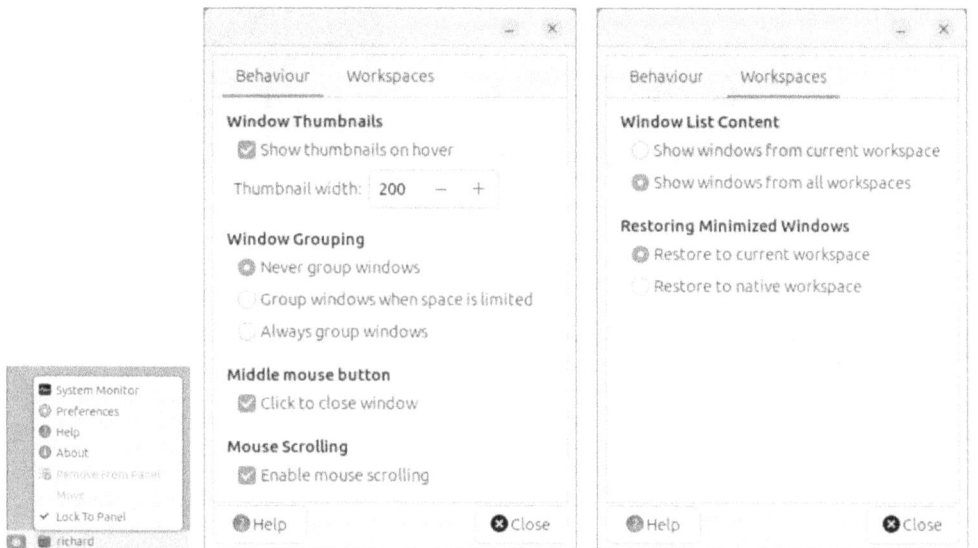

Figure 10-18: Window List Preferences

If you choose to group windows, then common windows are grouped under a button that will expand like a menu, listing each window in that group. For example, all open terminal windows would be grouped under a single button, which when clicked would pop up a list of their buttons. The button shows the number of open windows. You can also choose to group only if there is not enough space on the Window List applet to display a separate button for each window.

Workspace Switcher

The Workspace Switcher applet, located on the right side of the bottom panel, lets you switch to different virtual desktops (see Figure 10-19 You can add the Workspace Switcher to any panel by selecting it from that panel's Add To dialog. The Workspace Switcher shows your entire virtual desktop as separate rectangles listed next to each other. Open windows show up as small rectangles in these squares. You can move any window from one virtual desktop to another by clicking and dragging its image in the Workspace Switcher from one workspace to another.

Figure 10-19: Workspace switcher, one row and two rows

In addition to the Workspace Switcher, you can use the scroll button on your mouse, or the Ctrl-Alt-arrow keys to move from one workspace to another. When you use the Ctrl-Alt-arrow keys, the right and left arrows move you through a row, and the up and down keys move you from one row to another. A small workspace bar appears at the center of the screen, highlighting the current workspace and displaying its name (see Figure 10-20).

Figure 10-20: Switching workspaces, Ctrl-Alt-*arrow*

To configure the Workspace Switcher, right-click on the applet to display a menu, and then select Preferences to display the Workspace Switcher Preferences dialog box (see Figure 10-21). Here, you can select the number of workspaces and name them. The default is four. You can also choose the number of rows for the workspace and whether to show their names.

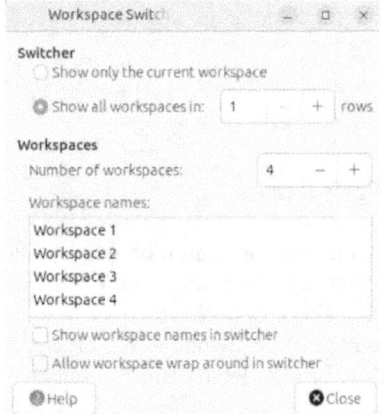

Figure 10-21: Workspace Switcher Preferences

MATE Panel Layouts

Ubuntu MATE provides a variety of panel layouts to choose from. You can choose the panel layout using the Panel tab on the MATE Tweak dialog (Preferences menu) (see Figure 10-22). Available layouts include Familiar (the default), Contemporary, Cupertino, Mutiny, Pantheon, Redmond, and Traditional. For a detailed description, check the online MATE Desktop Guide at:

https://guide.ubuntu-mate.org/#personalization-panel-layouts

You can activate certain features for a panel, as well as add applets to the panel, and then save it as your own, using the "Save as" button.

The Familiar layout is the default Ubuntu MATE layout with two panels, a top and bottom one. It uses the Brisk menu. The Traditional panel layout also has two panels, but use a Classic menu at the top. The Traditional layout is the one used in previous releases of Ubuntu MATE.

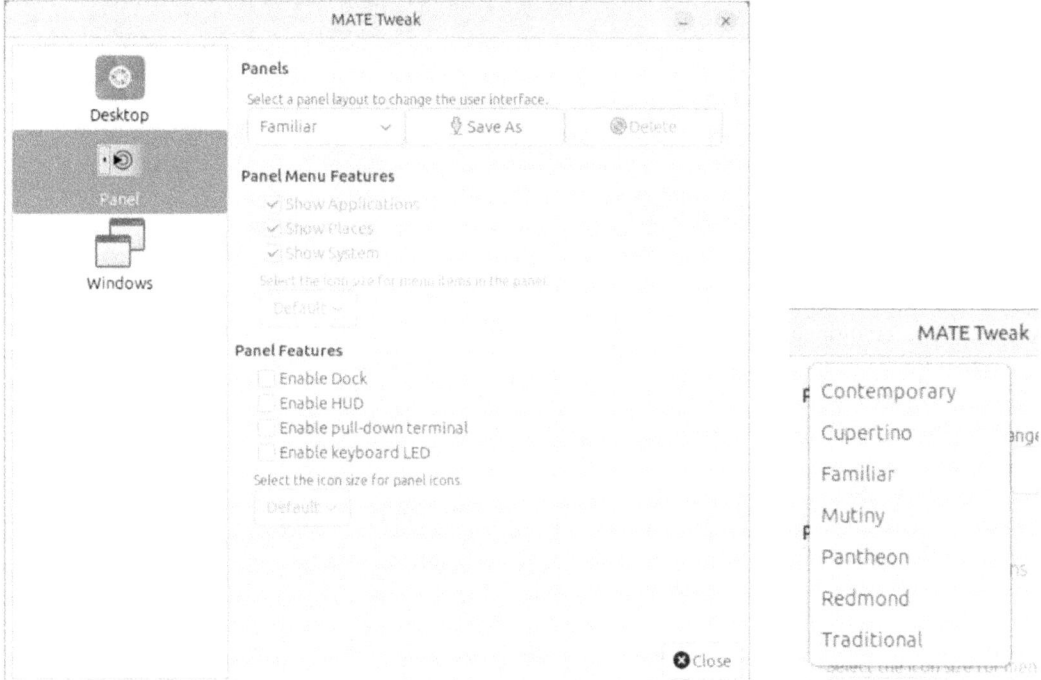

Figure 10-22: MATE Tweaks, Panel tab

The Cupertino, Pantheon, and Mutiny panel layouts all use the MATE Plank dock, which works similar to the dock on the MAC OS. Cupertino and Mutiny use the Brisk menu with a dash layout, whereas most of the others use the Brisk menu.

The Contemporary and Cupertino layouts feature an application menu on the top panel. For the currently active window, that application's menus are displayed on the top panel.

Familiar Layout

The Familiar layout is the default Ubuntu MATE layout, with two panels, top and bottom. It uses the Brisk menu, located at the left side of the top menu. (see Figure 10-23) .

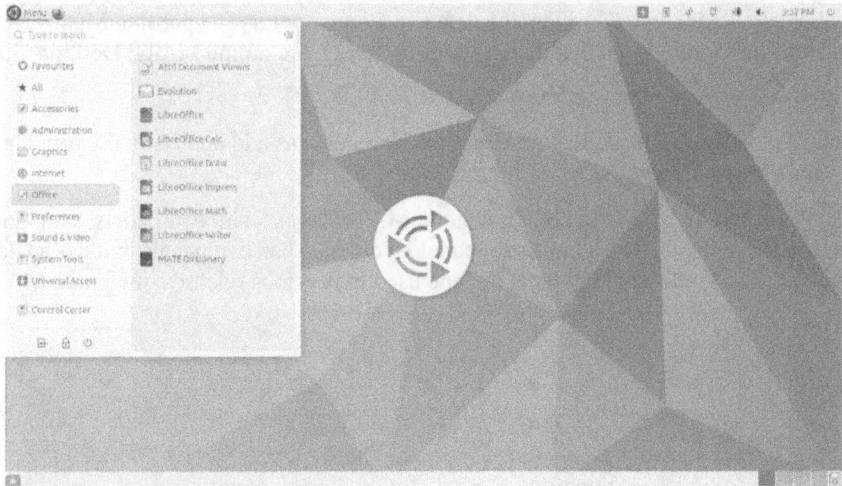

Figure 10-23: Familiar Panel Layout

Traditional Layout

The Traditional layout implements a top and bottom panel, but uses the Classic menu instead of the Brisk menu (see Figure 10-24). The Classic menu is the menu used in previous releases. On the Traditional panel layout you can use the MATE Tweak Panel tab to choose whether to show applications, places, or system menus. You can also set the icon size for icons in the menus.

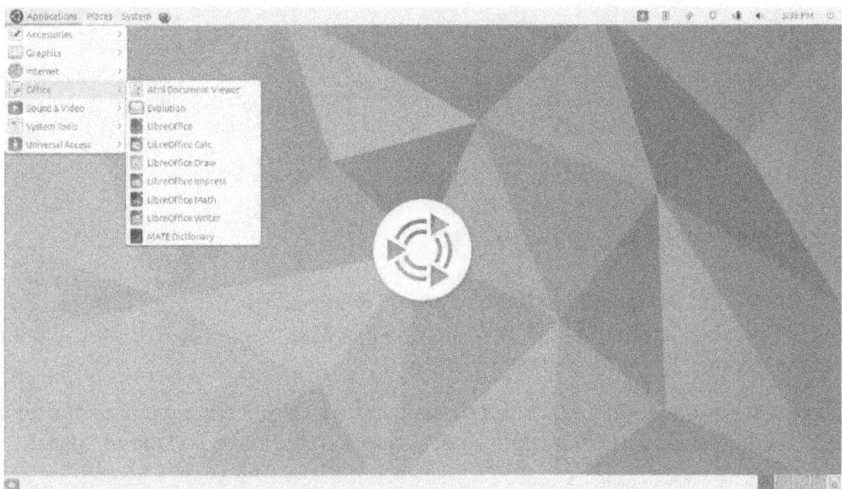

Figure 10-24: Traditional Panel Layout

Redmond Layout

The Redmond layout uses a standard Brisk menu but only one bottom panel. The Brisk menu is on the left side of the bottom panel (see Figure 10-25).

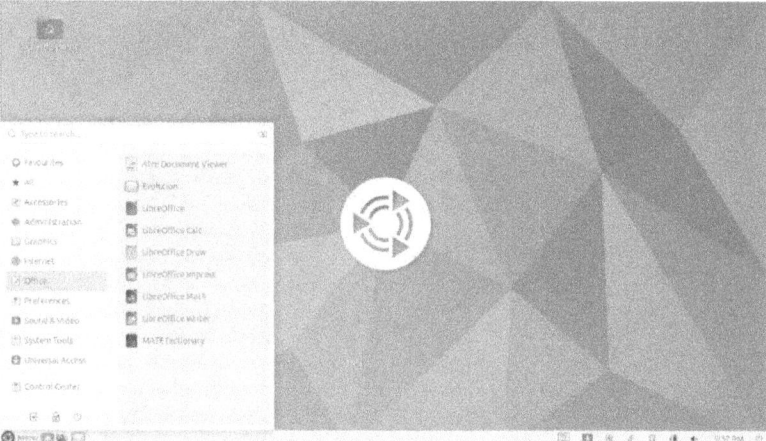

Figure 10-25: Redmond Panel Layout

Cupertino Layout

The Cupertino layout is modeled on the MAC OS and features the MATE Plank dock in place of the bottom panel (see Figure 10-26). The top panel uses the Brisk menu with the dash layout, using the entire screen and icons for menu entries. The top panel also implements an application menu. For the currently active window, its application menus are displayed on the top menu. Clicking on the desktop, displays a Desktop menu for desktop and system settings, a File menu of recently accessed files, and menus for the contents of the Documents, Music, Pictures, and Video folders.

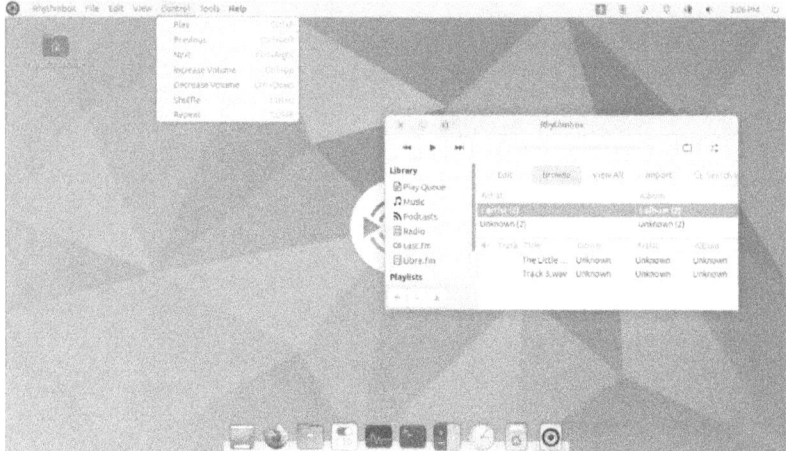

Figure 10-26: Cupertino Panel Layout

Mutiny Layout

The Mutiny layout is also modeled on the MAC OS and features the MATE Plank dock on the left side of the screen (see Figure 10-27). The top panel uses the Brisk menu with the dash layout, using the entire screen and icons for menu entries.

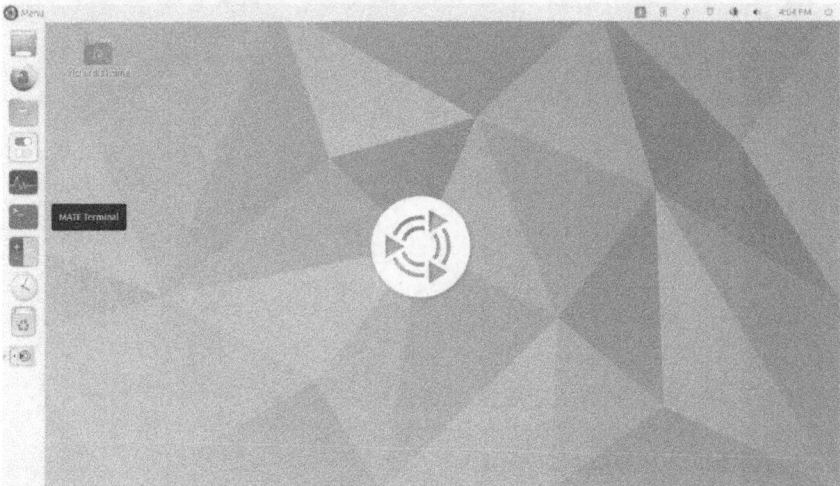

Figure 10-27: Mutiny Panel Layout

Pantheon Layout

The Pantheon layout uses a standard Brisk menu, but features the MATE Plank dock in place of the bottom panel (see Figure 10-28).

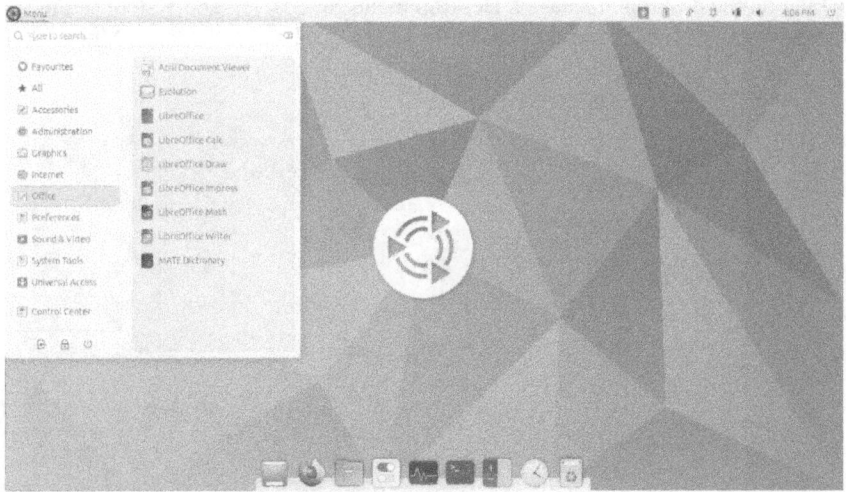

Figure 10-28: Pantheon Panel Layout

Contemporary Layout

The Contemporary layout uses a standard Brisk menu and a top and bottom panel (see Figure 10-29). The top panel also implements an application menu, like the Cupertino layout.

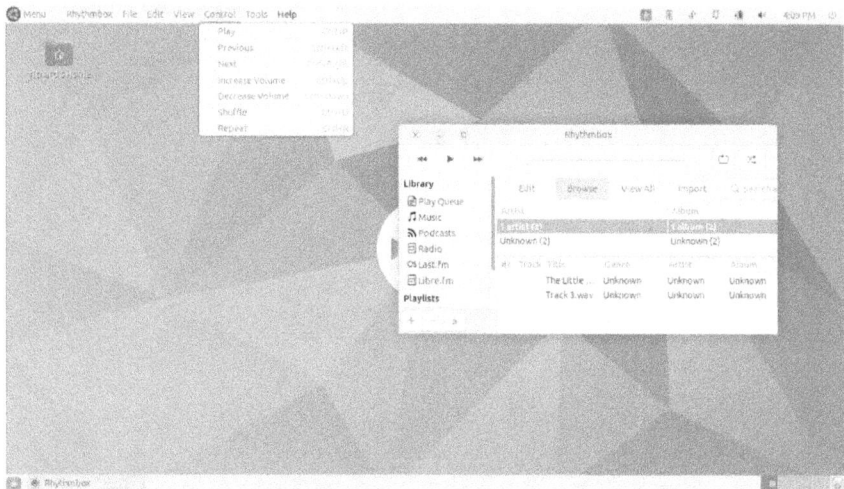

Figure 10-29: Contemporary Panel Layout

MATE Panel Menus

Several different types of menus are available for Ubuntu MATE. These are incorporated into the different panel layouts. The menus include Brisk menu on the top panel (Familiar, Contemporary, and Pantheon), Brisk menu on the bottom panel (Redmond), Classic and Compact menus (Traditional), and the Brisk menu with dash layout (Mutiny and Cupertino). You can add any of these menus to a panel by using the Add to Panel dialog. The Cupertino and Pantheon layouts will also include the MATE Dock, which operates much like the dock on Apple systems.

You can edit any of the menus using the Main Menu editor, with which you can add and remove applications from the menus, create new menus, and add or remove submenus (see Figure 10-30). You can open the editor by right-clicking on the menu button on the top bar and choosing "Edit Menus" from the pop-up menu. Menus are listed to left and items shown in a selected menu are check marked on the right. Click a checkmark to no longer display an entry. Click an empty checkbox to add a menu item.

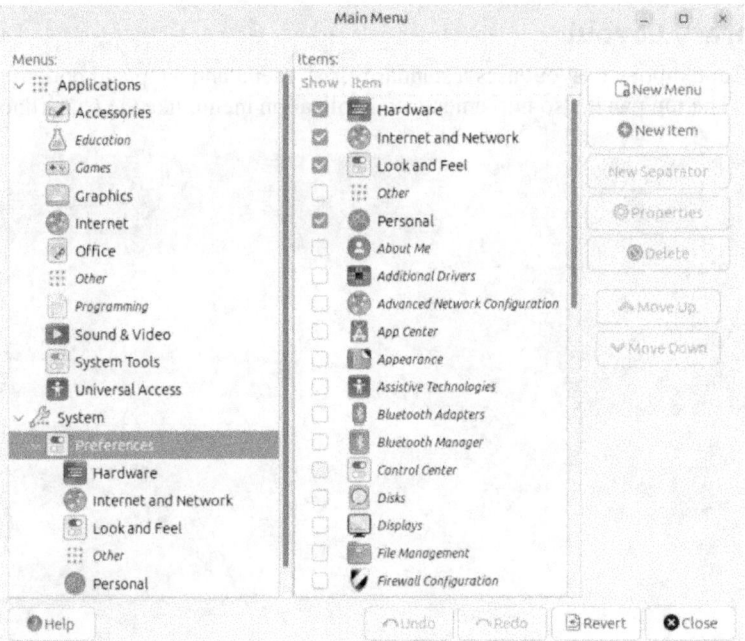

Figure 10-30: Main Menu Editor

Brisk Menu

Ubuntu MATE uses the Brisk menu on the top panel for the Familiar, Contemporary, Cupertino, and Pantheon panel layouts. On the Redmond layout the Brisk menu is placed on the single bottom panel. The Familiar panel layout is the default. Application categories are lists to the left and applications in a selected category are shown on the right (see Figure 10-31). The All category lists all the applications. The Favorites category lists only those application you have selected as your favorites. You can also access the Control Center and Universal Access dialog directly. Buttons at the bottom of the menu let you logout, lock, or shut down (power button) your system. At the top of the menu is a search box where you can search directly for an application. The search is dynamic, reducing the selection of found applications as you add more characters to the search pattern. If you right-click on an application, a menu is displayed with "Pin to favorites menu" and "Pin to desktop" options.

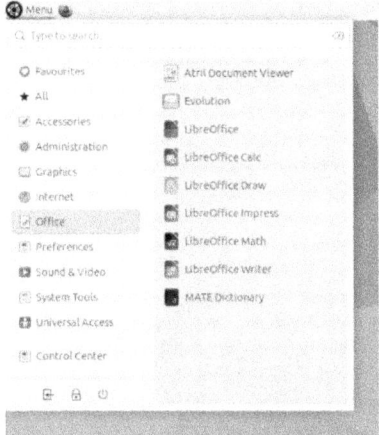

Figure 10-31: Brisk Menu - Applications

On the Redmond panel layout there is only one panel on the bottom edge of the screen. The Brisk menu is located on the left side of the panel (see Figure 10-32).

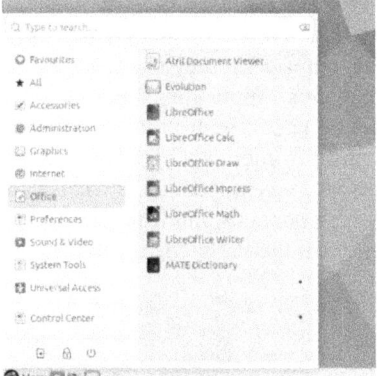

Figure 10-32: Brisk Menu - Redmond panel layout

Brisk Menu with dash layout

The Cupertino and Mutiny panel layouts (MATE-Tweak) use the Brisk Menu with a dash layout. Like GNOME, it displays an overview of icons for applications in different categories. Categories are listed at the top, along with a search box for locating applications (see Figure 10-33).

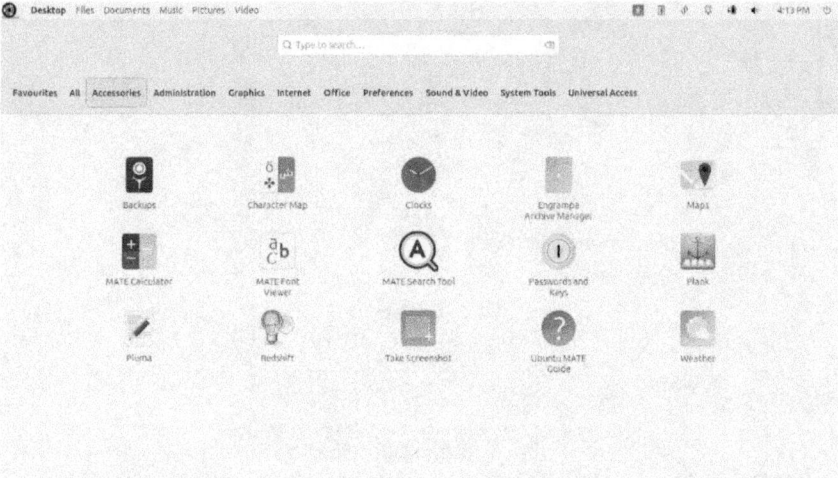

Figure 10-33: Brisk Menu with dash layout, Cupertino panel layout

Classic and Compact Menus

Ubuntu MATE uses the Classic Menu menu on the top panel for the Traditional panel layouts. It was the default panel layout used in previous release of Ubuntu MATE. The Classic Menu is a menubar that has three menus: Applications, Places, and System (See Figure 10-34). From the Applications menu, you can access your installed software applications. They are arranged by category with submenus for Internet, Graphics, Office, Sound & Video, and Accessories. The Places menu lets you access locations such as your home folder and removable devices. On the System menu you can access Administration tools from the Administration submenu, and Preferences dialogs from the Preferences submenu.

Figure 10-34: Classic Menu

The Compact menu combines the Classic menu into one menu, with the System and Places menus as submenus (see Figure 10-35). You can install the Compact menu on any panel using the "Add to Panel" dialog.

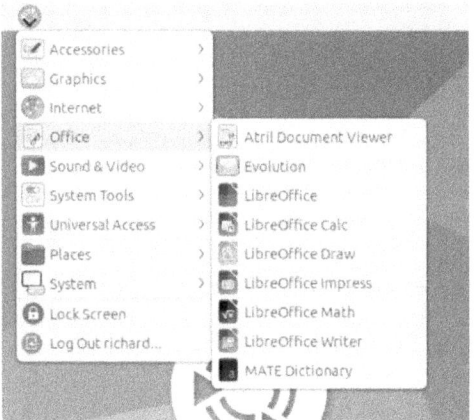

Figure 10-35: Compact Menu

Plank Applet (dock)

The Plank applet sets up a dock on the panel for applications. It initially shows a set of default applications (see Figure 10-36). As you open additional applications, icons for them appear on the panel (see Figure 10-37). In this way, the dock operates like the window list. If you minimize an application, you can maximize it again by clicking its icon. When the application closes, the icon disappears. Moving your mouse over an icon in the dock enlarges it and displays the name of the application. To have an application remain on the dock, you can right-click on it to display its menu and choose the "Keep in Dock" entry (see Figure 10-38). In effect, with the icons that remain, you can use the dock as a launcher for favorite applications. The menu also allows you to close added applications and well as perform some basic operations.

Figure 10-36: MATE Plank applet (dock) with default applications

Figure 10-37: MATE Plank on panel layout with additional applications

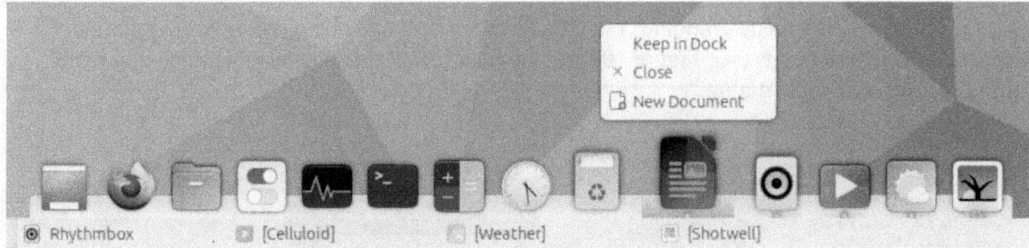

Figure 10-38: MATE Plank on panel layout docklet menu

You can set up the dock on any of the panel layouts by clicking the "Enable Dock" option in the MATE Tweaks Panel tab's Panel Features section (see Figure 10-39). A dock is set up at the bottom of the screen that operates more like docks in other operating systems. A set of favorite application docklets is already displayed. In the Cupertino, Pantheon, and Mutiny panel layouts, the "Enable Dock" option is selected by default. On the Mutiny panel layout the dock is placed on the left edge of the screen.

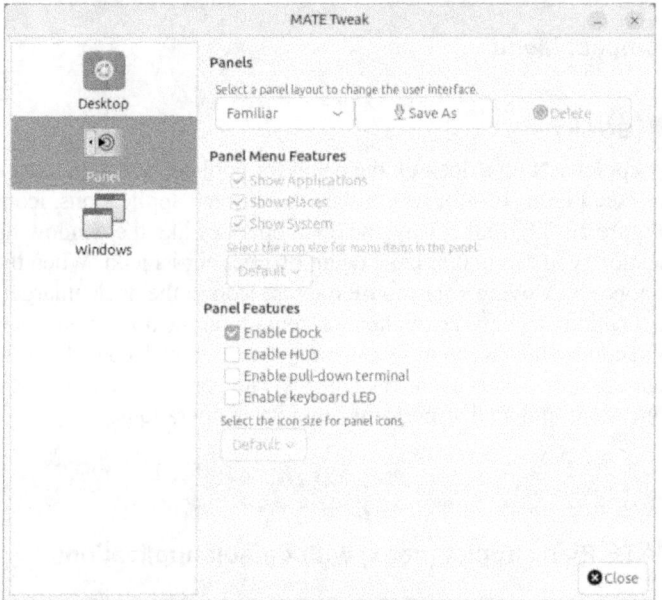

Figure 10-39: MATE Dock enabled on MATE Tweaks

You use the Plank Preferences dialog to configure your dock. It is accessible from the Preferences menu and from the Control Center | Look and Feel section as Plank Preferences. On the Plank Preferences dialog you configure the appearance, behavior, and the selection of default docklets. There are three tab: Appearance, Behavior, and Docklets. The Appearance tab lets you set the position and alignment of the dock, along with its theme (see Figure 10-40). The default theme is Yaru-light. You can position the dock on any edge of the screen: top, bottom, left, or right. The alignment can be at the center (the default), at the left of the start (left side or top), the end (right side or bottom) or fill (expands to entire edge. For fill you can align the docklets to the center, start, or end of the dock. You can also change the size of your icons making them larger or smaller. Icon zoom, where the icons enlarge when you pass your mouse over them, can be turned off. If you have multiple monitors you can choose which one to display the dock on.

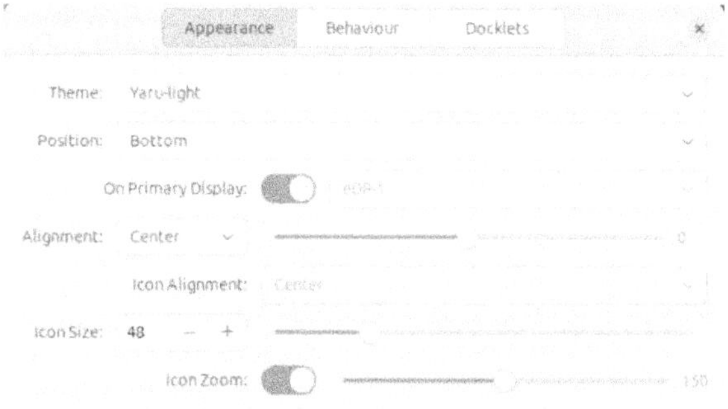

Figure 10-40: MATE Plank Preferences - Appearance

On the Behavior tab you can choose different ways to hide the dock, such as autohide when the dock is not used, or window dodge when a window covers it (see Figure 10-41). If you only want to show icons pinned to the dock, you can turn off the Show Unpinned option. To prevent icons from being removed, you can turn off the Lock Icons option. If you want to show only those icons open on a specific workspace, you can turn on the "Restrict to Workspace" option. Otherwise applications opened on one workspace are also displayed as icons in the docks shown on other workspaces.

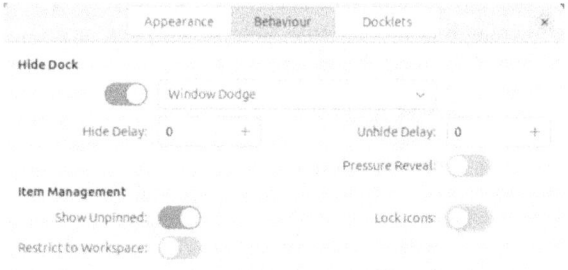

Figure 10-41: MATE Plank Preferences - Behavior

On the Docklets tab you have docklets you can add to your dock (see Figure 10-42). Shown on this tab are the docklets available for your docks. The Applications docklet manages the application icons added to the dock when you open an application or window. Other docklets you can add include the clock, battery, trash, and CPU monitor. To add one, just drag it to the dock. To remove one, just drag it from the dock. These docklets have no menu with a removal option.

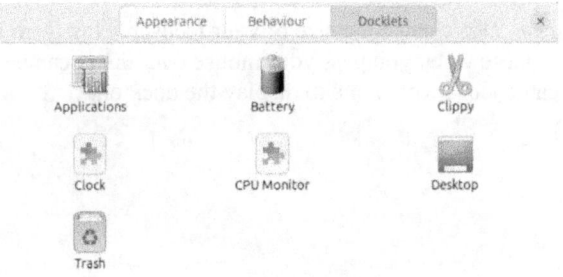

Figure 10-42: MATE Plank Preferences - Docklets

MATE Panel

The panel is the main component of the MATE desktop. Through it, you can start your applications, run applets, and access desktop areas. You can think of the MATE panel as a type of tool you can use on your desktop. You can have several MATE panels displayed on your desktop, each with applets and menus you have placed in them. In this respect, MATE is flexible, enabling you to configure your panels any way you want. The MATE panel works the same as the GNOME 2 panel. You can easily add applets to the panel, along with application launchers.

Ubuntu MATE uses the traditional GNOME 2 top and bottom panels by default, though you can add more. The top panel holds applets for the main menu (MATE Brisk menu), a launcher for the Firefox Web browser, and the indicator applet with several system buttons (see Figure 10-43). The indicator applet display buttons for Bluetooth, NetworkManager, notifications, the power manager, volume control, the clock, and shutdown.

Figure 10-43: MATE Top Panel

The bottom panel has applets for Show Desktop and the window list on the left, and the workspace switcher and the Trash on the right (see Figure 10-44).

Figure 10-44: MATE Panel

Panel configuration tasks such as adding applications, selecting applets, setting up menus, and creating new panels are handled from the Panel pop-up menu (see Figure 10-45). Right-click anywhere on the empty space of your panel to display a menu with entries for Properties, New Panel, Add To Panel, Reset Panel, and Delete This Panel, along with Help and About entries. New Panel lets you create other panels. Add To Panel lets you add items to the panel such as application launchers, applets for simple tasks like the Workspace Switcher, and menus like the MATE brisk or classic menus. The Reset Panel entry restores the panel to its desktop default state, removing any changes you made to it such as added applets, applications, or folders. The Properties entry will display a dialog for configuring the features for that panel, like the position of the panel and its hiding capabilities.

To add a new panel, select the New Panel entry in the Panel pop-up menu. A new expanded panel is automatically created and displayed at the top of your screen. You can then use the panel's Properties dialog to set different display and background features.

Figure 10-45: MATE Panel pop-up menu

Panel Properties

To configure individual panels, you use the Panel Properties dialog (see Figure 10-46). To display this dialog, you right-click a panel and select the Properties entry in the pop-up menu. For individual panels, you can set general configuration features and the background. The Panel Properties dialog displays two tabs, General and Background.

Displaying Panels

On the General tab of a panel's Properties dialog, you determine how you want the panel displayed. Here you have options for orientation, size, and whether to expand, auto-hide, or display hide buttons. The Orientation entry lets you select which side of the screen you want the panel placed on. You can then choose whether you want a panel expanded or not. An expanded panel will fill the edges of the screen, whereas a non-expanded panel is sized to the number of items in the panel and shows handles at each end. Expanded panels will remain fixed to the edge of the screen, whereas unexpanded panels can be moved.

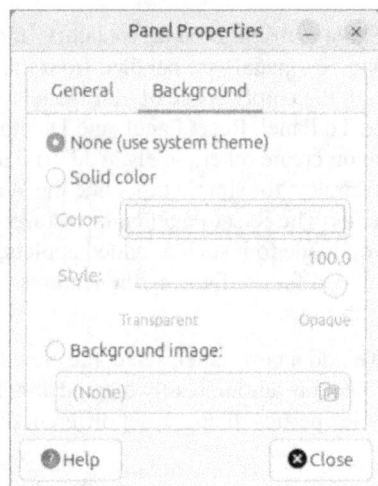

Figure 10-46: MATE Panel Properties

Moving and Hiding Expanded Panels

Expanded panels can be positioned at any edge of your screen. You can move expanded panels from one edge of a screen to another by selecting an edge from the Orientation menu on the Panel Properties General tab. If a panel is already there, the new one will stack on top of the current one. You cannot move unexpanded panels in this way. You can hide expanded panels either automatically or manually. These are features specified in the panel properties General box as the Autohide and "Show hide buttons" options. To automatically hide panels, select the Autohide feature. The panel will be hidden. To display the panel, move your mouse to the edge where the panel is located.

If you want to hide a panel manually, select the "Show hide buttons" option. Two hide buttons showing arrows will be displayed at either end of the panel. You can further choose whether to have these buttons display arrows or not (displaying arrows is the default). You can then hide the panel at any time by clicking either of the hide buttons located on each end of the panel. The arrows show the direction in which the panel will hide.

Unexpanded Panels: Movable and Fixed

Whereas an expanded panel is always located at the edge of the screen, an unexpanded panel is movable. It can be located at the edge of a screen, working like a shrunken version of an expanded panel, or you can move it to any place on your desktop, just as you would an icon.

An unexpanded panel will shrink to the number of its components, showing handles at either end (on the default Ambient-MATE theme for Ubuntu MATE, the handles show up as simply blank areas). You can then move the panel by dragging its handles. To access the panel menu with its properties entry, right-click either of its handles.

To fix an unexpanded panel at its current position, select the "Show hide buttons" option on the General tab of the panel Properties dialog. This will replace the handles with hide buttons and make the panel fixed. Clicking a Hide button will hide the panel to the edge of the screen, just as with expanded panels. If another expanded panel is already located on that edge, the button for a hidden unexpanded panel will be on top of it. The Autohide feature will also work for unexpanded panels placed at the edge of a screen.

If you want to fix an unexpanded panel to the edge of a screen, make sure it is placed at the edge you want, and then set its "Show hide buttons" option.

Panel Background

With a panel's Background tab on its Panel Properties dialog, you can change the panel's background color or image. For a color background, click the "Solid color" option, and then click the Color button to display a color selection window where you can choose a color from a color graph or a list of color boxes, or you can enter its number. Once your color is selected, you can use the Style slide bar to make it more transparent or opaque. To use an image instead of a color, select the "Background image" option and use the browse button to locate the image file you want. For an image, you can also drag and drop an image file from the file manager to the panel. That image then becomes the background image for the panel.

Panel Objects

A panel can contain several different types of objects. These include menus, launchers, applets, drawers, and special objects.

Menus   A panel menu has launchers that are buttons used to start an application or execute a command.

Launchers   You can select any application entry in the main menu and drag it to the panel, creating a launcher for it on the panel.

Applets   An applet is a small application designed to run within the panel. The Workspace Switcher showing the different desktops is an example of an applet.

Drawers   A drawer is an extension of the panel that can be opened or closed. You can think of a drawer as a shrinkable part of the panel. You can add anything to it that you can to a regular panel, including applets, menus, and even other drawers.

Special objects   These are used for special tasks not supported by other panel objects. For example, the Logout and Lock Screen buttons are special objects.

Moving, Removing, and Locking Objects

To move any object within the panel, right-click it and choose the Move entry. You can move it either to a different place on the same panel or to a different panel. For launchers, you can just drag the object directly where you want it to be. To remove an object from the panel, right-click it to display a pop-up menu for it, and then choose the "Remove From Panel" entry. To prevent an object from being moved or removed, you set its lock feature. Right-click the object and select the "Lock To Panel" entry. For a locked object, a checkmark appears before the "Lock to Panel" entry. To later allow it to be moved, you first have to unlock the object, Right-click it and select "Lock to Panel" to remove the checkmark and making the Move entry active.

Adding Objects

To add an object to a panel, select the object from the panel's "Add to Panel" dialog (see Figure 10-47). To display the Add To Panel dialog, right-click on the panel and select the "Add to Panel" entry. The "Add to Panel" dialog displays a lengthy list of common objects, such as the Classic Menu, Log Out, and Clock. For Application applets, you can click on the Applications Launcher entry and click the Add button to list all your installed applications. Launchers can also be added to a panel by just dragging them directly. Launchers include applications, folders, and files. The Custom Application Launcher lets you create a custom launcher, choosing an application or script.

Application Launchers

To add an application that already has an application launcher to a panel drag the application launcher to the panel. This will automatically create a copy of the launcher for use on that panel. Launchers may be menu items or desktop icons. All the entries in the main menu are application launchers. To add an application from the menu, just select it and drag it to the panel. For example, should you use the Pluma text editor frequently and want to add its icon to the panel, click and drag the Pluma menu entry in the Accessories menu to the panel. The Pluma text editor icon will appear in your panel. For any menu item, you can also go to its entry and right-click it, and then select the "Add to panel" entry. An application launcher for that application is then added to the panel. You can also drag any desktop application icon to a panel to add a copy of it to that panel.

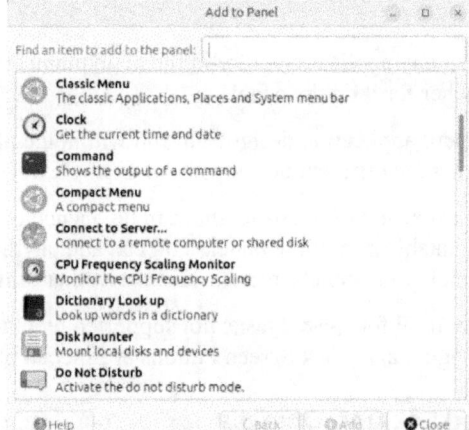

Figure 10-47: MATE Panel "Add to Panel" dialog for panel applets

Also, as previously noted, you can open the "Add to Panel" dialog, and then choose the Application Launcher entry and click the Add button. This will display a dialog with a listing of all the Application menu entries along with Preferences and Administration menus, expandable to their items. Just find the application you want added, select it, and click the Add button.

Adding Drawers

You can also group applications under a Drawer icon. Clicking the Drawer icon displays a list of the different application icons you can then select. To add a drawer to your panel, right-click the panel and select the "Add to panel" entry to display the "Add to Panel" dialog. From that list select the Drawer entry. This will create a drawer on your panel. You can then drag any items from desktop, menus, or windows (folders or launchers) to the drawer icon on the panel to have them listed in the drawer.

You can also add applets and applications to a drawer using the "Add to Drawer" dialog. Right-click on the drawer and choose the "Add to Drawer" entry to open the dialog. Then click the applet you want added to the drawer. To add applications, select the Applications Launcher entry and click Add to list your application menu categories, which are expandable to list applications. You can add an entire menu to the drawer by choosing the application category and clicking the Add button.

Adding Menus

A menu differs from a drawer in that a drawer holds application icons instead of menu entries. You can add application menus to your panel, much as you add drawers. To add an application menu to your panel, open the "Add to Panel" dialog and select the Application Launcher entry, clicking Forward to open the list of Application categories. Select the category you want, and click the Add button. That menu category with all its application items is added to your panel as a menu.

Adding Folders and Files

You can also add files and folders to a panel. For folders, click and drag the folder icon from the file manager window to your panel. Whenever you click this folder button, a file manager window opens, displaying that folder. You can also add folders to any drawer on your panel. To add a file, also drag it directly to the panel. To add a file (except for images, which, instead, change the background of the panel to that image), click and drag the file to the panel or drawer. When you click on the file icon, the file opens with its application.

Adding Applets

Applets are small programs that perform tasks within the panel. To add an applet, right-click the panel and select "Add to Panel" from the pop-up menu. This displays the "Add To Panel" dialog listing common applets along with other types of objects, such as launchers. Select the one you want. For example, to add the clock to your panel, select Clock. Once added, the applet will show up in the panel. If you want to remove an applet, right-click on the applet in the panel and select the "Remove From Panel" entry. To configure an applet, right-click on the applet and select the Preferences entry.

MATE features a number of helpful applets. Some applets monitor your system, such as the Battery Charge Monitor, which checks the battery in laptops, and System Monitor, which shows a graph indicating your current CPU and memory use.

Caja File Manager

The Caja file manager supports the standard features for copying, removing, and deleting items as well as setting permissions and displaying items. The program name for the file manager is **caja**. You can enhance Caja using extensions such as "Open terminal" to open the current folder in a new terminal window, and Engrampa that allows you to create (compress) and extract archives, including epub, arc, and rar files. Several extensions are already installed and enabled by default. They will display entries in appropriate menus. Extensions are enabled on the Extension tab of the File Management Preferences dialog (Edit | Preferences). To add more extension, use the Software Manager to install the caja extension packages. Extension packages have the prefix **caja-**, such as **caja-share**, **caja-dropbox**, and **caja-wallpaper**.

Home Folder Sub-folders and Bookmarks

Like Ubuntu, MATE uses the Common User Directory Structure (xdg-user-dirs at **https://freedesktop.org**) to set up sub-folders in the user home folder. Folders will include **Documents**, **Music**, **Pictures**, **Downloads**, and **Videos**. These localized user folders are used as defaults by many desktop applications. Users can change their folder names or place them within each other using the file browser. For example, Music can be moved into **Documents**, **Documents/Music**. Local configuration is held in the **.config/user-dirs.dirs** file. System-wide defaults are set up in the **/etc/xdg/user-dirs.defaults** file.

The folders are also default bookmarks. You can access a bookmarked folder directly from the Caja window side pane. You can also add your own bookmarks for folders by opening the folder and choosing "Add Bookmark" from the Bookmarks menu. Your folder will appear in the Bookmarks section of the Caja side pane (Places) and on the Bookmarks menu. Use the Edit Bookmarks dialog to remove bookmarks. Here you can remove a bookmark or change is name and location.

File Manager Windows

When you click your home folder icon on the desktop, a file manager window opens showing your home folder. The file manager window displays several components, including a menubar, a main toolbar, and a side pane (see Figure 10-48). The side pane works like the sidebar in the Nautilus (Ubuntu) file manager, but with a menu, like the file manager in GNOME 2. The file manager window's main pane (to the right) displays the icons or listing of files and sub-folders in the opened folder. When you select a file and folder, the status bar at the bottom of the window displays the name of the file or folder selected, and for files the size, and for folders the number of items contained. The status bar also displays the remaining free space on the current file system.

Chapter 10: Ubuntu MATE   **441**

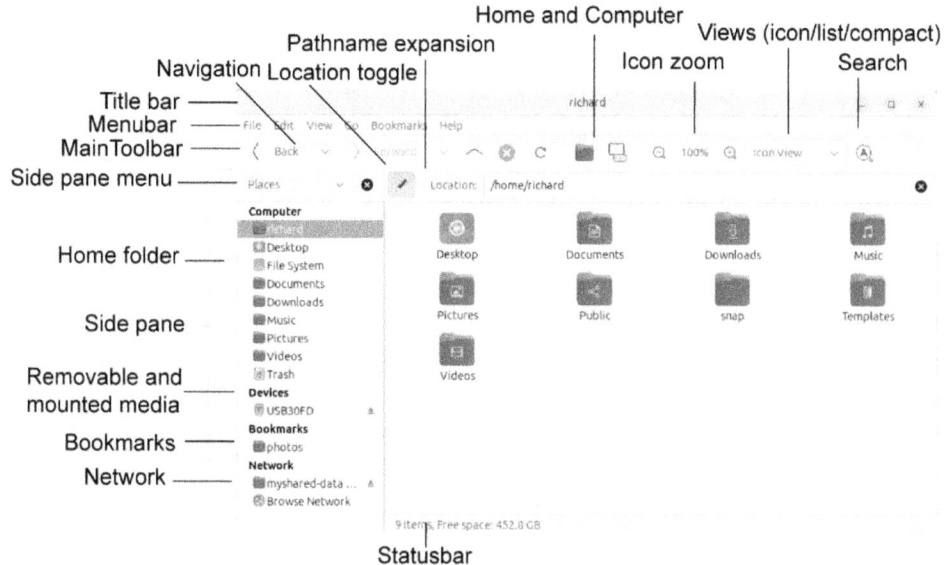

Figure 10-48: Caja file manager with side pane

Note: Caja works as an operational FTP browser. You can use the Connect to Server entry on the File menu to open a "Connect to Server" dialog, where you can enter the address for the FTP site.

When you open a new folder, the same window is used to display it, and you can use the Forward and Back buttons to move through previously opened folders (top left on the main toolbar) (see Figure 10-49). Down triangles to the right of the Back and Forward buttons display menus of previously accessed folders, which you can use to access a previous folder directly. There is also an up arrow to move to the parent folder, and a Home folder button to move directly to your home folder. The Computer button displays the computer window showing your file systems and attached devices. You can also access these operations from the file manager's Go menu (see Table 10-2). In addition there are reload and stop reload buttons to refresh the folder listing, should the list of files or folders change.

Figure 10-49: Caja navigation buttons: back, forward, parent, home, computer

As you open sub-folders, the main toolbar displays buttons for your current folder and its parent folders. You can click on a folder button to move to it directly. Initially, the button shows a path of sub-folders from your home folder. Clicking on the small triangle arrow to the left expands the path to the top level, from the root folder (the hard disk icon).

Menu Item	Description
Open Parent	Move to the parent folder
Back	Move to the previous folder viewed in the file manager window
Forward	Move to the next folder viewed in the file manager window
Paste	Paste files that you have copied or cut, letting you move or copy files between folders, or make duplicates.
Same Location as Other Pane	If you have two panes open on the window, you can make both panes view the same folder
Home Folder	Move to the Home folder
Computer	Move to the Computer folder, showing icons for your devices
Templates	Move to the Templates folder
Trash	Open the trash folder to see deleted files and folders, which can be restored.
Network	Move to the network folder showing connected systems on your network and open remote folders.
Location	Open the location navigation box for entering the path name of a file or folder
Search for Files	Search for files and folders using the file manager window

Table 10-2: File Manager Go Menu

You can also display a location URL text box instead of buttons, where you can enter the location of a folder, either on your system or on a remote system. To display the location text box, press **Ctrl-l**, or from the Go menu select Location, or click the Location toggle (pencil icon) at the beginning of the location path on the main toolbar (see Figure 10-50). These access methods operate as toggles that move you a back and forth from the location text box to the button path.

Figure 10-50: Caja locations: unexpanded, expanded, and location path

The File menu has entries for opening a new tab (Ctrl-t), opening a new file manager window (Ctrl-n), creating a new folder (Shift-Ctrl-n), connecting to a remote FTP server, and displaying the properties of the current folder (Alt-Return). Most have corresponding keys (see Table 10-3).

Menu Item	Description
New Tab	Creates a new tab.
New Window	Open a new file manager window
Create Folder	Creates a new subfolder in the folder.
Create Document	Creates a text document.
Connect to server	Connect to an FTP server using the file manager
Open in Terminal	Open the current folder in a new terminal window (Open Terminal extension)
Properties	Properties for the current open folder
Empty Trash	Empty the trash folder
Close All Windows	Close all file manage windows
Close	Close the file manager window.
Open With	When a file is selected the Open With item is displayed showing possible applications to open the file with
Open	When a folder is selected the Open item is displayed showing also the "Open in New Tab" and "Open in New Window" items, along with the Open With submenu.

Table 10-3: File Manager File Menu

File Manager Side Pane

The file manager side pane has a menu from which you can choose to display places (Places), the tree view of the file system (Tree), information on the current or selected folder or file (Information), the history of previously opened folders for that login session (History), notes (Notes), and emblems you can place on a file or folder (Emblems).

The default for the side pane is the Places view, which displays sections for Computer, Devices, Bookmarks, and Network items showing your file systems and default home folder sub-folders (see Figure 10-51). You can choose to display or hide the side pane by selecting the "Side Pane" entry in the View menu, or by clicking the close button on the right side of the side pane menu. You can also use F9 to toggle the side pane on and off.

444 Part 3: Desktops

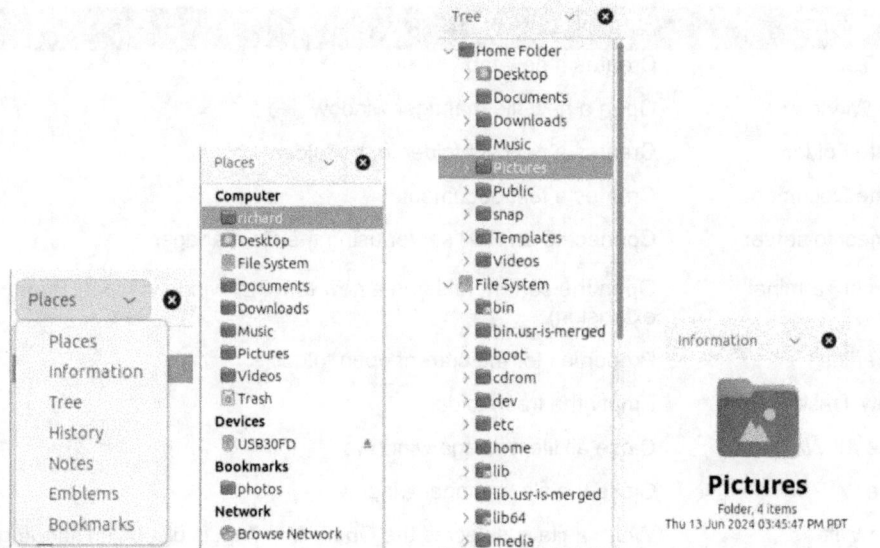

Figure 10-51: File manager side pane menu and views

Selecting the File System entry in the side pane places you at the top of the file system, letting you move to any accessible part of it. In the Computer section, you can search your default folders, such as Documents and Pictures. Should you bookmark a folder (Bookmarks menu, "Add Bookmark" entry (Ctrl-d)), a Bookmark section appears on the side pane with the bookmark. To remove or rename a bookmark, right-click on its entry in the side pane and choose Remove or Rename from the pop-up menu (see Figure 10-52). The bookmark name changes, but not the original folder name.

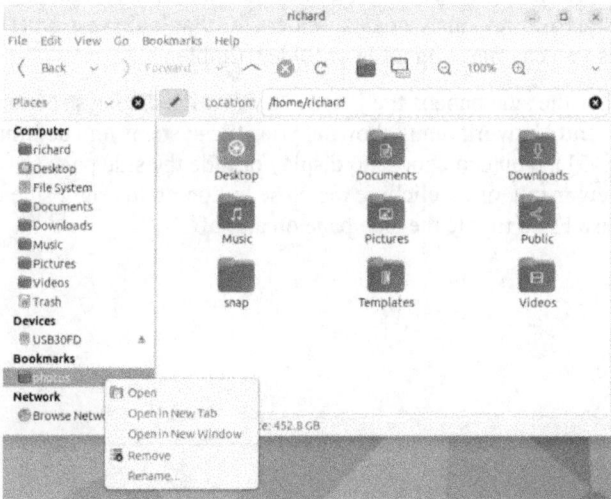

Figure 10-52: File manager side pane with bookmarks menu

Tabs

The Caja file manager supports tabs with which you can open up several folders in the same file manager window. To open a tab, select New Tab from the File menu or press **Ctrl-t**. A tab bar appears with tab buttons for each tab, displaying the name of the folder open, and an **x** close button (see Figure 10-53). You can re-arrange tabs by clicking and dragging their tabs to the right or left. You can also use the Ctrl-PageUp and Ctrl-PageDown keys to move from one tab to another. Use the Shift-Ctrl-PageUp and Shift-Ctrl-PageDown keys to rearrange the tabs. To close a tab, click its close **x** button on the right side of the tab.

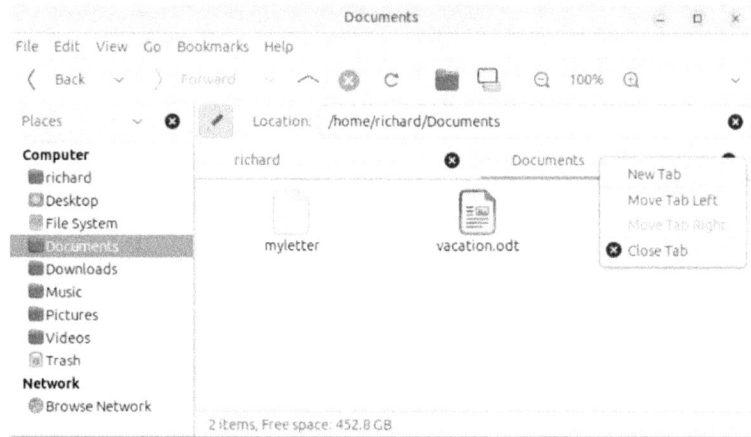

Figure 10-53: File manager window with tabs

Displaying Files and Folders

You can view a folder's contents as icons, a compact list, or as a detailed list, which you can choose from the menu on the right side of the main toolbar: icon, list, and compact views (see Figure 10-54).

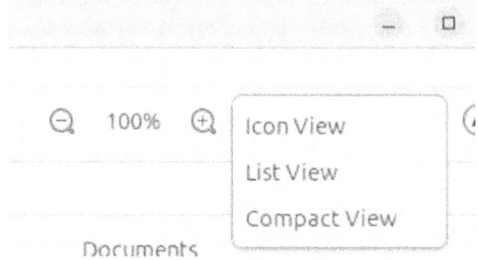

Figure 10-54: File manager file and folder views

Use the control keys to change views quickly: **Ctrl-1** for Icons, **Ctrl-2** for list, and **Ctrl-3** for the compact view. The List view provides the name, size, type, and date. Buttons are displayed for each field across the top of the main pane. You can use these buttons to sort the list according to that field. For example, to sort the files by date, click the Date Modified button; to sort by size, click Size button. Click again to alternate between ascending and descending order.

446 Part 3: Desktops

Certain types of file icons will display previews of their contents. For example, the icons for image files will display a thumbnail of the image. A text file will display in its icon the first few words of its text.

The View menu has entries for managing and arranging your file manager icons (see Table 10-4) (see Figure 10-55). You can choose Icons, List, and Compact views. In the Icon view, the "Arrange items" submenu appears, which provides entries for sorting icons by name, size, type, emblem, extension, and modification date. You can also simply reverse the order, or position icons manually.

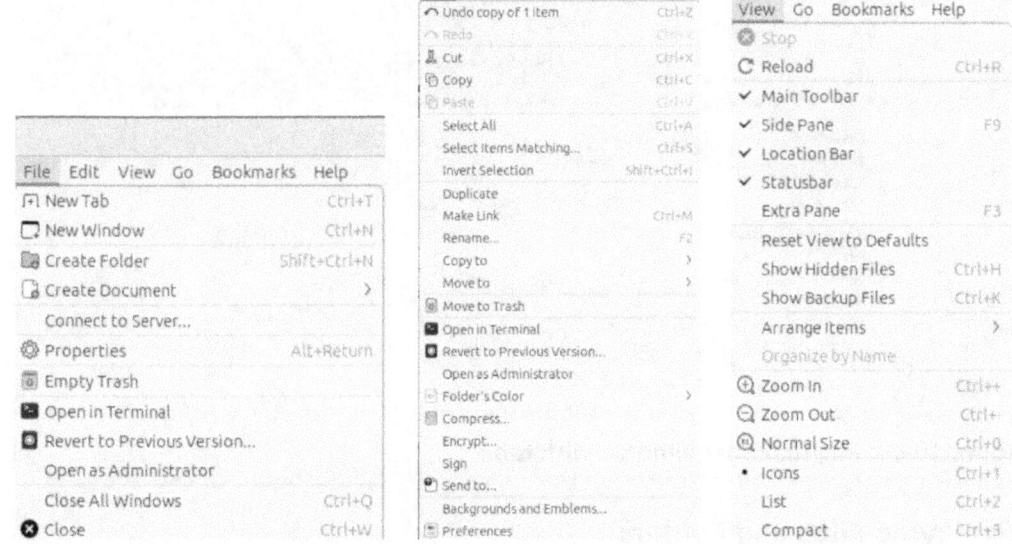

Figure 10-55: File manager File, Edit, and View menus

The View | Zoom In entry enlarges your view of the window, making icons bigger, and Zoom Out reduces your view, making them smaller. Normal Size restores icons to the standard size. You can also use the **Ctrl-+** and **Ctrl--** keys to zoom in and out.

File manager tools and menus

From the Edit menu, you can paste files you have cut or copied to move or copy them between folders, or make duplicates (see Table 10-5 and see Figure 10-50). The selection menu items let you select all files and folders, those matching a simple regular expression, and to invert a selection, choosing all those not selected. On the Files menu, the Properties entry opens the folder properties dialog with Basic and Permissions tabs.

In the icon view, you can right-click anywhere on the empty space on the main pane of a file manager window to display a pop-up menu with entries to create a new folder, arrange icons, zoom icons, and open the folder properties dialog (see Table 10-4).

Navigating in the file manager

The file manager operates similarly to a web browser, using the same window to display opened folders. It maintains a list of previously viewed folders, and you can move back and forth through that list using the toolbar navigation buttons (left side). The Back button with the left arrow moves you to the previously displayed folder, the Forward button with the right arrow moves you to the next previously displayed folder, and the up arrow moves to the parent folder. The home folder icon opens your home folder, and the computer icon (monitor) opens the Computer window, which lists icons for your file systems and removable devices.

Use the side pane's Places view to access your bookmarked folders, storage devices (USB, CD/DVD disc, and attached hard drives), and mounted network folders. On the Computer section of the side pane, you can access your home folders, trash, and the file system (root folder). On the Bookmarks section, you can access any additional bookmarks you created. Attached devices are listed in the Devices section, and mounted network folders are listed in the Network section.

Menu Item	Description
Stop	Stop current task
Reload	Refresh file and folder list
Main Toolbar	Displays main toolbar
Side Pane	Displays side pane
Location Bar	Displays location bar
Statusbar	Displays status bar at bottom of folder window
Extra Pane	Display dual panes for file manager window, with separate folders open in each
Reset View to Defaults	Displays files and folders in default view
Show Hidden Files	Show administrative dot files.
Arrange Items: By Name, Size, Type, Modification Date, and Emblems	Arrange files and folder by specified criteria
Organize by Name	Sort icons in Icon view by name
Zoom In	Provides a close-up view of icons, making them appear larger.
Zoom Out	Provides a distant view of icons, making them appear smaller.
Normal Size	Restores view of icons to standard size.
Icons	Displays icons
List	Displays file list with name, size, type, and date. Folders are expandable.
Compact	Displays compact file list using only the name and small icons

Table 10-4: File Manager View Menu

Menu Item	Description
Cut, Copy	Move or copy a file or folder
Paste	Paste files that you have copied or cut, letting you move or copy files between folders, or make duplicates.
Undo, Redo	Undo or Redo a paste operation
Select All	Select all files and folders in this folder
Select Items Matching	Quick search for files using basic pattern matching.
Invert Selection	Select all other files and folders not selected, deselecting the current selection.
Duplicate	Make a copy of a selected file
Make Link	Make a link to a file or folder
Rename	Rename a selected file or folder
Copy to	Copy a file or folder to one of the default bookmarks
Move to	Move a file or folder to one of the default bookmarks
Move To Trash	Move a file for folder to the trash folder for later deletion
Delete	Delete a file or folder immediately.
Compress	Compress selected files and folders to a compressed archive file such as a tar, cpio, or zip file (Engrampa extension).
Backgrounds and Emblems	Choose a background for the file manager windows. Add emblems to any folder or file in the file manager window.
Preferences	The Caja File Manager preferences for your account.

Table 10-5: File Manager Edit Menu

To open a subfolder, you can double-click its icon or right-click the icon and select Open from the menu. You can also open the folder in a new tab or a new window. The Open With submenu lists other possible file managers and applications to open the folder with such as Files (Caja). You can also click on the folder to select it, and then choose Open from the File menu (File | Open). The tab, new window, and Open With items are also listed when a folder is selected. Figure 10-56 shows the File menu with the different Open items for a folder and the Open With submenu for a file. Table 10-3 lists the File menu options.

Chapter 10: Ubuntu MATE   **449**

Figure 10-56: File manager File | Open

Menu Item	Description
Create Folder	Creates a new subfolder in the folder.
Create Document	Creates a text document.
Arrange Items: By Name, Size, Type, Modification Date, and Emblems	Arrange files and folder by specified criteria
Organize by Name	Sort icons in Icon view by name
Open in Terminal	Open a terminal window at that folder (Open terminal extension)
Zoom In	Provides a close-up view of icons, making them appear larger.
Zoom Out	Provides a distant view of icons, making them appear smaller.
Normal Size	Restores view of icons to standard size.
Properties	Opens the Properties dialog for the folder

Table 10-6: File Manager Pop-up Menu

You can open any folder or file system listed in the side pane Places view by clicking on its folder or bookmark. You can also right-click on a bookmark or folder to display a menu with entries to Open, "Open in a New Tab", and "Open in a New Window" (see Table 10-7). The "Open in a New Window" item is an easy way to access devices from the file manager. The menu for the Trash entry lets you empty the trash. For any bookmark, you can also remove and rename the entry. Entries for removable devices in the side pane such as USB drives also have a menu item for Eject. Internal hard drives have an Unmount entry instead.

Menu Item	Description
Open	Opens the file with its associated application. Folders are opened in the file manager. Associated applications are listed.
Open In A New Tab	Opens a folder in a new tab in the same window.
Open In A New Window	Opens a folder in a separate window, accessible from the toolbar, right-click.
Remove	Remove bookmark from the side pane.
Rename	Rename a bookmark.

Table 10-7: The File Manager Side Pane Pop-Up Menu

Caja File Manager Search

From a file manager window, click the Search button on the toolbar (Looking glass at right), or select Go | Search for Files, to open a Search box below the toolbar. Enter the pattern to search and press ENTER or click the looking glass button on the right side of the text box. The results are displayed.

Menus for location and file type will appear in the folder window, with + and - buttons for adding or removing search parameters, including location, file type, tags, modification time, size, and text in the content of the file. Click the plus + button to add more search parameters. The search begins from the folder opened, as specified by the first location parameter. But you can specify another folder to search, using the Location parameter's folder menu listing possible folders. To search multiple folders at once, click the + button to add a Location parameter, and specify the folder to be searched on that Location parameter's folder menu. You can do the same for multiple file types, specifying only files with certain types, as well as for modification times, file sizes, tags, and searched content.

Managing Files and Folders

As a GNOME-compliant file manager, Caja supports desktop drag-and-drop operations for copying and moving files. To move a file or folder, drag-and-drop from one folder to another. The move operation is the default drag-and-drop operation in GNOME. To copy a file to a new location, press the CTRL key as you drag.

Using a file's pop-up menu

You can also perform remove, rename, and link creation operations on a file by right-clicking its icon and selecting the action you want from the pop-up menu that appears (see Table 10-8). For example, to remove an item, right-click it and select the Move To Trash entry from the pop-up menu. This places it in the Trash folder, where you can later delete it. To create a link, right-click the file and select Make Link from the pop-up menu. This creates a new link file that begins with the term "Link." If you select an archive file, the pop-up menu also displays entries to "Extract Here" and "Extract to" (Engrampa extension).

Chapter 10: Ubuntu MATE **451**

Menu Item	Description
Open	Opens the file with its associated application. Folders are opened in the file manager. Associated applications are listed.
Open In A New Tab	Opens a folder in a new tab in the same window.
Open In A New Window	Opens a folder in a new window
Open With	Selects an application with which to open the file, or a file manager to use to open a folder.
Cut Copy	Entries to cut and copy the selected file.
Paste into Folder	Paste the selected folder
Make Link	Creates a link to that file in the same folder.
Rename (F2)	Renames the file.
Copy To	Copy a file to the Home Folder, Desktop, or to a folder displayed in another pane in the file manager window.
Move To	Move a file to the Home Folder, Desktop, or to a folder displayed in another pane in the file manager window.
Move To Trash	Moves a file to the Trash folder, where you can later delete it.
Delete	Delete the file or folder permanently
Compress	Archives files (Engrampa extension).
Extract Here Extract To	When an archive is selected, these entries appear (Engrampa extension).
Properties	Displays the Properties dialog.

Table 10-8: The File and Folder Pop-Up Menu

Renaming Files

To rename a file, you can either right-click the file's icon and select the Rename entry from the pop-up menu or click its icon and press the F2 function key. The name of the icon will be bordered, encased in a small text box. You can overwrite the old one, or edit the current name by clicking a position in the name to insert text, as well as use the backspace key to delete characters. You can also rename a file by entering a new name in its Properties dialog box (Basic tab).

Grouping Files

You can select a group of files and folders by clicking the first item and then hold down the SHIFT key while clicking the last item, or by clicking and dragging the mouse across items you want to select. To select separated items, hold the CTRL key down as you click the individual icons. If you want to select all the items in the folder, choose the Select All entry in the Edit menu (Edit | Select All) (**Ctrl-a**). You can then copy, move, or even delete several files at once. To select items that have a certain pattern in their name, choose Select Items Matching from the Edit menu to open a search box where you can enter the pattern (**Ctrl-s**). Use the * character to match partial patterns, as in *let* to match on all filenames with the pattern "let" in them. The pattern **my*** would match on filenames beginning with the "my" pattern, and ***png** would match on all PNG image files.

Opening Applications and Files MIME Types

You can start any application in the file manager by double-clicking either the application itself or a data file used for that application. If you want to open the file with a specific application, you can right-click the file and select one of the Open With entries. One or more Open with entries will be displayed for default and possible application, like "Open with Text Editor" for a text file. If the application you want is not listed, you can select "Open with Other Application" to open a dialog listing available applications.

Folders also have an Open With submenu, listing alternative file managers you can use to open the folder, should they be installed. Applications that work on folders are also listed such as the Shotwell image manager and the Rhythmbox music player.

To change or set the default application to use for a certain type of file, you open a file's Properties dialog and select the Open With tab. Here you can choose the default application to use for that kind of file. Possible applications will be listed with a button next to each entry. The default has its button turned on. Click the button of the one you want to change to the default. Once you choose the default, it will appear in the Open With item for this type of file. If there is an application on the Open With tab you do not want listed in the Open With menu, select it and click the Remove button.

If you want to add an application to the Open With menu, click the "Add" button to open the Add Application dialog, which lists possible applications. Select the one you want and click the Add button. You can use the "Use a custom command" text box to enter a command. The Browse button lets you locate a command.

File and Folder Properties

In a file's Properties dialog, you can view detailed information on a file and set options and permissions (see Figure 10-57). A file's Properties dialog has five tabs: Basic, Emblems, Permissions, Open With, and Notes. Folders do not have an Open With tab. Certain kinds of files will have additional tabs, providing information about the file. For example, an audio file will have an Audio tab listing the type of audio file and any other information like a song title or compression method used. An image file will have an Image tab listing the resolution and type of image. Folders also have an "Access Control List" and "Extended user attributes" tabs that you can use to control user access to a folder.

The Basic tab shows detailed information such as type, size, location, and date modified. The type is a MIME type, indicating the type of application associated with it. The file's icon is displayed at the top with a text box showing the file's name. You can edit the filename in the Name text box, changing that name.

If you want to change the icon image used for the file or folder, click the icon image (next to the name) to open a Select Custom Icon dialog to browse for the one you want. The **/usr/share/pixmaps** folder holds the set of current default images, though you can select your own images (click **pixmaps** entry in the side pane). Click an image file to see its icon displayed in the right pane. Double-click to change the icon image.

Figure 10-57: File properties on Caja

The Permissions tab for files shows the read, write, and execute permissions for owner, group, and others, as set for this file. You can change any of the permissions here, provided the file belongs to you. You configure access for the owner, the group, and others, using menus. You can set owner permissions as Read Only or Read And Write. For group and others, you can also set the None option, denying access. Clicking on the group name displays a menu listing different groups, allowing you to select one to change the file's group. If you want to execute the file as an application, you check the "Allow executing file as program" entry. This has the effect of setting the execute permission.

The Permissions tab for folders operates much the same way, but it includes two access entries: Folder Access and File Access. The Folder Access entry controls access to the folder with options for None, List Files Only, Access Files, and Create And Delete Files. These correspond to read, write, and execute permissions given to folders. The File Access entry lets you set permissions for all those files in the folder. They are the same as for files: for the owner Read or Read and Write, for the group and others the entry adds a None option to deny access. To set the permissions for all the files in the folder accordingly (not just the folder), you click the "Apply Permissions To Enclosed Files" button.

The Open With tab for files lists all the applications associated with this kind of file. You can select the one you want to use as the default. This can be particularly useful for media files, where you may prefer a specific player for a certain file or a particular image viewer for pictures. To add an applications that is not listed, click the Add button to open an "Add Application" dialog listing installed applications you can choose from.

The Notes tab lets you add notes about the file. A note emblem will then appear on the right top corner of the file's icon.

The Digest tab lets you easily perform checksum confirmations on downloaded files. Enter the checksum value into the Check text box. A green checkmark means it is confirmed. You can choose which hash functions to use.

For folders, the Access Control List tab lets you set ACL controls for a folder, specifying those users that can have access to a folder. This will afford you more refined control over access to a folder. In general, only the owner has write access and all other users have read and execute access (Other). Should you also want certain users to also have write access you could do so on this tab, selecting the users from the "Available participants" list. You could also change the current entry for Other, removing read an execute access, and then only allowing certain users to access the folder. To add a user to the "Current participants in ACL" list, select it in the "Available participants" list and click the "Add participant to ACL" button. To remove a user from the "Current participants in ACL" list, select it and click the "Remove participant from ACL" button. If a user is not listed in the "Available participants" list, click "Advanced features" to open a text box where you can search for the user. You can also choose to list system users.

The "Extended user attributes" tab lets you add ACL attributes to a folder. Click the Add button to create an attribute entry where you can enter its name and value. Use the Remove button to remove an attribute.

The Share tab for folders allows you to share folders as network shares. If you have Samba or NFS, these will allow your folders and files to be shared with users on other systems. Be sure to first install the Caja Share package. You have the option to specify whether the shared folder or file will be read-only or allow write access. To allow write access check the "Allow others to create and delete files in this folder" entry. To open access to all users, check the Guest access entry.

Caja Preferences

You can set preferences for your Caja file manager in the Preferences dialog, accessible by selecting the Preferences item in any Caja file manager window's Edit menu (Edit | Preferences). The File Management Preferences dialog has seven tabs: Views, Behavior, Display, List Columns, Preview, Media, and Extensions.

> The Views tab allows you to select how files are displayed by default, such as the list, icon, or compact view. You can set default zoom levels for icon, compact, and list views.

> Behavior lets you choose how to select files, manage the trash, and handle scripts.

> Display lets you choose what added information you want displayed in an icon caption, like the size or date. You can also specify the format of the date.

> The List Columns tab lets you choose both the features to display in the list view and the order in which to display them. In addition to the already-selected Name, Size, Date, and Type, you can add features such as permissions, group, MIME type, and owner. For folders you can also display a count of the number of items.

> The Preview tab lets you choose whether you want small preview content displayed in the icons, like beginning text for text files.

> The Media tab lets you choose what applications to run for certain media, such as run the Celluloid media player for DVD videos, or Rhythmbox for audio files.

Extensions lists extensions installed for Caja such as "Open Terminal" which lets you open a folder in a terminal window (Open in Terminal menu item), Engrampa which allows you to create and extract archives directly from the file manager window (Compress menu item), and caja-seahorse that allows you to encrypt files and folders (Encrypt menu item).

Control Center

Both Preference and Administration tools can be accessed either from the MATE menu or from the Control Center (see Figure 10-58). You can access the Control Center at the bottom of the MATE menu. The Control Center opens a window listing the different applications by section: Administration, Hardware, Internet and Network, Look and Feel, and Personal. Icons for the tools are displayed. Single-click on an icon to open it. The Control Center also has a dynamic search capability. A side pane holds a filter search box and links for the groups. As you enter a pattern in the Filter search box, matching applications appear at the right. Commonly used applications can be listed under Common Tasks. If you want an application to be started when your system starts, you can right-click on its icon and choose "Add to Startup Programs" to add it directly to the Startup Applications dialog. Several of the tools are administration applications such as App Center, MATE User Manager, and Printers. Others are GNOME preferences used for MATE, such as Appearance, About Me, Screensaver, and Keyboard.

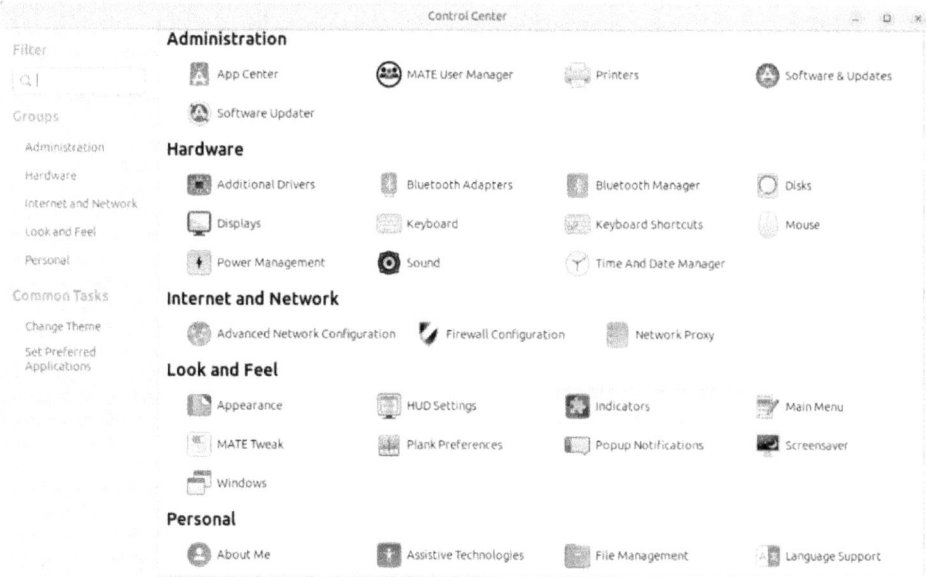

Figure 10-58: GNOME Control Center

MATE Preferences

You can configure different parts of your MATE interface using tools listed in the Preferences menu and from the Control Center. MATE provides several tools for configuring your MATE desktop. The MATE preferences are listed in Table 10-9. On some preferences tools, a Help button displays detailed descriptions and examples. Some of the more important tools are discussed here.

The keyboard shortcuts configuration (Keyboard Shortcuts) lets you map keys to certain tasks, like mapping multimedia keys on a keyboard to media tasks like play and pause. There are tasks for the desktop, multimedia, and window management. With window management, you can also map keys to perform workspace switching. The tasks and keys that are already assigned are listed. To change the keys used for a task, double click its shortcut entry and type the new keys. A task that has no assigned keys is disabled. Click the shortcut entry to enter a key sequence for it. To add a new task, click add to choose the application and a name for it. These are added under the Custom Shortcuts section. Click the new task's shortcut to add a key for it. To disable a shortcut, click the shortcut entry and press the backspace key.

The Windows configuration (Windows) is where you can enable features like window roll-up (Titlebar Action), window movement key, and mouse window selection.

Preferences	Description
About Me	Personal information like image, addresses, and password.
Additional Drivers	Ubuntu Software and Updates Additional Drivers tab for detecting and adding commercial drivers.
Advanced Network Configuration	NetworkManager Network Connections editor for managing and adding network devices.
Appearance	Desktop Appearance configuration: Themes, Fonts, Backgrounds, and Visual Effects.
Assistive Technologies	Enables features like accessible login and keyboard screen.
Bluetooth Adapters	Manage and connect Bluetooth devices.
Disks	Opens the GNOME Disks utility.
Displays	Opens the GNOME Monitor Preferences dialog for detecting monitors and setting resolution, with an option to show monitors in the panel.
File Management	File Manager options including media handling applications, icon captions, and the default view (also accessible from file manager window, Edit | Preferences).
Firewall Configuration	Gufw firewall management application for the Ubuntu ufw firewall
Indicators	Configure indicators in the Indicator applet (System Menu, Date, sound, power, and notifications)
Keyboard	Configure your keyboard: selecting options, models, and typing breaks, as well as accessibility features like slow, bounce, and sticky keys.
Keyboard Shortcuts	Configure keys for special tasks, like multimedia operations.
Language Support	Specify a language.
Main Menu	Add or remove categories and menu items for the Applications,

	Preferences, and System menus.
MATE Tweak	MATE Tweak application for configuring your desktop, panel, and windows.
MATE User Manager	MATE application for configuring and adding users on your system.
Mouse	Mouse and touchpad configuration: select hand orientation, speed, and accessibility.
Network Proxy	Specify proxy configuration if needed: manual or automatic
Onboard Settings	Options for the screen based keyboard.
Plank Preferences	Configure the MATE Plank dock
Popup Notifications	Placement and display theme for notifications.
Power Management	The GNOME power manager for configuring display, suspend, and shutdown options.
Preferred Applications	Set default Web browser, mail application, music player, and terminal window.
Screensaver	Select and manage your screen saver, including the activation time.
Sound	Configure sound effects, output volume, sound device options, input volume, and sound application settings (Pulseaudio).
Startup Applications	Manage your session with startup programs and save options.
Time and Date Manager	Set the time, date, and time zone.
Windows	Enable window abilities like roll up on the title bar, movement key, window selection.

Table 10-9: The MATE Preferences

About Me: photo, name, and password

To set up personal information, including the icon to be used for your login screen, you use the About Me preferences tool. You can access it from the Preferences menu (Preferences | About Me) and from the Control Center. The About Me preferences dialog lets you change your password (see Figure 10-59) and the icon or image used to represent the user. Should you want to change your password, you can click on the Change Password button to open a change password dialog.

Clicking on the image icon opens a browser window where you can select a personal image. The **/usr/share/pixmaps/faces** folder is selected by default, which displays several images. The selected image displays at the right on the browser window. For a personal photograph, you can select the Picture folder. This is the Pictures folder on your home folder. Should you place a photograph or image there, you could then select if for your personal image. The image will be used in the login screen when showing your user entry.

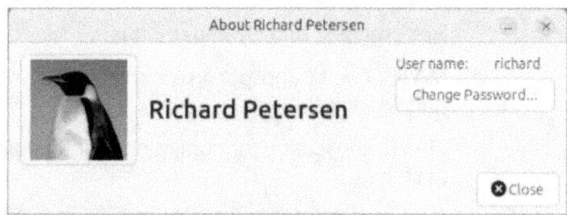

Figure 10-59: About Me: Preferences | About Me

Appearance

Several appearance-related configuration tasks are combined into the Appearance Preferences dialog (Appearance entry in the Preferences menu or Appearance icon on the Control Center's Personal section). You can change your theme, background image, or configure your fonts. The Appearance dialog shows four tabs: Theme, Background, Fonts, and Interface (see Figure 10-60). On the Interface tab, you can choose to show icons in menus and on buttons.

Desktop Background

You use the Background tab on the Appearance Preferences dialog to select or customize your desktop background image (see Figure 10-60). You can also access the Background tab by right-clicking the desktop background and select Change Desktop Background from the desktop menu. Installed backgrounds are listed, with the current background selected. To add your own image, either drag-and-drop the image file to the Background tab or click on the Add button to locate and select the image file. To remove an image, select it and click the Remove button.

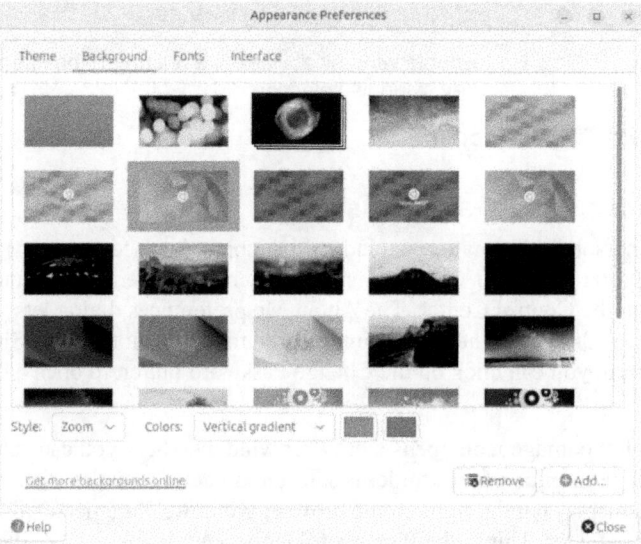

Figure 10-60: Choosing a desktop background, System | Preferences | Appearance

From the Style drop-down menu, you can choose display options such as Zoom, Centered, Scaled, Tiled, or Fill Screen. A centered or scaled image will preserve the image proportions. Fill screen may distort it. Any space not filled, such as with a centered or scaled images, will be filled in with the desktop color. From the Colors menu, you can set the desktop color to a solid color, horizontal gradient, or vertical gradient. Click on the color button next to the Colors menu to open a "Pick a Color" dialog where you can select a color from a selection of choices or add a new one from a graph or with the color number. For gradients, two color buttons are displayed for selecting a color at each end of the gradient.

Initially, the Ubuntu backgrounds are listed. Install the **gnome-backgrounds** package to add a collection of GNOME backgrounds. To download more backgrounds, click the "Get more backgrounds online" link.

Desktop Themes

You use the Themes tab on the Appearance Preferences dialog to select or customize a theme. Themes control your desktop appearance. The Themes tab will list icons for currently installed themes (see Figure 10-61). It features an extensive list of Yaru based themes, each with a different accent color. Yaru is the official theme for Ubuntu. The icons show key aspects for each theme such as window, folder, and button images, in effect previewing the theme for you.

The Ubuntu MATE custom theme is initially selected. You can select a different theme if you wish. If you have downloaded additional themes from **https://www.gnome-look.org/**, you can click the install button to locate and install them. Once installed, the additional themes will also be displayed in the Theme tab. If you download and install a theme or icon set from the Ubuntu repository, it will be automatically installed for you.

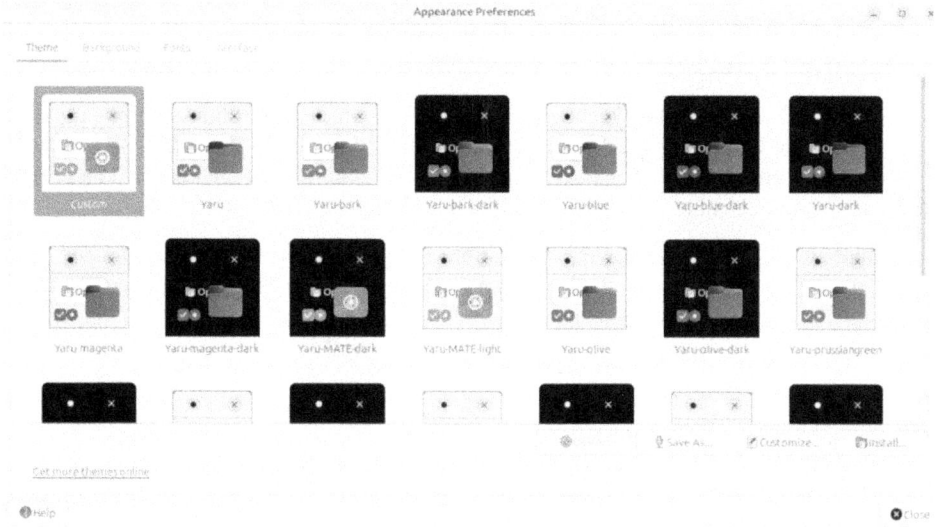

Figure 10-61: Appearance - Selecting GNOME themes

The true power of Themes is shown its ability to let users customize any given theme. Themes are organized into controls, window border, icons, and pointer. Controls covers the appearance of window and dialog controls like buttons and slider bars. Window border lets you choose title bars, borders, and window buttons sets. Icons lets you choose different icon sets. Pointers provides different pointer sets to use. You can even download and install separate components like specific icon sets, which you can then use in a customized theme.

Clicking the Customize button opens a Customize Theme dialog with tabs for different theme components. The components used for the current theme are selected by default. In the Controls, Window Border, Icons, and Pointer tabs you will see listings of the different themes. You can then mix and match different components from those themes, creating your own customized theme, using window borders from one theme and icons from another. Upon selecting a component, your desktop changes automatically showing you how it looks. If you have added a component, like a new icon set, it also is shown.

Once you have created a new customized theme, a Custom Theme icon appears in the list on the Theme tab. To save the customized theme, click the Save As button. This opens a dialog where you can enter the theme name, any notes, and specify whether you also want to keep the theme background.

Customized themes and themes installed directly by a user are placed in the **.themes** folder in the user's home folder. Should you want these themes made available for all users, you can move them from the **.themes** folder to the **/usr/share/themes** folder. In a terminal window run a **cp** command as shown here for the **mytheme** theme. The operation requires administrative access (**sudo**).

```
sudo cp -r .themes/mytheme   /usr/share/themes
```

You can do the same for icon sets you have downloaded. Such sets will be installed in the user's **.icons** folder. You can then copy them to the **/usr/share/icons** folder to make them available to all users.

Assistive Technologies

On MATE, the Assistive Technologies dialog is a simple set of buttons for accessing accessibility tabs for other tools (see Figure 10-62). In the Assistive Technologies section, use the "Enable assistive technologies" checkbox to turn assistive technologies on and off. The Preferred Applications button opens the Accessibility tab on the Preferred Applications dialog.

In the Preferences section, there are buttons to open the accessibility tabs for the keyboard and mouse preferences dialogs. On the keyboard accessibility tab, you can configure features such as sticky, slow, and bounce keys. The mouse button opens the mouse preferences dialog.

Chapter 10: Ubuntu MATE   **461**

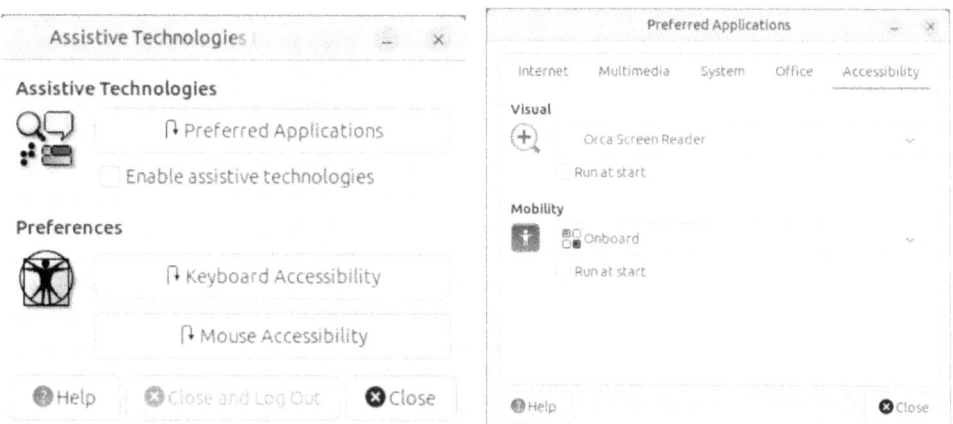

Figure 10-62: Assistive Technologies Preferences

Bluetooth Manager and Adapters

The Bluetooth Manager icon on the Control Center opens the Bluetooth Devices dialog where you can scan for and connect to Bluetooth devices (see Figure 10-63). Click the Search button to scan for and list available devices, and then click on the device you want to select it and click the plus button to connect to it.

The Bluetooth Adapters icon opens the Bluetooth Adapter dialog where you can set visibility settings (Hidden, Always visible, and Temporarily visible) and the name of the adapter. You can also access the Bluetooth Adapters dialog from the Adapter menu's Preferences entry on the Bluetooth Manager (Bluetooth Devices dialog).

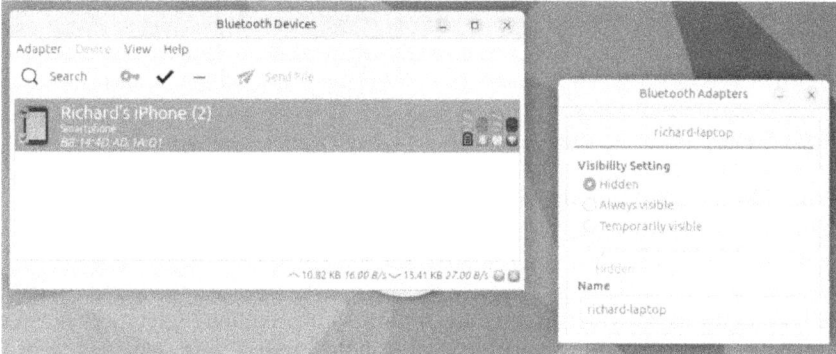

Figure 10-63: Bluetooth Manager and Adapters

You can quickly manage your Bluetooth devices from the Bluetooth Indicator menu on the right side of the top panel (see Figure 10-64). The Devices entry opens the Bluetooth Manager, and the Adapters entry opens Bluetooth Adapters. You can also turn Bluetooth off, list recently accessed devices (Recent Connections), and send files to a device.

462 Part 3: Desktops

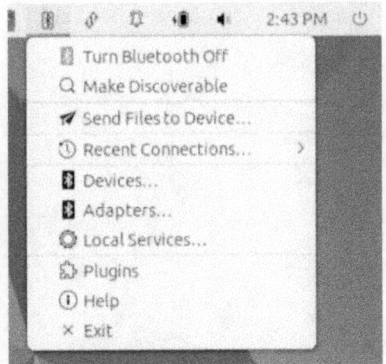

Figure 10-64: Bluetooth Indicator Menu

You can also choose what plugins you want to use for your Bluetooth connections, as well as configure specific plugins (see Figure 10-65). You can access the Plugins dialog from the View menu on the Bluetooth Manager dialog (Bluetooth Devices) and from the Bluetooth indicator menu. Most plugins do not support configuration options. Those that do will be in bold type and their configuration button will be active (not faded type). For the Discovery Manager plugin you can set the Discoverable timeout. RecentConns lets you set the number of recent connections to display on the Recent Connections menu and the PowerManager lets you choose whether to power Bluetooth adapters automatically.

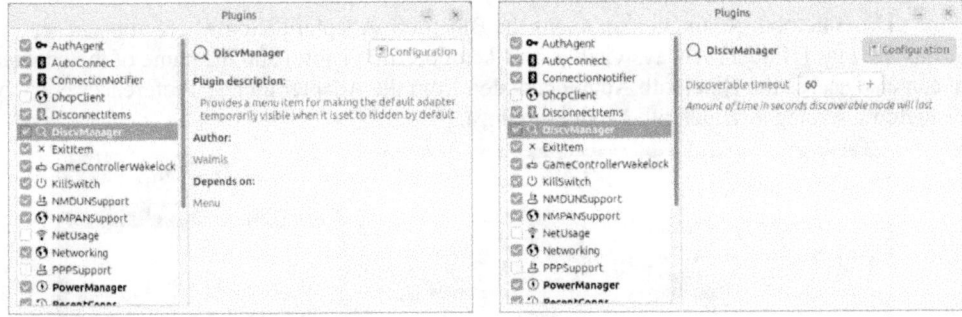

Figure 10-65: Bluetooth Plugins

Displays

Selecting the Displays icon on the Control Center or from the Preferences menu opens the Monitor Preferences dialog where you can set the resolution, refresh rate, and rotation of the monitor. Should you have multiple monitors, click the "Detect monitors" button to access them. Scaling can be set to auto, 100 percent, or 200 percent (see Figure 10-66). Click the Apply button to effect changes. The "Apply system-wide" button applies the changes for all users.

Figure 10-66: Monitor Preferences.

Note: To scale a HiDPI monitor such as smaller 4k monitors, be sure to set the HiDIPI option in the MATE Tweak Windows tab. Auto-detect will scale when needed, Regular does no scaling, and HiDPI will always scale.

File Management: Default Applications for Media

Caja handles preferences for media operations. You set the preferences using the File Management Preferences dialog. It is accessible from the Edit | Preferences menu item on any Caja file manager window, from the Preferences menu as File Management, or from the Control Center as File Management (in the Personal section).

The Media tab of the File Management Preferences dialog lists entries for CD Audio, DVD Video, Music Player, Photos, and Software. Menus let you select the application to use for the different media (see Figure 10-67). You also have options for Ask what to do, Do Nothing, and Open folder. The Open Folder options will just open a window displaying the files on the disc. A segment labeled "Other media" lets you set up an associations for less used media like Blu-Ray discs. Initially, the "Ask what to do" option will be set for all entries. Possible options are listed on each menu, like Rhythmbox Music Player for CD Audio discs and Celluloid for DVD Video. Photos can be opened with the Shotwell Photo-manager. Once you select an option, when you insert removable media, like a CD Audio discs, its associated application is automatically started.

If you just want to turn off the startup for a particular kind of media, you can select the Do Nothing entry from its application menu. If you want to be prompted for options, then set the "Ask what to do" entry. When you insert a disc, a dialog with a menu for possible actions is displayed. The default application is already selected. You can select another application or select the Do Nothing or Open Folder options.

You can turn off the automatic startup for all media by checking the box for "Never prompt or start programs on media insertion" at the bottom of the Media panel. You can also enable the option "Browse media when inserted" to just open a folder showing its files.

464 Part 3: Desktops

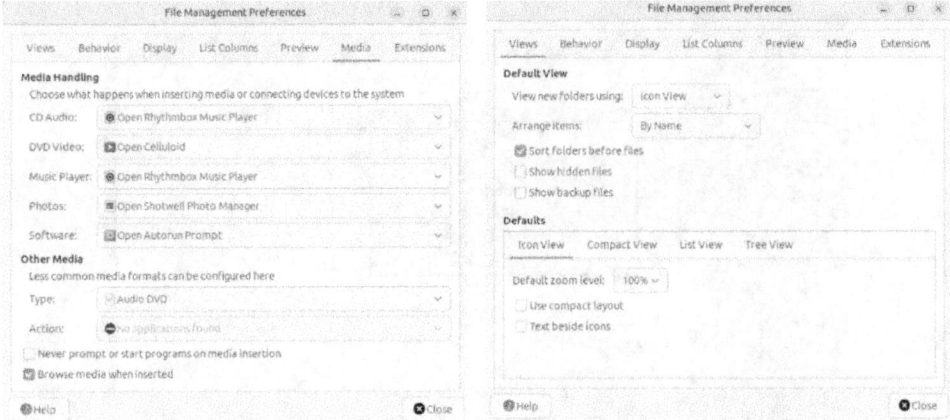

Figure 10-67: File Management Preferences for Media

Fonts

On the Font tab, you can change font sizes, select fonts, and configure rendering options (see Figure 10-68). Fonts are listed for Applications, Documents, Desktop, Window title, and Fixed width. Click on a font button to open a "Pick a Font" dialog where you can select a font, choose its style (regular, italic, or bold), and change its size. You can further refine your font display by clicking the Details button to open a window where you can set features like the dots-per-inch, hinting, and smoothing.

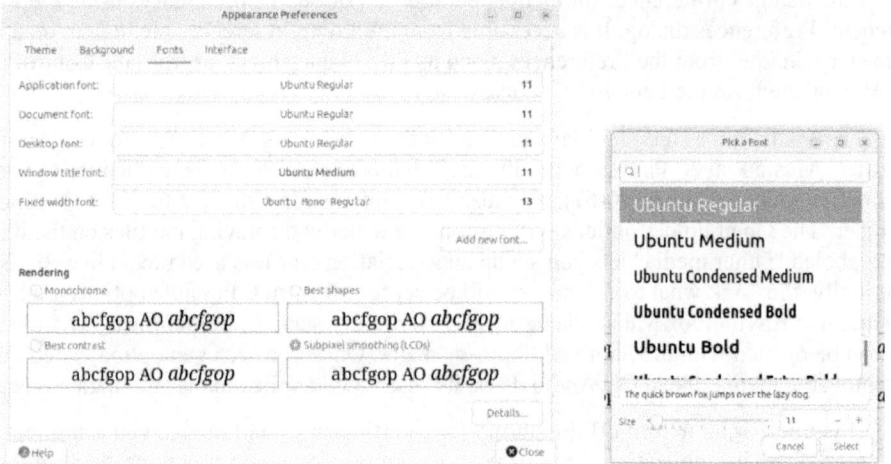

Figure 10-68: Fonts

With very large monitors and their high resolutions becoming more common, one feature users find helpful is the ability to increase the desktop font sizes. On a large widescreen monitor, resolutions less than the native one tend not to scale well. A monitor always looks best in its native resolution. With a large native resolution text sizes become so small they are hard to read. You can overcome this issue by increasing the font size. The default size is 10. Increasing it to 12 makes text in all desktop features like windows and menus much more readable.

Configuring Fonts

To refine your font display, you can use the font rendering features. Open the Fonts tab on the Appearance tool. In the Font Rendering section are basic font rendering features like Monochrome, Best contrast, Best shapes, and Subpixel smoothing. Choose the one that works best. For LCD monitors choose subpixel smoothing. For detailed configuration, click the Details button. Here you can set Smoothing, Hinting (anti-aliasing), and Subpixel color order features. The Subpixel color order is hardware dependent.

On MATE, clicking on a font button in the Appearance Fonts tab will open a "Pick a Font" dialog that lists all available fonts. You can also generate a listing by using the **fc-list** command. The list will be unsorted, so you should pipe it first to the sort command. You can use **fc-list** with any font name or name pattern to search for fonts, with options to search by language, family, or styles.

```
fc-list | sort
```

Adding Fonts

You can install a font from a font file you have downloaded or copied by clicking the "Add new font" button on the Appearance's Fonts tab. Numerous font packages are also available on the Linux repositories. When you install the font packages, the fonts are installed automatically on your system and ready for use. True type font packages begin with **ttf-** prefix. Microsoft true type fonts are available from the **ttf-mscorefonts-installer** package. Fonts are installed in the **/usr/share/fonts** folder. This folder will have subfolders for different font collections like **truetype** and **X11**. You can install fonts manually yourself by copying fonts to the **/user/share/fonts** folder (use the **sudo** command). For dual-boot systems, where Windows is installed as one of the operating systems, you can copy fonts directly from the Windows font folder on the Windows partition (which is mounted in **/media**) to **/usr/share/fonts**.

Mouse and Keyboard Preferences

The Mouse and Keyboard preferences are the primary tools for configuring your mouse and keyboard. Mouse preferences lets you choose speed, hand orientation, and double-click times. For laptops, you can configure your touchpad, enabling touchpad clicks and edge scrolling. Keyboard preferences shows several tabs for selecting your keyboard model (Layouts), configuring keys (Layouts tab, Options button), repeat delay (General tab), and enforcing breaks from power typing as a health precaution (Typing Break tab) (see Figure 10-69).

To configure your sound devices you use the Sound Preferences tool (Sound). MATE uses sound themes to specify an entire set of sounds for different effects and alerts. On the Hardware tab you select a device to use. The Input tab configures input volume, and the Output tab configures output. The Applications tab lets you adjust the output of running applications.

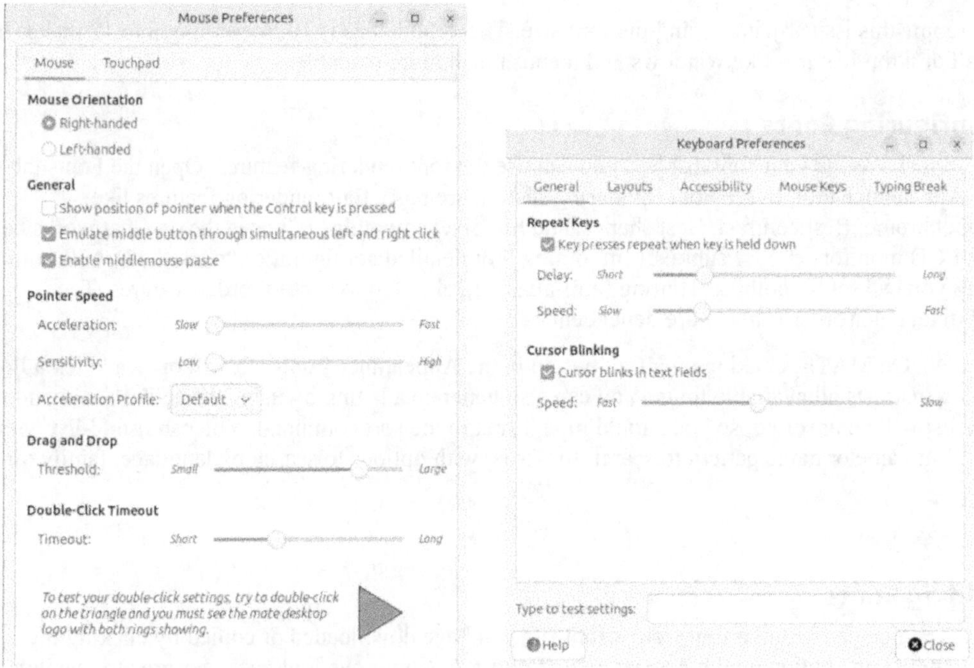

Figure 10-69: Mouse and Keyboard Preferences

MATE Power Management

For power management, MATE uses the MATE Power Manager, **mate-power-manager**, which makes use of Advanced Configuration and Power Interface (ACPI) support provided by a computer to manage power use. The MATE Power Manager can display an icon on the panel showing the current power source, a battery or plugin (lightning). Clicking on the battery icon displays a dialog showing the power charge of your laptop and any wireless devices like a wireless mouse.

The MATE Power manager is configured with Power Management Preferences (**mate-power-preferences**), accessible from Preferences | Power Management, and by clicking on the MATE Power Management panel icon and selecting Power Settings from the menu (also on the GNOME Control Center | Hardware section). Power Manager preferences can be used to configure both a desktop and a laptop (see Figure 10-70).

For a desktop, two tabs appear on the Power Management Preferences window, On AC Power and General. The AC Power tab offers two sleep options, one for the computer and one for the display screen. You can put each to sleep after a specified interval of inactivity. On the General tab, you set actions to take when you press the power button or the suspend button.

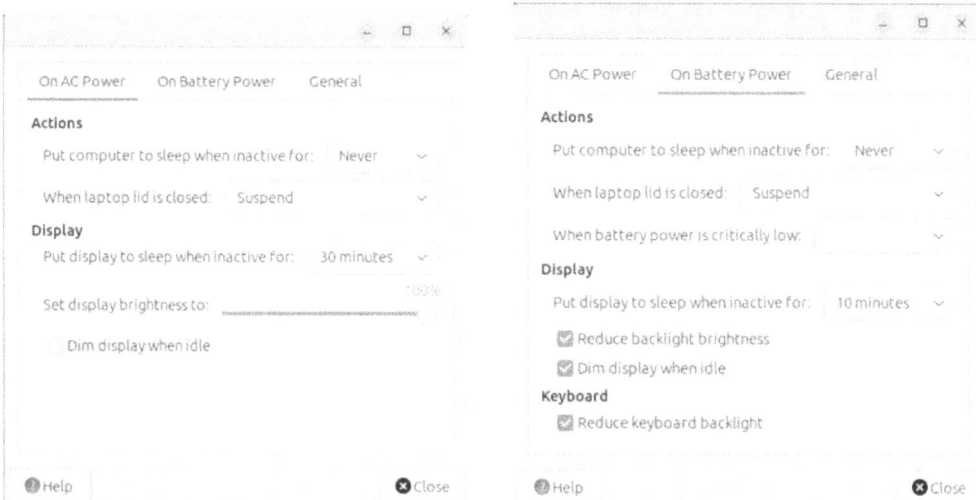

Figure 10-70: MATE Power Manager - AC and Battery

A laptop will also have an On Battery Power tab where you can set additional options for the battery and display, such as shutting down if the battery is too low, or dimming the display when the system is idle. On this tab you can also set the screen brightness. The laptop On AC Power tab will also have an Actions option for actions to take when the laptop lid is closed: suspend, blank screen, and shutdown.

To see how your laptop or desktop is performing with power, you can use Power statistics. This is accessible from the System Tool menus as Power Statistics. The Power Statistics window will display a sidebar listing your different power devices. A right pane will show tabs with power use information for a selected device. The Laptop battery device will display three tabs: Details, History, and Statistics. The History tab will show your recent use, with graph options (Graph type menu) for Time to empty (time left), Time to full (recharging), Charge, and Rate. The Statistics tab can show charge and discharge graphs.

Popup Notifications

The Popup Notifications dialog lets you choose what position on the screen you want your notifications displayed, as well as what theme to use (see Figure 10-71). The themes available are Slider (the default), Nodoka, Coco, and Standard theme. Should you have multiple monitors you can choose the one on which to display notifications, or just use the active monitor. To turn off notification click the "Enable Do Not Disturb" option. To see a preview of your configuration changes, click the Preview button.

Notifications can be quickly accessed from the Popup Indicator button (bell icon) on the Indicator applet on the right side of the top menu. Clicking the Popup indicator button displays a list of current notification, with and close box for each (x). At the bottom of the list is a "Do not disturb" switch you can use the turn off notifications. To remove all notifications at once select the Clear entry. You can configure the Notifications indicator menu using the Ayatana Indicators Settings dialog's Notifications tab, accessible from the Control Center (System Settings) as

Indicators in the Look and Feel section, and from the main menu's Preferences menu (see Indicator Applet Configuration at the beginning of this chapter).

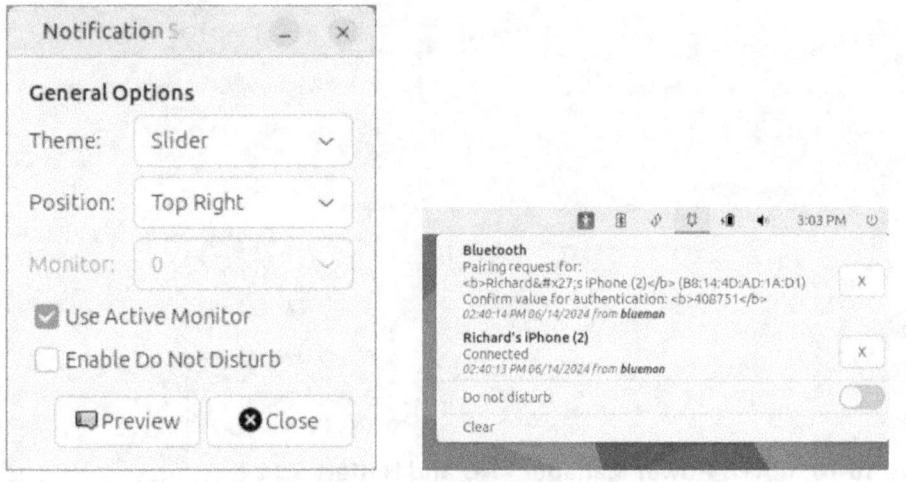

Figure 10-71: Pop-up Notifications

Preferred Applications for Web, Mail, Accessibility, and terminal windows

Certain types of files will have default applications already associated with them. For example, double-clicking a Web page file will open the file in the Firefox Web browser. If you prefer to set a different default application, you can use the Preferred Applications tool (see Figure 10-72) . You access the Preferred Applications tool from the Preferences menu (Preferences | Preferred Applications), and from the Control Center (Personal section). This tool will let you set default applications for Web pages, mail readers, accessibility tools, multimedia, office applications, and system-level tools. Available applications are listed in popup menus. The default mail reader is Evolution, and the default Web browser is Firefox. To make another application the default, click on the menu button to display a list of other possible installed applications. The Preferred applications tool has tabs for Internet, Multimedia, System, Office, and Accessibility. On the Multimedia tab, you can select the default image viewer, video player, and multimedia player. On the Office tab, you can specify the default document viewer, word processor, and spreadsheet application. On the System tab, you can choose the default text editor, terminal window application, file manager, and calculator. The Accessibility panel has options for selecting visual and mobility support such as a screen reader and onboard keyboard.

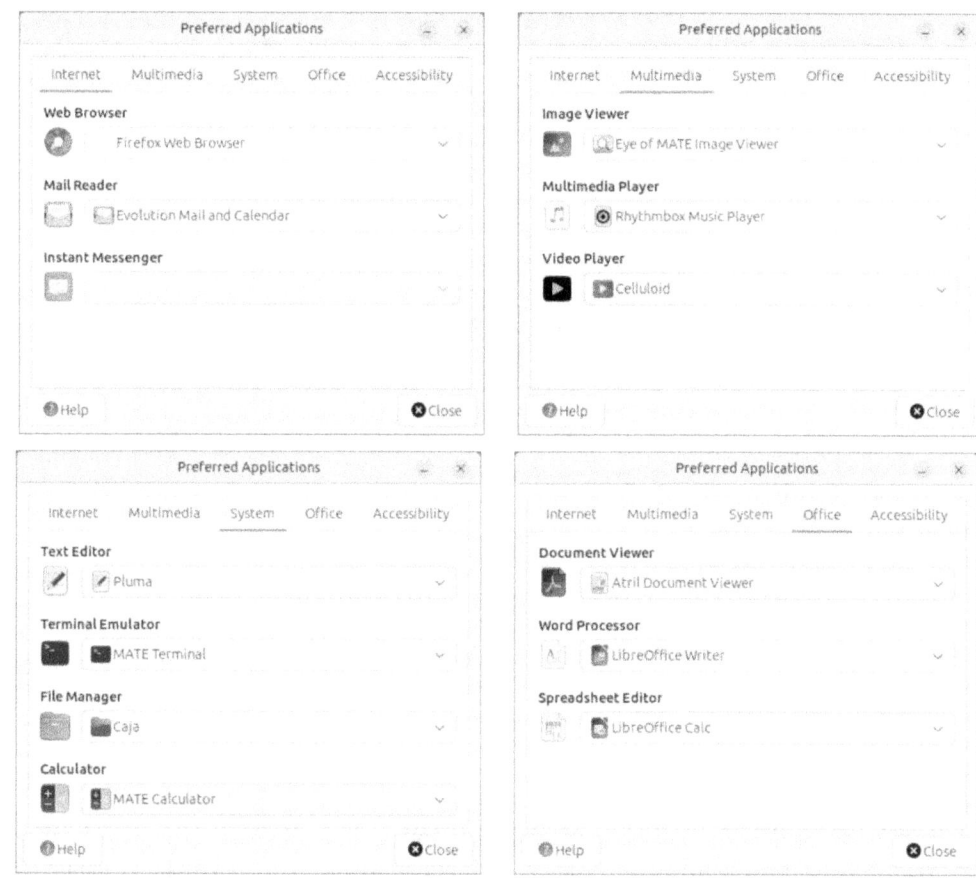

Figure 10-72: Preferred Applications tool

Screen Saver and Lock

With the Screensaver Preferences, you can control when the computer is considered idle and what screen saver to use if any (see Figure 10-73). You can access the Screensaver Preferences dialog from the Preferences menu as Screensaver, or from the Control Center in the Personal section. You can choose from various screen savers, using the scroll box to the left, with a preview displayed at the right. You can also control whether to lock the screen or not, when idle and for how long. You can turn off the Screensaver by unchecking the "Activate screensaver when computer is idle" box.

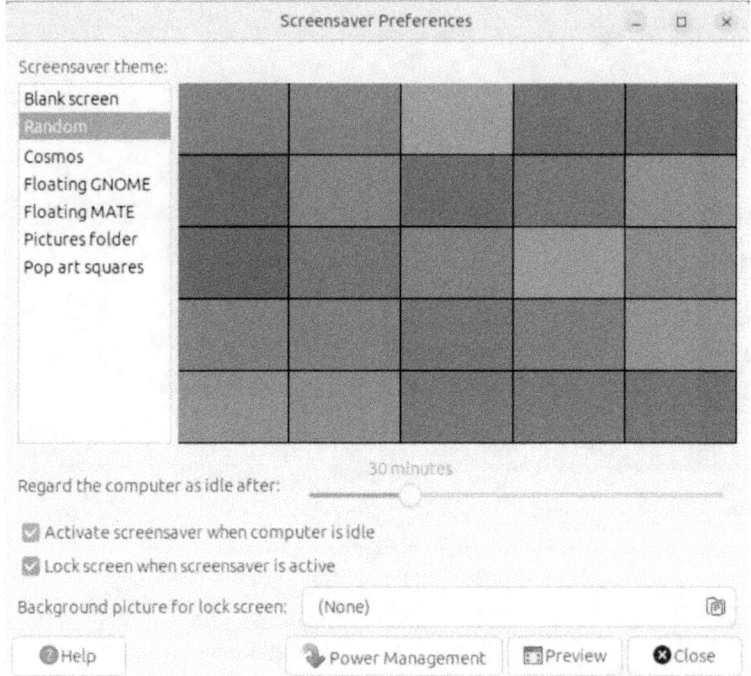

Figure 10-73: Screensaver Preferences

Sound

You can quickly manage the sound volume from the Sound Indicator menu on the right side of the top panel (see Figure 10-74). Adjust the sound using the slider. To mute the sound click the Mute switch. Current sound applications such as Rhythmbox and Celluloid will be listed. If you are playing a sound file (music or video) basic controls are displayed that you can use. The Sound Settings entry opens the Sound Preferences dialog, letting you configure your sound devices.

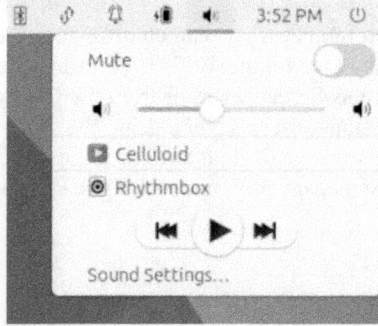

Figure 10-74: Sound Indicator Menu

You configure sound devices and set the volume for sound effects, input and output, and applications using Sound Preferences dialog. Choose Sound on the Preferences menu or select

Sound Settings from the panel sound indicator menu. This opens the Sound Preferences dialog, which has five tabs: Sound Effects, Output, Input, Sounds, and Applications (see Figure 10-75).

The Sound Effects tab lets you select the theme for an alert sound. A sliding bar lets you set the volume for your sound alerts, or turn them off by clicking the Mute option.

Volume Control is integrated into the Sound dialog. A sliding bar at the top of the dialog, above the tabs, lets you set the output volume.

The Hardware tab lets you choose a sound device to use, should you have several sound devices. You can then choose the sound format to configure the Profile menu such as Analog stereo output or Analog stereo input. Click the "Test Speakers" button to test the speakers.

On the Input tab, you set the input volume for an input device such as a microphone. A Mute option lets you disable it. When speaking or recording, the input level is displayed. If you have more than one input device, they will be listed in the Connector menu. Choose the one you want to configure.

On the Output tab, you can configure balance settings for a selected output device. If you have more than one device, it will be listed in the Connector menu. Choose the one you want to configure. The available settings will change according to the device selected. For a simple Analog Stereo Output, there is only a single balance setting

The Applications tab will show applications currently using sound devices. You can set the sound volume for each

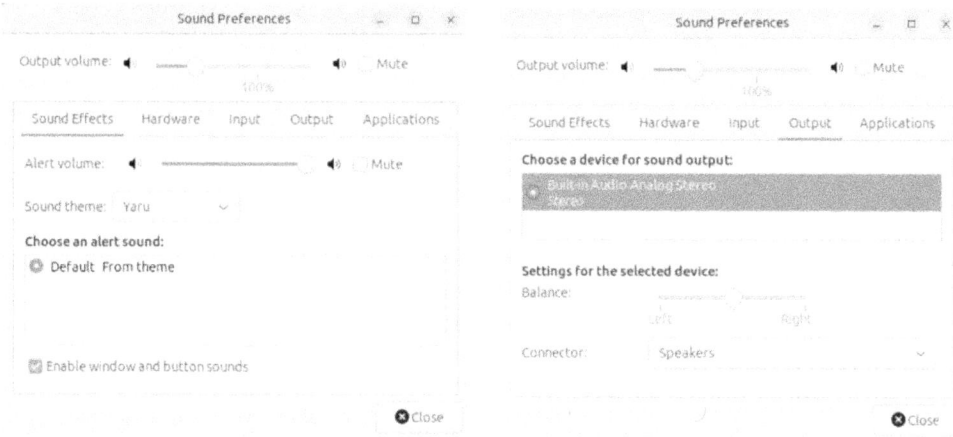

Figure 10-75: Sound Preferences - effects and output

Time and Date Manager

The Time and Date Indicator menu on the right side of the top panel (see Figure 10-76) shows the time on the panel. Clicking it displays the date and the calendar, location, and time. On the calendar you can click on a date and then click on the Add Event entry to open the Evolution calendar application where you can set an event reminder. The Time and Date Settings entry opens the Time and Date dialog, where you can configure the time and date.

472 Part 3: Desktops

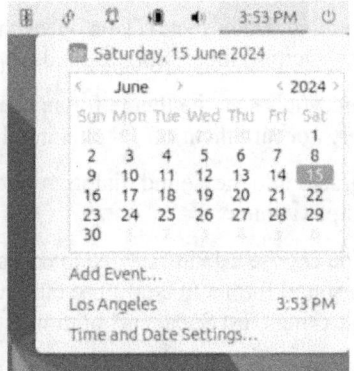

Figure 10-76: Time and Date Indicator Menu

The Time and Date Manager dialog lets you set the time either from a Network Time Protocol server (the NTP sync switch), or to set it manually (see Figure 10-77). The Network Time Protocol server is the default. Turn off the NTP sync switch to enable manual settings or the time and date. Use the Calendar to set the date.

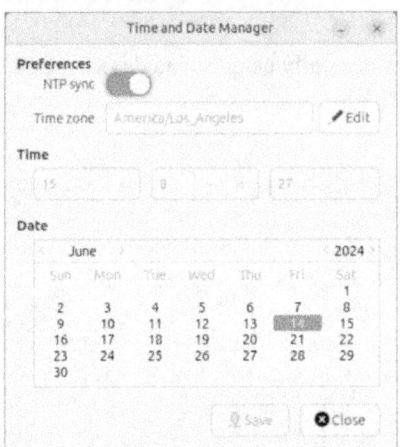 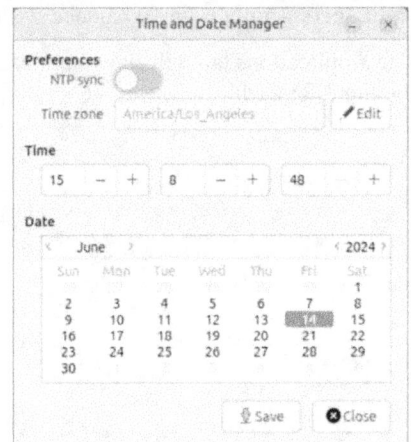

Figure 10-77: Time and Date Manager

You can also choose a time zone. Click the Edit button on the Time zone option to open a Time Zone Selection dialog where you can click on the time zone you want. You can use the search box to search for a time zone by city. A drop down menu will appear with city options as you enter the name.

The time and date are displayed on the Indicator applet on the right side of the top panel. You can configure the time and date Indicator menu using the Ayatana Indicators Settings dialog's "Date and Time" tab, accessible from the Control Center (System Settings) as Indicators in the Look and Feel section, and from the main menu's Preferences menu (see Indicator Applet Configuration at the beginning of this chapter).

ubuntu

11. Ubuntu Flavors

- Xubuntu (Xfce)
- Lubuntu (LXQT)
- Ubuntu Studio
- Ubuntu Budgie
- Ubuntu Cinnamon
- Ubuntu Unity

Ubuntu Flavors are based on the Ubuntu Linux distribution, but use different desktops and initial software collections. These are common desktops that are used for other Linux distribution, but have been adapted for Ubuntu and the Ubuntu software repositories, including Snap. These include Kubuntu based on the KDE Plasma desktop (see Chapter 9), Ubuntu MATE which uses the MATE desktop (see Chapter 10), Xubuntu which uses the Xfce desktop, Lubuntu adapts the LXDE desktop, Ubuntu Budgie uses the Budgie desktop, which is based on the Ubuntu GNOME desktop. Ubuntu Studio is a customized collection of multimedia production software from the Ubuntu repository and uses the Kubuntu desktop. Ubuntu Kylin is designed specifically for Chinese users.

The Ubuntu Flavors are available at:

https://ubuntu.com/download/flavours

They are also available at:

http://cdimage.ubuntu.com

Xubuntu (Xfce)

Xubuntu uses the Xfce desktop, with the Ubuntu repositories. The Xfce desktop is a lightweight desktop designed to run fast without the kind of overhead required for full featured desktops like KDE and GNOME. You can think of it as a window manager with desktop functionality. It includes its own file manager and panel, but the emphasis is on modularity and simplicity. Like GNOME, Xfce is based on GTK+ GUI tools. The desktop consists of a collection of modules like the thunar file manager, xfce4-panel panel, and the xfwm4 window manager. Keeping with its focus on simplicity, Xfce features only a few common applets on its panel. It's small scale makes it appropriate for laptops or dedicated systems, that have no need for complex overhead found in other desktops. Xfce is useful for desktops designed for just a few tasks, like multimedia desktops.

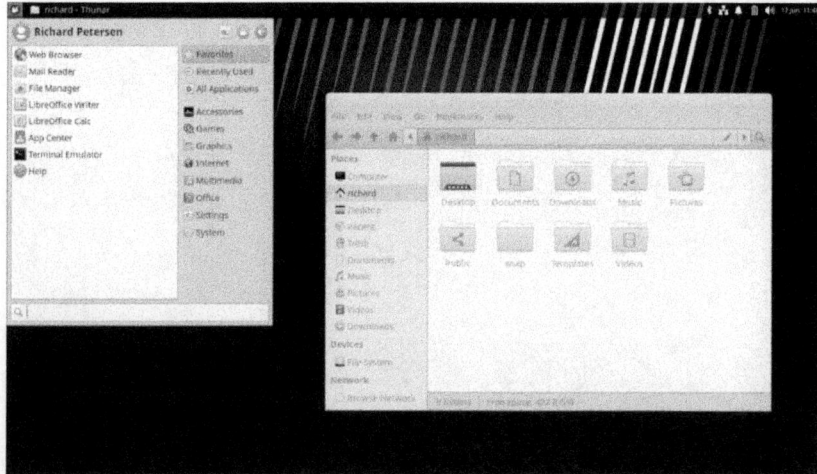

Figure 11-1: Xubuntu (Xfce) Desktop

You can find out more about Xubuntu and download it from:

`https://xubuntu.org`

You can find out more about Xfce from:

`https://xfce.org/`

To install Xubuntu as an alternative desktop on a system, select the **xubuntu-desktop** package in the Synaptic Package Manager or use the **apt** command.

The desktop displays icons for your Home folder and Trash (see Figure 11-1). The top panel holds a menu button on the left side for the Applications menu (Whisker menu). From the menu, you can access applications and administration tools. Next to the menu button are the window list buttons for open windows. The right side of the panel has buttons for the time and date (calendar), volume control, power manager, notifications, network connections, and power status. You can add more items by clicking on the panel and selecting Panel | Add new items. This opens a window with several applets like the clock and workspace switcher, as well as Action Buttons for logout and shutdown. To move an applet, right-click on it and choose Move from the pop-up menu, and then move the mouse to the new insertion location and click.

Right-clicking anywhere on the desktop background displays the desktop menu with options such as create folders, open a terminal window, and arrange icons.

Clicking the power button at the bottom right of the Applications menu, opens a dialog with buttons for logout, shut down, restart, suspend, and switch user. You can also choose to save your current session, restoring your open windows when you log back in.

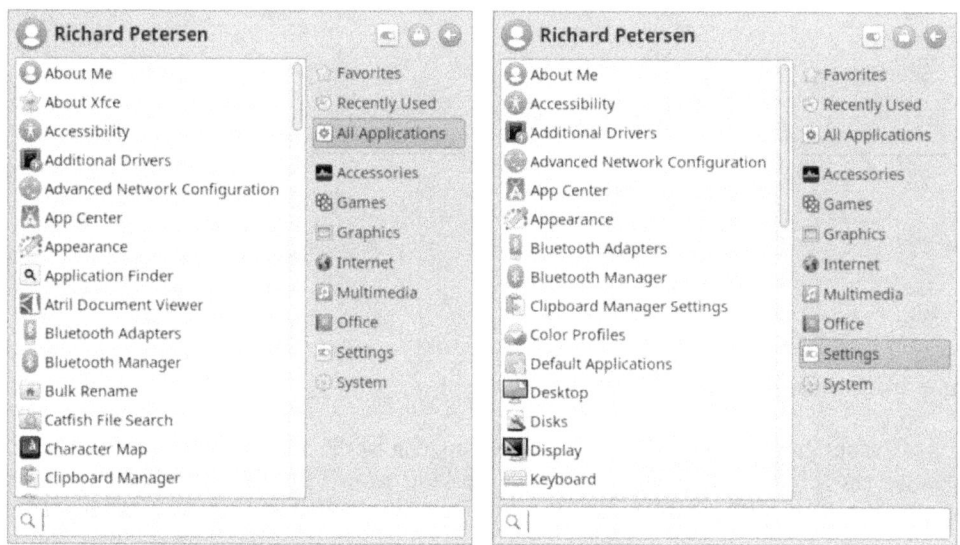

Figure 11-2: Xubuntu (Xfce) Applications Menu

You can access applications from the Applications menu (left side of the top panel). Categories are shown to the right, and the items in the category are listed to the left (see Figure 11-2). You can use a search box at the top to find an application. The name of the current user is listed

476 Part 3: Desktops

at the bottom of the menu. At the lower right are the Settings, Lock Screen, and Log Out buttons. Clicking the Log Out button displays a menu of log out, shut down, and restart buttons.

Xfce file manager is called Thunar. The file manager will open a side pane in the shortcuts view that lists entries for not just for the home folder, but also your file system, desktop, and trash folders (see Figure 11-1). The File menu lets you perform folder operations like creating new folders. From the Edit menu, you can perform tasks on a selected file like renaming the file or creating a link for it. You can change the side pane view to a tree view of your file system by selecting the option from the menubar View | Side Pane | Tree, (Ctrl-e). The Shortcuts entry changes the view back (Ctrl-b).

To configure the Xubuntu desktop, you use the Settings Manager, accessible from the Applications menu by clicking the Settings button at the bottom right of the Applications menu. This opens the Settings window, which shows icons for your desktop, display, panel, user interface, among others (see Figure 11-3). Use the Appearance tool to select themes, icons, fonts, and toolbar styles. The Panel tool lets you add new panels and control features like lock for freely movable and mode for horizontally or vertically positioned panels. You can also choose a background image and the items to include in the panel. You can also access the Settings Manager tools from the desktop menu by choosing Applications | Settings.

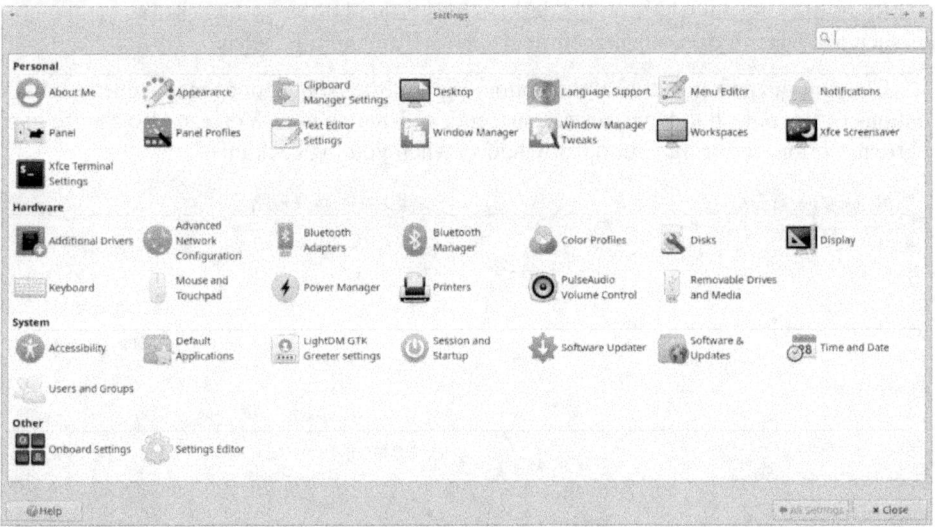

Figure 11-3: Xubuntu (Xfce) Settings Manager

To configure the desktop, select the Desktop icon on the Settings window or right-click on the desktop and select Desktop Settings from the desktop menu. This opens the Desktop window where you can select the background image, control menu behavior, and set icon sizes (see Figure 11-4).

Figure 11-4: Xubuntu (Xfce) Desktop Settings

Lubuntu (LXQT)

Lubuntu uses the LXQT desktop, the Lightweight QT Desktop Environment. The LXQT desktop provides a small desktop designed for use on minimal or low power systems like laptops, netbooks, or older computers.

You can find out more about Lubuntu and download it from:

https://lubuntu.me/

You can find out more about LXQT at:

https://lxqt.github.io/

To install Lubuntu as an alternative desktop on a system, select the **lubuntu-desktop** package on the Synaptic Package Manager or use the **sudo apt install** command to install it from a terminal window.

The desktop displays a single panel at the bottom with the application menu to the left, followed by the windows taskbar, and system applets to the right (see Figure 11-5). From the panel applications menu, you can access any applications. Next to the menu is a workspace switcher, Quicklaunch widget, and a taskbar for open windows. You can drag any application entry in the menu to the Quicklauch widget to have its icon displayed on the panel.

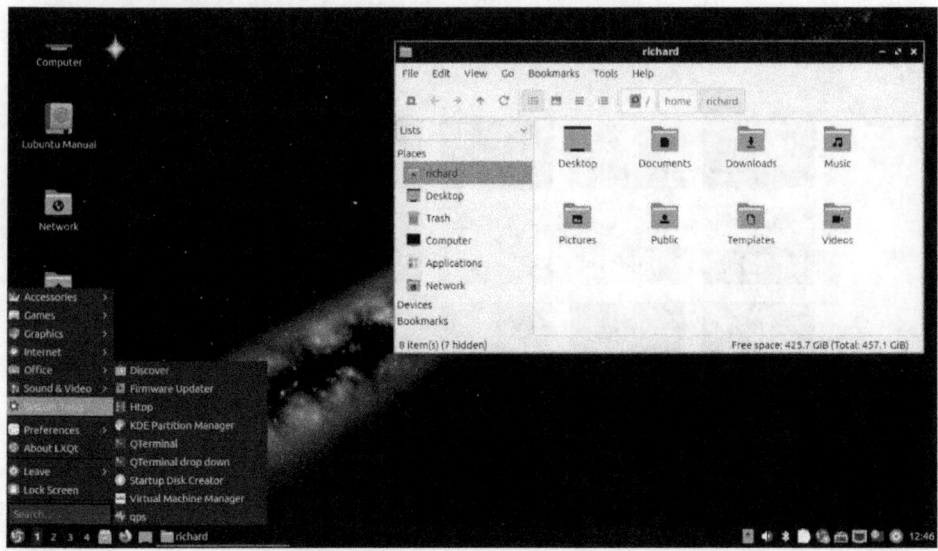

Figure 11-5: Lubuntu (LXQT) desktop

The bottom panel shows widgets for the applications menu, the workspace switcher, the PC-Man file manager, Web browser, minimize windows, and the window list. On the right side of the panel are widgets for the removeable device manager, volume control, clipboard, power management, NetworkManager, notifications, and the clock (see Figure 11-6).

Figure 11-6: Lubuntu (LXQT) panel

The Leave entry on the applications menu leave entry opens a dialog with buttons for logout, shutdown, suspend, hibernate, reboot, and leave.

Lubuntu uses the PC-Man file manager as shown in Figure 11-5. The toolbar performs browser tasks like moving backward and forward to previously viewed folders, as well as new tabs and icon and list views. The side pane has a location (Places) and folder tree view. You can switch between the two using the menu at the top of the pane.

To configure your panel, right-click on the panel and select Configure Panel to open the Configure Panel dialog at the Placement tab (see Figure 11-7). You can set the position and size of the panel, the autohide feature. On the Styling tab you can set the background and font color for the panel, as well as the icon theme.

Figure 11-7: Lubuntu (LXQT) Configure Panel

To manage your widgets on the panel, right-click on the panel and select Manage Widgets from the menu to open the Configure Panel dialog at the Widgets tab (see Figure 11-8). Buttons to the right let you add, remove, and configure your widgets. Loaded widgets are listed. To remove a widget, select it and click the minus button. To configure a widget, click the configure button (gear symbol) to open the widget's configuration dialog. This will vary among applets. To set the time display format, select the world clock and click configure button to open the clock settings dialog. Widget settings can also be configured directly from the panel. Right-click on the widget and choose the Configure entry, like Configure "World Clock " for the world clock widget.

To add a new applet to the panel, Click the Plus button to open the Add Plugins window, which will list all available applets and panel features like spaces. Select the one you want and click the Add Widget button (see Figure 11-8).

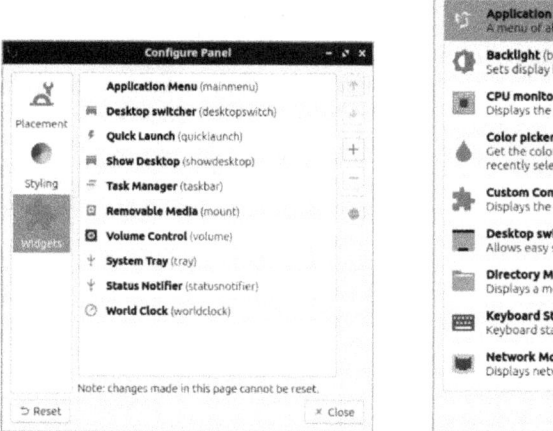 

Figure 11-8: Lubuntu (LXQT) Configure Panel Widgets tab and Plugins

Part 3: Desktops

To configure the desktop, right-click anywhere on the desktop and choose Desktop Preferences from the pop-up menu. This opens the Desktop Preferences window with tabs for General, Background, Slide Show, and Advanced (see Figure 11-9). The General tab lets you set the icon size, label text font and color, as well as the minimum item spacing. The Advanced tab lets you choose what icons to display on the desktop (home, trash, computer, and network). The Slide Show enables a wallpaper slideshow and lets you choose the folder for the slideshow images as well as the time intervals. The Background tab lets you select the background color, wallpaper mode, and wallpaper image file.

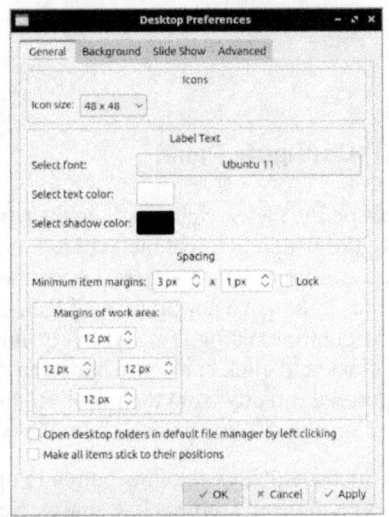

Figure 11-9: Lubuntu (LXQT) Desktop Preferences

Ubuntu Studio

Ubuntu Studio provides a collection of Linux-based multimedia software for graphic design, audio production, and video production (see Figure 11-10). Applications include Blender 3d modeling and the Audacity sound editor. Ubuntu Studio is based on Kubuntu and has the Kubuntu system tools such as the Dolphin file manager, the Discover software manager, and Kubuntu System Settings tools. The panel is at the top of the screen with button for popular applications such as Firefox, the Kdenlive video editor, and the Gimp image editor. The task manager uses the KDE Icon-only task manager. Buttons for open applications are displayed on the panel. Passing your mouse over an application button display icons you can choose for all the windows currently open with that application.

You can download Ubuntu Studio from:

https://ubuntustudio.org/

The site also has documentation and support links for applications.

Chapter 11: Ubuntu Flavors **481**

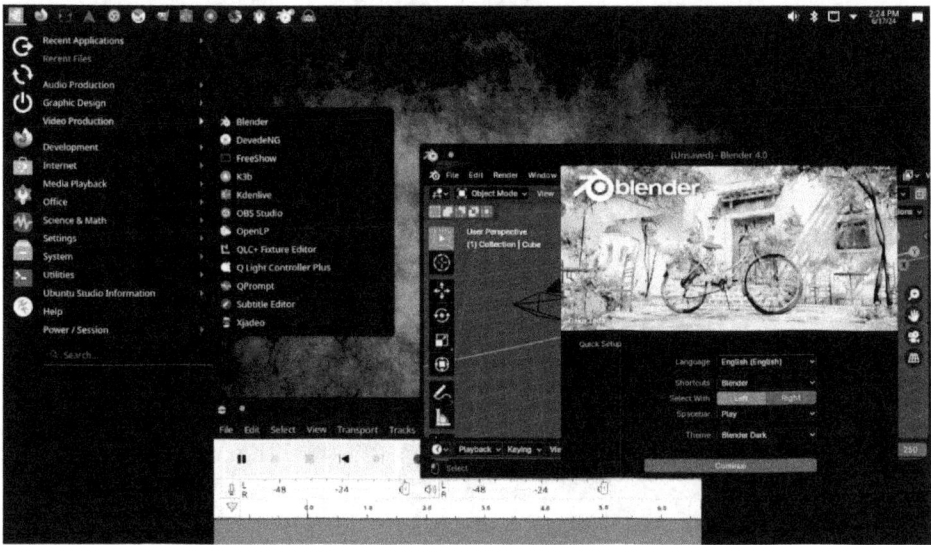

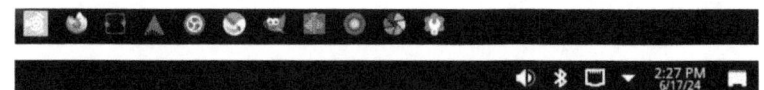

Figure 11-10: Ubuntu Studio

Ubuntu Budgie

Ubuntu Budgie uses the Budgie desktop, developed for the Solus Linux distribution (see Figure 11-11). It installs the full set of applications, though a few of the default applications are different. The media player is Parole instead of Videos and the Budgie Control Center is used instead of GNOME Settings. Ubuntu Budgie uses the same Apps Center for managing software. Ubuntu Budgie features immediate updates, as they become available. This ensures a more secure system.

The Plank dock at the bottom has favorite applications. The top panel has applets on the right and the time and date in the center. When you open an application, an icon for it appears on the dock. You can right-click on it to have it shown permanently.

Part 3: Desktops

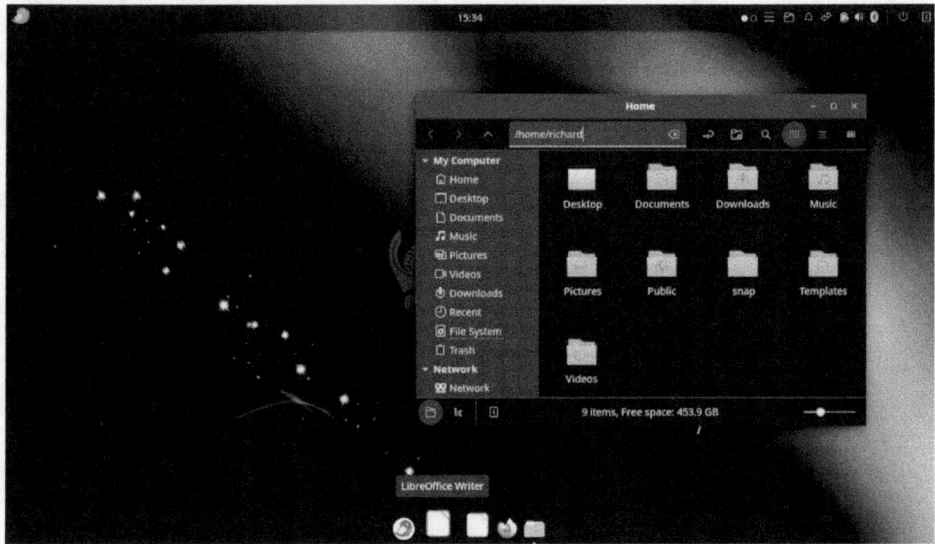

Figure 11-11: Ubuntu Budgie

You can download Ubuntu Budgie from:

https://ubuntubudgie.org/downloads

You can access applications from the menu at the top left of the panel. Buttons on the top left of the menu let you switch between an icon view of the menu and a list view with categories (see Figure 11-12).

 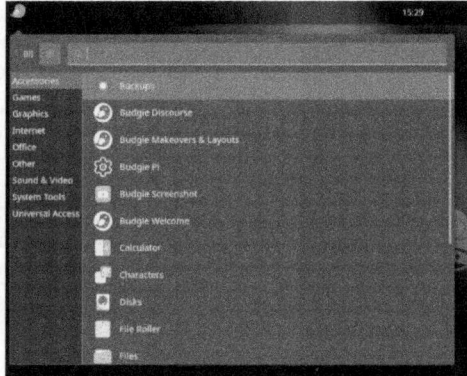

Figure 11-12: Ubuntu Budgie menu

The Welcome dialog's Getting Started dialog has links for common tasks such as updates, drivers, and customization (see Figure 11-13).

Chapter 11: Ubuntu Flavors **483**

Figure 11-13: Ubuntu Budgie Welcome

For Budgie Applets you can use the Budgie Extras dialog accessible from the INSTALL SOFTWARE menu (see Figure 11-14). Budgie applets include Hotcorners that set up corners to activate features when you move your mouse to one, Clockworks which provides a world clock display, Weather and Forecast applet, and Window Shuffler for moving and arranging windows.

484   Part 3: Desktops

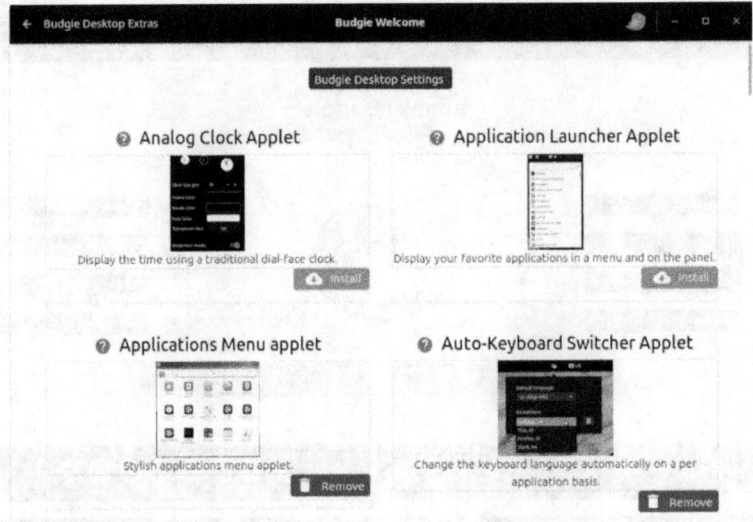

Figure 11-14: Budgie Applets

For Budgie themes you can use the Budgie Themes and dialog accessible from the MAKEOVERS & LAYOUTS button (see Figure 11-15).

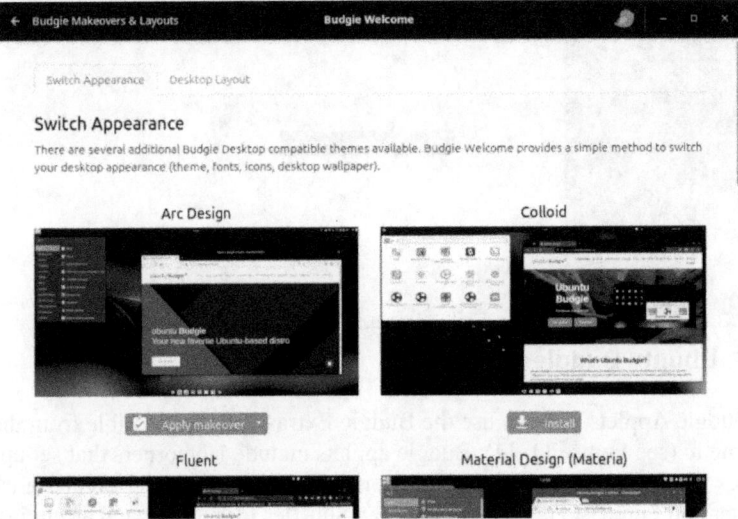

Figure 11-15: Budgie Themes

Ubuntu Cinnamon

Ubuntu Cinnamon uses the Cinnamon desktop, which was developed by Linux Mint. Though Cinnamon was originally derived from GNOME 3, its interface is similar to GNOME 2, using a simple panel with applets (see Figure 11-16). The Cinnamon desktop is designed for ease of use on desktop systems, using a traditional panel with applets for most desktop tasks. Applets for

Bluetooth, NetworkManager, sound volume, power, and time and date are placed on the right side of the panel. The left side of the panel is the Cinnamon menu, the panel launchers applet to quick start applications, and the Grouped Windows List applet for open windows. You can easily add and remove applets using the System Settings Applets dialog, accessible from the Panel applet. The Panel Edit mode (right-click on the panel) lets you reposition and remove applets. The system supported folders (Computer, Home, and Trash) are displayed on the desktop.

You can find out more about Ubuntu Cinnamon and download it from:

`https://ubuntucinnamon.org/`

Figure 11-16: Ubuntu Cinnamon desktop

When you open an application, a button for it is displayed on the bottom panel in the grouped window list applet. Each application button shows the number of windows open for that application. Moving your mouse over a Grouped Window List button displays thumbnails for any open windows for that application (see Figure 11-17). Moving the mouse over a window thumbnail highlights it and displays a close button in the upper right corner as well as briefly showing what the opened window would be on the desktop. Clicking on the thumbnail restores the window if it is minimized or makes that window the active window on your desktop.

Part 3: Desktops

Figure 11-17: Ubuntu Cinnamon Grouped Window List

The Cinnamon desktop features a Cinnamon menu for applications, places, and tasks, with a Favorites icon bar for the commonly used applications and tasks (see Figure 11-18). The Favorites icon bar shows icons for System Settings, chat, the terminal window, and the Nemo file manager. There are also icons for lock, logout, and shut down operations.

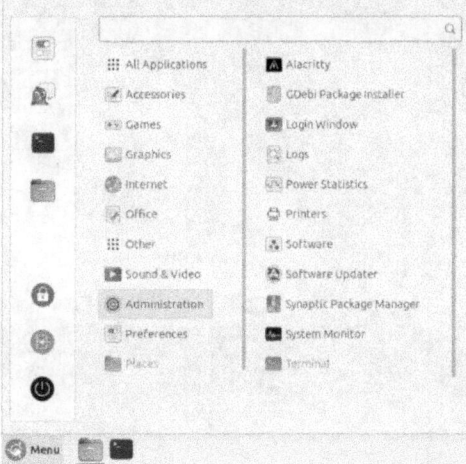

Figure 11-18: Ubuntu Cinnamon menu

Cinnamon uses the Nemo file manager. You can access your home folder by clicking the Home Folder icon on the desktop, the home folder button on the panel, or the home folder icon on the Cinnamon menu's Favorites icon bar. A file manager window opens showing your home directory. The file manager window displays several components, including a browser toolbar, location bar, and a sidebar showing devices, file systems, and folders. When you open a new folder, the same window is used to display it, and you can use the forward and back arrows to move through previously opened folders. The location bar displays either folder buttons or a pathname showing your current folder and its parent folders. You toggle between a button display or pathname. Figure 11-19 shows the file manager window.

Chapter 11: Ubuntu Flavors **487**

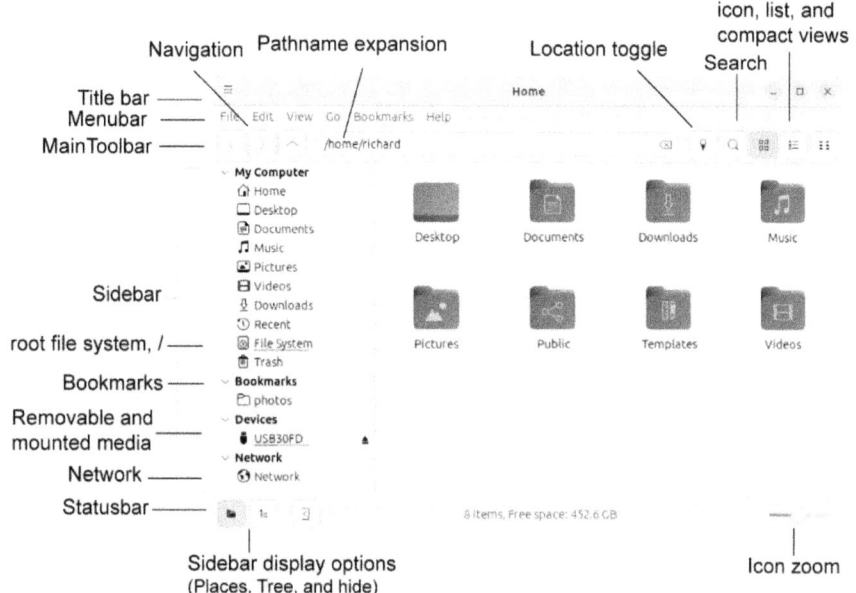

Figure 11-19: Ubuntu Cinnamon Nemo File manager

You can configure desktop settings and perform most administrative tasks using the administration tools listed in the System Settings dialog, accessible from the Preferences menu and from the menu Favorites icon bar. System Settings organizes tools into Appearance, Preferences, Hardware, and Administration categories (see Figure 11-20). For software management Ubuntu Cinnamon uses GNOME Software and the Synaptic Package Manager, instead of the Apps Center. For administration and preferences it uses different GNOME administrative tools such as those for printing, sound, and Bluetooth devices.

488 Part 3: Desktops

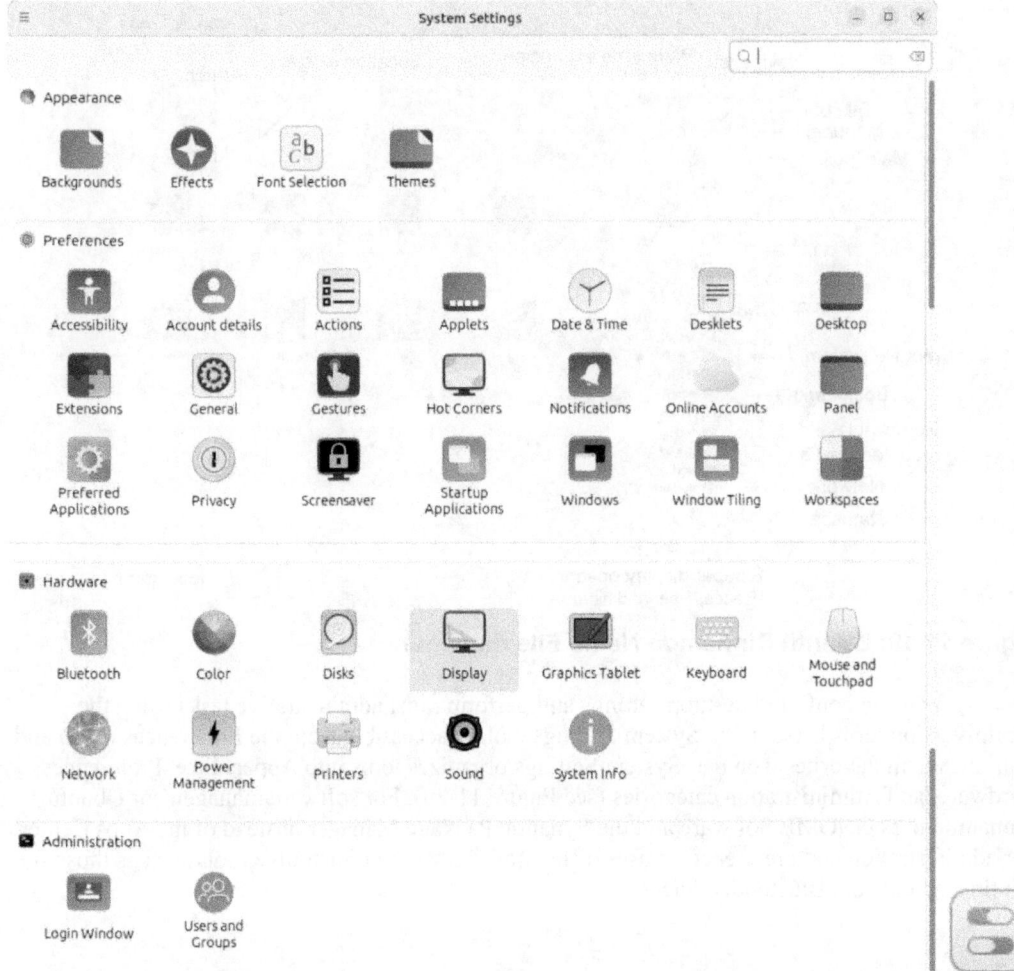

Figure 11-20: System Settings dialog (Appearance and Preferences)

Ubuntu Unity

Ubuntu Unity uses the older Ubuntu Unity desktop used up until Ubuntu 16.04. Unity is designed to make the best use of screen space, placing a launcher on the left side to free up vertical space, making the window menu bar part of the top panel, along with indicator menus for NetworkManager, sound volume, messaging, time and date, and the Session menu (see Figure 11-21).

You can find out more about Ubuntu Unity and download it from:

https://ubuntuunity.org/

The Unity interface features a Launcher for applications and tasks, with icons for the dash, the home folder, LibreOffice applications (Writer, Calc, and Impress), and System Settings. There are also icons for accessing mounted devices and the trash. You can use the System Setting's Appearance dialog to configure changes to your Unity interface, such as Launcher hiding options and the size of the Launcher icons.

The menu bar displays the applications menu and the indicator menus. The left side of the menu bar is the application menu, showing the menu bar for the currently selected open window. The right side of the menu bar holds indicator menus for desktop appearance, NetworkManager, notifications, keyboard, Bluetooth, power, sound volume, Date and time, and the Session menu (user switching and shut down options).

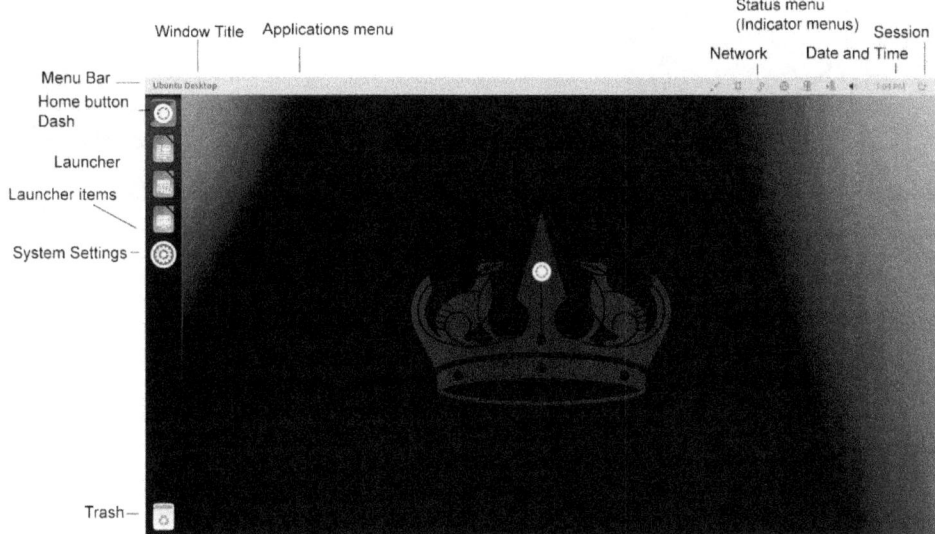

Figure 11-21: Ubuntu Unity interface

When you click on a window, its title is displayed on the top panel. When you move your mouse to the left side of the top panel, that window's menu bar is displayed in the applications menu (see Figure 11-22).

490 Part 3: Desktops

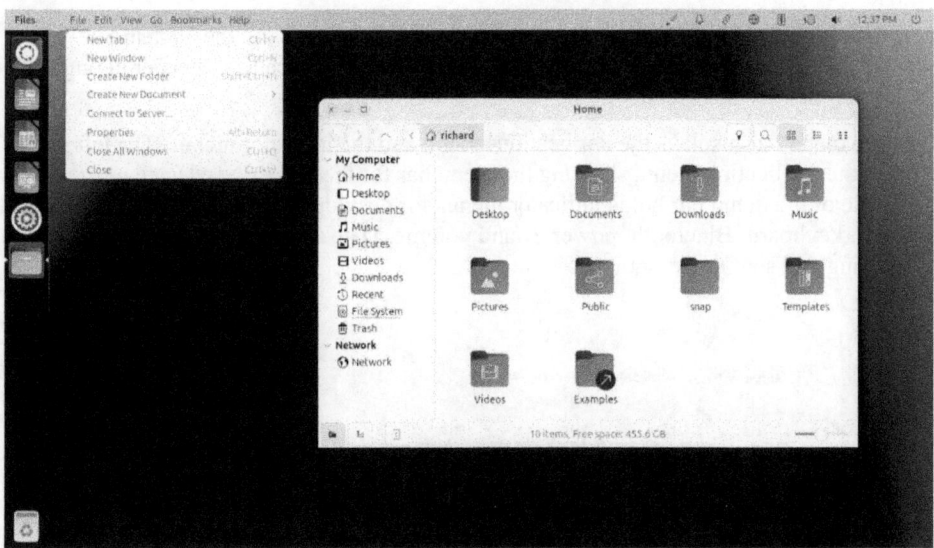

Figure 11-22: Ubuntu Unity interface with selected window and applications menu

The dash button at the top of the Launcher opens the dash, displaying a search box to let you search for applications (see Figure 11-23). At the top of the dash are icons for different lenses: home, applications, files & folders, music, pictures, and videos. Click on an icon to open that lens. Clicking on the applications button opens the Applications dash with a filter menu for accessing different application categories, such as Internet, Media, and System. Applications are organized into the recently used and those installed.

You can close the dash by clicking the dash icon, the close button (**x**) located at the top left side of the panel, or by pressing the ESC key. You can expand it to full-screen by clicking the square button at the top left, to the right of the **x** button.

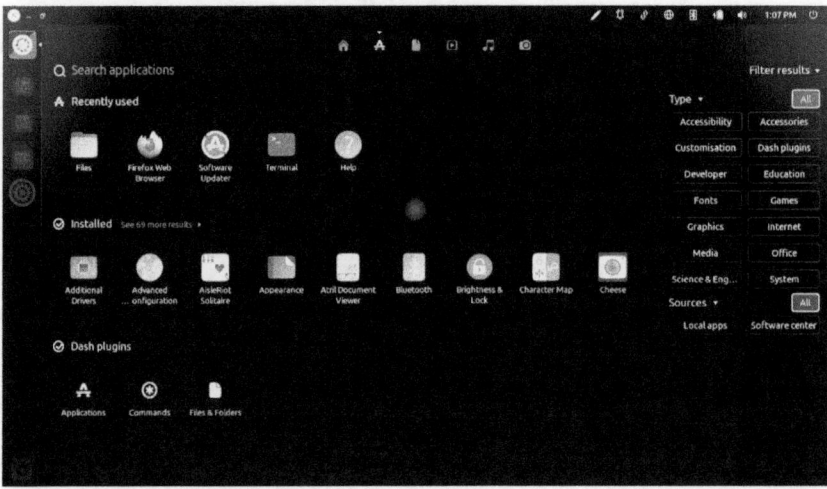

Figure 11-23: Ubuntu Unity dash

For folder and file access, Ubuntu Unity uses GNOME Files. You can access your home folder by clicking the Files application in the Dash (Applications lens). A file manager window opens showing your home folder. Your home folder will already have default folders created for commonly used files. These include Pictures, Documents, Music, Videos, and Downloads.

The file manager window displays several components, including a browser toolbar, location bar, and a sidebar showing devices, file systems, and folders. On Ubuntu Unity, the file menu is located in the applications menu on the top bar. When you open a new folder, the same window is used to display it, and you can use the forward and back arrows to move through previously opened folders. Figure 11-24 shows the file manager window.

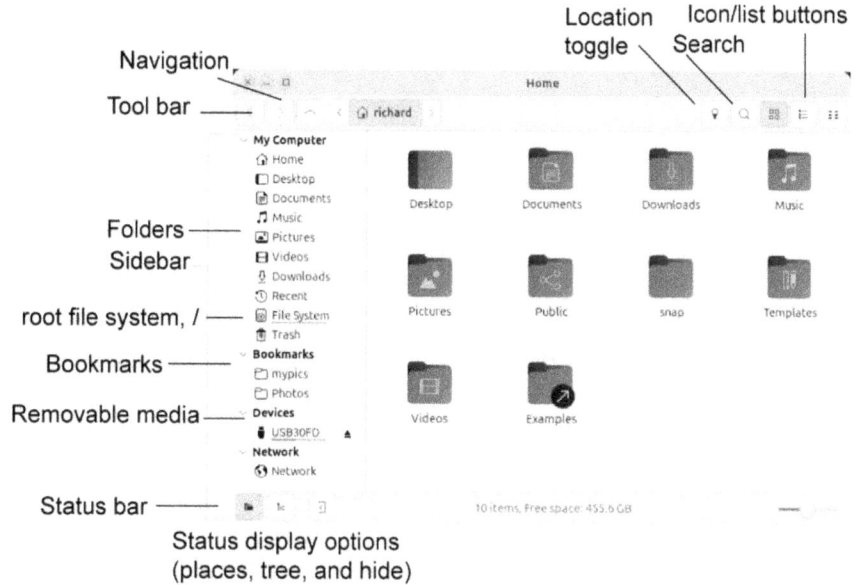

Figure 11-24: Ubuntu Unity File manager

For managing software, use the Synaptic Package Manager. To install individual packages, use the GDebi Package Installer.

You can configure desktop settings and perform most administrative tasks using the settings tools listed in the GNOME System Settings dialog, accessible from the session menu and the Launcher. System Settings organizes tools into Personal, Hardware, and System categories (see Figure 11-25). Some invoke the Ubuntu supported system tools available from previous releases such as Printers (system-config-printer). Others use older GNOME configuration and administrative tools such as Displays, User Accounts, and Power. System Settings tools will open with an "All Settings" button at the top left, which you can click to return to the System Settings dialog.

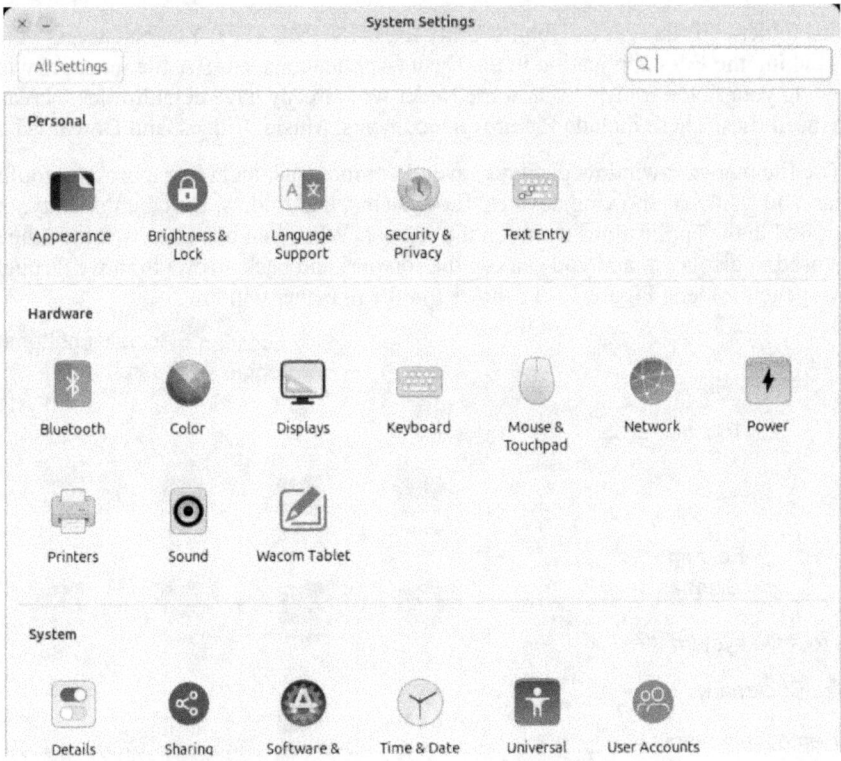
Figure 11-25: System Settings dialog

ubuntu

12. Shells

The Command Line
History
Filename Expansion: *, ?, [ ]
Standard Input/Output and Redirection
Linux Files
The File Structure
Listing, Displaying, and Printing Files
Managing Directories: mkdir, rmdir, ls, cd, pwd
File and Directory Operations: find, cp, mv, rm, ln

The shell is a command interpreter that provides a line-oriented interactive and non-interactive interface between the user and the operating system. You enter commands on a command line and they are interpreted by the shell and then sent as instructions to the operating system (the command line interface is accessible from GNOME, KDE, and MATE through a Terminal windows). You can also place commands in a script file to be consecutively executed, much like a program. This interpretive capability of the shell provides for many sophisticated features. For example, the shell has a set of file expansion characters that can generate filenames. The shell can redirect input and output, as well as display previously executed commands.

Shell	Web Site
www.gnu.org/software/bash	BASH website with online manual, FAQ, and current releases
www.gnu.org/software/bash/manual/bash.html	BASH online manual
www.zsh.org	Z shell website with referrals to FAQs and current downloads.
www.kornshell.com	Korn shell site with manual, FAQ, and references

Table 12-1: Linux Shells

Several different types of shells have been developed for Linux: the Bourne Again shell (BASH), the Korn shell, the TCSH shell, and the Z shell. All shells are available for your use, although the BASH shell is the default. You only need one type of shell to do your work. Ubuntu Linux includes all the major shells, although it installs and uses the BASH shell as the default. If you use the command line shell, you will be using the BASH shell unless you specify another. This chapter discusses the BASH shell, which shares many of the same features as other shells.

You can find out more about shells at their respective websites as listed in Table 12-1. In addition, a detailed online manual is available for each installed shell. Use the **man** command and the shell's keyword to access them, **bash** for the BASH shell, **ksh** for the Korn shell, **zsh** for the Z shell, and **tsch** for the TSCH shell. For example, the command **man bash** will access the BASH shell online manual.

Note: You can find out more about the BASH shell at www.gnu.org/software/bash. A detailed online manual is available on your Linux system using the **man** command with the **bash** keyword.

The Command Line

The Linux command line interface consists of a single line into which you enter commands with any of their options and arguments. From GNOME or KDE, you can access the command line interface by opening a terminal window (Applications Overview | Terminal). Should you start Linux with the command line interface, you will be presented with a BASH shell command line when you log in.

By default, the BASH shell has a dollar sign ($) prompt, but Linux has several other types of shells, each with its own prompt (like % for the C shell). The root user will have a different prompt, the #. A shell prompt, such as the one shown here, marks the beginning of the command line:

$

You can enter a command along with options and arguments at the prompt. For example, with an **-l** option, the **ls** command will display a line of information about each file, listing such data as its size and the date and time it was last modified. In the next example, the user enters the **ls** command followed by a **-l** option. The dash before the **-l** option is required. Linux uses it to distinguish an option from an argument.

```
$ ls -l
```

If you wanted only the information displayed for a particular file, you could add that file's name as the argument, following the **-l** option:

```
$ ls -l mydata
-rw-r--r-- 1 chris weather 207 Feb 20 11:55 mydata
```

Tip: Some commands can be complex and take some time to execute. When you mistakenly execute the wrong command, you can interrupt and stop such commands with the interrupt key, CTRL-C.

You can enter a command on several lines by typing a backslash just before you press ENTER. The backslash "escapes" the ENTER key, effectively continuing the same command line to the next line. In the next example, the **cp** command is entered on three lines. The first two lines end in a backslash, effectively making all three lines one command line.

```
$ cp -i \
mydata \
/home/george/myproject/newdata
```

You can also enter several commands on the same line by separating them with a semicolon (;). In effect, the semicolon operates as an execute operation. Commands will be executed in the sequence in which they are entered. The following command executes an **ls** command followed by a **date** command.

```
$ ls ; date
```

You can also conditionally run several commands on the same line with the **&&** operator. A command is executed only if the previous command is true. This feature is useful for running several dependent scripts on the same line. In the next example, the **ls** command is run only if the **date** command is successfully executed.

```
$ date && ls
```

TIP: Commands can also be run as arguments on a command line, using their results for other commands. To run a command within a command line, you encase the command in back quotes.

Command Line Editing

The BASH shell, which is your default shell, has special command line editing capabilities (see Table 12-2). You can easily modify commands you have entered before executing them, moving anywhere on the command line and inserting or deleting characters. This is very helpful for complex commands.

Movement Commands	Operation
CTRL-F, RIGHT-ARROW	Move forward a character
CTRL-B, LEFT-ARROW	Move backward a character
CTRL-A or HOME	Move to beginning of line
CTRL-E or END	Move to end of line
ALT-F	Move forward a word
ALT-B	Move backward a word
CTRL-L	Clear screen and place line at top
Editing Commands	**Operation**
CTRL-D or DEL	Delete character cursor is on
CTRL-H or BACKSPACE	Delete character before the cursor
CTRL-K	Cut remainder of line from cursor position
CTRL-U	Cut from cursor position to beginning of line
CTRL-W	Cut the previous word
CTRL-C	Cut entire line
ALT-D	Cut the remainder of a word
ALT-DEL	Cut from the cursor to the beginning of a word
CTRL-Y	Paste previous cut text
ALT-Y	Paste from set of previously cut text
CTRL-Y	Paste previous cut text
CTRL-V	Insert quoted text, used for inserting control or meta (Alt) keys as text, such as CTRL-B for backspace or CTRL-T for tabs
ALT-T	Transpose current and previous word
ALT-L	Lowercase current word
ALT-U	Uppercase current word
ALT-C	Capitalize current word
CTRL-SHIFT-_	Undo previous change

Table 12-2: Command Line Editing Operations

You can press CTRL-F or the RIGHT ARROW key to move forward a character, or the CTRL-B or LEFT ARROW key to move back a character. CTRL-D or DEL deletes the character the cursor is on, and CTRL-H or BACKSPACE deletes the character preceding the cursor. To add text, you use the arrow keys to move the cursor to where you want to insert text and type the new characters.

You can even cut words with the CTRL-W or ALT-D key, and then press the CTRL-Y key to paste them back in at a different position, effectively moving the words. As a rule, the CTRL version of the command operates on characters, and the ALT version works on words, such as CTRL-T to transpose characters and ALT-T to transpose words. At any time, you can press ENTER to execute the command. For example, if you make a spelling mistake when entering a command, rather than re-entering the entire command, you can use the editing operations to correct the mistake. The actual associations of keys and their tasks, along with global settings, are specified in the **/etc/inputrc** file.

The editing capabilities of the BASH shell command line are provided by Readline. Readline supports numerous editing operations. You can even bind a key to a selected editing operation. Readline uses the **/etc/inputrc** file to configure key bindings. This file is read automatically by your **/etc/profile** shell configuration file when you log in. Users can customize their editing commands by creating an **.inputrc** file in their home directory (this is a dot file). It may be best to first copy the **/etc/inputrc** file as your **.inputrc** file and then edit it. **/etc/profile** will first check for a local **.inputrc** file before accessing the **/etc/inputrc** file. You can find out more about Readline in the BASH shell reference manual at **www.gnu.org/software/bash**.

Command and Filename Completion

The BASH command line has a built-in feature that performs command line and filename completion. Automatic completions can be displayed by pressing the TAB key. If you enter an incomplete pattern as a command or filename argument, you can press the TAB key to activate the command and filename completion feature, which completes the pattern. A directory will have a forward slash (/) attached to its name. If more than one command or file has the same prefix, the shell simply beeps and waits for you to press the TAB key again. It then displays a list of possible command completions and waits for you to add enough characters to select a unique command or filename. For situations where you know multiple possibilities are likely, you can just press the ESC key instead of two TABs. In the next example, the user issues a **cat** command with an incomplete filename. When the user presses the TAB key, the system searches for a match and, when it finds one, fills in the filename. The user can then press ENTER to execute the command.

```
$ cat pre <tab>
$ cat preface
```

The automatic completions also work with the names of variables, users, and hosts. In this case, the partial text needs to be preceded by a special character, indicating the type of name. A listing of possible automatic completions follows:

Filenames begin with any text or /.

Shell variable text begins with a **$** sign.

Username text begins with a ~ sign.

Host name text begins with a **@**.

Commands, aliases, and text in files begin with normal text.

Variables begin with a **$** sign, so any text beginning with a dollar sign is treated as a variable to be completed. Variables are selected from previously defined variables, like system shell variables. Usernames begin with a tilde (~). Host names begin with a **@** sign, with possible names taken from the **/etc/hosts** file. For example, to complete the variable HOME given just $HOM, simply press a tab key.

```
$ echo $HOM <tab>
$ echo $HOME
```

If you entered just an **H**, then you could press TAB twice to see all possible variables beginning with H. The command line is redisplayed, letting you complete the name.

```
$ echo $H <tab> <tab>
$HISTCMD $HISTFILE $HOME $HOSTTYPE HISTFILE $HISTSIZE $HISTNAME
$ echo $H
```

You can also specifically select the kind of text to complete, using corresponding command keys. In this case, it does not matter what kind of sign a name begins with.

Command (CTRL-R for listing possible completions)	Description
TAB	Automatic completion
TAB TAB or ESC	List possible completions
ALT-/, CTRL-R-/	Filename completion, normal text for automatic
ALT-$, CTRL-R-$	Shell variable completion, $ for automatic
ALT-~, CTRL-R-~	Username completion, ~ for automatic
ALT-@, CTRL-R-@	Host name completion, @ for automatic
ALT-!, CTRL-R-!	Command name completion, normal text for automatic

Table 12-3: Command Line Text Completion Commands

For example, the pressing ALT-~ will treat the current text as a username. Pressing ALT-@ will treat it as a hostname, and ALT-$, as a variable. Pressing ALT-! will treat it as a command. To display a list of possible completions, press the CTRL-X key with the appropriate completion key, as in CTRL-X-$ to list possible variable completions. See Table 12-3 for a complete listing.

History

The BASH shell keeps a history list, of your previously entered commands. You can display each command, in turn, on your command line by pressing the UP ARROW key. Press the DOWN ARROW key to move down the list. You can modify and execute any of these previous commands when you display them on the command line.

Tip: The ability to redisplay a command is helpful when you have already executed a command you had entered incorrectly. In this case, you would be presented with an error message and a new, empty command line. By pressing the UP ARROW key, you can redisplay the previous command, make corrections to it, and then execute it again. This way, you would not have to enter the whole command again.

History Events

In the BASH shell, the history utility keeps a record of the most recent commands you have executed. The commands are numbered starting at 1, and a limit exists to the number of commands remembered. The default is 500. The history utility is a kind of short-term memory, keeping track of the most recent commands you have executed. To see the set of your most recent commands, type **history** on the command line and press ENTER. A list of your most recent commands is then displayed, preceded by a number.

```
$ history
1 cp mydata today
2 vi mydata
3 mv mydata reports
4 cd reports
5 ls
```

History Commands	Description
CTRL-N or DOWN ARROW	Moves down to the next event in the history list
CTRL-P or UP ARROW	Moves up to the previous event in the history list
ALT-<	Moves to the beginning of the history event list
ALT->	Moves to the end of the history event list
ALT-N	Forward Search, next matching item
ALT-P	Backward Search, previous matching item
CTRL-S	Forward Search History, forward incremental search
CTRL-R	Reverse Search History, reverse incremental search
fc *event-reference*	Edits an event with the standard editor and then executes it **Options** -l List recent history events; same as **history** command -e *editor event-reference* Invokes a specified editor to edit a specific event
History Event References	
!*event num*	References an event with an event number
!!	References the previous command
!*characters*	References an event with beginning characters
!?*pattern*?	References an event with a pattern in the event
!-*event num*	References an event with an offset from the first event
!*num-num*	References a range of events

Table 12-4: History Commands and History Event References

Each of these commands is technically referred to as an event. An event describes an action that has been taken, a command that has been executed. The events are numbered according to their sequence of execution. The most recent event has the highest number. Each of these events can be identified by its number or beginning characters in the command.

The history utility lets you reference a former event, placing it on your command line so you can execute it. The easiest way to do this is to use the UP ARROW and DOWN ARROW keys to place history events on the command line, one at a time. You need not display the list first with **history**. Pressing the UP ARROW key once places the last history event on the command line. Pressing it again places the next history event on the command line. Pressing the DOWN ARROW key places the previous event on the command line.

You can use certain control and meta keys to perform other history operations like searching the history list. A meta key is the Alt key, and the ESC key on keyboards that have no Alt key. The Alt key is used here. Pressing Alt-< will move you to the beginning of the history list. Alt-n will search it. Ctrl-s and Ctrl-r will perform incremental searches, displaying matching commands as you type in a search string. Table 12-4 lists the different commands for referencing the history list.

Tip: If more than one history event matches what you have entered, you will hear a beep, and you can then enter more characters to help uniquely identify the event.

You can also reference and execute history events using the ! history command. The ! is followed by a reference that identifies the command. The reference can be either the number of the event or a beginning set of characters in the event. In the next example, the third command in the history list is referenced first by number and then by the beginning characters:

```
$ !3
mv mydata reports
$ !mv my
mv mydata reports
```

You can also reference an event using an offset from the end of the list. A negative number will offset from the end of the list to that event, thereby referencing it. In the next example, the fourth command, **cd mydata**, is referenced using a negative offset, and then executed. Remember that you are offsetting from the end of the list, in this case event 5, up toward the beginning of the list, event 1. An offset of 4 beginning from event 5 places you at event 2.

```
$ !-4
vi mydata
```

To reference the last event, you use a following !, as in !!. In the next example, the command ! ! executes the last command the user executed, in this case, **ls**:

```
$ !!
ls
mydata today reports
```

Filename Expansion: *, ?, [ ]

Filenames are the most common arguments used in a command. Often you will know only part of the filename, or you will want to reference several filenames that have the same extension or begin with the same characters. The shell provides a set of special characters that search out, match, and generate a list of filenames. These are the asterisk, the question mark, and brackets (*, ?, []). Given a partial filename, the shell uses these matching operators to search for files and expand to a list of filenames found. The shell replaces the partial filename argument with the expanded list of matched filenames. This list of filenames can then become the arguments for commands such as **ls**, which can operate on many files. Table 12-5 lists the shell's file expansion characters.

Common Shell Symbols	Execution
ENTER	Execute a command line.
;	Separate commands on the same command line.
`command`	Execute a command.
$(command)	Execute a command.
[ ]	Match on a class of possible characters in filenames.
\	Quote the following character. Used to quote special characters.
|	Pipe the standard output of one command as input for another command.
&	Execute a command in the background.
!	Reference history command.
File Expansion Symbols	**Execution**
*	Match on any set of characters in filenames.
?	Match on any single character in filenames.
[ ]	Match on a class of characters in filenames.
Redirection Symbols	**Execution**
>	Redirect the standard output to a file or device, creating the file if it does not exist and overwriting the file if it does exist.
>!	The exclamation point forces the overwriting of a file if it already exists.
<	Redirect the standard input from a file or device to a program.
>>	Redirect the standard output to a file or device, appending the output to the end of the file.
Standard Error Redirection Symbols	**Execution**
2>	Redirect the standard error to a file or device.
2>>	Redirect and append the standard error to a file or device.
2>&1	Redirect the standard error to the standard output.

Table 12-5: Shell Symbols

Matching Multiple Characters

The asterisk (*) references files beginning or ending with a specific set of characters. You place the asterisk before or after a set of characters that form a pattern to be searched for in filenames.

If the asterisk is placed before the pattern, filenames that end in that pattern are searched for. If the asterisk is placed after the pattern, filenames that begin with that pattern are searched. Any matching filename is copied into a list of filenames generated by this operation.

In the next example, all filenames beginning with the pattern "doc" are searched for and a list generated. Then all filenames ending with the pattern "day" are searched for and a list is generated. The last example shows how the * can be used in any combination of characters.

```
$ ls
doc1 doc2 document docs mydoc monday tuesday
$ ls doc*
doc1 doc2 document docs
$ ls *day
monday tuesday
$ ls m*d*
monday
$
```

Filenames often include an extension specified with a period and followed by a string denoting the file type, such as **.c** for C files, **.cpp** for C++ files, or even **.jpg** for JPEG image files. The extension has no special status, and is only part of the characters making up the filename. Using the asterisk makes it easy to select files with a given extension. In the next example, the asterisk is used to list only those files with a **.c** extension. The asterisk placed before the **.c** constitutes the argument for **ls**.

```
$ ls *.c
calc.c main.c
```

You can use * with the **rm** command to erase several files at once. The asterisk first selects a list of files with a given extension, or beginning or ending with a given set of characters, and then it presents this list of files to the **rm** command to be erased. In the next example, the **rm** command erases all files beginning with the pattern "doc":

```
$ rm doc*
```

Caution: Use the * file expansion character carefully and sparingly with the **rm** command. The combination can be dangerous. A misplaced * in an **rm** command without the -i option could easily erase all the files in your current directory. The **-i** option will first prompt you to confirm whether the file should be deleted.

Matching Single Characters

The question mark (?) matches only a single incomplete character in filenames. Suppose you want to match the files **doc1** and **docA**, but not the file **document**. Whereas the asterisk will match filenames of any length, the question mark limits the match to one extra character. The next example matches files that begin with the word "doc" followed by a single differing letter:

```
$ ls
doc1 docA document
$ ls doc?
doc1 docA
```

Matching a Range of Characters

Whereas the * and ? file expansion characters specify incomplete portions of a filename, the brackets ([]) enable you to specify a set of valid characters to search for. Any character placed within the brackets will be matched in the filename. Suppose you want to list files beginning with "doc", but only ending in **1** or **A**. You are not interested in filenames ending in **2** or **B**, or any other character. This is how it is done.

```
$ ls
doc1 doc2 doc3 docA docB docD document
$ ls doc[1A]
doc1 docA
```

You can also specify a set of characters as a range, rather than listing them one by one. A dash placed between the upper and lower bounds of a range of characters selects all characters within that range. The range is usually determined by the character set in use. In an ASCII character set, the range "a-g" will select all lowercase alphabetic characters from **a** through **g**, inclusive. In the next example, files beginning with the pattern "doc" and ending in characters **1** through **3** are selected. Then, those ending in characters **B** through **E** are matched.

```
$ ls doc[1-3]
doc1 doc2 doc3
$ ls doc[B-E]
docB docD
```

You can combine the brackets with other file expansion characters to form flexible matching operators. Suppose you want to list only filenames ending in either a **.c** or **.o** extension, but no other extension. You can use a combination of the asterisk and brackets: * [co]. The asterisk matches all filenames, and the brackets match only filenames with extension **.c** or **.o**.

```
$ ls *.[co]
main.c   main.o   calc.c
```

Matching Shell Symbols

At times, a file expansion character is actually part of a filename. In these cases, you need to quote the character by preceding it with a backslash (\) to reference the file. In the next example, the user needs to reference a file that ends with the **?** character, called **answers?**. The **?** is, however, a file expansion character and would match any filename beginning with "answers" that has one or more characters. In this case, the user quotes the **?** with a preceding backslash to reference the filename.

```
$ ls answers\?
answers?
```

Placing the filename in double quotes will also quote the character.

```
$ ls "answers?"
answers?
```

This is also true for filenames or directories that have white space characters like the space character. In this case, you could either use the backslash to quote the space character in the file or directory name, or place the entire name in double quotes.

```
$ ls My\ Documents
My Documents
$ ls "My Documents"
My Documents
```

Generating Patterns

Though not a file expansion operation, {} is often useful for generating names that you can use to create or modify files and directories. The braces operation only generates a list of names. It does not match on existing filenames. Patterns are placed within the braces and separated with commas. Any pattern placed within the braces will be used to generate a version of the pattern, using either the preceding or following pattern, or both. Suppose you want to generate a list of names beginning with "doc", but ending only in the patterns "ument", "final", and "draft". This is how it is done.

```
$ echo doc{ument,final,draft}
document docfinal docdraft
```

Since the names generated do not have to exist, you could use the {} operation in a command to create directories, as shown here:

```
$ mkdir {fall,winter,spring}report
$ ls
fallreport springreport winterreport
```

Standard Input/Output and Redirection

The data in input and output operations is organized like a file. Data input at the keyboard is placed in a data stream arranged as a continuous set of bytes. Data output from a command or program is also placed in a data stream and arranged as a continuous set of bytes. This input data stream is referred to in Linux as the standard input, while the output data stream is called the standard output. A separate output data stream reserved solely for error messages is called the standard error.

Because the standard input and standard output have the same organization as that of a file, they can easily interact with files. Linux has a redirection capability that lets you easily move data in and out of files. You can redirect the standard output so that, instead of displaying the output on a screen, you can save it in a file. You can also redirect the standard input away from the keyboard to a file, so that input is read from a file instead of from your keyboard.

When a Linux command is executed it produces output, this output is placed in the standard output data stream. The default destination for the standard output data stream is a device, usually the screen. Devices, such as the keyboard and screen, are treated as files. They receive and send out streams of bytes with the same organization as that of a byte-stream file. The screen is a device that displays a continuous stream of bytes. By default, the standard output will send its data to the screen device, which will then display the data.

For example, the **ls** command generates a list of all filenames and outputs this list to the standard output. This stream of bytes in the standard output is directed to the screen device. The list of filenames is then printed on the screen. The **cat** command also sends output to the standard output. The contents of a file are copied to the standard output, whose default destination is the screen. The contents of the file are then displayed on the screen.

Command	Execution
ENTER	Execute a command line.
;	Separate commands on the same command line.
command\ opts args	Enter backslash before carriage return to continue entering a command on the next line.
`command`	Execute a command.
Special Characters for Filename Expansion	**Execution**
*	Match on any set of characters.
?	Match on any single characters.
[ ]	Match on a class of possible characters.
\	Quote the following character. Used to quote special characters.
Redirection	**Execution**
command > filename	Redirect the standard output to a file or device, creating the file if it does not exist and overwriting the file if it does exist.
command < filename	Redirect the standard input from a file or device to a program.
command >> filename	Redirect the standard output to a file or device, appending the output to the end of the file.
command 2> filename	Redirect the standard error to a file or device
command 2>> filename	Redirect and append the standard error to a file or device
command 2>&1	Redirect the standard error to the standard output in the Bourne shell.
command >& filename	Redirect the standard error to a file or device in the C shell.
Pipes	**Execution**
command | command	Pipe the standard output of one command as input for another command.

Table 12-6: The Shell Operations

Redirecting the Standard Output: > and >>

Suppose that instead of displaying a list of files on the screen, you would like to save this list in a file. In other words, you would like to direct the standard output to a file rather than the screen. To do this, you place the output redirection operator, the greater-than sign (>), followed by the name of a file on the command line after the Linux command. Table 12-6 lists the different ways you can use the redirection operators. In the next example, the output of the **ls** command is redirected from the screen device to a file:

```
$ ls -l *.c > programlist
```

The redirection operation creates the new destination file. If the file already exists, it will be overwritten with the data in the standard output. You can set the **noclobber** feature to prevent overwriting an existing file with the redirection operation. In this case, the redirection operation on an existing file will fail. You can overcome the **noclobber** feature by placing an exclamation point after the redirection operator. You can place the **noclobber** command in a shell configuration file to make it an automatic default operation. The next example sets the **noclobber** feature for the BASH shell and then forces the overwriting of the **oldarticle** file if it already exists:

```
$ set -o noclobber
$ cat myarticle >! oldarticle
```

Although the redirection operator and the filename are placed after the command, the redirection operation is not executed after the command. In fact, it is executed before the command. The redirection operation creates the file and sets up the redirection before it receives any data from the standard output. If the file already exists, it will be destroyed and replaced by a file of the same name. In effect, the command generating the output is executed only after the redirected file has been created.

In the next example, the output of the **ls** command is redirected from the screen device to a file. First, the **ls** command lists files, and in the next command, **ls** redirects its file list to the **listf** file. Then the **cat** command displays the list of files saved in **listf**. Notice the list of files in **listf** includes the **listf** filename. The list of filenames generated by the **ls** command includes the name of the file created by the redirection operation, in this case, **listf**. The **listf** file is first created by the redirection operation, and then the **ls** command lists it along with other files. This file list output by **ls** is then redirected to the **listf** file, instead of being printed on the screen.

```
$ ls
mydata intro preface
$ ls > listf
$ cat listf
mydata intro listf preface
```

Tip: Errors occur when you try to use the same filename for both an input file for the command and the redirected destination file. In this case, because the redirection operation is executed first, the input file, because it exists, is destroyed and replaced by a file of the same name. When the command is executed, it finds an input file that is empty.

You can also append the standard output to an existing file using the >> redirection operator. Instead of overwriting the file, the data in the standard output is added at the end of the file. In the next example, the **myarticle** and **oldarticle** files are appended to the **allarticles** file. The **allarticles** file will then contain the contents of both **myarticle** and **oldarticle**.

```
$ cat myarticle >> allarticles
$ cat oldarticle >> allarticles
```

The Standard Input

Many Linux commands can receive data from the standard input. The standard input itself receives data from a device or a file. The default device for the standard input is the keyboard. Characters typed on the keyboard are placed in the standard input, which is then directed to the

Linux command. Just as with the standard output, you can also redirect the standard input, receiving input from a file rather than the keyboard. The operator for redirecting the standard input is the less-than sign (<). In the next example, the standard input is redirected to receive input from the **myarticle** file, rather than the keyboard device. The contents of **myarticle** are read into the standard input by the redirection operation. Then the **cat** command reads the standard input and displays the contents of **myarticle**.

```
$ cat < myarticle
hello Christopher
How are you today
$
```

You can combine the redirection operations for both standard input and standard output. In the next example, the **cat** command has no filename arguments. Without filename arguments, the **cat** command receives input from the standard input and sends output to the standard output. However, the standard input has been redirected to receive its data from a file, while the standard output has been redirected to place its data in a file.

```
$ cat < myarticle > newarticle
```

Redirecting the Standard Error: >&, 2>, |&

When you execute commands, it is possible for an error to occur. You may give the wrong number of arguments or some kind of system error could take place. When an error occurs, the system will issue an error message. Usually, such error messages are displayed on the screen along with the standard output. Error messages are placed in another standard byte stream called the standard error. In the next example, the cat command is given as its argument the name of a file that does not exist, **myintro**. In this case, the **cat** command will simply issue an error. Redirection operators are listed in Table 12-6.

```
$ cat myintro
cat : myintro not found
```

Because error messages are in a separate data stream from the standard output, this means that if you have redirected the standard output to a file, error messages will still appear on the screen for you to see. Though the standard output may be redirected to a file, the standard error is still directed to the screen. In the next example, the standard output of the **cat** command is redirected to the file **mydata**. The standard error, containing the error messages, is still directed toward the screen.

```
$ cat myintro > mydata
cat : myintro not found
```

Like the standard output, you can also redirect the standard error. This means that you can save your error messages in a file for future reference. This is helpful if you need to save a record of the error messages. Like the standard output, the standard error's default destination is the display. Using special redirection operators, you can redirect the standard error to any file or device that you choose. If you redirect the standard error, the error messages will not be displayed on the screen. You can examine them later by viewing the contents of the file in which you saved them.

All the standard byte streams can be referenced in redirection operations with certain numbers. The numbers 0, 1, and 2 reference the standard input, standard output, and standard error respectively. By default an output redirection, >, operates on the standard output, 1. You can modify the output redirection to operate on the standard error by preceding the output redirection operator with the number 2, **2>**. In the next example, the **cat** command again will generate an error. The error message is redirected to the standard byte stream represented by number 2, the standard error.

```
$ cat nodata 2> myerrors
$ cat myerrors
cat : nodata not found
```

You can also append the standard error to a file by using the number 2 and the redirection append operator, >>. In the next example, the user appends the standard error to the **myerrors** file, which then functions as a log of errors.

```
$ cat nodata 2>> myerrors
$ cat compls 2>> myerrors
$ cat myerrors
cat : nodata not found
cat : compls not found
$
```

To redirect both the standard output as well as the standard error, you would need a separate redirection operation and file for each. In the next example, the standard output is redirected to the file **mydata**, and the standard error is redirected to **myerrors**. If nodata were to exist, then **mydata** would hold a copy of its contents.

```
$ cat nodata 1> mydata 2> myerrors
cat myerrors
cat : nodata not found
```

If you want to save a record of your errors in the same file as that used for the redirected standard output, you need to redirect the standard error into the standard output. You can reference a standard byte stream by preceding its number with an ampersand. **&1** references the standard output. You can use such a reference in a redirection operation to make a standard byte stream a destination file. The redirection operation **2>&1** redirects the standard error into the standard output. In effect, the standard output becomes the destination file for the standard error. Conversely, the redirection operation **1>&2** would redirect the standard input into the standard error.

Pipes: |

You may encounter situations in which you need to send data from one command to another. In other words, you may want to send the standard output of a command to another command, rather than to a destination file. Suppose you want to send a list of your filenames to the printer to be printed. You need two commands to do this: the **ls** command to generate a list of filenames and the **lpr** command to send the list to the printer. In effect, you need to take the output of the **ls** command and use it as input for the **lpr** command. You can think of the data as flowing from one command to another. To form such a connection in Linux, you use what is called a pipe. The pipe operator, the vertical bar character |, placed between two commands forms a connection between them. The standard output of one command becomes the standard input for the other. The pipe operation receives output from the command placed before the pipe and sends this data as input to the command placed after the pipe. As shown in the next example, you can connect the **ls** command and the **lpr** command with a pipe. The list of filenames output by the **ls** command is piped into the **lpr** command.

```
$ ls | lpr
```

You can combine the pipe operation with other shell features, such as file expansion characters, to perform specialized operations. The next example prints only files with a **.c** extension. The **ls** command is used with the asterisk and **.c** (***.c**) to generate a list of filenames with the **.c** extension. Then this list is piped to the **lpr** command.

```
$ ls *.c | lpr
```

In the preceding example, a list of filenames was used as input. What is important to note is that pipes operate on the standard output of a command, whatever that might be. The contents of whole files, or even several files, can be piped from one command to another. In the next example, the **cat** command reads and outputs the contents of the **mydata** file, which are then piped to the **lpr** command:

```
$ cat mydata | lpr
```

Linux has many commands that generate modified output. For example, the **sort** command takes the contents of a file and generates a version with each line sorted in alphabetic order. The **sort** command works best with files that are lists of items. Commands such as **sort** that output a modified version of its input are referred to as filters. Filters are often used with pipes. In the next example, a sorted version of **mylist** is generated and piped into the **more** command for display on the screen. The original file, **mylist**, has not been changed and is not sorted. Only the output of **sort** in the standard output is sorted.

```
$ sort mylist | more
```

The standard input piped into a command can be more carefully controlled with the standard input argument (-). When you use the dash as an argument for a command, it represents the standard input.

Linux Files

You can name a file using any letters, underscores, and numbers. You can also include periods and commas. Except in certain special cases, you should never begin a filename with a period. Other characters, such as slashes, question marks, or asterisks, are reserved for use as special characters by the system and should not be part of a filename. Filenames can be as long as 256 characters. Filenames can also include spaces, though to reference such filenames from the command line, be sure to encase them in quotes. On a desktop like GNOME or KDE, you do not need to use quotes.

You can include an extension as part of a filename. A period is used to distinguish the filename proper from the extension. Extensions can be useful for categorizing your files. You are probably familiar with certain standard extensions. For example, C source code files always have a **.c** extension. Files that contain compiled object code have an **.o** extension. You can make up your own file extensions. The following examples are all valid Linux filenames. Keep in mind that to reference the name with spaces on the command line, you would have to encase it in quotes as "New book review":

```
preface
chapter2
9700info
New_Revisions
calc.c
intro.bk1
New book review
```

Special configuration files are also used to hold shell configuration commands. These are the hidden, or dot, files, which begin with a period. Dot files used by commands and applications have predetermined names, such as the **.mozilla** directory used to hold your Mozilla data and configuration files. When you use **ls** to display your filenames, the dot files will not be displayed. To include the dot files, you need to use **ls** with the **-a** option.

The **ls -l** command displays detailed information about a file. First, the permissions are displayed, followed by the number of links, the owner of the file, the name of the group to which the user belongs, the file size in bytes, the date and time the file was last modified, and the name of the file. Permissions indicate who can access the file: the user, members of a group, or all other users. The group name indicates the group permitted to access the file. The file type for **mydata** is that of an ordinary file. Only one link exists, indicating the file has no other names and no other links. The owner's name is **chris**, the same as the login name, and the group name is **weather**. Other users probably also belong to the **weather** group. The size of the file is 207 bytes, and it was last modified on February 20 at 11:55 A.M. The name of the file is **mydata**.

If you want to display this detailed information for all the files in a directory, use the **ls -l** command without an argument.

```
$ ls -l
-rw-r--r-- 1 chris weather 207 Feb 20 11:55 mydata
-rw-rw-r-- 1 chris weather 568 Feb 14 10:30 today
-rw-rw-r-- 1 chris weather 308 Feb 17 12:40 monday
```

All files in Linux have one physical format, a byte stream, which is simply a sequence of bytes. This allows Linux to apply the file concept to every data component in the system. Directories are classified as files, as are devices. Treating everything as a file allows Linux to organize and exchange data more easily. The data in a file can be sent directly to a device such as a screen because a device interfaces with the system using the same byte-stream file format used by regular files.

This same file format is used to implement other operating system components. The interface to a device, such as the screen or keyboard, is designated as a file. Other components, such as directories, are themselves byte-stream files, but they have a special internal organization. A directory file contains information about a directory, organized in a special directory format. Because these different components are treated as files, they can be said to constitute different file types. A character device is one file type. A directory is another file type. The number of these file types may vary according to your specific implementation of Linux. Five common types of files exist: ordinary files, directory files, first-in first-out (FIFO) pipes, character device files, and block device files. Although you may rarely reference a file's type, it can be useful when searching for directories or devices.

Although all ordinary files have a byte-stream format, they may be used in different ways. The most significant difference is between binary and text files. Compiled programs are examples of binary files. However, even text files can be classified according to their different uses. You can have files that contain C programming source code or shell commands, or even a file that is empty. The file could be an executable program or a directory file. The Linux **file** command helps you determine what a file is used for. It examines the first few lines of a file and tries to determine a classification for it. The **file** command looks for special keywords or special numbers in those first few lines, but it is not always accurate. In the next example, the **file** command examines the contents of two files and determines a classification for them:

```
$ file monday reports
monday: text
reports: directory
```

If you need to examine the entire file byte by byte, you can do so with the **od** (octal dump) command, which performs a dump of a file. By default, it prints every byte in its octal representation. You can also specify a character, decimal, or hexadecimal representation. The **od** command is helpful when you need to detect any special character in your file or if you want to display a binary file.

The File Structure

Linux organizes files into a hierarchically connected set of directories. Each directory may contain either files or other directories. In this respect, directories perform two important functions. A directory holds files, much like files held in a file drawer, and a directory connects to other directories, much as a branch in a tree is connected to other branches. Because of the similarities to a tree, such a structure is often referred to as a tree structure.

The Linux file structure branches into several directories beginning with a root directory, /. Within the root directory, several system directories contain files and programs that are features of the Linux system. The root directory also contains a directory called **home** that contains the home directories of all the users in the system. Each user's home directory, in turn, contains the directories the user has made for their own use. Each of these can also contain directories. Such nested directories branch out from the user's home directory.

Note: The user's home directory can be any directory, though it is usually the directory that bears the user's login name. This directory is located in the directory named **/home** on your Linux system. For example, a user named dylan will have a home directory called **dylan** located in the system's **/home** directory. The user's home directory is a subdirectory of the directory called **/home** on the system.

Home Directories

When you log in to the system, you are placed within your home directory. The name given to this directory by the system is the same as your login name. Any files you create when you first log in are organized within your home directory. Within your home directory, you can create more directories. You can then change to these directories and store files in them. The same is true for other users on the system. Each user has a home directory, identified by the appropriate login name. Users, in turn, can create their own directories.

You can access a directory either through its name or by making it your working directory. Each directory is given a name when it is created. You can use this name in file operations to access files in that directory. You can also make the directory your working directory. If you do not use any directory names in a file operation, the working directory will be accessed. The working directory is the one from which you are currently working. When you log in, the working directory is your home directory, which usually has the same name as your login name. You can change the working directory by using the **cd** command to move to another directory.

Directory	Function
/	Begins the file system structure, called the *root*.
/home	Contains users' home directories.
/bin	Holds all the standard commands and utility programs.
/usr	Holds those files and commands used by the system; this directory breaks down into several subdirectories.
/usr/bin	Holds user-oriented commands and utility programs.
/usr/sbin	Holds system administration commands.
/usr/lib	Holds libraries for programming languages.
/usr/share/doc	Holds Linux documentation.
/usr/share/man	Holds the online Man files.
/var/spool	Holds spooled files, such as those generated for printing jobs and network transfers.
/sbin	Holds system administration commands for booting the system.
/var	Holds files that vary, such as mailbox files.
/dev	Holds file interfaces for devices such as the terminals and printers (dynamically generated by udev, do not edit).
/etc	Holds system configuration files and any other system files.

Table 12-7: Standard System Directories in Linux

Pathnames

The name you give to a directory or file when you create it is not its full name. The full name of a directory is its pathname. The hierarchically nested relationship among directories forms paths, and these paths can be used to identify and reference any directory or file uniquely or absolutely. Each directory in the file structure can be said to have its own unique path. The actual name by which the system identifies a directory always begins with the root directory and consists of all directories nested below that directory.

In Linux, you write a pathname by listing each directory in the path separated from the last by a forward slash. A slash preceding the first directory in the path represents the root. The pathname for the **chris** directory is **/home/chris**. If the **chris** directory has a subdirectory called **reports**, then the full the pathname for the **reports** directory would be **/home/chris/reports**. Pathnames also apply to files. When you create a file within a directory, you give the file a name. The actual name by which the system identifies the file is the filename combined with the path of directories from the root to the file's directory. As an example, the pathname for **monday** is **/home/chris/reports/monday** (the root directory is represented by the first slash). The path for the **monday** file consists of the root, **home**, **chris**, and **reports** directories and the filename **monday**.

Pathnames may be absolute or relative. An absolute pathname is the complete pathname of a file or directory beginning with the root directory. A relative pathname begins from your working directory. It is the path of a file relative to your working directory. The working directory is the one you are currently operating in. Using the previous example, if **chris** is your working directory, the relative pathname for the file **monday** is **reports/monday**. The absolute pathname for **monday** is **/home/chris/reports/monday**.

The absolute pathname from the root to your home directory can be especially complex and, at times, even subject to change by the system administrator. To make it easier to reference, you can use the tilde (~) character, which represents the absolute pathname of your home directory. You have to specify the rest of the pathname for a file from your home directory. In the next example, the user references the **monday** file in the **reports** directory. The tilde represents the path to the user's home directory, **/home/chris**, and then the rest of the path to the **monday** file is specified, **/reports/monday**.

```
$ cat ~/reports/monday
```

System Directories

The root directory that begins the Linux file structure contains several system directories that contain files and programs used to run and maintain the system. Many also contain other subdirectories with programs for executing specific features of Linux. For example, the directory **/usr/bin** contains the various Linux commands that users execute, such as **lpr**. The directory **/bin** holds system level commands. Table 12-7 lists the basic system directories.

Listing, Displaying, and Printing Files: ls, cat, more, less, and lpr

One of the primary functions of an operating system is the management of files. You may need to perform certain basic output operations on your files, such as displaying them on your screen or printing them. The Linux system provides a set of commands that perform basic file-management operations, such as listing, displaying, and printing files, as well as copying, renaming, and erasing files. These commands are usually made up of abbreviated versions of words. For example, the **ls** command is a shortened form of "list" and lists the files in your directory. The **lpr** command is an abbreviated form of "line print" and will print a file. The **cat**, **less**, and **more** commands display the contents of a file on the screen. Table 12-8 lists these commands with their different options.

When you log in to your Linux system, you may want a list of the files in your home directory. The **ls** command, which outputs a list of your file and directory names, is useful for this. The **ls** command has many possible options for displaying filenames according to specific features.

Displaying Files: cat, less, and more

You may also need to look at the contents of a file. The **cat** and **more** commands display the contents of a file on the screen. The name **cat** stands for concatenate.

```
$ cat mydata
computers
```

The **cat** command outputs the entire text of a file to the screen at once. This presents a problem when the file is large because its text quickly speeds past on the screen. The **more** and **less** commands are designed to overcome this limitation by displaying one screen of text at a time. You can then move forward or backward in the text at your leisure. You invoke the **more** or **less** command by entering the command name followed by the name of the file you want to view (**less** is a more powerful and configurable display utility).

```
$ less mydata
```

When **more** or **less** invoke a file, the first screen of text is displayed. To continue to the next screen, you press the **f** key or the SPACEBAR. To move back in the text, you press the **b** key. You can quit at any time by pressing the **q** key.

Command or Option	Execution
`ls`	This command lists file and directory names.
`cat` *filenames*	This filter can be used to display a file. It can take filenames for its arguments. It outputs the contents of those files directly to the standard output, which, by default, is directed to the screen.
`more` *filenames*	This utility displays a file screen by screen. Press the SPACEBAR to continue to the next screen and **q** to quit.
`less` *filenames*	This utility also displays a file screen by screen. Press the SPACEBAR to continue to the next screen and **q** to quit.
`lpr` *filenames*	Sends a file to the line printer to be printed; a list of files may be used as arguments. Use the **-P** option to specify a printer.
`lpq`	Lists the print queue for printing jobs.
`lprm`	Removes a printing job from the print queue.

Table 12-8: Listing, Displaying, and Printing Files

Printing Files: lpr, lpq, and lprm

With the printer commands such as **lpr** and **lprm**, you can perform printing operations such as printing files or canceling print jobs (see Table 12-8). When you need to print files, use the **lpr** command to send files to the printer connected to your system. In the next example, the user prints the **mydata** file:

```
$ lpr mydata
```

If you want to print several files at once, you can specify more than one file on the command line after the **lpr** command. In the next example, the user prints out both the **mydata** and **preface** files:

```
$ lpr mydata preface
```

Printing jobs are placed in a queue and printed one at a time in the background. You can continue with other work as your files print. You can see the position of a particular printing job at any given time with the **lpq** command, which displays the owner of the printing job (the login name of the user who sent the job), the print job ID, the size in bytes, and the temporary file in which it is currently held.

If you need to cancel an unwanted printing job, you can do so with the **lprm** command, which takes as its argument either the ID number of the printing job or the owner's name. It then removes the print job from the print queue. For this task, **lpq** is helpful, for it provides you with the ID number and owner of the printing job you need to use with **lprm**.

Managing Directories: mkdir, rmdir, ls, cd, pwd

You can create and remove your own directories, as well as change your working directory, with the **mkdir**, **rmdir**, and **cd** commands. Each of these commands can take as its argument the pathname for a directory. The **pwd** command displays the absolute pathname of your working directory. In addition to these commands, the special characters represented by a single dot, a double dot, and a tilde can be used to reference the working directory, the parent of the working directory, and the home directory, respectively. Taken together, these commands enable you to manage your directories. You can create nested directories, move from one directory to another, and use pathnames to reference any of your directories. Those commands commonly used to manage directories are listed in Table 12-9.

Creating and Deleting Directories

You create and remove directories with the **mkdir** and **rmdir** commands. In either case, you can also use pathnames for the directories. In the next example, the user creates the directory **reports**. Then the user creates the directory **articles** using a pathname.

```
$ mkdir reports
$ mkdir /home/chris/articles
```

You can remove a directory with the **rmdir** command followed by the directory name. In the next example, the user removes the directory **reports** with the **rmdir** command.

```
$ rmdir reports
```

To remove a directory and all its subdirectories, you use the **rm** command with the **-r** option. This is a very powerful command and could be used to erase all your files. You will be prompted for each file. To remove all files and subdirectories without prompts, add the **-f** option. The following example deletes the **reports** directory and all its subdirectories.

```
rm -rf reports
```

Displaying Directory Contents

To distinguish between file and directory names, you need to use the **ls** command with the **-F** option. A slash is then displayed after each directory name in the list.

```
$ ls
weather reports articles
$ ls -F
weather reports/ articles/
```

The **ls** command also takes as an argument any directory name or directory pathname. This enables you to list the files in any directory without first having to change to that directory. In the next example, the **ls** command takes as its argument the name of a directory, **reports**. Then the **ls** command is executed again, only this time the absolute pathname of **reports** is used.

```
$ ls reports
monday tuesday
$ ls /home/chris/reports
monday tuesday
$
```

Command	Execution
`mkdir` *directory*	Creates a directory.
`rmdir` *directory*	Erases a directory.
`ls -F`	Lists directory name with a preceding slash.
`ls -R`	Lists working directory as well as all subdirectories.
`cd` *directory name*	Changes to the specified directory, making it the working directory. `cd` without a directory name changes back to the home directory: $ cd reports
`pwd`	Displays the pathname of the working directory.
directory name / *filename*	A slash is used in pathnames to separate each directory name. In the case of pathnames for files, a slash separates the preceding directory names from the filename.

`..`	References the parent directory. You can use it as an argument or as part of a pathname:
	$ cd ..
	$ mv ../larisa oldarticles

`.`	References the working directory. You can use it as an argument or as part of a pathname: $ ls .
`~/`*pathname*	The tilde is a special character that represents the pathname for the home directory. It is useful when you need to use an absolute pathname for a file or directory: $ cp monday ~/today

Table 12-9: Directory Commands

Moving Through Directories

The **cd** command takes as its argument the name of the directory to which you want to move. The name of the directory can be the name of a subdirectory in your working directory or the full pathname of any directory on the system. If you want to change back to your home directory, you need to enter only the **cd** command by itself, without a filename argument.

```
$ cd reports
$ pwd
/home/chris/reports
```

Referencing the Parent Directory

A directory always has a parent (except, of course, for the root). For example, in the preceding listing, the parent for **reports** is the **chris** directory. When a directory is created, two entries are made: one represented with a dot (.), and the other with double dots (..). The dot represents the pathname of the directory, and the double dots represent the pathname of its parent directory. Double dots, used as an argument in a command, references the parent directory. The single dot references the directory itself.

You can use the single dot to reference your working directory, instead of using its pathname. For example, to copy a file to the working directory retaining the same name, the dot can be used in place of the working directory's pathname. In this sense, the dot is another name for the working directory. In the next example, the user copies the **weather** file from the **chris** directory to the **reports** directory. The **reports** directory is the working directory and can be represented with the single dot.

```
$ cd reports
$ cp /home/chris/weather .
```

The .. symbol is used to reference files in the parent directory. In the next example, the **cat** command displays the **weather** file in the parent directory. The pathname for the file is the .. symbol (for the parent directory) followed by a slash and the filename.

```
$ cat ../weather
raining and warm
```

Tip: You can use the **cd** command with the .. symbol to step back through successive parent directories of the directory tree from a lower directory.

File and Directory Operations: find, cp, mv, rm, ln

As you create more files, you may want to back them up, change their names, erase some of them, or even give them added names. Linux provides several file commands that you can use to search for files, copy files, rename files, or remove files (see Table 12-5). If you have a large number of files, you can also search them to locate a specific one. The commands are shortened forms of full words, consisting of only two characters. The **cp** command stands for "copy" and copies a file, **mv** stands for "move" and renames or moves a file, **rm** stands for "remove" and erases a file, and **ln** stands for "link" and adds another name for a file, often used as a shortcut to the original. One exception to the two-character rule is the **find** command, which performs searches of your filenames to find a file. All these operations can be handled by desktops, such as GNOME and KDE.

Searching Directories: find

Once a large number of files have been stored in many different directories, you may need to search them to locate a specific file, or files, of a certain type. The **find** command enables you to perform such a search from the command line. The **find** command takes as its arguments directory names followed by several possible options that specify the type of search and the criteria for the search. It then searches within the directories listed and their subdirectories for files that meet these criteria. The **find** command can search for a file by name, type, owner, and even the time of the last update.

```
$ find directory-list -option criteria
```

The **-name** option has as its criteria a pattern and instructs **find** to search for the filename that matches that pattern. To search for a file by name, you use the **find** command with the directory name followed by the **-name** option and the name of the file.

```
$ find directory-list -name filename
```

Command or Option	Execution
`find`	Searches directories for files according to search criteria. This command has several options that specify the type of criteria and actions to be taken.
`-name` pattern	Searches for files with the pattern in the name.
`-lname` pattern	Searches for symbolic link files.
`-group` name	Searches for files belonging to the group name.
`-gid` name	Searches for files belonging to a group according to group ID.
`-user` name	Searches for files belonging to a user.
`-uid` name	Searches for files belonging to a user according to user ID.
`-mtime` num	Searches for files last modified num days ago.
`-context` scontext	Searches for files according to security context (SE Linux).
`-print`	Outputs the result of the search to the standard output. The result is usually a list of filenames, including their full pathnames.
`-type` filetype	Searches for files with the specified file type. File type can be **b** for block device, **c** for character device, **d** for directory, **f** for file, or **l** for symbolic link.
`-perm` permission	Searches for files with certain permissions set. Use octal or symbolic format for permissions.
`-ls`	Provides a detailed listing of each file, with owner, permission, size, and date information.
`-exec` command	Executes command when files found.

Table 12-10: The find Command

The **find** command also has options that merely perform actions, such as outputting the results of a search. If you want **find** to display the filenames it has located, you simply include the **-print** option on the command line along with any other options. The **-print** option is an action that instructs **find** to write to the standard output the names of all the files it locates (you can also use the **-ls** option instead to list files in the long format). In the next example, the user searches for all the files in the **reports** directory with the name **monday**. Once located, the file, with its relative pathname, is printed.

```
$ find reports -name monday -print
reports/monday
```

The **find** command prints out the filenames using the directory name specified in the directory list. If you specify an absolute pathname, the absolute path of the found directories will be output. If you specify a relative pathname, only the relative pathname is output. In the preceding example, the user specified a relative pathname, **reports**, in the directory list. Located filenames were output beginning with this relative pathname. In the next example, the user specifies an absolute pathname in the directory list. Located filenames are then output using this absolute pathname.

```
$ find /home/chris -name monday -print
/home/chris/reports/monday
```

Tip: Should you need to find the location of a specific program or configuration file, you could use **find** to search for the file from the root directory. Use **/** as the directory. This command searched for the location of the **more** command and files on the entire file system: **find / -name more -print**.

Searching the Working Directory

If you want to search your working directory, you can use the dot in the directory pathname to represent your working directory. The double dots would represent the parent directory. The next example searches all files and subdirectories in the working directory, using the dot to represent the working directory. If your working directory is your home directory, this is a convenient way to search through all your own directories. Notice that the located filenames that are output begin with a dot.

```
$ find . -name weather -print
./weather
```

You can use shell wildcard characters as part of the pattern criteria for searching files. The special character must be quoted to avoid evaluation by the shell. In the next example, all files (indicated by the asterisk, *) with the **.c** extension in the **programs** directory are searched for and then displayed in the long format using the **-ls** action:

```
$ find programs -name '*.c' -ls
```

Locating Directories

You can also use the **find** command to locate other directories. In Linux, a directory is officially classified as a special type of file. Although all files have a byte-stream format, some files, such as directories, are used in special ways. In this sense, a file can be said to have a file type. The **find** command has an option called **-type** that searches for a file of a given type. The **-type** option takes a one-character modifier that represents the file type. The modifier that represents a directory is a **d**. In the next example, both the directory name and the directory file type are used to search for the directory called **travel**:

```
$ find /home/chris -name travel -type d -print
/home/chris/articles/travel
```

File types are not so much different types of files, as they are the file format applied to other components of the operating system, such as devices. In this sense, a device is treated as a type of file, and you can use **find** to search for devices and directories, as well as ordinary files. Table 12-10 lists the different types available for the **find** command's **-type** option.

You can also use the find operation to search for files by ownership or security criteria, like those belonging to a specific user or those with a certain security context. The **-user** option lets you locate all files belonging to a certain user. The following example lists all files that the user

chris has created or owns on the entire system. To list those just in the users' home directories, you would use **/home** for the starting search directory. This would find all those in a user's home directory as well as any owned by that user in other user directories.

```
$ find /home -user chris -print
```

Copying Files

To make a copy of a file, you give the **cp** command two filenames as its arguments (see Table 12-11). The first filename is the name of the file to be copied, the one that already exists. This is often referred to as the source file. The second filename is the name you want for the copy. This will be a new file containing a copy of all the data in the source file. This second argument is referred to as the destination file. The syntax for the **cp** command follows:

```
$ cp source-file destination-file
```

Command	Execution
cp *filename filename*	Copies a file. **cp** takes two arguments: the original file and the name of the new copy. You can use pathnames for the files to copy across directories:
cp -r *dirname dirname*	Copies a subdirectory from one directory to another. The copied directory includes all its own subdirectories:
mv *filename filename*	Moves (renames) a file. The **mv** command takes two arguments: the first is the file to be moved. The second argument can be the new filename or the pathname of a directory. If it is the name of a directory, then the file is moved to that directory, changing the file's pathname:
mv *dirname dirname*	Moves directories. In this case, the first and last arguments are directories:
ln *filename filename*	Creates added names for files referred to as links. A link can be created in one directory that references a file in another directory:
rm *filenames*	Removes (erases) a file. Can take any number of filenames as its arguments. Literally removes links to a file.

Table 12-11: File Operations

In the next example, the user copies a file called **proposal** to a new file called **oldprop**:

```
$ cp proposal oldprop
```

You could unintentionally destroy another file with the **cp** command. The **cp** command generates a copy by first creating a file and then copying data into it. If another file has the same name as the destination file, that file is destroyed and a new file with that name is created. By default, Ubuntu configures your system to check for an existing copy by the same name (**cp** is aliased with the **-i** option). To copy a file from your working directory to another directory, you need to use that directory name as the second argument in the **cp** command. In the next example, the **proposal** file is overwritten by the **newprop** file. The **proposal** file already exists.

```
$ cp newprop proposal
```

You can use any of the wildcard characters to generate a list of filenames to use with **cp** or **mv**. For example, suppose you need to copy all your C source code files to a given directory. Instead of listing each one individually on the command line, you could use an * character with the **.c** extension to match on and generate a list of C source code files (all files with a **.c** extension). In the next example, the user copies all source code files in the current directory to the **sourcebks** directory:

```
$ cp *.c sourcebks
```

If you want to copy all the files in a given directory to another directory, you could use * to match on and generate a list of all those files in a **cp** command. In the next example, the user copies all the files in the **props** directory to the **oldprop** directory. Notice the use of a **props** pathname preceding the * special characters. In this context, **props** is a pathname that will be appended before each file in the list that * generates.

```
$ cp props/* oldprop
```

You can use any of the other special characters, such as **.**, **?**, or **[]**. In the next example, the user copies both source code and object code files (**.c** and **.o**) to the **projbk** directory:

```
$ cp *.[oc] projbk
```

When you copy a file, you can give the copy a name that is different from the original. To do so, place the new filename after the directory name, separated by a slash.

```
$ cp filename directory-name/new-filename
```

Moving Files

You can use the **mv** command to either rename a file or to move a file from one directory to another. When using **mv** to rename a file, you use the new filename as the second argument. The first argument is the current name of the file you are renaming. If you want to rename a file when you move it, you can specify the new name of the file after the directory name. In the next example, the **proposal** file is renamed with the name **version1**:

```
$ mv proposal version1
```

As with **cp**, it is easy for **mv** to erase a file accidentally. When renaming a file, you might accidentally choose a filename already used by another file. In this case, that other file will be erased. The **mv** command also has an **-i** option that checks first to see if a file by that name already exists.

You can also use any of the special characters to generate a list of filenames to use with **mv**. In the next example, the user moves all source code files in the current directory to the **newproj** directory:

```
$ mv *.c newproj
```

If you want to move all the files in a given directory to another directory, you can use * to match on and generate a list of all those files. In the next example, the user moves all the files in the **reports** directory to the **repbks** directory:

```
$ mv reports/* repbks
```

Note: The easiest way to copy files to a CD-R/RW or DVD-R/RW disc is to use the built-in GNOME Files burning capability. Just insert a blank disk, open it as a folder, and drag-and-drop files on to it.

Copying and Moving Directories

You can also copy or move whole directories at once. Both **cp** and **mv** can take as their first argument a directory name, enabling you to copy or move subdirectories from one directory into another (see Table 12-11). The first argument is the name of the directory to be moved or copied, and the second argument is the name of the directory within which it is to be placed. The same pathname structure used for files applies to moving or copying directories.

You can just as easily copy subdirectories from one directory to another. To copy a directory, the **cp** command requires you to use the **-r** option, which stands for "recursive." It directs the **cp** command to copy a directory, as well as any subdirectories it may contain. In other words, the entire directory subtree, from that directory on, will be copied. In the next example, the **travel** directory is copied to the **oldarticles** directory. Now two **travel** subdirectories exist, one in **articles** and one in **oldarticles**.

```
$ cp -r articles/travel oldarticles
$ ls -F articles
/travel
$ ls -F oldarticles
/travel
```

Erasing Files and Directories: the rm Command

As you use Linux, you will find the number of files you use increases rapidly. Generating files in Linux is easy. Applications such as editors, and commands such as **cp**, can easily be used to create files. You can remove them with the **rm** command. The **rm** command can take any number of arguments, enabling you to list several filenames and erase them all at the same time. In the next example, the file **oldprop** is erased:

```
$ rm oldprop
```

Be careful when using the **rm** command, because it is irrevocable. Once a file is removed, it cannot be restored (there is no undo). With the **-i** option, you are prompted separately for each file and asked whether you really want to remove it. If you enter **y**, the file will be removed. If you enter anything else, the file is not removed. In the next example, the **rm** command is instructed to erase the files **proposal** and **oldprop**. The **rm** command then asks for confirmation for each file. The user decides to remove **oldprop**, but not **proposal**.

```
$ rm -i proposal oldprop
Remove proposal? n
Remove oldprop? y
$
```

Links: the ln Command

You can give a file more than one name using the **ln** command. You might do this because you want to reference a file using different filenames to access it from different directories. The added names are often referred to as *links*. Linux supports two different types of links, hard and symbolic. Hard links are literally another name for the same file, whereas symbolic links function like shortcuts referencing another file. Symbolic links are much more flexible and can work over many different file systems, while hard links are limited to your local file system. Furthermore, hard links introduce security concerns, as they allow direct access from a link that may have public access to an original file that you may want protected. Links are usually implemented as symbolic links.

Symbolic Links

To set up a symbolic link, you use the **ln** command with the **-s** option and two arguments: the name of the original file and the new, added filename. The **ls** operation lists both filenames, but only one physical file will exist.

```
$ ln -s original-file-name added-file-name
```

In the next example, the **today** file is given the additional name **weather**. It is just another name for the **today** file.

```
$ ls
today
$ ln -s today weather
$ ls
today weather
```

You can give the same file several names by using the **ln** command on the same file many times. In the next example, the file **today** is assigned the names **weather** and **weekend**:

```
$ ln -s today weather
$ ln -s today weekend
$ ls
today weather weekend
```

If you list the full information about a symbolic link and its file, you will find the information displayed is different. In the next example, the user lists the full information for both **lunch** and **/home/george/veglist** using the **ls** command with the **-l** option. The first character in the line specifies the file type. Symbolic links have their own file type, represented by an l. The file type for **lunch** is l, indicating it is a symbolic link, not an ordinary file. The number after the term "group" is the size of the file. Notice the sizes differ. The size of the **lunch** file is only 4 bytes. This is because **lunch** is only a symbolic link, a file that holds the pathname of another file and a pathname takes up only a few bytes. It is not a direct hard link to the **veglist** file.

```
$ ls -l lunch /home/george/veglist
lrw-rw-r-- 1 chris group 4 Feb 14 10:30 lunch
-rw-rw-r-- 1 george group 793 Feb 14 10:30 veglist
```

To erase a file, you need to remove only its original name (and any hard links to it). If any symbolic links are left over, they will be unable to access the file. In this case, a symbolic link would hold the pathname of a file that no longer exists.

Hard Links

You can give the same file several names by using the **ln** command on the same file many times. To set up a hard link, you use the **ln** command with no **-s** option and two arguments: the name of the original file and the new, added filename. The **ls** operation lists both filenames, but only one physical file will exist.

```
$ ln original-file-name added-file-name
```

In the next example, the **monday** file is given the additional name **storm**. It is just another name for the **monday** file.

```
$ ls
today
$ ln monday storm
$ ls
monday storm
```

To erase a file that has hard links, you need to remove all its hard links. The name of a file is actually considered a link to that file. Hence the command **rm** removes the link to the file. If you have several links to the file and remove only one of them, the others stay in place and you can reference the file through them. The same is true even if you remove the original link, the original name of the file.

Part 4: Administration

System Tools
System Administration
Network Connections

ubuntu

13. System Tools

System Monitor
Scheduling Tasks
System Log
Disk Usage Analyzer
Virus Protection
Hardware Sensors
Disk Utility
Plymouth
Logical Volume Management
OpenZFS

Useful system tools, as well as user specific configuration tools, can be found in the Applications overview and its Utilities application folder (see Table 13-1). The Utilities application folder lists specialized tools like the Disk Utility, System Monitor, and the Disk Usage Analyzer.

Ubuntu System Tools	Name	Description
`gnome-system-monitor`	System Monitor	GNOME System Monitor
`gnome-logs`	Logs	GNOME Logs
`gnome-terminal`	Terminal	GNOME Terminal Window
`baobab`	Disk Usage Analyzer	Disk usage analyzer with graphic representation
`gnome-nettool`	Network Tools	Network analysis
`KDE task scheduler`	Task Scheduler	KDE schedule manager (KDE desktop only)
`ClamTK`	Virus Scanner	Clam Virus scanner
`Disk Utility`	Disk Utility	Udisks utility for managing hard disks and removable drives

Table 13-1: Ubuntu System Tools

GNOME System Monitor

Ubuntu provides the GNOME System Monitor for displaying system information and monitoring system processes, accessible from the Applications overview. There are three tabs: Processes, Resources, and File Systems (see Figure 13-1).

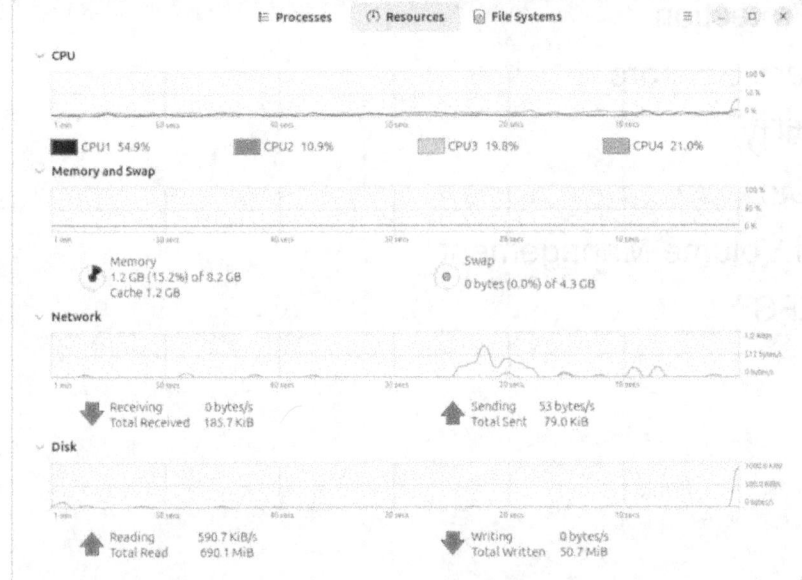

Figure 13-1: GNOME System Monitor: Resources

The Resources tab displays graphs for CPU, Memory and Swap, Network, and Disk history. If your system has a multi-core CPU, the CPU History graph shows the usage for each CPU. The Memory and Swap Memory graph shows the amount of memory in use. The Network History graph displays both the amount of sent and received data, along with totals for the current session. The File Systems tab lists your file systems, where they are mounted, and their type, as well as the amount of disk space used and how much is free. Double clicking on a file system entry will open that file system in a file manager window.

The Processes tab lists your processes, letting you sort and search processes. You can use field buttons to sort by name (Process Name), process ID (ID), percentage of use (%CPU), and memory used (Memory), among others. The menu (right side of the menu bar) lets you select all processes, just your own (My Processes), or active processes. You can stop any process by selecting it and then clicking the End Process button (lower-right corner) or by right-clicking on it and choosing End. You can right-click a process entry to display a menu with actions you can take on the selected process, such as stopping (Stop), ending (End), killing (Kill), and continuing a process (Continue), as well as changing the priority of the process (Change Priority). The Open Files entry opens a dialog listing all the files, sockets, and pipes the process is using. The Properties entry displays a dialog showing all the details for a process, such as the name, user, status, memory use, CPU use, and priority. The Memory Maps display, selected from the Memory Maps entry, shows information on virtual memory, inodes, and flags for a selected process.

Display features such as the colors used for CPU graphs can be set using the dconf editor's gnome-system-monitor keys at org | gnome | gnome-system-monitor.

Managing Processes

Should you have to force a process or application to quit, you can use the Gnome System Monitor Processes tab to find, select, and stop the process. You should be sure of the process you want to stop. Ending a critical process could cripple your system. Application processes will bear the name of the application, and you can use those to force an application to quit. Ending processes manually is usually performed for open-ended operations that you are unable to stop normally. In Figure 13-2, the Firefox application has been selected. Clicking the End Process button on the lower left will then force the Firefox Web browser to end.

The pop-up menu for a process (right-click) provides several other options for managing a selected process: stop, continue, end, kill, and change priority. There are corresponding keyboard keys for most options. The stop and continue operations work together. You can stop (Stop) a process, and then later start it again with the Continue option. The End option stops a process safely, whereas a Kill option forces an immediate end to the process. The End option is preferred, but if it does not work, you can use the Kill option. Change Priority can give a process a lower or higher priority, letting it run faster or slower. The Properties option opens a dialog listing process details such as the name, user, status, different types of memory used, CPU usage, start time, process id, and priority. The Open Files option lists all the files, sockets, and pipes the process is using.

You can also use the **pkill** command with a process name or a process ID to end a process. To use a process name, enter the process name with the **-n** option for the most recent process for that name.

```
pkill -n firefox
```

You can use the **kill** command in a terminal window to end a process. The **kill** command takes as its argument a process number. Be sure you obtain the correct one. Use the **ps** command to display a process id. Entering in the incorrect process number could cripple your system. The **ps** command with the **-C** option searches for a particular application name. The **-o pid=** option will display only the process id, instead of the process id, time, application name, and tty. Once you have the process id, you can use the **kill** command with the process id as its argument to end the process.

```
$ ps -C firefox -o pid=
5555
$ kill 5555
```

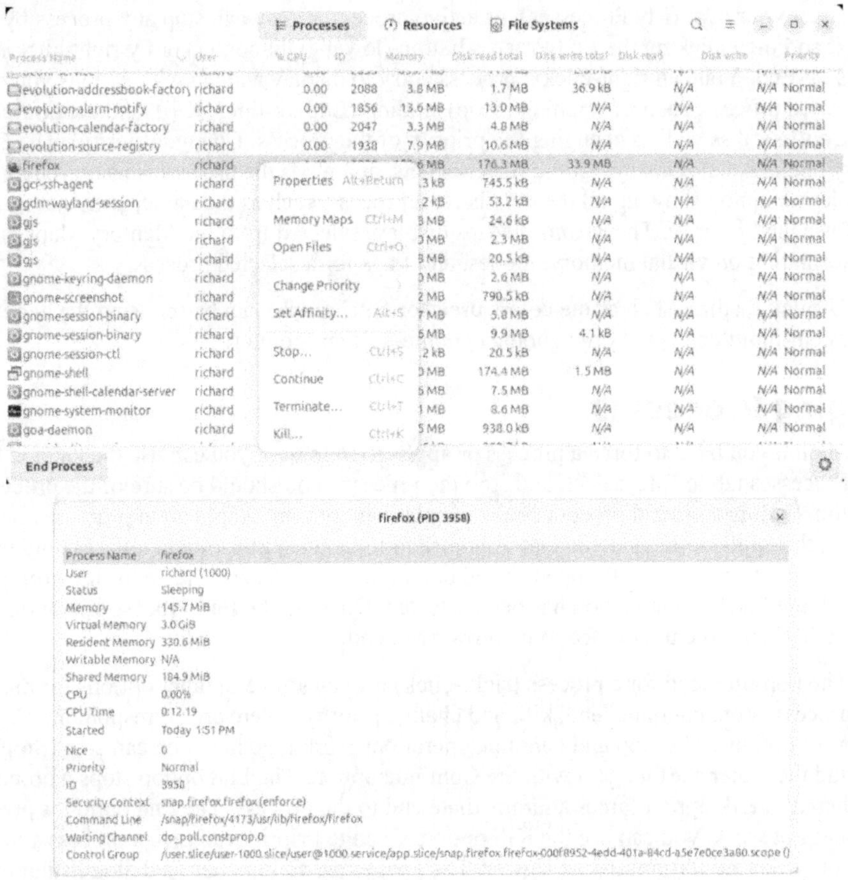

Figure 13-2: GNOME System Monitor: Processes

One way to ensure the correct number is to use the **ps** command to return the process number directly as an argument to a **kill** command. In the following example, an open-ended process was started with the **mycmd** command. An open-ended process is one that will continue until you stop it manually.

```
mycmd > my.ts
```

The process is then ended by first executing the **ps** command to obtain the process id for the **mycmd** process (back quotes), and then using that process id in the **kill** command to end the process. The **-o pid=** option displays only the process id.

```
kill `ps -C mycmd -o pid=`
```

Glances

Glances is a comprehensive system monitoring tool run from the command line in a terminal window with the **glances** command.

You can install glances with the App Center as a Snap package. Alternatively, you can install the APT version (Debian) in a terminal window with the **apt** command (**glances** and **glances-doc** packages).

```
sudo apt install glances
```

Glances shows detailed resource use for the system, network, disk, file system, sensors, and processes. (see Figure 13-3). It also warns you of any critical alerts. The system section covers detailed memory, CPU, swap and load usage. The network section shows the activity on each network device. The Disk I/O section lists your storage devices and their read/write usage. The File Sys section shows all your partitions and how much memory is used. The Sensors section shows the temperature detected by your sensors such as those for CPU, GPU, and the ambient temperature. The Tasks section lists your active processes by CPU usage, showing memory used, pid, user and the command. Press **q** to end your glances session.

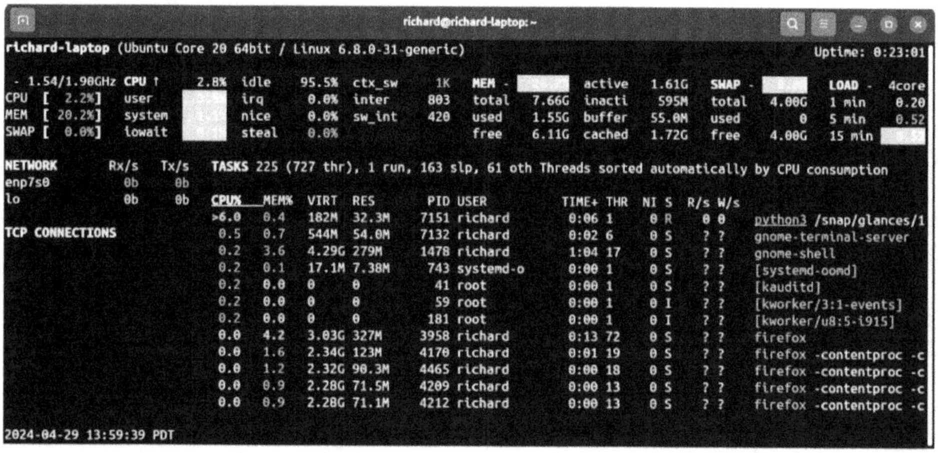

Figure 13-3: Glances System Monitor

Glances is organized into modules which you can disable to show only a limited set of reports. For example, if you are not interested in the disk I/O reports, you can disable the diskio module with the **--disable-diskio** option. See the **glances** man page for a complete list of module options you can use.

```
glances --disable-diskio.
```

There are also several runtime commands you can use to show and hide modules, such as **f** to toggle the file system reports on an off, **d** to toggle disk I/O, **n** for network stats, **s** for showing sensors, and **p** to sort processes by name.

Scheduling Tasks

Scheduling regular maintenance tasks, such as backups, can be managed either by using the systemd timers or by the cron service. The systemd timers are systemd files that run service files. Check the man page for **systemd.timer** for a detailed description of timers. They have the extension **.timer**. A timer file will automatically run a corresponding service file that has the same name. For example, the **dnf-automatic.timer** will run the **dnf-automatic.service** file. The timer file only contains scheduling information. Its filename determines which service file to run. It is possible to designate a different service file with the Unit directive in the timer file. If you want to run a command line operation for which there is no service file, you can create your own with an ExecStart entry for that command.

The timer files have a timer section in which you define when the service file is run. There are options that are relative to certain starting points like when system booted up, and the **OnCalendar** option that reference calendar dates. The **OnCalendar** option uses calendar event expressions as defined on the **systemd.time** man page. A calendar event expression consists of a weekday, year, month, and time. The time is specified in hour, minute, and second, separated by colons. A range of weekdays is separated by two periods, and specific weekdays by commas. Leaving out the year or month selects any year or month. The following references weekdays in May at 2 pm.

```
OnCalendar=Mon..Fri 05 14:00
```

You can create timer files and place them in the **/etc/systemd/system** folder. If you also have to set up a service file for it, you can place it in the same folder. To activate a timer be sure to enable it with **systemctl**. If you created a service file, be sure to enable that also.

You can still use the older cron service to schedule tasks. The cron service is implemented by the **cron** daemon that constantly checks for certain actions to take. These tasks are listed in the **crontab** file. The **cron** daemon constantly checks the user's **crontab** file to see if it is time to take these actions. Any user can set up a **crontab** file. An administrative user can set up a **crontab** file to take system administrative actions, such as backing up files at a certain time each week or month.

Creating cron entries can be a complicated task, using the **crontab** command to make changes to crontab files in the **/etc/crontab** folder. Instead, you can use desktop cron scheduler tools to set up cron actions.

KDE Task Scheduler

On KDE you can use the KDE Task Scheduler to set up user and system-level scheduled tasks (install the **kde-config-cron** package). You access the Task Scheduler on the KDE System Settings window in the System Administration section as Task Scheduler. The Task Scheduler window will list your scheduled tasks. Tasks can be either personal or system-wide. Click the New Task button to open a New Task window where you can enter the command to run, add comments, and then specify the time in months, days, hours, and minutes from simple arranged buttons. On the Task Scheduler window, you can select a task and use the side buttons to modify it, delete the task, run it now, or print a copy of it. For tasks using the same complex commands or arguments, you can create a variable, and then use that variable in a command. Variables are listed in the Environment Variables section. To use a variable in a scheduled task, precede its name with the $ character when you enter the command. Entering just the $ symbol in the Command text box will display a drop-down list of pre-defined system variables you can use like **$PATH** and **$USER**.

Logs

Various system logs for tasks performed on your system are stored in the **/var/log** folder. Here you can find logs for mail, news, and all other system operations, such as Web server logs (see Figure 8-4). This usually includes startup tasks, such as loading drivers and mounting file systems. If a driver for a device failed to load at startup, you will find an error message for it here. Logins are also recorded in this file, showing you who attempted to log into what account. The **/var/log/mail.log** file logs mail message transmissions and news transfers.

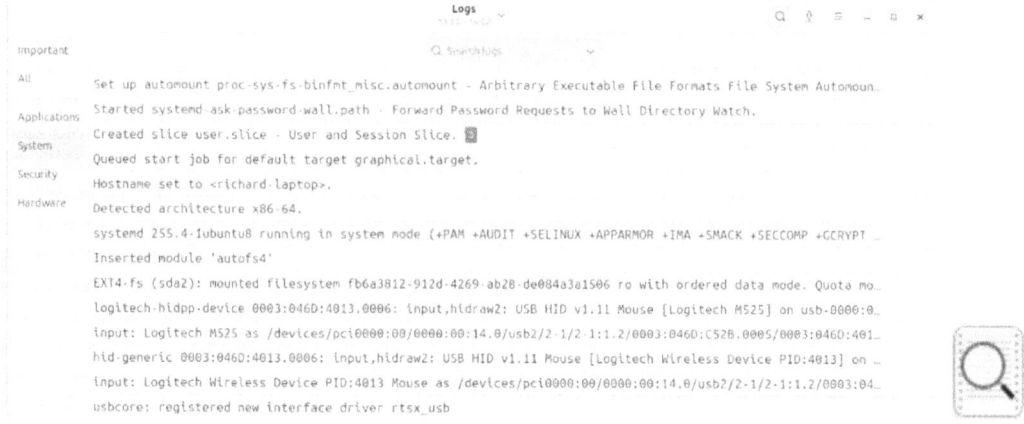

Figure 13-4: System Log

To view logs, you can use Gnome Logs accessible as Logs on the Applications overview's Utility folder (see Figure 13-4). A side panel lists different log categories. Selecting one displays the log messages to the right. Critical messages are listed under the Important category. The "Logs" label on the title bar is a button you can click to display a list of recent boot sessions. You can select one to refine the messages displayed. By default, the most recent one is chosen. A search button on the top right opens a search box where you can search for messages in the selected log. Search has options (menu to the right) for refining the search by fields and by time.

Disk Usage Analyzer

The disk usage analyzer lets you see how much disk space is used and available on all your mounted hard disk partitions (see Figure 13-5). It will also check all LVM and RAID arrays. You can access it from the Applications overview Utilities application folder.

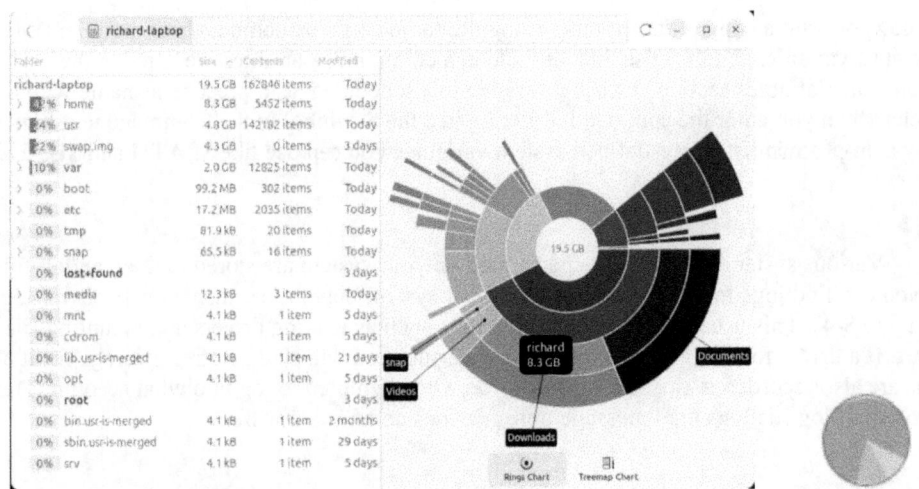

Figure 13-5: Disk Usage Analyzer

Usage is shown in a simple graph, letting you see how much overall space is available and where it is. On the scan dialog, you can choose to scan your home folder (Home Folder, your entire file system (disk drive icon), an attached device like a USB drive, or a specific or remote folder (see Figure 13-6). To scan a folder click the gear button (top right) to open a menu with the option "Scan Folder." When you scan a folder or a file system, disk usage for your folder is analyzed and displayed. Each file system is shown with a graph for its usage, as well as its size and the number of top-level folders and files. Then the folders are shown, along with their size and contents (files and folders).

A representational graph for disk usage is displayed on the right pane. The graph can be either a Ring Chart or a Treemap. The Ring Chart is the default. Choose the one you want from the buttons on the lower right. For the Ring Chart, folders are shown, starting with the top level folders at the center and moving out to the subfolders. Passing your mouse over a section in the graph displays its folder name and disk usage, as well as all its subfolders. The Treemap chart shows a box representation, with greater disk usage in larger boxes, and subfolders encased within folder boxes.

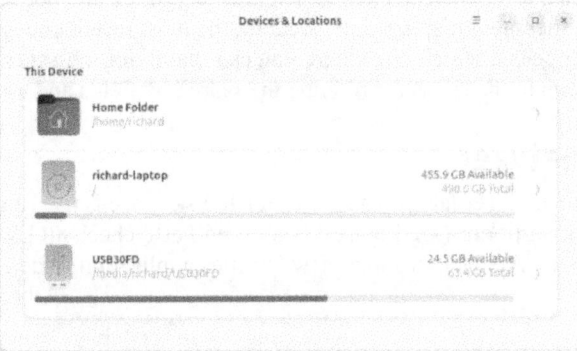

Figure 13-6: Disk Usage Analyzer: Scan dialog

Virus Protection

For virus protection, you can use the Linux version of ClamAV, which uses a GNOME front-end called ClamTk, **https://www.clamav.net**. This Virus scanner is included on the Ubuntu main repository. You can install ClamTk as a Debian package from the App Center. The supporting ClamAV packages will also be selected and installed for you (clamav-base and clamav-freshclam). You can also install ClamAV using the Synaptic Package Manager, choose the clamav, clamav-base, clamav-freshclam (online virus definitions), and ClamTK packages (Klamav for KDE). Selecting just ClamTk will automatically select the other clamav packages for installation. The **clamav-freshclam** package retrieves current virus definitions from the ClamAV servers. For ClamAV to check your mail messages automatically, you need to install the ClamAV scanner daemon (**clamav-daemon** and **clamdscan** packages).

You can access ClamTk from the Applications overview as ClamTk. With ClamTk, you can scan specific files and folders, as well as your home folder (see Figure 13-7). Searches can be recursive, including subfolders (Settings). You have the option to check configuration files (scan dot files). You can also perform quick or recursive scans of your home folder. Infected files are quarantined.

Figure 13-7: The ClamTK tool for ClamAV virus protection

Your virus definitions will be updated automatically. If you want to check manually for virus definitions, you need to click Update Assistant and choose to update the signatures yourself and click the Apply button and then the Back button. Then click the Updates icon and click the Yes button next to "Check for updates."

Hardware Sensors

A concern for many users is the temperatures and usage of computer components. You can install different software packages to enable certain sensors (see Table 13-2).

Sensor application	Description
lm-sensors	Detects and accesses computer (motherboard) sensors like CPU and fan speed. Run **sensors-detect** once to configure.
hddtemp	Detects hard drive temperatures (also detected by Disk Utility)
Disk Utility	Disk Utility provides SMART information for hard disks showing current hard disk temperatures as well as detailed disk health information and checks.
Psensor	Application to detect and display system and hard drive temperatures.
Xsensors	Application to detect and display system temperatures and fans.
Sensors Unity	Application to detect and display system temperatures and fans.

Table 13-2: Sensor packages and applications

For CPU, system, fan speeds, and any other motherboard supported sensors, you can use Psensor, Xsensors, Sensors Unity, and the **lm-sensors** tools, along with several other sensor apps. Psensors installs the hddtemp hard drive temperature server and displays your CPU, graphics card, and hard drive temperatures. You can set temperature thresholds for alerts. Sensors Unity and Xsensors display your CPU temperatures, fan speeds, and voltages. Install with the App Center. For Sensors Unity set permissions to allow access to hardware information.

If not already installed, install the **lm-sensors** package. Then you have to configure your sensor detection. In a terminal window enter the following command and press ENTER to answer yes to the prompts.

```
sudo sensors-detect
```

Disk Utility lets you know your hard disk temperature. Disk Utility uses Udisks to access SMART information about the disk drive, including the temperature and overall health. Open Disk Utility, select the hard disk to check, and then, click on the "SMART Data and Tests" entry from the task menu (ellipses) in the upper right. This opens a SMART Data & Self-Tests dialog with hardware information about the hard disk (see Figure 13-11) including temperature, power cycles, bad sectors, and the overall health of the disk.

Disk Utility and Udisks

Disk Utility is a Udisks supported user configuration interface for your storage media, such as hard disks, USB drives, and DVD/CD drives (**gnome-disk-utility** package, installed by default). Tasks supported include disk labeling, mounting disks, disk checks, and encryption. You can also perform more advanced tasks, like managing RAID and LVM storage devices, as well as partitions. Disk Utility is accessible on GNOME from the Applications overview Utility folder. Users can use Disk Utility to format removable media like USB drives. Disk Utility is also integrated into GNOME Files, letting you format removable media directly.

Chapter 13: System Tools **537**

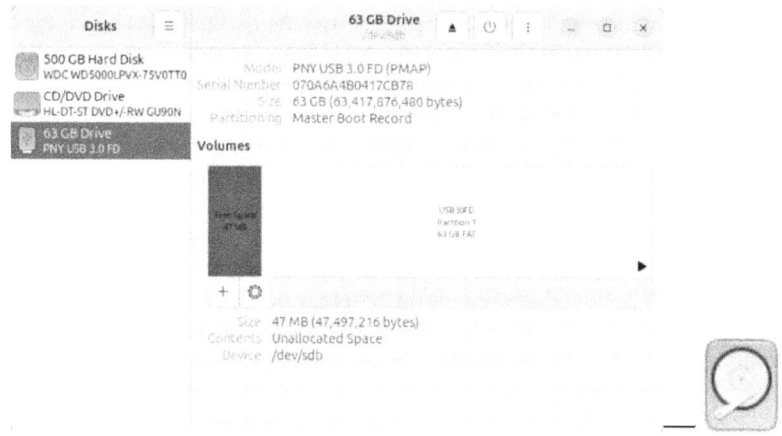

Figure 13-8: Disk Utility

The Disk Utility window shows a sidebar with entries for your storage media (see Figure 13-8). Clicking on an entry displays information for the media on the right pane. Removable devices such as USB drives display power and eject buttons on the title bar, along with a task menu with an entry to format the disk. If you are formatting a partition, like that on removable media, you can specify the file system type to use.

Warning: Disk Utility will list your fixed hard drives and their partitions, including the partitions on which your Ubuntu Linux system is installed. Be careful not to delete or erase these partitions.

If you select a hard disk device, information about the hard disk is displayed on the right pane at the top, such as the model name, serial number, size, partition table type, and SMART status (Assessment) (see Figure 13-9). Click the menu button to display a menu on the upper right with tasks you can perform on the hard drive: Format, Benchmark, and SMART Data.

Figure 13-9: Disk Utility, hard drive

The Volumes section on the hard disk pane shows the partitions set up on the hard drive (see Figure 13-10). Partitions are displayed in a graphical icon bar, which displays each partition's size and location on the drive. Clicking on a partition entry on the graphical icon bar displays information about that partition such as the file system type, device name, partition label, and partition size. The "Contents" entry tells if a partition is mounted. If in use, it displays a "Mounted at:" entry with a link consisting of the path name where the file system is mounted. You can click on this path name to open a folder with which you can access the file system. The button bar below the Volumes images provides additional tasks you can perform, such as unmounting a file system (square button) and deleting a partition (minus button). From the more tasks menu (gear button), you can choose entries to check and repair the file system, resize or format it, and change the partition label (Edit Filesystem), partition type (Edit partition), and mount options (Edit Mount Options). Certain partitions, like extended partitions, display limited information and have few allowable tasks.

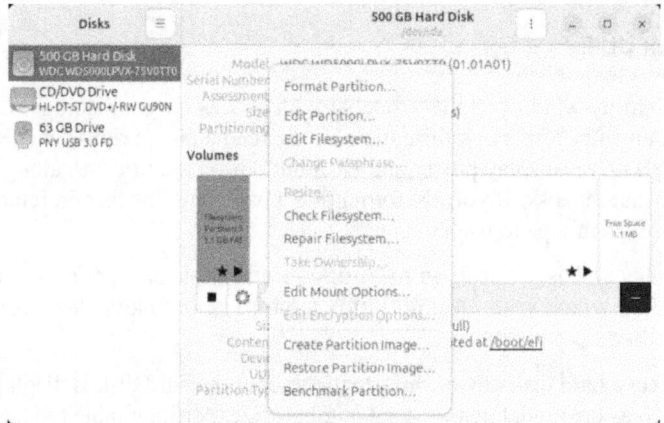

Figure 13-10: Disk Utility, Volumes

For more detailed hardware information about a hard drive, you can click on the "SMART Data and Tests" entry from the task menu (ellipses) in the upper right. This opens a SMART Data & Self-Tests dialog with hardware information about the hard disk (see Figure 13-11) including temperature, power cycles, bad sectors, and the overall health of the disk. The Attributes section lists SMART details such as the Read Error Rate, Spinup time, temperature, and write error rate. Click the switch on to enable the self-tests, and off to disable testing. Click the "Refresh" button to manually run the tests. Click the "Start Self-test" button to open a menu with options for short, extended, and conveyance tests.

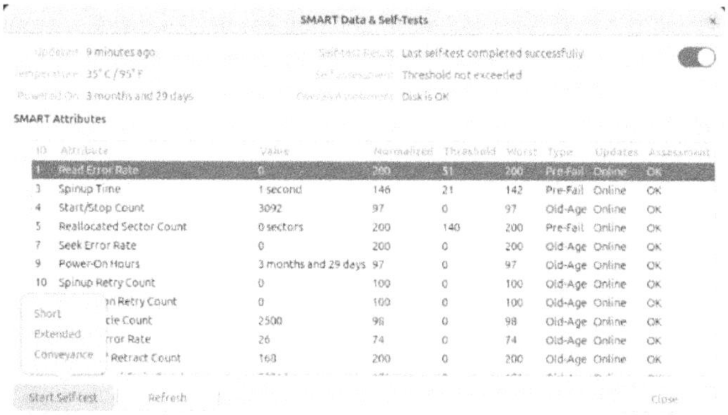

Figure 13-11: Disk Utility: Hard Disk hardware SMART data

Plymouth

Plymouth provides a streamlined, efficient, and faster graphical boot that does not require X server support. It relies on the kernel's Kernel Modesettings (KMS) feature that provides direct support for basic graphics. With the Direct Rendering Manager driver, Plymouth can make use of different graphical plugins. KMS support is currently provided for AMD, Nvidia, and Intel graphics cards.

The Plymouth Ubuntu text theme is installed by default. You can install others like ubuntu-logo, breeze, or kubuntu-logo. The theme packages begin with the prefix **plymouth-theme**. You can search for them on the Synaptic Package Manager or with the **apt** command. The default theme package is **plymouth-theme-ubuntu-text**, which install the bgrt.plymouth theme.

Choosing to use a Plymouth theme involves using the Debian alternatives system, which is designed to designate an application to use when there are several alternative versions to select. A link is set up for the application to use in the **/etc/alternatives** folder. For Plymouth, this link is named **default.plymouth**. You can choose a Plymouth theme by entering the **update-alternatives** command with the **--config** option, the **default.plymouth** link, and the **sudo** command in a terminal window as shown here.

```
sudo update-alternatives --config default.plymouth
```

This displays a numbered menu listing your installed themes. An asterisk indicates the current theme. Enter the number of the theme you want to use. The **default.plymouth** link is then set to the theme you choose. When your system starts up again, it will use that Plymouth theme.

Some of the non-Ubuntu themes may hang on start up. In that case, you can edit the boot kernel line to remove the **splash** option and then boot to your system (see Chapter 3). Then use **update-alternatives** to change your Plymouth theme.

Managing keys with Seahorse

For GPG and SSH encryption, signing, and decryption of files and text, GNOME provides Seahorse. With Seahorse you can manage your encryption keys stored in keyrings as well as SSH keys and passphrases. You can import keys, sign keys, search for remote keys, and create your own keyrings, as well as specify keyservers to search and publish to. All these operations can also be performed using the **gpg** command. Seahorse is installed by default.

Passwords and Keys

To import, sign, and locate keys you use the Password and Keys application, accessible from the Utilities application folder on the applications overview (Utilities | Passwords and Keys). The Passwords and Keys window displays a sidebar with three sections: Passwords, Keys, and Certificates (see Figure 13-12). The Seahorse menu on the right side of the Seahorse header bar shows options for viewing keys (personal, trusted, and any) and the "Password and Keys" folder menu (left side) shows options for finding remote keys, syncing and publishing keys, preferences, and help.

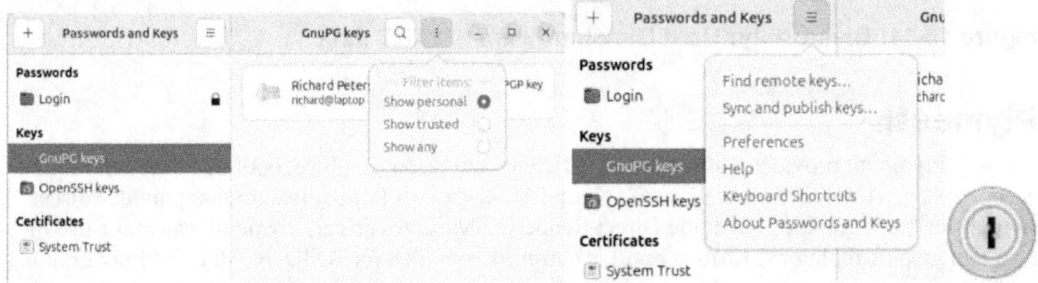

Figure 13-12: Seahorse Passwords and Keys (version 3.3)

Keyrings

The Passwords section lists your keyrings. Keyrings store network and application passwords. A login keyring is set up for you. You can create new keyrings by clicking the plus button on the left of the "Passwords and Keys" title bar and select Password keyring. An "Add password keyring" dialog prompts you for the name of the keyring, and then a "New keyring password" dialog prompts you to enter the keyring password. The strength of the password is indicated. The new keyring is listed in the Passwords section.

To manage keys in your keyring, right-click on the key entry and choose Properties from the menu (see Figure 13-13). Here you can change the description, password for accessing the key, and delete the key. Information about the key's use, type, login, and additional details. A key used to access a network would have the server accessed, protocol used, domain, and the user needed.

Chapter 13: System Tools 541

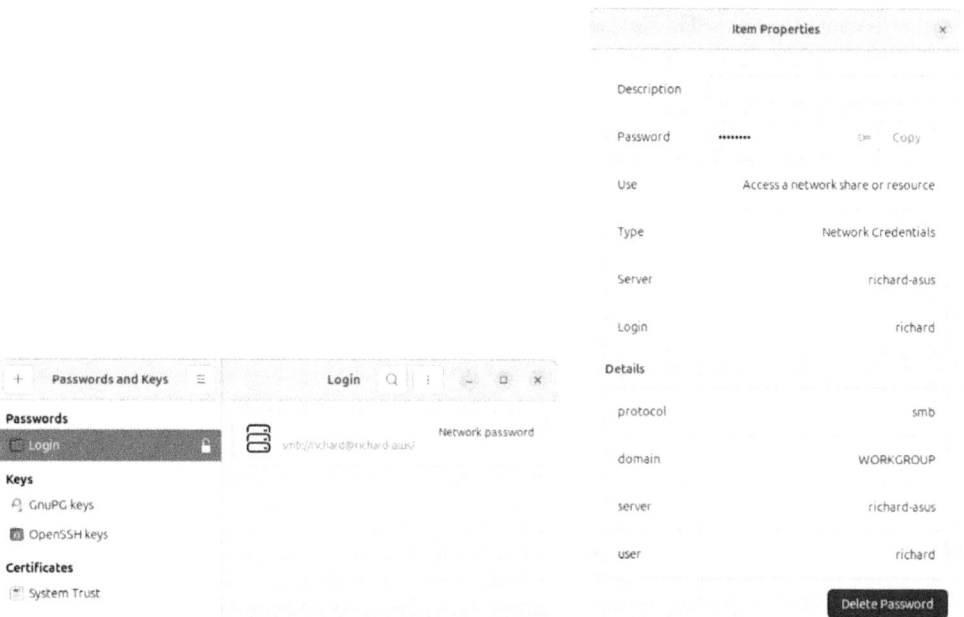

Figure 13-13: Seahorse Keyring key Properties dialog

Creating a new GPG key

Your personal encryption keys are displayed on the PGP Keys section. The entry "GnuPG keys" in the sidebar displays your GPG keys. To create your own private/public click the plus button (+) on the left side of the title bar. You can choose whether to set up a GPG, Private, or Secure Shell key. Choose the "GPG key" entry and click Continue (see Figure 13-14). Keep in mind that before you can perform any encryption, you first have to set up your own GPG key pair, private and public.

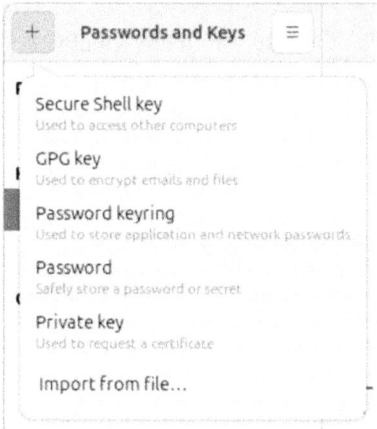

Figure 13-14: Choose Encryption key type

This opens a New PGP Key window where you enter your name and email address. In the "Advanced key options" section you can set Encryption type (DSA, RSA, or the signature only for each), Key strength, and Expiration Date (see Figure 13-15). You can also choose to never have it expire. Then click the Create button.

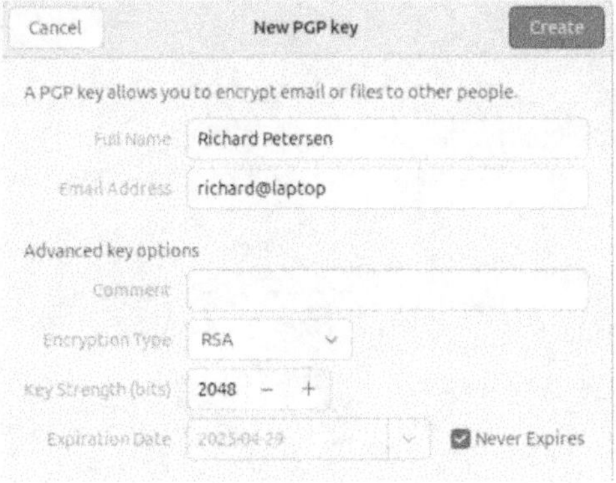

Figure 13-15: Create Encryption key

You are then asked to enter a passphrase (password) for the encryption key (see Figure 13-16). This passphrase will allow you to decrypt any data encrypted by your key.

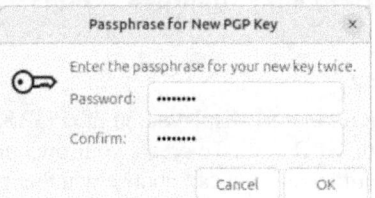

Figure 13-16: Passphrase for encryption key

The key is then generated. This can take a few moments.

Once your key is created, it will appear in the "GnuPG keys" tab of the Passwords and Keys dialog (see Figure 13-17).

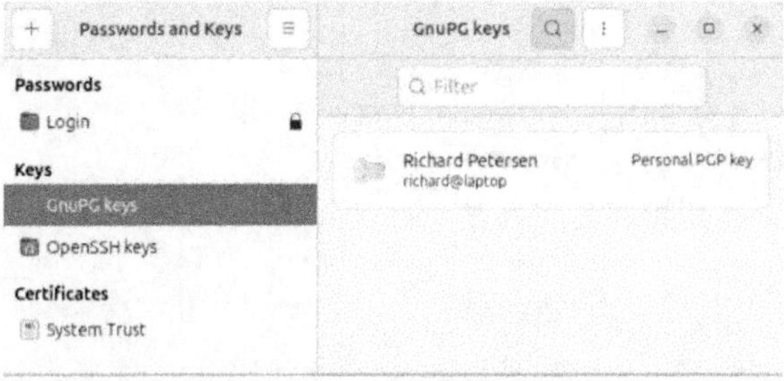

Figure 13-17: My Personal Keys

Right-clicking on the key and selecting Properties, displays a dialog titled with the name of the key and showing three sections: User IDs, Subkeys, and Trust. The Owner section shows the key type and ID, as well as a photo for the key and a button to allow you to change the passphrase for the key (see Figure 13-18). Click the plus button to select a new image file for the photo. Clicking on the calendar button on the Expires entry opens a calendar where you can set an expiration date. The menu on the top left side of the titlebar lists entries for changing the passphrase for the key and exporting the key to a file as a public or secret key.

Any subkeys are also listed, which you can expire, revoke, or delete. You can add new subkeys, specifying a key type, length, and expiration date. Expanding a subkey shows the key's fingerprint, type, and creation date. Buttons allow you to change the expiration date, revoke the key, and delete it.

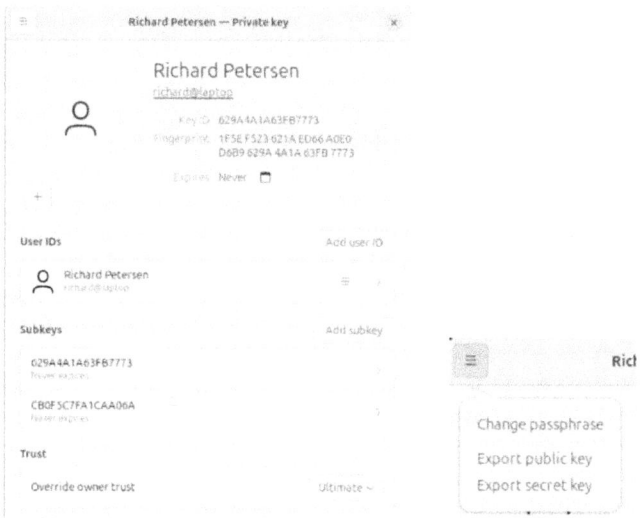

Figure 13-18: GnuPGP key dialog: Owner tab

In the User IDs section, you can expand the key to show its signatures. The entry for the key shows a menu to the right with entries for "Make primary", Sign, and Delete. Selecting the Sign entry opens the Sign Key dialog where you can sign the key (see Figure 13-19), choose how much you trust the key, and whether others can see it and if you want to be able to revoke it. Then click the Sign button to sign the key.

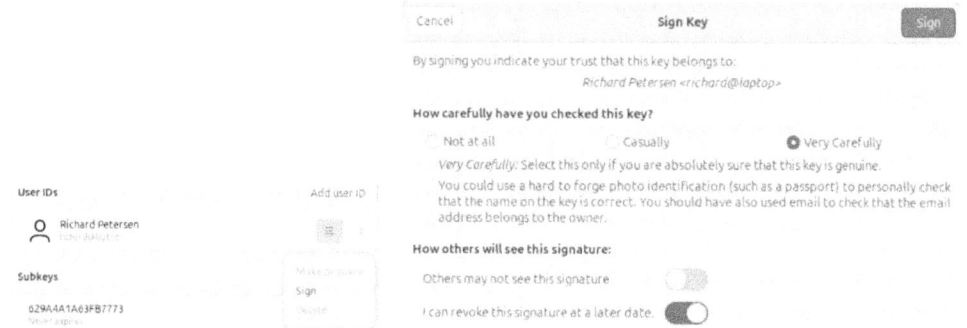

Figure 13-19: GnuPGP key dialog: Details tab

Keyservers

When you created your own private key, you also generated a corresponding public key that others can use to encrypt data they send to you and decrypt signatures of messages you send to them. Many applications will publish public keys that you can download and import to your system with Seahorse. The keys are available on keyservers. To manage your keyservers, choose Preferences from the Seahorse folder menu to open the Preferences dialog (see Figure 13-20). Here you can specify the keyservers to access. Two default servers are listed: **hkp://keyserver.ubuntu.com:11371** and **ldap://keyserver.pgp.com**. To add a keyserver, click the Add button to open a dialog where you enter the keyserver address and port. You will see the keyserver added to the list.

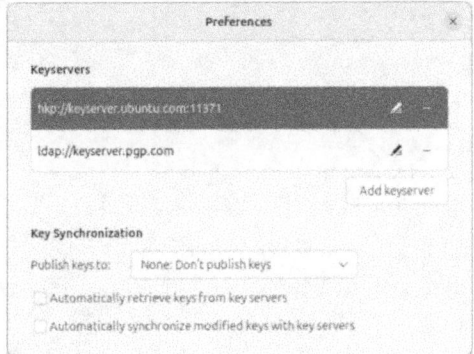

Figure 13-20: Seahorse Preferences - Keyservers

Importing Public Keys

In the "Passwords and Keys" dialog, press **Ctrl-i** to import a public key from a file you have already downloaded to your system. Alternatively, if you know the name of the key, you can try searching the keyservers for it. Choose "Find remote keys" from the "Passwords and Keys" folder menu on the left side of the header bar to open the Find Remote Keys dialog where you can enter a search string for the key (see Figure 13-21). The search term is treated as a prefix, matching on all possible completions. The keyservers to search are listed in the "Where to search" section, with checkboxes to choose those you want searched.

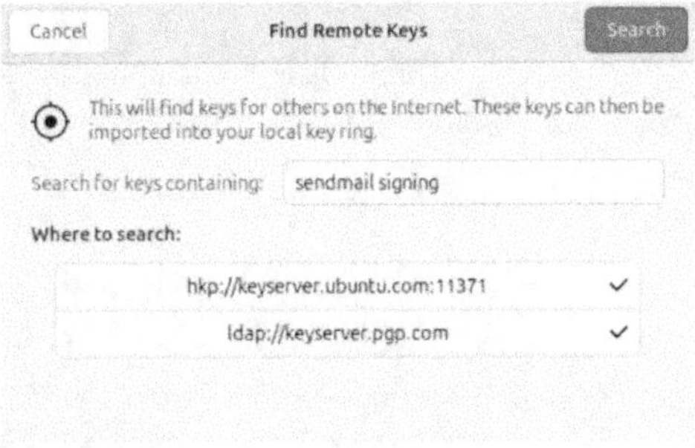

Figure 13-21: Searching for keys

Chapter 13: System Tools **545**

Results are listed in a new window labeled "Remote keys containing" (see Figure 13-22). Select the one you want, and then click the download/import button to the right of the key entry to import the key. To see information about a key, double click the entry (see Figure 13-23). Information about the owner, the trust level, and details about the key such as type and strength are displayed.

Figure 13-22: Importing keys

Figure 13-23: Key information

Once you have imported the key, it will appear in the "GnuPG keys" tab in the Passwords And Keys window (see Figure 13-24). The Seahorse menu on the right side of the header bar lists the types of keys to display: Show personal, Show trusted, and Show any. For newly imported keys, be sure to choose the "Show any" option otherwise the new entry will not be displayed.

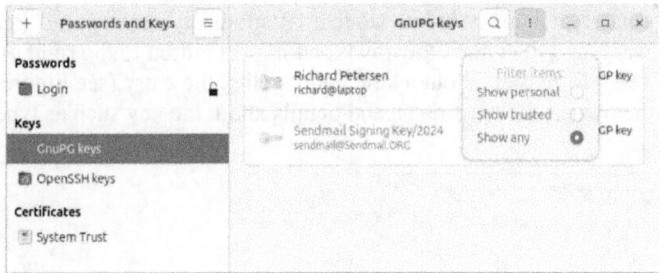

Figure 13-24: Imported keys

If you know that you can trust the key, you can sign it, making it a valid key. Double click on its entry, or right-click and select Properties, to open its Properties dialog, and in the Trust section (see Figure 13-25), click the "Signature trust" switch. Then click the "Sign Key" button to open the Sign key dialog (see Figure 13-26). You are asked how carefully you have checked the key: Not at all, Casually, or Very Carefully. You also choose whether others can see your signature and if you can revoke it later. Then click the Sign button. A dialog appears prompting you to enter your GPG passphrase. On the Properties dialog, the Sign entry is replaced by a "Revoke key signature" entry, and the User ID section lists the key signatures (see Figure 13-27). The key is then listed as a trusted key when you choose the "Show trusted" option in the Seahorse menu (see Figure 13-28).

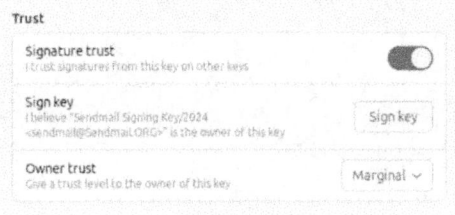

Figure 13-25: Imported key Trust tab for an unsigned key

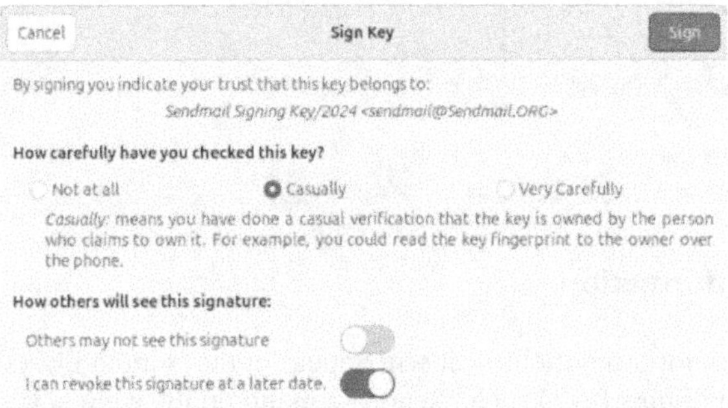

Figure 13-26: Signing a key

Chapter 13: System Tools **547**

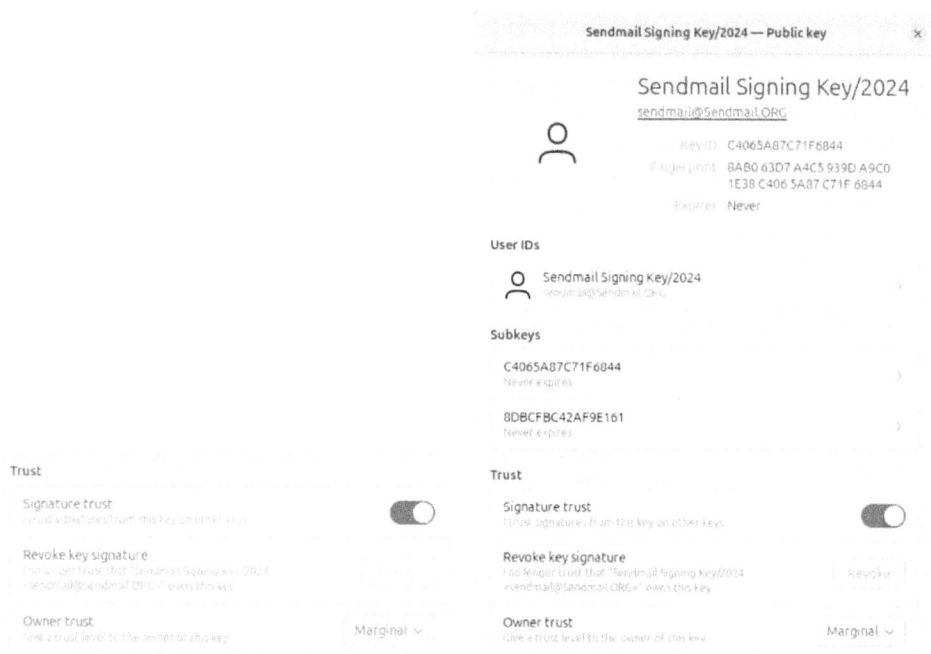

Figure 13-27: Signed key

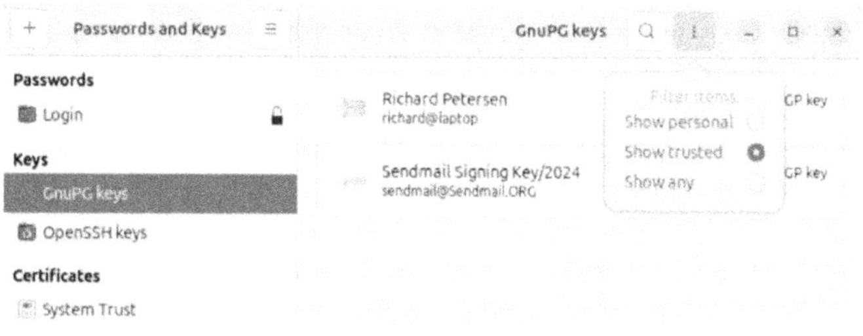

Figure 13-28: Trusted keys

Sharing Keys

To make your public key available to others, you can export it to a file to send directly to other users, automatically share it with other users on your system, or publish on a keyserver. You export your public key to a **.pgp** binary file by right-clicking on it and choosing Export from the pop-up menu. Alternatively, you can export the public key to an ASCII-armored coded **.asc** text file by opening the key's Properties dialog, selecting the Details tab, and then clicking the "Export" button and selecting "Export public key." You can do this for your private (secret) key also.

You can also share your key by publishing it on a public keyserver for anyone to download and import. On the Seahorse Preferences dialog (folder menu), from the "Publish Keys to:" menu you can choose the keyserver to publish to or choose not to publish (the default) (see Figure 13-29). You also have the options to automatically retrieve keys and synchronize modified keys. To then publish a key choose "Sync and publish keys" from the Seahorse folder menu to open the Sync Keys dialog and click the Sync button. The Key Servers button opens the Preferences dialog showing the keyservers, letting you choose the one you want to publish to ("Publish keys to" menu).

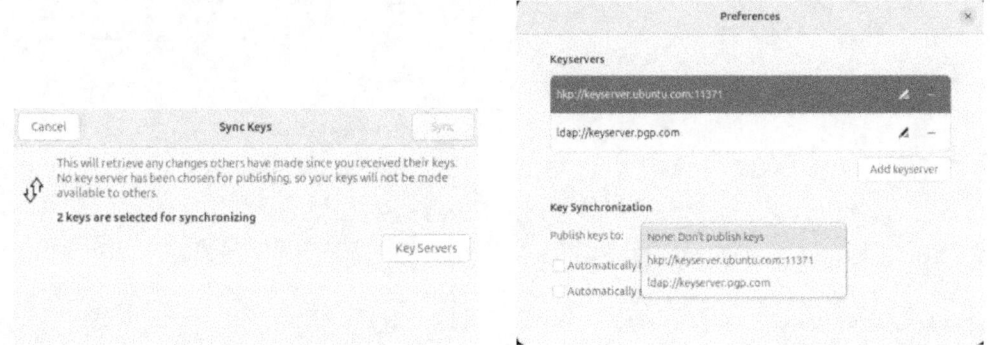

Figure 13-29: Seahorse Preferences

Seahorse integrates support for GPG. Should you import a key with the **gpg** command, it will appear in the GnuPG keys tab. Also, you can sign a key using the **gpg** command with the --**sign-key** option and the key is validated.

Logical Volume Manager

For easier hard disk storage management, you can set up your system to use the Logical Volume Manager (LVM), creating LVM partitions that are organized into logical volumes, to which free space is automatically allocated. Logical volumes provide a more flexible and powerful way of dealing with disk storage, organizing physical partitions into logical volumes in which you can easily manage disk space. Disk storage for a logical volume is treated as one pool of memory, though the volume may, in fact, contain several hard disk partitions spread across different hard disks. Adding a new LVM partition merely increases the pool of storage accessible to the entire system. Check the LVM HOWTO at **www.tldp.org** for detailed examples.

LVM Structure

In an LVM structure, LVM physical partitions, also known as extents, are organized into logical groups, which are, in turn, used by logical volumes. In effect, you are dealing with three different levels of organization. At the lowest level, you have physical volumes. These are physical hard disk partitions that you create with partition creation tools such as **Gparted** or **fdisk**. The partition type will be a Linux LVM partition, **fdisk** code **8e**. These physical volumes are organized into logical groups, known as volume groups, that operate much like logical hard disks. You assign collections of physical volumes to different logical groups.

Once you have your logical groups, you can then create logical volumes. Logical volumes function much like hard disk partitions on a standard setup. For example, on the **turtle** group volume, you could create a **/var** logical volume, and on the **rabbit** logical group, you could create **/home** and **/projects** logical volumes. You can have several logical volumes on one logical group, just as you can have several partitions on one hard disk.

You treat the logical volumes as you would any ordinary hard disk partition. Create a file system on it with the **mkfs** command, and then you can mount the file system to use it with the mount command. For Ubuntu, the file system type would be **ext4**.

Storage on logical volumes is managed using what are known as extents. A logical group defines a standard size for an extent, say 4MB, and then divides each physical volume in its group into extents of that size. Logical volumes are, in turn, divided into extents of the same size, which are then mapped to those on the physical volumes.

Logical volumes can be linear, striped, or mirrored. The mirror option will create a mirror copy of a logical volume, providing a restore capability. The striped option lets you automatically distribute your Logical volume across several partitions, as you would a RAID device. This adds better efficiency for very large files but is complicated to implement. Like a RAID device, stripe sizes have to be consistent across partitions. As LVM partitions can be of any size, the stripes sizes have to be carefully calculated. The simplest approach is just to use a linear implementation, much like a RAID 0 device, just treating the storage as one large ordinary drive, with storage accessed sequentially.

There is one restriction and recommendation for logical volumes. The boot partition cannot be part of a logical volume. You still have to create a separate hard disk partition as your boot partition with the **/boot** mountpoint in which your kernel and all needed boot files are installed. This is why a default partition configuration set up during Ubuntu installation for LVM will include a separate **/boot** partition of type **ext4**, whereas the root partition will be installed on Logical volumes. There will be two partitions, one for the logical group (LVM physical volume, **pv**) holding the root volume, and another for the boot partition (**ext4**). The logical volumes will in turn both be **ext4** file systems.

LVM Tools: using the LVM commands

To use LVM be sure that the **lvm2** package is installed (Ubuntu repository). Use the App Center, the Synaptic Package Manager, or the **apt** command. You can then use a collection of LVM tools to manage your LVM volumes, adding new LVM physical partitions and removing current ones. For the LVM tools, you can either use LVM tools directly or use the **lvm** command to generate an interactive shell from which you can run LVM commands. There are Man pages for all the LVM commands. LVM maintains configuration information in the **/etc/lvm/lvm.conf** file, where you can configure LVM options such as the log file, the configuration backup folder, or the folder for LVM devices (see the **lvm.conf** Man page for more details).

You can use the **pvdisplay**, **vgdisplay**, and **lvdisplay** commands to show detailed information about a physical partition, volume groups, and logical volumes. The **pvscan**, **vgscan**, and **lvscan** commands list your physical, group, and logical volumes.

Managing LVM Physical Volumes with the LVM commands

A physical volume can be any hard disk partition or RAID device. A RAID device is seen as a single physical volume. You can create physical volumes either from a single hard disk or from partitions on a hard disk. On very large systems with many hard disks, you would more likely use an entire hard disk for each physical volume.

You would first use a partition utility like **fdisk**, **parted**, or **gparted** to create a partition of the LVM partition type (**8e**). Then, you can initialize the partition as a physical volume using the **pvcreate** command.

To initialize a physical volume on an entire hard disk, you use the hard disk device name, as shown here:

```
pvcreate /dev/sdc
```

This will initialize one physical partition, **pv**, called **sdc1** on the **sdc** hard drive (the third Serial ATA drive, c).

If you are using a particular partition on a drive, you create a new physical volume using the partition's device name, as shown here:

```
pvcreate /dev/sda3
```

To initialize several drives, just list them. The following create two physical partitions, sdc1 and sdd1.

```
pvcreate /dev/sdc /dev/sdd
```

You could also use several partitions on different hard drives. This is a situation in which your hard drives each hold several partitions. This condition occurs often when you are using some partitions on your hard drive for different purposes like different operating systems, or if you want to distribute your Logical group across several hard drives. To initialize these partitions at once, you simply list them.

```
pvcreate /dev/sda3 /dev/sdb1 /dev/sdb2
```

Once you have initialized your partitions, you have to create LVM groups on them.

Managing LVM Groups

Physical LVM partitions are used to make up a volume group. You can manually create a volume group using the **vgcreate** command and the name of the group along with a list of physical partitions you want in the group.

If you are then creating a new volume group to place these in, you can include them in the group when you create the volume group with the **vgcreate** command. The volume group can use one or more physical partitions. The configuration described in the following example used only one physical partition for the **VolGroup00**. In the following example, a volume group called **mymedia** that is made up two physical volumes, **sdc** and **sdd**.

```
vgcreate mymedia /dev/sdc /dev/sdd
```

The previous example sets up a logical group on two serial ATA hard drives, each with its own single partition. Alternatively, you can set up a volume group to span partitions on several hard drives. If you are using partitions for different functions, this approach gives you the flexibility for using all the space available across multiple hard drives. The following example creates a group called **mygroup** consisting of three physical partitions, **/dev/sda3**, **/dev/sdb2**, and **/dev/sdb4**:

```
vgcreate mygroup /dev/sda3 /dev/sdb2 /dev/sdb4
```

If you later want to add a physical volume to a volume group you would use the **vgextend** command. The **vgextend** command adds a new partition to a logical group. In the following example, the partition **/dev/sda4** is added to the volume group **mygroup**. In effect, you are extending the size of the logical group by adding a new physical partition.

```
vgextend mygroup   /dev/sda4
```

To add an entire new drive to a volume group, you would follow a similar procedure. The following example adds a fifth serial ATA hard drive, **sde**, first creating a physical volume on it and then adding that volume, **sde**, to the **mymedia** volume group.

```
pvcreate /dev/sde
vgextend mymedia /dev/sde
```

To remove a physical partition, first, remove it from its logical group. You may have to use the **pmove** command to move any data off the physical partition. Then use the **vgreduce** command to remove it from its logical group.

You can remove an entire volume group by first deactivating it with **vgchange -a n** and then using the **vgremove** command.

Activating Volume Groups

Whereas in a standard file system structure you mount and unmount hard disk partitions, with an LVM structure, you activate and deactivate entire volume groups. The group volumes are accessible until you activate them with the **vgchange** command with the **-a** option. To activate a group, first, reboot your system, and then enter the **vgchange** command with the **-a** option and the y argument to activate the logical group (an **n** argument will deactivate the group).

```
vgchange -a  y  mygroup
```

Managing LVM Logical Volumes

To create logical volumes, you use the **lvcreate** command and then format your logical volume using the standard formatting command like **mkfs.ext4**. With the **-n** option you specify the volume's name, which functions like a hard disk partition's label. You use the **-L** or **--size** options to specify the size of the volume. Use a size suffix for the measure, **G** for Gigabyte, **M** for megabyte, and **K** for kilobytes. There are other options for implementing features like whether to implement a linear, striped, or mirrored volume, or to specify the size of the extents to use. Usually, the defaults work well. The following example creates a logical volume named **projects** on the **mygroup** logical group with a size of 20GB.

```
lvcreate -n projects   -L 20GB mygroup
```

The following example sets up a logical volume on the **mymedia** volume group that is 540GB in size. The **mymedia** volume group is made up of two physical volumes, each on 320GB hard drives. In effect, the two hard drives are logically seen as one.

```
lvcreate -n myvideos   -L 540GB mymedia
```

Once you have created your logical volume, you then need to create a file system to use on it. The following creates an **ext4** file system on the **myvideos** logical volume.

```
mkfs.ext4 myvideos
```

You could also use:

```
mkfs -t ext4 myvideos
```

With **lvextend**, you can increase the size of the logical volume if there is unallocated space available in the volume group.

Should you want to reduce the size of a logical volume, you use the **lvreduce** command, indicating the new size. Be sure to reduce the size of any file systems (**ext4**) on the logical volume, using the **resize2fs** command.

To rename a logical volume use the **lvrename** command. If you want to completely remove a logical volume, you can use the **lvremove** command.

Steps to create a new LVM group and volume

Physical Partition First create a physical partition on your hard drive. You can use GParted or fdisk with the disk device name to create the partition. For example, to use fdisk to create a new partition on a new hard drive, whose device name is **/etc/sde**, you would enter:

```
fdisk /etc/sde
```

Then, in the fdisk shell, use the **fdisk n** command to create a new partition, set it as a primary partition (**p**), and make it the first partition. If you plan to use the entire hard drive for your LVM, you would need only one partition that would cover the entire drive.

Then use the **t** command to set the partition type to 8E. The 8E type is the LVM partition type. To make your changes, enter **w** to write changes to the disk.

Physical Volume Next create a physical volume (pv) on the new and empty LVM partition, using the **pvcreate** command and the device name.

```
pvcreate /dev/sde
```

Volume Group Then, create your volume group with **vgcreate** command, with the volume group name and the hard disk device name.

```
vgcreate mynewgroup /dev/sde
```

Be sure the volume group is activated. Use the **vgs** command to list it. If not listed, use the following command to activate it.

```
vgchange -a y mynewgroup
```

Logical Volume Then, create a logical volume, or volumes, for the volume group, using the **lvcreate** command. The **--size** or **-L** options determines the size and the **--name** option specifies the name. To find out the available free space, use the **vgs** command. You can have more than one logical volume in a volume group, or just one if you prefer. A logical volume is conceptually similar to logical volumes in an extended partition on Windows systems.

```
lvcreate --size --name mynewvol1
```

Format the Logical volume. You then use the **mkfs** command with the **-t** option to format the logical volume. The logical volume will be listed in a folder for the LVM group, within the **/dev** folder, **/dev/mynewgroup/mynewvol1**.

```
mkfs -t ext4 /dev/mynewgroup/mynewgroup-mynewvol1
```

Steps to add a new drive to an LVM group and volume

Physical Partition First create a physical partition on your hard drive. You can use GParted or **fdisk** with the disk device name to create the partition. For the type specify LVM (**8E**).

Physical Volume Next, create a physical volume (pv) on the new and empty LVM partition, using the **pvcreate** command and the device name.

```
pvcreate /dev/sdf
```

Add to Logical Group Use the **vgextend** command to add the new physical volume to your existing logical group (LG).

```
vgextend mynewgroup /dev/sdf
```

Add to Logical Volume Then, you can create new logical volumes in the new space, or expand the size of a current logical volume. To expand the size of a logical volume to the new space, first, unmount the logical volume. Then use the **lvextend** command to expand to the space on the new hard drive that is now part the same logical group. With no size specified, the entire space on the new hard drive will be added.

```
umount /dev/mynewgroup/mynewvol1
lvextend /dev/mynewgroup/mynewvol /dev/sdf
```

Use the **-L** option to specify a particular size, **-L +250G** . Be sure to add the + sign to have the size added to the current logical volume size. To find out the available free space, use the **vgs** command.

Add to file system Use the **resize2fs** command to extend the Linux file system (ext4) on to logical volume to include the new space, formatting it. Unless you specify a size (second parameter), all the available unformatted space is used.

```
resize2fs /dev/mynewgroup/mynewvol1
```

LVM Device Names: /dev/mapper

The **device-mapper** driver is used by LVM to set up tables for mapping logical devices to hard disk. The device name for a logical volume is kept in the **/dev/mapper** folder and has the format *logical group –logical volume*. The default LVM setup for Ubuntu has the name **ubuntu-root**. The **mypics** logical volume in the **mymedia** logical group would have the device name, **/dev/mapper/mymedia-mypics**. In addition, there will be a corresponding device folder for the logical group, which will contain logical volume names. For the **ubuntu** logical group, there is a device folder called **/dev/ubuntu**.

Note: You can backup volume group metadata (configuration) using the **vgcfgbackup** command. This does not backup your logical volumes (no content). Metadata backups are stored in **/etc/lvm/backup**, and can be restored using **vgcfgrestore**.

Using LVM to replace drives

LVM can be very useful when you need to replace an older hard drive with a new one. Hard drives are expected to last about six years on the average. You could want to replace the older drive with a larger one (hard drive storage sizes double every year or so). Replacing additional hard drives is easy. To replace a boot drive is much more complicated.

To replace the drive, simply incorporate the new drive to your logical volume (see Steps to add a new drive to an LVM group and volume). The size of your logical volume will increase accordingly. You can use the **pmove** command to move data from the old drive to the new one. Then, issue commands to remove the old drive (**vgreduce**) from the volume group. From the user and system point of view, no changes are made. Files from your old drive will still be stored in the same folders, though the actual storage will be implemented on the new drive.

Replacement with LVM becomes more complicated if you want to replace your boot drive, the hard drive from which your system starts up and which holds your Linux kernel. The boot drive contains a special boot partition and the master boot record. The boot partition cannot be part of any LVM volume. You would first have to create a boot partition on the new drive using a partition tool such as Parted or fdisk, labeling it as boot (the boot drive is usually very small, about 200 MB). Then mount the partition on your system, and copy the contents of your **/boot** folder to it. Then add the remainder of the disk to your logical volume and logically remove the old disk, copying the contents of the old disk to the new one. You would still have to boot with the install USB/DVD and issue the **grub-install** command to install the master boot record on your new drive. You can then boot from the new drive.

LVM Snapshots

A snapshot records and defines the state of the logical volume at a designated time. It does not create a full copy of data on the volume, but only just changes since the last snapshot. A snapshot defines the state of the data at a given time. This allows you to back up the data in a consistent way. Should you need to restore a file to its previous version, you can use the snapshot of it. Snapshots are treated as a logical volume and can be mounted, copied, or deleted.

To create a snapshot, use the **lvcreate** command with the **-s** option. In this example, the snapshot is given the name mypics-snap1 (**-n** option). You need to specify the full device name for the logical group you want to create the snapshot for. Be sure there is enough free space available in the logical group for the snapshot. In this example, the snapshot logical volume is created in the **/dev/mymedia** logical group. It could just as easily be created in any other logical group. Though a snapshot normally uses very little space, you have to guard against overflows. If the snapshot is allocated the same size as the original, it will never overflow For systems where little of the original data changes, the snapshot can be very small. The following example allocates one-third the size of the original (60GB).

```
sudo lvcreate -s -n mypics-snap1 -l 20GB /dev/mymedia
```

You can then mount the snapshot as you would any other file system.

```
sudo mount /dev/mymedia/mypic-snap1 /mysnaps
```

To delete a snapshot you use the **lvremove** command, removing it like you would any logical volume.

```
sudo lvremove -f /dev/mymedia/mypics-nap1
```

Snapshots are very useful for making backups while a system is still active. You can use tar or dump to back up the mounted snapshot to a disk or tape. All the data from the original logical volume will be included, along with the changes noted by the snapshot.

Snapshots also allow you to perform effective undo operations. You can create a snapshot of a logical volume, then unmount the original and mount the snapshot in its place. Any changes you make will be performed on the snapshot, not the original. Should problems occur, unmount the snapshot and then mount the original. This restores the original state of your data. You could also do this using several snapshots, restoring to a previous snapshot. With this procedure, you could test new software on a snapshot, without endangering your original data. The software would be operating on the snapshot, not the original logical volume.

You can also use them as alternative versions of a logical volume. You can read and write to a snapshot. A write will change only the snapshot volume, not the original, creating, in effect, an alternate version.

OpenZFS

The ZFS file system incorporates the features of a logical volume manager (LVM), RAID systems, and file systems. It is now an experimental option in the install process ("Advanced features" button on the "Installation type" screen). ZFS abstracts a file system, much like LVM, setting up a pool of storage from which a file system can be generated. Checksums for data blocks are saved outside the data blocks and are checked for any corruption within the blocks. This makes ZFS effective in protecting against silent data corruption from problems such as write interrupts, driver bugs, and access failures. If RAID-Z support has been set up, corrupted blocks can be recovered. RAID-Z implements a data-oriented RAID-like support with automatic mirroring of your data within the file system. In addition, the LVM-like abstraction of ZFS allows for large files. Writes are performed with a copy-on-write transaction method, where data is not overwritten directly, but added.

ZFS was developed by SUN, which is now controlled by Oracle. Since 2010, OpenZFS provides an open source version of ZFS for Linux systems. Ubuntu now supports the ZFS file system, using the OpenZFS kernel module. Tools to manage ZFS file systems can be installed with the **zfsutils-linux** package (the App Center, Synaptic Package Manager, or **apt** command). See the following for more information:

https://wiki.ubuntu.com/Kernel/Reference/ZFS

Much like an LVM system, you have the physical devices (called virtual devices, VDEVs) that are combined and striped into a data pool (**zpool** command), which can then be used to create the ZFS file system. At the pool level, you can implement RAIDZ options. With the **zfs** command, you can then create file systems in your pool, as well as create snapshots (read-only copy) of a ZFS file system, or a clone (writeable copy). To perform an integrity check of the pool, use the **zpool** command's **scrub** option.

Use **zfs-auto-snapshots** to have ZFS automatically generate snapshots as you update your system.

sudo apt install zfs-auto-snapshot

To restore your system to one of these snapshots, you would access the History entry in the Grub boot menu when you start your system. This opens a list of previous snapshots. Choose the one you want to open options for restoring the system with or without user data, or to a recovery state.

Ubuntu also provides the ZSys system tool (**zsys** package) for easily managing your ZFS file systems. ZSys implements the **zsysctl** command that interfaces with ZFS through the **zsysd** daemon. You can use the **zsysctl** command to perform operations on your ZFS file systems. The **list** command lists your file systems and the **show** command shows their status.

```
zsysctl list
```

```
zsysctl show
```

If you choose the ZFS install option during installation, both the **zfsutils-linux** and **zsys** packages are installed for you. You can find out more about ZSys at:

`https://github.com/ubuntu/zsys`

ubuntu

14. System Administration

Ubuntu Administrative Tools
Controlled Administrative Access
Users and Groups
Bluetooth
File System Access
Shared Folders and Samba
GRUB Bootloader
Editing Configuration Files Directly
Backup Management

Most administrative configurations tasks are performed for you automatically. Devices like printers, hard drive partitions, and graphics cards are detected and set up for you. There are cases where you may need to perform tasks manually like adding new users and installing software. Such administrative operations can be performed with user-friendly system tools. Most administration tools are located in Settings or listed on the Applications overview and its Utilities application folder.

Ubuntu Administration Tools	Description
App Center	Software management using online repositories (GNOME Software)
Software Updater	Update tool using Ubuntu repositories
Synaptic Package Manager	Software management using online repositories (no longer supported by Ubuntu, available on the Universe repository)
NetworkManager	Detects, connects, and configures your network interfaces
clock	GNOME Time & Date tool (see Chapter 3)
Users	GNOME User configuration tool
users-admin	Older User and Group configuration tool, install gnome-system-tools.
system-config-printer	Printer configuration tool used for additional printer configuration
Gufw and FirewallD	Configures your network firewall
Deja-dup	Backup tool using rsync

Table 14-1: Ubuntu Administration Tools

Ubuntu Administrative Tools

On Ubuntu, administration is handled by a set of specialized administrative tools, such as those for user management and printer configuration (see Table 14-1). To access the desktop-based administrative tools, you need to log in as a user who has administrative access. You created such a user when you first installed Ubuntu. On the Ubuntu desktop, system administrative tools are accessed from the Applications overview and from Settings. Here you will find tools to set the time and date, manage users, configure printers, and install software. Settings Users lets you create and modify users. Setting Printers lets you install and reconfigure printers. All tools provide easy-to-use and intuitive desktop interfaces. Tools are identified by simple descriptive terms.

TIP: If you have difficulties with your system configuration, check the **https://v** and the **https://askubuntu.com/** sites for possible solutions. The site offers helpful forums ranging from desktop and installation problems to games, browsers, and multimedia solutions. Also, check the Community tab at **https://ubuntu.com** for documentation and tutorials.

Ubuntu uses the GNOME administrative tools and independent tools developed by open source projects. PolicyKit is used for device authorizations, and the App Center, the Synaptic Package Manager, and the **apt** command provide software management. In addition, Virus protection is handled by the third party application ClamAV. The older GNOME administrative tools such as Users and Groups are also available, but not installed by default (**gnome-system-tools** package).

/etc/hostname and hostnamectl

The **/etc/hostname** file contains your hostname. You can use the **hostnamectl** command in a terminal window to display your current hostname and all information pertaining to it such as the machine ID, the kernel used, the architecture, chassis (type of computer), and the operating system (you can add the **status** option if you want). Three different kinds of hostnames are supported: static, pretty, and transient. You can set each with the **hostnamectl**'s **set-hostname** command with the corresponding type. The static hostname is used to identify your computer on the network (usually a fully qualified host name). You can use the **--static** option to set it. The pretty hostname is a descriptive hostname made available to users on the computer. This can be set by **set-hostname** with the **--pretty** option. The transient hostname is one allocated by a network service such as DHCP, and can be managed with the **--transient** option. Without options, the **set-hostname** command will apply the name to all the host name types.

```
hostnamectl set-hostname --pretty "my computer"
```

The **set-chassis** command sets the computer type, which can be desktop, laptop, server, tablet, handset, and vm (virtual system). Without a type specified it reverts to the default for the system. The **set-icon-name** command sets the name used by the graphical applications for the host.

Controlled Administrative Access

To access administrative tools, you have to log in as a user who has administrative permissions. The user that you created during installation is given administrative permissions automatically. Log in as that user. When you attempt to use an administrative tool, a dialog opens prompting you to enter your user password. As an administrative user, this is the password you logged in with. Some tools will open without authorization but remain locked, preventing any modifications. These tools, like Settings Users have an Unlock button you can press to gain access. You can use the Settings Users tool to grant or deny particular users administrative access.

To perform system administration operations, you must first have the access rights enabling you to perform administrative tasks. There are several ways to gain such access: login as a **sudo** supported user, unlocking an administrative tool for access with PolicyKit, or logging in as the root user. PolicyKit is the preferred access method and is used on many administrative tools. The **sudo** granted access method was used in previous Ubuntu releases, and is still used for many tasks including software upgrade and installation. The **root** user access is still discouraged but provides complete control over the entire system.

> PolicyKit: Provides access only to specific applications and only to users with administrative access for that application. It requires that the specific application be configured for use by PolicyKit. Ubuntu 24.04 LTS uses the policykit-1 version of PolicyKit (Ubuntu repository). It is installed by default and fully supported.

> **sudo** and **pkexec**: Provides access to any application with full administrative authorization. It imposes a time limit to reduce risk. The **pkexec** command is used for graphical administrative tools like the Synaptic Package Manager. You will still need to

use **sudo** to perform any command-line Linux commands at the root level, like moving files to an administrative folder or running the **systemctl** command to start or stop servers.

root user access, **su**: Provides complete direct control over the entire system. This is the traditional method for accessing administrative tools. It is disabled by default on Ubuntu, but can be enabled. The **su** command will allow any user to log in as the root user if they know the root user password. It is considered a serious security risk.

sudo

The sudo service provides administrative access to specific users. You have to be a user on the system with a valid username and password that has been authorized by the sudo service for administrative access. This allows other users to perform specific super user operations without having full administrative level control such as **root** user access. You can find more about sudo at **https://www.sudo.ws**.

sudo command

Some administrative operations require access from the command line in the terminal window. For such operations, you would use the **sudo** command. You can open a terminal window from the Applications overview. For easier access, you can pin the Terminal icon to the dock (right-click and choose "Pin to Dash").

To use **sudo** to run an administrative command, you would precede the command with the **sudo** command. You are then prompted to enter your password. You will be issued a time-restricted ticket to allow access. The following example sets the system date using the **date** command.

```
sudo date 0406165908
password:
```

You can also use the **sudo** command to run an application with administrative access. From the terminal window, you would enter the **sudo** command with the application name as an argument. For example, to use the **nano** editor to edit a system configuration file, you would start **nano** using the **sudo** command in a terminal window, with the **nano** command and the filename as its arguments. This starts up **nano** editor with administrator privileges. The following example will allow you to edit the **/etc/fstab** file to add or edit file system entries. You will be prompted for your user password.

```
sudo nano /etc/fstab
```

sudo configuration

Access for **sudo** is controlled by the **/etc/sudoers** file. This file lists users and the commands they can run, along with the password for access. If the NOPASSWD option is set, then users will not need a password. The ALL option, depending on the context, can refer to all hosts on your network, all root-level commands, or all users. See the Man page for **sudoers** for detailed information on all options.

```
man sudoers
```

To make changes or add entries, you have to edit the file with the special sudo editing command **visudo**. This invokes the **nano** editor (see Chapter 5) to edit the **/etc/sudoers** file. Unlike a standard editor, **visudo** will lock the **/etc/sudoers** file and check the syntax of your entries. You are not allowed to save changes unless the syntax is correct. If you want to use a different editor, you can assign it to the EDITOR shell variable. Use Ctrl-x to exit and Ctrl-o to save. Be sure to invoke **visudo** with the **sudo** command to gain authorized access.

```
sudo visudo
```

A **sudoers** entry has the following syntax.

```
user    host=command
```

The *host* is a host on your network. You can specify all hosts with the ALL term. The *command* can be a list of commands, some or all qualified by options such as whether a password is required. To specify all commands, you can also use the ALL term. The following gives the user **georgep** full root-level access to all commands on all hosts.

```
georgep  ALL = ALL
```

In addition, you can let a user run as another user on a given host. Such alternate users are placed within parentheses before the commands. For example, if you want to give **georgep** access to the **beach** host as the user **mydns**, you use the following.

```
georgep beach = (mydns) ALL
```

To specify a group name, you prefix the group with a **%** sign, as in **%mygroup**. This way, you can give the same access to a group of users. By default, **sudo** will grant access to all users in the **admin** group. These are user granted administrative access. The ALL=(ALL) ALL entry allows access by the administrative group users to all hosts as all users to all commands.

```
%admin   ALL=(ALL)   ALL
```

With the NOPASSWD option, you can allow members of a certain group access without a password. A commented **sudo** group is provided in the **/etc/sudoers** file.

```
%sudo    ALL=NOPASSWD:   ALL
```

Though on Ubuntu, **sudo** is configured to allow **root** user access, Ubuntu does not create a **root** user password. This prevents you from logging in as the **root** user, rendering the sudo root permission useless. The default **/etc/sudoers** file does configure full access for the root user to all commands. The ALL=(ALL:ALL) ALL entry allows access by the root user to all hosts as all users to all commands. If you were to set up a password for the root user, the root user could then log in and have full administrative access.

```
root    ALL=(ALL:ALL)   ALL
```

The sudo group also has the same permissions, allow execution of any commands.

```
sudo    ALL=(ALL:ALL)   ALL
```

If you want to see what commands you can run, you use the **sudo** command with the **-l** option. The **-U** option to specifies a particular user. In the following example, the user **richard** has full administrative access.

```
$ sudo -U richard -l
User richard may run the following commands on this host:
    (ALL : ALL) All
```

The **/etc/sudoers.d** folder holds configuration files for **sudo** that are included in the sudoers file. They usually hold permissions for applications to have **sudo** access such as the Snap server.

Root User Access: root and su

You can access the root user from any normal terminal window using the **sudo** command on the **su** command. The **su** command is the superuser command. Superuser is another name for the **root** user. A user granted administrative access by **sudo** could then become the **root** user. The following logs into the root user.

```
sudo su
```

Ubuntu is designed never to let anyone directly log in as the root user. The **root** user would have total control over the entire system. Instead, certain users are given administrative access with which they can separately access administrative tools, performing specific tasks. Even though a **root** user exists, a password for the root user is not defined, never allowing access to it.

Should you want to for some reason, it is possible to activate the root user by using the **passwd** command to create a root user password. Keep in mind that having a root user is a serious security risk. To activate the root user, enter the **passwd** command with the **root** username in a **sudo** operation.

```
sudo passwd root
```

You are prompted for your administrative password, and then prompted by the **passwd** command to enter a password for the **root** user. You are then prompted to repeat the password.

```
Enter new UNIX password:
Retype new UNIX password:
passwd: password updated successfully
```

You can then log in with the **su** command as the root user, making you the superuser (you still cannot login as the root user from the display manager login screen). Because a superuser has the power to change almost anything on the system, such a password is usually carefully guarded, changed very frequently, and given only to those whose job it is to manage the system. With the correct password, you can log in to the system as a system administrator and configure the system any way you want.

```
su root
```

The **su** command alone will assume the root username.

```
su
```

The **su** command can be used to login to any user, provided you have that user's password.

```
su georgep
```

To exit from an **su** login operation, just enter **exit**.

```
exit
```

PolicyKit

PolicyKit controls access to certain applications and devices. It is one of the safest ways to grant a user direct access. PolicyKit configuration and support is already set up for you. The PolicyKit-1version of PolicyKit is used for PolicyKit operations. Configuration files for these operations are held in **/usr/share/polkit-1**. There is, as yet, no desktop tool you can use to configure these settings.

Difficulties occur if you want to change the authorization setting for certain actions, like mounting internal hard drives. Currently, you can change the settings by manually editing the configuration files in the **/usr/share/polkit-1/actions** folder. To make changes, you first have to know the action to change and the permission to set. The man page for **polkit** will list possible authorizations. The default authorizations are **allow_any** for anyone, **allow_inactive** for a console, and **allow_active** for an active console only (user logged in). These authorizations can be set to the following specific values.

auth_admin	Administrative user only, authorization required always
auth_admin_keep	Administrative user only, authorization kept for a brief period
auth_self	User authorization required
auth_self_keep	User authorization required, authorization kept for a brief period
yes	Always allow access
no	Never allow access

You will need to know the PolicyKit action to modify and the file to edit. The action is listed in the PolicyKit dialog that prompts you to enter the password (expand the Details arrow) when you try to use an application. The filename will be the first segments of the action name with the suffix "policy" attached. For example, the action for mounting drives is:

```
org.freedesktop.udisks2.filesystem-mount-system
```

Its file is:

```
org.freedesktop.UDisks2.policy
```

The file is located in the **/usr/share/polkit-1/actions** folder. It's full path name is:

```
/usr/share/polkit-1/actions/org.freedesktop.UDisks2.policy
```

Users with administrative access, like your primary user, can mount partitions on your hard drives automatically. However, users without administrative access require authorization using an administrative password before they can mount a partition (see Figure 14-13). Should you want to allow non-administrative users to mount partitions without an authorization request, the **org.freedesktop.UDisks2.policy** file in the **/usr/share/polkit-1** folder has to be modified to change the **allow_active** default for **filesystem-mount-system** action from **auth_admin_keep** to **yes**. The **auth_admin_keep** option requires administrative authorization.

Enter the following to edit the **org.freedesktop.UDisks2.policy** file in the **/usr/share/polkit-1/actions** folder with the **nano** editor, or open it with Text Editor.

```
sudo nano /usr/share/polkit-1/actions/org.freedesktop.UDisks2.policy
```

Locate the **action id** labeled as:

```
<action id ="org.feedesktop.udisks2.filesystem-mount-system">
  <description>Mount a filesystem on a system device</description>
```

This is usually the second action id. At the end of that action section, you will find the following entry. It will be located within a defaults subsection, <defaults>.

```
<allow_active>auth_admin_keep</allow_active>
```

Replace **auth_admin_keep** with **yes**.

```
<allow_active>yes</allow_active>
```

Save the file. Non-administrative users will no longer have to enter a password to mount partitions.

Users (Settings | System | Users)

You can configure and create user accounts using the Settings Users tool accessible from Settings as Users link in the System tab. Users does not provide any way to control groups. If you want group control and more configuration options, you can use the Users and Groups application (**gnome-system-tools** package).

You can access the Settings Users tab from the Users link on Settings System tab. The Users tab opens to the user tab for the primary user, the one you set up when you installed your Ubuntu (see Figure 14-1). To return to the System tab, click the left arrow displayed at the top left on the header bar, before the sidebar.

The primary user, the one you set up when installing your Ubuntu system, is displayed, showing the user settings: the user full name, a link to a dialog for changing a name, switches for automatic login and administrator status, a link to a dialog for changing variations of the selected language if available, links to tabs for other users you have added, and an Add User button at the bottom for opening a tab where you can add a new user. To access the settings for another user, click on its link in the Other Users section. Tabs for added users will have the same settings, but there will be no Other Users section. Instead of an Add User button, it will have a Remove User button. To return to the primary user's tab, click the left arrow button on the left side of the header bar before the sidebar. From the primary user's tab you can then link to tabs for other users if you wish.

Initially, at the top of the Users tab is an Unlock button. Click on this button to open an authentication dialog, prompting for your password (see Figure 14-2). Once authentication is accepted, the Unlock button and its warning banner disappears. You can then change the password, account type, icon, or name for the currently selected user, as well as add new users.

Chapter 14: System Administration **565**

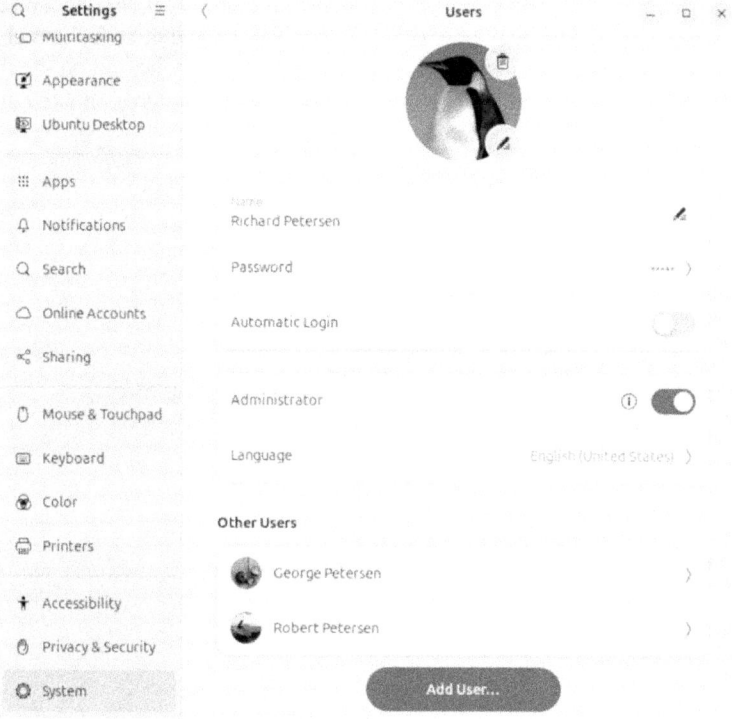

Figure 14-1: Users - Settings | System | Users

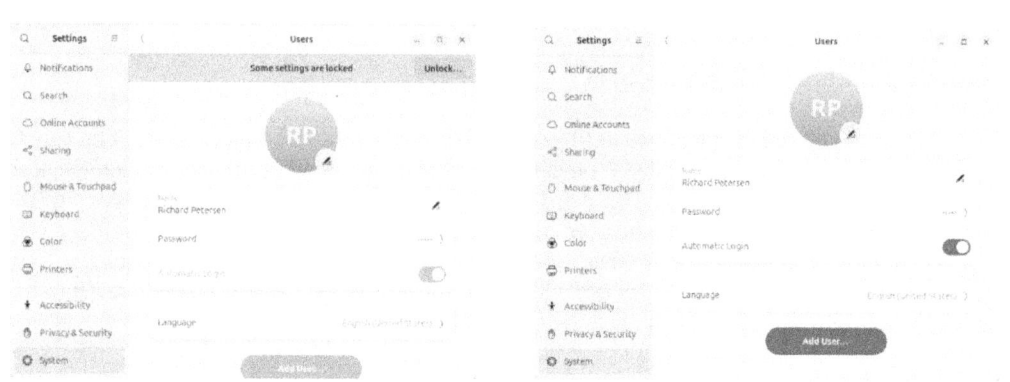

Figure 14-2: Users - unlock

Add User button, which you click to add a new user. When you add a new account, the Add User tab opens, allowing you to set the account type (standard or administrator), the full name of the user, and the username (see Figure 14-3). For the username, you can enter a name or choose from a recommended list of options. You can also choose to set the password at this time. Click the Add button on the upper right to create the user. The new account appears as a link in the Other Users section of the primary administrative user's tab, showing the name and icon. Selecting the user shows its account type, language, password, an automatic login option, and the Account activity showing if the user is logged in or when they last logged out. You can change the account type, language, password, and icon by clicking on their entries. Clicking on the Account Activity link open and Account Activity dialog showing when a user previously logged in and logged out.

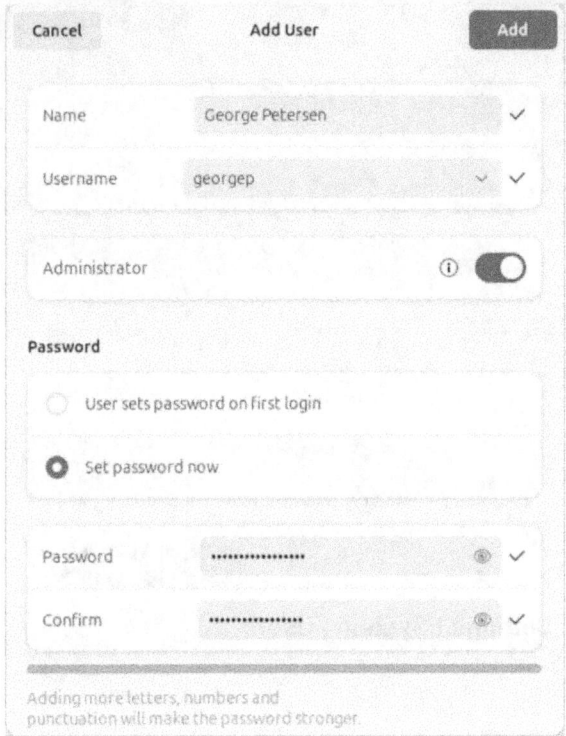

Figure 14-3: Users - Add a new user

The account remains inactive until you specify a password (see Figure 14-4). You can do this when you add the account or later. You can also change the password for an account. Click the password entry to open the "Change Password" dialog where you can enter the new password (see Figure 14-5). You can choose to let the user enter the new password on a user's next login, or you can change it now. To change it now, select the "Set a password now" option. Then click the New Password text box to enter a new password. Click the Confirm Password text box to enter the password again, confirming it. Then click the Change button on the upper right.

Chapter 14: System Administration **567**

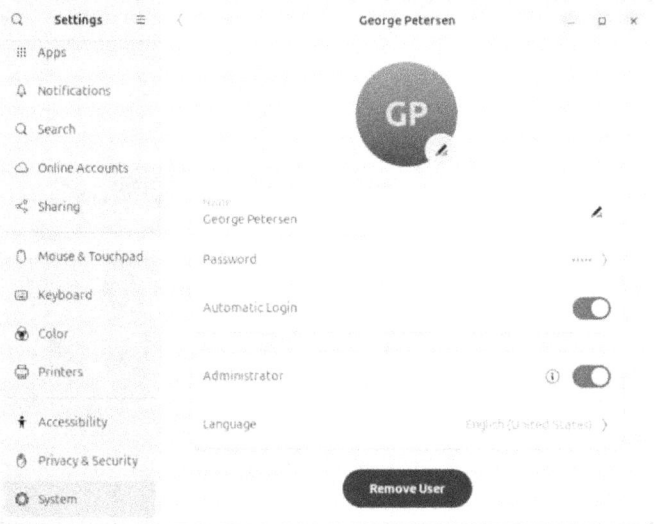

Figure 14-4: Users

Figure 14-5: Users, password dialog

To change the user icon (avatar), click the edit button (pencil) on the user's icon image to display a pop-up dialog showing available images you can use (see Figure 14-6). You can also select a picture from a folder (Select a File). The Select a File button opens to your Pictures folder, but you can navigate to other folders. Many of the photos used in previous releases are at **/usr/share/pixmaps/faces**. Once selected, the image appears along with the a trash can button for removing the icon. You can also use the edit button on the icon to change it.

Currently, group configuration is not supported.

568 Part 4: Administration

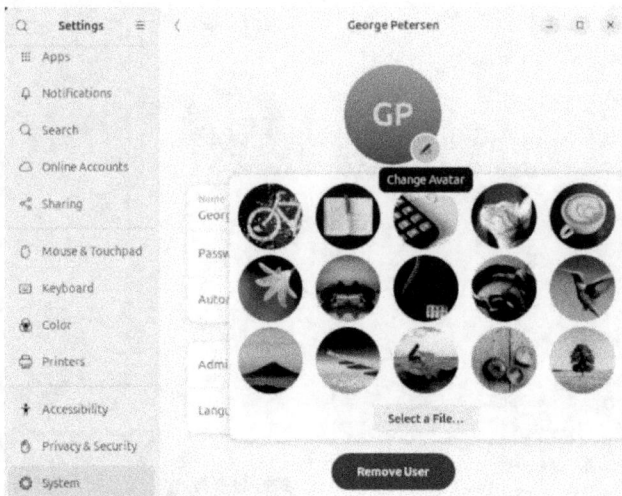

Figure 14-6: **User - Selecting User Icon**

Users and Groups

Alternatively, you can install the older "Users and Groups" application, which you can install as a Debian package on the App Center. Users and Groups is part of the **gnome-system-tools** package and is named **users-admin**. It will be accessible from "User and Groups" on the Applications overview (The **gnome-system-tools** package is no longer supported by Ubuntu). This opens a User Settings window, which displays two panes, a left scrollable pane for a list of users, showing their icon and login name, and a right pane showing information about a selected user. Below the left pane are buttons for adding and deleting users, as well as Managing Groups.

When you start up the users-admin application, only read access is allowed, letting you scroll through the list of users, but not make any changes or add new ones (see Figure 14-7). Read-only access is provided to all users. Users will be able to see the list of users on your system, but they cannot modify their entries, add new ones, or delete current users. Administrative access is required to perform these operations.

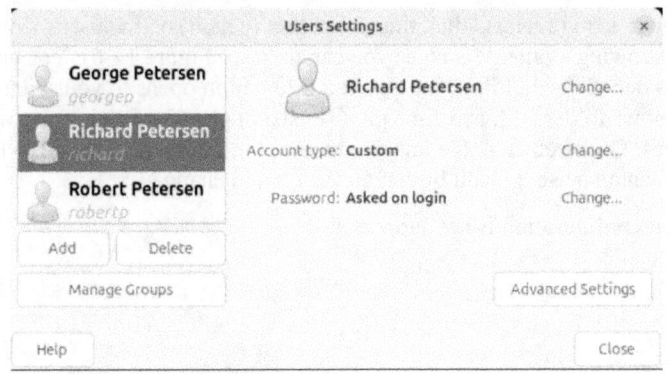

Figure 14-7: **Users and Groups**

When you first click a task button, such as Add, Delete, or Advanced Settings, an Authenticate dialog will open and prompt you to enter your user password. You will also be prompted to authenticate if you click a Change link to change a user password, account type, or name.

To change settings for a user, select the user in the User Settings window. On the left pane the username, account type and password access are listed with a Change link to the right of each. Clicking on a Change link lets you change that property. When you click a Change link, an authentication dialog will prompt you to enter an administrative user password. To change a username, click the Change link to the right of the username to open the "Change User Name" dialog with a text box for entering the new name.

To change a user password, you would click the Change link to the right of the Password entry to open the "Change User Password" dialog with entries for the current password and the new password (see Figure 14-8). You can also choose to generate a random password.

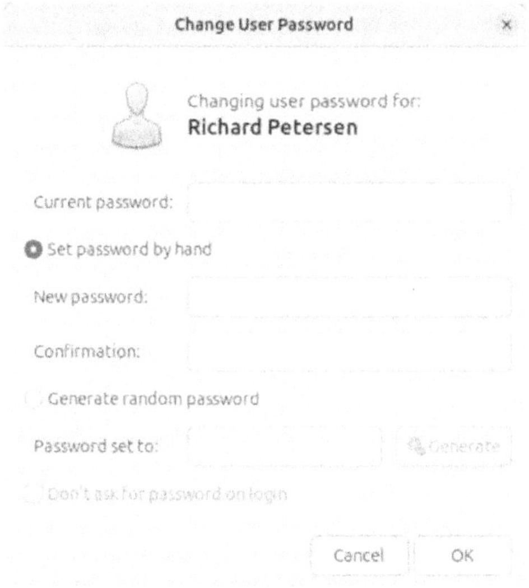

Figure 14-8: User Settings: Change User Password dialog

An account type can be Administrator, Desktop User, or Custom. When you click the Change link for the Account type, the "Change User Account Type" dialog opens with options for each.

For more detailed configuration, you click the Advanced Settings button to open the "Change Advanced User Settings" dialog, which has tabs for Contact Information, User Privileges, and Advanced (see Figure 14-9). On the Contact tab, you can add basic contact information if you wish, for an office address, as well as work and home phones.

On the User Privileges tab you can control device access and administrative access (see Figure 14-10). You can restrict or allow access to CD-ROMs, scanners, and external storage like USB drives.

The Advanced tab lets you select a home folder, the shell to use, a main group, and a user ID. Defaults are already chosen for you. A home folder in the name of the new user is specified and the shell used is the BASH shell. Normally you would not want to change these settings, though you might prefer to use a different shell, like the C-Shell. For the group, the user has a group with its own username (same as the short name).

For a Desktop user to create a share, they have to have permission to do so (administrative users already have this permission). On the Users and Groups's Advanced dialog's Privileges tab set the "Share files with the local network" option.

Figure 14-9: Users and Groups: Change User Privileges

Should to you decide to delete a user, you are prompted to keep or delete the user's home folder along with the user's files.

New Users (Users and Groups)

To create a new user, click the Add button in the Users Settings window to open a "Create New User" dialog, where you can enter the username. You enter the full name of the User in the Name textbox. Select a possible user name from the menu by the Username label. The user name is also the name of the new user's main group (see Figure 14-10). The new user is then added to the User Settings window.

The "Change User Password" dialog is then displayed, with entries for the new password and confirmation. You can also choose to use a randomly generated password instead (see Figure 14-11). Click the Generate button generate a password.

If you decide not to enter a password (click Cancel), the account will remain disabled. To enable it later, click on the Enable Account button to open the "Change User Password" dialog where you can add the password.

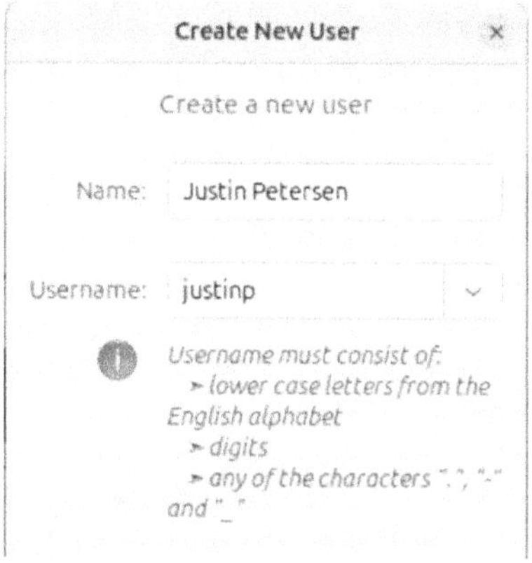

Figure 14-10: Users and Groups: Create New User

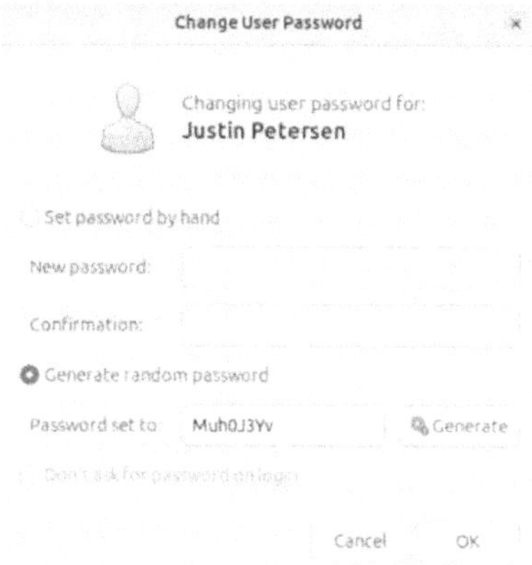

Figure 14-11: Users and Groups: new user password

The Account type is set initially to Desktop user, restricting access by the new user. Should you want to enable administrative access for this user, click the Change link to the right of the Account type entry to open the "Change User Account Type" dialog, where you can change the account type to Administrator. To set more specific privileges and for key user configuration settings such as the home folder and user id, click the Advanced Settings button to open the "Change Advanced User Settings" dialog with Contact Information, User Privileges, and Advanced tabs.

The icon used for a user is chosen by the user from their Preference's About dialog.

Alternatively, you can use the **useradd** command in a terminal window or command line to add user accounts and the **userdel** command to remove them. The following example adds the user **dylan** to the system:

```
$ sudo useradd dylan
```

Groups (Users and Groups)

To manage groups, click the Manage Groups button in the Users Settings window. This opens a Group Settings window that lists all groups (see Figure 14-12). To add or remove users to or from a group, click the group name in the Group Settings window and click Properties. You can then check or uncheck users from the Group Members listing.

To add a new group, click the Add Group button in the Group Settings window to open a New Group dialog, where you can specify the group name, its id, and select the users to add to the group (see Figure 14-13). If you want to remove a group, just select its entry in the Groups Settings window and click the Delete button.

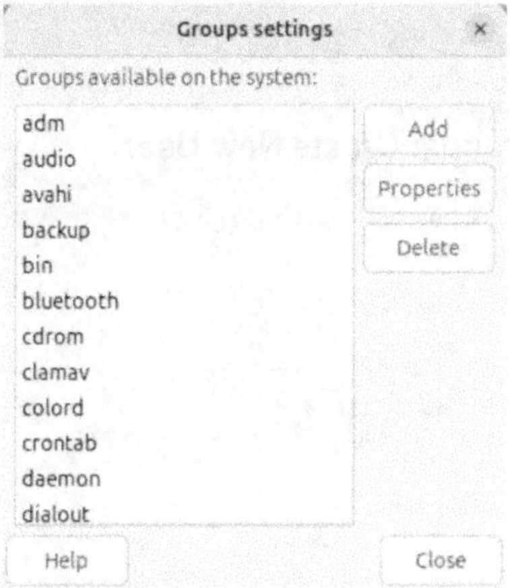

Figure 14-12: Users and Groups: Groups settings

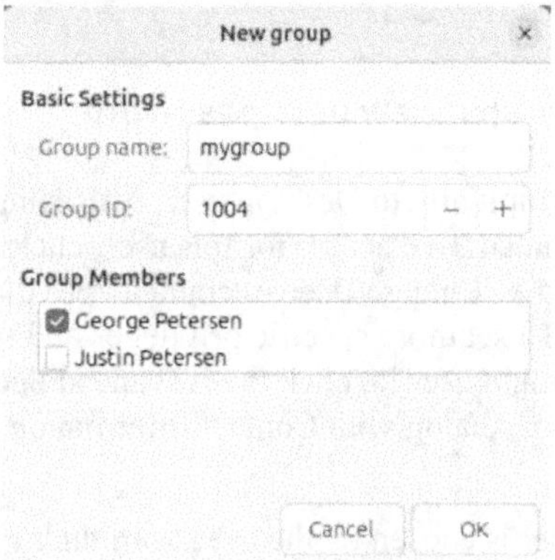

Figure 14-13: Group Properties: Group Users panel

Passwords

The easiest way to change your password is to use the Users dialog available from Settings as User. Select your username, then click the Password entry to open the Change User Password dialog (see Figure 14-5).

Alternatively, you can use the **passwd** command. In a terminal window enter the **passwd** command. The command prompts you for your current password. After entering your current password and pressing ENTER, you are then prompted for your new password. After entering the new password, you are asked to re-enter it. This makes sure you have actually entered the password you intended to enter.

```
$ passwd
Changing password for richard.
(current) UNIX password:
Enter new UNIX password:
Retype new UNIX password:
passwd: password updated successfully
$
```

Managing Services

Many administrative functions operate as services that need to be turned on. They are daemons, constantly running and checking for requests for their services. When you install a service, its daemon is normally turned on automatically. You can start, stop, and restart a service from a terminal window using the **systemctl** command with the service name and the commands: **start**, **stop**, **restart**, and **status**. The **status** command tells you if a service is already running. To restart the Samba file sharing server (**smbd**) you would use the following command. Use the **status** command to see if it is enabled. You will need administrative access for all these command, except for the **status** command. To provide that access include the **sudo** command.

```
sudo systemctl restart smbd
```

To disable a service so that it is not turned on automatically, you would use the **disable** command. To have it turned on, you use the **enable** command. The **enable** command starts up the service when you system starts. If you enable before a restart and want to run the service, you would use the **start** command.

```
sudo systemctl disable smbd
sudo systemctl enable smbd
sudo systemctl start smbd
```

Ubuntu uses systemd to manage services. The systemd services are managed using **.service** configuration files in the **/lib/systemd/system** and **/etc/systemd/system** folders.

File System Access

Various file systems can be accessed on Ubuntu. Any additional internal hard drive partitions on your system, both Linux and Windows NTFS, will be detected automatically, but not mounted. In addition, you can access remote Windows shared folders and make your shared folders accessible to other hosts on your network.

Access to Internal Linux File Systems

Ubuntu will automatically detect other Linux file systems (partitions) on all your internal hard drives. Entries for these partitions are displayed on a file manager Other Locations folder. Initially, they are not mounted. Administrative users can mount internal partitions by clicking on its entry or icon, which mounts the file system and displays an icon for it on the Ubuntu dock. A file manager window opens displaying the top-level contents of the file system. The file system is mounted under the /**media** folder, in a sub-folder with the username, and then in a folder named with the file system (partition) label, or, if unlabeled, with the device UUID name.

Non-administrative users (users you create and do not specify as administrators), cannot mount internal partitions unless the task is authenticated using an administrative user's password. An authorization window will appear. You will be asked to choose a user who has administrative access from a drop-down menu, and then enter that user's password. If there is only one administrative user, that user is selected automatically and you are prompted to enter that user's password. Whenever you start up your system again, you will still have to mount the file system, again providing authorization.

Access to Windows NTFS File Systems on Local Drives

If you have installed Ubuntu on a dual-boot system with Windows, Linux NTFS file system support is installed automatically. Your NTFS partitions are mounted using Filesystem in Userspace (FUSE). The same authentication control used for Linux file systems applies to NTFS file systems. Entries for the NTFS partitions are listed on the Other Locations folder of any file manager window. Click on an NTFS partition to mount it. If you are a user with administrative access, the file system is mounted automatically. If you are a user without administrative access, you will be asked to choose a user that has administrative access from a drop-down menu, and then enter that user's password, providing authorization. The NTFS file system is then mounted with an Eject button displayed at the right side of its entry on the Other Locations folder and an icon for it is displayed on the Ubuntu dock with an umount option. You can access the file system by clicking on its entry in a file manager Other Locations folder or by clicking on its icon on the Ubuntu dock. The partitions will be mounted under the /**media** folder with their UUID numbers or labels used as folder names. The NTFS partitions are mounted using **ntfs-3g** drivers.

Zero Configuration Networking: Avahi and Link Local Addressing

Zero Configuration Networking (Zeroconf) allows the setup of non-routable private networks without the need of a DHCP server or static IP addresses. A Zeroconf configuration lets users automatically connect to a network and access all network resources, such as printers, without having to perform any configuration. On Linux, Zeroconf networking is implemented by Avahi (**http://avahi.org**), which includes multicast DNS (mDNS) and DNS service discovery (DNS-SD) support that automatically detects services on a network. IP addresses are determined using either IPv6 or IPv4 Link Local (IPv4LL) addressing. IPv4 Link Local addresses are assigned from the 168.254.0.0 network pool. Derived from Apple's Bonjour Zeroconf implementation, it is a free and open source version currently used by desktop tools, such as the GNOME virtual file system. Ubuntu implements full Zeroconf network support with the Avahi daemon that implements multicast DNS discover, and **avahi-autoipd** that provides dynamic configuration of local IPv4 addresses. Both are installed as part of the desktop configuration. Avahi support tools like **avahi-browse** and **avahi-publish** are located in the **avahi-utils** package.

Access to Linux Local Network Shared File Systems with mDNS

Once configured, shared Windows folders and printers on any of the computers connected to your local network are accessible from any file manager window sidebar. The multicast DNS discovery service, mDNS (called Avahi in Linux), automatically detects hosts on your home or local network. Supporting Samba libraries are already installed and will let you directly access any shared folders.

You can use the multicast DNS discovery service to access any shared Linux folders on Linux systems that are running a Samba server. For such Linux system network browsing is enabled. You can open the Other Locations folder on the file manager to see the other Linux systems on your network (see Figure 14-14). Double click on the one you want to access to open a listing of the shared folders on that system. The shared folders are then displayed. Double click on the folder you want to open. You are first asked to login using the remote systems user name and password. It is mounted on your system, with and entry for it on the file manager sidebar and on the Other Locations folder. When finished, you can eject the folder using either the sidebar entry (eject button) or, on the Other Locations folder, the shared folder's context menu's (right-click) Disconnect entry.

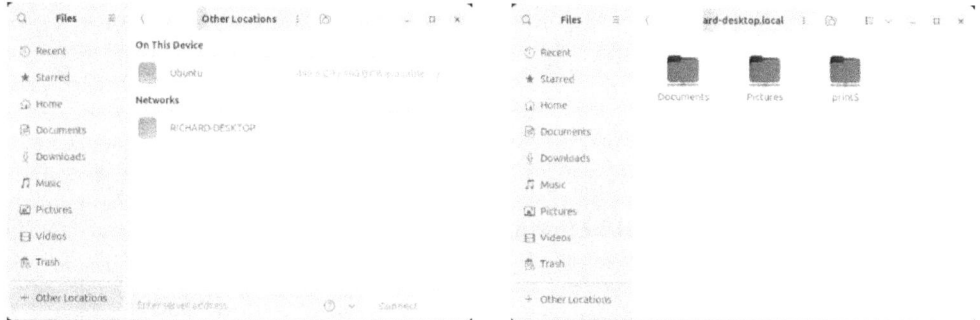

Figure 14-14: Accessing shared folders using multicast DNS discovery (Avahi)

If you are using a firewall, be sure that it is configured for access to allow multicast DNS discovery. For the UFW firewall installed with Ubuntu, access for multicast DNS discovery service can be configured with Gufw by selecting the Multicast DNS application when adding a rule from the Preconfigured tab (UDP port 5353). For FirewallD, on firewall-config (Administration | Firewall), be sure that the **mdns** service is enabled, both runtime and permanent (Zones | Services tab) (see Figure 14-15).

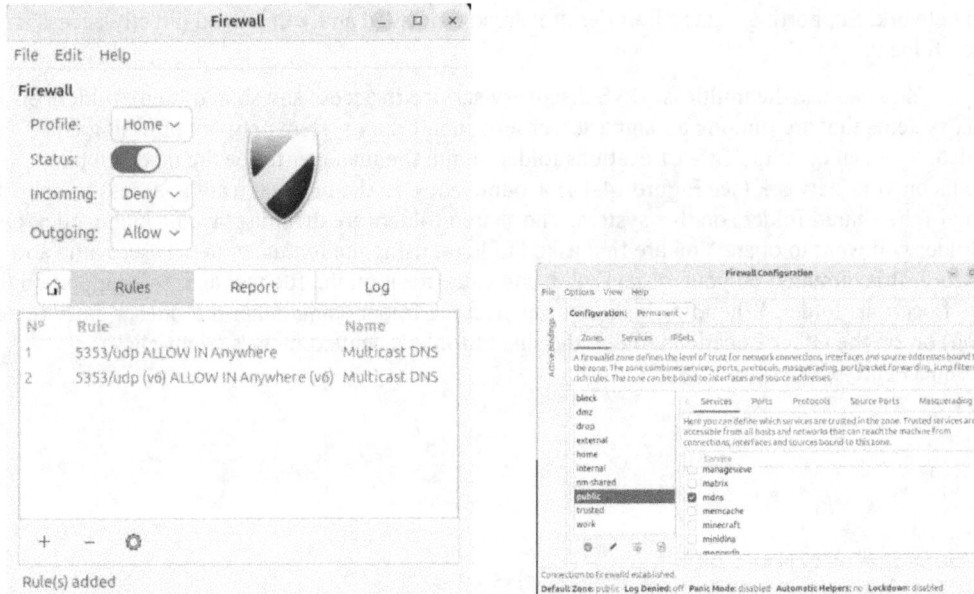

Figure 14-15: Gufw and FirewallD configuration for multicast DNS discovery (Avahi), mdns service

Problems can occur if the discovery process is not able to resolve the names of the hosts on your network. The multicast DNS discovery (mdns) service will append a **.local** to your host name for use by mdns, such as **richard-laptop.local**. If your host has the **.local** extension added irregularly or if it is missing, you will not be detected on your network. The way to ensure that your host is referenced is to create a **/etc/mdns.allow** file with entries for the **.local** and **.local.** which will remove the strict mdns requirement for the **.local** part of the host name. In the **/mdns.allow** file place the two lines as shown here.

/etc/mdns.allow

```
.local
.local.
```

In addition, you have to use **mdns4** instead of **mdns4_minimal** in the **/etc/nsswitch.conf** file. **mdns4_minimal** does not check the **/etc/mdns.allow** file, whereas **mdns4** does check it. In the **/etc/nsswitch.conf** file, modify the current hosts line:

```
hosts      files mdsn4_minimal [NOTFOUND=return] dns
```

to the following:

```
hosts      files mdsn4 [NOTFOUND=return] dns
```

Discovery is handled by the **nss-mdns** tool. For more information check:

https://github.com/lathiat/nss-mdns

Access to Windows Local Network Shared File Systems

You can access Windows shares directly using the Samba support for accessing Windows shares, which is already installed. This is not the Samba server. You can access Windows shares using the Connect text box on the file manager's Other Locations window. Enter in the **smb://** protocol (the Samba protocol) and the name of the shared folder or that of the remote Windows system you want to access. A dialog opens prompting you to specify either an Anonymous connection or that of a Registered User. For the Registered User enter your Windows user name, network domain, and Windows password (see Figure 14-16).

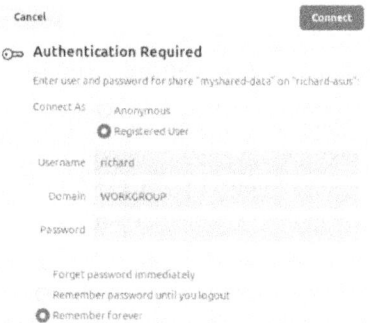

Figure 14-16: User Authentication dialog

You have the option to forget the password, in which case you will have to re-enter it each time you want to access the shared folder. The "Remember password" option remembers the username and password during your current session, and the "Remember forever" option lets you add the username and password to your password keyring (see Figure 14-17). Whenever you try to access the shared folder again for the first time during a new session, you are simply asked for your Ubuntu user password.

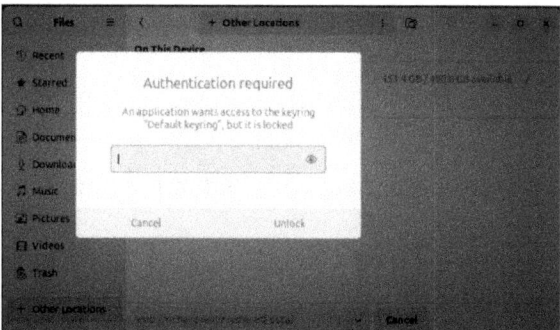

Figure 14-17: Keyring Authentication

Click the Connect button and then the particular shared folder or the shared folders on that host will be displayed. You can then access the shared folder and it is mounted automatically on your desktop. The file manager sidebar will show an entry for the folder with an eject button for un-mounting it. Figure 14-18 shows the **myshared-data** shared folder on a Windows system mounted with an eject button on the sidebar.

Part 4: Administration

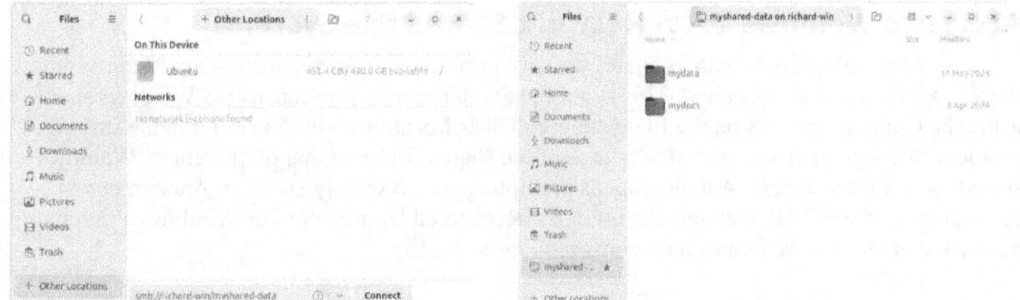

Figure 14-18: Other Locations - shared Windows folders

You can quickly access previously shared folders from the Connect bar's textbox in Other Locations. Click on the Connect textbox's menu button (up-arrow to the right) to display a list of previously accessed shared folders (see Figure 14-19). Click on the one you want, to access it immediately. If this is the first time in this session that you have accessed a shared folder, you will be prompted to enter your user password to activate your login keyring.

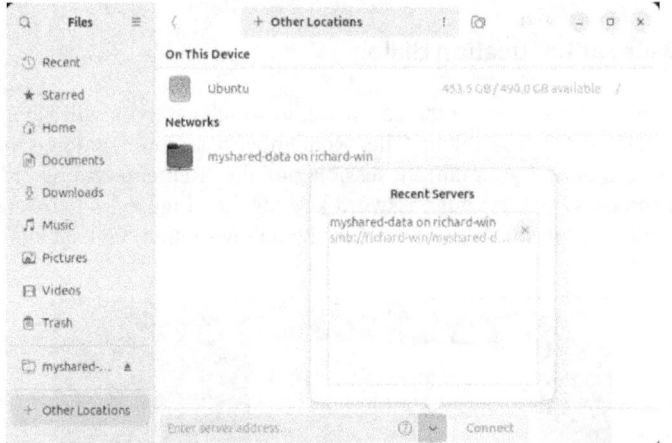

Figure 14-19: Other Locations Connect bar - List of previously accessed shared folders

Shared Folders for your network (nautilus-share, Samba, and smbpasswd)

Your default configuration of Ubuntu does not let you share folders on a network. This is true even for those upgrading from a previous release. To enable the sharing of folders on Ubuntu 24.04, you have to install the **nautilus-share** and Samba server package (**samba**). Then, for a user to be allowed to share their folders, you use the **smbpasswd -a** command to give that user a Samba password and add that user to the **sambashare** group. Other local computers cannot access the shared folders on your Linux system until you install a sharing server, Samba for Windows systems and Linux/Unix systems. Be sure also to allow firewall access for Samba (see Chapter 15, Firewalls).

In previous releases the **nautilus-share** package was installed when you installed Ubuntu. It no longer is. You have to install the **nautilus-share** package yourself using the **sudo apt install** command in a terminal window.

```
sudo apt install nautilus-share
```

The **nautilus-share** package requires that the Samba server be installed. If Samba is not already installed, it will install it. You can also install the Samba server (**samba** package) directly with the Synaptic Package Manager or the **apt install** command. The Samba server is not installed with installation and you cannot install it from the App Center. Instead, you have to open a terminal window (Terminal application) and enter the **apt install** command on the command line as an administrator (**sudo**).

```
sudo apt install samba
```

Two servers are installed and run using the **smbd** and **nmbd** systemd service scripts. The **smbd** server is the Samba server, and the **nmbd** server is the network discovery server. Should the Samba server fail to start, you can start it manually in a terminal window with the commands:

```
sudo systemctl start nmbd
sudo systemctl start smbd
```

You can check the current status with the **status** option and restart with the **restart** option:

```
systemctl status nmbd
systemctl status smbd
```

When first installed, Samba imports the user accounts already configured on your Ubuntu system. Corresponding Windows users with the same username and password as an Ubuntu account on your Ubuntu system are connected automatically to the Ubuntu shared folders. Should the Windows user have a different password, that user is prompted on Windows to enter a username and password. This is an Ubuntu username and password. In the case of a Windows user with the same username but different password, the user would enter the same username with an Ubuntu user password, not the Windows password.

Each user attempting to access a Samba server will need a Samba server user name and a Samba password for that user. Such user-level security requires that this username and Samba password be stored in the Samba password database, which is maintained separately by the Samba server. To add a user Samba password, in a terminal window, enter the **smbpasswd** command with the **-a** option and the username you want to add. You are then prompted to enter a Samba password for that user.

```
richard@richard-laptop:~$ sudo smbpasswd -a richard
[sudo] password for richard:
New SMB password:
Retype new SMB password:
Added user richard.
richard@richard-laptop:~$
```

To enable sharing on a particular user account, including your own, you have to first give the user permission to share folders on a local network by adding the user to the **sambashare** group. The user that installed the **nautilus-share** packages is automatically added to the **sambashare** group. For other users, the **smbpasswd** operation not only creates a Samba password for the user, but should also add the user to the **sambashare** group. If it fails to add the user to the **sambashare** group, you can do so manually by opening a terminal window and use the **adduser** command to add a user to a group. The first argument is the user name and the second argument is the group name. To add the richard user to the **sambashare** group you would enter.

```
sudo adduser richard sambashare
```

You could also use **useradd** with the **-G** option, or **usermod** with the **-a** and **-G** options.

```
sudo useradd -G richard sambashare
```

```
sudo usermod -a -G richard sambashare
```

With these three elements in place (**nautilus-share**, **samba**, and setting up a Samba password for your user) you can now share your folders. You have to logout and login to your system for the changes to take effect.

The **nautilus-share** package adds a "Sharing Options" entry to the context menu for a folder. To share a folder on your Ubuntu system, right-click on it and select Sharing Options from the context menu. This opens a Folder Sharing dialog where you can allow sharing, and choose whether to permit modifying, adding, or deleting files in the folder (see Figure 14-20). You can also allow access to anyone who does not also have an account on your system (guest). Once you have made your selections, click the Create Share button. You can later change the sharing options if you want.

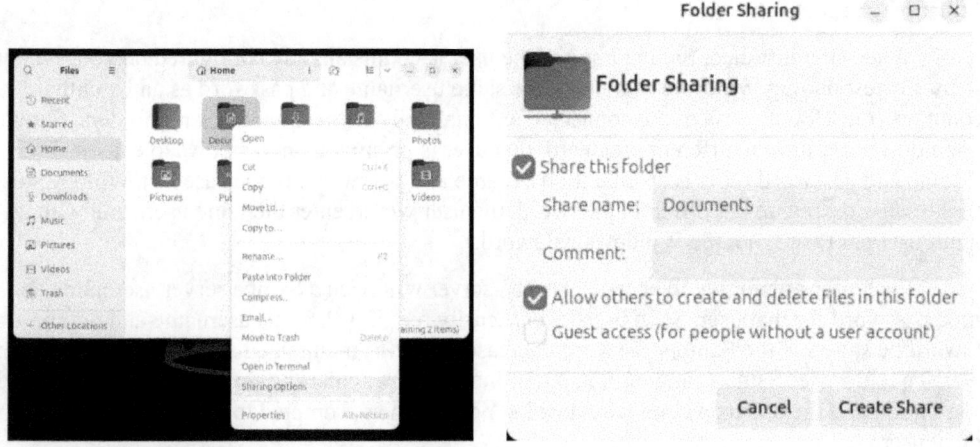

Figure 14-20: Folder Sharing Options

To allow access by other users, permissions on the folder will have to be changed. You will be prompted to allow the file manager to make these changes for you. Just click the "Add the permissions automatically" button (see Figure 14-21).

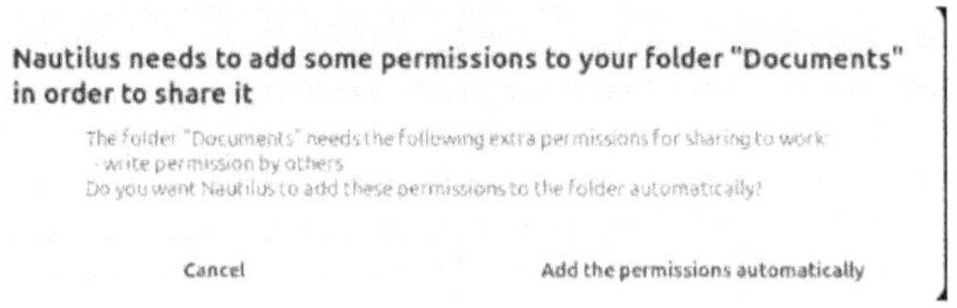

Chapter 14: System Administration **581**

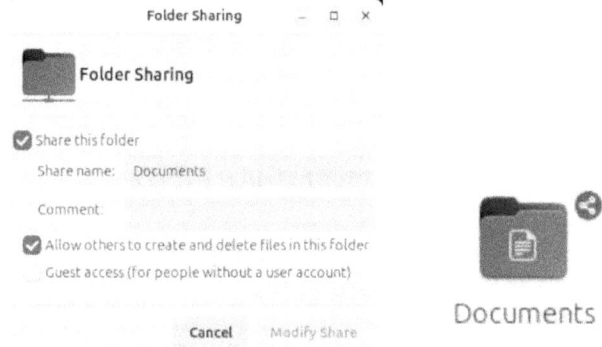

Figure 14-21: Folder Sharing permissions prompt

Note: If you are running a firewall, be sure to configure access for the NFS and Samba services, including browsing support. Otherwise, access to your shared folders by other computers may be blocked (see Chapter 15).

Once you click the Create Share button, the share is created and the button changes to a Modify Share button (see Figure 14-22). Folders that are shared display a sharing emblem next to their icon on a file manager window. To make changes, select the Sharing Options entry from the folder's context menu to open the Folder Sharing dialog. Make your selections, and then click the Modify Share button to make the changes.

Figure 14-22: Folder Sharing dialog

Once sharing is enabled, the Files file manager will display your system in the Networks entry of the Other Locations tab. You can click on it to display the shares on your system (see Figure 14-23).

Figure 14-23: Other Locations with sharing enabled

If you are using a firewall, be sure that it is configured for access by Samba to allow multicast DNS discovery. For Gufw (Firewall Configuration), be sure that the rules are added for

Part 4: Administration

Samba. For FirewallD, on firewall-config (Firewall), be sure that the mdns, samba, and samba-client services are enabled (Zones | Services tab) (see Figure 14-24).

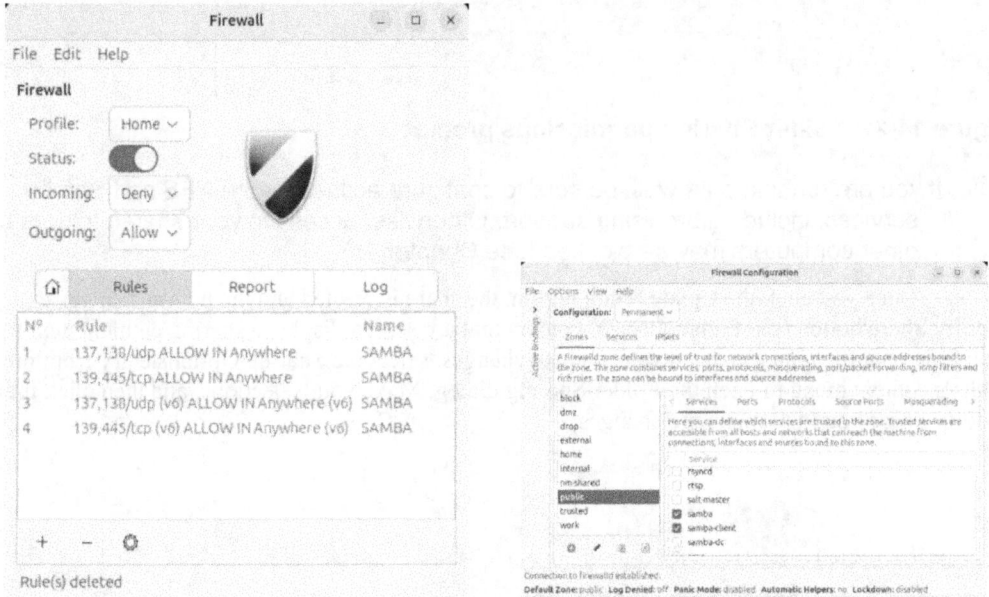

Figure 14-24: Samba Firewall Configuration, Gufw (UFW) and firewall-config (FirewallD)

Accessing Samba Shares from Windows

You can browse Samba Shares from a Windows network window. On a Windows window, click the Network entry in the sidebar to open a list or icons for available systems on your network (see Figure 14-25). Click on system to display the shares available from that system. The first time you access the share, you may be prompted to enter your Samba password. The folder shares for that system are then displayed (see Figure 14-26).

Figure 14-25: Samba shares on Windows

Chapter 14: System Administration   **583**

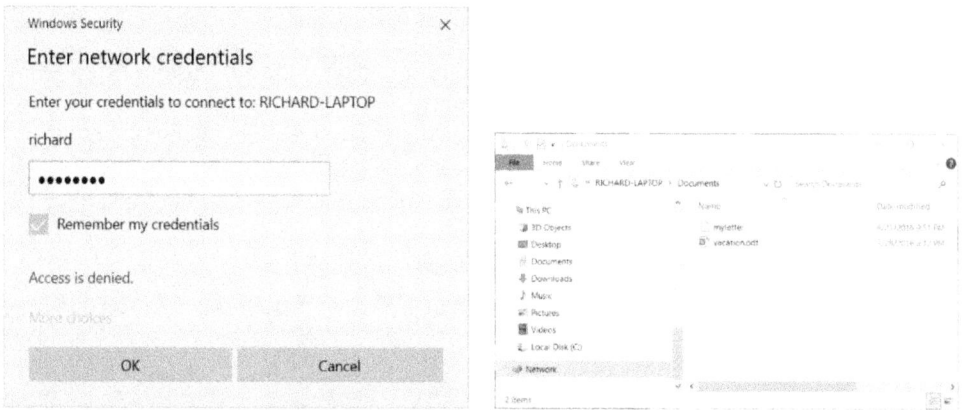

Figure 14-26: Accessing a Samba share on Windows

If you are having difficulty accessing a Samba share, you can use an alternative method using Windows network location shortcuts. You can add a new network location for it, that will be accessible from a shortcut you can set up for it on your Windows file manager "This PC" folder. To set up the shortcut, open the Windows file manager to any folder and right-click on the "This PC" entry in the sidebar to display a menu. Click on the "Add a network location" entry to open the "Add Network Location Wizard" and click Next. Click on the "Choose a custom network location" entry and click Next. In the text box labeled "Internet or network address:" enter the host name of your Linux system that holds the shares you want to access, beginning with the two backward slashes and followed by a backward slash (you may have to also enter the name of one of the shared folders on that system).

\\richard-laptop\

You can then click the Browse button to open a dialog showing a tree of all the shared folders on that host. You can choose a share, or any of a share's subfolders. Their file pathname is automatically added to the address textbox. Alternatively, you could enter the folder path name in the text box directly with the subfolders separated by single backward slashes. If you are sharing your Linux home folders, then the shared folder is the name of the user's Home folder, the user name. Samples are shown here.

\\richard-laptop\richard

\\richard-laptop\richard\Pictures

\\richard-laptop\mydocs

Once the locations for your shared folders are set up in Windows, you can access them again quickly from their shortcuts in the "This PC" folder.

File and Folder Permissions

On the desktop, you can set a folder or file permission using the Permissions tab in its Properties window (see Figure 14-27). For Files, right-click the icon (icon view) or entry (list view) for the file or folder in the file manager window and select Properties to open the Properties dialog. If you want to execute this file as an application (say, a shell script) click the "Executable as Program" switch. This has the effect of setting the execute permission.

To change permissions, click the Permissions link to open the Set Custom Permissions dialog. Here you will find Access pop-up menus for read and write permissions for Owner, Group, and Others. You can set owner permissions as Read Only or Read And Write. For the group and others, you can also set the None option, denying access. In the Group section, the group name expands to a menu listing different groups. Select one to change the file's group. From the menu you can also search for a group.

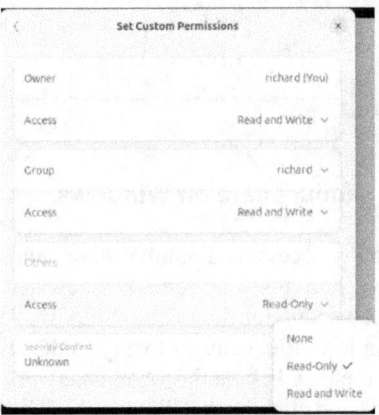

Figure 14-27: File Permissions

The Permissions tab for folders (folders) operates much the same way, with Access menus for Owner, Group, and Others (see Figure 14-28). For subfolders, right-click on the folder and choose Properties from the menu. For the current open folder, choose Properties from the folder's menus on the location bar. Click on the Permissions link to open the Set Custom Permissions dialog where you can change the folder's permissions. The Access menus controls access to the folder with options for List Files Only, Access Files, and Create And Delete Files. These correspond to the read, read and execute, and read-write-execute permissions given to folders. To set the permissions for all the files and folders in the folder accordingly (not just the folder), click the "Change Permissions for Enclosed Files" button to open a dialog where you can specify the owner, group, and others permissions for files and folders in the folder (see Figure 14-28). The access options are the same as for files: for the owner, there are Read or Read and Write permissions for files and List Files Only, Access Files, and "Create and Delete Files" for folders. The group and others access menus add a None option to deny access.

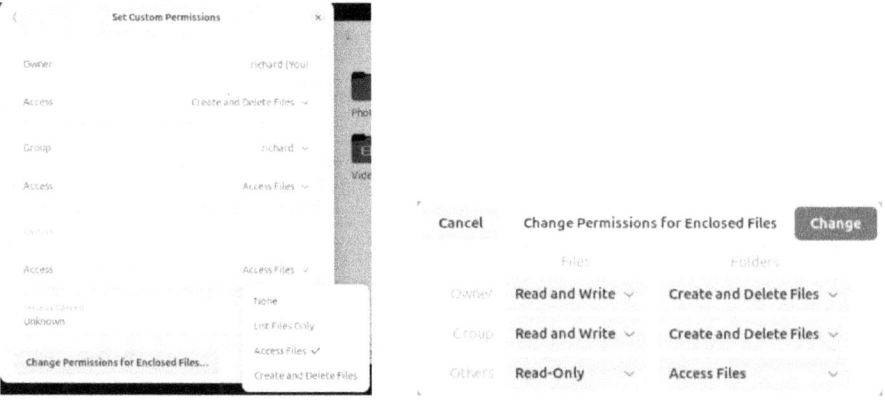

Figure 14-28: Folder Permissions

Automatic file system mounts with /etc/fstab

Though most file systems are automatically mounted for you, there may be instances where you need to have a file system mounted manually. Using the **mount** command you can do this directly, or you can specify the **mount** operation in the **/etc/fstab** file to have it mounted automatically. Ubuntu file systems are uniquely identified with their UUID (Universally Unique IDentifier). These are listed in the **/dev/disk/by-uuid** folder (or with the **sudo blkid** command). In the **/etc/fstab** file, the file system disk partitions are listed as a comment, and then followed by the actual file system mount operation using the UUID. The following example mounts the file system on partition **/dev/sda3** to the **/media/sda3** folder as an **ext4** file system with default options (**defaults**). The UUID for device **/dev/sda3** is b8c526db-cb60-43f6-b0a3-5c0054f6a64a.

```
# /dev/sda3
UUID=b8c526db-cb60-43f6-b0a3-5c0054f6a64a /media/sda3 ext4 defaults 0 2
```

You can also identify your file system by giving it a label. You can use the **ext2label** command to label a file system. In the following **/etc/fstab** file example, the Linux file system labeled **mydata1** is mounted to the **/mydata1** folder as an **ext4** file system type.

To find out the UUID of any device you use the **blkid** command.

```
blkid
```

/etc/fstab

```
# /etc/fstab: static file system information.
#
# <file system> <mount point>   <type>  <options>       <dump>  <pass>
# / was on /dev/sda2 during installation
UUID=a179d6e6-b90c-4cc4-982d-a4cfcedea7df / ext4 errors=remount-ro 0 1
# /boot/efi was on /dev/sda1 during installation
UUID=7982-2520 /boot/efi vfat umask=0077 0 1
# /dev/sda3
UUID=b8c526db-cb60-43f6-b0a3-5c0054f6a64a /media/sda3 ext4 defaults 0 2
/swapfile           none    swap    sw      0 0
LABEL=mydata1 /newdata          ext4          defaults                1 1
```

Should you have to edit your **/etc/fstab** file, you can use Text Editor on the desktop or, in a terminal window, an editor such as **nano** or **vi** with the **sudo** command.

To mount a partition manually, use the **mount** command and specify the type with the **-t** option. Use the **-L** option to mount by label. List the file system first, and then the folder name to which it will be mounted. For an NTFS partition, you would use the type **ntfs**. For partitions with the Ext4 file system you would use **ext4**, and for older Linux partitions you would use **ext3**. The mount option has the format:

```
mount -t type  file-system  folder
```

The following example mounts the **mydata1** file system to the **/newdata** folder

```
mount -t ext4  -L mydata1  /newdata
```

Bluetooth

Bluetooth is a wireless connection method for locally connected devices such as keyboards, mice, printers, and Bluetooth-capable cell phones. BlueZ is the official Linux Bluetooth protocol and is integrated into the Linux kernel. The BlueZ protocol was developed originally by Qualcomm and is now an open source project, located at **http://www.bluez.org/**. It is included in the bluez and bluez-libs packages, among others. Check the BlueZ site for a complete list of supported hardware.

A Bluetooth button and link is displayed on the system menu on the top panel (see Figure 14-29). If you have Bluetooth devices attached to your system, the button will display a message showing the number of connected devices. Clicking the Bluetooth button will turn off Bluetooth, graying the button. Click on it again to turn Bluetooth on. You can also use the Bluetooth tab on Settings to turn it on again. Click the link button (right arrow) to the right of the Bluetooth button to display Bluetooth devices to turn off or on. There is also a link to open Bluetooth Settings.

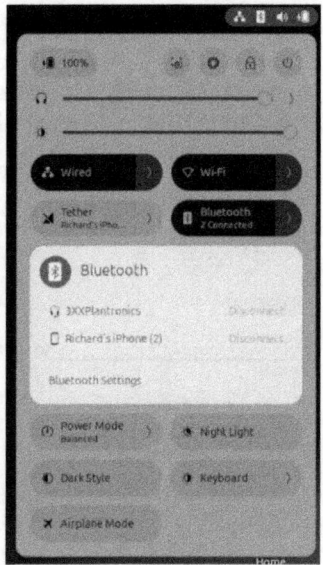

Figure 14-29: System menu Bluetooth button's menu

Chapter 14: System Administration **587**

This Bluetooth Settings link opens Settings to the Bluetooth tab (see Figure 14-30). You can also access Bluetooth tab on Settings directly. On the Bluetooth settings tab, a Bluetooth switch at the top right lets you turn Bluetooth on or off. Detected devices are listed in the Devices section. Initially, devices are disconnected. Click on a device entry to connect it. A dialog opens with a detected pin number, which you confirm. Then the device configuration dialog is displayed, with a switch to connect or disconnect the device (see Figure 14-31). Pair, type, and address information are also displayed. If the device supports sound, a Sound Setting button is shown, which opens the Sound tab in Settings which displays that device (see Figure 14-32). To remove the device configuration, click the Forget Device button.

Figure 14-30: Bluetooth Settings

Figure 14-31: Bluetooth Device Configuration

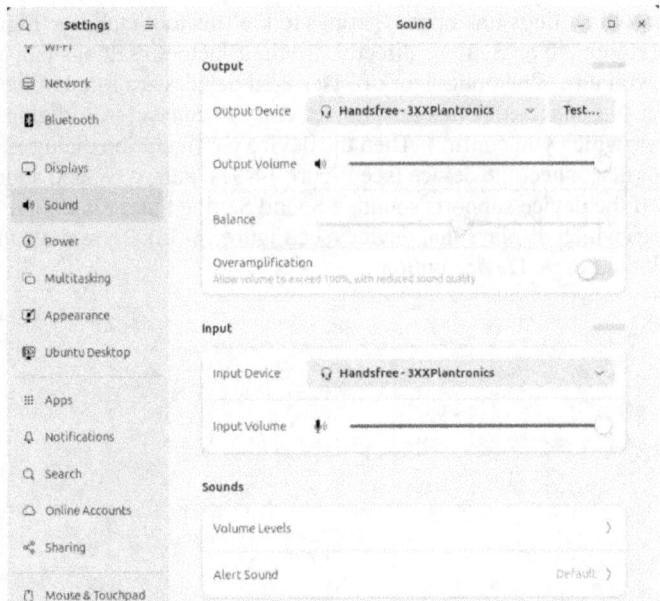

Figure 14-32: Bluetooth Sound

When connecting to a phone (see Figure 14-33), a pin number is detected and displayed. On the configuration dialog, you can choose to connect or disconnect. The phone address is shown. Click the Forget Device button to remove the phone from your Bluetooth system. You can reconnect later by locating the device in the list of possible device on the Settings Bluetooth tab. Once connected, the phone is listed in the System menu's Bluetooth link as one of your Bluetooth devices that you can disconnect or connect to.

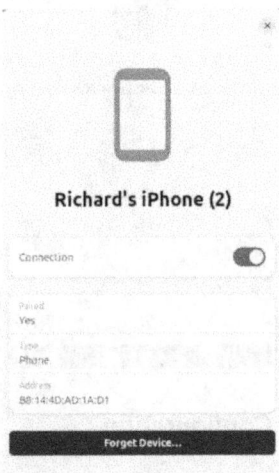

Figure 14-33: Bluetooth for phones

You can configure a phone to operate as a personal Hotspot using your phone's Bluetooth connection. This is referred to as a Bluetooth tether. The phone operates as a mobile phone network device (PAN/NAP). A Tether entry appears for the phone in the system menu (see Figure 14-34). The Tether button is initially grayed. Click on it to activate the connection. Clicking on the Tether button's link to the right (right arrow), displays a list of Bluetooth Tethers you can connect to. Your phone should be listed. Click on its entry to connect or disconnect the tether.

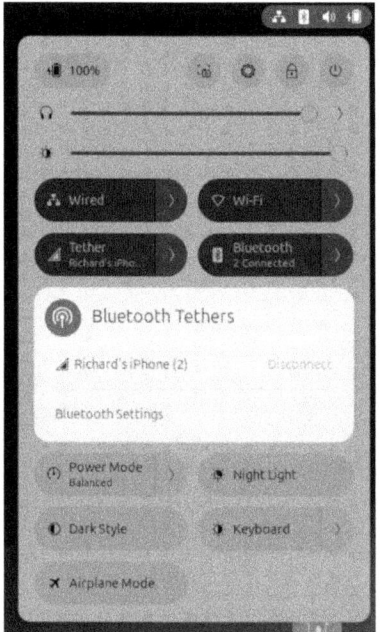
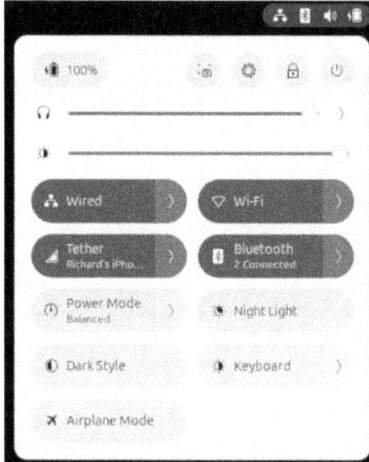

Figure 14-34: Bluetooth Tether in System menu

When you set up a Bluetooth tether, an entry for it will appear in the Settings Network tab in a Bluetooth section (see Figure 14-35). There is a switch to turn the tether on or off. Clicking on the configuration button open a Bluetooth network dialog similar to other network dialogs, with tabs for Details, Identity, IPV4, and Ipv6 (see Figure 14-36). The Details tab will list your phone's hardware address, last use, and options to connection automatically, make available to other users, and specify if the phone has data limits. There is also a button to remove the connection. The Identity tab just lists your phone. IPv4 and IPv6 have automatic connections, but you can enter manual settings.

590 Part 4: Administration

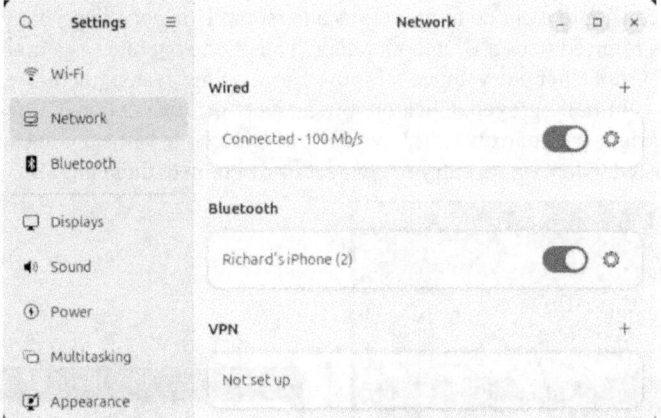

Figure 14-35: Bluetooth Tethers in Settings Network tab

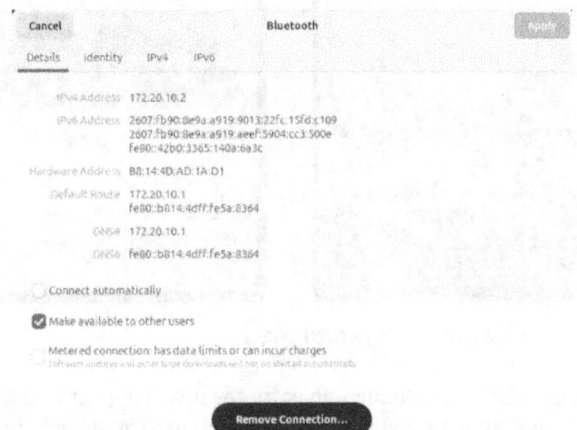

Figure 14-36: Settings Network Bluetooth Tethers Configuration dialog

If you turn off Bluetooth for your system, the Tether button is removed from the System menu. If you choose to remove your phone from Bluetooth by Clicking on its Forget Device button on its configuration dialog (Setting Bluetooth tab, click on phone entry), the Tether button is removed from the System menu. If you reconnect to your phone, the Tether button is also displayed (see Figure 14-37).

Chapter 14: System Administration 591

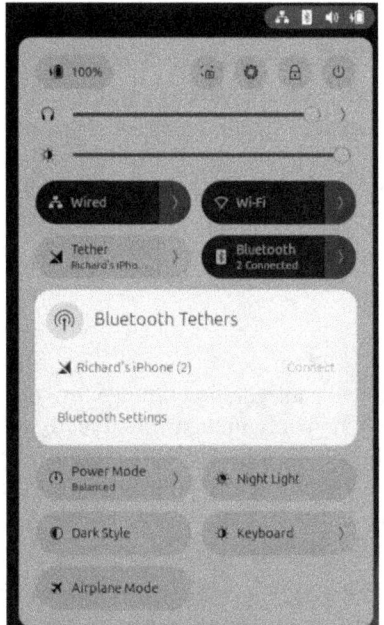
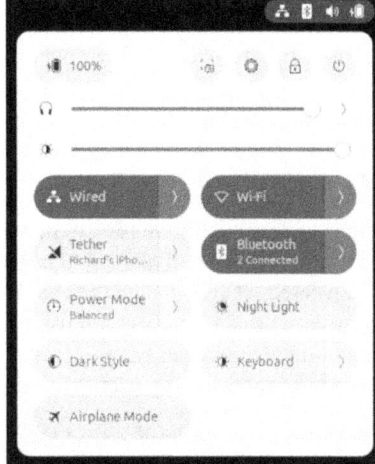

Figure 14-37: Bluetooth Tether inactive

DKMS

DKMS is the Dynamic Kernel Module Support originally developed by DELL. DKMS enabled device drivers can be generated automatically whenever your kernel is updated. This is helpful for proprietary drivers like the Nvidia and AMD proprietary graphics drivers (the X11 open source drivers, Xorg, are automatically included with the kernel package). In the past, whenever you updated your kernel, you also had to download and install a separate proprietary kernel module compiled just for that new kernel. If the module was not ready, then you could not use a proprietary driver. To avoid this problem, DKMS was developed, which uses the original proprietary source code to create new kernel modules as they are needed. When you install a new kernel, DKMS detects the new configuration and compiles a compatible proprietary kernel module for your new kernel. This action is fully automatic and entirely hidden from the user.

On Ubuntu both the Nvidia and AMD proprietary graphics drivers are DKMS enabled packages that are managed and generated by the DKMS service. The generated kernel modules are placed in the **/lib/modules/***kernel-version***/kernel/updates** folder. When you install either a graphics proprietary package, their source code is downloaded and used to create a graphics driver for use by your kernel. The source code is placed in the **/usr/src** folder. The DKMS configuration files and build locations for different DKMS-enabled software are located in subfolders in the **/var/lib/dkms** folder.

DKMS is not installed by default. Use the Synaptic Package Manager or the **apt** command to install it. DKMS configuration files are located in the **/etc/dkms** folder. The **/etc/dkms/framework.conf** file holds DKMS variable definitions for folders that DKMS uses, like the source code and kernel module folders. The **/etc/init.d/dkms_autoinstaller** is a script the runs the DKMS operations to generate and install a kernel module. DKMS removal and install directives for kernel updates are maintained in the **/etc/kernel** folder.

Should DKMS fail to install and update automatically, you can perform the update manually using the **dkms** command. The **dkms** command with the **build** action creates the kernel module, and then the **dkms** command with the **install** action installs the module to the appropriate kernel module folder. The **-m** option specifies the module you want to build and the **-k** option is the kernel version (use **uname -r** to display your current kernel version). Drivers like Nvidia and AMD release new versions regularly. You use the **-v** option to specify the driver version you want. See the man page for **dkms** for full details.

Editing Configuration Files

Though the administrative tools will handle all configuration settings for you, there may be times when you will need to make changes by editing configuration files directly. Most system configuration files are text files located in the **/etc** folder. To change any of these files, you will need administrative access, requiring you use the Text Editor or the **sudo** command. Text Editor will automatically detect the need for administrative access and prompt you to enter your password. Such files can only be modified by users with administrative access.

Caution: Be careful when editing your configuration files. Editing mistakes can corrupt your configurations. It is advisable to make a backup of any configuration files you are working on first, before making major changes to the original.

Text Editor will let you edit several files at once, opening a tab for each. You can use Text Editor to edit any text file, including ones you create yourself. Two commonly edited configuration files are **/etc/default/grub** and **/etc/fstab**. The **/etc/fstab** file lists all your file systems and how they are mounted, and **/etc/default/grub** file is the configuration file for your Grub 2 boot loader.

You can also use other standard editors, such as **nano** or **vi**, to edit such files. Be sure to use the **sudo** command for administrative access.

```
sudo nano /etc/default/grub
```

User configuration files, dot files, can be changed by individual users directly without administrative access. An example of a user configuration file is the **.profile** file, which configures your login shell. To access dot files, first configure the file manager to display dot files by selecting the Show Hidden Files entry in the sidebar menu of any file manager window. This displays the dot files in your file manager window and in the Text Editor open file dialog.

GRUB 2

The Grand Unified Bootloader (GRUB) is a multiboot boot loader used for most Linux distributions. Linux and Unix operating systems are known as multiboot operating systems and take arguments passed to them at boot time. With GRUB, users can select operating systems to run from a menu interface displayed when a system boots up. Use arrow keys to move to an entry and press ENTER. If instead, you need to edit an entry, press **e**, letting you change kernel arguments or specify a different kernel. The **c** command places you in a command line interface. Provided your system BIOS supports very large drives, GRUB can boot from anywhere on them. For detailed information and instructions on Grub2 on Ubuntu, check the Ubuntu Grub2 Wiki at:

```
https://help.ubuntu.com/community/Grub2
```

Check the GRUB Man page for GRUB options. GRUB is a GNU project with its home page at **https://www.gnu.org/software/grub/**, the manual at **https://www.gnu.org/software/grub/manual/grub/**.

Grub2 detects and generates a menu for you automatically. You do not have to worry about keeping a menu file updated. All your operating systems and Ubuntu kernels are detected when the system starts up, and a menu to display them as boot options is generated at that time.

With Grub2, configuration is placed in user-modifiable configuration files held in the **/etc/default/grub** file and in the **/etc/grub.d** folder. There is a Grub2 configuration file called **/boot/grub/grub.cfg**, but this file is generated by Grub each time the system starts up, and should never be edited by a user. Instead, you would edit the **/etc/default/grub** file to set parameters like the default operating system to boot. To create your own menu entries, you create entries for them in the **/etc/grub.d/40_custom** file.

Grub options are set by assigning values to Grub options in the **/etc/default/grub** file. You can edit the file directly with the Text Editor to change these options. Open the Text Editor and click the Open menu on the left side of the header, then click the files button (labeled "Open New Document) to the right of the Search box. This opens a file manager location window (see Figure 14-38). Click on Other Locations, then Computer, then the **etc** folder, then the **default** folder. In that folder select the **grub** file and click the Open button on the right side of the header. This will open the **/etc/default/grub** file (see Figure 14-39).

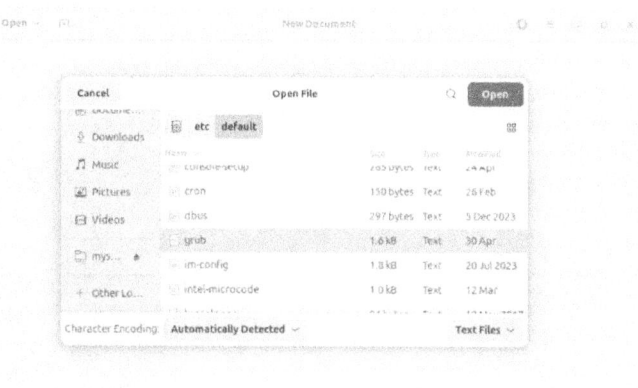

Figure 14-38: Opening the /etc/default/grub file in Text Editor

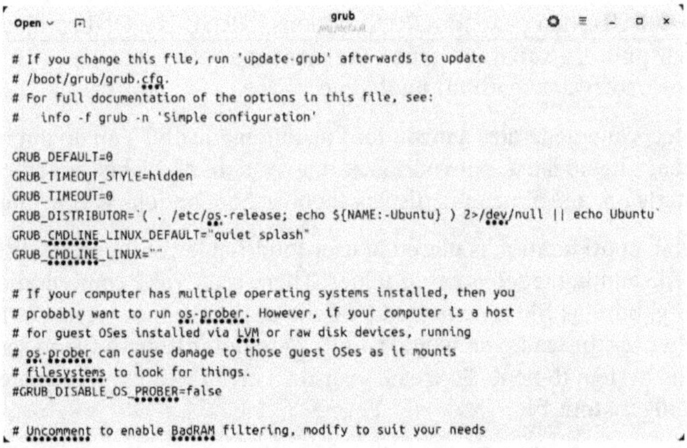

Part 4: Administration

Figure 14-39: Editing the /etc/default/grub file in Text Editor

You can then edit it. When you first try to save it, you prompted to enter your administrative password (for administrative users, this is just their password). Once authenticated, the file is saved and the name of the file in the header now has "(Administrator)" attached to it (see Figure 14-40). You can continue to make further changes and saving them.

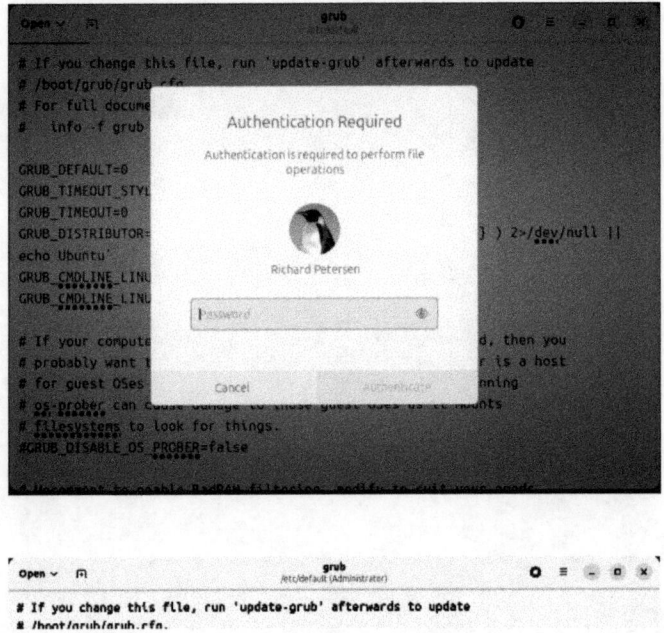

Figure 14-40: Saving the /etc/default/grub file in Text Editor, authenticated as Administrator

You could also edit the file with the older Gedit editor. Open a terminal window and enter the following command. You will be prompted to enter your password. If **sudo** is not already installed, you will have to install it.

```
sudo gedit /etc/default/grub
```

The **grub** file used on Ubuntu 24.04 LTS is shown here:

/etc/default/grub

```
# If you change this file, run 'update-grub' afterwards to update
# /boot/grub/grub.cfg.
# For full documentation of the options in this file, see:
#   info -f grub -n 'Simple configuration'

GRUB_DEFAULT=0
GRUB_TIMEOUT_STYLE=hidden
GRUB_TIMEOUT=1
GRUB_DISTRIBUTOR=`( . /etc/os-release; echo ${NAME:-Ubuntu} ) 2>/dev/null || echo Ubuntu`
GRUB_CMDLINE_LINUX_DEFAULT="quiet splash"
GRUB_CMDLINE_LINUX=""

# If your computer has multiple operating systems installed, then you
# probably want to run os-prober. However, if your computer is a host
# for guest OSes installed via LVM or raw disk devices, running
# os-prober can cause damage to those guest OSes as it mounts
# filesystems to look for things.
#GRUB_DISABLE_OS_PROBER=false

# Uncomment to enable BadRAM filtering, modify to suit your needs
# This works with Linux (no patch required) and with any kernel that obtains
# the memory map information from GRUB (GNU Mach, kernel of FreeBSD ...)
#GRUB_BADRAM="0x01234567,0xfefefefe,0x89abcdef,0xefefefef"

# Uncomment to disable graphical terminal
#GRUB_TERMINAL=console

# The resolution used on graphical terminal
# note that you can use only modes which your graphic card supports via VBE
# you can see them in real GRUB with the command `vbeinfo'
#GRUB_GFXMODE=640x480

# Uncomment if you don't want GRUB to pass "root=UUID=xxx" parameter to Linux
#GRUB_DISABLE_LINUX_UUID=true

# Uncomment to disable generation of recovery mode menu entries
#GRUB_DISABLE_RECOVERY="true"

# Uncomment to get a beep at grub start
#GRUB_INIT_TUNE="480 440 1"
```

For dual boot systems (those with both Ubuntu and Windows or Mac), the option that users are likely to change is GRUB_DEFAULT, which sets the operating system or kernel to boot automatically if one is not chosen. The option uses a line number to indicate an entry in the Grub boot menu, with numbering starting from 0 (not 1). First, check your Grub menu when you boot up (press the ESC key on boot to display the Grub menu), and then count to where the entry of the operating system you want to make the default is listed. If the Windows entry is at 4th, which would be line 3 (counting from 0), to make it the default you would set the GRUB_DEAULT option to 3.

```
GRUB_DEFAULT=3
```

Should you want to change the default frequently, you would have to edit the **/etc/default/grub** file each time to change it. A safer way to set the default is to configure GRUB to use the **grub-set-default** command. First, edit the **/etc/default/grub** file and change the option for GRUB_DEFAULT to **save**.

```
GRUB_DEFAULT=saved
```

Then update GRUB.

```
sudo update-grub
```

The **grub-set-default** command takes as its option the number of the default you want to set (numbering from 0) or the name of the kernel or operating system. The following sets the default to 0, the first kernel entry.

```
sudo grub-set-default 0
```

For a kernel name or operating system, you can use the name as it appears on the GRUB menu (enclosing the name in quotes), such as:

```
sudo grub-set-default 'Windows (loader) (on /dev/sda1)'
```

The GRUB_TIMEOUT option sets the number of seconds Grub will wait to allow a user to access the menu, before booting the default operating system. The default options used for Ubuntu kernels are listed by the GRUB_CMDLINE_LINUX_DEFAULT option. Currently, these include the **splash** and **quiet** options to display the Ubuntu emblem on startup (**splash**), but not the list of startup tasks being performed (**quiet**).

The GRUB_TIMEOUT_STYLE option sets whether the menu is displayed or not during the timeout period. Options can be **menu**, which displays the Grub menu, **countdown**, which only displays a countdown timer for the timeout period, and **hidden**, which does not display the menu unless the user presses the ESC key. On Ubuntu this option is set to **hidden** by default.

```
GRUB_TIMEOUT_STYLE=hidden
```

The following would always display the Grub menu.

```
GRUB_TIMEOUT_STYLE=menu
```

Should you have other operating systems on your computer such as Windows, and GRUB fails to detect them, it could be that the **os-prober** application has been disabled. You can enable it with the following option added to the **/etc/default/grub** file.

```
GRUB_DISABLE_OS_PROBER=false
```

Once you have made your changes, you have to run the **update-grub** command with **sudo**, as noted in the first line of the **/etc/default/grub** file. Otherwise, your changes will not take effect. This command will generate a new **/etc/grub/grub.cfg** file, which determines the actual Grub 2 configuration.

```
sudo update-grub
```

You can add your own Grub2 boot entries by placing them in the **/etc/grub.d/40_custom** file. The file is nearly empty except for an initial **exec tail** command that you must take care not to change. Samples of added entries are shown on the Ubuntu Grub2 Wiki, **https://help.ubuntu.com/community/Grub2**. After you make your additions to the **40_custom** file, you have to run **sudo update-grub** to have the changes take effect.

When the GRUB package is updated by Ubuntu, you will be given the choice to keep your current local version or use the maintainer's version. Keeping the local version is selected by default. However, unless you have extensively customized your configuration, it is always advisable to select the maintainer's version. The maintainer's version is the most up-to-date. If you had made any changes previously to the **/etc/default/grub** file, you will have to edit that file and make the same changes again, such as setting the default operating system to load. Be sure to run **sudo update-grub** to make the changes take effect.

Backup Management: Deja Dup, rsync, BackupPC, and Amanda

Backup operations have become an important part of administrative duties. Several backup tools are provided on Linux systems, including Amanda and the traditional dump/restore tools, as well as the **rsync** command used for making individual copies. Deja Dup is a front end for the duplicity backup tool, which uses **rsync** to generate backup archives. Deja Dup is the recommended default backup tool, available from the Applications overview's Utilities group as Backups. Amanda provides server-based backups, letting different systems on a network backup to a central server. BackupPC provides network and local backup using configured **rsync** and **tar** tools. The dump tools let you refine your backup process, detecting data changed since the last backup. Table 14-2 lists websites for Linux backup tools.

Website	Tools
`https://rsync.samba.org`	rsync remote copy backup
`https://launchpad.net/deja-dup` `http://www.nongnu.org/duplicity`	Deja Dup frontend for duplicity which uses rsync to perform basic backups
`http://www.amanda.org`	Amanda network backup
`https://sourceforge.net/projects/dump/`	dump and restore tools
`https://backuppc.github.io/backuppc/`	BackupPC network or local backup using configured rsync and tar tools.

Table 14-2: Backup Resources

Deja Dup (Backups)

Deja Dup is a front end for the duplicity backup tool, which uses rsync to generate backup archives (**http://www.nongnu.org/duplicity/**). Once installed, you can access Deja Dup on the Applications overview in the Utilities application folder as Backups.

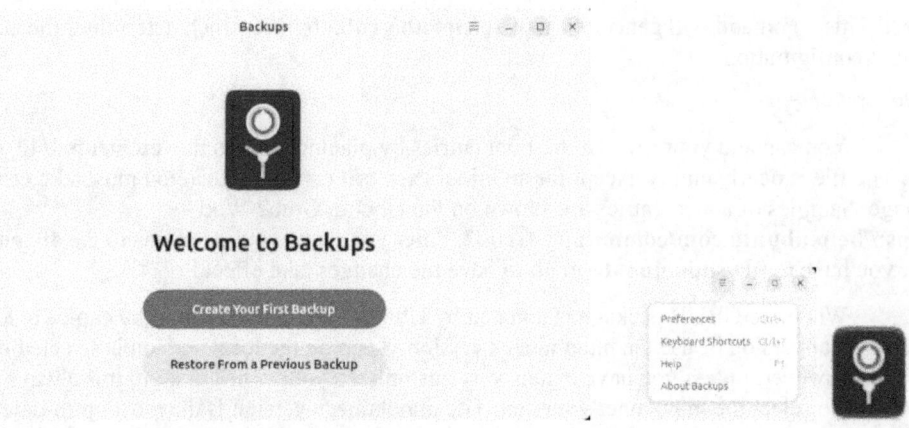

Figure 14-41: Deja Dup settings - overview

The default backup setting for Deja Dup is to store your backups on Google Drive. However, you can change this setting to a local folder or a network share (General tab in Preferences). Should you want to use Google Drive, you will also have to install the **python3-pydrive** package, which will manage access to your Google drive account.

The deja-dup dialog shows buttons for backing up and restoring backups (see Figure 14-41). A menu on the upper right of the titlebar has entries for Preferences, Help, and Keyboard shortcuts. Select the Help entry on the titlebar menu to display the Deja Dup manual.

The deja-dup Preferences dialog shows tabs for General and Folders (see Figure 14-42). A switch in the Schedule section of the dialog allows you to turn automatic backups on and off. The General tab provides storage and scheduling settings with buttons to automatically perform a backup and a menu for selecting the time interval for your backups.

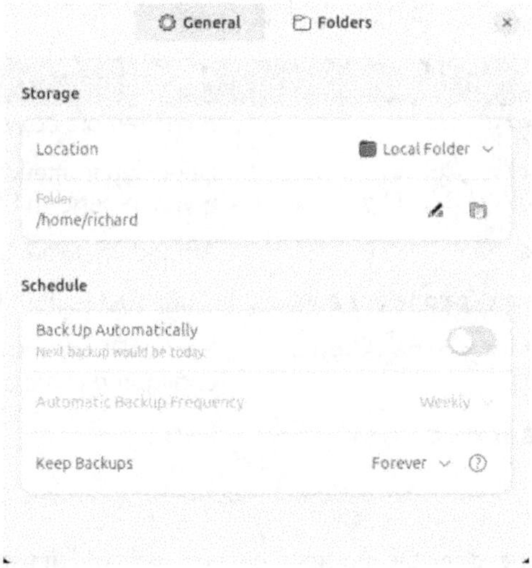

Figure 14-42: Deja Dup Preferences

The Storage section lets you specify the location (see Figure 14-43). You can choose different locations, such as an FTP account, a cloud account, SSH server, Samba (Windows) share, or a local folder. Choose the one you want from the Location menu. With each choice, you are prompted for the appropriate configuration information.

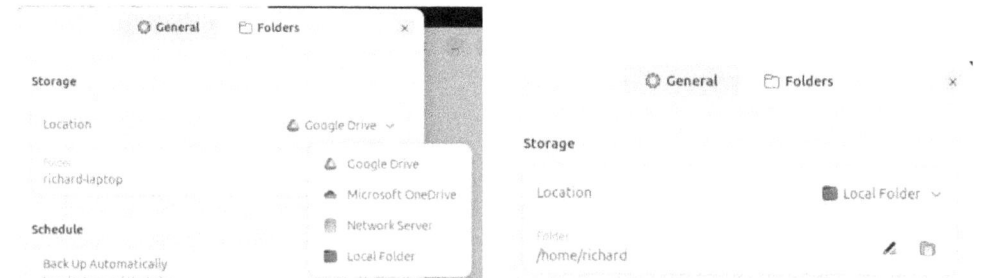

Figure 14-43: Deja Dup settings - storage for Windows share and Local folder

In the Schedule section, the Automatic Backup Frequency menu lets you specify the frequency of your backups. The Keep Backups menu specifies how long to keep them (see Figure 14-44). First turn on Automatic backup. Backups can be performed daily, weekly, every two weeks, or monthly. They can be kept for a week, month, several months, a year, or forever.

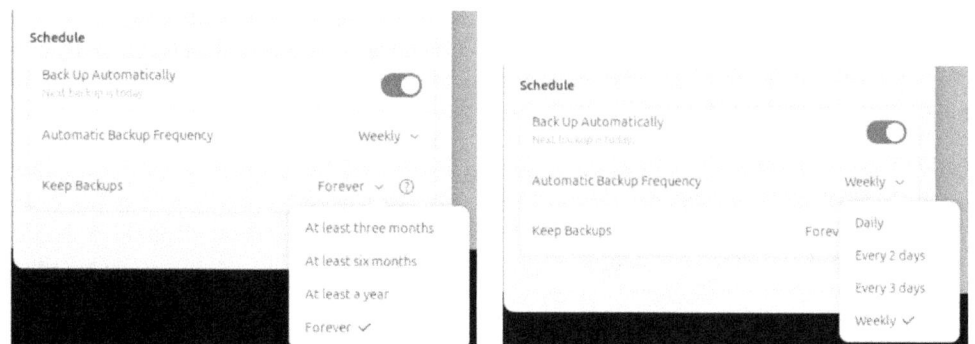

Figure 14-44: Deja Dup settings - backup times

The Folders tab has sections for "Folders to Back Up" and "Folders to Ignore" (see Figure 14-45). Click the plus button (+) at the bottom of the folders list to add a new folder for backup. Do the same to specify folders to ignore. The trash button at the right of each entry removes selected folders from the list. Your home folder has been added already. The "Folders to ignore" section specifies folders you do not want to back up. The Downloads and Trash folders are already specified.

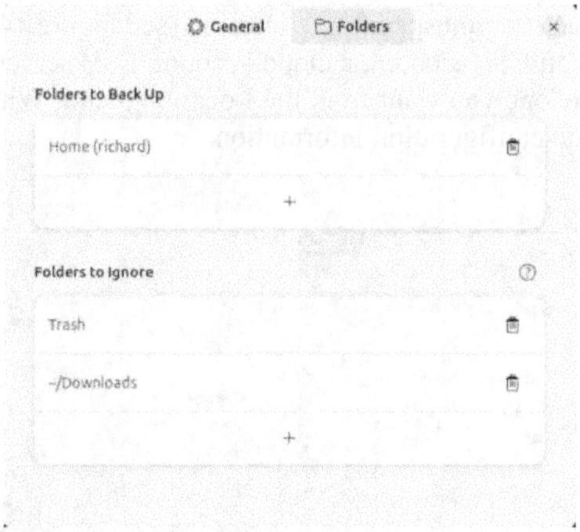

Figure 14-45: Deja Dup settings - Folders to save and ignore

When you perform a backup, you first choose the folders to backup and to ignore. Click the Forward button to continue. Next you choose a storage location. You are prompted to backup with or without encryption. For encrypted backups, you are prompted to enter a password, which you will need to restore the files (see Figure 14-46). You are then asked to select the date of the backup to use, the most recent being the default.

To restore a backup, click on the Restore tab on the Deja-dup window. This displays all the folders in your current backup (see Figure 14-47). Click on the ones you want to restore. The Restore button on the lower left becomes active. Click it to the start the restore process. You can choose what backup to use from the Date menu on the lower right. To automatically choose all the folders and files either press Ctrl-a or select the Select All entry from the menu on the right side of the Deja-dup window header bar. You can also search for files and folders by clicking the Search button (looking glass) on the right side of the Deja-dup header bar.

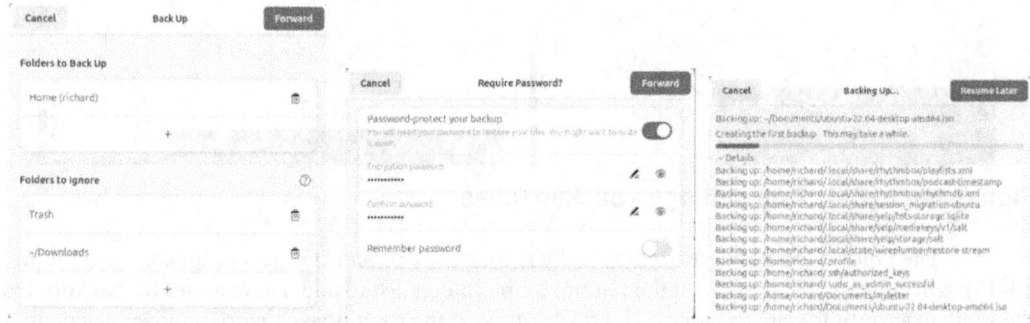

Figure 14-46: Deja Dup backup: encryption

Chapter 14: System Administration   **601**

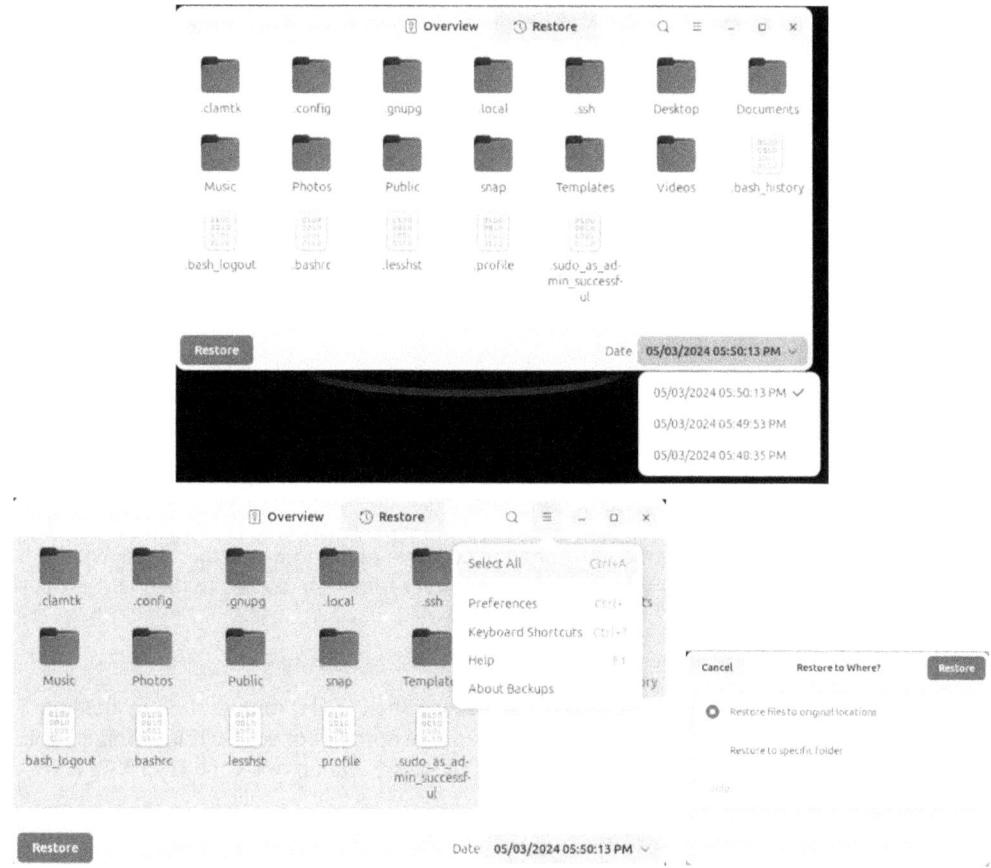

Figure 14-47: Deja Dup restore

Once you have selected the files to restore and have clicked the Restore button, you can choose whether to restore to the original location or a specific folder. The backup restore operation is then performed. When restoring, you are prompted to specify the location you are backing up from, the backup date to restore from, and whether to restore to the original location or a specific folder.

Individual Backups: archive and rsync

You can backup and restore particular files and folders with archive tools like **tar**, restoring the archives later. For backups, **tar** is used usually with a tape device. To schedule automatic backups, you can schedule appropriate **tar** commands with the **cron** utility. The archives can be also compressed for storage savings. You can then copy the compressed archives to any medium, such as a DVD disc, USB drive, external hard drive, or tape. On GNOME you can use File Roller to create archives easily.

File Roller also supports LZMA compression, a more efficient and faster compression method. On File Roller, when creating a new archive, select "Tar compressed with lzma (.tar.lzma)" for the Archive type. When choosing Create Archive from GNOME Files file manager window on selected files, on the Create Archive dialog, choose the **.lzma** file type for just compression, and the **.tar.lzma** type for a compressed archive.

If you want to remote-copy a folder or files from one host to another, making a particular backup, you can use **rsync**, which is designed for network backups of particular folders or files, intelligently copying only those files that have been changed, rather than the contents of an entire folder. In archive mode, it can preserve the original ownership and permissions, providing corresponding users exist on the host system. The following example copies the **/home/george/myproject** folder to the **/backup** folder on the host **rabbit**, creating a corresponding **myproject** subfolder. The **-t** specifies that this is a transfer. The remote host is referenced with an attached colon, **rabbit:**

```
rsync -t /home/george/myproject    rabbit:/backup
```

If instead, you wanted to preserve the ownership and permissions of the files, you would use the **-a** (archive) option. Adding a **-z** option will compress the file. The **-v** option provides a verbose mode.

```
rsync -avz /home/george/myproject    rabbit:/backup
```

A trailing slash on the source will copy the contents of the folder, rather than generating a subfolder of that name. Here the contents of the **myproject** folder are copied to the **george-project** folder.

```
rsync -avz /home/george/myproject/    rabbit:/backup/george-project
```

The **rsync** command is configured to use Secure Shell (SSH) remote shell by default. You can specify it or an alternate remote shell to use with the **-e** option. For secure transmission, you can encrypt the copy operation with SSH. Either use the **-e ssh** option or set the **RSYNC_RSH** variable to ssh.

```
rsync -avz -e ssh  /home/george/myproject    rabbit:/backup/myproject
```

You can copy from a remote host to the host you are on.

```
rsync -avz lizard:/home/mark/mypics/  /pic-archive/markpics
```

You can also run **rsync** as a server daemon. This will allow remote users to synchronize copies of files on your system with versions on their own, transferring only changed files rather than entire folders. Many mirror and software FTP sites operate as **rsync** servers, letting you update files without have to download the full versions again. Configuration information for rsync as a server is kept in the **/etc/rsyncd.conf** file.

Tip: Though it is designed for copying between hosts, you can also use **rsync** to make copies within your own system, usually to a folder in another partition or hard drive. Check the **rsync** Man page for detailed descriptions of each.

BackupPC

BackupPC provides an easily managed local or network backup of your system or hosts, on a system using configured rsync or tar tools. There is no client application to install, just configuration files. BackupPC can backup hosts on a network, including servers, or just a single system. Data can be backed up to local hard disks or to network storage such as shared partitions or storage servers. You can configure BackupPC using your Web page configuration interface. This is the host name of your computer with the **/backuppc** name attached, like **http://richard1/backuppc**. Detailed documentation is installed at **/usr/share/doc/BackupPC**. You can find out more about BackupPC at **https://backuppc.github.io/backuppc/**. You can install BackupPC using the Synaptic Package Manager and with the **apt install** command (**backuppc** package). Canonical provides critical updates. Configuration files are located at **/etc/BackupPC**. The **config.pl** file holds BackupPC configuration options and the **hosts** file lists hosts to be backed up.

BackupPC uses both compression and detection of identical files to reduce the size of the backup, allowing several hosts to be backed up in limited space. Once an initial backup is performed, BackupPC will only backup changed files, reducing the time of the backup significantly.

Amanda

To back up hosts connected to a network, you can use the Advanced Maryland Automatic Network Disk Archiver (Amanda) to archive hosts. Amanda uses **tar** tools to back up all hosts to a single host operating as a backup server. Backup data is sent by each host to the host operating as the Amanda server, where they are written out to a backup medium such as tape. With an Amanda server, the backup operations for all hosts become centralized in one server, instead of each host having to perform its backup. Any host that needs to restore data simply requests it from the Amanda server, specifying the file system, date, and filenames. Backup data is copied to the server's holding disk and from there, to tapes. Detailed documentation and updates are provided at **http://www.amanda.org**. For the server, be sure to install the **amanda-server** package, and for clients you use the **amanda-clients** package. Also install the **amanda-common** package. You can install Amanda using the apt install command or the Synaptic Package Manager, Utilities (universe) section. Canonical does not provide critical updates.

Printing

This section covers the printing-configuration tools: the GNOME Printers tool (Settings Printers) and the older **system-config-printer** tool. Most printers are detected for you automatically. You can use the Settings Printers tab to turn them on or off and access their print queues. As an alternative, you can still use the older **system-config-printer**, available as Printer Settings as a Debian package on the Apps Center. Both are front ends for the Common UNIX Printing System (CUPS), which provides printing services (**www.cups.org**).

When you attach a local printer to your system for the first time, the GNOME Printers tool automatically detects the printer and installs the appropriate driver. A message appears briefly in the notifications dialog, indicating that a new printer has been detected. The printer is then listed in both the GNOME Settings Printers tool and in the older **system-config-printer**. If the detection fails, you can use the GNOME Settings Printers tool, accessible from GNOME Settings, to set up your printer.

Most newer printer models support driverless printing. Instead of installing a driver, the printer supports a driverless driver. You can print to any of these printers without first downloading and installing a driver for them. The printers are automatically detected through DNS Service Discovery (DNS-SD). The CUPS Web configuration interface, system-config-printer, GNOME printers, and **lpadmin** already support driverless printing.

CUPS uses the driverless utility to detect available driverless printers and to generate PPD configuration files for them. The drivers may not be as complete in features as their official drivers, but will print. Currently printers compatible with IPP Anywhere and Apple Raster supported printers can make use of driverless drivers, usually newer printers. GNOME Printer, system-config-printer, and the CUP Web interface all use the driverless tool to detect and configure driverless printers. See the man page for **driverless** for more information.

KDE provides support for adding and configuring CUPS printers through the KDE System Settings Printer Configuration dialog. Select the Printer Configuration icon under Hardware. USB printers that are automatically detected will be listed in the KDE Printer Configuration dialog.

Printers can be local or remote. Both are referenced using Universal Resource Identifiers (URI). URIs support both network protocols used to communicate with remote printers and device connections used to reference local printers.

Remote printers are referenced by the protocol used to communicate with them, including **ipp** for the Internet Printing Protocol used for UNIX network printers, **smb** for the Samba protocol used for Windows network printers, and **lpd** for the older LPRng UNIX print servers. Their URIs are similar to a web URL, indicating the network addresses of the system the printer is connected to.

```
ipp://mytsuff.com/printers/queue1
smb://guest@lizard/myhp
```

For attached local printers, the URI will use the device connection and the device name. The **usb:** prefix is used for USB printers; **parallel:** is used for older printers connected to a parallel port; **serial:** is used for printers connected to a serial port; **scsi:** is used for SCSI-connected printers. For a locally attached USB printer, the URI would be something like the following:

```
usb://Canon/S330
```

Settings Printers tab

The Printers tool is accessible from the Settings Printers tab. It lists installed printers, letting you configure them and access their job queues (see Figure 14-48). If no printers are detected, an Add button is displayed on the tab, which you can use to detect your printer. Once you have added a printer, the Add Printer button is displayed in the Printers tab's header, which you can use to detect additional printers. The Printers tab will list entries for detected and configured printers. A printer entry displays the printer name, model, status, a jobs button with the number of jobs, and a configuration button (gear icon). Click the jobs button to open a dialog listing active jobs for this printer (see Figure 14-49). For each job entry there are buttons to the right to pause or remove the job.

Chapter 14: System Administration **605**

Figure 14-48: Settings Printers tab

Figure 14-49: Settings Printers - Jobs

    To configure a printer, click the ellipsis button to display a menu with entries for the printer's options, details, default, and removal (see Figure 14-50). Choosing the "Use Printer by Default", makes it your default printer. The "Remove Printer" entry removes the printer configuration from your system. The "Printer Details" entry opens a dialog with printer's details, such as the name, location, address, and driver. There are buttons for selecting a driver from a search, database, or a PPD file. Clicking on the "Printing Options" entry open the printer's options dialog (see Figure 14-50). You can configure printer features, such as page setup, image quality, and color. The Advanced tab lets you set specialized options, such as contrast, ink type, and saturation.

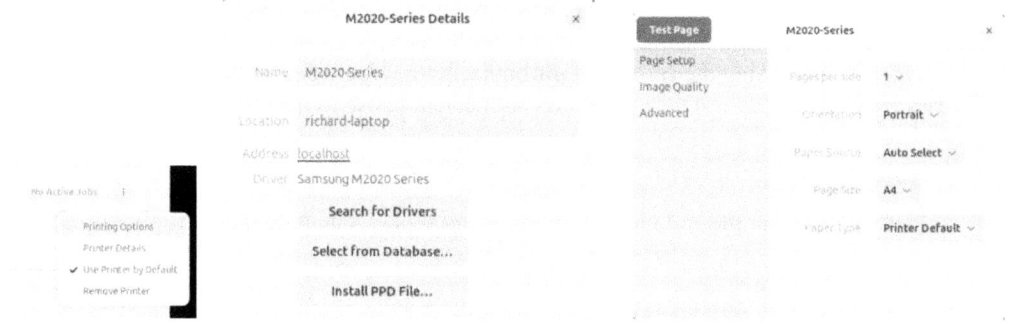

Figure 14-50: Settings Printers - Details and Options

On the Settings Printers tab, you can click the Add button to open the Add Printer dialog, which lists printers attached to your system (see Figure 14-51). They are detected automatically. If you know the address of a printer on your network, you can enter it in the search box at the bottom to have it detected and displayed.

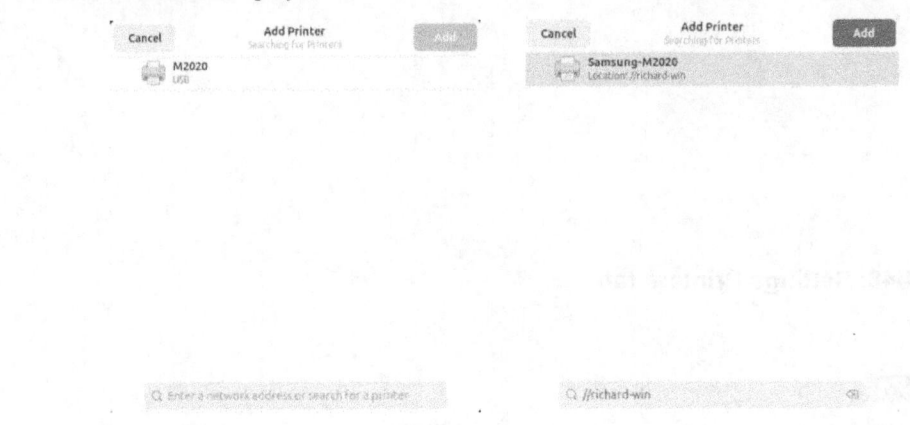

Figure 14-51: Settings Printers - add printer

Remote Printers

Most newer printers support driverless printing. Available remote printers are detected automatically, and driverless configurations generated by CUPS. To manually search for a remote printer remote printer that is attached to a Windows system or another Linux system running CUPS, you specify its location, using special URL protocols. For another CUPS printer on a remote host, the protocol used is **ipp**, for Internet Printing Protocol, whereas for a Windows printer, it would be **smb**. Older Unix or Linux systems using LPRng would use the **lpd** protocol. Be sure your firewall is configured to allow access to remote printers.

Shared Windows printers on any of the computers connected to your local network are automatically accessible once configured. Be sure the Samba server is installed to let you access directly any of shared Windows printers.

Should you want to share a printer on your Ubuntu computer with users on other computers, you need to install the Samba server (Samba package) and have the Server Message Block services enabled using the **smbd** and **nmbd** daemons. You would then configure the printer as a shared device. You can use the **systemctl** command to restart, stop, and start the services.

```
sudo systemctl restart smbd
sudo systemctl restart nmbd
```

Also, be sure that the **smbclient** package is installed. Ubuntu does not install it by default.

```
sudo apt install smbclient
```

On the GNOME Settings Printers tab, click the Add button to open the Add Printer dialog listing Printers attached to your system. Remote printers will be automatically detected and listed. To manually add a remote printer and you know the address of the printer on your network, you can enter it in the search box at the bottom to have it detected and displayed.

Print Settings (system-config-printer)

You can also use the older **system-config-printer** tool to edit a printer configuration or to add a remote printer. You can install **system-config-printer** from the App Center as a Debian package named "Print Settings". You can open the Print Settings application from the Applications overview as Printers. A printer configuration window is displayed, showing icons for installed printers. As you add printers, icons for them are displayed in the Printer configuration window (see Figure 14-52).

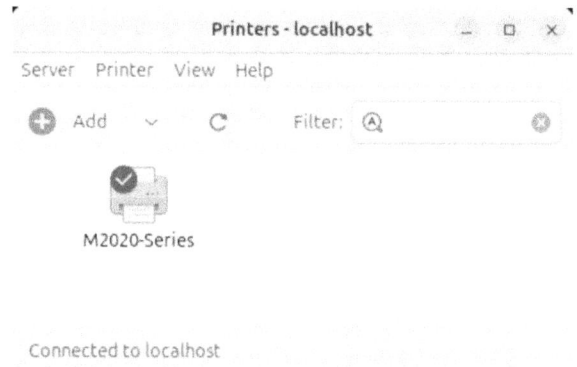

Figure 14-52: Print Settings (system-config-printer0

To see the printer settings, such as printer and job options, access controls, and policies, double-click the printer icon or right-click and select Properties. The Printer Properties window opens with six tabs: Settings, Policies, Access Control, Printer Options, Job Options, and Ink/Toner Levels (see Figure 14-53).

Figure 14-53: Printer Properties window

The Printer configuration window Printer menu lets you rename the printer, enable or disable it, and make it a shared printer. Select the printer icon and then click the Printer menu. The Delete entry will remove a printer configuration. Use the Set As Default entry to make the printer a system-wide or personal default printer. There are also entries for accessing the printer properties and viewing the print queue.

The Printer icon menu is accessed by right-clicking the printer icon. If the printer is already a default, there is no Set As Default entry. The Properties entry opens the printer properties window for that printer.

The View Print Queue entry opens the Document Print Status window, which lists the jobs for that printer. You can change the queue position as well as stop or delete jobs. From the toolbar, you can choose to display printed jobs and reprint them. You will be notified if a job should fail.

To check the server settings, select Settings from the Server menu. This opens a new window showing the CUPS printer server settings. The Common UNIX Printing System (CUPS) is the server that provides printing services (**www.cups.org**).

To select a particular CUPS server, select the Connect entry in the Server menu. This opens a Connect to CUPS Server window with a drop-down menu listing all current CUPS servers from which to choose.

Again, when you edit any printer's configuration settings, you will be prompted for authorization. Whenever you try to change a printer setting, such as its driver or URI, you are prompted to enter the administrative password for device authorization.

To make a printer the default, either right-click the printer icon and select Set As Default or single-click the printer icon and then, from the Printer configuration window's Printer menu, select the Set As Default entry. A Set Default Printer dialog opens with options for setting the system-wide default or setting the personal default. The system-wide default printer is the default for your entire network served by your CUPS server, not just your local system. The system-wide default printer will have a green check mark emblem on its printer icon in the Printer configuration window (see Figure 14-54).

Figure 14-54: Default Printer

Should you wish to use a different printer as your default, you can designate it as your personal default. To make a printer your personal default, select the entry Set as My Personal Default Printer in the Set Default Printer dialog. A personal emblem, a heart, will appear on the printer's icon in the Printer configuration window.

If you have more than one printer on your system, you can make one the default by clicking the Make Default Printer button in the printer's properties Settings pane.

The Class entry lets you create a printer class. You can access the New menu from the Server menu or from the Add button. This feature lets you select a group of printers to print a job, instead of selecting just one. That way, if one printer is busy or down, another printer can be automatically selected to perform the job. Installed printers can be assigned to different classes.

To edit an installed printer, double-click its icon in the Printer configuration window or right-click and select the Properties entry. This opens a Printer Properties window for that printer. A sidebar lists the configuration tabs. Click one to display that tab. There are configuration entries for Settings, Policies, Access Control, Printer Options, Job Options, and Ink/Toner Levels.

To install a new printer, choose the Server | New | Printer menu entry or click the Add button on the toolbar (see Figure 14-55). A New Printer window opens and displays a series of dialog boxes from which you select the connection, model, drivers, and printer name with location.

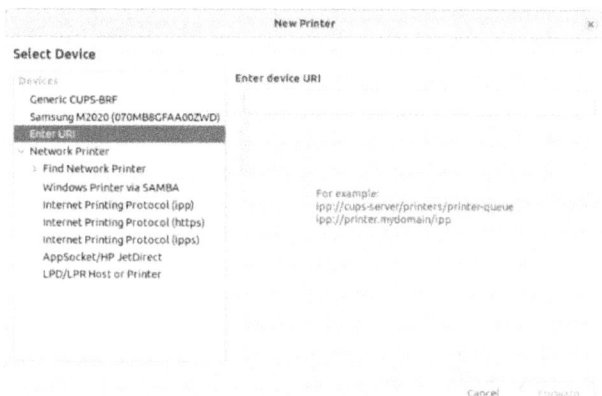

Figure 14-55: New Printer

The location is specified using special URI protocols. For another CUPS printer on a remote host, the protocol used is **ipp**, for Internet Printing Protocol, whereas for a Windows printer, it is **smb**. Older UNIX and Linux systems using LPRng use the **lpd** protocol.

You can also use system-config-printer to set up a remote printer on Linux, UNIX, or Windows networks. When you add a new printer or edit one, the New Printer dialog will list possible remote connection types under the Network entry. When you select a remote connection entry, a pane will be displayed to the right where you can enter configuration information.

First, you need to install the **smbclient** package along with **python3-smbc**, using the **apt install** command. This package is currently not installed by default. Be sure your user is added to the **sambashare** group.

```
sudo adduser richard sambashare
```

To find a connected printer on your network automatically, click the Find Network Printer entry. This is a simple easy way to find a printer for a small network. Enter the hostname of the system the remote printer is connected to, then click the Find button. The host is searched and the detected printers are displayed as entries under the Network Printer heading (see Figure 14-56). You may be asked to login as a qualified user. You can then click the Find button to open a dialog listing shared printers on the host. Choose the one you want. For more refined access you can use the "Windows Printer via Samba" operation. The selected printer will appear under the Network Printer heading in the sidebar (see Figure 14-57).

610 Part 4: Administration

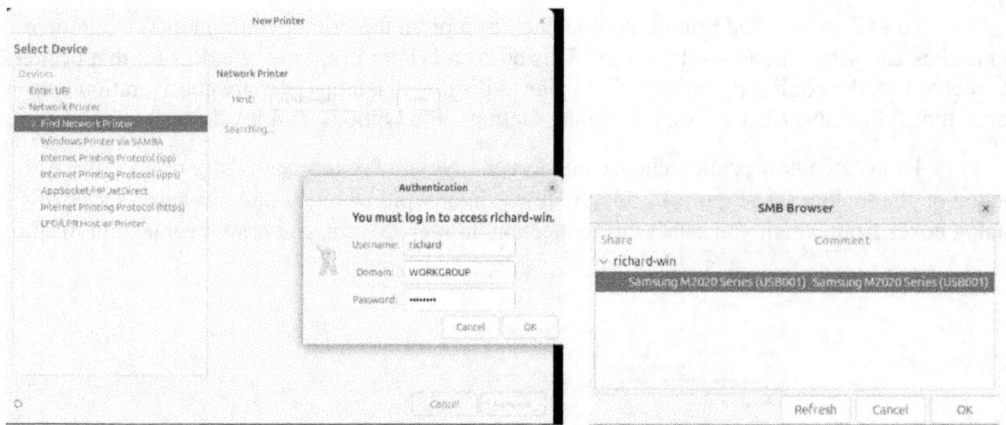

Figure 14-56: Finding a network printer

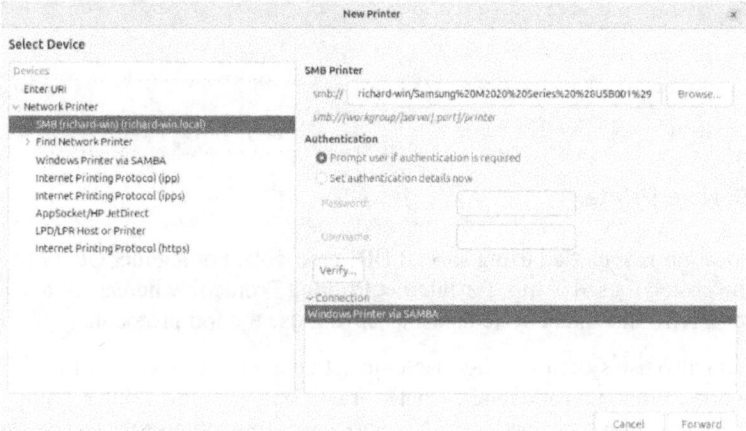

Figure 14-57: Selecting a network printer

      To configure a specific type of printer, choose from the available entries. For a remote Linux or UNIX printer, select either Internet Printing Protocol (ipp), which is used for newer systems, or LPD/LPR Host or Printer, which is used for older systems. Both panes display entries for the Host name and the queue. For the Host name, enter the hostname of the system that controls the printer. For an Apple or HP jet direct printer on your network, select the AppSocket/HP jetDirect entry.

      A "Windows printer via Samba" printer is one located on a Windows network, and provides more refined access than the Find Network Printer operation. You need to specify the Windows server (hostname or IP address), the name of the share, the name of the printer's workgroup, and the username and password. The format of the printer SMB URL is shown on the SMP Printer pane. The share is the hostname and printer name in the **smb** URI format *//workgroup/hostname/printername.* The workgroup is the windows network workgroup that the printer belongs to. On small networks, there is usually only one. The hostname is the computer where the printer is located. The username and password can be for the printer resource itself, or for access by a particular user. The pane will display a box at the top where you can enter the share host and printer name as an **smb** URI. Click the Browse button to open a dialog that will list shared printers on the host. Choose the one you want.

If the Browse operation accessed by the Browse button does not work, you may have to enter the exact name of the printer, including special characters such as spaces and parenthesis. These special characters are referenced with a preceding percent sign, **%**, followed by the ASCII hexadecimal value for the character. A space is referenced as **%20**, an open parenthesis as **%28**, and a close parenthesis as **%29**. In these examples, the Windows name of the Samsung M2020 printer is:

`Samsung M2020 Series (USB001)`

This would be:

`Samsung%20M2020%20Series%20%28USB001%29`

Be sure to also include your host name. If you have multiple workgroups on your network, include the workgroup name also. The full entry for the previous example, with the host 'richard-win" would be:

`richard-win/Samsung%20M2020%20Series%20%28USB001%29`

With the workgroup name "workgroup" it would be:

`workgroup/richard-win/Samsung%20M2020%20Series%20%28USB001%29`

You also can enter in any needed Samba authentication, if required, such as a username and password. Check "Authentication required" to allow you to enter the Samba Username and Password. The Connections section to the lower right will list "Windows Printer via Samba" as the connection. With the current version of Samba, if you do not enter it now, it will prompt you for a user name and password when you try to use the printer. This may not work. To be sure of access you should enter the user and password on this dialog now.

You then continue with install screens for the printer model, driver, and name. Once installed, you can then access the printer properties just as you would any printer (see Figure 14-58).

Figure 14-58: Remote Windows printer Settings

The configured remote printer is then listed in the system-config-printer window, along with other printers (see Figure 14-59). When you choose to print from an application, the remote printer will be listed along with your local printers.

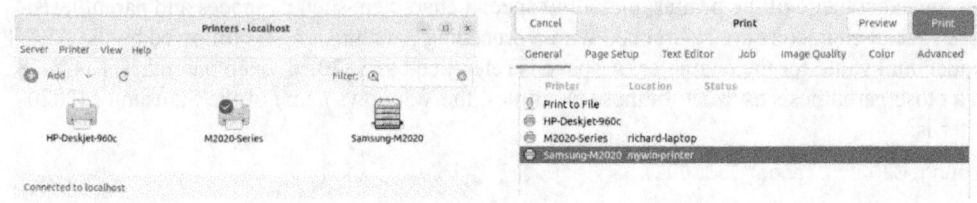

Figure 14-59: Remote Windows Printers

15. Network Connections

NetworkManager

Settings: WiFi and Network

NetworkManager manual configuration

Wired Configuration

Wireless Configuration

VPN Configuration

Dial-up PPP Access: wvdial

Network Configuration with systemd-networkd

Setting up a firewall with Gufw and ufw

Setting up Your Firewall with FirewallD

Network Information

Ubuntu will automatically detect and configure your network connections with NetworkManager. Should the automatic configuration either fail or be incomplete for some reason, you can perform a manual configuration using the Settings Wi-Fi and Network tabs. If you want to make a simple dial-up modem connection, you can use WvDial. Your network will also need a firewall. UFW (with the Gufw interface) or FirewallD is recommended. Table 15-1 lists several network configuration tools.

Network Connections: Dynamic and Static

If you are on a network, you may need to obtain certain information to configure your connection interface. Most networks now support dynamic configuration using either the older Dynamic Host Configuration Protocol (DHCP) or the IPv6 Protocol and its automatic address configuration. In this case, you need only check the DHCP entry in most network configuration tools. If your network does not support DHCP or IPv6 automatic addressing, or you are using a static connection (DCHP and IPv6 connections are dynamic), you will have to provide detailed information about your connection. For a static connection, you would enter your connection information manually such as your IP address and DNS servers, whereas in a dynamic connection this information is provided automatically to your system by a DHCP server or generated by IPv6 when you connect to the network. For DHCP, a DHCP client on each host will obtain the information from a DHCP server serving that network. IPv6 generates its addresses directly from the device and router information such as the device hardware MAC address.

Network Configuration Tool	Description
NetworkManager	Used for all network connections including wired, wireless, mobile broadband, VPN, and DSL. **nmcli** is the command line interface version of NetworkManager.
Network (Settings)	Network connection preferences, allowing quick connection to wired networks, VPN connections, and proxies.
Wi-Fi (Settings)	Wi-Fi connection preferences, allowing quick connection to wireless networks.
ufw	Sets up a network firewall.
Gufw	GNOME interface for UFW firewall
FirewallD	Sets up a network firewall.
wvdial	PPP dial-up modem connection
systemd-networkd	systemd-based network configuration

Table 15-1: Ubuntu Network Configuration Tools

In addition, if you are using a dynamic DSL, ISDN, or a modem connection, you will also have to supply provider, login, and password information, and specify whether your system is dynamic or static. You may also need to supply specialized information such as DSL or modem compression methods or dialup number.

You can obtain most of your static network information from your network administrator, or from your ISP (Internet Service Provider). You would need the following information:

The device name for your network interface   For LAN and wireless connections, this is the network device name, which you can find using the **ifconfig** or **ip l** commands. For a modem, DSL, or ISDN connection, this is a PPP device named **ppp0** (**ippp0** for ISDN). Virtual private network (VPN) connections are also supported.

Hostname   Your computer will be identified by this name on the Internet. Do not use localhost; that name is reserved for special use by your system. The name of the host should be a simple word, which can include numbers, but not punctuation such as periods and backslashes. On a small network, the hostname is often a single name. On a large network that could have several domains, the hostname includes both the name of the host and its domain.

Domain name   This is the name of your network.

The Internet Protocol (IP) address assigned to your machine   This is needed only for static Internet connections. Dynamic connections use the DHCP protocol to assign an IP address for you automatically. Every host on the Internet is assigned an IP address. Small and older network addresses might still use the older IPv4 format consisting of a set of four numbers, separated by periods. The IP protocol version 6, IPv6, uses a new format with a complex numbering sequence that is much more automatic.

Your network IP address   Static connections only. This address is similar to the IP address but lacks any reference to a particular host.

The netmask   IPv4 Static connections only. This is usually 255.255.255.0 for most networks. If, however, you are part of a large network, check with your network administrator or ISP.

The broadcast address for your network, if available (optional)   IPv4 Static connections only. Usually, your broadcast address is the same as your IP address with the number 255 added at the end.

The IP address of your network's gateway computer   Static connections only. This is the computer that connects your local network to a larger one like the Internet.

Name servers   The IP address of the name servers your network uses. These enable the use of URLs.

NIS domain and IP address for an NIS server   Necessary if your network uses an NIS server (optional).

User login and password information   Needed for dynamic DSL, ISDN, and modem connections.

NetworkManager

NetworkManager detects your network connections automatically, both wired and wireless. It uses the automatic device detection capabilities of udev to configure your connections. Should you instead need to configure your network connections manually, you can also use NetworkManager to enter the required network connection information. NetworkManager operates as a daemon with the name NetworkManager. It will automatically scan for both wired and wireless connections. Information provided by NetworkManager is made available to other applications.

NetworkManager is designed to work in the background, providing status information for your connection and switching from one configured connection to another as needed. For an initial configuration, it detects as much information as possible about a new connection.

NetworkManager is also user specific. When a user logs in, wireless connections the user prefers will start up (wired connections are started automatically).

User and System-Wide Network Configuration: NetworkManager

NetworkManager will automatically detect your network connections, both wired and wireless. It is the default method for managing your network connections. NetworkManager makes use of the automatic device detection capabilities of udev to configure your connections. Should you instead have to configure your network connections manually, you would use the Settings Wi-Fi and Network tabs.

NetworkManager is user specific. When a user logs in, it selects the network connection preferred by that user. For wireless connections, the user can choose from a list of current possible connections. For wired connections, a connection can be started automatically, when the system starts up. Initial settings will be supplied from the system-wide configuration.

Configurations can also be applied system-wide to all users. When editing or adding a network connection, the edit or add dialog displays a "Make available to other user" check box in the lower-left corner. Click this check box and then click the Apply button to make the connection configuration system-wide. An authentication dialog will first prompt you to enter your administrative password.

NetworkManager can configure any network connection. This includes wired, wireless, and all manual connections. Network Interface Connection (NIC cards) hardware is detected using udev. Information provided by NetworkManager is made available to other applications over D-Bus.

With multiple wireless access points for Internet connections, a system could have several different network connections to choose from, instead of a single-line connection such as DSL or fiber. This is particularly true for notebook computers that access different wireless connections at different locations. Instead of manually configuring a new connection each time one is encountered, the NetworkManager tool can automatically configure and select a connection to use.

By default, an Ethernet connection will be preferred, if available. For wireless connections, you will have to choose the one you want.

NetworkManager is designed to work in the background, providing status information for your connection and switching from one configured connection to another, as needed. For initial configuration, it detects as much information as possible about the new connection.

NetworkManager operates as a daemon with the name **NetworkManager**. If no Ethernet connection is available, NetworkManager will scan for wireless connections, checking for Extended Service Set Identifiers (ESSIDs). If an ESSID identifies a previously used connection, then it is automatically selected. If several are found, then the most recently used one is chosen. If only a new connection is available, the NetworkManager waits for the user to choose one. A connection is selected only if the user is logged in. If an Ethernet connection is later made, the NetworkManager will switch to it from wireless.

The NetworkManager daemon can be turned on or off, using the **systemctl** command as the root user.

```
sudo systemctl start NetworkManager
sudo systemctl stop NetworkManager
```

NetworkManager Manual Configuration using GNOME Settings

The Network configuration is available on Settings, can be used to configure all your network connections manually. Automatic wireless and wired connections were covered in Chapter 3.

Settings Wi-Fi tab

On the Settings dialog there is a Wi-Fi tab for wireless configuration and a Network tab for wired, VPN, and proxy configurations (see Figure 15-1). On the Wi-Fi tab, an Airplane Mode switch and a list of visible wireless connections are listed. The currently active connection will have a "Connected" label. At the top of the tab is a switch for turning Wi-Fi on and off. Below this switch are a Saved Networks link that lists previously accessed Wi-Fi Networks, a "Connect to Hidden Network" link for connections to hidden networks, and a "Turn On Wi-Fi Hotspot" link for turning on your computer's Wi-Fi hotspot capability.

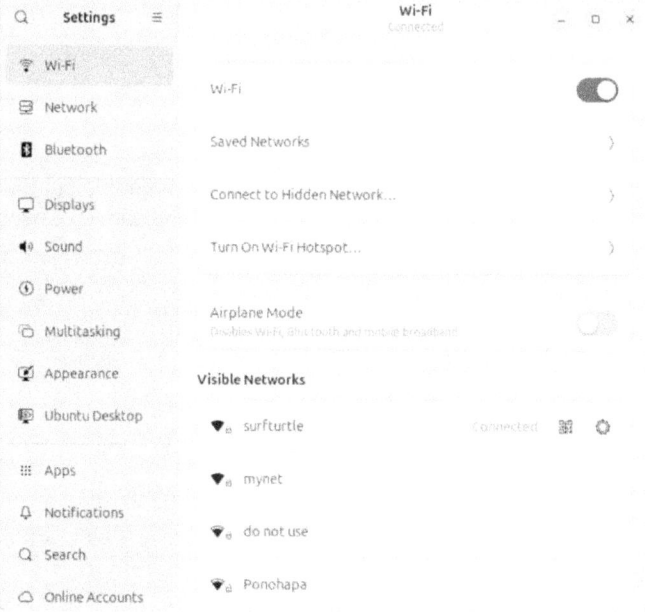

Figure 15-1: Settings Wi-Fi

Selecting an entry in the Visible Networks list will create a gear button for it, which you can click to open the network configuration dialog with tabs for Details, Security, Identity, IPv4, IPv6, and Reset. The Details tab show strength, speed, security methods, IP and hardware

618 Part 4: Administration

addresses, routes, and the DNS server IP address (see Figure 15-2). You can choose to connect automatically and whether to make the connection system-wide. You can also choose to impose data limits. It also has a "Forget Connection" button for removing this Wi-Fi connection information.

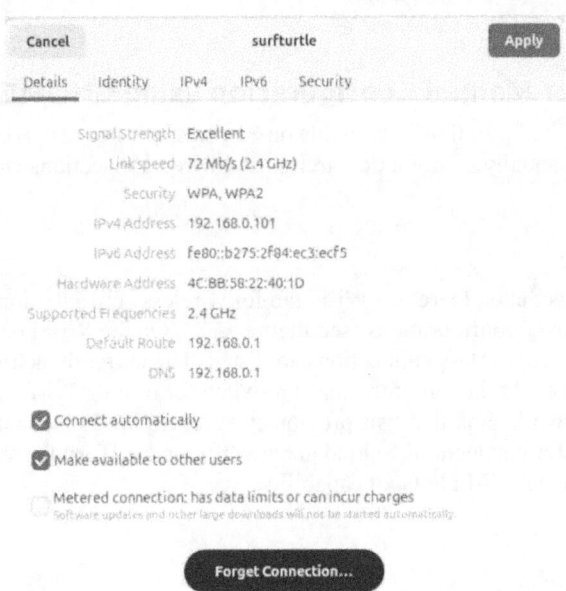

Figure 15-2: Wi-Fi - Details tab

To edit the connection manually, you use the Security, Identity, and IP tabs. The Security tab displays a menu from which you can choose a security method and a password (see Figure 15-3).

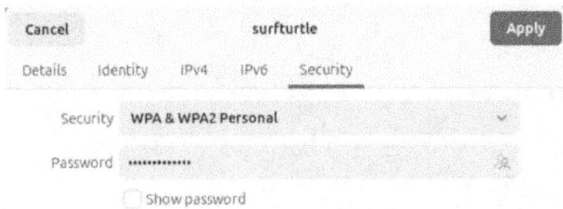

Figure 15-3: Wi-Fi - Security tab

On the Identity tab, you can specify the SSID name and MAC Address (see Figure 15-4).

Chapter 15: Network Connections   **619**

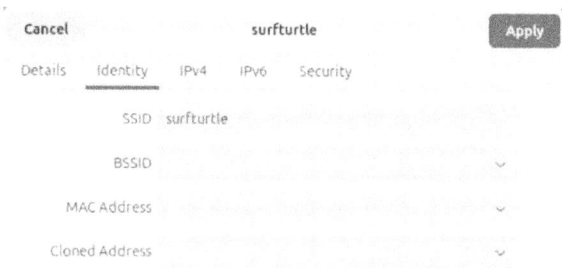

Figure 15-4: Wi-Fi - Identity tab

On the IPv4 and IPv6 Settings tabs, there are sections for Method, Addresses, the DNS servers, and Routes. In the Method section you can choose the type connection you want. By default, it is set to Automatic. If you change it to Manual, the Address section appears for the address, netmask, and gateway (see Figure 15-5). On the IPv6 tab, the netmask in the Address section is replaced by prefix. The Disable option turns off the connection. You can turn off Automatic switches for the DNS and Routes sections to make them manual. Separate multiple DNS IP addresses with a comma.

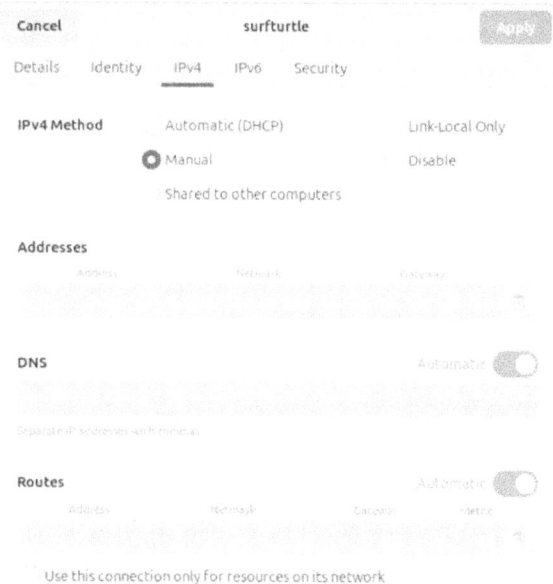

Figure 15-5: Wi-Fi - IPv4 tab, Manual

Once you have configured a Wi-Fi connection, a Saved Network link appears on the Settings Wi-Fi tab. Clicking on the link open a Saved Wi-Fi Networks dialog that list all the Wi-Fi connections you have configured (see Figure 15-6). Clicking on the configuration button opens that Wi-Fi connection's configuration dialog. Clicking on the Forget Network button (trash can) removes the Wi-Fi connection and its configuration.

620 Part 4: Administration

Figure 15-6: Saved Networks

Settings Network tab (wired)

For a wired connection, click the Network tab on Settings to display lists for Wired, VPN, and Network Proxy. The Wired list shows your current wired connections with on and off switches for each. A plus button at the top right of the Wired list lets you add more wired connections. Next to a connection's switch a gear button is displayed (see Figure 15-7). Clicking the gear button opens a configuration dialog with tabs for Details, Identity, IPv4, IPv6, and Security (see Figure 15-8).

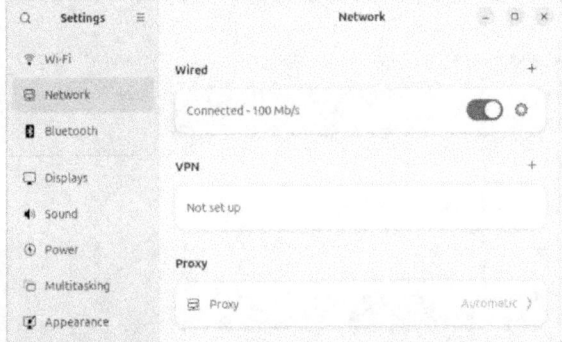

Figure 15-7: Settings Network

The Details tab list the connection information such as the IP addresses, hardware addresses, route, and DNS server. You can choose to connect automatically and whether to make the connection system-wide. You can also choose to impose data limits.

Chapter 15: Network Connections   621

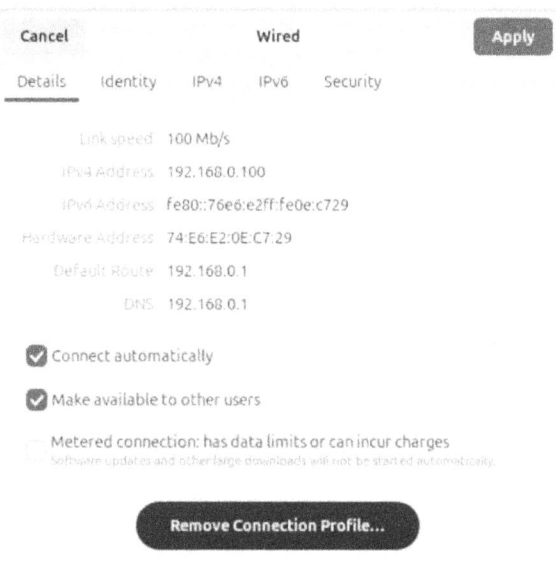

Figure 15-8: Wired Configuration -Details tab

On the Settings Network tab you can add a new configuration for a network connection, Click on the plus button above the connected entry to open the New Profile dialog where you can enter different identity, IPv4, IPv6, and security configurations (see Figure 15-9). On the Identity tab you can enter a profile name.

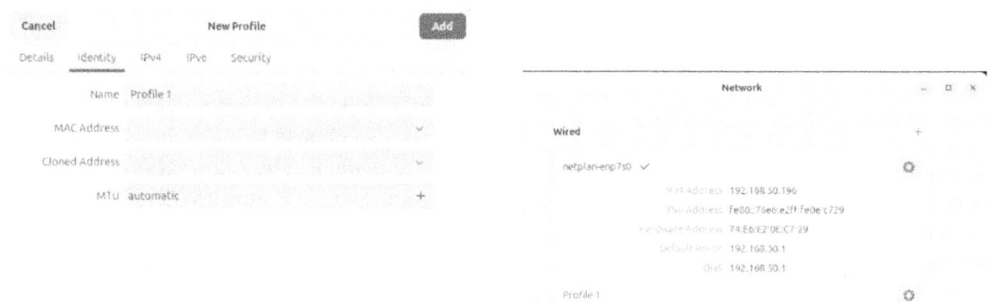

Figure 15-9: Wired Configuration - New Profile

You can use the Security, Identity, and IP tabs to manually configure the connection. The Security tab lets you turn on 802.1x security and choose an authentication method, as well as provide a username and password (see Figure 15-10).

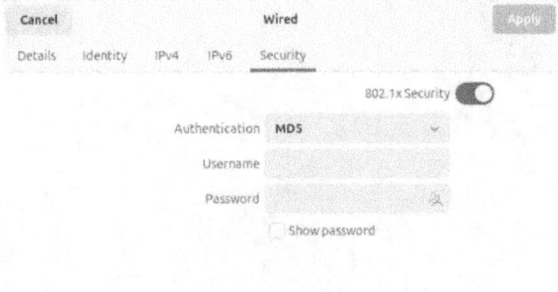

Figure 15-10: Wired Configuration - Security tab

On the Identity tab, you can set the name, choose the hardware address and set the MTU blocks (see Figure 15-11).

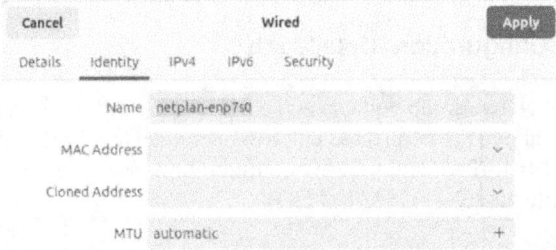

Figure 15-11: Wired Configuration - Identity tab

The IPv4 and IPv6 Settings tabs have sections for Method, Addresses, DNS servers, and Routes. From the Method set of options at the top, you can also choose to make the connection automatic, manual, link-local, or to disable it. If you choose manual, The Addresses section appears, which lets you enter the address, netmask, and gateway (see Figure 15-12). On the IPv6 tab, the netmask entry is replaced by a prefix entry. DNS and Routes have a switch for automatic. Turning the switch off allows you to manually enter a DNS server address or routing information.

Chapter 15: Network Connections   **623**

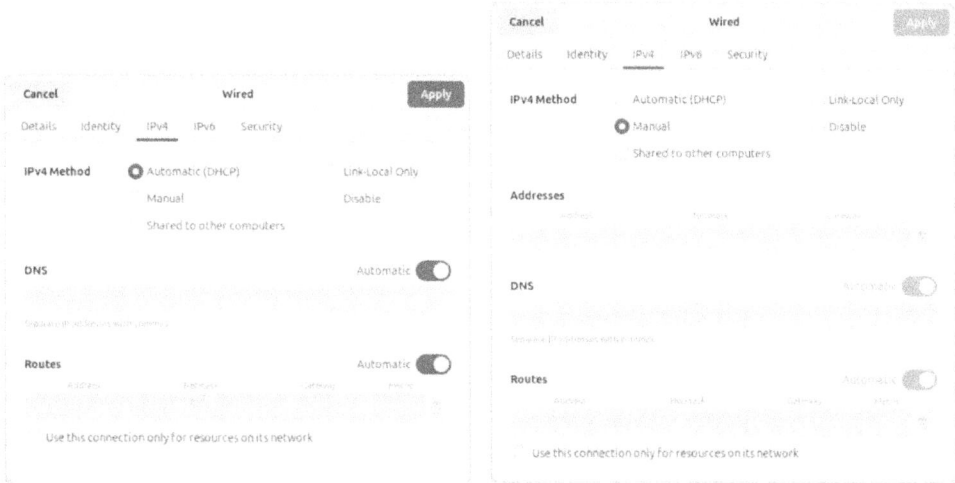

Figure 15-12: Wired Configuration - IPv4 tab

For VPN connections, click the plus button at the top right of the VPN list in the Settings Network tab to open an Add VPN dialog. The dialog lists supported VPN connection types, such as Point-to-Point, OpenVPN, and WireGuard (see Figure 15-13). The Bond, Bridge, and VLAN entries open the Network Connections dialogs for those connections.

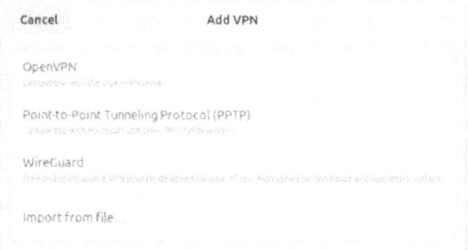

Figure 15-13: Settings Network - add VPN connections

You can then configure the VPN connections in the "Add VPN" dialog, which, for OpenVPN, shows tabs for Details, Identity, IPv4, and IPv6 (see Figure 15-14). The IP tabs are the same as for wireless and wired configuration dialogs. On the Identity tab, you can enter the name, gateway, and authentication information. Click the Advanced button for detailed connection configuration.

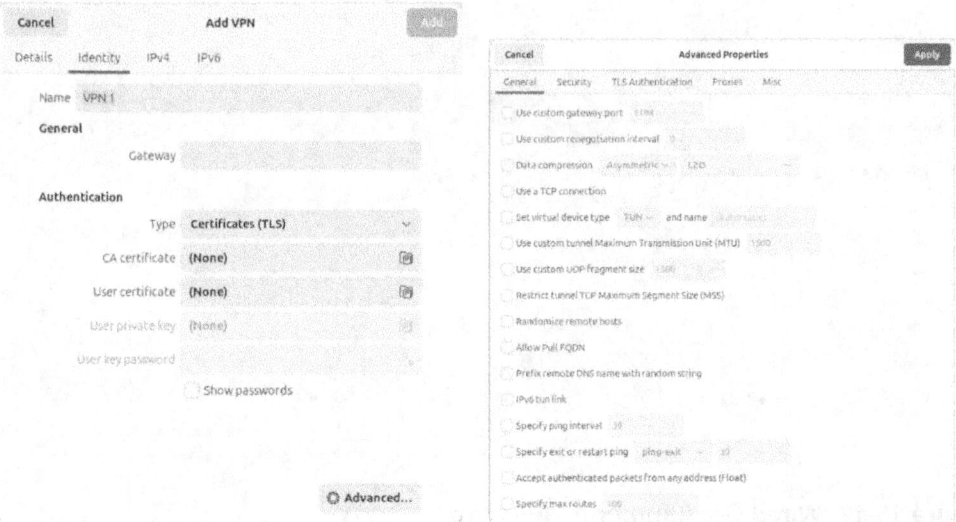

Figure 15-14: OpenVPN connection

Ubuntu supports the new WireGuard virtual network manager, which provides better encryption and efficiency than the older IPsec and OpenVPN tools. WireGuard works by setting up dedicated network interfaces (**wg**), which are then used for the VPN connections. Check the WireGuard Web site for information on how to configure and manage a Wireguard connection (**https://www.wireguard.com**).

You can configure a WireGuard VPN connection with NetworkManager on the Settings Network tab's VPN section. Click on the plus sign to display a list of possible VPN connections and select WireGuard. This opens an Add VPN dialog with a WireGuard tab that you can use to configure your WireGuard connection, with a WireGuard tab instead of an Identity tab (see Figure 15-15).

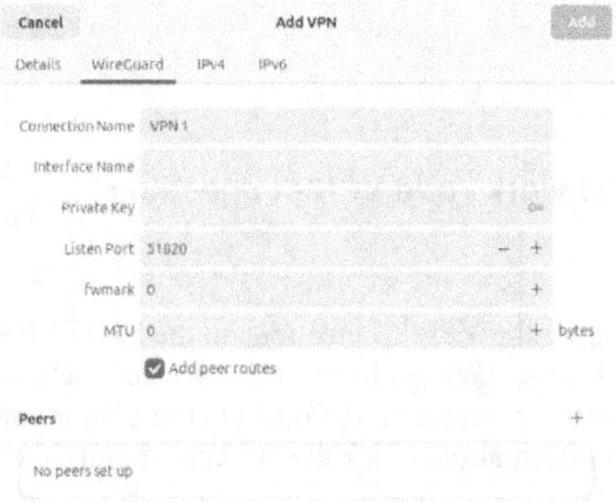

Figure 15-15: WireGuard connection

You can also install the WireGuard package directly with the App Center (Snap repository), the **apt** command (Universe repository), or with the Synaptic Package Manager (Universe repository).

```
sudo apt install wireguard
```

Additional VPN services are available from the Debian (Universe) repository. You can install them with the Ubuntu Apps Center (Debian repository), the Synaptic Package Manager (search on network-manager), or the **apt** command. The PPTP service for Microsoft VPN connections and OpenVPN are installed by default. Other popular VPN services include Fortinet (SSL), OpenConnect (SSL), Layer 2 Tunneling Protocol (IPSec encryption), Cisco Concentrator, Iodine (DNS tunneling), and Openswan (IPSec). NetworkManager support is installed using the corresponding NetworkManager plugin for these services. The plugin packages begin with the name **network-manager**. OpenVPN, which uses the **openvpn** software along with the **network-manager-openvpn** plugin, is install be default. For the Layer 2 Tunneling Protocol VPN install the **network-manager-l2tp** plugin. For the Fortinet SSL VPN install the **network-manager-fortisslvpn** plugin. For the OpenConnect VPN (Juniper SSL client) install the **network-manager-openconnect** plugin. For Cisco Concentrator based VPN, install the **network-manager-vpnc** plugin. Strongswan uses the **network-manager-strongswan** plugin. For the Iodine VPN (DNS tunneling) install the **network-manager-iodine** plugin.

NetworkManager Manual Configuration Using Network Connections: nm-connection-editor

You can also use the older Network Connections utility (**nm-connection-editor**) to edit any network connection. It is part of the **network-manager-gnome** package, which is installed by default. You can run it from a terminal window with the following command.

```
sudo nm-connection-editor
```

Established connections are listed, with at toolbar at the bottom for adding, removing, and editing network connections (see Figure 15-16). Your current network connections should already be listed.

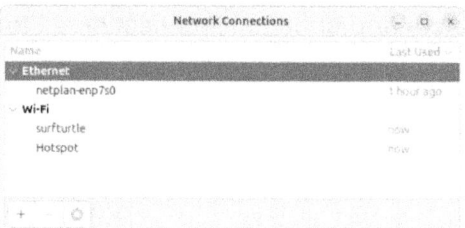

Figure 15-16: Network Connections (nm-connection-editor)

When you add a connection, you can choose its type from a drop-down menu. The menu organizes connection types into three categories: Hardware, Virtual, and VPN. Hardware connections cover both wired (Ethernet, DSL, and InfiniBand) and wireless (Wi-Fi, WiMAX, and Mobile Broadband) connections. VPN lists the supported VPN types, such as OpenVPN, PPTP, and Cisco. You can also import a previously configured connection. Virtual supports VLAN and Bond virtual connections.

Configuration editing dialogs display a General tab from which you can make your configuration available to all users and automatically connect when the network connection is available. You can also choose to use a VPN connection and whether to use a metered connection.

Click the edit button (Gear button) to edit an Ethernet connection, opening an Editing window. Click the add button (plus button) to open the "Choose a Connection Type" dialog, where you can click the Create button to add a new connection and opens a similar window, with no settings. The Ethernet tab lists the MAC hardware address and the MTU. The MTU is usually set to automatic. The standard default configuration for a wired Ethernet connection uses DHCP. Connect automatically will set up the connection when the system starts up. There are seven tabs, General, Ethernet, 8.02.1x Security, DCB, Proxy, IPv4 Settings, and IPv6 Settings. The IPv4 Settings tab lets you select the kind of wired connection you have. The manual configuration entries for an IPv4 connection are shown in Figure 15-17. Click the Add button to enter the IP address, network mask, and gateway address. Then enter the address for the DNS servers and your network search domains. The Routes button will open a window in which you can manually enter any network routes.

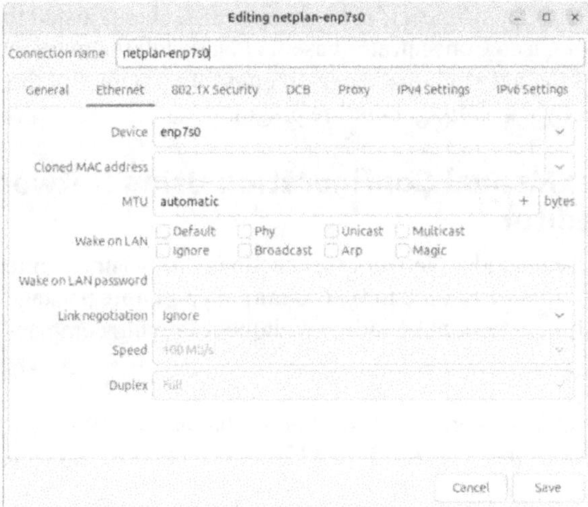

Figure 15-17: IPv4 wired configuration (nm-connection-editor)

For a wireless connection, you enter wireless configuration data, such as your ESSID, password, and encryption method. For wireless connections, you choose Wi-Fi or WiMAX as the connection type. The Editing Wi-Fi connection window opens with tabs for general configuration, your wireless information, security, proxy, and IP settings (see Figure 15-18). On the Wi-Fi tab, you specify your SSID, along with your mode and MAC address.

On the Wi-Fi Security tab, you enter your wireless connection security method. The commonly used method, WPA Personal, is supported, along with WPA3 personal. The WPA personal method only requires a password. More secure connections, such as Dynamic WEP and Enterprise WPA, are also supported. These will require much more configuration information, such as authentication methods, certificates, and keys.

For a new broadband connection, choose the Mobile Broadband entry in the connection type menu. A 3G wizard starts up to help you set up the appropriate configuration for your particular 3G service. Configuration steps are listed on the left pane. If your device is connected, you can select it from the drop-down menu on the right pane.

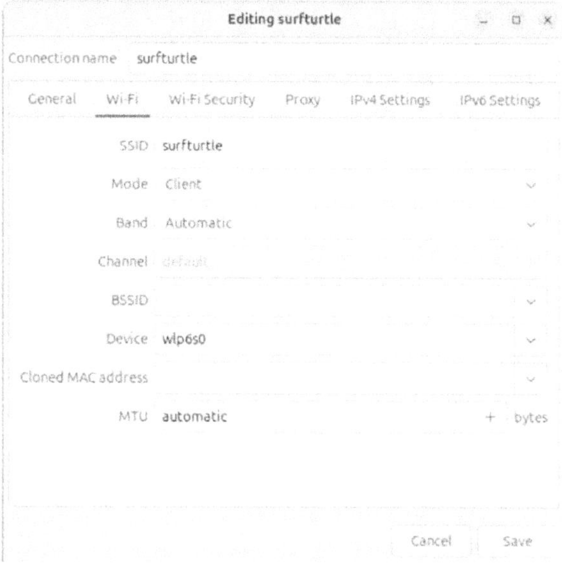

Figure 15-18: Wireless configuration (nm-connection-editor)

Once a service is selected, you can further edit the configuration by clicking its entry in the Mobile Broadband tab and clicking the Edit button. The Editing window opens with tabs for Mobile Broadband, PPP, IPv4, and IPv6 settings. On the Mobile Broadband tab, you can enter your number, username, and password. Advanced options include the APN, Network, and PIN. The APN should already be entered.

On the NetworkManager panel applet menu, the VPN Connection entry submenu will list configured VPN connections for easy access. The Configure VPN entry will open the Network Connections window to the VPN section, from which you can then add, edit, or delete VPN connections. The Disconnect VPN entry will end the current active VPN connection. To add a VPN connection, choose a VPN connection type from the connection type menu.

The Editing VPN Connection dialog opens with tabs such as General, VPN, Proxy, IPv4, and IPv6 Settings. On the VPN tab, you enter VPN connection information, such as the gateway address and any additional VPN information that may be required. For an OpenVPN connection, you will have to provide the authentication type, certificates, and keys. Clicking the Advanced button opens the Advanced Options dialog. An OpenVPN connection will have tabs for General, Security, and TLS Authentication. On the Security tab, you can specify the cipher to use.

Note: If your system detects a cellular network modem (Wireless WAN Cellular device), you can use the System Settings Mobile Network tab to configure it.

NetworkManager wireless router, using your wireless connection as a Hotspot and for a Hidden Network.

You can set up your wireless connection as a wireless router for your own wireless network. The "Turn On Wi-Fi Hotspot" link in the Settings Wi-Fi tab, opens a dialog letting you set up your computer as a wireless router that other computers can connect to (see Figure 15-19). Once the hotspot is active, mobile devices can scan a QR code displayed on the Wi-Fi tab to quickly connect to it. You can also display the QR code by clicking on the QR code button on the network's entry in the Wi-Fi tab to display a Share Network dialog with a Scan to Connect QR code.

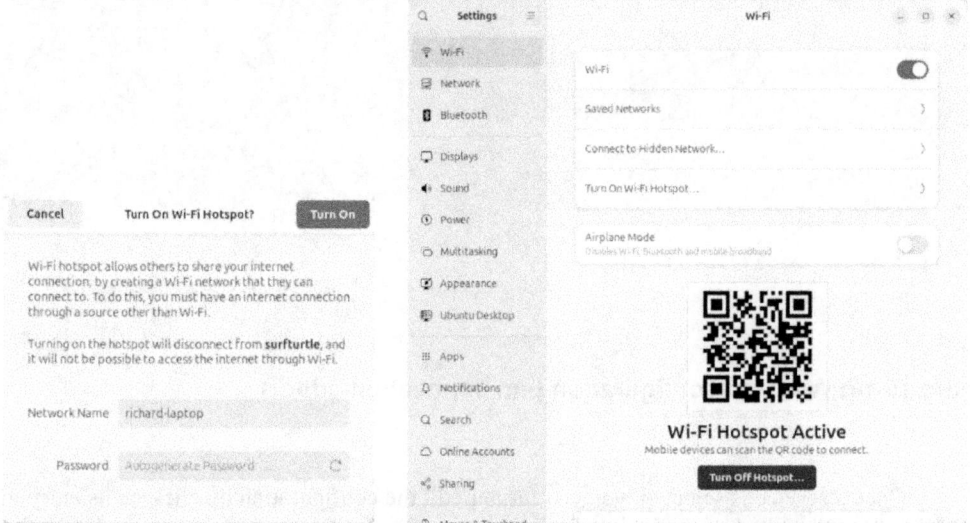

Figure 15-19: Turn on Wi-Fi Hotspot

A hidden wireless network will not perform any SSID broadcasting, keeping its SSID private. You access it through the "Connect to Hidden Network" link on the Settings Wi-Fi tab. This opens the "Connect to Hidden Wi-Fi Network" window (see Figure 15-20).

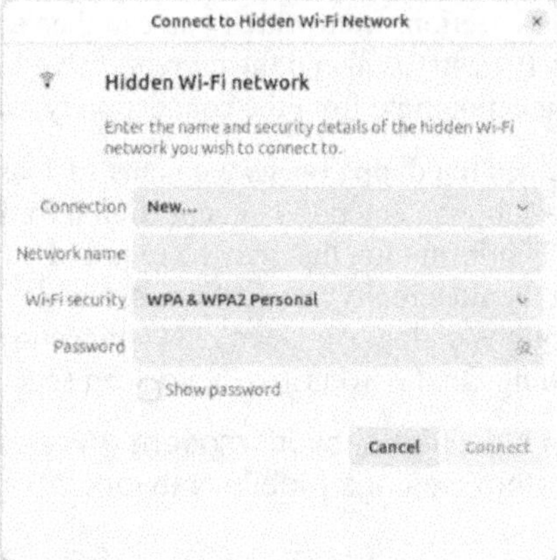

Figure 15-20: Connect to a Hidden Wi-Fi Network

Managing Network Connections with nmcli

The **nmcli** command is NetworkManager Command Line Interface command. Most network configuration tasks can be performed by **nmcli**. The **nmcli** command manages NetworkManager through a set of objects: general (**g**), networking (**n**), radio (**r**), connection (**c**), device (**d**), and agent (**a**). Each can be referenced using the full name or a unique prefix, such as **con** for connection or **dev** for device. The unique prefix can be as short as a single character, such as **g** for general, **c** for connections, or **d** for device. See Table 15-2 for a list of the objects and commonly used options. The **nmcli** man page provides a complete listing with examples.

The general object shows the current status of NetworkManager and what kind of devices are enabled. You can limit the information displayed using the **-t** (terse) and **-f** (field) options. The STATE field show the connection status, and the CONNECTIVITY field the connection.

```
$ nmcli general
STATE       CONNECTIVITY  WIFI-HW  WIFI     WWAN-HW  WWAN
connected   full          enabled  enabled  enabled  enabled

$ nmcli -t -f STATE general
connected
```

The **connection** object references the network connection and the **show** option displays that information. The following example displays your current connection.

```
nmcli connection show
```

You can use **c** instead of **connection** and **s** instead of show.

```
$ nmcli c s
NAME        UUID                                  TYPE            DEVICE
enp7s0      f7202f6d-fc66-4b81-8962-69b71202efc0  802-3-ethernet  enp7s0
AT&T LTE 1  65913b39-789a-488c-9559-28ea6341d9e1  gsm             --
```

As with the general object, you can limit the fields displayed using the **-f** option. The following only list the name and type fields.

```
$ nmcli -f name,type c s
NAME        TYPE
enp7s0      802-3-ethernet
AT&T LTE 1  gsm
```

Adding the **--active** option will only show active connections.

```
nmcli c s --active
```

To start and stop a connection (like **ifconfig** does), use the **up** and **down** options.

```
nmcli con up enp7s0.
```

Use the **device** object to manage your network devices. The **show** and **status** options provide information about your devices. To check the status of all your network devices use the **device** object and **status** options:

Object	Description
`general`	NetworkManager status and enabled devices. Use the terse (**-t**) and field (**-f**) option to limit the information displayed.
`networking`	Manage networking, use `on` and `off` to turn networking on or off, and `connectivity` for the connection state.
`radio`	Turns on or off the wireless networking (on or off). Can turn on or off specific kinds of wireless: `wifi`, `wwan` (mobile broadband), and `wimax`. The `all` option turns on or off all wireless.
`connection`	Manage network connections. `show` List connection profiles. With `--active` show only active connections. `up` Activate a connection `down` Deactivate a connection `add` Add a new connection, specifying `type`, `ifname`, `con-name` (profile). `modify` Edit an existing connection, use + and - to add new values to properties `edit` Add a new connection or edit an existing one using the interactive editor `delete` Delete a configured connection (profile) `reload` Reload all connection profiles `load` Reload or load a specific
`device`	Manage network interfaces (devices). `status` Display device status `show` Display device information `connect` Connect the device `disconnect` Disconnect the device `delete` Delete a software device, such as a bridge. `wifi` Display a list of available wifi access points `wifi rescan` Rescan for and display access points `wifi connect` Connect to a wifi network; specify `password`, `wep-key-type`, `ifname`, `bssid`, and `name` (profile name) `wimax` List available WiMAX networks
`agent`	Run as a NetworkManager secret agent or polkit agent. `secret` As a secret agent, nmcli listens for secret requests. `polkit` As a polkit agent it listens for all authorization requests.

Table 15-2: The nmcli objects

```
nmcli device status
DEVICE  TYPE      STATE         CONNECTION
enp7s0  ethernet  connected     enp7s0
wlp6s0  wifi      disconnected  --
lo      loopback  unmanaged     --
```

You can abbreviate **device** and **status** to **d** and **s**.

`nmcli d s`

You also use the **device** object to connect and disconnect devices. Use the **connect** or **disconnect** options with the interface name (ifname) of the device, in this example, **enp7s0**. With the **delete** option, you can remove a device.

```
nmcli device disconnect enp7s0
nmcli device connect enp7s0
```

To turn networking on or off you use the **networking** object and the **on** and **off** options. Use the **connectivity** option to check network connectivity. The networking object alone tells you if it is enabled or not.

```
$ nmcli networking
enabled

$ nmcli networking on

$ nmcli networking connectivity
full
```

Should you want to just turn on or off the Wifi connection, you would use the **radio** object. Use **wifi**, **wwan**, and **wimax** for a specific type of wifi connection and the **all** option for all of them. The radio object alone shows wifi status of all your wifi connection types.

```
$ nmcli radio
WIFI-HW  WIFI     WWAN-HW  WWAN
enabled  enabled  enabled  enabled

$ nmcli radio wifi on

$ nmcli radio all off
```

nmcli Wired Connections

You can use **nmcli** to add connections, just as you can with the desktop NetworkManager tool. To add a new static connection use the connection object with the **add** option. Specify the connection's profile name with the **con-name** option, the interface name with the **ifname** option, the **type**, such as ethernet. For a static connection you would add the IP address (**ipv4** or **ipv6**), and the gateway address (**gw4** or **gw6**). For a DHCP connection simply do not list the IP address and gateway options. The profile name can be any name. You could have several profile names for the same network device. For example, for your wireless device, you could have several wireless connection profiles, depending on the different networks you want to connect to. Should you connect your Ethernet device to a different network, you would simply use a different connection profile that you have already set up, instead of manually reconfiguring the connection. If you do not specify a connection name, one is generated and assigned for you. The connection name can be the same as the device name as shown here, but keep in mind that the connection name refers to the profile and the device name refers to the actual device.

```
$ nmcli c s
NAME          UUID                                    TYPE            DEVICE
enp7s0        f7202f6d-fc66-4b81-8962-69b71202efc0    802-3-ethernet  enp7s0
```

For a DHCP connection, specify the profile name, connection type, and ifname. The following example creates an Ethernet connection with the profile name "my-wired."

```
nmcli con add con-name my-wired type ethernet ifname enp7s0
```

For a static connection add the IP (**ip4** or **ip6**) and gateway (**gw4** or **gw6**) options with their addresses.

```
nmcli con add con-name my-wired-static ifname enp7s0 type ethernet ip4 192.168.1.0/24 gw4 192.168.1.1
```

In most cases, the type is Ethernet (wired) or wifi (wireless). Check the **nmcli** man page for a list of other types, such as gsm, infiniband, vpn, vlan, wimax, and bridge.

You can also add a connection using the interactive editor. Use the **edit** instead of the **add** option, and specify the **con-name** (profile) and connection type.

```
nmcli con edit type ethernet con-name my-wired
```

To modify an existing connection, use the **modify** option. For an IP connection, the property that is changed is referenced as part of the IP settings, in this example, **ip4**. The IP properties include addresses, gateway, and method (ip4.addresses, ip4.gateway, and ip4.method).

```
nmcli con mod my-wired ip4.gateway 192.168.1.2
```

To add or remove a value for a property use the + and - signs as a prefix. To add a DNS server address you would use **+ip4.dns**. To remove one use **-ip4.dns**.

```
nmcli con mod my-wired +ip4.dns 192.168.1.5
```

You can also modify a connection using the interactive editor. Use the **edit** instead of the **modify** option with the connection name.

```
nmcli con edit enp7s0
```

You are then placed in the interactive editor with an **nmcli>** prompt and the settings you can change are listed. The **help** command lists available commands. Use the **describe** command to show property descriptions.

Use **print** to show the current value of a property and **set** to change its value. To see all the properties for a setting, use the **print** command and the setting name. Once you have made changes, use the **save** command to effect the changes.

```
print ipv4
print ipv4.dns
print connection
set ipv4.address 192.168.0.1
```

The **edit** option can also reference a profile using the **id** option. The Name field in the connection profile information is the same as the ID. Also, each profile is given a unique system UUID, which can also be used to reference the profile.

Once you are finished editing the connection, enter the **quit** command to leave the editor.

nmcli Wireless Connections

To see a list of all the available wifi connections in your area, you use the **wifi** option with the **device** object. You can further qualify it by interface (if you have more than one) by adding the **ifname** option, and by BSSID adding the **bssid** option.

```
nmcli device wifi
```

To connect to a new Wifi network, use the **wifi connect** option and the SSID. You can further specify a password, wep-key-type, key, ifname, bssid, name (profile name), and if it is private. If you do not provide a name (profile name), nmcli will generate one for you.

```
nmcli dev wifi connect surfturtle password mypass wep-key-type wpa ifname wlp6s0 name my-wireless1
```

To reconnect to a Wifi network for which you have previously set up a connection, use the **connection** object with the **up** command and the **id** option to specify the profile name.

```
nmcli connection up id my-wireless1
```

You can also add a new wireless connection using the **connection** object and the **wifi** type with the **ssid** option.

```
nmcli con add con-name my-wireless2 ifname wlp6s0 type wifi ssid ssidname
```

Then, to set the encryption type use the **modify** command to set the **sec.key-mgmt** property, and for the passphrase set the **wifi-sec.psk** property.

```
nmcli con mod my-wirless2 wifi-sec.key-mgmt wpa-psk
nmcli con modify my-wireless2 wifi-sec.psk mypassword
```

Dial-up PPP Modem Access: wvdial

For direct dial-up PPP modem connections, you can use the wvdial dialer, an intelligent dialer that, not only dials up an ISP service but also performs login operations, supplying your username and password. The wvdial tool runs on the command line using the **wvdial** command, and on the desktop with the GNOME PPP application. The wvdial program first loads its configuration from the **/etc/wvdial.conf** file. In this file, you can place modem and account information, including modem speed, ISP phone number, username, and password.

The **wvdial.conf** file is organized into sections, beginning with a section label enclosed in brackets. A section holds variables for different parameters that are assigned values, such as **username = chris**. The default section holds default values inherited by other sections, so you need not repeat them. Table 15-3 lists the wvdial variables.

You can use the **wvdialconf** utility to create a default **wvdial.conf** file, detecting your modem and setting default values for basic features automatically. You can then edit the **wvdial.conf** file and modify the Phone, Username, and Password entries entering your dial-up information. Remove the preceding semicolon (;) to unquote the entry. Any line beginning with a semicolon is ignored as a comment.

You can also create a named dialer. This is helpful if you have different location or services you log in to.

To start wvdial, enter the command **wvdial** in a terminal window, which then reads the connection configuration information from the **/etc/wvdial.conf** file; wvdial dials the location and initiates the PPP connection, providing your username and password when requested.

You can set up connection configurations for any number of connections in the **/etc/wvdial.conf** file. To select one, enter its label as an argument to the **wvdial** command, as shown here:

```
wvdial mylocation
```

Variable	Description
Inherits	Explicitly inherits from the specified section. By default, sections inherit from the [Dialer Defaults] section.
Modem	The device wvdial should use as your modem. The default is **/dev/modem**.
Baud	The speed at which wvdial communicates with your modem. The default is 57,600 baud.
Init1...Init9	Specifies the initialization strings to be used by your modem; wvdial can use up to 9. The default is "ATZ" for Init1.
Phone	The phone number you want wvdial to dial.
Area Code	Specifies the area code, if any.
Dial Prefix	Specifies any needed dialing prefix—for example, 70 to disable call waiting or 9 for an outside line.
Dial Command	Specifies the dial operation. The default is "ATDT".
Login	Specifies the username you use at your ISP.
Login Prompt	If your ISP has an unusual login prompt, you can specify it here.
Password	Specifies the password you use at your ISP.
Password Prompt	If your ISP has an unusual password prompt, you can specify it here.
Force Address	Specifies a static IP address to use (for ISPs that provide static IP addresses to users).
Auto Reconnect	If enabled, wvdial attempts to reestablish a connection automatically if you are randomly disconnected by the other side. This option is on by default.

Table 15-3: Variables for wvdial

Netplan

Netplan is used to configure and set up your network connections. The **/etc/netplan** folder holds network service and interface information for configuring your network device. The actual configuration file is generated when the system starts up and, for NetworkManager, is placed in the **/run/NetworkManager/system-connections** folder (for systemd-networkd it is placed in the **/var/run/systemd/network** folder). There is no fixed configuration file in the **/etc** folder. Instead a simple Netplan configuration file in the **/etc/netplan** folder is used to generate the network configuration file. The **/etc/netplan** files are written using YAML (YAML Ain't Markup Language) and have the extension **.yaml**. This method provides a level of abstraction that make configuration of different available network devices much more flexible. The default network service for the Ubuntu desktop is NetworkManager and for the Ubuntu server it is **networkd**. You can use networkd on the Ubuntu desktop, instead of NetworkManager if you want. You can find out more about Netplan at:

https://netplan.io

Detailed examples of Netplan configurations files can be found at:

/usr/share/doc/netplan/examples

These include examples for static, wireless, NetworkManager, dhcp, bridge, bonding, and vlans.

Netplan configuration file

The Netplan configuration files are located in the **/etc/netplan** folder. The Ubuntu Desktop version generates a Netplan configuration file for NetworkManager that is now located in **/lib/netplan/00-network-manager-all.yaml**. It is not to be modified. A copy is still placed in **/etc/netplan/01-network-manager-all.yaml**. NetworkManager is the default for the Ubuntu desktop. You can edit this file to add configuration for more devices, or you can add more configuration files, each of which will be read by Netplan and a corresponding runtime configuration file generated in the **/run/NetworkManager/system-connections** folder. As NetworkManager is designed to configure multiple devices, you only need the one Netplan configuration file. But for other network managers such as **systemd-network**, you could have files for different types of network devices such as ethernet and Wi-Fi, or a different file for each device. Configuration file names usually begin with a number, starting with **1-** for the default, though they can be any name. An easy way to create a new file is to copy the default or an example file from **/usr/share/doc/netplan/examples** and then edit it.

A Netplan configuration file is organized into keys consisting of upper level configuration definitions that apply to different types of devices such as ethernets, and lower level IDs that are used to configure devices. The file begins with the top-level **network:** key followed by the Netplan version, in this case, version 2. The **renderer:** ID specifies the network service to use. For the Ubuntu desktop this is **NetworkManager**. Ubuntu uses NetworkManager by default instead of systemd-networkd, which simplifies the default Netplan configuration file. The file holds only the renderer information, as NetworkManager handles all the details. You would use the Settings Network tab to configure your network.

/etc/netplan/00-network-manager-all.yaml

```
# Let NetworkManager manage all devices on this system
network:
  version: 2
  renderer: NetworkManager
```

For other types of connections such as Wi-Fi connections, wired profiles, and systemd-networkd, there are additional keys that are used. For a wired connection, the configuration type is **ethernets:** and for Wi-Fi the configuration type is **wifis:**. Under the configuration type the keys for the available network devices are listed. Under each device are the IDs used to configure it. In the case of a DHCP connection you usually only need one, **dhcp:** Other IDs such as **address:** for a static connection or **gateway:** for a gateway address could also be listed.

Additional configuration files for Wi-Fi connections and wired profiles are configured and managed by the Ubuntu Settings Wi-Fi and Network tabs. Settings saves the connection configuration in NetworkManager **.yaml** files in the **/etc/netplan** folder. These files should not be edited directly. They should be modified through the Settings Wi-Fi and Network tabs. The names for these connections consist of a number such as 90, **NM** for NetworkManager, and the UUID of the connection. The following is a name for the Wi-Fi connection.

```
90-NM-45c9495b-38c3-418f-9ce6-f0f70bf2f244.yaml
```

A copy of the file is shown here. The **match: name:** key references the wireless device, **wlp6s0**, instead of the wired device, **enp7s0**.

90-NM-45c9495b-38c3-418f-9ce6-f0f70bf2f244.yaml

```
network:
  version: 2
  wifis:
    NM-45c9495b-38c3-418f-9ce6-f0f70bf2f244:
      renderer: NetworkManager
      match:
        name: "wlp6s0"
      dhcp4: true
      dhcp6: true
      access-points:
        "surfturtle":
          auth:
            key-management: "psk"
            password: "Neptune102219&"
          networkmanager:
            uuid: "45c9495b-38c3-418f-9ce6-f0f70bf2f244"
            name: "surfturtle"
            passthrough:
              wifi-security.auth-alg: "open"
              ipv6.addr-gen-mode: "default"
              ipv6.ip6-privacy: "-1"
              proxy._: ""
      networkmanager:
        uuid: "45c9495b-38c3-418f-9ce6-f0f70bf2f244"
        name: "surfturtle"
```

Netplan configuration files for profiles are generated by the Settings Network tab. The netplan files for Profile-1 is shown here. The wired device is referenced, **enp7s0**.

90-NM-26145cf5-8c3e-4ba3-844a-164208293f9c.yaml

```
network:
  version: 2
  ethernets:
    NM-26145cf5-8c3e-4ba3-844a-164208293f9c:
      renderer: NetworkManager
      match:
        name: "enp7s0"
      dhcp4: true
      dhcp6: true
      wakeonlan: true
      networkmanager:
        uuid: "26145cf5-8c3e-4ba3-844a-164208293f9c"
        name: "Profile 1"
        passthrough:
          ethernet._: ""
          ipv6.addr-gen-mode: "default"
          ipv6.ip6-privacy: "-1"
          proxy._: ""
```

The run time configuration files for NetworkManager are in the **/run/NetworkManager/system-connections** folder and have names beginning with **netplan** and have the extension **.nmconnection**, such as **netplan-enp7s0.nmconnection** for a wired connection.

Configure a network with systemd-networkd

The systemd based network manager called **systemd-networkd** can currently be used for basic operations. You would use it as a small, fast, and simple alternative to a larger manager such as NetworkManager. The service, target, and socket files for systemd-networkd are located in the **/lib/systemd/system**, systemd-networkd.service and systemd-networkd.socket. Network resolvconf operations are handled with **systemd-resolved.service**. User configuration files for **systemd-networkd** are located in **/etc/systemd/network**.

In the **systemd-networkd.service** file several security features are enabled. A capability bounding set (CapabilityBoundingSet) lets you limit kernel capabilities to those specified. The man page for **capabilities** list the available capabilities. The CAP_NET capabilities limit the networkd service to network operations such as interface configuration, firewall administration, multicasting, sockets, broadcasting, and proxies. The CAP_SET capabilities allow for file and process GID and UIDs. The CAP_CHOWN, CAP_DAC_OVERRIDE, and CAP_FOWNER capabilities deal with bypassing permission checks for files. The CAP_SYS capabilities that provide system administrative capabilities are not included. In addition, the ProtectSystem option (**systemd.exec**) prevents the service from making any changes to the system (**/usr**, **/boot**, and **/etc** folders are read only for this service). The ProtectHome option makes the **/home**, **/root**, and **/run/user** folders inaccessible. WatchdogSec sets the watchdog timeout for the service. Check the **systemd.directives** man page for a list of all systemd directives.

```
ExecStart=!!/usr/lib/systemd/systemd-networkd
CapabilityBoundingSet=CAP_NET_ADMIN CAP_NET_BIND_SERVICE CAP_NET_BROADCAST
CAP_NET_RAW CAP_SETUID CAP_SETGID CAP_SETPCAP CAP_CHOWN CAP_DAC_OVERRIDE
CAP_FOWNER
ProtectSystem=strict
ProtectHome=yes
WatchdogSec=3min
```

The **systemd-networkd.socket** file sets **systemd.socket** options for buffer size (ReceiveBuffer), network link (ListenNetlink), passing credentials (PassCredentials). As a condition for starting the service, the CAP_NET_ADMIN capability needs to be set in the capability bounding set (ConditionCapability).

systemd-networkd.socket

```
[Unit]
Description=Network Service Netlink Socket
Documentation=man:systemd-networkd.service(8) man:rtnetlink(7)
ConditionCapability=CAP_NET_ADMIN
DefaultDependencies=no
Before=sockets.target shutdown.target
Conflicts=shutdown.target

[Socket]
ReceiveBuffer=128M
ListenNetlink=route 1361
PassPacketInfo=yes

[Install]
WantedBy=sockets.target
```

The **systemd-resolved.service** provides for the resolvconf operations (DNS server information). It has the same capabilities as **systemd-neworkd.service**, except for the network capabilities.

In addition, the **systemd-networkd-resolvconf-update.service** updates the DNS information. The **systemd-networkd-wait-online.service** delays activation of other services, until **systemd-networkd** service comes online.

The systemd-networkd Netplan configuration file

You have to create a Netplan configuration file for the systemd-networkd service. You could have files for different types of network devices such as ethernet and Wi-Fi, or a different file for each device. Configuration file names usually begin with a number, starting with **1-** for the default, though they can be any name.

You would then have to know how networking on your system is configured. For many systems, especially those using DHCP, this is a simple configuration, but for others, such as a static connection, it can be complex. For a system using a standard DHCP connection, as shown in this chapter, you can simply copy the **dhcp.yaml** file from the **/usr/share/doc/netplan/examples** folder to the **/etc/netplan** folder. Prefix the file name with a number, such as **2-**. You can leave the **01-network-manager-all.yaml** file in **/etc/netplan** in case you should want to switch back to using NetworkManager

```
cd /usr/share/doc/netplan/examples
sudo cp dhcp.yaml /etc/netplan/02-dhcp.yaml
```

If you do not know it already, find out the name of your Ethernet device with **ip link** command. Then use a text editor like **nano** to edit the **02-dhcp.yaml** and replace the name of ethernet device, **enp3s0**, with the name of the one on your system. You can use the **ifconfig** command to find the name or your device. Be sure to use the **sudo** command to start the editor.

```
cd /etc/netplan
sudo nano 02-dhcp.yaml
```

A Netplan configuration file is organized into keys consisting of upper level configuration definitions that apply to different types of devices such as ethernets, and lower level IDs that are used to configure devices. The file begins with the top-level **network:** key followed by the Netplan version, in this case, version 2. The **renderer:** ID specifies the network service to use. For the Ubuntu server this is the netplan default, **networkd**. For a wired connection, the configuration type is **ethernets:**, as shown in this example. Under **ethernets:** the keys for the available network devices are listed. Under each device are the IDs used to configure it. In the case of a DHCP connection you usually only need one, **dhcp:** Other IDs such as **address:** for a static connection or **gateway:** for a gateway address could also be listed. The final would look something like the following.

/etc/netplan/02-dhcp.yaml

```
network:
  version: 2
  renderer: networkd
  ethernets:
    enp7s0:
      dhcp4: true
```

The runtime file generated by Netplan for network configuration will be located in **/var/run/systemd/network** and will have a name that includes "netplan" and the network device name, such as **10-netplan-enp7s0.network**. This file is generated automatically at startup. If you have edited the Netplan configuration file or added a new one, and do not wish to restart your system, you can use the Netplan **generate** command to create the run time configuration file directly, and then use the **apply** command to have Netplan apply that configuration to your network connections.

```
sudo netplan generate
sudo netplan apply
```

You then have to shut down and disable NetworkManager. The service script for managing NetworkManager is **network-manager**.

```
sudo systemctl stop network-manager
sudo systemctl disable network-manager
```

Then enable and start **systemd-networkd**.

```
sudo systemctl enable systemd-networkd
sudo systemctl start systemd-networkd
```

Use the **networkctl status** command to check on the status of your network connections.

```
networkctl status
```

For information about a specific device add the device name to the status command.

```
networkctl status enp7s0
```

Netplan wireless configuration for systemd-networkd

For systemd-networkd wireless devices you have to edit your Netplan configuration file to add your wireless device name, the wireless network you want to access, and the password for that network. Instead of editing the default file directly, you can copy the **02-dhcp.yaml** file with the 2 changed to 3 and give it a name such as **03-wireless.yaml**. Netplan will read any **yaml** file in the **/etc/netplan** folder. You can find an example of a wireless configuration file at **/usr/share/doc/netplan/examples**, but it is for the network that does not support dhcp and is more complicated.

```
cd /etc/netplan
sudo cp 2-dhcp.yaml 03-wireless.yaml
```

Then edit the file to add keys for Wi-Fi, accesspoints, the SSID, and the password.

```
sudo nano 3-wireless.yaml
```

An example of a wireless Netplan configuration is shown below. Instead of the **ethernets:** definition you use the **wifis:** definition. This is followed by a key consisting of the wireless device name, such as **wlp6s0:**. Below that key is the **dhcp4:** ID and the **accesspoints:** ID, used to configure the Wi-Fi device. Under the **accesspoints:** ID you add an ID consisting of the SSID of the wireless network you want to connect to (the wireless network's name). The SSID must be within quotes. Under this ID you add the **password:** ID and the password for accessing that wireless network. The password must be within quotes.

/etc/netplan/03-wireless.yaml

```
network:
  version: 2
  renderer: networkd
  wifis:
    wlp6s0:
      dhcp4: true
      accesspoints:
        "SSID":
          password: "password"
```

Netplan generates a wireless configuration file at startup in **/run/netplan**. A wireless file will have the name of the device added along with the name of wireless network (SSID), such as **netplan-wlp6s0-surfturtle**.

This file is then used by the **wpa_supplicant@service** to submit the SSID and password to **wpa_supplicant**, which then accesses the wireless network. The **wpa_supplicant@.service** file is shown here.

wpa_supplicant@.service

```
[Unit]
Description=WPA supplicant daemon (interface specific version)
Requires=sys-subsystem-net-devices-%i.device
After=sys-subsystem-net-devices-%i.device
Before=network.target
Wants=network.target

[Service]
Type=simple
ExecStart=/sbin/wpa_supplicant -c /etc/wpa_supplicant/wpa_supplicant-%I.conf -i%I
ExecReload=/bin/kill -HUP $MAINPID

[Install]
WantedBy=multi-user.target
```

If you reboot, the wireless netplan file will be read and your wireless device configured. To configure your device without rebooting, you can use the Netplan **generate** command to create the run time configuration file directly (**/var/run/systemd/network**), and then use the **apply** command to have Netplan apply that configuration to your network connection.

```
sudo netplan generate
sudo netplan apply
```

Then restart systemd-networkd.

```
sudo systemctl restart systemd-networkd
```

You can use the **networkctl** command to see if your wireless device has been properly configured and is connected. The **networkctl** command works only for systemd-networkd..

```
$ networkctl
IDX LINK          TYPE        OPERATIONAL  SETUP
  1 lo            loopback    carrier      unmanaged
  2 enp7s0        ether       routable     configured
  3 wlp6s0        wlan        routable     configured

3 links listed.
```

Switching between systemd-networkd and network-manager

Your original Netplan configuration file for NetworkManager, **01-network-manager-all.yaml**, should still be in your **/etc/netplan** folder.

To change from systemd-networkd back to NetworkManager, first stop and disable systemd-networkd with the **systemctl** command.

```
sudo systemctl stop systemd-networkd
sudo systemctl disable systemd-networkd
```

Then enable and start NetworkManager. Use the service name for NetworkManager, **network-manager**. Also, remove or move the systemd-networkd netplan file in the **/etc/netplan** folder so that it is not read. You could also just rename the extension.

```
sudo systemctl enable network-manager
sudo systemctl start network-manager
sudo mv /etc/netplan/netplan/02-dhcp.yaml /home
```

You can use the **status** command for **systemctl** to see if your network device is active or inactive.

```
systemctl status systemd-networkd
systemctl status network-manager
```

To change back to systemd-networkd, disable NetworkManager and enable systemd-networkd. Also add your systemd-networkd netplan file back to the **/etc/netplan** folder.

```
sudo systemctl stop network-manager
sudo systemctl disable network-manager
sudo systemctl enable systemd-networkd
sudo systemctl start systemd-networkd
```

If your NetworkManager file is, for some reason, missing from the **/etc/netplan** folder, you can just copy the **network_manager.yaml** file from the **netplan.io** doc folder, **/usr/share/doc/netplan/examples**.

```
cd /usr/share/doc/netplan/examples
sudo cp network_manager.yaml   /etc/netplan/1-network-manager-all.yaml
```

Then use the **netplan** command with the **apply** option to generate a new network configuration file.

```
sudo netplan generate
sudo netplan apply
```

Firewalls

You can choose from several different popular firewall management tools. Ubuntu provides a firewall management tool called the Uncomplicated Firewall (ufw), which is a frontend for IPtables. You can also choose to use other popular management tools like FirewallD or Fwbuilder. Both ufw and FirewallD are covered in this chapter. Search Synaptic Package Manager for "firewall" to see a complete listing.

IPtables has been replaced by nftables. Whereas IPtables works like an interpreter, processing each individual rule one at a time, nftables operates more like a programming language, able to handle many rules at once on incoming packets. On Ubuntu 24.04, the **/sbin/iptables** command is a link to the **/etc/alternatives/iptables** command, which, in turn, is a link to the **/usr/sbin/iptables-nft**, which, in turn, is a link to **xtables-nft-multi** command. The **/usr/sbin/xtables-nft-multi** command implements the **iptables-nft** commands such as **iptables-nft**, **iptables-nft-save**, and **iptables-nft-restore**. The commands **/sbin/iptables-save** and **/sbin/iptables-restore** are links to **/etc/alternatives/iptables-save** and **/etc/alternative/iptables-restore**, which are links to **/sbin/iptables-nft-save** and **/sbin/iptables-nft-restore**, both of which are links to **xtables-nft-multi**. The **xtables-nft-multi** command reads IPtables rules and convert them to nftables format using the **nft_compat** module. Though the ufw frontend manages IPtables rules, these rules are converted and used by nftables. FirewallD, on the other hand, operates as a frontend for nftables directly. Also, if you have to add rules directly to your firewall and need to convert from IPtables to nftables, you can use the **iptables-translate** command. The **iptables-**

translate command takes as its argument an IPtables rule and generates the nftables equivalent. You can find out more about nftables at: **https://wiki.nftables.org/**.

Important Firewall Ports

Commonly used services like Linux and Windows file sharing (Samba), FTP servers, BitTorrent, and Secure SHell remote access, use certain network connection ports on your system (see Table 15-4). A default firewall configuration will block these ports. You have to configure your firewall to allow access to the ports these services use before the services will work.

For example, to access a Windows share, you not only have to have the Samba service running, but also have to configure your firewall to allow access on ports 135, 137, 138, and 445 (the ports Samba services use to connect to Windows systems), and port 5353 used for multicast DNS discovery. Most can be selected easily as preconfigured items in firewall configuration tools, like Gufw and FirewallD. Some, though, may not be listed.

Port number	Service
135,137,138,and 445	Samba ports 135 and 445 use the TCP Protocol, and 137 and 138 use the UDP protocol.
139	Netbios-ssn
22	Secure SHell, ssh
2049	NFS, Linux and Unix shares
631	IPP, Internet Printing Protocol, access to remote Linux/Unix printers
21	FTP
25	SMTP, forward mail
110	POP3, receive mail
143	IMAP, receive mail
5353	multicast DNS discovery service (mdns), Zeroconf

Table 15-4: Service ports

Setting up a firewall with ufw

The Uncomplicated Firewall, ufw, is the supported firewall application for Ubuntu. It provides a simple firewall that can be managed with the Gufw desktop interface or with **ufw** commands. ufw uses the IPtables format to define rules and run the firewall. The ufw application is just a management interface for IPtables rules. The IPtables rule files are held in the **/etc/ufw** directory. Default IPtables rules are kept in **before** and **after** files, with added rules in user files. Firewall configuration for certain packages will be placed in the **/usr/share/ufw.d** directory. Keep in mind, that these IPtable rules are automatically converted for use by nftables. nftables is the actual firewall backend for Ubuntu 24.04. You can find out more about ufw at the Ubuntu Firewall site at **https://wiki.ubuntu.com/UncomplicatedFirewall** and at the Ubuntu firewall section in the Ubuntu Server Guide at **https://ubuntu.com/server/docs**. The Server Guide also shows information on how to implement IP Masquerading on ufw.

Gufw

Gufw provides an easy to use desktop interface for managing your ufw firewall. A simple interface lets you add rules, both custom and standard. You can install Gufw from the App Center as a Debian packages named Firewall Configuration (Universe repository, **gufw** package). On the Applications overview, search on firewall and choose Firewall Configuration.

Gufw will initially open with the firewall disabled, with no ports configured. The application is locked initially. The Status button is set to off, and the shield image will be gray. To enable the firewall, click the left side of the Status button, setting the status to on. The shield image will be colored and the firewall rules will be listed. Figure 15-21 shows the firewall enabled and several rules listed. Rules for both IPv4 and IPv6 (**v6**) network protocols are listed.

The Gufw dialog has a Firewall section and three tabs: Rules, Report, and Log. The Firewall section has a Status button for turning the firewall on or off. There is a Profile menu for Home, Office, and Public configurations. The Incoming and Outgoing drop down menus are for setting the default firewall rules. Available options are Deny, Reject, or Allow, and are applied to incoming and outgoing traffic, respectively. By default, incoming traffic is denied (Deny), and outgoing traffic is allowed (Allow). Rules you specified in the Rules tab will make exceptions, allowing only certain traffic in or out. Should you select the Allow option, the firewall accepts all incoming traffic. In this case you should set up rules to deny access to some traffic, otherwise, the firewall becomes ineffective, allowing access to all traffic. The Report tab lists active services and ports such as the Samba server on port 139. The Log tab list firewall notices. You can copy notices, as well as delete a log. The Home tab provides basic help on how to use Gufw.

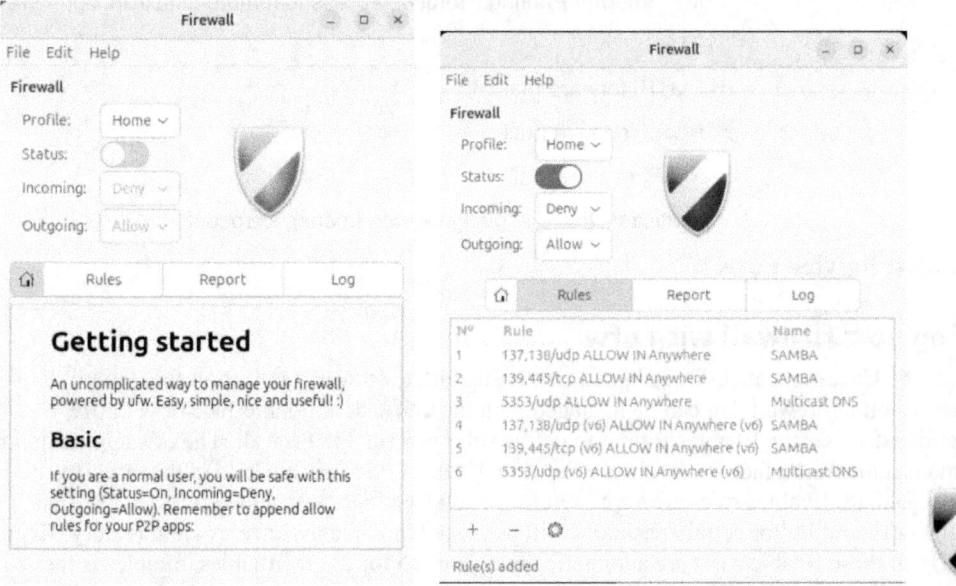

Figure 15-21: Gufw

To add a rule, click the Rules tab, and then click the plus button (+) on the lower left corner of the Rules tab to open the "Add a Firewall Rule" dialog, which has three tabs for managing rules: Preconfigured, Simple, and Advanced. The Preconfigured tab provides five menus: the first for the policy (Allow, Deny, Reject, and Limit), the second for the traffic direction (In or Out), the third for the category of the application and the fourth for a subcategory, and the fifth for the particular application or service for the rule. The list of possible applications is extensive. You can narrow the list down by using the Category and Subcategory menus. The main categories are Audio video, Games, Network, Office, and System. The Network category with the Services subcategory lists most network services like SSH, Samba, and FTP. You could also simply use the search box (Application Filter) to search for a service.

If there is a security issue with the rule, a warning is displayed. Should you need to modify the default rule for an application, you can click on the arrow button to the right of the search box to open the Advanced tab for that rule.

Click the Add button to add the rule. Once added, a port entry for the rule appears in the Rules section. In Figure 15-22 the Samba service has been selected and then added, showing up in the Rules section as "137,138/udp ALLOW IN Anywhere."

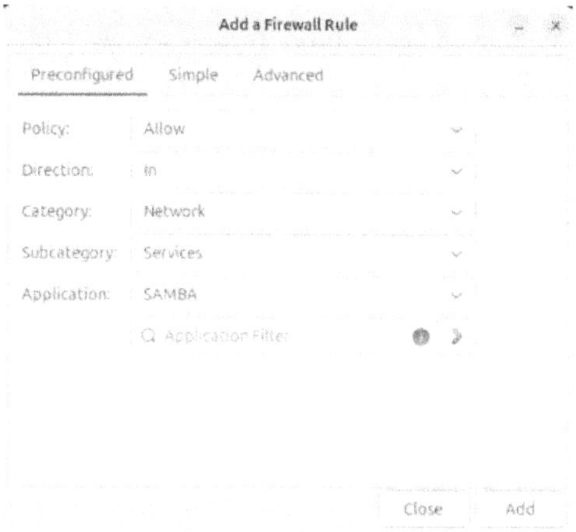

Figure 15-22: Gufw Preconfigured rules

Applications and services can also be blocked. To prevent access by the FTP service, you would first select Deny as the Policy, then Services as the Category, and then FTP as the Application.

Besides Allow and Deny, you can also choose a Limit option. The Limit option will enable connection rate limiting, restricting connections to no more than 6 every 30 seconds for a given port. This is meant to protect against brute force attacks.

Should there be no preconfigured entry, you can use the Simple tab to allow access to a port (see Figure 15-23). The first menu is for the rule (Allow, Deny, Reject, and Limit), and the second for the protocol (TCP, UDP, or both). In the Port text box, you enter the port number.

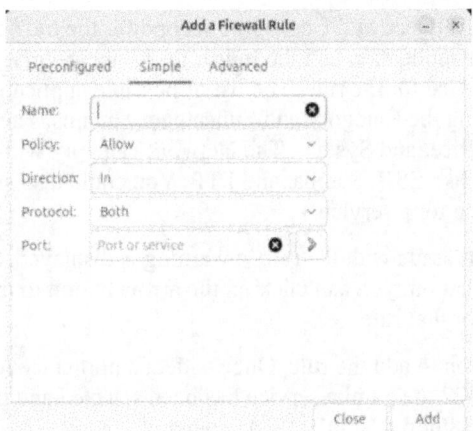

Figure 15-23: Gufw Simple rules

On the Advanced tab, you can enter more complex rules. You can set up allow or deny rules for tcp or udp protocols, and specify the incoming and outgoing host (ip) and port (see Figure 15-24).

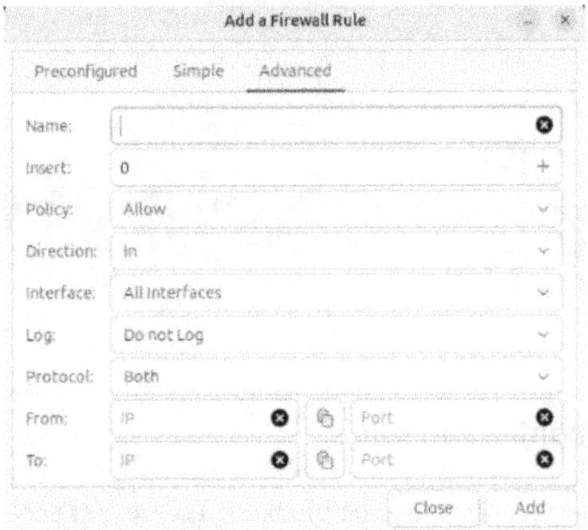

Figure 15-24: Gufw Advanced rules

If you decide to remove a rule, select it in the Rules section and then click the minus button on the lower left corner (-). To remove several rules, click and press Shift-click or use Ctrl-click to select a collection of rules, and then click the minus button.

You can edit any rule by selecting it and clicking the edit button (gear image) to open an "Update a Firewall Rule" dialog (see Figure 15-25). For a default or simple rule, you can only change a few options, but you can turn on logging.

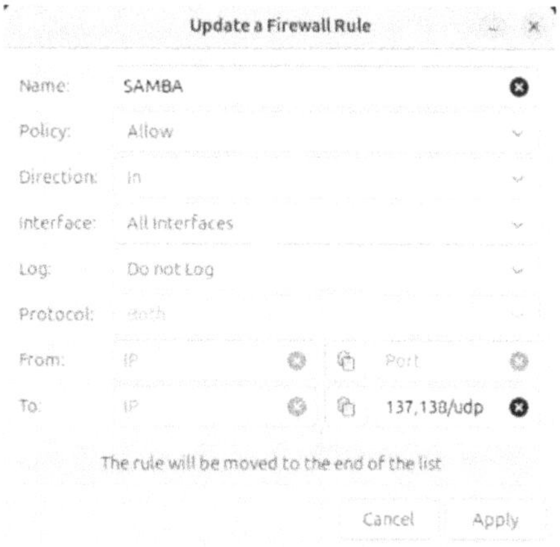

Figure 15-25: Gufw edit a rule

You can also create rules for detected active ports. Click the Report tab and then select a port and click on the plus button at the bottom of the tab. An "Add a Firewall Rule" dialog opens to the Advanced tab with the name of the service active on that port and the port number (see Figure 15-26). You can change any of the options. The port number is already entered.

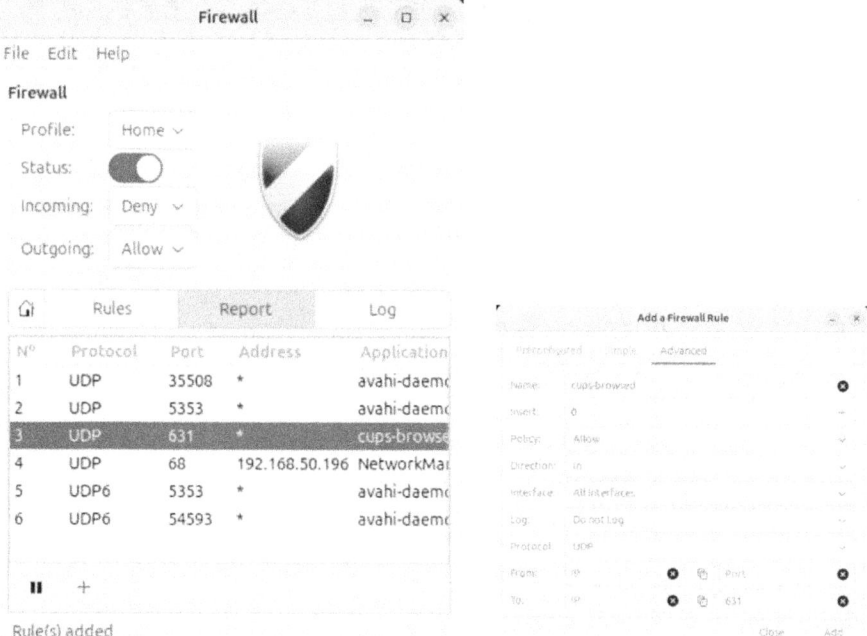

Figure 15-26: Gufw create a rule for an active port

Should you want to you can pause any activity on a port by selecting it and clicking the pause button at the bottom of the tab. The button will change to a play button. Select the port and click the play button to activate the port.

ufw commands

You can also manage your ufw firewall using **ufw** commands entered on a command line in a Terminal window. A **ufw** command requires administrative access and must be run with the **sudo** command. To check the current firewall status, listing those services allowed or blocked, use the **status** command.

```
sudo ufw status
```

If the firewall is not enabled, you first will have to enable it with the **enable** command.

```
sudo ufw enable
```

You can restart the firewall, reloading your rules, using the **systemctl** command with the **restart** option.

```
sudo systemctl restart ufw
```

You can add rules using **allow** and **deny** rules and their options as listed in Table 15-5. To allow a service, specify the **allow** rule and the service name. This is the name for the service listed in the **/etc/services** file. For connection rate limiting, use the **limit** option in place of **allow**. The following allows the ftp service.

```
sudo ufw allow ftp
```

Commands	Description
enable | disable	Turn the firewall on or off
status	Display status along with services allowed or denied.
logging on | off	Turn logging on or off
default allow | deny	Set the default policy, allow is open, whereas deny is restrictive
allow *service*	Allow access by a service. Services are defined in **/etc/services**, which specify the ports for that service.
allow *port /protocol*	Allow access on a particular port using specified protocol.
deny *service*	Deny access by a service
delete *rule*	Delete an installed rule, use allow, deny, or limit and include rule specifics.
proto *protocol*	Specify protocol in allow, deny, or limit rule
from *address*	Specify source address in allow, deny, or limit rule
to *address*	Specify destination address in allow, deny, or limit rule
port *port*	Specify port in allow, deny, or limit rule for from and to address

Table 15-5: UFW firewall operations

If the service you want is not listed in **/etc/services**, and you know the port and protocol it uses, you can specify the port and protocol directly. For example, the Samba service uses port 445 and protocol tcp (among others, see Table 15-4).

```
sudo ufw allow 445/tcp
```

The status operation shows what services the firewall rules allow.

```
sudo ufw status
To                      Action          From
21:tcp                  ALLOW           Anywhere
21:udp                  ALLOW           Anywhere
139,445:tcp             ALLOW           Anywhere
```

To remove a rule, prefix it with the **delete** command.

```
sudo ufw delete allow 445/tcp
```

More detailed rules can be specified using address, port, and protocol commands. These are very similar to the actual IPtables commands. Packets to and from particular networks, hosts, and ports can be controlled. The following denies ssh access (port 22) from host 192.168.03.

```
sudo ufw deny proto tcp from 192.168.03 to any port 22
```

ufw rule files

The rules you add are placed in the **/etc/ufw/user.rules** file as IPtables rules. The ufw program is just a front end for **iptables-restore**, which will read this file and set up the firewall using **iptables** commands. **ufw** will also have **iptables-restore** read the **before.rules** and **after.rules** files in the /etc/ufw folder. These files are considered administrative files that include needed supporting rules for your IPtables firewall. Administrators can add their own IPtables rules to these files for system specific features like IP Masquerading. The **before.rules** file will specify a table with the * symbol, as in ***filter** for the netfilter table. For the NAT table, you would use ***nat**. At the end of each table segment, a COMMIT command is needed to instruct ufw to apply the rules. Rules use **-A** for allow and **-D** for deny, assuming the **iptables** command.

Default settings for ufw are placed in **/etc/default/ufw**. Here you will find the default INPUT, OUTPUT, and FORWARD policies specified by setting associated variables, like DEFAULT_INPUT_POLICY for INPUT and DEFAULT_OUTPUT_POLICY for OUTPUT. The DEFAULT_INPUT_POLICY variable is set to DROP, making DROP the default policy for the INPUT rule. The DEFAULT_OUTPUT_POLICY variable is set to ACCEPT, and the DEFAULT_FORWARD_POLICY variable is set to DROP. To allow IP Masquerading, DEFAULT_FORWARD_POLICY would have to be set to ACCEPT. These entries set default policies only. Any user rules you have set up would take precedence.

FirewallD and firewall-config

Though not supported by Ubuntu, you can use the FirewallD dynamic firewall daemon to set up a firewall. FirewallD operates as a frontend for nftables, directly. To configure FirewallD you use the **firewalld-config** desktop interface. You can also use the **firewalld-cmd** command from the command line. You can install **firewalld-config** as a Debian package named Firewall on the App Center. Both the FirewallD daemon and the firewalld-config packages are installed. To set up your firewall, run **firewall-config** (the Firewall icon in the Applications overview) (see Figure 15-27).

Part 4: Administration

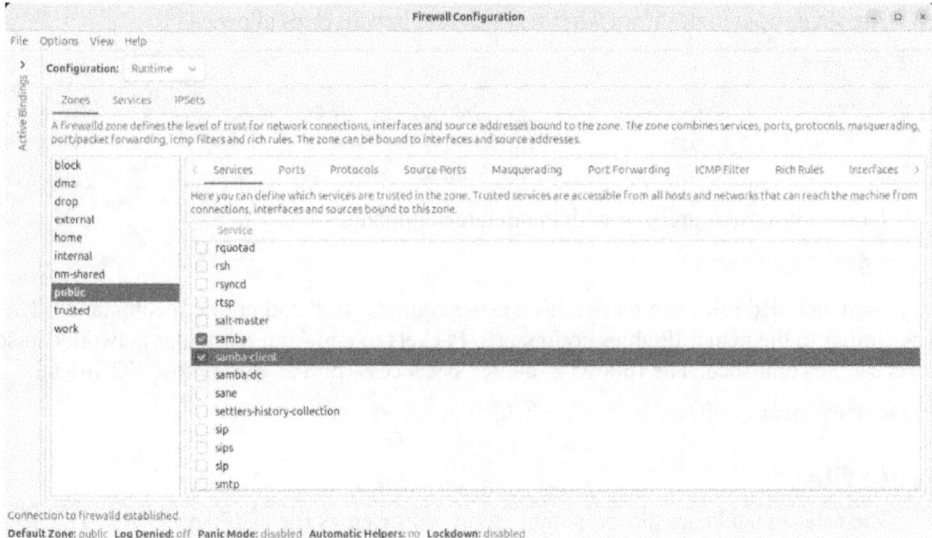

Figure 15-27: Firewall (firewall-config, FirewallD) - Runtime Configuration

You can also start and stop the FirewallD daemon in a terminal window with the following command.

```
sudo systemctl start firewalld
sudo systemctl stop firewalld
```

With **firewall-config,** you can configure either a Runtime or Permanent configuration. Select one from the Configuration menu. The Runtime configuration shows your current runtime set up, whereas a Permanent configuration does not take effect until you reload or restart. If you wish to edit your zones and services, you need to choose the Permanent Configuration (see Figure 15-28). This view displays a zone toolbar for editing a zone at the bottom of the zone scroll box, and an Edit Services button on the Services tab for editing service protocols, ports, and destination addresses.

Additional tabs can be displayed from the View menu for configuring ICMP types, and for adding firewall rules directly (Direct Configuration).

From the Options menu, you can reload your saved firewall.

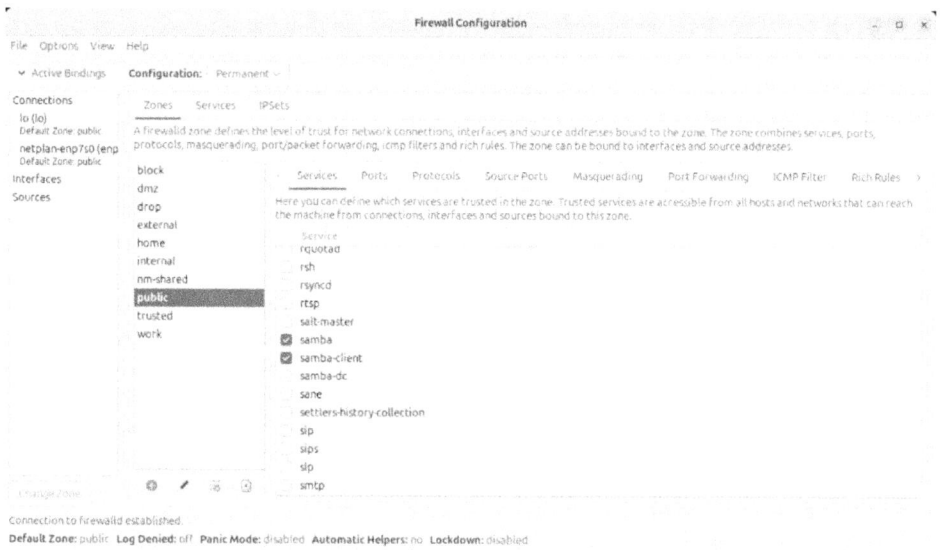

Figure 15-28: Permanent Configuration

A firewall configuration is set up for a given zone, such as a home, work, internal, external, or public zone. Zones provide an added level of protection by the firewall. They divide the network protected by the Firewall into separate segments, which can only communicate as permitted by the firewall. In effect, zones separate one part of your network from another. Each zone has its own configuration. Zones are listed in the Zone scroll box on the left side of the firewall-config window. Select the one you want to configure. The firewall-config window opens to the default zone, Public. You can choose the default zone from the System Default Zone dialog (see Figure 15-29), which you open from the Options menu as "Change Default Zone."

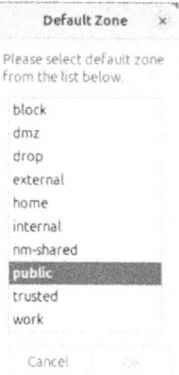

Figure 15-29: Default Zone

To the left of the Zones tab is the Active Bindings section, which lists the network connections, interfaces, and sources on your system. For each active connection the zone bound to it is listed, such as the public zone bound to the wired connection in Figure 15-28. To change the zone bound to a connection you select the entry and click the Change Zone button at the bottom of the Active Binding section. This open a Select zone dialog where you can choose a different zone to be bound to a connection. You can choose from any of the zones in the zones tab. You can also change a connection binding from the Options menu by choosing "Change Zones of Connections."

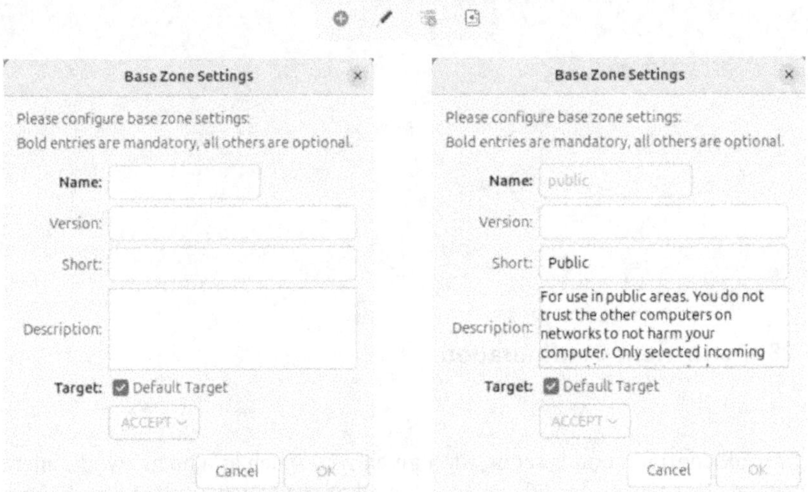

Figure 15-30: Base Zone Settings

If you choose Permanent Configuration from the Current View Menu, a toolbar for zones is displayed below the Zone scroll box. The plus button lets you add a zone and the minus button removes a zone. The pencil button lets you edit a zone. The add and edit buttons open the Base Zone Settings dialog, where you enter or edit the zone name, version, description, and the target (see Figure 15-30). The default target is ACCEPT. Other options are REJECT and DROP. The Load Zone Defaults button (yellow arrow) loads default settings, removing any changes you have made.

Each zone, in turn, can have one or more network connections. From the Options menu choose "Change Zones of Connections" to select a network connection for the zone.

For a given zone you can configure services, ports, masquerading, port forwarding, and ICMP filter. A Linux system is often used to run servers for a network. If you are creating a strong firewall but still want to run a service such as a Web server, an FTP server, Samba desktop browsing, or SSH encrypted connections, you must specify them in the Services tab. Samba desktop browsing lets you access your Samba shares, like remote Windows file systems, from your Linux desktop.

For a selected service, you can specify service settings such as ports and protocols it uses, any modules, and specific network addresses. Default settings are already set up for you such as port 139 for Samba, using the TCP protocol. To modify the settings for a service, click the Services tab on the Firewall Configuration window to list your services (see Figure 15-31). Choose the service you want to edit from the Service scroll box at the left. For a given service you can then use the Ports, Protocols, Source Port, Modules, and Destination tabs to specify ports, protocols, modules, and addresses. On the Ports tab, click the Add button to open the Port and Protocol dialog where you can add a port or port range, and choose a protocol from the Protocol menu (see Figure 15-32). On the Destination tab, you can enter an IPv4 or IPv6 destination address for the service.

Figure 15-31: Service Settings

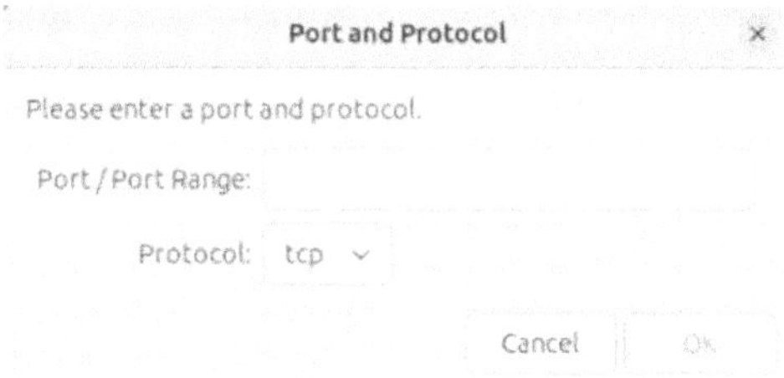

Figure 15-32: Service Protocols and Ports

On the Zones tab, the Ports tab lets you specify ports that you may want opened for certain services, like BitTorrent. Click the Add button to open a dialog where you can select the port number along with the protocol to control (tcp or udp), or enter a specific port number or range.

If your system is being used as a gateway to the Internet for your local network, you can implement masquerading to hide your local hosts from outside access from the Internet. This also requires IP forwarding which is automatically enabled when you choose masquerading. Local hosts will still be able to access the Internet, but they will masquerade as your gateway system. You would select for masquerading, the interface that is connected to the Internet. Masquerading is available only for IPv4 networks, not IPv6 networks.

The Port Forwarding tab lets you set up port forwarding, channeling transmissions from one port to another, or to a different port on another system. Click the Add button to add a port, specifying its protocol and destination (see Figure 15-33).

654 Part 4: Administration

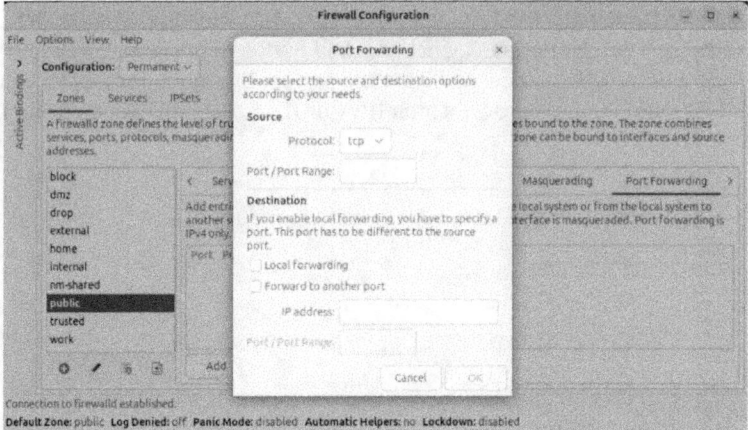

Figure 15-33: Port Forwarding

The ICMP Filters tab allows you to block ICMP messages. By default, all ICMP messages are allowed. Blocking ICMP messages makes for a more secure system. Certain types of ICMP messages are often blocked as they can be used to infiltrate or overload a system, such as the ping and pong ICMP messages (see Figure 15-34).

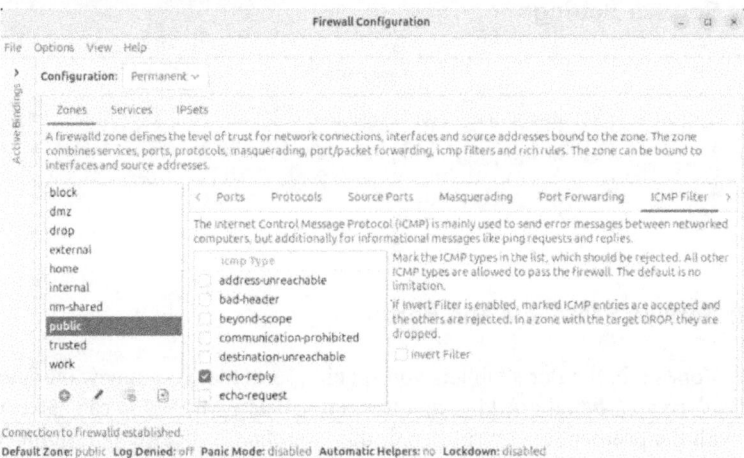

Figure 15-34: ICMP Filters

If you have specific firewall rules to add, use the Direct Configuration tab (displayed from the View | Direct Configuration menu).

GNOME Nettool

The GNOME Nettool utility (**gnome-nettool**) provides a GNOME interface for network information tools like the ping and traceroute operations as well as Finger, Whois, and Lookup for querying users and hosts on the network (see Figure 15-35). You can install it from the Ubuntu App Center as a Debian package named Network Tools. Nettool is then accessible from the

Applications overview as Network Tools. The first tab, Devices, describes your connected network devices, including configuration and transmission information about each device, such as the hardware address and bytes transmitted. Both IPv4 and IPv6 host IP addresses are listed.

You can use the ping, finger, lookup, whois, and traceroute operations to find out status information about systems and users on your network. The ping operation is used to check if a remote system is up and running. You use finger to find out information about other users on your network, seeing if they are logged in or if they have received mail. The traceroute tool can be used to track the sequence of computer networks and systems your message passed through on its way to you. Whois will provide domain name information about a particular domain, and Lookup will provide both domain name and IP addresses. Netstat shows your network routing (addresses used) and active service (open ports and the protocols they use). Port Scan lists the ports and services they use on a given connection (address).

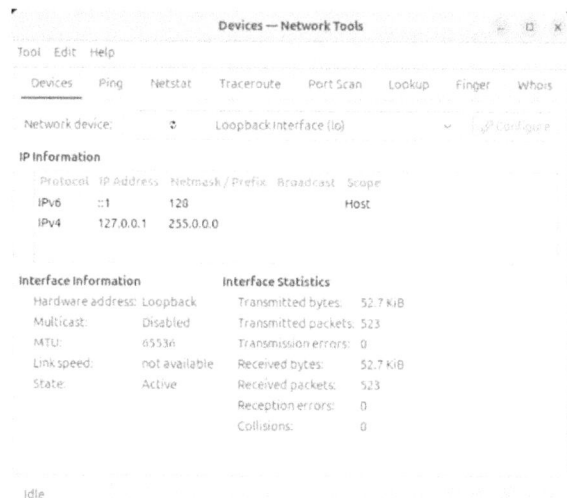

Figure 15-35: Gnome network tool

Predictable and unpredictable network device names

Network devices now use a predictable naming method that differs from the older naming method. Names are generated based on the specific device referencing the network device type, its hardware connection and slot, and even its function. The traditional network device names used the **eth** prefix with the number of the device for an Ethernet network device. The name **eth0** referred to the first Ethernet connection on your computer. This naming method was considered unpredictable as it did not accurately reference the actual Ethernet device. The old system relied on probing the network driver at boot, and if your system had several Ethernet connections, the names could end up being switched, depending you how the startup proceeded. With systemd udev version 197, the naming changed to a predictable method that specifies a particular device. The predictable method references the actual hardware connection on your system.

Name	Description
en	Ethernet
sl	serial line IP (slip)
wl	wlan, wireless local area network
ww	wwan, wireless wide area network (mobile broadband)
p	pci geographical location (pci-e slot)
s	hotplug slot index number
o	onboard cards
f	function (used for cards with more than one port)
u	USB port
i	USB port interface

Table 15-6: Network Interface Device Naming

The name used to reference a predictable device name connection has a prefix for the type of device followed by several qualifiers such as the type of hardware, the slot used, and the function number. Instead of the older unpredictable names like **eth0**, the first Ethernet device is referenced by a name like **enp7s0**. The interface name **enp7s0** references an Ethernet (en) connection, at pci slot 7 (p7) with the hotplug slot index number 0 (s0). **wlp6s0** is a wireless (wl) connection, at pci slot 6 (p6) with the hotplug slot index number 0 (s0). **virvb0** is a virtual (vir) bridge network (vb) interface. Table 15-6 lists predictable naming prefixes. Unlike the older unpredictable names, the predictable names will most likely be different for each computer. Predictable network names, along with alternatives, are discussed at:

https://www.freedesktop.org/wiki/Software/systemd/PredictableNetworkInterfaceNames/

The naming is carried out by the kernel and is describe in the comment section of the kernel source's **systemd/src/udev/udev-bultin-net_id.c** file.

Network device path names

The folder **/sys/devices** lists all your devices in subfolders, including your network devices. The path to the devices progresses through subfolders named for the busses connecting the device. To quickly find the full path name, you can us the **/sys/class** folder instead. For network devices use **/sys/class/net**. Then use the **ls -l** command to list the network devices with their links to the full pathname in the **/sys/devices** folder (the **../..** path references a cd change up two folders (class/net) to the **/sys** folder).

```
$ cd /sys/class/net
$ ls
enp7s0   lo   wlp6s0
$ ls -l
total 0
lrwxrwxrwx 1 root root 0 Feb 19 12:27 enp7s0 ->
../../devices/pci0000:00/0000:00:1c.3/0000:07:00.0/net/enp7s0
lrwxrwxrwx 1 root root 0 Feb 19 12:27 lo -> ../../devices/virtual/net/lo
lrwxrwxrwx 1 root root 0 Feb 19 12:28 wlp6s0 ->
../../devices/pci0000:00/0000:00:1c.2/0000:06:00.0/net/wlp6s0
```

So the full path name in the **/sys/devices** folder for **enp7s0** is:

/sys/devices/pci0000:00/0000:00:1c.3/0000:07:00.0/net/enp7s0

You can find the pci bus slot used with the **lspci** command. This command lists all your pci connected devices. In this example, the pci bus slot used 7, which is why the pci part of the name **enp7s0** is **p7**. The **s** part refers to a hotplug slot, in this example **s0**.

```
$ lspci
06:00.0 Network controller: Qualcomm Atheros QCA9565 / AR9565 Wireless Network
Adapter (rev 01)
07:00.0 Ethernet controller: Realtek Semiconductor Co., Ltd. RTL8101/2/6E PCI
Express Fast/Gigabit Ethernet controller (rev 07)
```

Devices have certain properties defined by udev, which manages all devices. Some operations, such as systemd link files, make use these properties. The ID_PATH, ID_NET_NAME_MAC, and INTERFACE properties can be used to identify a device to udev. To display these properties, you use the **udevadm** command to query the udev database. With the **info** and **-e** options, properties of all active devices are displayed. You can pipe (|) this output to a **grep** command to display only those properties for a given device. In the following example, the properties for the **enp7s0** device are listed. Preceding the properties for a given device is a line, beginning (^) with a "P" and ending with the device name. The **.*** matching characters match all other intervening characters on that line, **^P.*enp7s0**. The **-A** option displays the specified number of additional lines after that match, **-A 22**.

```
$ udevadm info -e | grep -A 22 ^P.*enp7s0
P: /devices/pci0000:00/0000:00:1c.3/0000:07:00.0/net/enp7s0
E: DEVPATH=/devices/pci0000:00/0000:00:1c.3/0000:07:00.0/net/enp7s0
E: ID_BUS=pci
E: ID_MM_CANDIDATE=1
E: ID_MODEL_FROM_DATABASE=RTL8101/2/6E PCI Express Fast/Gigabit Ethernet
controller
E: ID_MODEL_ID=0x8136
E: ID_NET_DRIVER=r8169
E: ID_NET_LINK_FILE=/lib/systemd/network/99-default.link
E: ID_NET_NAME_MAC=enx74e6e20ec729
E: ID_NET_NAME_PATH=enp7s0
E: ID_OUI_FROM_DATABASE=Dell Inc.
E: ID_PATH=pci-0000:07:00.0
E: ID_PATH_TAG=pci-0000_07_00_0
E: ID_PCI_CLASS_FROM_DATABASE=Network controller
E: ID_PCI_SUBCLASS_FROM_DATABASE=Ethernet controller
E: ID_VENDOR_FROM_DATABASE=Realtek Semiconductor Co., Ltd.
E: ID_VENDOR_ID=0x10ec
E: IFINDEX=2
E: INTERFACE=enp7s0
E: SUBSYSTEM=net
E: SYSTEMD_ALIAS=/sys/subsystem/net/devices/enp7s0
E: TAGS=:systemd:
E: USEC_INITIALIZED=1080179
```

For certain tasks, such as renaming, you many need to know the MAC address. You can find this with the **ip link** command, which you can abbreviate to **ip l**. The MAC address is before the brd string. In this example, the MAC address for **enp7s0** is 74:e6:e2:0e:c7:29. The **ip link** command also provides the MTU (Maximum Transmission Unit) and the current state of the connection.

```
$ ip link
1: lo: <LOOPBACK,UP,LOWER_UP> mtu 65536 qdisc noqueue state UNKNOWN mode DEFAULT
group default qlen 1 link/loopback 00:00:00:00:00:00 brd 00:00:00:00:00:00
2: enp7s0: <BROADCAST,MULTICAST,UP,LOWER_UP> mtu 1500 qdisc fq_codel state UP
mode DEFAULT group default qlen 1000 link/ether 74:e6:e2:0e:c7:29 brd
ff:ff:ff:ff:ff:ff
3: wlp6s0: <BROADCAST,MULTICAST> mtu 1500 qdisc noop state DOWN mode DEFAULT
group default qlen 1000 link/ether 4c:bb:58:22:40:1d brd ff:ff:ff:ff:ff:ff
```

Renaming network device names with udev rules

If you should change your hardware, like your motherboard with its Ethernet connection, or, if you use an Ethernet card and simply change the slot it is connected to, then the name will change. For firewall rules referencing a particular Ethernet connection, this could be a problem. You can, if you wish, change the name to one of your own choosing, even using the older unpredictable names. This way you would only have to update the name change, rather than all your rules and any other code that reference the network device by name.

You can change a device name by adding a user udev rule for network device names. Changes made with udev rules work for both NetworkManager and systemd-networkd. In the **/etc/udev/rules.d** folder, create a file with the **.rules** extension and prefixed by a number less than

80, such as **70-my-net-names.rules**. The .rules files in **/etc/udev/rules.d** take precedence over those in the udev system folder, **/lib/udev/rules.d**.

In the udev rule, identify the subsystem as net (SUBSYSTEM=="net"), the action to take as add (ACTION=="add")), then the MAC address (ATTR[address}, the address attribute). Use **ip link** to obtain the mac address. The MAC address is also listed as the ID_NET_NAME_MAC entry in the **udevadm info** output (be sure to remove the prefix and add intervening colons). Use the NAME field to specify the new name for the device. Use the single = operator to make the name assignment.

/etc/udev/rules.d/70-my-net-names.rules

SUBSYSTEM=="net", ACTION=="add", ATTR{address}=="74:e6:e2:0e:c7:29", NAME="eth0"

To further specify the device you can add the kernel name (KERNEL) of the device. The kernel name is the INTERFACE entry.

SUBSYSTEM=="net", ACTION=="add", ATTR{address}=="74:e6:e2:0e:c7:29", KERNEL=="enp7s0", NAME="eth0"

Renaming network device names for systemd-networkd with systemd.link

The systemd-networkd manager provides an alternate way to change network device names (keep in mind that an udev rule will also work for systemd-networkd). To change the name you would set up a systemd link file in the **/etc/systemd/network** folder. The **systemd.link** man page shows how to do this. A systemd link file consists of Match and Link sections. In the Match section you specify the network device, and in the Link section specify the name you want to give it. The network device can be referenced by its predictable name (Path) or MAC address (MACAddress).

The default systemd link file is **/lib/systemd/network/99-default.link**. The file has a Link section which lists policies to use in determining the name. The NamePolicy key lists the policies to be checked, starting with the kernel, then the udev database, udev firmware onboard information, udev hot-plug slot information, and the device path. In most cases, the slot policy is used. The MACAddressPolicy is set to persistent, for devices that have or need fixed MAC addresses.

99-default.link

```
[Link]
NamePolicy=keep kernel database onboard slot path
AlternativeNamesPolicy=database onboard slot path
MACAddressPolicy=persistent
```

To rename a device, you would set up a systemd link file in the **/etc/systemd/network** folder. The **/etc/systemd** folder takes precedence over the **/lib/systemd** folder. A link file consists of a priority number, any name, and the **.link** extension. Lower numbers have a higher priority. In this example, the network device **enp7s0** has its named changed to **eth0**. The Match section uses the Path key to match on the device path, using the ID_PATH property for the device provided by udev.

You can query the udev database for information on your network device using the **udevadm info** command and match on the device. An added **grep** operation for ID_PATH= will display only the ID_PATH property.

```
$ udevadm info -e | grep -A 22 ^P.*enp7s0 | grep ID_PATH=
E: ID_PATH=pci-0000:07:00.0
```

For the Path key, use the udev ID_PATH value and a * glob matching character for the rest of the path. The Link section uses the Name key to specify the new name. The MacAddressPolicy should be set to persistent, indicating a fixed connection. Start the name of the link file with a number less than 99, so as to take precedence over the **99-default.link** file.

10-my-netname.link

```
[Match]
Path=pci-0000:07:00.0-*

[Link]
Name=eth0
MacAddressPolicy=persistent
```

Instead of the Path key, you could use the MACAddress key to match on the hardware address of the network device. The MAC address is udev ID_NET_NAME_MAC property without the prefix and with colons separation. The MAC address in this example is 74:e6:e2:0e:c7:29. You can also use **ip link** to find the MAC address (the numbers before **brd**).

10-my-netname.link

```
[Match]
MACAddress=74:e6:e2:0e:c7:29

[Link]
Name=eth0
MacAddressPolicy=persistent
```

Alternatively, you could use the OriginalName key in the Match section instead of the Path. The original name is the udev INTERFACE property, which is also the name of the device as displayed by **ifconfig**.

10-my-netname.link

```
[Match]
OriginalName=enp7s0*

[Link]
Name=eth0
MacAddressPolicy=persistent
```

Table Listing

Table 1-1: Ubuntu DVD ISO Image locations 35
Table 1-2: Ubuntu Flavors 36
Table 1-3: Ubuntu help and documentation 40
Table 2-1: Ubuntu releases 46
Table 3-1: Window and File Manager Keyboard shortcuts 90
Table 3-2: Settings 105
Table 4-1: Linux Software Package File Extensions 160
Table 4-2: snap commands 164
Table 4-3: apt-get commands 197
Table 5-1: Linux Office Suites 214
Table 5-2: LibreOffice Applications 215
Table 5-3: Calligra Applications 216
Table 5-4: Office Applications for GNOME 217
Table 5-5: PostScript, PDF, and DVI viewers 220
Table 5-6: E-book Readers 222
Table 5-7: Desktop Editors 227
Table 5-8: Vi Editor Commands 231
Table 5-9: Database Management Systems for Linux 233
Table 5-10: Linux Mail Clients 235
Table 5-11: Linux Newsreaders 245
Table 6-1: Linux and Ubuntu Multimedia Sites 248
Table 6-2: Graphics Tools for Linux 249

Table 6-3: Multimedia third-party codecs	256
Table 6-4: Music players, editors, and rippers	259
Table 6-5: CD/DVD Burners	261
Table 6-6: Video and DVD Projects and Applications	263
Table 6-7: Sound device and interface tools	270
Table 6-8: PulseAudio commands (command-line)	273
Table 7-1: Web browsers	277
Table 7-2: Java Packages and Java Web Applications	283
Table 7-3: Linux FTP Clients	285
Table 7-4: Instant Messenger, Talk, and VoIP Clients	291
Table 8-1: GNOME Resources	296
Table 8-2: File Manager Folder Menu	325
Table 8-3: File Manager Pop-up Menu	325
Table 8-4: File Manager Sidebar Tools Menu	328
Table 8-5: File Manager View Menu	330
Table 8-6: The File and Folder Pop-up Menu	331
Table 8-7: The File Manager Sidebar Pop-up Menu	331
Table 9-1: KDE Web Sites	342
Table 9-3: KWin desktop effects keyboard shortcuts	390
Table 9-4: KDE File Manager Keyboard Shortcuts	395
Table 10-1: The MATE Desktop Menu	418
Table 10-2: File Manager Go Menu	442
Table 10-3: File Manager File Menu	443
Table 10-4: File Manager View Menu	447
Table 10-5: File Manager Edit Menu	448
Table 10-6: File Manager Pop-up Menu	449
Table 10-7: The File Manager Side Pane Pop-Up Menu	450
Table 10-8: The File and Folder Pop-Up Menu	451
Table 10-9: The MATE Preferences	457
Table 12-1: Linux Shells	494
Table 12-2: Command Line Editing Operations	496

Table 12-3: Command Line Text Completion Commands	498
Table 12-4: History Commands and History Event References	499
Table 12-5: Shell Symbols	501
Table 12-6: The Shell Operations	505
Table 12-7: Standard System Directories in Linux	512
Table 12-8: Listing, Displaying, and Printing Files	514
Table 12-9: Directory Commands	516
Table 12-10: The find Command	518
Table 12-11: File Operations	520
Table 13-1: Ubuntu System Tools	528
Table 13-2: Sensor packages and applications	536
Table 14-1: Ubuntu Administration Tools	558
Table 14-2: Backup Resources	597
Table 15-1: Ubuntu Network Configuration Tools	614
Table 15-2: The nmcli objects	630
Table 15-3: Variables for wvdial	634
Table 15-4: Service ports	643
Table 15-5: UFW firewall operations	648
Table 15-6: Network Interface Device Naming	656

Figure Listing

Figure 1-1: Ubuntu 24.04 LTS Ubuntu Desktop 31
Figure 1-2: Ubuntu 24.04 LTS Ubuntu Desktop, Default selection 32
Figure 1-3: Ubuntu Live USB/DVD 38
Figure 2-1: Ubuntu Live session System menu and Wired Network configuration 50
Figure 2-2: Install screen for Ubuntu Desktop USB/DVD 51
Figure 2-3: Live USB/DVD (Desktop) with Install icon 52
Figure 2-4: Install Welcome and Language screen 52
Figure 2-5: Accessibility screen 53
Figure 2-6: Keyboard Layout 53
Figure 2-7: Internet connection 54
Figure 2-8: Try or install Ubuntu 55
Figure 2-9: Type of Installation, interactive or automatic 55
Figure 2-10: Applications, Default and Extended software selections 56
Figure 2-11: Recommended proprietary software 56
Figure 2-12: Disk setup, No detected operating systems 58
Figure 2-13: Advanced features 59
Figure 2-14: LVM selection 59
Figure 2-15: LVM with encryption 60
Figure 2-16: Security key for encrypted system 61
Figure 2-17: Security key login 61
Figure 2-18: Manual Installation (manual partitioning) 64
Figure 2-19: Manually partitioning a new hard drive 64
Figure 2-20: Create a new partition table on a blank hard drive 65
Figure 2-21: Select free space on a blank hard drive 65
Figure 2-22: Automatically created EFI boot partition 66

Figure 2-23: Create a new root partition 66
Figure 2-24: Manual partitions 67
Figure 2-25: Ready to install 67
Figure 2-26: Select your timezone 68
Figure 2-27: Create your account 69
Figure 2-28: Install progress slide show 70
Figure 2-29: Installation completed 71
Figure 2-30: Upgrade message and authentication 72
Figure 2-31: Distribution Upgrade dialog 73
Figure 2-32: Grub advanced options menu with recovery kernels 74
Figure 2-33: Recovery options 74
Figure 3-1: Ubuntu GRUB menu 79
Figure 3-2: Editing a GRUB menu item 79
Figure 3-3: The GDM user listing 80
Figure 3-4: GDM login 81
Figure 3-5: GDM Session menu 82
Figure 3-6: System menu 83
Figure 3-7: System menu power profile modes 84
Figure 3-8: Lock Screen 84
Figure 3-9: Power Off menu with Log Out entry 85
Figure 3-10: Log Out dialog 85
Figure 3-11: Power Off menu and Power Off dialog 86
Figure 3-12: Window header bar and buttons 88
Figure 3-13: The Ubuntu desktop 88
Figure 3-14: Activities overview 89
Figure 3-15: Applications Overview 90
Figure 3-16: Files File manager 91
Figure 3-17: File manager grid/list button 91
Figure 3-18: File manager folder, view, and tools menus 92
Figure 3-19: GNOME Tweaks - Appearance tab (themes) 93
Figure 3-20: GNOME Tweaks - Fonts tab 94

Figure 3-21: GNOME Tweaks - Startup Applications tab 95
Figure 3-22: System menu with network Quick Settings buttons, on and off 96
Figure 3-23: System Menu Wi-Fi button's menu showing Wi-Fi connections 97
Figure 3-24: Wi-Fi authentication 97
Figure 3-25: System menu with Wi-Fi button on and off 98
Figure 3-26: Settings Wi-Fi tab 98
Figure 3-27: Settings Wi-Fi entry with scan button and Scan dialog 99
Figure 3-28: Settings Wi-Fi connection - Details tab 99
Figure 3-29: Settings Network tab with Wired connection 100
Figure 3-30: Settings Network tab with proxy settings 101
Figure 3-31: Ubuntu (GNOME) Settings 102
Figure 3-32: Settings Sidebar 103
Figure 3-33: Accessibility 105
Figure 3-34: Accessibility - Seeing 106
Figure 3-35: Appearance 107
Figure 3-36: Apps 108
Figure 3-37: Default Applications 108
Figure 3-38: Removable Media defaults 109
Figure 3-39: Apps - permissions (not sandboxed) 110
Figure 3-40: Apps - Permissions (sandboxed apps) 111
Figure 3-41: Apps - File Type and Link Types 112
Figure 3-42: Apps - Storage 113
Figure 3-43: Color management dialog 113
Figure 3-44: Displays 114
Figure 3-45: Displays - scaling and multiple displays (join) 115
Figure 3-46: Displays - multiple displays (mirror) 115
Figure 3-47: Displays - Night Light 116
Figure 3-48: Keyboard 117
Figure 3-49: Mouse 118
Figure 3-50: Touchpad 119
Figure 3-51: Multitasking 121

Figure 3-52: Notifications dialog 122

Figure 3-53: Notification settings for an application 122

Figure 3-54: Search 123

Figure 3-56: Online Accounts 124

Figure 3-57: System menu button with battery indicator and System menu with Battery button 124

Figure 3-58: System menu Quick Settings Power Mode button and menu 125

Figure 3-59: Power 126

Figure 3-60: Power Statistics 127

Figure 3-70: Privacy & Security 128

Figure 3-71: Privacy & Security - Connectivity 128

Figure 3-72: Privacy & Security - Screen Lock configuration 129

Figure 3-73: Privacy & Security - File History & Trash 129

Figure 3-74: Sharing 130

Figure 3-75: Sharing - Media Sharing dialog 130

Figure 3-76: System 131

Figure 3-77: System - Region & Language 132

Figure 3-78: Region & Language - Language Support 132

Figure 3-79: Region & Language - Your Account Language and Formats 133

Figure 3-80: System - Date & Time Settings dialog 134

Figure 3-81: Date & Time manual settings 134

Figure 3-82: Time Zone dialog 135

Figure 3-83: Date & Time dialog on the top bar of your desktop 135

Figure 3-84: System - Users 136

Figure 3-85: System - Remote Desktop - Desktop Sharing 137

Figure 3-86: System - Remote Desktop - Remote Login 138

Figure 3-87: System - Secure Shell 138

Figure 3-88: System - About 139

Figure 3-89: System - About - System Details 140

Figure 3-90: Ubuntu Desktop 141

Figure 3-91: Ubuntu Desktop - Configure Desktop Behavior dialog 142

Figure 3-92: Gnome File Manager Search 142

Figure 3-93: Devices sidebar in the file manager window and icons on the dock 143
Figure 3-94: Removable Devices notifications 143
Figure 3-95: File manager window, writing to blank DVD disc... 144
Figure 3-96: Disk Writer, writing ISO image to USB drive.. 145
Figure 3-97: Startup Applications Preferences 145
Figure 3-98: Hardware Drivers: Software & Updates, Additional Drivers tab 146
Figure 3-99: Ubuntu Desktop Guide... 148
Figure 3-100: Ubuntu Desktop Guide topics... 148
Figure 3-101: Ubuntu Desktop Guide page 149
Figure 3-102: Ubuntu Help, All Documents.. 149
Figure 3-103: Terminal Window 151
Figure 3-104: Terminal Window menu 151
Figure 3-105: Terminal Window Search dialog 152
Figure 3-106: Terminal Window with tabs showing tabs menu 153
Figure 3-107: Terminal Window Profile configuration 153
Figure 3-108: GNOME Console 154
Figure 4-1: App Center - Snap Package 163
Figure 4-2: Listing of popular available Snaps: find 165
Figure 4-3: Listing of installed snaps: list.. 166
Figure 4-4: App Center - Snap Tracks and Risk Levels 168
Figure 4-5: Snap application permissions - Settings 171
Figure 4-6: App Center 176
Figure 4-7: App Center Categories 177
Figure 4-8: App Center category with Sort menu.. 177
Figure 4-9: App Center, using the search box... 178
Figure 4-10: App Center, software descriptor page 179
Figure 4-11: App Center, Snap package channels.. 180
Figure 4-12: App Center, installing applications 180
Figure 4-13: App Center, removing applications 180
Figure 4-14: App Center, Manage tab... 181
Figure 4-15: Software & Updates - Ubuntu software repository sections 185

Figure 4-16: Software & Updates - Other Software configuration 186
Figure 4-17: Software & Updates - Authentication, package signature keys 186
Figure 4-18: Software & Updates - Developer Options 187
Figure 4-19: App Center, APT (DEB) package 188
Figure 4-20: App Center, APT (DEB) package application page 188
Figure 4-21: App Center, APT and Snap package versions 189
Figure 4-22: GNOME Software 190
Figure 4-23: GNOME Software Addons for codecs 191
Figure 4-24: Synaptic Package Manager 192
Figure 4-25: Synaptic Package Manager: Sections 192
Figure 4-26: Synaptic Package Manager: Status 193
Figure 4-27: Software Updater with selected packages 202
Figure 4-28: Details of updates 203
Figure 4-29: Details of updates, Technical description 203
Figure 4-30: Downloading updates 204
Figure 4-31: Downloaded updates 204
Figure 4-32: Software & Updates Update configuration 205
Figure 4-33: Software & Updates - Ubuntu Pro (Livepatch) 206
Figure 4-34: Firmware Updater 206
Figure 4-35: GNOME Software Flatpak 207
Figure 5-1: LibreOffice Writer word processor 215
Figure 5-2: FBReader E-book reader - library window 221
Figure 5-3: FBReader E-book reader - book dialog 221
Figure 5-4: Calibre E-book reader, organizer, and converter 222
Figure 5-5: Gnote 222
Figure 5-6: GNOME Clocks: World tab 223
Figure 5-7: GNOME Weather: city with forecast 224
Figure 5-8: GNOME Characters 225
Figure 5-9: Fonts 225
Figure 5-10: GNOME Calendar 226
Figure 5-11: GNOME Text Editor 227

Figure 5-12: GNOME Gedit 228
Figure 5-13: Editing with nano 228
Figure 5-14: Thunderbird Email client 236
Figure 5-15: Evolution Email client 238
Figure 5-16: Evolution Calendar 239
Figure 6-1: Shotwell Photo Management 250
Figure 6-2: Shotwell Photo Editing 251
Figure 6-3: digiKam Photo Manager 251
Figure 6-4: Image Viewer (Eye of Gnome) 252
Figure 6-5: GIMP 253
Figure 6-6: Inkscape 254
Figure 6-7: Gwenview 254
Figure 6-8: GNOME Software's codec wizard 257
Figure 6-9: Rhythmbox GNOME Multimedia Player 259
Figure 6-10: Elisa KDE Multimedia Player 260
Figure 6-11: GNOME Music 260
Figure 6-12: GNOME Videos: Videos tab 262
Figure 6-13: GNOME Videos, playing a video 262
Figure 6-14: GNOME Videos Search 263
Figure 6-15: VLC Video Player (VideoLAN) 265
Figure 6-16: Celluloid on Ubuntu 265
Figure 6-17: Videos (Totem) Movie Player plugins 266
Figure 6-18: Pitivi video editor 267
Figure 6-19: Shotcut video editor 267
Figure 6-20: System menu Volume Control 270
Figure 6-21: Settings Sound tab 271
Figure 6-22: Volume Levels and Alert Sound dialogs 272
Figure 7-1: Firefox Web Browser 278
Figure 7-2: Firefox Settings 279
Figure 7-3: Firefox Add-ons Management 280
Figure 7-4: Web (Epiphany) Web browser 281

Figure 7-5: Chromium Web Browser (Google Chrome) 282
Figure 7-6: Transmission BitTorrent client 283
Figure 7-7: Transmission BitTorrent client properties 284
Figure 7-8: GNOME FTP access with the file manager 286
Figure 7-9: GNOME FTP access with the file manager Other Locations Connect bar 287
Figure 7-10: GNOME FTP file download 287
Figure 7-11: GNOME Maps 292
Figure 8-1: Ubuntu Desktop 297
Figure 8-2: System menu 299
Figure 8-3: Desktop Menu 300
Figure 8-4: Desktop folder 300
Figure 8-5: Activities Overview 301
Figure 8-6: Settings Multitasking tab Hot Corner option 301
Figure 8-7: Activities Overview with workspace selector (multiple workspaces) 302
Figure 8-8: Dock/Dash with favorites and running applications 303
Figure 8-9: Dock Configuration on Settings Appearance 304
Figure 8-10: Window thumbnails (Activities and single click on application dock icon) .305
Figure 8-11: Workspace thumbnails with workspace selector 305
Figure 8-12: Applications overview 306
Figure 8-13: Creating Overview Application Folders 307
Figure 8-14: Changing Overview Application Folder Names 308
Figure 8-15: Adding Icons to an Overview Application Folder 308
Figure 8-16: Overview Application Folders 309
Figure 8-17: Activities - search box 310
Figure 8-18: Activities - Search configuration 310
Figure 8-19: Window colors, Settings | Appearance 311
Figure 8-20: Settings Multitasking Active Screen Edges option 311
Figure 8-21: Favorites window thumbnails 312
Figure 8-22: Window Tiling 313
Figure 8-23: Enhanced Tiling option in Settings Ubuntu Desktop 313
Figure 8-24: Tiling Popup option showing apps to tile 313

Figure 8-25: Window Switcher (ALT+TAB) 314
Figure 8-26: GNOME Tweaks, Windows configuration 315
Figure 8-27: Activities button showing number of workspaces and the current one used
.... 316
Figure 8-28: Settings Multitasking tab Dynamic and Fixed workspaces 316
Figure 8-28: Workspaces, dynamic and fixed 316
Figure 8-30: Workspaces on the activities overview, dynamic and fixed 316
Figure 8-31: Settings Multitasking - workspaces on multiple monitors 317
Figure 8-32: Workspace selector on the Applications overview - dynamic and fixed 317
Figure 8-33: Workspace selector on the Applications and Activities overviews 318
Figure 8-34: Notifications 319
Figure 8-35: GNOME Tweaks Tool - Appearance tab (themes) 319
Figure 8-36: Accessing and copying application launchers 320
Figure 8-37: Application Launchers on the Desktop 321
Figure 8-38: GNOME Help browser - Ubuntu Desktop Guide 321
Figure 8-39: GNOME Help - All Documents 322
Figure 8-40: File manager with sidebar 323
Figure 8-41: File manager folder menu 324
Figure 8-42: File manager folder menu - Open in Terminal 324
Figure 8-43: File manager New Folder 325
Figure 8-44: File manager adaptive narrow width, notifications and no sidebar 326
Figure 8-45: File manager adaptive narrow width, sort menu and navigation 326
Figure 8-46: File manager adaptive narrow width, displayed sidebar 327
Figure 8-47: File manager sidebar menus 327
Figure 8-48: File manager sidebar Tools menu 328
Figure 8-49: File manager window with tabs 329
Figure 8-50: File manager View and Tools menus 330
Figure 8-51: File manager Rename dialog 332
Figure 8-52: File manager - Renaming several files at once - template 333
Figure 8-53: File manager - Renaming several files at once - Find and Replace 333
Figure 8-54: File manager - Compress and Archive dialogs 334
Figure 8-55: File manager - Copying files 334

Figure 8-56: File manager - Open File dialog (Open With) 335
Figure 8-57: File properties and permissions 336
Figure 8-58: File properties and permissions for executable file 336
Figure 8-59: File manager Preferences 337
Figure 8-60: File manager search 338
Figure 8-61: File manager search with no results 339
Figure 8-62: File manager sidebar Search Everywhere search 339
Figure 9-1: SDDM Display Manager, login screen 344
Figure 9-2: SDDM Display Manager, Desktop Session menu 345
Figure 9-3: The KDE desktop 345
Figure 9-3: KDE Keyboard Shortcuts 346
Figure 9-4: KDE Help Center 347
Figure 9-5: Desktop Menu 348
Figure 9-6: Display Settings 348
Figure 9-7: Edit Mode 349
Figure 9-8: Desktop Settings, wallpaper 349
Figure 9-9: Desktop Settings, Get New Wallpapers 350
Figure 9-10: System Settings | Appearance | Global Theme | Get New Themes 351
Figure 9-11: Log Out dialog 351
Figure 9-12: Application Launcher leave buttons 352
Figure 9-13: Application Menu Power/Session menu 352
Figure 9-14: Application Dashboard Power/Session 353
Figure 9-15: Shut Down dialog 353
Figure 9-16: Application menu alternatives 354
Figure 9-17: Application Launcher 354
Figure 9-18: Application Launcher Applications 355
Figure 9-19: Application Launcher Places 356
Figure 9-20: Application Launcher Settings 356
Figure 9-21: Application Launcher Power and Session buttons 357
Figure 9-22: Application Menu 358
Figure 9-23: Application Menu Settings 358

Figure 9-24: Application Dashboard 359
Figure 9-25: Application Dashboard - All Applications 359
Figure 9-26: Application Dashboard Settings 360
Figure 9-27: KRunner application search 361
Figure 9-28: Device Notifier 361
Figure 9-29: Device Notifier menu and its panel icon..362
Figure 9-30: NetworkManager connections and panel icons: 362
Figure 9-31: KDE NetworkManager connection information - speed and details:...........363
Figure 9-32: KDE connection editor and KDE NetworkManager 363
Figure 9-33: Clock Widget with task sidebar and configuration dialog 364
Figure 9-34: Adding a widget - Widgets dialog 365
Figure 9-35: Folder View, Calculator, Digital Clock, Individual Cores Usage, Hard Disk Activity, and Sticky Notes widgets: 366
Figure 9-36: Folder and Icon widgets: 366
Figure 9-37: Activities menu entry and the Activities widget 367
Figure 9-38: Activities Manager 368
Figure 9-39: Create an activity...368
Figure 9-40: stop Activity icons 369
Figure 9-41: Activity Manager and screen of selected activity 369
Figure 9-42: Window Activity menu 370
Figure 9-43: System Settings | Workspace Behavior | Activities....................................370
Figure 9-44: Activity Switcher Widgets for Desktop and Panel 371
Figure 9-45: Activities button for desktop and panel..371
Figure 9-46: Activity Pager for the desktop and panel 372
Figure 9-47: Activity Bar for desktop and panel 372
Figure 9-48: Activity Switcher widget alternatives selection 373
Figure 9-49: Window tiles 374
Figure 9-50: Choosing a task manager from panel menu 375
Figure 9-51: Application panel menus 375
Figure 9-52: Application panel menus Application section 376
Figure 9-53: Icon-only Task Manager, application icons 376
Figure 9-54: Icon-only Task Manager, application thumbnails for open windows 377

Figure 9-55: Icon-only Task Manager, maximizing a minimized window using thumbnails 377
Figure 9-56: Task Manager panel applications with unopened and opened windows....378
Figure 9-57: Task Manager..378
Figure 9-58: Window List...379
Figure 9-59: Icon-only Task Manager Applications 379
Figure 9-60: Task Manager Applications and opened buttons.......................................380
Figure 9-61: Virtual Desktops configuration with System Settings and the Pager widget 381
Figure 9-62: Pager Panel and Desktop widgets 381
Figure 9-63: Pager Widget Settings: 382
Figure 9-64: Overview effect 382
Figure 9-65: Overview effect virtual desktops 383
Figure 9-66: Overview effect managing desktops..383
Figure 9-67: Overview effect configuration on System Settings....................................384
Figure 9-68: KDE panel with Icon-only Task Manager and open window 384
Figure 9-69: KDE panel with Task Manager and open window 385
Figure 9-70: KDE Add Widgets option on panel...385
Figure 9-71: KDE Add Widgets dialog for panel...386
Figure 9-72: Displaying panel widget information 386
Figure 9-73: Removing a widget from the panel in edit mode......................................386
Figure 9-74: System Tray..387
Figure 9-75: KDE panel system tray settings 388
Figure 9-76: KDE Panel Configuration, Edit Mode..388
Figure 9-77: KDE Panel Configuration details and display features 389
Figure 9-78: Desktop Effects selection 390
Figure 9-79: Desktop Effects configuration 390
Figure 9-80: Window Management | Task Switcher 391
Figure 9-81: Thumbnail Switch - ALT-TAB 391
Figure 9-82: Thumbnail Breeze Switch - ALT-TAB 392
Figure 9-83: Present Windows (Windows effects) CTRL-F9 and CTRL-F10 392
Figure 9-84: Desktop Grid - META-F8...393

Figure 9-85: The KDE file manager (Dolphin) 393
Figure 9-86: The KDE file manager menus 394
Figure 9-87: The KDE file manager with panels 395
Figure 9-88: The KDE file manager panel Recent 396
Figure 9-89: The KDE file manager with split views..396
Figure 9-90: The KDE file manager share dialog for folders...397
Figure 9-91: The KDE file manager Samba password creation..397
Figure 9-92: Dolphin file manager configuration 398
Figure 9-93: The KDE Search Bar..400
Figure 9-94: The KDE Filter Bar 401
Figure 9-95: Plasma System Settings - Sidebar view..402
Figure 9-96: Plasma System Settings - Sidebar icon list..403
Figure 9-97: KDE System Settings | Appearance | Global Theme | Application Style 403
Figure 9-98: KDE System Settings | Users..404
Figure 9-99: Plasma System Settings - Icon view 404
Figure 9-100: Plasma System Settings - Icon view (Workspace Behavior) 405
Figure 9-101: Discover Software Manager 406
Figure 9-102: Discover Software Manager - Application Description 406
Figure 10-1: Ubuntu MATE Guide 408
Figure 10-2: Webcamoid webcam application 409
Figure 10-3: Celluloid on MATE 410
Figure 10-4: MATE desktop and panel..411
Figure 10-5: MATE system menu 412
Figure 10-6: Indicator Applet Complete 412
Figure 10-7: MATE Indicator Applet Configuration - Sessions (System Menu) 413
Figure 10-8: MATE Indicator Applet Configuration - Date and Time 413
Figure 10-9: MATE Indicator Applet Configuration - Notifications 414
Figure 10-10: MATE with Brisk Menu and Caja file manager 415
Figure 10-11: Run Application dialog, Alt-F2 415
Figure 10-12: Application desktop menu, Alt-F1 416
Figure 10-13: MATE Tweak...417

Figure 10-14: MATE Desktop Menu 418
Figure 10-15: MATE window and window menu 419
Figure 10-16: Switching Windows with thumbnails (Alt-Tab) 420
Figure 10-17: Window List applet 421
Figure 10-18: Window List Preferences 421
Figure 10-19: Workspace switcher, one row and two rows 422
Figure 10-20: Switching workspaces, Ctrl-Alt-*arrow* 422
Figure 10-21: Workspace Switcher Preferences 422
Figure 10-22: MATE Tweaks, Panel tab 423
Figure 10-23: Familiar Panel Layout 424
Figure 10-24: Traditional Panel Layout 424
Figure 10-25: Redmond Panel Layout 425
Figure 10-26: Cupertino Panel Layout 425
Figure 10-27: Mutiny Panel Layout 426
Figure 10-28: Pantheon Panel Layout 426
Figure 10-29: Contemporary Panel Layout 427
Figure 10-30: Main Menu Editor 428
Figure 10-31: Brisk Menu - Applications 429
Figure 10-32: Brisk Menu - Redmond panel layout 429
Figure 10-33: Brisk Menu with dash layout, Cupertino panel layout 430
Figure 10-34: Classic Menu 430
Figure 10-35: Compact Menu 431
Figure 10-36: MATE Plank applet (dock) with default applications 431
Figure 10-37: MATE Plank on panel layout with additional applications 431
Figure 10-38: MATE Plank on panel layout docklet menu 432
Figure 10-39: MATE Dock enabled on MATE Tweaks 432
Figure 10-40: MATE Plank Preferences - Appearance 433
Figure 10-41: MATE Plank Preferences - Behavior 433
Figure 10-42: MATE Plank Preferences - Docklets 434
Figure 10-43: MATE Top Panel 434
Figure 10-44: MATE Panel 434

Figure 10-45: MATE Panel pop-up menu 435
Figure 10-46: MATE Panel Properties...436
Figure 10-47: MATE Panel "Add to Panel" dialog for panel applets 438
Figure 10-48: Caja file manager with side pane 441
Figure 10-49: Caja navigation buttons: back, forward, parent, home, computer.............441
Figure 10-50: Caja locations: unexpanded, expanded, and location path 442
Figure 10-51: File manager side pane menu and views...444
Figure 10-52: File manager side pane with bookmarks menu 444
Figure 10-53: File manager window with tabs...445
Figure 10-54: File manager file and folder views..445
Figure 10-55: File manager File, Edit, and View menus...446
Figure 10-56: File manager File | Open...449
Figure 10-57: File properties on Caja..453
Figure 10-58: GNOME Control Center 455
Figure 10-59: About Me: Preferences | About Me 458
Figure 10-60: Choosing a desktop background, System | Preferences | Appearance 458
Figure 10-61: Appearance - Selecting GNOME themes..459
Figure 10-62: Assistive Technologies Preferences 461
Figure 10-63: Bluetooth Manager and Adapters 461
Figure 10-64: Bluetooth Indicator Menu 462
Figure 10-65: Bluetooth Plugins 462
Figure 10-66:Monitor Preferences. 463
Figure 10-67: File Management Preferences for Media 464
Figure 10-68: Fonts..464
Figure 10-69: Mouse and Keyboard Preferences..466
Figure 10-70: MATE Power Manager - AC and Battery...467
Figure 10-71: Pop-up Notifications 468
Figure 10-72: Preferred Applications tool..469
Figure 10-73: Screensaver Preferences..470
Figure 10-74: Sound Indicator Menu 470
Figure 10-75: Sound Preferences - effects and output 471

Figure 10-76: Time and Date Indicator Menu 472
Figure 10-77: Time and Date Manager 472
Figure 11-1: Xubuntu (Xfce) Desktop 474
Figure 11-2: Xubuntu (Xfce) Applications Menu 475
Figure 11-3: Xubuntu (Xfce) Settings Manager 476
Figure 11-4: Xubuntu (Xfce) Desktop Settings 477
Figure 11-5: Lubuntu (LXQT) desktop 478
Figure 11-6: Lubuntu (LXQT) panel 478
Figure 11-7: Lubuntu (LXQT) Configure Panel 479
Figure 11-8: Lubuntu (LXQT) Configure Panel Widgets tab and Plugins 479
Figure 11-9: Lubuntu (LXQT) Desktop Preferences 480
Figure 11-10: Ubuntu Studio 481
Figure 11-11: Ubuntu Budgie 482
Figure 11-12: Ubuntu Budgie menu 482
Figure 11-13: Ubuntu Budgie Welcome 483
Figure 11-14: Budgie Applets 484
Figure 11-15: Budgie Themes 484
Figure 11-16: Ubuntu Cinnamon desktop 485
Figure 11-17: Ubuntu Cinnamon Grouped Window List 486
Figure 11-18: Ubuntu Cinnamon menu 486
Figure 11-19: Ubuntu Cinnamon Nemo File manager 487
Figure 11-20: System Settings dialog (Appearance and Preferences) 488
Figure 11-21: Ubuntu Unity interface 489
Figure 11-22: Ubuntu Unity interface with selected window and applications menu.....490
Figure 11-23: Ubuntu Unity dash 490
Figure 11-24: Ubuntu Unity File manager 491
Figure 11-25: System Settings dialog 492
Figure 13-1: GNOME System Monitor: Resources 528
Figure 13-2: GNOME System Monitor: Processes 530
Figure 13-3: Glances System Monitor 531
Figure 13-4: System Log 533

Figure 13-5: Disk Usage Analyzer 534
Figure 13-6: Disk Usage Analyzer: Scan dialog 534
Figure 13-7: The ClamTK tool for ClamAV virus protection 535
Figure 13-8: Disk Utility 537
Figure 13-9: Disk Utility, hard drive 537
Figure 13-10: Disk Utility, Volumes 538
Figure 13-11: Disk Utility: Hard Disk hardware SMART data 539
Figure 13-12: Seahorse Passwords and Keys (version 3.3) 540
Figure 13-13: Seahorse Keyring key Properties dialog 541
Figure 13-14: Choose Encryption key type 541
Figure 13-15: Create Encryption key 542
Figure 13-16: Passphrase for encryption key 542
Figure 13-17: My Personal Keys 542
Figure 13-18: GnuPGP key dialog: Owner tab 543
Figure 13-19: GnuPGP key dialog: Details tab 543
Figure 13-20: Seahorse Preferences - Keyservers 544
Figure 13-21: Searching for keys 544
Figure 13-22: Importing keys 545
Figure 13-23: Key information 545
Figure 13-24: Imported keys 546
Figure 13-25: Imported key Trust tab for an unsigned key 546
Figure 13-26: Signing a key 546
Figure 13-27: Signed key 547
Figure 13-28: Trusted keys 547
Figure 13-29: Seahorse Preferences 548
Figure 14-1: Users - Settings | System | Users 565
Figure 14-2: Users - unlock 565
Figure 14-3: Users - Add a new user 566
Figure 14-4: Users 567
Figure 14-5: Users, password dialog 567
Figure 14-6: User - Selecting User Icon 568

Figure 14-7: Users and Groups 568
Figure 14-8: User Settings: Change User Password dialog 569
Figure 14-9: Users and Groups: Change User Privileges 570
Figure 14-10: Users and Groups: Create New User 571
Figure 14-11: Users and Groups: new user password 571
Figure 14-12: Users and Groups: Groups settings 572
Figure 14-13: Group Properties: Group Users panel 572
Figure 14-14: Accessing shared folders using multicast DNS discovery (Avahi) 575
Figure 14-15: Gufw and FirewallD configuration for multicast DNS discovery (Avahi), mdns service 576
Figure 14-16: User Authentication dialog 577
Figure 14-17: Keyring Authentication 577
Figure 14-18: Other Locations - shared Windows folders 578
Figure 14-19: Ober Locations Connect bar - List of previously accessed shared folders 578
Figure 14-20: Folder Sharing Options 580
Figure 14-21: Folder Sharing permissions prompt 581
Figure 14-22: Folder Sharing dialog 581
Figure 14-23: Other Locations with sharing enabled 581
Figure 14-24: Samba Firewall Configuration, Gufw (UFW) and firewall-config (FirewallD) 582
Figure 14-25: Samba shares on Windows 582
Figure 14-26: Accessing a Samba share on Windows 583
Figure 14-27: File Permissions 584
Figure 14-28: Folder Permissions 585
Figure 14-29: System menu Bluetooth button's menu 586
Figure 14-30: Bluetooth Settings 587
Figure 14-31: Bluetooth Device Configuration 587
Figure 14-32: Bluetooth Sound 588
Figure 14-33: Bluetooth for phones 588
Figure 14-34: Bluetooth Tether in System menu 589
Figure 14-35: Bluetooth Tethers in Settings Network tab 590
Figure 14-36: Settings Network Bluetooth Tethers Configuration dialog 590

Figure 14-37: Bluetooth Tether inactive 591

Figure 14-38: Opening the /etc/default/grub file in Text Editor 593

Figure 14-39: Editing the /etc/default/grub file in Text Editor 594

Figure 14-40: Saving the /etc/default/grub file in Text Editor, authenticated as
    Administrator 594

Figure 14-41: Deja Dup settings - overview 598

Figure 14-42: Deja Dup Preferences 598

Figure 14-43: Deja Dup settings - storage for Windows share and Local folder 599

Figure 14-44: Deja Dup settings - backup times 599

Figure 14-45: Deja Dup settings - Folders to save and ignore 600

Figure 14-46: Deja Dup backup: encryption 600

Figure 14-47: Deja Dup restore 601

Figure 14-48: Settings Printers tab 605

Figure 14-49: Settings Printers - Jobs..605

Figure 14-50: Settings Printers - Details and Options 605

Figure 14-51: Settings Printers - add printer 606

Figure 14-52: Print Settings (system-config-printer0 607

Figure 14-53: Printer Properties window 607

Figure 14-54: Default Printer..608

Figure 14-55: New Printer 609

Figure 14-56: Finding a network printer 610

Figure 14-57: Selecting a network printer...610

Figure 14-58: Remote Windows printer Settings 611

Figure 14-59: Remote Windows Printers 612

Figure 15-1: Settings Wi-Fi...617

Figure 15-2: Wi-Fi - Details tab 618

Figure 15-3: Wi-Fi - Security tab 618

Figure 15-4: Wi-Fi - Identity tab 619

Figure 15-5: Wi-Fi - IPv4 tab, Manual..619

Figure 15-6: Saved Networks 620

Figure 15-7: Settings Network 620

Figure 15-8: Wired Configuration -Details tab 621

Figure 15-9: Wired Configuration - New Profile 621

Figure 15-10: Wired Configuration - Security tab 622

Figure 15-11: Wired Configuration - Identity tab 622

Figure 15-12: Wired Configuration - IPv4 tab 623

Figure 15-13: Settings Network - add VPN connections 623

Figure 15-14: OpenVPN connection 624

Figure 15-15: WireGuard connection 624

Figure 15-16: Network Connections (nm-connection-editor) 625

Figure 15-17: IPv4 wired configuration (nm-connection-editor) 626

Figure 15-18: Wireless configuration (nm-connection-editor) 627

Figure 15-19: Turn on Wi-Fi Hotspot 628

Figure 15-20: Connect to a Hidden Wi-Fi Network 628

Figure 15-21: Gufw 644

Figure 15-22: Gufw Preconfigured rules 645

Figure 15-23: Gufw Simple rules 646

Figure 15-24: Gufw Advanced rules 646

Figure 15-25: Gufw edit a rule 647

Figure 15-26: Gufw create a rule for an active port 647

Figure 15-27: Firewall (firewall-config, FirewallD) - Runtime Configuration 650

Figure 15-28: Permanent Configuration 651

Figure 15-29: Default Zone 651

Figure 15-30: Base Zone Settings 652

Figure 15-31: Service Settings 653

Figure 15-32: Service Protocols and Ports 653

Figure 15-33: Port Forwarding 654

Figure 15-34: ICMP Filters 654

Figure 15-35: Gnome network tool 655

Index

.local
　Avahi, 576
.torrent, 283
.wine, 208
/etc/apt/sources.list.d/ubuntu.sources, 183
/etc/hostname, 559
/media, 574

A

AbiWord, 217
Activities
　GNOME, 300
　　Activities button, 297
　　dynamic workspace indicator, 297
　　hot corner, 301
　　workspaces, 301
　KDE, 367
　　activites pager, 370
　　switching, 370
additional printer settings, 607
　remote printers, 609
Administration
　Disk Usage Analyzer, 533
　glances, 531
　GNOME System Monitor, 528
　KDE System Settings, 402
　Logs, 533
　MATE Control Center, 455
　PolicyKit, 563
　root user, 562
　services, 573
　su, 562
　sudo, 560

System Settings, 492
systemd, 573
Tools
　Gufw, 644
　NetworkManager, 616
　Services, 573
　Software updater, 202
　System Monitor, 528
　terminal window, 150
　virus protection, 535
Ubuntu Administrative Tools, 558
Ubuntu System Tools, 527
Administrative Tools, 558
Advanced Linux Sound Architecture, 270
Advanced Package Tool, 39, 158, 181
alien, 200
ALSA
　alsamixer, 270
　amixer, 270
alsamixer, 270
Amanda, 603
amixer, 270
App Center, 175
　APT, 187
　Snap, 175
Appearance, 458
Apple, 35
applets, 439
Application Dashboard, 359
　shutdown, 353
Application Launcher, 354
　shutdown, 351
Application Menu, 357, 374
　shutdown, 352
Applications

administration, 558
burners, 261
email, 234
FTP, 284
GNOME
   overview, 306
IM, 290
Internet, 276
KDE, 380
KRunner, 360
mail, 234
MATE
   defaults, 452
multimedia, 255
music, 258
networks, 614
newsreaders, 243
Office, 214
TV, 268
Video, 261
applications overview
   GNOME, 306
Apps
   Settings, 110
APT, 158
   apt-get, 196
   updates, 202
apt cache tools, 198
apt-cache, 199
apt-get, 196
   install, 196
   update, 198
   upgrade, 73, 198
Archive Manager, 143
Assistive technologies
   MATE, 460
auth_admin_keep, 563
Authentication
   root user, 562
   su, 562
   sudo, 560
Avahi, 574
   FirewallD, 575
   mdns.allow, 576
   mdns4, 576
   shared file systems, 574
Ayatana Indicators, 412

Date and Time, 413
session menu, 413

B

backgrounds
   GNOME, 107
   KDE, 349
   MATE, 458
Backports
   repository, 182
backup, 597
   Amanda, 603
   BackupPC, 602
   Deja Dup, 597
      restore, 600
   duplicity, 597
   rsync, 602
   tar, 601
BackupPC, 602
bad
   Gstreamer, 257
base
   Gstreamer, 257
battery, 467
BitTorrent, 47, 283
   Transmission, 283
Bluetooth, 586
   MATE, 461
bookmarks
   Caja, 440
   Files, 327
Bootloader
   configuration, 593
   edit, 78
   GRUB, 592
   GRUB_DEFAULT, 595
   grub-install, 75
   Plymouth, 80, 539
   re-install, 74
   update-grub, 596
brightness
   KDE, 387
   MATE, 467
   Ubuntu, 298
Budgie, 481

C

Caja, 439
  bookmarks, 440
  copy, 450
  displaying files and folders, 445
  file management, 463
  file properties, 452
  folder properties, 453
  FTP, 441
  media, 463
  navigation, 447
  permissions, 454
  preferences, 454
  side pane, 443
  tabs, 445
  xdg-user-dirs, 440
calendar, 225
Calibre
  E-book reader, 221
Calligra Suite, 216
Calligra Words, 217
Camera, 249, 252
CD Burners and Rippers, 261
CD burning, 144
CD/DVD disc images
  Archive Manager, 143
Celluliod, 264, 410
channels
  Snap, 167
characters
  GNOME Characters, 224
Characters, 224
Chromium, 281
Cinnamon, 485
ClamAV
  virus protection, 535
Clementine, 259
clocks
  GNOME Clocks, 223
codecs
  DVB, 256
  ffmpeg, 256
  installation, 55, 56
  lame, 256
  libdvbpsi, 256
  Matroska, 269
  MPEG-4, 269
  Multimedia third-party, 255
  Xvid, 269
  xvidcore, 256
command line, 154, 494
  date, 135
  editing, 495
  terminal window, 150
command line interface, 86
commands, 154
  shell, 497
Common Unix Printing System (CUPS), 608
Common User Directory Structure, 440
compress
  GNOME, 333
compression
  LZMA, 601
configuration
  nano, 229
  networks, 615, 616
configuration files
  editing, 592
confinement
  Snap, 168
Connect bar
  FTP, 286
Console, 154
  GNOME Console, 154
Contemporary
  desktop layouts, 427
Control Center
  MATE, 455
copy
  GNOME, 334
  KDE, 399
  MATE, 416, 450
  shell, 520
cron, 532
  KDE Task Scheduler, 532
CrossOver, 218
Cupertino
  desktop layouts, 425
CUPS, 608
curl, 288
customization
  application launchers, 320
  GNOME, 319

D

Database Management Systems, 233
database servers
   MySQL, 233
   PostgreSQL, 233
Databases
   LibreOffice, 233
   MariDB, 234
   MySQL, 234
   PostgreSQL, 234
   SQL Databases, 233
date, 135
   date, 135
Date & Time
   GNOME, 135
   MATE, 472
      Indicators, 413
dconf editor
   Software updater, 204
DEB, 195
Debian alternatives system, 539
default applications
   GNOME, 108
   MATE, 463
default.plymouth, 539
Deja Dup, 597
   restore, 600
Desktop
   actvities
      GNOME, 300
   application launchers, 320
   backgrounds
      GNOME, 107
      KDE, 349
      MATE, 458
   Bluetooth
      MATE, 461
   Cinnamon, 485
   copy files, 450
      GNOME, 334
      KDE, 399
      MATE, 416
   customization, 319
   Date & Time
      GNOME, 135
      MATE, 472
   default applications

      GNOME, 108
      MATE, 452
   displaying files and folders
      Caja), 445
      GNOME, 329
   displays
      GNOME, 114
      MATE, 462
   Dolphin, 393
   favorites
      GNOME, 303
   file manager, 491
   GNOME, 337
   file properties
      Caja, 452
      GNOME, 335
   flavors, 474
   fonts
      GNOME, 320
      KDE, 402
      MATE, 464
   GNOME, 296
      applications overview, 306
      Apps, 110
      compress files, 333
      Date & Time, 135
      Desktop folder, 300, 320
      desktop menu, 299
      display, 114
      file manager, 322
      folder properties, 337
      keyboard, 116
      language, 116
      mouse, 117
      overview, 306
      power management, 124
      privacy, 127
      removable devices, 142
      rename files, 332
      search, 338
      security, 127
      sharing, 130
      touchpad, 117
      universal access, 105
      windows overview, 304
   GNOME Tweaks, 92
   Help, 147

icons
  GNOME, 320
  MATE, 417
KDE, 342
  Activities, 367
  configuration, 346
  desktop menu, 347
  edit mode, 348
  lock, 351
  logout, 351
  menus, 354, 357, 359
  Shut down, 351
  task managers, 374
keyboard
  MATE, 465
Lubuntu, 477
MATE
  Brisk Menu, 428
  desktop menu, 418
  desktop settings, 417
  dock
    Plank, 431
  menus, 427
    classic, 430
    compact, 431
  notifications, 467
  panel menus, 427
  Power Manager, 466
  preferred applications, 468
  Tweak, 417
  window list, 420
  workspace switcher applet, 422
mouse MATE, 465
notifications
  GNOME, 121, 123, 318
panel
  MATE, 434
Plasma, 343
power management
  power profiles, 83
removable media
  GNOME, 109
sound
  MATE, 470
System menu
  power profiles, 83
System Settings, 492

themes
  MATE, 459
Tweak Tool, 319
Ubuntu, 88, 296
Ubuntu Administrative Tools, 558
Ubuntu Budgie, 481
Ubuntu MATE, 408, 410
Ubuntu Studio, 480
Ubuntu Unity, 488
universal access
  MATE, 460
Wi-Fi
  GNOME, 96, 617
  KDE, 362
windows
  GNOME, 310
  KDE, 373
  MATE, 419
wired
  GNOME, 100, 620
workspaces
  GNOME, 315
  KDE, 380
    Overview effect, 382
    pager, 380
  MATE, 421
XFce, 474
Xubuntu, 474
desktop effects
  desktop grid, 392
  KDE, 389
  present windows, 392
desktop grid, 392
desktop layouts
  MATE, 423
    Contemporary, 427
    Cupertino, 425
    Familiar, 424
    Mutiny, 426
    Pantheon, 426
    Redmond, 425
    Traditional, 424
desktop publishing
  Scribus, 216
Devices
  GNOME, 142
    removable devices, 142

KDE
  device notifier, 361
  Udisks, 536
Dia, 218
diagrams
  Dia, 218
digiKam, 251
Directories, 515
  copy, 522
  erase, 522
Discover software manager
  KDE, 405
Disk Usage Analyzer, 533
display
  configuration, 146
  Displays, 146
  GNOME, 114
  MATE, 462
  vendor drivers, 146
display manager
  GDM, 80
  SDDM, 344
distribution upgrade, 71
DivX, 269
  Xvid, 269
  xvidcore, 256
dkms, 592
DKMS, 591
  dkms command, 591
dock
  MATE
    docklets, 433
    plank, 431
    preferences, 432
  Ubuntu, 302
docklets
  MATE
    Plank, 433
Document Viewers, 219
  Okular, 219
documentation
  GNOME, 147
  info pages, 150
  Man pages, 150
  Ubuntu, 40
  Ubuntu Desktop Guide, 147
Dolphin, 393

copy, 399
move, 399
preferences, 398
Samba, 396
download, 283
dpkg, 196, 198, 199
  alien, 200
dpkg-query, 199
Dragon Player, 263
drawers, 438
drawing
  LibreOffice Draw, 216
dual-booting, 47
duplicity, 597
DVB
  dvb-apps, 268
  dvbscan, 268
  Kaffeine, 268
dvb-apps, 268
dvbscan, 268
DVD
  burning, 144, 261
  libdvdcss, 256
DVD Video, 266
  libdvdcss, 266
DVI, 219
  Okular, 219
  TeX, 219
Dynamic IP Address, 614
Dynamic Kernel Module Support, 591
dynamic workspace indicator, 297

E

E-book reader
  Calibre, 221
  FBReader, 220
  Foliate, 220
edit
  GRUB, 78
Editors, 213, 226
  Emacs, 229
  Gedit, 227
  Gvim, 229
  Kate, 229
  nano, 228
  Pluma, 409

Index

Text Editor, 226
Vi Editor, 229
Vim, 229
Elisa, 259
Emacs, 229
Email, 234
Encryption
   importing public keys, 544
   installation, 60
   keyrings, 540
   Seahorse, 539
   sharing keys, 547
Epiphany, 280
Evince
   DVI, 219
Evolution, 237

F

faac, 256
faad2, 256
Familiar
   desktop layouts, 424
Favorites
   GNOME, 303
FBReader, 220
fetchmail, 242
ffmpeg, 256
File Management
   MATE, 463
File Manager, 142, 491
   bookmarks
      Caja, 440
      GNOME, 327
   Caja, 439
      side pane, 443
   Caja preferences, 454
   displaying files and folders
      Caja, 445
      GNOME, 329
   Dolphin preferences, 398
   FTP, 286
   GNOME
      Files, 322
      search, 338
      sidebar, 327
   KDE, 401
   Dolphin, 393
   Samba, 396
   Lubuntu, 478
   navigation (Caja), 447
   PC-Man, 478
   preferences
      GNOME, 337
   tabs
      Caja, 445
      GNOME, 329
   Thunar, 476
   xdg-user-dirs, 440
   Xubuntu, 476
file permission
   GNOME, 583
File Roller, 601
File Systems, 573
   encryption, 60
   fstab, 585
   Linux, 573
   LVM, 548
   NTFS, 574
   Windows, 573
   ZFS, 548, 555
filename completion, 497
filename expansion, 500
Filenames, 509
Files, 509, 513
   compress, 333
   Connect bar, 286
   copy, 334, 520
   default applications
      GNOME, 108
      MATE, 452
   display
      Caja, 445
      GNOME, 329
   FTP, 286
   move, 521
   properties
      Caja, 452
      GNOME, 335
   rename, 332, 399
Files file manager
   GNOME, 322
Filezilla, 287
filter bar

Index

KDE, 401
find, 517
Firefox, 277
   FTP, 285
Firewall, 642
   Avahi, 575
   firewall-config, 649
   FirewallD, 649
   Gufw, 644
   iptables-nft, 642
   masquerading, 653
   nftables, 642
   ports, 643
   Ports, 653
   ufw, 643, 648
firewall-config, 649
FirewallD, 649
   Avahi, 575
   mdns, 575
   nftables, 642
   samba, 582
Flatpak, 207
Flavors, 474
flowchart
   Dia, 218
folders
   display
      Caja, 445
      GNOME, 329
   GNOME
      Desktop folder, 300, 320
   permissions
      Caja, 454
   properties
      Caja, 453
      GNOME, 337
   Samba, 578, 579
   sambashare, 580
   sharing, 578
Foliate
   E-book reader, 220
Fonts, 225
   GNOME Tweaks, 93
   MATE, 464
fstab, 585
ftp, 289
FTP, 285

Caja, 441
Connect bar, 286
curl, 288
file manager, 286
Files, 286
Filezilla, 287
ftp, 289
gFTP, 288
lftp, 290
Nautilus, 286
wget, 288
FTP Clients, 284

G

GDM, 80
Gedit, 227
gFTP, 288
GIMP, 253
Glances, 531
GNOME, 88, 296
   application launchers, 320
   applications overview, 306
   calendar, 225
   Characters, 224
   Clocks, 223
   compress, 333
   copy, 334
   customization, 319
   desktop, 296
   desktop backgrounds, 107
   Desktop folder, 300, 320
   desktop icons, 320
   desktop menu, 299
   display configuration, 146
   display manager, 80
   dock, 302
   documentation, 147
   DVD/CD burner, 144
   Favorites, 303
   file manager, 322, 491
      preferences, 337
      search, 142, 338
   file permission, 583
   file properties, 335
   Files, 322
   Flatpak, 207

folder properties, 337
Foliate, 220
fonts, 93, 225, 320
Gedit, 227
GNOME Tweaks, 92
GNOME Videos, 261
Graphics, 252
groups, 572
Gufw, 644
Help, 147, 321
lock screen, 84
login screen, 80
logs, 533
Music, 260
NetworkManager, 96, 617
Network tab, 100, 620
Notes, 223
notifications, 318
overview, 300
photos, 249
printers, 604
remote printers, 606, 609
rename, 332
search, 338
startup applications, 94, 320
   preferences, 145
System menu, 82, 298
tiles, 312
Tweak Tool, 319
Ubuntu Desktop Guide, 147
Users, 564
wallpaper, 107
Wi-Fi, 96, 617
window colors, 310
windows, 310
windows overview, 304
wired, 100, 620
workspace selector, 317
workspaces, 315
GNOME Console, 154
GNOME Control Center, 455
GNOME Music, 260
GNOME office applications, 217
GNOME Software, 189
GNOME System Monitor, 528
   Processes, 529
GNOME Text Editor, 226

GNOME Tweaks, 92
GNOME Videos, 261, 264
GNOME Web browser
   Epiphany (GNOME Web), 280
gnome-nettool, 654
GNU General Public License, 43
gnubiff, 241
Gnumeric, 217
good
   Gstreamer, 257
Google
   Chromium, 281
GPG keys
   Passwords and Keys, 541
Grand Unified Bootloader, 592
Graphics, 247, 252
   GIMP, 253
   GNOME, 252
   Inkscape, 253
   KDE, 254
   Krita, 254
groups
   GNOME
      Users and Groups, 572
   managing, 572
GRUB, 592
   configuration, 593
   editing, 78
   grub-install, 75
   grub-set-default, 596
   History (ZFS), 555
   re-installing the boot loader, 74
   update-grub, 596
GRUB 2, 592
GRUB_DEFAULT, 595
grub-install, 75
grub-set-default, 596
GStreamer, 257
   bad, 257
   base, 257
   good, 257
   MP3, 258
   Plug-ins, 257
   ugly, 257
gstreamer-bad, 256
gstreamer-ugly, 256
Gufw, 644

Gvim, 229

H

hard drives
    SMART information, 536, 538
hardware sensors, 536
HDTV, 268
    audio, 256
    Kaffeine, 268
    liba52, 268
Help, 40, 147
    GNOME, 321
    info pages, 150
    Man pages, 150
    Ubuntu Desktop Guide, 147
help.ubuntu.com, 41
hidden wireless networks, 628
history
    shell, 498
Home Directories, 511
hostname, 559
hostnamectl, 559
hot corner, 301

I

Icon-only Task Manager, 376, 379
icons
    desktop
        GNOME, 320
        MATE, 417
IMAP, 241
importing public keys, 544
Indicators
    Date and Time, 413
    session menu, 413
    Ubuntu MATE, 412
info, 150
info pages, 150
Inkscape, 253
install, 196
Installation
    BitTorrent, 47
    computer name, 68
    encryption, 60
    Live DVD, 52

LVM, 59
minimal installation, 55, 56
multimedia codecs, 55, 56
overview, 48
partitions, 57
Prepare disk space, 57
specify partitions manually (advanced), 63
Ubuntu, 46
updates, 55, 56
USB, 38
user, 68
Welcome, 52
Instant Messenger, 290
    Pidgin, 291
interfaces
    Snap, 168
iptables
    nftables, 642
iptables-nft, 642

J

Java, 282
    APT
        OpenJDK-21, 282
    OpenJDK, 282
    Snap
        OpenJDK-22, 282
Java 2 Runtime Environment, 282
JRE, 282

K

K3b, 261
Kaffeine, 263, 264, 268
Kate, 229
KDE, 36, 342
    Activities, 367
        activites bar, 372
    Application Launcher, 352
    Application Menu, 352
    applications, 380
    brightness, 387
    configuration, 346
    copy, 399
    desktop backgrounds, 349
    desktop effects, 389

desktop grid, 392
desktop menu, 347
desktop pager, 380
device notifier, 361
Discover software manager, 405
Dolphin, 393
edit mode, 348
filter bar, 401
graphics, 254
Help Center, 347
Kaffeine, 264
KMail, 239
KRunner, 360
Kubuntu, 343
lock, 351
log out, 351
mail client, 239
menus
   Application Dashboard, 359
   Application Launcher, 354
   Application Menu, 357
   selection, 353
move, 399
NetworkManager, 362
Overview effect, 382
pager, 380
panel, 384
   task managers, 374
panel configuration, 388
photos, 251
Plasma, 343, 384
present windows, 392
rename, 399
Samba, 396
SDDM, 344
search, 400
search bar, 400
Shut down, 351
shutdown, 353
task managers
   Icon-only Task Manager, 376, 379
   Task Manager, 378
   Window List, 379
Task Scheduler, 532
themes, 350
tiles, 374
Ubuntu, 342

Users, 404
virtual desktops, 380
   Overview effect, 382
   pager, 380
wallpaper, 349
Widgets, 364
Wi-Fi, 362
windows, 373
workspaces, 380
   overview effect, 382
   pager, 380
keyboard, 52, 53, 54
   GNOME, 116
   MATE, 456, 465
keyrings, 540
   Passwords and Keys, 540
keyservers
   Passwords and Keys, 544
kill, 530
KMail, 239
Krita, 254
KRunner, 360
Kubuntu, 36, 343
KWin
   desktop grid, 392
   present windows, 392
Kylin, 36

L

lame, 256
language
   GNOME, 116
laptop
   brightness
      KDE, 387
      MATE, 467
      Ubuntu, 298
lftp, 290
liba52, 268
libdvbpsi, 256
libdvdcss, 266
libmad, 256
LibreOffice, 214
LibreOffice Base, 233
libxvidcore, 269
Links, 282

hard links, 523
symbolic, 523
Linux, 43
Man pages, 150
Linux file structure, 511
Linux Mint
Cinnamon, 485
Live USB/DVD, 50
Livepatch, 205
Software & Updates, 205
lm-sensors, 536
lock screen
GNOME, 84
KDE, 351
MATE, 469
Logical Volume Manager, 548
login
GDM, 80
logind, 81
SDDM, 344
logind, 81
logout
KDE, 351
logs
GNOME Logs, 533
ls, 510
Lubuntu, 36, 477
configuration, 478
panel, 478
PC-Man, 478
LVM, 548
/dev/mapper, 553
commands, 549
device names, 553
encryption, 60
groups, 550
installation, 59
Logical Volumes, 551
physical volume, 549
snapshots, 554
vgcreate, 550
LXQT
configuration, 478
panel, 478
PC-Man, 478
Lynx, 282
LZMA, 601

M

Mail, 234, 240
Evolution, 237
fetchmail, 242
gnubiff, 241
IMAP, 241
KMail, 239
mail, 240
MIME, 242
Mutt, 240
notification, 241
POP servers, 241
remote mail servers, 241
Thunderbird, 235
Mail applications, 234
mailing lists, 242
main
repository, 182
man, 150
Man pages, 150
maps, 292
MariaDB, 234
masquerading, 653
MATE, 407, 408
adding panel objects, 438
Appearance, 458
Applets, 439
applications, 409
assistive technologies, 460
backgrounds, 458
Bluetooth, 461
brightness, 467
Brisk Menu, 428
Caja, 439
Celluloid, 264, 410
copy, 416, 450
default applications, 463
desktop, 410
desktop icons, 417
desktop layouts, 423
Contemporary, 427
Cupertino, 425
Familiar, 424
Mutiny, 426
Pantheon, 426

Redmond, 425
Traditional, 424
desktop settings, 417
displays, 462
drawers, 438
file management, 463
folder properties, 453
fonts, 464
Indicators, 412
keyboard, 456, 465
lock screen, 469
menus
    Brisk Menu dash layout, 429
    classic, 430
    Compact, 431
mouse, 465
notifications, 467
panel, 434
panel menus, 427
panel objects, 437
Plank dock, 431, 433
    preferences, 432
Power Manager, 466
preferences, 455
preferred applications, 468
screensaver, 469
sound, 470
themes, 459
Time and Date Manager, 472
Tweak, 417
Ubuntu MATE Guide, 408
universal access, 460
Webcamoid, 409
window list, 420
windows, 419
workspace switcher applet, 422
workspaces, 421
MATE Tweak
    desktop, 417
    desktop layouts, 423
Matroska, 269
mdns
    FirewallD, 575
    Gufw, 575
    mdns4, 576
mdns.allow, 576
menus

GNOME
    desktop menu, 299
    System menu, 82
KDE
    Application Dashboard, 359
    Application Launcher, 354
    Application Menu, 357
MATE, 427
    Brisk Menu, 428
    Brisk Menu dash layout, 429
    compact, 431
    panel, 439
messenger
    Pidgin, 291
Metalinks, 47
Microsoft Office, 218
MIME, 242
mkdir, 515
mkv
    Matroska, 269
Monitoring
    Disk Usage Analyzer, 533
    Disk Utility, 536, 538
    glances, 531
    Nettool, 654
mouse
    GNOME, 117
    MATE, 465
move
    shell, 521
MP3, 258, 261
    lame, 256
mpeg2dec, 256
MPEG-4, 269
    Matroska, 269
MPlayer, 263, 264
MPV, 264
multicast DNS discovery, 574
    FirewallD, 575
    Gufw, 575
    mdns.allow, 576
Multimedia, 247, 255
    applications, 261
    Camera, 249
    CD Burners and Rippers, 261
    Celementine, 260
    Celluloid, 264, 410

codecs, 255, 256
digiKam, 251
DVD, 261
DVD Video, 266
Elisa, 259
GNOME Music, 260
GNOME Videos, 261
GStreamer, 257
HDTV, 268
installation, 55, 56
Kaffeine, 264, 268
Matroska, 269
MP3, 261
MPEG-4, 269
MPlayer, 264
mpv, 264
PiTiVi Video editor, 266
Rhythmbox, 258
Shotcut Video editor, 267
Shotwell, 249
Sound Preferences, 269
third-party codecs, 255
TV Players, 268
Ubuntu Studio, 269, 480
VideoLAN, 264
vlc, 264
Webcamoid, 409
Xvid, 269
multiverse
  repository, 182
music
  Clementine, 259
  Elisa, 259
  GNOME Music, 260
  MP3, 258, 261
  Rhythmbox, 258
Music Applications, 258
Mutiny
  desktop layouts, 426
Mutt, 240
Mysql, 234
MySQL, 233, 234
MythTV, 263, 268

N

nano, 228

Nautilus
  FTP, 286
nautilus-share
  shared folders, 578
Netplan, 638
  configuration, 635
  networkctl, 639, 641
  NetworkManager, 641
  systemd-networkd, 634
  Wi-Fi, 640
Nettool, 654
Network Configuration, 613
Network Information, 614
Network Object Model Environment, 296
Network tab
  GNOME, 100, 620
networkctl, 639, 641
Networking
  link files, 659
  Netplan, 634, 638
  Network tab, 620
  networkctl, 639, 641
  NetworkManager, 641
  nmcli, 629
  predictable network device names, 655
  renaming device names, 658
  renaming network device names, 658, 659
  systemd-networkd, 637, 659
  udev, 658
  Wi-Fi, 640
  Wi-Fi tab, 617
  Zeroconf, 574
NetworkManager, 615, 616
  device names, 655
  GNOME, 96, 617
  hidden wireless network, 628
  KDE, 362
  manual configuration, 617, 625
  Netplan, 635
  networkctl, 639, 641
  network-manager, 641
  nmcli, 629
  systemd-networkd, 641
  udev, 658
  Virtual Private Networks, 623
  WireGuard, 624
  wireless router, 628

wireless security, 626
NetworkManager Command Line Interface
  (**nmcli**), 629
Networks
  Avahi, 574
  configuration, 615, 616
  device names, 655
  firewall, 649
  Glances, 531
  hidden wireless networks, 628
  manual configuration, 617, 625
  multicast DNS discovery, 574
  Nettool, 654
  networkctl, 639, 641
  NetworkManager, 615, 616
  nmcli, 629
  renaming device names, 658, 659
  renaming network device names, 658
  shared file systems, 574, 577
  shared folders, 578
  systemd link files, 659
  udev, 658
  wireless router, 628
  Zero Configuration Networking, 574
news transport agents, 246
newsreaders, 244
  binary, 245
  news transport agents, 246
  NNTPSERVER, 244
  NZB, 245
  par2, 245
  slrn, 245
nftables, 642
  iptables-nft, 642
nmbd, 579, 606
nmcli, 629
NNTPSERVER, 244
notes
  GNOME Notes, 223
notifications, 318
  GNOME, 121, 123
  MATE, 467
NTFS, 574
nvidia-settings, 147
NZB, 245

O

Office
  fonts, 225
  GNOME Calendar, 225
  GNOME Characters, 224
  GNOME Clocks, 223
  GNOME Notes, 223
Office Suites, 214
  Calligra, 216
  GNOME office applications, 217
  LibreOffice, 214
  OpenOffice, 214
Okular, 219
  DVI, 219
Open Source, 42
OpenJDK, 282
OpenOffice, 214
OpenZFS, 555
Overview
  GNOME, 300

P

Package Management Software, 160
packages
  Ubuntu
    software, 39
packages.ubuntu.com, 159
pager
  KDE
    activities pager, 370
  MATE
    workspace switcher, 422
Panel
  KDE, 384
    Icon-only Task Manager, 376, 379
    Task Manager, 378
    Window List, 379
  KDE configuration, 388
  Lubuntu, 478
  LXQT, 478
  MATE, 434
    adding objects, 438
    Brisk Menu, 428
    dock
      Plank, 431

drawers, 438
menus, 439
  Brisk Menu dash layout, 429
panel menus, 427
panel objects, 437
menus
  KDE, 353
  MATE, 430
    compact menu, 431
panel objects
  MATE, 437
Pantheon
  desktop layouts, 426
par2, 245
Partitions, 57
  blank hard drive, 63
  new partitions, 63
passwd, 573
Passwords, 572
  keyrings, 540
Passwords and Keys
  GPG keys, 541
  importing keys, 544
  keyrings, 540
  keyservers, 544
  Seahorse, 540
  sharing keys, 547
Pathnames, 512
PC-Man, 478
PDF
  Okular, 219
  pdfedit, 219
pdfedit, 219
permissions
  Caja, 454
  GNOME
    files, 583
Photos
  Camera, 252
  digiKam, 251
  Shotwell, 249
  webcam, 252
Photoshop, 208
physical volume, 549
Pidgin, 291
pipes
  shell, 508

Pipewire, 269
PiTiVi Video editor, 266
Plank dock, 431, 433
  preferences, 432
Plasma, 343, 384
Plymouth, 80, 539
  default.plymouth, 539
  update-alternatives, 539
PolicyKit, 563
  auth_admin_keep, 563
  PolicyKit-1, 563
polkit-1, 563
POP, 241
ports
  firewall, 643, 653
PostgreSQL, 233, 234
power management
  GNOME, 124
  MATE, 466, 467
  power profiles, 83
  Power Statistics, 126
  powertop, 127
  tuned, 127
power profiles, 83
Power Statistics, 126
powertop, 127
PPP, 633
predictable network device names, 655, 658, 659
  link files, 659
  systemd-networkd, 659
  udev, 658
Preferences
  file manager
    Caja, 454
    Dolphin, 398
    GNOME, 337
    MATE, 455
      Control Center, 455
  monitors, 146
  Software & Updates, 185
  sound, 269, 270
preferred applications
  MATE, 468
present windows, 392
presentation
  Calligra Sheets, 217

Index

LibreOffice Impress, 215
print servers
    CUPS, 608
Printers, 603
    additional printer settings, 607
    remote printers, 606, 609
    Samba, 610, 611
    Settings, 604
    Windows, 610, 611
Printing
    default printer, 608
    lpr, 514
    personal default printer, 608
privacy
    GNOME, 127
processes, 529
    Gnome System Monitor, 529
    kill, 530
    ps, 530
properties
    files
        Caja, 452
        GNOME, 335
    folders
        Caja, 453
        GNOME, 337
proprietary graphics drivers, 591
ps, 530
Psensor, 536
public keys
    importing, 544
PulseAudio, 272
    PulseAudio Volume Control, 273
    PulseAudio Volume Meter, 274
PulseAudio Volume Control, 273

R

Recovery, 73
redirection
    shell, 504
    standard error, 507
Redmond
    desktop layouts, 425
re-install bootloader, 74
remote printers, 606, 609
    Samba, 611

Windows, 611
removable media
    GNOME, 109
rename
    GNOME, 332
    KDE, 399
repositories, 182
    /etc/apt/sources.list.d/ubuntu.sources, 183
    Backports, 182
    Flatpak, 207
    main, 182
    multiverse, 182
    restricted, 182
    Security updates, 183
    ubuntu.sources, 185
    universe, 182
    Updates, 182
restricted
    repository, 182
revisions
    Snap, 172
Rhythmbox, 258
risk levels
    Snap, 167
root user, 562
    su, 562
    sudo, 560
router
    wireless, 628
rsync, 602

S

Samba, 579, 610
    Dolphin, 396
    FirewallD, 582
    folders, 578
    KDE, 396
    nautilus-share, 579
    nmbd, 579
    printers, 610
    sambashare, 580
    shared folders, 579
    smbd, 579
    smbpasswd, 579
    UFW, 582

Windows, 582
sambashare
   shared folders, 580
scanner, 219, 220
schedule tasks
   cron, 532
   KDE Task Scheduler, 532
   systemd timers, 532
Scribus, 216
SDDM, 344
Seahorse, 539
   importing keys, 544
   keyrings, 540
   Passwords and Keys, 540
   sharing keys, 547
search
   file manager
      search, 142
   filter bar, 401
   GNOME, 338
   KDE, 400
   software, 194
search bar
   KDE, 400
Security
   GNOME, 127
   PolicyKit, 563
   virus protection, 535
Security updates
   repository, 183
sensors, 536
   Disk Utility, 536
   lm-sensors, 536
   Psensor, 536
   Xsensors, 536
services, 573
   Snap, 174
   systemctl command, 573
   systemd, 573
session menu
   MATE
      Indicators, 413
sessions
   Startup Applications Preferences, 145
Settings
   additional printer settings, 607
   Apps, 110

Default Apps, 108, 109
background, 107
Date & Time, 135
display, 114
keyboard, 116
language, 116
mouse, 117
Network tab, 100, 620
notifications, 121, 123
Power (power management), 124
Printers, 604
privacy, 127
remote printers, 609
security, 127
sharing, 130
Sound Preferences, 269
touchpad, 117
universal access, 105
Wi-Fi tab, 96
shared file systems, 574, 577
   Avahi, 574
   FirewallD, 575, 582
   mdns.allow, 576
   multicast DNS discovery, 574
   UFW, 582
   Windows
      GNOME, 582
shared folders, 578
   GNOME, 578, 579
   KDE, 396
   nautilus-share, 578
   Samba, 579
   sambashare, 580
   smbpasswd, 579
   Windows, 582
sharing
   GNOME, 130
shell, 493
   commands, 497
   copy, 520
   cp, 520
   filename completion, 497
   filename expansion, 500
   history, 498
   matching multiple characters, 502
   move, 521
   mv, 521

pipes, 508
range of characters, 503
redirection, 504, 507
standard error, 507
standard input, 506
standard output, 505
Shotcut Video editor, 267
Shotwell, 249
   editing photos, 250
Shut down
   GNOME
      Poweroff, 86
   KDE, 351, 353
side pane
   MATE
      Caja, 443
sidebar
   GNOME
      Files, 327
Simple Desktop Display Manager (SDDM), 344
Skype, 291
slrn, 245
slrnpull, 245
SMART, 536, 538
smbd, 579, 606
smbpasswd
   GNOME, 579
   shared folders, 579
snap, 163
Snap, 159
   App Center, 175
   channels, 167
   confinement, 168
   interfaces, 168
   revisions, 172
   risk levels, 167
   services, 174
   snap command, 163
   snaps, 40
   systemd, 174
   tracks, 167
   Ubuntu **snap-store**, 175
   updates, 200
Snap Store
   App Center, 175
Snapshot

Camera, 252
snapshots
   LVM, 554
   ZFS, 555
Social networking, 290
software
   /etc/apt/sources.list.d/ubuntu.sources, 183
   alien, 200
   App Center, 175
      APT, 187
      Snap, 175
   APT, 158
   apt-cache, 199
   apt-get, 196
   confinement, 168
   DEB, 195
   dpkg, 199
   Flatpak, 207
   GNOME
      GNOME Software, 189
   KDE
      Discover, 405
   Livepatch, 205
   Metalinks, 47
   open source, 42
   search, 194
   Snap, 40, 159
   Software & Updates, 185
   Synaptic Package Manager, 191
   Ubuntu
      packages, 39
   Zsync, 47
Software & Updates, 185
software package types, 159
Software updater, 200, 202
   dconf, 204
   upgrade, 71
sound
   alsamixer, 270
   amixer, 270
   MATE, 470
   Pipewire, 269
   PulseAudio, 272
   PulseAudio Volume Control, 273
   PulseAudio Volume Meter, 274
   sound interfaces, 272

704 Index

Sound Preferences, 269
    SPDIF, 272
Sound Effects, 272, 471
Sound Preferences, 269, 270
Source code, 195
SPDIF, 272
spreadsheet
    Calligra Sheets, 217
    Gnumeric, 217
    LibreOffice Calc, 215
SQL Databases, 233
SSID, 628
standard error, 507
standard input, 506
standard input/output
    shell, 504
standard output, 505
Startup Applications
    GNOME
        Preferences, 145
    GNOME Tweaks, 94
startup-animation
    Plymouth, 80, 539
Static IP address, 614
su, 562
sudo, 560
    configuration, 560
Symbolic Links, 523
Synaptic Package Manager, 191
system administration, 557
    KDE System Settings, 402
    MATE Control Center, 455
system directories, 513
System menu, 82, 297, 298
    power profiles, 83
System Settings, 492
    KDE, 402
System Tools, 527
    Disk Usage Analyzer, 533
    Disk Utility, 536
    GNOME System Monitor, 528
    KDE Task Scheduler, 532
    Logs, 533
system-config-printer
    remote printers, 609
    Samba, 611
systemctl, 573

systemd, 573
    logind, 81
    Netplan, 634
    Snap, 174
    systemd timers, 532
    systemd-networkd, 637
    Wi-Fi, 640
systemd timers, 532
systemd-networkd
    configuration, 638
    Netplan, 634
    networkctl, 639, 641
    NetworkManager, 641
    renaming device names, 659
    Wi-Fi, 640

T

tabs
    configuration, 153
    file manager
        Caja, 445
        GNOME, 329
    terminal window, 152
tar, 601
Task Manager, 378
task managers
    KDE, 374
        Icon-only Task Manager, 376, 379
        Task Manager, 378
        Window List, 379
temperature
    Disk Utility, 536
terminal window, 150
    cut and paste, 152
    GNOME Console, 154
    tabs, 152, 153
TeX, 219
    Evince, 219
    Okular, 219
Text Editor, 226
themes
    KDE, 350
    MATE, 459
    Yaru theme, 87
Thunar, 476
Thunderbird, 235

tiles
    GNOME, 312
    KDE, 374
time
    date, 135
    GNOME
        Date & Time, 135
    GNOME Clocks, 223
    MATE, 472
Time and Date Manager, 472
timer
    GNOME Clocks, 223
Totem, 261, 263
    totem plugins, 265
touchpad
    GNOME, 117
tracks
    Snap, 167
Traditional
    desktop layouts, 424
Transmission, 47, 283
tuned, 127
TV Players, 268
    Kaffeine, 268
    MythTV, 268
    tvtime, 268
Tweak
    MATE, 423
Tweak Tool, 319

U

Ubuntu, 30, 36
    Administrative Tools, 558
    brightness, 298
    documentation, 40
    Flatpak, 207
    flavors, 36
    GNOME, 88, 296
    GNOME Software, 189
    GNOME Tweaks, 92
    help, 40, 41
    hot corner, 301
    Installation, 46
    Introduction, 29
    Kubuntu, 343
    language, 30
    Live USB/DVD, 37
    Livepatch, 205
    MATE, 408, 410
    news, 42
    power profiles, 83
    printers, 604
    recovery, 73
    releases, 34
    System Settings, 492
    Tweak Tool, 319
    Ubuntu Desktop, 34
    Ubuntu dock, 302
    Ubuntu Studio, 269
    discource.ubuntu.com, 41
    update, 200
    workspaces, 301
    Yaru theme, 87
Ubuntu 20.04 LTS, 31
Ubuntu Budgie, 481
Ubuntu Cinnamon, 485
Ubuntu Desktop, 34, 88, 296
    display configuration, 146
    Displays, 146
    documentation, 147
    Help, 147
    startup applications, 145
    Ubuntu Desktop Guide, 147
Ubuntu Desktop Guide, 147
Ubuntu download
    BitTorrent, 47
    Metalinks, 47
    Zsync, 47
Ubuntu Flavors, 473, 474
    Kubuntu, 343
    Lubuntu, 477
    Ubuntu Budgie, 481
    Ubuntu Cinnamon, 485
    Ubuntu MATE, 408
    Ubuntu Studio, 480
    Ubuntu Unity, 488
    Xubuntu, 474
Ubuntu Font Family, 3
Ubuntu Live USB/DVD, 37, 50
Ubuntu MATE, 407
Ubuntu repository, 182
Ubuntu Studio, 269, 480
Ubuntu Unity, 488

ubuntu.sources, 183, 185
discourse.ubuntu.com, 41
ubuntustudio-desktop, 269
ubuntustudio-video, 263
udev
    predictable network device names, 655, 658
Udisks, 536
    SMART, 536, 538
ufw, 643, 648
    commands, 648
    Gufw, 644
    samba, 582
ugly
    Gstreamer, 257
unexpanded panels
    movable and fixed, 436
Unity, 488
universal access
    GNOME, 105
    MATE, 460
universe
    repository, 182
update, 198
update-alternatives, 539
update-grub, 596
Updates, 55, 56
    APT, 202
    dconf, 204
    Livepatch, 205
    repository, 182
    Snap, 200
    software, 200
    Software updater, 202
upgrade, 198
    apt-get, 73
    distribution, 71
    Software updater, 71
URL Addresses, 276
USB
    installation, 38
    Live drive, 38
    Live USB/DVD, 50
Usenet News, 243
useradd, 571
Users, 568
    GNOME, 564

groups, 572
installation, 68
KDE, 404
managing users, 568
new users, 570
Passwords, 572
root user, 562
su, 562
sudo, 560
Users and Groups, 568
users-admin, 568

V

vendor display drivers, 146
vgcreate, 550
Vi Editor, 229
video
    Celluloid, 264, 410
    DVD Video, 266
    GNOME Videos, 261, 264
    Kaffeine, 264
    MPEG-4, 269
    MPlayer, 264
    mpv, 264
    PiTiVi Video editor, 266
    Shotcut Video editor, 267
    VideoLAN, 264
    vlc, 264
VideoLAN, 263, 264
videolan.org
    libdvdcss, 266
Videos, 261
Vim, 229
virtual desktops
    GNOME, 315
        dynamic workspace indicator, 297
        workspace selector, 317
    KDE, 380
        Overview effect, 382
        pager, 380
    MATE, 421
Virtual Private Networks
    NetworkManager, 623
    OpenVPN, 623
    PPTP, 625
    WireGuard, 624

virus protection, 535
vlc, 264
VoIP
   Skype, 292

W

w_scan, 268
wallpaper
   GNOME, 107
   KDE, 349
Web, 280
Web browser, 277
   Chromium, 281
   Firefox, 277
   Links, 282
   Lynx, 282
   Web (Epiphany), 280
webcam
   Camera, 252
Webcamoid, 409
Welcome, 52
wget, 288
widgets, 364
Wi-Fi
   GNOME, 96, 617
   KDE, 362
   Netplan, 640
Wi-Fi tab
   GNOME, 96
window colors, 310
   GNOME, 310
window list
   MATE, 420
Window List, 379
windows
   file systems, 574
   GNOME, 310
      overview, 304
   KDE, 373
      tiles, 374
   MATE, 419
   window colors, 310
   Windows compatibility layer, 208
   Wine, 208
Windows
   printers (Samba), 610

remote printers, 611
   Samba, 582
   shared file systems, 582
   system-config-printer, 611
Windows compatibility layer
   Wine, 208
Wine, 208
wired
   GNOME, 100, 620
   KDE, 362
   Network Connections, 626
   Network tab, 100, 620
   nmcli, 631
   systemd-networkd, 639
WireGuard, 624
wireless
   GNOME, 96, 617
   hidden network, 628
   hotspot, 628
   KDE, 362
   Network Connections, 626
   nmcli, 633
   systemd-networkd, 640
   Wi-Fi tab, 98, 617
wireless router, 628
wireless security, 626
wordprocessing
   AbiWord, 217
   Calligra Words, 217
   LibreOffice Writer, 215
workspace selector
   GNOME, 317
      dynamic workspace indicator, 297
workspaces
   GNOME, 301, 315
      dynamic workspace indicator, 297
      workspace selector, 317
   KDE, 380
      Overview effect, 382
      pager, 380
   MATE, 421
      workspace switcher applet, 422
wvdial, 633

X

X Window System
  Displays, 146
  RandR, 146
  vendor drivers, 146
XFce, 474, 477
Xine, 264
Xsensors, 536
Xubuntu, 36, 474
  Thunar, 476
Xvid, 269
xvidcore, 256

Y

Yaru theme, 87

Z

Zero Configuration Networking, 574
Zeroconf, 574
  Avahi, 574
zfs, 555
ZFS, 555
  History, 555
  snapshots, 555
  zfs, 555
  zfsutil-linux, 555
  zsysctl, 556
Zsync, 47
zsysctl, 556